# Contents

iii

# DIGITAL LOGIC AND COMPUTER ORGANIZATION

**V. RAJARAMAN**

Honorary Professor
Supercomputer Education and Research Centre
Indian Institute of Science, Bangalore

**T. RADHAKRISHNAN**

Professor of Computer Science and Software Engineering
Concordia University
Montreal, Canada

**Prentice-Hall of India Private Limited**
New Delhi - 110001
2006

**Rs. 295.00**

**DIGITAL LOGIC AND COMPUTER ORGANIZATION**
V. Rajaraman and T. Radhakrishnan

**ISBN-81-203-2979-1**

The export rights of this book are vested solely with the publisher.

Published by Asoke K. Ghosh, Prentice-Hall of India Private Limited, M-97, Connaught Circus, New Delhi-110001 and Printed by Rajkamal Electric Press, B-35/9, G.T. Karnal Road Industrial Area, Delhi-110033.

# Preface

This book is an elementary introduction to Digital Logic and Computer Organization. It does not assume extensive knowledge of electronics or mathematics. A student in final year of B.Sc., second year of B.E. in Indian Universities or a first-year engineering student in Canadian Universities would be able to follow this book. Knowledge of programming in a higher level programming language such as Java, C++, or Pascal will be useful to give the student a good perspective on the current development of the subject.

This book is logically in two parts. The first six chapters are primarily concerned with Digital Logic. Chapters 7 to 13 are devoted to Computer Organization. The background provided by the first part is essential to follow the second part of the book. The first part can be studied independently for a course on Digital Logic.

The book begins with a chapter on representation of data in digital form that is required in all software systems and other digital systems. Number systems for enumeration, binary codes for representing decimals and character data are described. This chapter also describes digital representation of multimedia data such as graphics, audio and video. It is followed by a chapter on Boolean Algebra. Application of Boolean Algebra in minimizing Boolean expressions is described in this chapter. Veitch-Karnaugh map method and Quine-McCluskey chart method which are scalable beyond four variables are presented. We found that most students were able to use mechanically the minimization methods but experienced difficulty in formulating truth tables from problem specifications written in plain English. We thus devote most of Chapter 3 to combinatorial circuits to illustrate how a given specification is interpreted, appropriate Boolean variables selected, inputs and outputs identified, and a combinatorial logic circuit designed. Synthesis of combinatorial circuits with NAND/NOR gates, with multiplexers and programmable logic arrays (PLA) are also discussed in this chapter. Besides these topics, this chapter also describes the functioning of CMOS gates and their use in designing open-drain and tri-state gates. The applications of tri-state and open-drain gates in digital systems are also described.

Chapter 4 is on the design of sequential switching circuits. We describe in this chapter how flip-flops, registers and counters are designed. We describe Mealy and Moore models for sequential machines. These models introduce the students to the concepts of abstraction and modeling of a complex digital system. We design various sequential circuits such as counters using flip-flops. We also illustrate in this chapter the method of designing sequential machines from the given requirement specifications. Chapter 5 is on designing the Arithmetic Logic Unit or ALU of a computer. ALU is one of the three important subsystems of a computer system, the other two being memory and control. We describe algorithms for the four basic arithmetic operations: addition, subtraction, multiplication and division. Apart from integer arithmetic we also discuss the representation of floating point numbers using IEEE754 standard and algorithms for carrying out arithmetic operations using floating point numbers. The chapter concludes with a description of MSI chips used to carry out arithmetic and logic operations. In Chapter 6 we present applications of sequential circuits. Specifically we describe the use of Algorithmic State Machine (ASM) charts to express sequential algorithms relevant to the design of digital systems and ALU. We present a Hardware Description Language (HDL) to express those algorithms represented by ASM charts. We use HDL description of ALUs to design them.

The computer organization aspect of this book starts in Chapter 7. In Chapter 7 we present a layered view of a computer system. This chapter lays the foundation to our later discussions on software-hardware trade-off which is the major theme of this part of the book. In Chapter 8 we discuss the logical organization of a hypothetical small computer we call SMAC. SMAC is iteratively improved to SMAC+ and SMAC++ by introducing new instructions and new hardware features in each iteration of development. At each stage we discuss why new features are introduced and how they make programming easier for more complex applications. SMAC++ may be simulated using a language such as C++ or Java and machine language programs may be written and tested to be interpreted by such a simulator. Chapter 9 discusses general features of typical Central Processing Units. Various instruction formats, addressing modes and register sets are described. This chapter also examines processor bus structure, data and control paths in a CPU. We introduce microprogram control of CPU and relate it to HDL described in Chapter 6.

Chapter 10 is concerned with the organization of the main memory of a computer. We present the design of random access memories such as SRAMs and DRAMs. We describe how larger memories can be constructed using smaller IC chip memory blocks. We also describe other memories such as Read Only Memory (ROM) and dual ported RAM. The second part of this chapter describes the need for cache and its design. We also discuss the need for a large address space needed to support modern applications and how a large address space can be achieved, in a cost effective manner, using a combination of a main memory with a secondary memory. This forms a basis for understanding the trade-off between cost and performance.

Chapter 11 describes several devices used for input and output of computers. We consider I/O devices such as VDU, flat panel displays, keyboards and several types of printers. We also describe secondary memory devices such as hard disk, floppy disk, flash memory, CD-ROM, archival memory, namely, Ultrium high capacity tapes and digital audio tapes. The methods used to interface peripheral devices with CPU/Memory and procedures to efficiently transfer data to and from peripherals to memory are described in Chapter 12. Various methods of data transfer such as program controlled, interrupt controlled and DMA are discussed. The structure of I/O bus and bus protocols are also described.

The last chapter, namely, Chapter 13 looks at a real-life computer, namely, Intel's Pentium which is the most popular processor used in desktop computers. The intention of this chapter is to put the various concepts learnt in the previous chapters in perspective by examining how they are applied in practice.

We feel strongly that a laboratory should run concurrently with the lectures and appropriate experiments should be planned. We present in Appendix A, six experiments. They can be used to teach how to use IC chips to build gates, registers, counters and a small memory on a bread-board. The last experiment is to build a toy computer with 4 instructions. This can be improved if there is sufficient time and other resources, to build SMAC (which has 8 instructions, 2 registers and 16 byte memory).

We have written the book in a style that a student can read and understand the essential concepts with minimal help from outside. However, it should be kept in mind that no textbook can 100% replace good classroom teaching. We would like to thank all our students, readers, reviewers, copy editors and colleagues for the many constructive suggestions given by them which have greatly improved the book. We would like to thank Ms. T. Mallika for an excellent job of typing and other secretarial assistance. Thanks are due to Director, Indian Institute of Science for providing the infrastructure which allowed the first author to write this book. Radhakrishnan profoundly thanks his wife, the Concordia University and its Dean of Faculty of Engineering and Computer Science for their support in several ways in co-authoring this book. He cannot find suitable words to express thanks for the unbounded love and support given by Mrs. Rajaraman while he was writing in Bangalore.

Finally we have great pleasure in acknowledging the dedicated support of Mrs. Dharma Rajaraman. She checked the manuscript and the proofs with great care and supported this project in every possible way. Mere words are not adequate to express our heartfelt thanks to her.

**V. Rajaraman**
**T. Radhakrishnan**

———————————— Chapter ————————————

# 1

# Data Representation

---

## Learning Goals

In this chapter we will learn:

☞ Why binary digits are used to represent, store and process data in computers.

☞ How decimal numbers are converted to binary numbers and vice versa.

☞ Why number systems other than binary are used to represent numbers.

☞ How a decimal number is coded as a binary string and the different codes used and their features.

☞ Why redundant bits are introduced in codes and how they are used to detect and correct errors.

☞ Coding methods used to represent characters such as English letters, mathematical symbols, etc.

☞ How monochrome and colour pictures, video data and audio data are coded as binary strings and why there is a need to compress the resulting strings.

## 1.1  INTRODUCTION

We may define a digital computer or a digital system as a machine which accepts a stream of symbols, stores them, processes them according to precise rules and produces a stream of symbols at its output. At the simplest level, a digital processor may accept a single number at its input, perform an operation on it and produce another number at its output.

1

For example, a processor to find the square of a one digit number would fall in this category. At a more complex level a large number of symbols may be processed using extensive rules. As an example consider a digital system to automatically print a book. Such a system should accept a large text or the typewritten material. Given the number of letters which could be accommodated on a line (page width) and the rules for hyphenating a word, it should determine the space to be left between words on a line so that all lines are aligned on both the left and right hand sides of a page. The processor should also arrange lines into paragraphs and pages as directed by commands. Decisions to leave space for figures should be made. A multitude of such decisions are to be taken before a well laid out book is obtained. Such complex processing would require extensive special facilities such as a large amount of storage, electronic circuits to count and manipulate characters, and a printer which has a complete assortment of various sizes and styles of letters. Regardless of the complexity of processing, there are some basic features which are common to all digital processing of information which enable us to treat the subject in a unified manner. These features are:

1. All streams of input symbols to a digital system are encoded with two distinct symbols. These symbols, 0 (zero) and 1 (one), are known as binary digits or **bits.** Bits can be stored and processed reliably and inexpensively with currently available electronic circuits.

2. Instructions for manipulating symbols are to be precisely specified such that a machine can be built to execute each instruction. The instructions for manipulation are also encoded using binary digits.

3. A digital computer has a storage unit in which the symbols to be manipulated are stored. The encoded instructions for manipulating the symbols are also stored in the storage unit.

4. Bit manipulation instructions are realized by electronic circuits. Examples of simple manipulation instructions are: add two bits, compare two bits and move one bit from one storage unit to another. Complex manipulation instructions maybe built using simple instructions. A sequence of instructions for accomplishing a complex task may be stored in the storage unit and is called a **program.** The idea of building a complex instruction with a sequence of simple instructions is important in building digital computers.

The logic design of digital computers and systems consists of implementing the four basic steps enumerated above keeping in view the engineering constraints such as the availability of processing elements, their cost, reliability, maintainability and ease of fabrication.

At this stage, we should distinguish between the design of a general purpose digital computer and that of a specialized digital subsystem. Even though the four basic steps in design are common to both, the constraints which are peculiar to each of these lead to a difference in the philosophy of design.

A general purpose machine is designed to perform a variety of tasks. Each task requires the execution of a different sequence of processing rules. The processing rules to be followed vary widely. At the outset one may not be able to predict all the tasks he may like to do with a machine. A flexible design is thus required. This flexibility is achieved by carefully selecting the elementary operations to be implemented through electronic circuits.

These electronic circuits are together called **hardware.** One may realize a complex operation by using various sequences of elementary operations. For example, one may realize a multiplication operation by repeated use of addition operation, which may be thought of as a *macro* operation. A set of macros could be used to perform more complex tasks. One can thus build up a hierarchy of programs, all stored in the computer's memory, which can be invoked by any user to perform a very complex task. A user need not work only with the elementary operations available as hardware functions. He can use the hierarchy of programs which constitute the **software** of a computer and which is an integral part of a general purpose digital computer.

It should be observed that it is possible to perform macro operations entirely by specially designed electronic circuits rather than by using programs. Thus, software can be replaced by hardware and vice versa. What basic tasks are to be performed by hardware and what are to be done by combined software and hardware is an engineering design decision which depends on cost versus speed requirements and other constraints prevailing at a given time. One of the purposes of this book is to bring out the hardware-software trade-off, which is important in the design of general purpose computers.

This book deals with two aspects of digital computer design namely, computer logic and computer organization. There are three layers in computer design as shown in Figure 1.1. The bottom-most layer deals with digital circuits, which are used for arithmetic and logic operations. It deals with combining these logic blocks to perform more complex logical functions. Important topics that computer logic covers are representation of data (numerical, character, graphics, audio and video) as strings of binary digits, use of Boolean algebra as a modelling tool, physical realization of Boolean functions using logic gates, combinational and sequential logic circuits and how to realize a digital processing requirement specification using combinational and sequential logic circuits.

| | |
|---|---|
| Top Layer | Computer Architecture |
| Middle Layer | Computer Organization |
| Bottom Layer | Computer Logic |

**Fig. 1.1  Layered view of computer design.**

**Computer organization** primarily deals with combining building blocks described in computer logic as a programmable computer system. Besides arithmetic logic unit it is also about designing memory, I/O systems and ensuring their cooperative operation to carry out a sequence of instructions namely, a program. In this book we will also be describing important hardware-software trade-offs to ensure optimal functioning of a computer.

**Computer architecture** primarily deals with methods of alleviating speed mismatch between CPU, Memory and I/O units by a combination of hardware and software methods. It also deals with the interaction of the hardware with the operating system to ensure easy and optimal operation of a computer. We will not discuss this aspect of computer design in this book.

This chapter discusses the representation of data in digital systems. The five main categories of data are:

1. Numbers
2. Characters
3. Pictures or Images
4. Video
5. Audio

As was stated earlier in this section, in a digital system all data to be processed or stored are represented by strings of symbols where each symbol, called a bit, is either a 0 or a 1. The primary reasons for choosing to represent all data using only zeros or ones are:

1. Physical devices used for operating on data in digital systems perform most reliably when operated in one out of two distinct states. For example, circuits designed with transistors operate with maximum reliability when used in the "two state" namely, binary mode.

2. Most devices which are currently available to store data, do so by being in one out of two stable states. For example, magnetic discs store information by being magnetized in a specified direction or in an opposite direction.

We will present in the next section how numbers are represented using binary digits.

## 1.2 NUMBERING SYSTEMS

The most widely used number system is the positional system. In this system the position of various digits indicates the significance to be attached to that digit. For example, the number 8072.443 is taken to mean

| $8 \times 10^3$ | $+0 \times 10^2$ | $+7 \times 10^1$ | $+2 \times 10^0$ | $+4 \times 10^{-1}$ | $+4 \times 10^{-2}$ | $+3 \times 10^{-3}$ |
|---|---|---|---|---|---|---|
| 1000th | 100th | Tenth | Unit | 1/10th | 1/100th | 1/1000th |
| position | position | position | position | position | position | position |

In this notation the zero in the number 8072 is significant as it fixes the position and consequently, the weights to be attached to 8 and 7. Thus, 872 does not equal 8072.

An example of a non-positional number system is the Roman numeral system. This number system is quite complicated due to the absence of a symbol for zero.

Positional number systems have a *radix* or a *base*. In the decimal system the radix is 10. A number system with radix $r$ will have $r$ symbols and would be written as:

$$a_n\ a_{n-1}\ a_{n-2}\ \cdots\ a_0 \cdot a_{-1}\ a_{-2}\ \ldots\ a_{-m}$$

and would be interpreted to mean:

$$a_n r^n + a_{n-1}\ r^{n-1} + \cdots + a_0 r^0 + a_{-1} r^{-1} + a_{-2} r^{-2} + \cdots + a_{-m} r^{-m}$$

The symbols $a_n, a_{n-1}, \ldots, a_{-m}$ used in the above representation should be one of the $r$ symbols allowed in the system. In the above representation $a_n$ is called the most significant digit of the number and $a_{-m}$ (the last digit) is called the least significant digit.

In digital systems and computers, the number system used has a radix 2 and is called the **binary system.** In this system only two symbols namely, 0 and 1 are used. The symbol is called a **bit,** a shortened form for **binary digit.**

A number in the binary system will be written as a sequence of 1s and 0s. For example, 1011.101 is a binary number and would mean:

$$1 \times 2^3 + 0 \times 2^2 + 1 \times 2^1 + 1 \times 2^0 + 1 \times 2^{-1} + 0 \times 2^{-2} + 1 \times 2^{-3}$$

The equivalent number in decimal is thus:

$$8 + 0 + 2 + 1 + 1/2 + 0 + 1/8 = 11.625$$

Table 1.1 gives the decimal numbers from 0 to 17 and their binary equivalents.

**TABLE 1.1**
**Binary Equivalents of Decimal Numbers**

| Decimal | Binary | Decimal | Binary | Decimal | Binary |
|---------|--------|---------|--------|---------|--------|
| 0 | 0 | 6 | 110 | 12 | 1100 |
| 1 | 1 | 7 | 111 | 13 | 1101 |
| 2 | 10 | 8 | 1000 | 14 | 1110 |
| 3 | 11 | 9 | 1001 | 15 | 1111 |
| 4 | 100 | 10 | 1010 | 16 | 10000 |
| 5 | 101 | 11 | 1011 | 17 | 10001 |

It is seen that the length of binary numbers can become quite long and cumbersome for human use. Hexadecimal system (base 16) is thus often used to convert binary to a form requiring lesser number of digits. The **hexadecimal system** uses the 16 symbols 0, 1, 2, ..., 7, ..., 9, A, B, C, D, E. As its radix 16 is a power of 2, namely $2^4$, each group of four bits has hexadecimal equivalent. This is shown in Table 1.2. It is, therefore, fairly simple to convert binary to hexadecimal and vice versa. (One must contrast this with conversion of binary to decimal.)

**TABLE 1.2**
**Binary Numbers and Their Hexadecimal and Decimal Equivalents**

| Binary | Hexadecimal | Decimal | Binary | Hexadecimal | Decimal |
|--------|-------------|---------|--------|-------------|---------|
| 0000 | 0 | 0 | 1000 | 8 | 8 |
| 0001 | 1 | 1 | 1001 | 9 | 9 |
| 0010 | 2 | 2 | 1010 | A | 10 |
| 0011 | 3 | 3 | 1011 | B | 11 |
| 0100 | 4 | 4 | 1100 | C | 12 |
| 0101 | 5 | 5 | 1101 | D | 13 |
| 0110 | 6 | 6 | 1110 | E | 14 |
| 0111 | 7 | 7 | 1111 | F | 15 |

As illustrated in Example 1.1, one may convert a binary number to hexadecimal by grouping together successive **four bits** of the binary number starting with its least significant bit. These four bit groups are then replaced by their hexadecimal equivalents.

Because of the simplicity of binary to hexadecimal (abbreviated as Hex) conversion, when converting from binary to decimal, it is often faster to first convert from binary to Hex and then convert the Hex to decimal.

*Example 1.1.* Convert the following binary number to hexadecimal:

| **Binary number:** | 101 | 1010 | 1011 | 0111 |
|--------------------|-----|------|------|------|
| **Hexadecimal:** | 2 | A | B | 7 |

*Example 1.2.*   Convert the following binary number to Hexadecimal

| **Binary number:** | 11 | 1011 | 0101 | • | 1101 | 11 |
|---|---|---|---|---|---|---|
| **Hex number:** | 3 | B | 5 | • | D | C |

Observe that groups of four bits in the integral part of the binary number are formed starting from the right most bit as leading 0s here are not significant. On the other hand, bits on the fractional part are grouped from left to right as the right most bits of the fractional part are not significant.

The decimal equivalent of $(3B5.DC)_{Hex}$ is (using Table 1.2)

$$3 \times 16^2 + B \times 16^1 + 5 \times 16^0 \cdot D \times 16^{-1} + C \times 16^{-2}$$
$$= 3 \times 256 + 11 \times 16 + 5 \times 1 \cdot 13 \times 16^{-1} + 12 \times 16^{-2}$$
$$= 768 + 176 + 5 \cdot 13/16 + 12/256$$
$$= 949.859375$$

## 1.3   DECIMAL TO BINARY CONVERSION

In addition to knowing how to convert binary numbers to decimal, it is also necessary to know the technique of changing a decimal number to a binary number. The method is based on the fact that a decimal number may be represented by:

$$d = a_n 2^n + a_{n-1} 2^{n-1} + \cdots + a_1 2^1 + a_0 2^0 \qquad (1.1)$$

If we divide $d$ by 2, we obtain:

$$\text{Quotient } q = d/2 = a_n 2^{n-1} + a_{n-1} 2^{n-2} + \cdots + a_1 2^0 \qquad (1.2)$$

and remainder $r = a_0$.

Observe that $a_0$ is the least significant bit of the binary equivalent of $d$. Dividing the quotient by 2, we obtain:

$$q/2 = d/(2 \times 2) = a_n 2^{n-2} + a_{n-1} 2^{n-3} + \cdots + a_2 2^0 \qquad (1.3)$$

and the remainder equals $a_1$.

Thus, successive remainders obtained by division yield the bits of the binary number. Division is terminated when $q = 0$. The procedure is illustrated in Example 1.3.

*Example 1.3.*   Convert the decimal number 19 to binary.

```
2 | 19              Remainder
   2 | 9        1    Least significant bit
      2 | 4     1
         2 | 2  0
            2 | 1  0
               0  1    Most significant bit
```

Thus, $19 = 10011$. Check: $10011 = 1 \times 16^1 + 3 \times 16^0 = 16 + 3 = 19$.

Decimal to Hex conversion is similar. In this case 16 is used as the divisor instead of 2. For example, the decimal number 949 is converted to Hex in Example 1.4.

*Example 1.4.*

|  |  | **Decimal Remainder** | **Hex. Equivalent** |
|---|---|---|---|

$$16 \overline{\smash{\big)}\, 949} \qquad 5 \qquad 5 \uparrow$$

$$16 \overline{\smash{\big)}\, 59} \qquad 11 \qquad \text{B} \quad \text{Most}$$

$$16 \overline{\smash{\big)}\, 3} \qquad 3 \qquad 3 \quad \text{significant}$$

$$0 \qquad\qquad\qquad\qquad \text{digit}$$

Thus, $(949)_{10} = (3B5)_{16} = (3B5)_{Hex}$

Check: $(3B5)_{16} = 3 \times 16^2 + 11 \times 16^1 + 5 \times 16^0 = 768 + 176 + 5 = (949)_{10}$.

Observe the notation used to represent the base of a number. The number 16 or Hex used outside the parentheses in $(3B5)_{16}$ indicates that 3B5 is to be interpreted as a number in base 16.

The method used for decimal to binary conversion is expressed as Algorithm 1.1.

---

ALGORITHM 1.1. **Decimal to binary conversion**

*var*

  D: integer {D is the given decimal integer to be converted to binary};

  B: *bitstring* {B stores the binary equivalent of D};

  Q, R: integer {Intermediate variables used in conversion};

*begin* {of algorithm}

 *Input* D;

 B: *null;* {*null* is a null string}

 *if* (D = 0) *then begin* B:= 0; *goto* 10 *end;*

 *While* (D ≠ 0) *do*

  *begin*

   Q:= D *div* 2 {D *div* 2 gives the integer quotient of D/2};

   R:= D *mod* 2; {D *mod* 2 gives the remainder when D is divided by 2}

   B:= *Concatenate to left* (R, B)

   {If R = 1 and B = 01 then

   *Concatenate to left* (R, B) yields B = 101};

     D:= Q

  *end;*

10: *Output* B;

*end* {of algorithm}.

---

The procedure discussed above is to convert a decimal integer to binary. Decimal fractions may also be converted to binary. The method is based on observing that a decimal fraction may be represented in the form shown in Equation (1.4). In order to find its binary equivalent, we have to find the coefficients $a_{-1}, a_{-2}, \ldots$ .

$$d = a_{-1}2^{-1} + a_{-2}\,2^{-2} + \cdots + a_{-n}\,2^{-n} \tag{1.4}$$

$$2 \times d = a_{-1} + \underbrace{a_{-2}\,2^{-1} + \cdots + a_{-n}2^{-n+1}}_{d_1 < 1} \tag{1.5}$$

$$\underset{\text{0 or 1}}{\downarrow}$$

$$2 \times d_1 = a_{-2} + \underbrace{a_{-3}\,2^{-1} + \cdots + a_{-n}2^{-n+2}}_{d_2 < 1} \tag{1.6}$$

$$\underset{\text{0 or 1}}{\downarrow}$$

Thus, if we multiply a fraction by 2, the integral part of the product is the most significant bit of the binary equivalent of the fraction. The fractional part of the product may be multiplied again by 2 to obtain the next significant bit. The procedure is continued till the fractional part of the product is zero. The method is given as Example 1.5

*Example 1.5.*   Convert 0.859375 to binary.

| Decimal | Product | Binary | |
|---------|---------|--------|---|
| 0.859375 | $0.859375 \times 2 = 1.71875$ | 1 | |
| 0.71875 | $0.71875 \times 2 = 1.4375$ | 1 | |
| 0.4375 | $0.4375 \times 2 = 0.875$ | 0 | Most |
| 0.875 | $0.875 \times 2 = 1.75$ | 1 | significant |
| 0.75 | $0.75 \times 2 = 1.5$ | 1 | bit |
| 0 | $0.5 \times 2 = 1.0$ | 1 | |

Binary equivalent = 0.110111.

The method is given as Algorithm 1.2.

---

ALGORITHM 1.2. **Conversion of decimal fraction to binary fraction**

*var*

   D: *real* {D is the decimal fraction to be converted to a binary fraction};
   B: *bitstring* {B is the binary fraction equivalent of D};
   P: *real* {P is an intermediate variable used during conversion};
   INTP: *bit* {Integer part of P which can be either 0 or 1};
   *begin* {of algorithm}
                        *Input*   D;
                           B:= 0. *null* {*null* is a null string};
      *if* (D = 0) *then begin* B:= 0; *goto* 10 *end*;
      *While* (D ≠ 0) *and* length (B) ≤ 9 *do*
            {length (B) returns the number of bits in B and we have limited it to 9}
            *begin*
               P:= D * 2:
               INTP:= *Trunc* (P) {Trunc(P) returns the integer part of P};
               B:= *Concatenate to right* (INTP, B)
               {If INTP = 1 and B = 0.01 then

> *Concatenate to right* (INTP, B) yields 0.011}
>           D:= P − INTP
>       *end;*
>   10: *Output* B;
> *end* {of algorithm}.

This algorithm is used in Example 1.6 to convert 0.3 to binary. Observe that a terminating decimal fraction might lead to a non-terminating binary fraction. Thus, in the algorithm we have developed the binary fraction only up to a length of 9 bits.

*Example 1.6.*

| Decimal | Product | Binary |
|---------|---------|--------|
| 0.3 × 2 | 0.6 | 0 |
| 0.6 × 2 | 1.2 | 1 |
| 0.2 × 2 | 0.4 | 0 |
| 0.4 × 2 | 0.8 | 0 |
| 0.8 × 2 | 1.6 | 1 |
| recurs beyond this point | | |
| 0.6 × 2 | 1.2 | 1 |

Thus, 0.3 = 0.0100(1100)
                    ↓
                recurring

A similar procedure may be used to convert a decimal fraction to its Hex equivalent as illustrated in Example 1.7.

*Example 1.7.*

| Decimal | Product | Hex |
|---------|---------|-----|
| 0.3 × 16 | 4.8 | 4 |
| 0.8 × 16 | 12.8 | C |
| 0.8 × 16 | 12.8 | C |

Thus, $(0.3)_{10}$ = $(0.4 \text{ C})_{Hex}$
                          ↓
                      recurring

## 1.4 BINARY CODED DECIMAL NUMBERS

We considered in the previous sections the methods of converting decimal numbers to binary form and vice versa. There is another method of representing decimal numbers using binary digits. This method is called **binary coded decimal** (BCD) representation.

There are 10 symbols in the decimal system namely, 0, 1, ..., 9. **Encoding** is the procedure of representing each one of these 10 symbols by a unique string consisting of the two symbols of the binary system namely, 0 and 1. It is further assumed that the same number of bits are used to represent any digit. The number of symbols which could be represented using $n$ bits is $2^n$. Thus, in order to represent the 10 decimal digits we require at least four bits as three bits will allow only $2^3 = 8$ possible distinct three-bit groups.

The method of encoding decimal numbers in binary is to make up a table of 10 unique four-bit groups and allocate one four-bit group to each decimal digit as shown in Table 1.3.

**TABLE 1.3**

**Encoding Decimal Digits in Binary**

| Decimal Digit | Binary Code |
|:---:|:---:|
| 0 | 0000 |
| 1 | 0001 |
| 2 | 0010 |
| 3 | 0011 |
| 4 | 0100 |
| 5 | 0101 |
| 6 | 0110 |
| 7 | 0111 |
| 8 | 1000 |
| 9 | 1001 |

If we want to represent a decimal number, for example, 15, using the code given in Table 1.3 we look up the table and get the binary code for 1 as 0001 and that for 5 as 0101 and code 15 by the binary code 00010101.

We must at this point distinguish carefully between encoding and conversion. For example, 15 when converted to binary would be 1111. On the other hand, when it is encoded each digit must be represented by a four-bit code and an encoding is 00010101. It should be observed that encoding requires more bits compared to conversion. On the average $\log_2 10 = 3.32$ bits are required when decimal numbers are converted to binary; as compared with this 4 bits per digit are needed in encoding. The ratio $(4/3.3) = 1.2$ is a measure of the extra bits (and consequently extra storage) required if an encoding is used. On the other hand, conversion of decimal to binary is slower compared to encoding. This is due to the fact that an algorithm involving successive division is needed for conversion whereas encoding is by straightforward table look-up. The slowness of conversion is not a serious problem in computations in which the volume of input/output is small. In business computers, where input/output dominates, it is necessary to examine BCD representation. In smaller digital systems such as desk calculators, digital clocks, etc., it is uneconomical to incorporate complex electronic circuits to convert decimal to binary and vice versa. Thus, BCD representation should be considered.

We saw that we need at least 4 bits to represent a decimal digit. There are, however, 16 four-bit groups. We need only 10 of these 16 for encoding decimal digits. There are 30 billion ways we can pick an ordered sequence of 10 out of 16 items (in other words there are 16!/6! permutations of selecting 10 out of 16 items). These many codes can thus be constructed.

Fortunately, all these $3 \times 10^{10}$ possible codes are not useful. Only a small number of these are used in practice and they are chosen from the viewpoint of ease in arithmetic, some error detection property, ease in coding, and any other property useful in a given application. The useful codes may be divided broadly into four classes:

1. Weighted codes
2. Self complementing codes
3. Cyclic, Reflected or Gray codes and
4. Error detecting and correcting codes.

## 1.4.1   Weighted Codes

In a weighted code the decimal value of a code is the algebraic sum of the weights of those columns in which a 1 appears. In other words, $d = \Sigma\ w(i)b(i)$ where w(i)s are the weights and b(i)s are either 0 or 1. Three weighted codes are given in Table 1.4.

### TABLE 1.4
### Examples of Weighted Codes

| Decimal Digit | Weights | Weights* | Weights |
|:---:|:---:|:---:|:---:|
| | 8 4 2 1 | 8 4 $\overline{2}$ $\overline{1}$ | 2 4 2 1 |
| 0 | 0 0 0 0 | 0 0 0 0 | 0 0 0 0 |
| 1 | 0 0 0 1 | 0 1 1 1 | 0 0 0 1 |
| 2 | 0 0 1 0 | 0 1 1 0 | 0 0 1 0 |
| 3 | 0 0 1 1 | 0 1 0 1 | 0 0 1 1 |
| 4 | 0 1 0 0 | 0 1 0 0 | 0 1 0 0 |
| 5 | 0 1 0 1 | 1 0 1 1 | 1 0 1 1 |
| 6 | 0 1 1 0 | 1 0 1 0 | 1 1 0 0 |
| 7 | 0 1 1 1 | 1 0 0 1 | 1 1 0 1 |
| 8 | 1 0 0 0 | 1 0 0 0 | 1 1 1 0 |
| 9 | 1 0 0 1 | 1 1 1 1 | 1 1 1 1 |

*An overbar is used to indicate a negative weight ($\overline{2}$ = –2)

In a weighted code we may have negative weights. Further, the same weight may be repeated twice as in the 2, 4, 2, 1 code. The criterion in choosing weights is that we must be able to represent all the decimal digits from 0 through 9 using these weights.

The 8, 4, 2, 1 code uses the natural weights used in binary number representation. Thus, it is known as Natural Binary Coded Decimal or NBCD for short. The first 10 groups of four bits represent 0 through 9. The remaining six groups are unused and are illegal combinations. They may be used sometimes for error detection.

## 1.4.2   Self-Complementing Codes

If a code is constructed such that when we replace a 1 by a 0 and a 0 by a 1 in the four-bit code representation of a digit $d$ we obtain the code for (9-$d$), it is called a **self-**

**complementing code.** For example, the 2, 4, 2, 1 and the 8, 4, $\overline{2}, \overline{1}$ codes are self-complementing. A necessary condition for a self-complementing weighted code is that the sum of its weights would be 9. Table 1.5 depicts a self-complementing code.

**TABLE 1.5**

**A Self-Complementing Weighted Code**

| $d$ | Code for $d$<br>2 4 2 1 | Code for 9-$d$<br>2 4 2 1 | 9-$d$ |
|---|---|---|---|
| 0 | 0 0 0 0 | 1 1 1 1 | 9 |
| 1 | 0 0 0 1 | 1 1 1 0 | 8 |
| 2 | 0 0 1 0 | 1 1 0 1 | 7 |
| 3 | 0 0 1 1 | 1 1 0 0 | 6 |
| 4 | 0 1 0 0 | 1 0 1 1 | 5 |
| 5 | 1 0 1 1 | 0 1 0 0 | 4 |
| 6 | 1 1 0 0 | 0 0 1 1 | 3 |
| 7 | 1 1 0 1 | 0 0 1 0 | 2 |
| 8 | 1 1 1 0 | 0 0 0 1 | 1 |
| 9 | 1 1 1 1 | 0 0 0 0 | 0 |

## 1.4.3 Cyclic Codes

A special problem arises when we want to code a continuously varying analog signal into a digital form. An example of this would be the reading of a shaft angle of a rotating machine when it is in motion. One way of digitizing the shaft positions would be to attach a wiper with three brushes to the shaft and let this sweep a circular disc which has insulating and conducting parts to represent the binary 1 and 0. Figure 1.2 shows such a disc. If the disc is coded such that two brushes simultaneously change from conducting to non-conducting segments (or vice versa) there is a possibility (due to misalignment, wearing out of brushes, etc.) that one brush may touch the non-conducting segment earlier than the other. This would give a wrong output for a short time and may not be allowed in some situations. So a coding technique is used such that not more than one bit varies from one code to the next. Such a code is called **Gray code, cyclic code** or a **reflected code.** In a cyclic code, each code group does not differ from its neighbour in more than one bit. To formalize this concept we will define what is known as the Hamming distance after its inventor, R.W. Hamming. The **Hamming distance** between two equal length binary sequences of 1s and 0s is the number of positions in which they differ. For example, if A = 0 1 1 0 and B = 1 0 1 0, the Hamming distance between A and B is two as they differ in their first and second positions counting from the left.

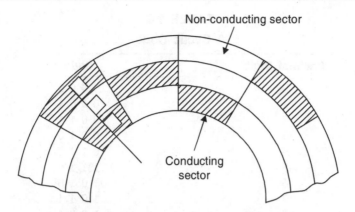

**Fig. 1.2 Digital encoding of a shaft position.**

Hamming distance between two successive code groups in a cyclic code is unity. In other words, each code group is adjacent to the next in sequence. Consider the map or grid shown in Figure 1.2. Each square in this map represents a four-bit code. For example, the square in the second row, third column represents the code 0 1 1 1. This map is coded to ensure that each square is at a unit distance from its adjacent square. Squares in the *n*th column of the top row are adjacent to those in the same column in the bottom row. For example, the fourth square in the top row is 0 0 1 0 and the fourth square in the bottom row is 1 0 1 0 and the Hamming distance between them is unity. Similarly, squares in the first column are adjacent to the squares in the last column. Thus, in this map each square has four neighbours. The four neighbours of 0 0 0 0 for example, are 0 0 0 1, 0 1 0 0, 0 0 1 0 and 1 0 0 0. This map is called **Karnaugh map** and can be used to construct a large number of cyclic codes. One such code can be constructed as shown in Figure 1.3. Start assigning the code to a decimal digit, say, 0 0 0 0, and proceed as indicated by the arrow and the mark 'o' in Figure 1.3. This gives the coding scheme shown in Table 1.6.

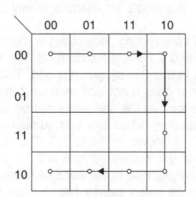

**Fig. 1.3  A Karnaugh map depicting a cyclic code.**

**TABLE 1.6**

**A Cyclic Code**

| Decimal Digit | Code |
|:---:|:---:|
| 0 | 0 0 0 0 |
| 1 | 0 0 0 1 |
| 2 | 0 0 1 1 |
| 3 | 0 0 1 0 |
| 4 | 0 1 1 0 |
| 5 | 1 1 1 0 |
| 6 | 1 0 1 0 |
| 7 | 1 0 1 1 |
| 8 | 1 0 0 1 |
| 9 | 1 0 0 0 |

## 1.4.4 Error Detecting Codes

Extremely reliable storage and transmission of data between units is required in digital computing systems. For example, storage of data in magnetic tapes is prone to error due to uneven magnetic surface, dust, etc. When data is transmitted between units in the system some bits might be corrupted due to noise. Thus, some method of detection of error in codes is commonly used in digital systems.

The main principle used in constructing error detecting codes is to use redundant bits in codes with the specific purpose of detecting errors. The method used is to ensure that the Hamming distance between any two codes in the set of codes is a pre-assigned minimum. If the minimum Hamming distance between any two codes is two, then if a single error occurs in one of the codes this can be detected because the corrupted code will be different from any of the codes allowed in the group. For example, the minimum distance between any two 5 bit codes obtained by concatenating the 4 bits of column 1 with 1 bit is column 2 in Table 1.7 is 2. If a single bit changes in any code it will be different from all other codes in this set.

One common method of constructing such codes is the introduction of an extra bit in the code. For example, suppose 0 0 1 1 is the code for 3. We may introduce a fifth bit such that the total number of ones in this five-bit group is odd. This bit is called the **parity bit.** If in a code, the total number of ones is not odd then we can conclude that it has a single error. We cannot detect two errors, as the odd parity will be satisfied with two or any even number of errors. We can, however, detect any odd number of errors. An 8, 4, 2, 1 code with an added odd parity bit is shown in Table 1.7. The reader should check that the minimum Hamming distance of this coding scheme is 2.

We may also introduce an extra bit in the code to make the total number of ones in the code even. This is called an **even parity bit.** A code with an even parity is also illustrated in Table 1.7.

Parity checking codes, as these are called, have found widespread application, because checking can be easily mechanized by them.

**TABLE 1.7**

**Illustrating Codes with Odd and Even Parity**

|   | 8 4 2 1<br>Code | Odd<br>Parity Bit | Non-Weighted<br>Code | Even<br>Parity Bit |
|---|---|---|---|---|
| 0 | 0 0 0 0 | 1 | 1 1 0 0 | 0 |
| 1 | 0 0 0 1 | 0 | 0 0 0 1 | 1 |
| 2 | 0 0 1 0 | 0 | 0 0 1 0 | 1 |
| 3 | 0 0 1 1 | 1 | 0 0 1 1 | 0 |
| 4 | 0 1 0 0 | 0 | 0 1 0 0 | 1 |
| 5 | 0 1 0 1 | 1 | 0 1 0 1 | 0 |
| 6 | 0 1 1 0 | 1 | 0 1 1 0 | 0 |
| 7 | 0 1 1 1 | 0 | 1 0 0 0 | 1 |
| 8 | 1 0 0 0 | 0 | 1 0 0 1 | 0 |
| 9 | 1 0 0 1 | 1 | 1 0 1 0 | 0 |

## 1.4.5   Error Correcting Codes

Coding schemes may be devised which not only detect errors, but also automatically correct them. Consider, for example, 36 bits recorded on a magnetic tape in six tracks with six bits along each track. Suppose an extra code group is recorded on a seventh track and it is devised to give an odd parity on the columns. Further, suppose that each code word has a seventh bit added as an odd parity bit. If any bit in the group is erroneously transmitted, it will cause simultaneous failure of parity on a row and a column. The row and the column automatically fix the position of the erroneous bit and thus it can be corrected. Table 1.8 illustrates this.

**TABLE 1.8**

**Illustrating an Error Correcting Code**

| | Sent Data | Row Parity<br>Bits | Received<br>Data | |
|---|---|---|---|---|
| | 0 0 0 0 0 0 | 1 | 0 0 0 0 0 0 | 1 |
| | 0 0 0 0 1 0 | 0 | 0 0 0 0 1 0 | 0 |
| | 0 0 1 1 0 0 | 1 | 0 0 1 0 0 0 | 1 ← Parity failure |
| | 0 0 0 1 1 0 | 1 | 0 0 0 1 1 0 | 1 |
| | 0 1 0 0 1 0 | 1 | 0 1 0 0 1 0 | 1 |
| | 0 1 0 0 0 0 | 0 | 0 1 0 0 0 0 | 0 |
| Column →<br>parity bits | 1 1 0 1 0 1 | | 1 1 0 1 0 1<br>↓<br>Parity failure | |

## 1.5  HAMMING CODE FOR ERROR CORRECTION

In the last section we saw that by adding a single parity bit to a code we can detect a single error in the code. The error detection is possible as the addition of the parity bit creates a minimum Hamming distance of two between any two codes. Thus, a single error will not map a code into any one of the other legitimate codes in the group. Hamming showed that by systematically introducing more parity bits in the code it is not only possible to detect an error, but also find out where the error occurred and correct it. More than one error can also be detected and corrected by increasing the code length with more parity bits and thereby, increasing the minimum Hamming distance between codes.

We will now examine how a Hamming code to detect and correct one error can be constructed. Suppose we want to add parity bits to 8, 4, 2, 1 code to make it a single error correction code. In order to correct a single error we should know where the error occurred in the composite code, including the parity bits. With four data bits we need at least three parity bits, so that the parity bits can be used to find out the error position in the seven-bit code. The code is constructed as follows: The individual bits in the seven-bit code are numbered from 1 to 7 as shown in Table 1.9. Bit positions 1, 2 and 4 are used as parity check bits and bits 3, 5, 6, 7 as data bits. The bit at position 1 is set so that it satisfies an even parity for bits 1, 3, 5, 7. Bit 2 is set to satisfy an even parity on bits 2, 3, 6, 7. Bit 4 is set so that it satisfies an even parity on bits 4, 5, 6, 7.

### TABLE 1.9
### A Single Error Correcting Hamming Code
### ($D_i$: Data bits. $P_i$: Parity bits)

| 1 | 2 | 3 | 4 | 5 | 6 | 7 | ←——— bit position |
|---|---|---|---|---|---|---|---|
| $P_1$ | $P_2$ | $D_3$ | $P_4$ | $D_5$ | $D_6$ | $D_7$ | |
| 0 | 0 | 0 | 0 | 0 | 0 | 0 | |
| 1 | 1 | 0 | 1 | 0 | 0 | 1 | |
| 0 | 1 | 0 | 1 | 0 | 1 | 0 | |
| 1 | 0 | 0 | 0 | 0 | 1 | 1 | |
| 1 | 0 | 0 | 1 | 1 | 0 | 0 | |
| 0 | 1 | 0 | 0 | 1 | 0 | 1 | |
| 1 | 1 | 0 | 0 | 1 | 1 | 0 | |
| 0 | 0 | 0 | 1 | 1 | 1 | 1 | |
| 1 | 1 | 1 | 0 | 0 | 0 | 0 | |
| 0 | 0 | 1 | 1 | 0 | 0 | 1 | |

When a code is received the following procedure is used to detect and correct the error:

1. Check even parity on positions 1, 3, 5, 7. If it passes, then $C_1 = 0$ else $C_1 = 1$.

2. Check even parity on positions 2, 3, 6, 7. If it passes, then $C_2 = 0$ else $C_2 = 1$.

3. Check even parity on positions 4, 5, 6, 7. If it passes, then $C_4 = 0$ else $C_4 = 1$.

4. The decimal equivalent of $C_4C_2C_1$ gives the position of the incorrect bit and that bit is corrected. If $C_4C_2C_1 = 0$ then there is no error in the code.

*Example 1.8.*    Suppose the following code is received:

```
0 1 1 0 1 1 0                               Received code
1 2 3 4 5 6 7                               Bit positions
```

Even parity in positions 1, 3, 5, 7 passes. Thus, $C_1 = 0$
Even parity in positions 2, 3, 6, 7 fails. Thus, $C_2 = 1$
Even parity in positions 4, 5, 6, 7 passes. Thus, $C_4 = 0$
The position of the error is thus $C_4C_2C_1 = 010 = 2$.
The correct code is thus:

$$0\ 0\ 1\ 0\ 1\ 1\ 0$$

The bit positions, which are checked by the individual parity bits, may be derived by observing that the decimal equivalent of $C_4C_2C_1$ should specify the position of the error in the code. Thus, by examining Table 1.10 we see that $C_1$ will be 1 whenever bits 1, 3, 5, or 7 is wrong. Similarly, $C_2$ will be 1 whenever 2, 3, 6 or 7 is incorrect and $C_4$ will be 1 whenever 4, 5, 6, or 7 is incorrect. Thus, these bits are used as check bits for the corresponding group of bits.

### TABLE 1.10
#### Illustrating Check bit Construction in Hamming Code

| Error in bit number | $C_4$ | $C_2$ | $C_1 \longleftarrow$ Check bits |
|---|---|---|---|
| No error | 0 | 0 | 0 |
| 1 | 0 | 0 | 1 |
| 2 | 0 | 1 | 0 |
| 3 | 0 | 1 | 1 |
| 4 | 1 | 0 | 0 |
| 5 | 1 | 0 | 1 |
| 6 | 1 | 1 | 0 |
| 7 | 1 | 1 | 1 |
| | ↓ | ↓ | └─→ Check on bits 1, 3, 5, 7 |
| | Check on bits 4, 5, 6, 7 | Check on bits 2, 3, 6, 7 | |

Observe that the method of construction of the Hamming code illustrated above ensures that there is a minimum distance of three between any two codes in the group. Thus, if two errors occur it can be detected as parity or parities will fail. The error cannot, however, be corrected. Only a single error can be detected and corrected.

In general, if a code group has a minimum distance of $L$ then the following inequality holds:

$$(C + D) \leq (L - 1)$$

where $D$ is the number of errors detected and $C$ is the number of errors corrected. (Remember that an error cannot be corrected unless it is first detected!) Thus, a distance of four code can correct at most one error and detect two errors.

The number of parity bits $k$ required to detect and/or correct errors in codes with $i$ data bits is given by the inequality

$$(2^k - 1) \geq (i + k)$$

As the $k$ parity bits must give the position of the error, the maximum decimal number which can be represented by $k$ bits should at least equal the total length of the code namely, the sum of data bits and check bits.

It should be remembered that Hamming codes are designed to guard against errors occurring at random positions in the code. Very often, while data is transmitted between different points, a burst of errors occur due to reasons such as voltage fluctuation, lightning, etc. Errors in reading from tapes and discs may also often have bursts of error due to dust particles, etc. Special coding methods for burst error correction are needed in such cases, but that is not discussed in this book.

## 1.6 ALPHANUMERIC CODES

In the previous sections we saw how numerical data is represented in computers. This is the simplest data type. Historically, it was the first type of data processed by digital computers. The versatility of modern computers arises due to its ability to process a variety of data types.

Types of data may be classified as shown in Figure 1.4.

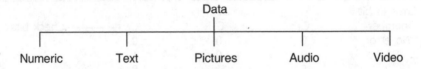

**Fig. 1.4 Types of data.**

**Textual data** consists of alphabets, special characters and numbers when not used in calculations (e.g., Telephone number).

**Picture data** are line drawings, photographs (both monochrome and colours), hand-written data, fingerprints, medical images, etc. They are two dimensional and time invariant.

**Audio data** are sound waves such as speech and music. They are continuous and time varying signals.

**Video data** are moving pictures such as that taken by movie cameras. They are actually a sequence of moving pictures. Like audio, video data is also time varying. In this section we will describe the representation of textual data. We will describe other data types and their representation in the next section.

As stated, textual data consists of alphabets and special characters besides decimal numbers. These are normally the 26 English letters, the 10 decimal digits and several special characters such as +, −, ×, /, $, etc. In order to code these with binary numbers one needs a string of binary digits. In the older computers the total number of characters was less than 64 and a string of six bits was used to code a character. In all current machines the number of characters has increased. Besides capital letters of the alphabet, the lower case letters are also used and several mathematical symbols such as >, <, ≥, etc., have been introduced. This has made the six-bit byte inadequate to code all characters. New coding schemes use seven or eight bits to code a character. With seven bits we can code 128 characters, which is quite adequate. In order to ensure uniformity in coding characters, a standard seven bit code, ASCII (American Standard Code of Information Interchange) has been evolved.

## 1.6.1 ASCII Code

The ASCII code is used to code two types of data. One type is the **printable characters** such as digits, letters and special characters. The other set is known as **control characters,** which represent coded data to control the operation of digital computers and are not printed. The ASCII code (in Hexadecimal) is given as Table 1.11.

### TABLE 1.11
### ASCII Code for Characters
### (Most significant hex digit)

| Hex | 0 | 1 | 2 | 3 | 4 | 5 | 6 | 7 |
|-----|-----|-----|-----|-----|-----|-----|-----|-----|
| 0 | NUL | DLE | SP | 0 | @ | P | ` | p |
| 1 | SOH | DC1 | ! | 1 | A | Q | a | q |
| 2 | STX | DC2 | " | 2 | B | R | b | r |
| 3 | ETX | DC3 | # | 3 | C | S | c | s |
| 4 | EOT | DC4 | $ | 4 | D | T | d | t |
| 5 | ENQ | NAK | % | 5 | E | U | e | u |
| 6 | ACK | SYN | & | 6 | F | V | f | v |
| 7 | BEL | ETB | ` | 7 | G | W | g | w |
| 8 | BS | CAN | ( | 8 | H | X | h | x |
| 9 | HT | EM | ) | 9 | I | Y | i | y |
| A | LF | SUB | * | : | J | Z | j | z |
| B | VT | ESC | + | ; | K | [ | k | { |
| C | FF | FS | , | < | L | \ | l | | |
| D | CR | GS | - | = | M | ] | m | } |
| E | SO | RS | . | > | N | ^ | n | ~ |
| F | SI | US | / | ? | O | – | o | DEL |

It may be observed from Table 1.11 that the codes for the English letters are in the same sequence as their lexical order, that is, the order in which they appear in a dictionary. The hexadecimal codes of A, B, C, ... Z, in ASCII are respectively 41, 42, 43, 44, 45, ..., 5A. This choice of codes is useful for alphabetical sorting, searching, etc.

A parity bit may be added to the seven-bit ASCII character code to yield an eight-bit code. A group of eight bits is known as a **byte.** A byte would be sufficient to represent a character or to represent two binary coded decimal digits. An abbreviation B is universally used for bytes. We will henceforth use B for byte.

It is possible to add redundant bits to a seven-bit ASCII code to make an error correcting code. At least four check bits are required to detect and correct a single error. The construction of Hamming codes for characters is left as an exercise to the reader.

### 1.6.2 Indian Script Code for Information Interchange (ISCII)

ASCII has been standardized for English letters. It is necessary to have a standard coding scheme for the Indian scripts to use computers to process information using Indian languages. This has been done by the Indian Standard Organization, who have published a document IS: 13194-91 on this. This standard conforms to International Standard ISO 2022: 1982 entitled "7-bit and 8-bit coded character set code extension technique". The Indian Standard maintains the seven-bit code for English letters exactly as in ASCII and allows eight-bit codes extensions for other scripts. Thus, English can co-exist with Indian scripts.

The approach followed in the Indian Standard is to have a common code and keyboard for all the Indian scripts. The standard English keyboard of terminals is maintained for English. An overlay is designed on this keyboard for Indian scripts. An optimal keyboard overlay for all Indian scripts has been designed keeping in view the phonetic nature of Indian languages.

In Table 1.11 we see that ASCII code starts with 00 and is specified up to 7F hexadecimal. The extension for Indian scripts starts from hexadecimal A1 and extends up to hexadecimal FA. The code is given in Table 1.12. More details regarding the code and the standard used in keyboard layout may be obtained from reference given at the end of the book [See 14].

**TABLE 1.12**
**ISCII Code for Devnagari Characters**
**(Most significant hex digit)**

| Hex | A | B | C | D | E | F |
|-----|-----|-----|-----|-----|-----|-----|
| 0 |  | ओ | ढ | .र | ॕ | EXT |
| 1 | = | औ | ण | ल | ॓ | ० |
| 2 | — | ऑ | त | ळ | ॔ | १ |
| 3 | ा | क | थ | ऴ | ॖ | २ |
| 4 | अ | ख | द | व | ंॅ | ३ |
| 5 | आ | ग | ध | श | ाॅ | ४ |
| 6 | इ | घ | न | ष | ाॅ | ५ |
| 7 | ई | ड़ | ऩ | स | ाॅ | ६ |
| 8 | उ | च | प | ह | ॒ | ७ |
| 9 | ऊ | छ | फ | INV | ि | ८ |
| A | ऋ | ज | ब | ी | | ९ |
| B | ऍ | झ | भ | ी | | |
| C | ए | ञ | म | ी | | |
| D | ऐ | ट | य | ृ | | |
| E | ऑ | ठ | य | ॖ | | |
| F | ओ | ड | र | ॗ | ATR | |

Recently, a new coding scheme for characters called **Unicode** has been standardized specifically to accommodate a large number of symbols of languages other than English and mathematical symbols such as ⇒ . It uses 16 bits (two bytes) for each character. As $2^{16}$ = 65536, the number of different types of characters which can be coded in Unicode is enormous. Thus, virtually every character of every language in the world can be represented in this international standard code. The first 128 codes of Unicode are identical to ASCII. It is thus compatible with ASCII. Details of Unicode may be obtained from the website www.standard.com/unicode.htm.

## 1.7 REPRESENTATION OF MULTIMEDIA DATA

As we pointed out earlier, computers nowadays are used not only to process numerical and character data, but also pictures, audio and video data. All data are internally represented as binary strings. We thus have to convert pictures, audio and video data into equivalent string of bits without losing the information contained in them. Of these three data types, pictures are static, that is, time is not a variable. Audio and video, however, vary with time, that is, time is an important independent variable. We will first examine how pictures (also known as images) are represented as binary strings.

### 1.7.1 Representation of Pictures

Pictures are static and two dimensional. There are two types of pictures, monochrome and colour. In both cases, to represent a picture as a binary string we assume the picture to be overlaid on a graph sheet (see Figure 1.5). Each $(x, y)$ coordinate of the graph sheet is called a **pixel** (or pel), an abbreviation for a picture element. If a picture is black in an $(x, y)$ coordinate it is represented by a 1, and if it is white it is represented by 0. Referring to Figure 1.5, the picture (a) is represented by a grid of 0s and 1s as shown in part (b). In this example, there are 100 $(x, y)$ coordinates and thus, 100 pixels are used to represent it. In practice, $(10 \times 10)$ is too small for a faithful representation of figures. For example, $(640 \times 480)$ is the grid size used to represent pixels on a VDU screen. The larger the number of pixels, the better is the resolution of the picture.

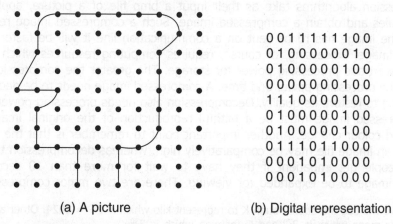

(a) A picture                 (b) Digital representation

**Fig. 1.5   A picture and its digital representation.**

In this example, we have assumed that the picture is black and white, e.g., a line drawing. In practice, monochrome pictures have several tones of grey. Thus, pictures such as a monochrome, X-ray films, etc. use several bits per pixel.

If eight bits are used per pixel then it can represent $2^8 = 256$ grey tones, which is quite adequate for human perception. Thus, $(640 \times 480)$ bytes $= 300$ KB* are needed to represent monochrome picture on a VDU screen. Nowadays colour pictures are more common. All VDUs are colour VDUs. Digital cameras take colour pictures.

Colour pictures are created by adding different proportions of the three primary colours— Red, Green and Blue (called RGB). Colour is usually represented by using eight bits per each primary colour. The number of bits used for each colour determines its intensity. Thus, if we use eight bits to represent Red, $2^8 = 256$ different intensities of red are seen. If eight bits each is used for R, G and B, then different intensity combinations of each colour will be seen as a different colour. For example, high intensity of blue and lower intensity of green and red will be seen as violet. With 256 intensity levels for each colour, a total of $256 \times 256 \times 256$, which is nearly 16 million colours, can be represented. Currently, the standard used in VDU screens and digital cameras is to allocate eight bits for colour. Thus, a $640 \times 480$ pixel colour picture will require $640 \times 480 \times 3$ bytes $= 900$ KB storage.

*Example 1.9.* A postcard size colour photo is 12 cm $\times$ 8 cm. A good photo quality resolution will require $(240 \times 480)$ pixels per sq. cm. If each pixel is represented by three bytes what is the storage needed for a postcard size colour picture?

*Solution.* Storage needed is: $240 \times 480 \times 12 \times 8 \times 3$ bytes $= 31.64$ MB.

This representation of pictures is called **bit map**, abbreviated as **bmp.** If a single picture takes 31.64 MB to store in bmp format, an album of 100 photos will need 316.4 MB – a huge memory. Thus, in practice bmp file is compressed to reduce storage requirements. The two general principles used to compress image files are:

(i) *Redundancy:* In an image, neighbouring pixels are highly correlated. Given a pixel, it is easy to guess its neighbours.

(ii) *Irrelevancy:* Our eyes cannot distinguish a million colours. They also extrapolate neighbouring pixels.

Compression algorithms take as their input a bmp file of a picture, apply a set of processing rules and obtain a compressed image. Such a compressed image requires less storage. If the image has to be sent on a communication line it will be faster to send a compressed image. Processing, of course, requires computing resources which also takes time. Thus, we trade processing power for storage. The greater the compression needed, the more is the processing power and time. A compressed image needs to be decompressed before viewing to restore its quality. Decompression also needs processing power and time. The decompressed image must be a faithful reproduction of the original image without distortion and colour change. Another important point to remember is that the time taken to compress an image file may be comparatively high, whereas decompression time should be small; people get impatient if they have to wait for more than 10 seconds for a compressed image to be expanded for viewing. There are two major compressed picture

---

*Henceforth we will use the abbreviation K to represent kilo which is $2^{10} = 1024$. Other abbreviations used are M for mega which is $2^{20}$ and G for giga which is $2^{30}$.

file formats known as **gif** (graphical image format) and **jpeg** (Joint Photographic Experts Group format). gif file attains a compression of 1:10. In jpeg we can trade compression ratio for quality. For moderate quality image a 1:64 compression ratio is obtained and for a good quality 1:20 compression is attained. Details of compression algorithms is outside the scope of this book. Hence, one may refer to the reference [22] given at the end of this chapter.

## 1.7.2 Respresentation of Video

A video consists of a succession of still pictures projected at intervals of less than (1/30) second. Due to persistence of our vision we have the illusion of seeing a moving picture with continuous movement of subjects in the picture. Each 640 × 480 pixel picture requires, if in bmp format (i.e., uncompressed and in colour), 900 KB storage. Thus, the storage needed to store 1 second video is 30 × 900 KB = 26.36 MB. If a 2-hour video is to be stored, it will need 2 × 60 × 60 × 26.36 MB = 185.4 GB. This is large storage and it is not possible to store it in a secondary storage device such as VCD or DVD. (We will discuss VCDs and DVDs later.) It is suffice to say that VCD can store about 600 MB and DVD about 7 GB. It is thus needed to compress a video if it is to be stored for use.

To begin with, we have to compress each still picture in the sequence of pictures. The preferred compression is jpeg, which reduces the size of a bmp file by about 20. If only jpeg compression is used we will still need 9.27 GB to store a two hour movie. Even this is impractical. Thus, further compression is needed. Such a compression is achieved by remembering that a video consists of a succession of pictures. The interval between successive pictures is only (1/30) second. This is exploited in compressing video. For example, in a scene where a bus is going on a road, most of the background such as the sky, hills, etc., will not change; only a small part of the video corresponding to the moving bus will change from frame to frame. Thus, only the changing part needs to be stored. If the bus occupies (1/8)$^{th}$ of the picture area then we need to store only (1/8)$^{th}$ of the picture. The rest can be ignored. Thus, only the first picture and changes in subsequent pictures need to be stored.

This is the main principle used in a compression algorithm standardized by an international committee known as the **Motion Picture Experts Group** (abbreviated MPEG). This algorithm works as follows:

A jpeg compressed picture is used to begin the process. This is called the **I-Picture or intracoded picture.** It is the key picture which is used to compress subsequent pictures in the group. A group of pictures **(GOP)** consists of 12 to 20 pictures. This GOP is kept in temporary storage. I-picture is divided into tiles of 16 × 16 pixels and is primarily used to index and retrieve subsequent pictures from the GOP (see Figure 1.6). Corresponding tiles in the next picture and the difference in pixel values of these tiles are calculated. For most of the tiles this difference will be very small, as the background such as sky or hills remain unchanged. Only a small part of the picture will be different. The difference will be two or four bits instead of 24 bits per pixel. This is a reduction by a factor of 12. When the difference in pixel values change substantially between successive pictures, it implies that there is a significant change in the scene. When this happens, this picture is taken as a new I-picture and the process is started again. What we have said so far is a very simplified explanation. The actual MPEG compression algorithm uses this idea, known as **motion prediction,** to account for change of position of moving objects. If jpeg compression is used for I-pictures and motion compression for a group of pictures, a reduction between 100 to 150 in bits, which is needed to store a video, is achieved. This is, in brief, the idea in MPEG compression. Thus, a two hour video will require approximately 1.8 GB storage. This is feasible as DVDs store over 7 GB.

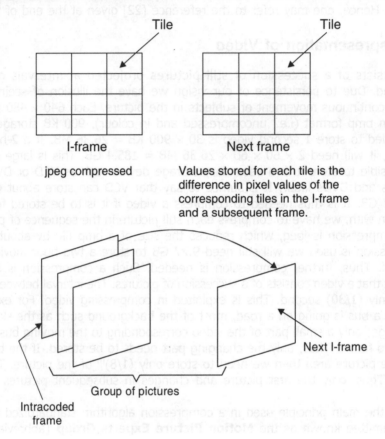

Tile                                    Tile

I-frame                                Next frame

jpeg compressed

Values stored for each tile is the
difference in pixel values of the
corresponding tiles in the I-frame
and a subsequent frame.

Next I-frame

Group of pictures

Intracoded
frame

**Fig. 1.6   MPEG compression principles.**

We saw that jpeg allows trade-off between the quality of the picture and the amount of compression. As MPEG uses jpeg it also allows variable compression.

The compression method we have discussed so far is called MPEG-1. This standard is for TV quality video with 640 × 480 pixels resolution. A standard called MPEG-2 supports high definition TV (HDTV) which provides 16:9 aspect ratio and 60 frames/second. MPEG-4 addresses the problem of transmitting video on low quality telephone lines. It is used in video conferencing. MPEG-10 is on the horizon for transmitting video on wireless infrastructure such as cell phones and wireless LANs.

## 1.7.3   Representation of Audio

Audio signals are continuous waveforms with time as the independent variable and amplitude of the signal as the dependent variable (see Figure 1.7). They are analog signals. If they are to be represented in digital form we should take samples of the signal at regular intervals. Each sample will have a value. For example, in Figure 1.7 the analog signal has been sampled every s seconds. The amplitudes of the samples are shown in Figure 1.8.

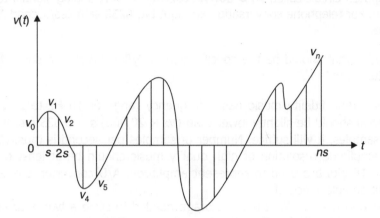

**Fig. 1.7  An analog signal.**

Two questions to be answered to digitally represent the analog signal are:

1.  How often should samples be taken? In other words, what should be the intervals between samples?
2.  How many bits should be used to represent the amplitude?

The first question is answered by a theorem called **Nyquist's sampling theorem.** It states that if $f_h$ is the highest frequency present in the signal, the sampling internal should be slightly lower than ($1/2 f_h$). Using this sampling will guarantee that all the information in the audio is preserved.

| Time    | 0     | s     | 2s    | 3s    | 4s    | 5s    | . . . | ns    |
|---------|-------|-------|-------|-------|-------|-------|-------|-------|
| Voltage | $v_0$ | $v_1$ | $v_2$ | $v_3$ | $v_4$ | $v_5$ | . . . | $v_n$ |

**Fig. 1.8  Digital values representing the analog signal of Fig. 1.7.**

*Example 1.10.*   Find the sampling interval to be used for representing telephone conversations.

*Solution.*   The highest frequency of normal human conversation is 3000 Hz. Thus, the sampling interval should be slightly lower than ($1/2 \times 3000$) s = 0.1667 ms. If we use 0.16 ms between samples it will suffice. Number of samples per second is thus, (1000/0.16) = 6250.

The second question is how many bits we should use to represent the amplitude. The number of bits depends upon the range of amplitudes and the smallest amplitude difference that we need to distinguish. If we use eight bits, we can represent 256 levels. If the amplitude is 5 V, the difference between two levels will be 5/256 ≈ 0.02 V. This is quite appropriate for human conversation. Thus, for telephone conversation eight bits are adequate.

An integrated circuit called **A/D convertor** will convert analog signals to their digital representation. For telephone conversation an eight bit, 6250 samples/second A/D convertor is appropriate.

*Example 1.11.*    What should be the specification of A/D convertor to convert high fidelity music to digital form?

*Solution.*    High fidelity music has a frequency range of 10 Hz to 20,000 Hz. Thus sampling interval should be slightly lower than (½ × 20,000) s = 0.025 ms. If we use 0.02 ms between samples, it will suffice. Number of samples per second is thus, (1000/0.02) = 50,000. The amplitude resolution of high quality music should be at least double that of speech. Thus, 16 bits are used to represent amplitude. A/D convertor is one which takes 50,000, 16 bit samples/second.

The next question is: What is the storage needed to store a two hour concert? It is: (50,000 × 2 × 2 × 60 × 60 ) = 700 MB. Normally, a CDROM will store about 500 MB. Thus, two CDs will be needed.

Just as in video, audio files are compressed before storage to save storage space. The compression standard is called **MP3,** the short form for MPEG–Version 2–Layer 3 audio compression standard, which is an international standard. This compression algorithm uses the fact that human ears hear the louder sound rather than softer ones. Further, in any audio signal there are periods when the frequency is low. During these periods the number of samples can be reduced. Using these facts MP3 algorithm reduces the number of samples and the storage requirement by a factor of 10 to 14. Thus, two hour high fidelity music may be stored in about 60 MB storage. An audio CD which normally stores 60 minutes of high fidelity music can now be used to store 720 minutes of music in MP3 format. This is an enormous amount of music. Audio music players are now available in the market which can accept music CDs stored in MP3 format, expand it and play it with high fidelity.

## SUMMARY

1. In a digital system all data is represented by a string of 0s and 1s called bits (binary digits).

2. Binary representation is used because electronic circuits perform most reliably when processing data in one out of two distinct states. Most physical devices available today to store data do so by being in either one of the two stable states.

3. A number: $a_n\ a_{n-1},\ a_{n-2} \dots a_1\ a_0,\ a_{-1}\ a_{-2} \dots a_{-m}$ in a positional number system is interpreted as: $a_n r^n + a_{n-1}\ r^{n-1} \dots a_1 r + a_0 r^0 + a_{-1} r^{-1} + a_{-2}\ r^{-2} + \dots + a_{-m} r^{-m}$ where $r$ is called the radix of the system and $a_0, a_1$, etc. are symbols chosen from a set of $r$ symbols (0, 1, 2, ..., $r - 1$). For decimal system the radix $r$ is 10 and the symbols are 0, 1, 2, ..., 9.

4. In binary number system, radix *r* is 2 and the symbols are 0 and 1.

5. In hexadecimal number system the radix *r* is 16 and the symbols are 0, 1, 2, ..., 9, A, B, C, D, E, F.

6. A decimal integer is converted to its binary equivalent by dividing it and successive quotients by 2 until the last quotient is 0. The first remainder is the least significant bit of the binary equivalent and the last remainder is the most significant bit.

7. Conversion of decimal integer to hexadecimal is similar but instead of dividing by 2, we divide by 16.

8. A decimal fraction is converted to its binary equivalent by multiplying it by 2. The integer part of first product is the most significant bit of the binary fraction. A terminating decimal function need not have a terminating binary fractional equivalent.

9. Conversion of decimal fraction to hexadecimal is done by multiplying the fraction with 16 instead of 2.

10. A decimal number is coded to its binary equivalent by picking 10 out of 16, four bit strings to code each digit.

11. The four important codes are: weighted codes, self-complementing codes, cyclic codes and error detecting/correcting codes.

12. In weighted codes each bit position has a weight. If the weights are 8, 4, 2 and 1, it is called Natural Binary Coded Decimal Digits.

13. In self-complementing codes, the code of (9-*d*) (where *d* is a decimal digit) is obtained by complementing each bit of the code for *d*.

14. The Hamming distance between two binary codes is the number of corresponding bits in which they differ. For example, the distance between 01010 and 11001 is $1 + 0 + 0 + 1 + 1 = 3$.

15. In cyclic codes, the distance between successive codes is exactly 1.

16. An even/odd parity bit is a bit appended to a code group to make the total number of 1s in the code even/odd. For example, even parity bit to be appended to code 01000 is 1 and the code with even parity is 010001.

17. Appending a parity bit to group of codes makes the distance between the codes at least 2. A single error in any of the codes can be detected if parity fails.

18. Hamming codes are used to not only detect, but also to correct errors. The number of bits *k* required to detect/correct errors in codes with *i* data bits is given by the inequality $(2^k - 1) \geq (i + k)$. The bits in each code group is $i + k$.

19. English characters A, B, C, ..., Z (both upper and lower case), numbers and special symbols such as @, +, etc., are represented by a standard code called ASCII (American Standard Code for Information Interchange). Each code consists of seven bits. Besides printable characters mentioned above, ASCII also has codes for non-printable control characters such as enter, escape, etc., found in a standard keyboard.

20. ASCII characters with an added parity bit gives eight bits and is called a byte.

21. Characters of Indian languages are coded using a code called ISCII (Indian Standard Code for Information Interchange). It is an eight bit code and maintains the seven bit code for English letters and other characters exactly as in ASCII.

22. Recently, a new coding scheme called Unicode has been standardized specifically to accommodate many languages such as Chinese, Japanese and many special characters such as symbol $\Rightarrow$ used in mathematics. ASCII is a subset of Unicode.

23. Besides processing numbers and characters, computers are now also used to process picture, audio and video data. It is thus necessary to code these data types also.

24. Pictures are represented by a two-dimensional grid of picture elements called pixels. Higher the resolution needed, finer the grid becomes and pixels increase. Eight bits per pixel are used for monochrome pictures. $2^8 = 256$ shades of grey can be represented with eight bits. All 0s represent black and all 1s represent white.

25. Colour pictures use 24 bits/pixels, eight bits each for each of the primary colours red, green and blue. Intensity of each colour is coded using these eight bits. Intensity variation of each colour leads to a large number of colours, such as violet, indigo, brown, etc.

26. As the number of bits needed to represent one (1024 × 1024) pixel picture is 3 MB, there is a need to compress the data. Different compression formats such as gif and jpeg have been standardized.

27. A video is a succession of pictures repeated every (1/30) second. Each picture is coded using the methods presented in the last three summary points.

28. If still pictures are compressed using jpeg compression, a two hour video will need approximately 9 GB of storage. Since this is very large, this is further compressed using the fact that the difference between successive frames in a video is not large. A set of compression algorithms called MPEG-1, MPEG-2, etc., have been standardized for compressing video for various applications.

29. Audio data is a function of time (called a waveform) represented by $a(t)$ where $a$ is the amplitude and $t$ the time. To represent audio using bits the waveform has to be sampled at regular intervals, and each sample represented by a bit string has to be proportional to its amplitude at the sampling time.

30. The number of samples should be slightly greater than $1/(2f_h)$, where $f_h$ is the highest frequency of the audio signal. The number of bits used to represent the amplitude depends on the resolution required for the application. For high quality audio 16 bits are used for amplitude and 50,000 samples are taken per second. For one-hour audio recording 350 MB of store is needed, which is very high.

31. To reduce the number of bits needed to represent audio, a compression algorithm called MP3 has been standardized. It reduces the storage needed by a factor of 10 to 14.

## EXERCISES

1. Convert the following decimal numbers to binary:
   (a) 49.32
   (b) 0.83
   (c) 94.00625

2. Convert the following binary numbers to decimal and octal forms:
   (a) 101101110
   (b) 11011.0101
   (c) 1.011101

3. Convert the following decimal numbers to base three and to base five:
   (a) 73
   (b) 10.333
   (c) 21.25

4. Convert the following binary numbers to their equivalent decimal and hexadecimal (base 16) representation:
   (a) 101101.0101
   (b) 1010.0111
   (c) 10.01

5. Obtain an algorithm to find all allowable weights for a weighted BCD code. Assume that all weights are positive integers. Use the algorithm to obtain all such sets of weights. (Observe that sets of weights such as 4, 3, 1, 1 and 3, 4, 1, 1 should be taken to be one set of weights.)

6. Obtain an algorithm to find all allowable weights for a weighted self-complementing BCD code. The weights may be positive or negative. Use the algorithm to obtain all such sets of weights. (Permutations of weights should not be taken to be distinct.)

7. Code base five numbers in a cyclic code.

8. Using a Karnaugh map construct a cyclic code for decimal digits such that the total number of 1s in the code is minimum.

9. Base four numbers are coded by the following codes. What is the minimum distance of this code group?

   000, 101, 011, 110

   How many errors can be detected if the coding scheme is used? How many errors may be corrected?

10. Estimate the number of words in a printed page and determine the number of bits required to encode the information in ASCII.

11. There are four types of nucleotides named A, C, G and T. A DNA molecule is made up of a linear sequence of any four nucleotides picked from this group. How many bits of information can be stored in a DNA molecule?

12. Decode the following ASCII text:

    | 1000010 | 1001100 | 1001100 | 1001001 | 1010011 |
    |---------|---------|---------|---------|---------|
    | 1010111 | 1000101 | 1001100 | 1001100 |         |

13. Device a single error correcting code for ASCII coded characters.

14. Obtain an algorithm to detect and correct single errors in Hamming coded ASCII characters.

15. Device a single error correcting Hamming code for decimal numbers represented in 8421 code.

16. How many parity bits are required for a double error correcting code for ASCII characters?

17. Decode the following ISCII coded text (in Hex) in Hindi:

   D0 A5 BA A5 D0 A5 CC A4 C6

18. Device a single error correcting code for ISCII coded characters.

19. What are the major differences between ASCII and Unicode. What are the advantages and disadvantages of using Unicode instead of ASCII?

20. You have an old photo album with 500 black and white photos of size 6 cm × 4 cm. You want to digitize and store them in a digital store. Assume (240 × 120) pixels resolution/cm². Find out how much storage is needed if the photos are stored in an uncompressed bit map form. What is the storage needed for gif file of these photos.

21. Repeat Exercise 20 for colour pictures. Find storage for moderate quality jpeg file of these pictures.

22. If colour pictures are stored using 12 bits per pixel, how many colours does this represent? If these colour pictures are stored with (200 × 100) pixel/cm² resolution, how much storage is needed to store 100 colour pictures of (10 cm × 10 cm)?

23. Colour moving pictures are to be displayed on a VDU screen with (1280 × 960) pixel. How much storage is needed to store a 90 minute video pictures in an uncompressed form. If the movie is stored using MPEG-4 compression, how much storage is needed?

24. What is an I-picture used in video compression? What are the main requirements for a picture to be classified as an I-picture?

25. Repeat Exercise 23 for MPEG compressed movie of 90 minutes duration.

26. Distinguish between pictures and audio.

27. Why should one digitize an analog audio signal to digital form? Assume that the highest frequency of an audio signal to be converted to digital form is 5000 Hz. How many samples must be taken per second? If amplitude resolution required is 0.5 per cent of the maximum amplitude, how many bits should be used to represent the amplitude? If 90 minutes of this digitized signal is to be stored, how much storage is needed? If it is compressed in MP3, how much storage is needed?

28. What is MP3 compression? Why is MP3 compression used? What principles are used in MP3 to compress audio signals?

29. A student tapes 10 lectures, each of 50 minutes duration, given by his Professor. He digitizes the tapes and stores them in MP3 compressed form on his hard disk. How much storage will it occupy?

# 2

# Boolean Algebra and Logic Gates

## 2.1 INTRODUCTION

In the last chapter we discussed how numbers may be represented in a binary form and in a binary coded decimal form in order to process them in digital systems. We also saw why binary system is used to represent data in digital computers. We need an appropriate tool to model operations using binary representation. For this purpose, Switching Algebra, which is a subset of a more general algebra known as Boolean Algebra, has been found most suitable. We will introduce Boolean algebra in this chapter and see how operations of this algebra can be realized by electronic circuits.

*Example 2.1.* Let us consider a simple single error correcting code. In this coding scheme, it is assumed that a 0 is coded as 0 0 0 and a 1 as 1 1 1 at the transmitting end of the signal. If a single error occurs during transmission, changing a 0 0 0 to a 0 0 1, 1 0 0 or 0 1 0, then the receiver is designed to decode (or interpret) any of these as 0. Similarly, when a 1 1 1 becomes a 1 0 1, 0 1 1 or 1 1 0 any of these bit strings is to be decoded as a 1. Figure 2.1 is a block diagram depicting this decoder.

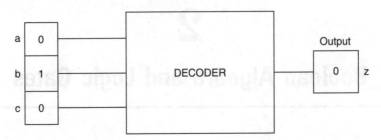

**Fig. 2.1   Block diagram of a single error corrector.**

The input-output relationship to be satisfied by the decoder is represented in Table 2.1. Observe that this table exhaustively lists all possible sets of values of *a*, *b* and *c* constituting the input, and for each such set gives the value of the output *z*. The first step in designing a decoder is to express the value of *z* as a function of *a*, *b*, *c* namely, $z = f(a, b, c)$. Observe that the variables *a*, *b*, *c* and *z* are two-valued, that is, they assume a value from a set consisting of two elements 0 and 1. In all digital systems we will be considering two-valued inputs and outputs. To obtain a closed form expression for $f(a, b, c)$ Switching algebra is useful.

**Switching algebra** was developed by Shannon in 1938 for designing telephone switching systems. It is a subset (for two-valued variables) of a more general algebra known as **Boolean algebra** developed by Boole (1815–64). Switching algebra uses a limited number of operators to connect variables together to form expressions and makes it easy to build electronic circuits to implement these operators. It is thus necessary to learn this algebra as it is the appropriate modelling tool to design digital systems.

**TABLE 2.1**

**Input-Output Relationship of the Single Error Corrector**

| Input | | | Output |
|:---:|:---:|:---:|:---:|
| *a* | *b* | *c* | *z* |
| 0 | 0 | 0 | 0 |
| 0 | 0 | 1 | 0 |
| 0 | 1 | 0 | 0 |
| 0 | 1 | 1 | 1 |
| 1 | 0 | 0 | 0 |
| 1 | 0 | 1 | 1 |
| 1 | 1 | 0 | 1 |
| 1 | 1 | 1 | 1 |

## 2.2 POSTULATES OF BOOLEAN ALGEBRA

Boolean algebra is introduced by first defining a set of elements allowed in this algebra, a set of operators which operate with the elements as operands and a set of axioms or postulates. Postulates are not proved but assumed to be true. The theorems of the algebra are derived from these postulates.

A **set** of elements is any collection of objects having a common property. If **K** is a set and *a* and *b* are objects, then the notation *a*, *b* ∈ **K** is used to indicate that *a* and *b* are members of the set **K.** The notation *a* ∉ **K,** indicates that *a* is not a member of the set **K.** A **binary operator** defined over a set **K** is a rule that assigns to each pair of elements taken from **K.** For example, if *a* ∗ *b* = *c* then, ∗ is a binary operator if for every *a*, *b* ∈ **K,** *c* ∈ **K.** If *c* ∉ **K,** then ∗ is not a binary operator. A **unary operator** is a rule that assigns for any element belonging to **K** another element in **K.** For example, if @ *d* = *h*, then @ is a unary operator if for every *d* ∈ **K,** *h* ∈ **K.**

For the formal definition of Boolean algebra we will use the postulates given by Huntington. Boolean algebra is defined on a set of elements **K,** together with two binary operators + and · , and unary operator - ( a bar over the variable), for which the following postulates are satisfied. Let *a*, *b* be two elements belonging to **K.**

POSTULATE 1:   (a) An operator '+' is defined such that if *c* = *a* + *b*, then *c* ∈ **K** for every pair of elements *a*, *b* ∈ **K.**

             (b) An operator '·' is defined such that if *d* = *a*·*b*, then *d* ∈ **K** for every pair of elements *a*, *b* ∈ **K.**

POSTULATE 2:   (a) There exists an element 0 in **K** such that *a* + 0 = *a* for every element *a* ∈ **K.**

             (b) There exists an element 1 in **K** such that *a* · 1 = *a* for every element *a* ∈ **K.**

POSTULATE 3:   For *a*, *b* ∈ **K,** the following commutative laws hold:

             (a) *a* + *b* = *b* + *a*

             (b) *a* · *b* = *b* · *a*

POSTULATE 4:   For *a*, *b*, *c* ∈ **K,** the following distributive laws hold:

             (a) *a* · (*b* + *c*) = *a* · *b* + *a* · *c*

             (b) *a* + (*b* · *c*) = (*a* + *b*) · (*a* + *c*)

POSTULATE 5:   For every element *a* ∈ **K,** there exists an element $\bar{a}$ (read a bar) such that

             (a) *a* + $\bar{a}$ = 1 and

             (b) *a* · $\bar{a}$ = 0

             (Observe that ⁻ (bar) is a unary operator operating on the element *a*)

POSTULATE 6:   There are at least two elements *a*, *b* ∈ **K** such that *a* ≠ *b*.

It is interesting to compare at this point the basic differences between Boolean algebra (based on Huntington's postulates) and the algebra of real numbers we are used to from school days. The basic differences are:

1. Boolean algebra does not have operations equivalent to division and subtraction. This is due to the absence of the definition of an inverse for the '+' and '.' operations.

2. Ordinary algebra deals with real numbers, which constitute a set with an infinite number of elements. Boolean algebra has only a finite set of elements. Switching algebra, which is a special Boolean algebra, deals with sets that have only two elements namely, 0 and 1.

3. In ordinary algebra, there is no equivalent of the unary operation of bar over a variable known as **complementing.**

4. The distributive law [**Postulate 4(b)**] $a + (b \cdot c) = (a + b) \cdot (a + c)$ does not hold in ordinary algebra.

However, Boolean algebra resembles ordinary algebra in some respects. This resemblance is due to the choice of symbols '+' and '.' for the two operators. This choice facilitates manipulation of Boolean algebra. A beginner should, however, be careful to remember that this resemblance is superficial.

## 2.3 BASIC THEOREMS OF BOOLEAN ALGEBRA

We will consider a special case of Boolean algebra with the following definitions:

**Definition 1:** The set **K** has two elements: 0 and 1.

**Definition 2(a):** The rules of operation with the operator '.' are given in Table 2.2(a).

<table>
<tr><td colspan="3">**TABLE 2.2(a)**<br>**Rules for '.' Operator**</td><td colspan="3">**TABLE 2.2(b)**<br>**Rules for '+' Operator**</td></tr>
<tr><td>*a*</td><td>*b*</td><td>*a* · *b*</td><td>*a*</td><td>*b*</td><td>*a* + *b*</td></tr>
<tr><td>0</td><td>0</td><td>0</td><td>0</td><td>0</td><td>0</td></tr>
<tr><td>0</td><td>1</td><td>0</td><td>0</td><td>1</td><td>1</td></tr>
<tr><td>1</td><td>0</td><td>0</td><td>1</td><td>0</td><td>1</td></tr>
<tr><td>1</td><td>1</td><td>1</td><td>1</td><td>1</td><td>1</td></tr>
</table>

**Definition 2(b):** The rules of operation with the operator '+' are given in Table 2.2(b).

**Definition 3:** The complement operation is defined as:

$$\overline{0} = 1; \quad \overline{1} = 0$$

The student can verify that the above definition of the set **K** and the operators '+', '.' and complementing, satisfy Huntington's postulates (see Exercise 2.1). As we will be exclusively dealing with Switching algebra in this book, we will use the terms Boolean algebra and Switching algebra as synonyms.

The two binary operators '.' and '+' are known as 'AND' operator and 'OR' operator respectively. The unary operator is known as 'NOT' operator. This algebra is useful in digital system mainly because simple electronic circuits exist to implement the AND, OR and NOT operations. We will introduce these circuits later in this chapter.

## 2.3.1 Duality Principle

Observe that in Section 2.2 the first five postulates of Huntington were listed in two parts (a) and (b). One part may be obtained from the other if '+' is interchanged with '·' and '0' is interchanged with '1'. This important property of Boolean algebra is known as the **duality principle.** This principle ensures that if a theorem is proved based on the postulates of the algebra, then a dual theorem obtained by interchanging '+' with '·' and '0' with '1' automatically holds and need not be proved separately.

## 2.3.2 Theorems

As Boolean algebra deals with a set consisting of only two elements, it is, in principle, possible to prove every theorem by considering all possible cases, that is, by exhaustive enumeration. Sometimes it is easier to prove a theorem using the postulates and some of the theorems proved earlier. Every theorem will have a dual which is presented without proof due to the fact that duality principle holds.

**Theorem 1(a):** $a + a = a$

    *Proof:* When $a = 0$, $0 + 0 = 0 = a$                by definition 2(b)

    And $a = 1$, $1 + 1 = 1 = a$                  by definition 2(b)

    As $a = 0$ or $a = 1$ and in both cases $a + a = a$, the theorem holds.

**Theorem 1(b)**: $a \cdot a = a$ (Dual theorem)

**Theorem 2(a):** $a + 1 = 1$

    When $a = 0$, $0 + 1 = 1$                   by definition 2(b)

    When $a = 1$, $1 + 1 = 1$                   by definition 2(b)

    Thus, $a + 1 = 1$

**Theorem 2(b):** $a \cdot 0 = 0$ (Dual theorem)

**Theorem 3(a):** $a + (a \cdot b) = a$

    *Proof:*

$$\begin{aligned} a + (a \cdot b) &= a \cdot 1 + a \cdot b && \text{by Postulate 2(b)}\\ &= a \cdot (1 + b) && \text{by Postulate 4(a)}\\ &= a \cdot 1 && \text{by Postulate 3(a) and Theorem 2(a)}\\ &= a && \text{by Postulate 2(b)} \end{aligned}$$

**Theorem 3(b):** $a \cdot (a + b) = a$ (Dual theorem)

**Theorem 4:** $\bar{\bar{a}} = a$

    When $a = 0$, $\bar{a} = 1$, $\bar{\bar{a}} = \bar{1} = 0 = a$

    When $a = 1$, $\bar{a} = 0$, $\bar{\bar{a}} = \bar{0} = 1 = a$

    Thus, $\bar{\bar{a}} = a$

**Theorem 5(a):** $a + (\bar{a} \cdot b) = a + b$

*Proof:*

| | |
|---|---|
| $a + (\bar{a} \cdot b) = (a + \bar{a}) \cdot (a + b)$ | by Postulate 4(b) |
| $= 1 \cdot (a + b)$ | by Postulate 5(a) |
| $= 1 \cdot a + 1 \cdot b$ | by Postulate 4(a) |
| $= a \cdot 1 + b \cdot 1$ | By Postulate 3(b) |
| $= (a + b)$ | By Postulate 2(b) |

**Theorem 5(b):** $a \cdot (\bar{a} + b) = a \cdot b$ (Dual theorem)

**Theorem 6(a):** $\overline{a + b} = \bar{a} \cdot \bar{b}$

*Proof:* Table 2.3 is used to show that the left-hand side equals the right-hand side for all values of $a$ and $b$ (columns 4 and 7 are identical).

**TABLE 2.3**

**Proof of Theorem 6(a)**

| $a$ | $b$ | $a + b$ | $\overline{a + b}$ | $\bar{a}$ | $\bar{b}$ | $\bar{a} \cdot \bar{b}$ |
|-----|-----|---------|--------------------|-----------|-----------|--------------------------|
| 0 | 0 | 0 | 1 | 1 | 1 | 1 |
| 0 | 1 | 1 | 0 | 1 | 0 | 0 |
| 1 | 0 | 1 | 0 | 0 | 1 | 0 |
| 1 | 1 | 1 | 0 | 0 | 0 | 0 |

**Theorem 6(b):** $\overline{a \cdot b} = \bar{a} + \bar{b}$ (Dual theorem)

Theorems 6(a) and (b) are important theorems and are very useful. They are known as **DeMorgan's Laws.** They can be extended to $n$ variables as given below:

$$\overline{a_1 + a_2 + a_3 + \cdots + a_n} = \bar{a}_1 \cdot \bar{a}_2 \cdot \bar{a}_3 \cdot \cdots \cdot \bar{a}_n$$

$$\overline{a_1 \cdot a_2 \cdot a_3 \cdot \cdots \cdot a_n} = \bar{a}_1 + \bar{a}_2 + \bar{a}_3 + \cdots + \bar{a}_n$$

**Theorem 7(a):** $a + (b + c) = (a + b) + c$  (Associative law)

This is proved by forming truth tables for the left-hand side and the right-hand side and showing they are identical.

**Theorem 7(b):** $a \cdot (b \cdot c) = (a \cdot b) \cdot c$ (Dual theorem)

All the important postulates and theorems of Boolean algebra are listed in Table 2.4. The student should become thoroughly conversant with this table in order to use the algebra effectively.

**TABLE 2.4**
**Summary of Postulates and Theorems**

| Reference | Primary | Dual |
|---|---|---|
| Postulate 2 | $a + 0 = a$ | $a \cdot 1 = a$ |
| Postulate 3 | $a + b = b + a$ | $a \cdot b = b \cdot a$ |
| Postulate 4 | $a \cdot (b + c) = a \cdot b + a \cdot c$ | $a + (b \cdot c) = (a + b) \cdot (a + c)$ |
| Postulate 5 | $a + \bar{a} = 1$ | $a \cdot \bar{a} = 0$ |
| Theorem 1 | $a + a = a$ | $a \cdot a = a$ |
| Theorem 2 | $a + 1 = 1$ | $a \cdot 0 = 0$ |
| Theorem 3 | $a + (a \cdot b) = a$ | $a \cdot (a + b) = a$ |
| Theorem 4 | $\bar{\bar{a}} = a$ | |
| Theorem 5 | $a + \bar{a} \cdot b = a + b$ | $a \cdot (\bar{a} + b) = a \cdot b$ |
| Theorem 6 | $\overline{a + b} = \bar{a} \cdot \bar{b}$ | $\overline{a \cdot b} = \bar{a} + \bar{b}$ |
| Theorem 7 | $a + (b + c) = (a + b) + c$ | $a \cdot (b \cdot c) = (a \cdot b) \cdot c$ |

## 2.3.3  Precedence of Operators

In order to evaluate Boolean expressions it is necessary to define the precedence of operators. The precedence is:

1. Scan the expression from left to right.
2. First evaluate the expressions enclosed in parentheses.
3. Perform all the complement (NOT) operations.
4. Perform all '·' (AND) operations in the order in which they appear.
5. Perform all '+' (OR) operations last.

*Example 2.2*   $x \cdot \bar{x} = y \cdot (\overline{x + z}) + (x \cdot z)$

| | |
|---|---|
| $\overline{x + z}, x \cdot z$ | First scan (Evaluate expressions in parentheses) |
| $\bar{x} \cdot \bar{z}$ | Second scan (Perform NOT operations) |
| $0, y \cdot \bar{x} \cdot \bar{z}, x \cdot z$ | Third scan (Perform AND operations) |
| $0 + y \cdot \bar{x} \cdot \bar{z} + x \cdot z$ | Last scan (Perform OR operations) |

## 2.3.4  Venn Diagram

To confirm our ideas of Boolean algebra, a pictorial model known as the **Venn diagram** is useful. This diagram consists of a rectangle inside which a number of circles are drawn— one circle for each variable. Points inside a circle are defined as belonging to the variable. Figure 2.2 shows a Venn diagram for two variables $x, y$. Points inside the circle named $x$

are assumed to represent $x = 1$ and those outside $x = 0$. With two intersecting circles $x$ and $y$, we have four areas corresponding to $x \cdot \bar{y}, x \cdot y, \bar{x} \cdot y, \bar{x} \cdot \bar{y}$ respectively as shown in the figure.

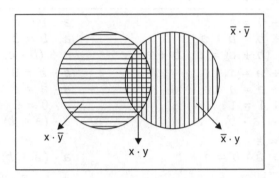

**Fig. 2.2   Venn diagram for two variables.**

Venn diagrams may be used to illustrate postulates and theorems of Boolean algebra. Figure 2.3 illustrates Postulate 4(b). In part (i) of Figure 2.3 the area covered by the slant lines corresponds to the expression $a + b \cdot c$. In part (ii) of Figure 2.3 area $(a + b)$ is marked by horizontal lines and area $(a + c)$ is marked by vertical lines. The area intersected by the horizontal and the vertical lines correspond to the expression $(a + b) \cdot (a + c)$ and this is identical to the area in part (i) of the figure. Venn diagrams thus provide an aid to remember the postulates and theorems of Boolean algebra.

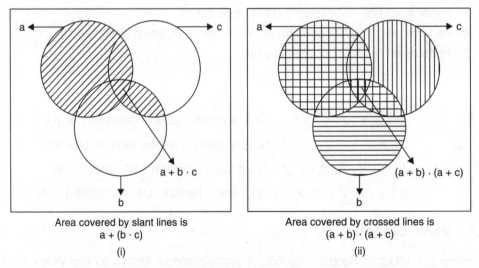

Area covered by slant lines is
$a + (b \cdot c)$

(i)

Area covered by crossed lines is
$(a + b) \cdot (a + c)$

(ii)

**Fig. 2.3   Venn diagram illustrating Postulate 4(b).**

## 2.4  BOOLEAN FUNCTIONS AND TRUTH TABLES

A Boolean function is defined as follows:

1. A set of Boolean variables is taken as independent variables.
2. Another Boolean variable is assigned the role of a dependent variable.
3. A rule is formulated which assigns a value to the dependent variable for each set of values of the independent variables. In mathematical notation we may write:

$$z = f(a, b, c) \tag{2.1}$$

where $a$, $b$, $c$ are the independent variables, $z$ is the dependent variable and the rule assigning values to $z$ for each set of values of $a$, $b$, $c$ is denoted by $f$. If $z = \bar{a} + b \cdot c$, then the rule denoted by $f$ is "NOT $a$ first; AND $b$, $c$ next; OR these two expressions". (In other words form $\bar{a} + b \cdot c$ ).

The value of $z$ for each combination (or set) of values of $a$, $b$ and $c$ may also be given as a table. That is, for each one of the eight sets of values of $a$, $b$ and $c$, a value of $z$ is given. It is feasible in Boolean algebra to define a function in this manner, as each independent variable can assume only one of two values (0 or 1) and exhaustive enumeration is feasible. It is important to note that $z$ can also assume only one of two values namely, 0 or 1.

A table which lists the value of the dependent variable for each set of values of the independent variables is known as a **truth table.** We will now obtain a truth table for the function $z = \bar{a} + b \cdot c$. The method of obtaining the table is to follow the steps enumerated below:

*Step 1:*  Form a table with one column for each of the independent variables and one column for the dependent variable. Use a vertical double line to separate the dependent and the independent variables.

*Step 2:*  Assuming there are $n$ independent variables, start with $0 \cdots 0$ ($n$ bits) as values of the independent variables and form successive rows (each containing $n$ bits) using the natural binary counting sequence till the count becomes ($2^n - 1$).

*Step 3:*  Substitute the values of the independent variables given in each row and evaluate the value of the dependent variable. Enter this value in the appropriate row to the right of the double vertical line which separates the dependent and independent variables.

*Example 2.3.*   For the function $z = \bar{a} + b \cdot c$, the truth table is developed following the above steps in Table 2.5.

**TABLE 2.5**

**Truth Table for** $z = \bar{a} + b \cdot c$

| a | b | c | z |
|---|---|---|---|
| 0 | 0 | 0 | 1 |
| 0 | 0 | 1 | 1 |
| 0 | 1 | 0 | 1 |
| 0 | 1 | 1 | 1 |
| 1 | 0 | 0 | 0 |
| 1 | 0 | 1 | 0 |
| 1 | 1 | 0 | 0 |
| 1 | 1 | 1 | 1 |

It is thus easy to obtain a truth table given a Boolean function. Some interesting questions we may ask are:

1. Given a truth table for a Boolean function, how can we obtain an expression to represent the dependent variable in terms of the independent variables?

2. Is this expression unique?

3. If it is not unique, are there any criteria which would allow us to choose one among them to represent the function?

We will devote the rest of this chapter to answering these questions.

## 2.5 CANONICAL FORMS FOR BOOLEAN FUNCTIONS

Tables 2.6(a)–2.6(c) give the truth tables of two variable functions. Table 2.6(a) is a table for the function $z_1 = \bar{x} \cdot \bar{y}$ and Table 2.6(b) is a table for the function $z_2 = x \cdot \bar{y}$. If we 'OR' the corresponding elements of the $z_1$ and $z_2$ columns of Tables 2.6(a) and (b), we obtain the last column of Table 2.6(c) which is the truth table for $z$. Thus, we may write:

$$z = z_1 + z_2 = \bar{x} \cdot \bar{y} + x \cdot \bar{y} \tag{2.2}$$

| **TABLE 2.6(a)** | | | **TABLE 2.6(b)** | | |
|---|---|---|---|---|---|
| **Truth Table for function** $z_1 = \bar{x} \cdot \bar{y}$ | | | **Truth Table for function** $z_2 = x \cdot \bar{y}$ | | |
| x | y | $z_1 = \bar{x} \cdot \bar{y}$ | x | y | $z_2 = x \cdot \bar{y}$ |
| 0 | 0 | 1 | 0 | 0 | 0 |
| 0 | 1 | 0 | 0 | 1 | 0 |
| 1 | 0 | 0 | 1 | 0 | 1 |
| 1 | 1 | 0 | 1 | 1 | 0 |

**TABLE 2.6(c)**

**Truth Table for function $z = z_1 + z_2$**

| $x$ | $y$ | $z = z_1 + z_2$ |
|-----|-----|-----------------|
| 0 | 0 | 1 |
| 0 | 1 | 0 |
| 1 | 0 | 1 |
| 1 | 1 | 0 |

Observe that each term on the right-hand side of Eq. (2.2) assumes a value of 1 for one and only one set of values of $x$ and $y$. For example, the first term $\bar{x} \cdot \bar{y}$ assumes a value 1 for $x = 0$, $y = 0$ and the second term $x \cdot \bar{y}$ assumes a value 1 for $x = 1$, $y = 0$. Each such set leads to a value of 1 in the corresponding row of the truth table for $z$.

The above observation is used for obtaining the Boolean expression corresponding to any truth table. The method is as follows:

*Step 1:* Inspect the column corresponding to $z$ starting from the top row. Pick the row with a 1 entry for $z$.

*Step 2:* A term in the Boolean expression corresponding to this row is obtained by applying 'AND' operation to all the independent variables in the truth table; the independent variables with a 0 entry appear in the complement form and those with a 1 entry appear as they are.

*Step 3:* Repeat step 1 and step 2 till all the entries in the $z$ column are exhausted. Obtain an expression by applying 'OR' operation to the terms corresponding to the 1 entries of $z$.

*Example 2.4.* We will now apply the above procedure to the Truth Table 2.7.

*Step 1:* Row 2 of the fourth column, namely the column giving $z$, is a 1.

*Step 2:* The term corresponding to this 1 in the Boolean expression for $z$ is $\bar{a} \cdot \bar{b} \cdot c$

*Step 3:* Rows 5, 6, 7, 8 have 1 as entries for $z$. The corresponding terms are: $a \cdot \bar{b} \cdot \bar{c}, a \cdot \bar{b} \cdot c, a \cdot b \cdot \bar{c}$ and $a \cdot b \cdot c$. Thus,

$$z = \bar{a} \cdot \bar{b} \cdot c + a \cdot \bar{b} \cdot \bar{c} + a \cdot \bar{b} \cdot c + a \cdot b \cdot \bar{c} + a \cdot b \cdot c \qquad (2.3)$$

The expression for $z$ obtained above is said to be in the **canonical (or standard) sum of products form.** Each term in the expression is said to be a **standard product** or **a minterm.**

The minterms and the notation used are illustrated in Table 2.8 for Boolean functions of three variables.

**TABLE 2.7**

**Truth Table for an Error Corrector**

| a | b | c | z | $\bar{z}$ |
|---|---|---|---|---|
| 0 | 0 | 0 | 0 | 1 |
| 0 | 0 | 1 | 1 | 0 |
| 0 | 1 | 0 | 0 | 1 |
| 0 | 1 | 1 | 0 | 1 |
| 1 | 0 | 0 | 1 | 0 |
| 1 | 0 | 1 | 1 | 0 |
| 1 | 1 | 0 | 1 | 0 |
| 1 | 1 | 1 | 1 | 0 |

The expression for $z$ (Eq. (2.3)) may be expressed in a number of equivalent forms using the notation of Table 2.8 as:

$$z = m_1 + m_4 + m_5 + m_6 + m_7 \qquad (2.4)$$

$$z = \Sigma\ 1,\ 4,\ 5,\ 6,\ 7 \qquad (2.5)$$

**TABLE 2.8**

**Illustrating Minterm Notation**

| Independent Variables | | | Minterm Notation | | |
|---|---|---|---|---|---|
| a | b | c | Term | Designation | Decimal Form |
| 0 | 0 | 0 | $\bar{a} \cdot \bar{b} \cdot \bar{c}$ | $m_0$ | 0 |
| 0 | 0 | 1 | $\bar{a} \cdot \bar{b} \cdot c$ | $m_1$ | 1 |
| 0 | 1 | 0 | $\bar{a} \cdot b \cdot \bar{c}$ | $m_2$ | 2 |
| 0 | 1 | 1 | $\bar{a} \cdot b \cdot c$ | $m_3$ | 3 |
| 1 | 0 | 0 | $a \cdot \bar{b} \cdot \bar{c}$ | $m_4$ | 4 |
| 1 | 0 | 1 | $a \cdot \bar{b} \cdot c$ | $m_5$ | 5 |
| 1 | 1 | 0 | $a \cdot b \cdot \bar{c}$ | $m_6$ | 6 |
| 1 | 1 | 1 | $a \cdot b \cdot c$ | $m_7$ | 7 |

The last notation is quite convenient to use. The symbol $\Sigma$ indicates that the OR of minterms are to be taken. These decimal numbers, if expanded to their binary form, indicate the values of the independent variables.

There is another standard form which may also be used to express Boolean functions. In order to express functions in this form one may use a step-by-step procedure similar to the one given at the beginning of this section. Instead of considering the rows of the truth table for $z$ with a 1 entry, the rows with zero entries are used. The individual term is formed by taking the sum (or OR) of the independent variables. A variable with a 0 entry is used as it is and a variable with a 1 entry is complemented. The individual terms are then ANDed. For the function of Table 2.7 the expression is:

$$z = (a + b + c) \cdot (a + \bar{b} + c) \cdot (a + \bar{b} + \bar{c}) \tag{2.6}$$

This expression is said to be in the **canonical (or standard) product of sums form.** Each term in the expression is said to be a **standard sum** or a **maxterm.**

A table similar to Table 2.8 may be formed to explain the maxterm notation. It is shown in Table 2.9. Using this notation $z$ may be expressed as:

$$z = M_0 \cdot M_2 \cdot M_3 \tag{2.7}$$
$$= \Pi\ 0,\ 2,\ 3 \tag{2.8}$$

**TABLE 2.9**

**Maxterms for Three Variables**

| Independent Variables | | | | Maxterm Notation | | |
|:---:|:---:|:---:|:---:|:---:|:---:|:---:|
| $a$ | $b$ | $c$ | Term | Designation | | Decimal Form |
| 0 | 0 | 0 | $a + b + c$ | $M_0$ | | 0 |
| 0 | 0 | 1 | $a + b + \bar{c}$ | $M_1$ | | 1 |
| 0 | 1 | 0 | $a + \bar{b} + c$ | $M_2$ | | 2 |
| 0 | 1 | 1 | $a + \bar{b} + \bar{c}$ | $M_3$ | | 3 |
| 1 | 0 | 0 | $\bar{a} + b + c$ | $M_4$ | | 4 |
| 1 | 0 | 1 | $\bar{a} + b + \bar{c}$ | $M_5$ | | 5 |
| 1 | 1 | 0 | $\bar{a} + \bar{b} + c$ | $M_6$ | | 6 |
| 1 | 1 | 1 | $\bar{a} + \bar{b} + \bar{c}$ | $M_7$ | | 7 |

As $z$ can be either 0 or 1, this expression derived from using the combinations of variables making $z = 0$ is equivalent to the expression of Eq. (2.3).

This equivalence may be shown by considering Table 2.7 again and writing the expression for $\bar{z}$ in the canonical sum of products form. By inspection of Table 2.7 we obtain:

$$\bar{z} = (\bar{a} \cdot \bar{b} \cdot \bar{c}) + (\bar{a} \cdot b \cdot \bar{c}) \cdot (\bar{a} \cdot b \cdot c) \tag{2.9}$$

Taking the complement of both sides of Eq. (2.9) we obtain:

$$z = (a + b + c) \cdot (a + \bar{b} + c) \cdot (a + \bar{b} + \bar{c}) \tag{2.10}$$

Equation (2.10) is identical to Eq. (2.6). Thus, it is clear that the expression for $z$ given in Eq. (2.3) and Eq. (2.10) are equivalent.

The illustrations used above also give a method of obtaining the canonical product of sums form, given the canonical sum of products. For a function of three variables, for example, if

$$z = \Sigma \ 1, 4, 5, 6, 7 \tag{2.11}$$

The complement is

$$\bar{z} = \Sigma 0, 2, 3 \tag{2.12}$$

and

$$z = \Pi 0, 2, 3 \tag{2.13}$$

Thus, to convert from the sum of products form to the product of sums form, change $\Sigma$ to $\Pi$, list as arguments in $\Pi$ those numbers missing in the $\Sigma$ form. (Remember that for an $n$ variable truth table the decimal equivalents of rows range from 0 to $2^n - 1$.)

To conclude this section we observe that there is no unique representation of truth tables in terms of Boolean expressions. These standard forms are convenient to obtain, but are not always useful for hardware implementation. Other equivalent forms are necessary for some practical implementations. This will be discussed later.

## 2.6 BINARY OPERATORS AND LOGIC GATES

So far we have considered three Boolean operators namely the AND, OR and NOT operators. The reason we use these three operators is because all Boolean expressions may be realized using these operators. Among these AND, OR are binary operators. There are many other binary operators which will now be introduced.

With two Boolean variables as inputs we know that a truth table has four rows. Corresponding to each row the output variable may be assigned a value 0 or 1. Thus, 16 distinct truth tables may be constructed with two variables as inputs as shown in Table 2.10. [In general for $N$ input variables $2**(2**N)$ truth tables may be constructed. We have used $**$ to represent an exponentiation operation.] In other words, 16 Boolean functions of two variables may be formed. By inspection of Table 2.10 we see that one may define eight different binary operators and one unary operator. The binary operators are: AND ($\cdot$), INHIBITION (/), EXCLUSIVE-OR ($\oplus$), OR (+), NOR ($\downarrow$), EQUIVALENCE ($\odot$), IMPLICATION ($\supset$) and NAND ($\uparrow$). The unary operator is COMPLEMENT (-). The 16 functions of two variables are given in Table 2.11. Boolean expressions, which describe these operators in terms of the familiar AND, OR, NOT operators, are also shown in this table.

**TABLE 2.10**

**Truth Tables for 16 Functions of Two Variables**

| $x$ | $y$ | $f_0$ | $f_1$ | $f_2$ | $f_3$ | $f_4$ | $f_5$ | $f_6$ | $f_7$ | $f_8$ | $f_9$ | $f_{10}$ | $f_{11}$ | $f_{12}$ | $f_{13}$ | $f_{14}$ | $f_{15}$ |
|---|---|---|---|---|---|---|---|---|---|---|---|---|---|---|---|---|---|
| 0 | 0 | 0 | 0 | 0 | 0 | 0 | 0 | 0 | 0 | 1 | 1 | 1 | 1 | 1 | 1 | 1 | 1 |
| 0 | 1 | 0 | 0 | 0 | 0 | 1 | 1 | 1 | 1 | 0 | 0 | 0 | 0 | 1 | 1 | 1 | 1 |
| 1 | 0 | 0 | 0 | 1 | 1 | 0 | 0 | 1 | 1 | 0 | 0 | 1 | 1 | 0 | 0 | 1 | 1 |
| 1 | 1 | 0 | 1 | 0 | 1 | 0 | 1 | 0 | 1 | 0 | 1 | 0 | 1 | 0 | 1 | 0 | 1 |

**TABLE 2.11**

**Sixteen Functions of Two Variables**

| Function | Name | Symbol | Word description |
|---|---|---|---|
| $f_0 = 0$ | NULL | | Always 0 |
| $f_1 = x \cdot y$ | AND | $x \cdot y$ | $x$ and $y$ |
| $f_2 = x \cdot \bar{y}$ | INHIBITION | $x/y$ | $x$ and not $y$ |
| $f_3 = x$ | | | Always $x$ |
| $f_4 = \bar{x} \cdot y$ | INHIBITION | $y/x$ | $y$ and not $x$ |
| $f_5 = y$ | | | Always $y$ |
| $f_6 = \bar{x} \cdot y + x \cdot \bar{y}$ | EXCLUSIVE-OR | $x \oplus y$ | $x$ or $y$ but not both |
| $f_7 = x + y$ | OR | $x + y$ | or |
| $f_8 = \overline{(x + y)}$ | NOR | $x \downarrow y$ | not ($x$ or $y$) |
| $f_9 = \bar{x} \cdot \bar{y} + x \cdot y$ | EQUIVALENCE | $x \odot y$ | $x$ equals $y$ |
| $f_{10} = \bar{y}$ | COMPLEMENT | $\bar{y}$ | Not $y$ |
| $f_{11} = x + \bar{y}$ | IMPLICATION | $y \supset x$ | If $y$ then $x$ |
| $f_{12} = \bar{x}$ | COMPLEMENT | $\bar{x}$ | Not $x$ |
| $f_{13} = \bar{x} + y$ | IMPLICATION | $x \supset y$ | If $x$ then $y$ |
| $f_{14} = \overline{(x \cdot y)}$ | NAND | $x \uparrow y$ | not ($x$ and $y$) |
| $f_{15} = 1$ | IDENTITY | | Always 1 |

Four of the 16 functions shown in Table 2.11 are normally useful in obtaining logic circuits. These are the Exclusive-OR which is similar to OR but assigns a 0 when both $x$ and $y$ are 1. (This function is the strict OR, that is, $x$ or $y$ but not both.) The EQUIVALENCE function gives a 1 if $x$ and $y$ are equal. The NOR function is the NOT of OR and the NAND function is the NOT of AND.

The question which arises now is the feasibility of using these binary operators to construct logic circuits. This depends on the following factors:

1. The mathematical property of the operator such as commutativity and associativity.
2. The ability of the gate by itself or in conjunction with a small set of other gates to realize expressions for all Boolean functions.
3. The feasibility and cost of making these gates with physical components.
4. Number of inputs that could be fed to the gate.

Of the eight binary operators discussed earlier Inhibition and Implication are not commutative. The Exclusive-OR and EQUIVALENCE satisfy factors 1, 2, 4 given above but are expensive to construct with presently available physical devices. The NAND and NOR satisfy all the 4 criteria and are now almost universally used, in preference to AND, OR, NOT gates since the advent of integrated circuits. We will discuss their properties and use in the next chapter. In this chapter we will primarily use AND, OR and NOT gates as they are appropriate for simplifying Boolean functions. We will see later that AND, OR and NOT gates may be realized using only NAND or NOR gates.

As we saw in the last section the three logical connectives, AND, OR and NOT are said to be logically complete as any Boolean function can be realized using these three connectives. In the development of computers a number of devices have been used to realize these functions. Currently, electronic circuits known as **Integrated Circuits (IC)** are used to implement these connectives. In implementation we first consider how we can represent the logical 1 and the logical 0 by electrical voltages. In IC implementation using gates the specifications used are to ensure that the logic levels are interpreted correctly inspite of noise in the system. A band of voltages is thus used to represent a 1 and another band to represent a 0. The standard specification used by IC manufacturers is illustrated in Figure 2.4(a) and 2.4(b). A voltage output of a gate is assumed to be a 1 if it lies in range $V_{out H}$ to $V_{cc}$ where $V_{cc}$ is the supply voltage. The output is assumed to be 0 if it lies in the range 0 to $V_{out L}$. These are the worst case values. In other words, in the worst possible case, with the gate loaded to its maximum the output voltage representing 1 should not be below $V_{out H}$ and that for 0 not above $V_{out L}$.

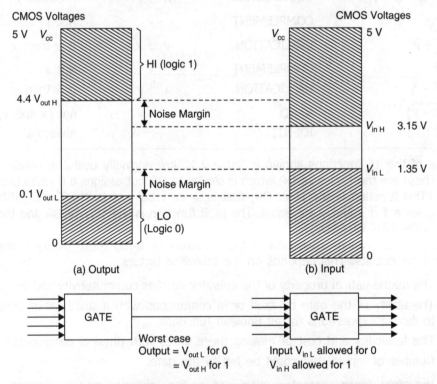

**Fig. 2.4   Range of voltages of HI and LO levels in CMOS gates. (The drawing is not to scale it is a sketch)**

The voltage at the input of a gate should adhere to the following specifications:

Voltage between $V_{cc}$ and $V_{in H}$ for 1 and 0 V to $V_{in L}$ for a 0.

Observe from the figure that $V_{in\,H} < V_{out\,H}$ and $V_{in\,L} > V_{out\,L}$. Thus, the input specifications allow a narrower gap separating 1 and 0 compared to the output. This implies that a gate output can be corrupted by noise whose magnitude at the Low (or 0) level can be up to $(V_{in\,L} - V_{out\,L})$ and at the High (or 1) level up to $(V_{out\,H} - V_{in\,H})$ and it can still be used as input to another gate (see Figure 2.5).

An IC technology which is commonly used nowadays is called **Complementary Metal Oxide Silicon (CMOS)**. In CMOS typically $V_{cc} = 5$ V, $V_{out\,H} = 4.4$ V, $V_{out\,L} = 0.1$ V and $V_{in\,L} = 1.35$V. Thus, the specification guarantees noise immunity of 1.25 V, which is excellent. Exact values for $V_{out\,H}$ etc. are given in the data sheets of the manufacturers and depends on the specific gate. What we have illustrated are only rough typical values.

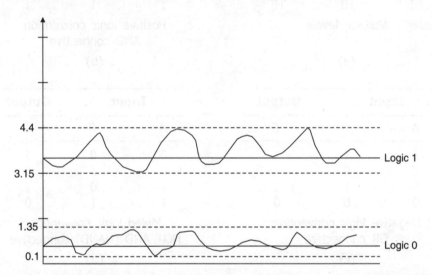

**Fig. 2.5 Illustrating the concept of noise immunity in CMOS gates.**

The convention of using HI voltage level to represent a 1 and LO voltage level to represent a 0 is known as **positive logic.** This is currently used widely in digital systems.

Another convention one may use is to assign a logical 0 to HI level and a logical 1 to LO level. This is known as **negative logic.** This convention is not popular with current electronic hardware.

One may also use a **mixed logic** convention in which the HI may be taken as 1 at the input of a gate and as 0 at the output.

In Table 2.12(a) we have depicted the input and output voltage levels of a gate. Table 2.12(b) assigns 0 to LO and 1 to HI as per positive logic convention and with this assignment the gate is an AND gate. In Table 2.12(c) the assignment of 1 to LO and 0 to HI follows the negative logic convention. With this assignment the gate is an OR gate. Lastly, in Table 2.12(d) the assignment of 0 to LO and 1 to HI at input and the reverse assignment namely, 1 to LO and 0 to HI leads to a gate which achieves a NOT of the AND operation. Such a gate is called a **NAND gate.**

**TABLE 2.12**

**Voltage Levels at Input and Output of a Gate and Interpretation According to Logic Convention Used**

| Input | | Output | Input | | Output |
|-------|-------|--------|-------|-------|--------|
| A | B | C | A | B | C |
| LO | LO | LO | 0 | 0 | 0 |
| LO | HI | LO | 0 | 1 | 0 |
| HI | LO | LO | 1 | 0 | 0 |
| HI | HI | HI | 1 | 1 | 1 |
| Voltage levels | | | Positive logic convention AND connective | | |
| (a) | | | (b) | | |

| Input | | Output | Input | | Output |
|-------|-------|--------|-------|-------|--------|
| A | B | C | A | B | C |
| 1 | 1 | 1 | 0 | 0 | 1 |
| 1 | 0 | 1 | 0 | 1 | 1 |
| 0 | 1 | 1 | 1 | 0 | 1 |
| 0 | 0 | 0 | 1 | 1 | 0 |
| Negative logic convention OR connective | | | Mixed logic convention NOT AND (NAND) connective | | |
| (c) | | | (d) | | |

Table 2.13(a) represents another gate whose input and output voltage levels are as shown. This gate is interpreted as an OR gate with positive logic, as an AND gate, with negative logic and as a NOT of the OR gate or **NOR** gate with a mixed logic assignment.

**TABLE 2.13**

**Voltage Levels at Input and Output of a Gate and Different Interpretations**

| Input | | Output | Input | | Output |
|-------|-------|--------|-------|-------|--------|
| A | B | C | A | B | C |
| LO | LO | LO | 0 | 0 | 0 |
| LO | HI | HI | 0 | 1 | 1 |
| HI | LO | HI | 1 | 0 | 1 |
| HI | HI | HI | 1 | 1 | 1 |
| Voltage levels | | | Positive logic OR | | |
| (a) | | | (b) | | |

| Input | | Output |
|:---:|:---:|:---:|
| A | B | C |
| 1 | 1 | 1 |
| 1 | 0 | 0 |
| 0 | 1 | 0 |
| 0 | 0 | 0 |

Negative logic AND

(c)

| Input | | Output |
|:---:|:---:|:---:|
| A | B | C |
| 0 | 0 | 1 |
| 0 | 1 | 0 |
| 1 | 0 | 0 |
| 1 | 1 | 0 |

Mixed logic NOR

(d)

Lastly, in Table 2.14(a) we show the input and output voltage levels of a gate with one input and one output. This represents a NOT gate with both positive and negative logic assignments. It is an identity operation with mixed logic convention.

### TABLE 2.14
**A One Input One Output Gate for NOT Operation with Mixed Logic Convention**

| Input | Output | Input | Output | Input | Output | Input | Output |
|:---:|:---:|:---:|:---:|:---:|:---:|:---:|:---:|
| A | B | A | B | A | B | A | B |
| LO | HI | 0 | 1 | 1 | 0 | 0 | 0 |
| HI | LO | 1 | 0 | 0 | 1 | 1 | 1 |
| (a) | | (a) | | (a) | | (a) | |

The symbols used for OR, AND and NOT gates with positive or negative logic convention are shown in Figure 2.6. When mixed logic convention is used, a polarity indicator as shown in Figure 2.7 is used.

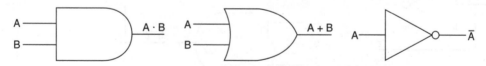

**Fig. 2.6  Symbols for AND, OR and NOT gates.**

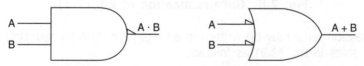

**Fig. 2.7  Symbols for mixed logic AND and OR gates.**

## 2.7  SIMPLIFYING BOOLEAN EXPRESSIONS

In Section 2.5 we obtained a Boolean expression for the truth Table 2.7 and it is reproduced as follows:

$$z = \bar{a} \cdot \bar{b} \cdot c + a \cdot \bar{b} \cdot \bar{c} + a \cdot \bar{b} \cdot c + a \cdot b \cdot \bar{c} + a \cdot b \cdot c \qquad (2.3)$$

Using AND, OR and NOT gates we may realize the Boolean expression for *z*, when the input variables *a*, *b* and *c* are given as shown in Figure 2.8. Observe that this realization of *z* requires three NOT gates, five three input AND gates and one five input OR gate, a total of nine gates.

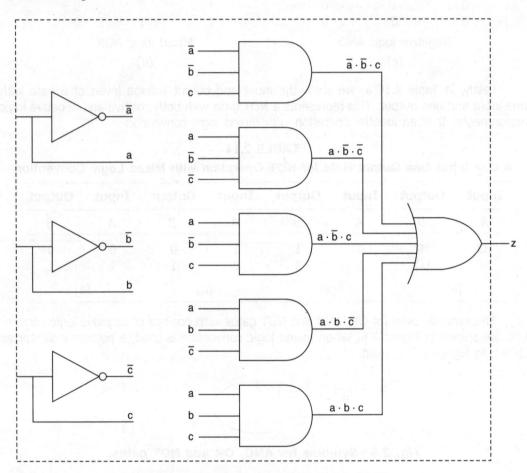

**Fig. 2.8   Gate realization of Eq. (2.3).**

The expression for *z* may be written in an alternate form by reducing the number of terms and variables in Eq. (2.3) as follows:

$$z = (\bar{a} + a) \cdot \bar{b} \cdot c + a \cdot \bar{b} \cdot \bar{c} + a \cdot b \cdot (\bar{c} + c) \qquad \text{By Postulate 4(a)}$$

$$= \bar{b} \cdot c + a \cdot \bar{b} \cdot \bar{c} + a \cdot b \qquad \text{By Postulates 3(a), 5(a)}$$

$$= \bar{b} \cdot (c + \bar{c} \cdot a) + a \cdot b \qquad \text{By Postulates 4(a), 3(b)}$$

$$= \bar{b} \cdot (c + a) + a \cdot b \qquad \text{By Theorem 5(a)}$$

$$= \bar{b} \cdot c + \bar{b} \cdot a + a \cdot b \qquad \text{By Postulate 4(a)}$$

$$= \bar{b} \cdot c + a \cdot (\bar{b} + b) \qquad \text{By Postulates 3(b), 4(a)}$$

$$= \bar{b} \cdot c + a \qquad \text{By Postulates 3(b), 5(a)}$$

This expression may be realized using AND, OR, NOT gates as shown in Figure 2.9. Observe that this realization uses only one NOT gate, one two input AND gate and one two input OR gate, a total of three gates as compared to nine gates used in the previous implementation.

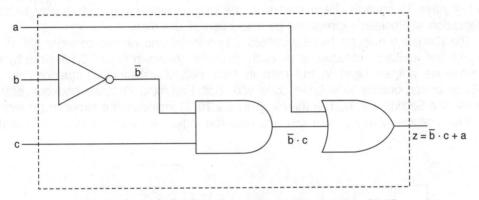

**Fig. 2.9   A minimal gate realization of Eq. (2.3).**

This example illustrates the value of simplifying Boolean expressions. Almost any Boolean expression obtained by inspection from a truth table such as Table 2.7 will be excessively complex and we must analyze such expressions with the objective of simplifying them. By simplifying we mean optimizing some engineering criteria such as minimizing the number of components, maximizing speed of operation, maximizing reliability, etc. Unfortunately, there are no simple techniques of manipulating Boolean expressions to directly achieve such engineering goals. But simple methods do exist to manipulate Boolean expressions to minimize the number of variables and complements of variables appearing in it. (The term **literal** will be used from now on to denote variables or their complements.) Because there is a close correlation between the number of literals in a Boolean expression and the total cost and reliability of the switching circuit derived from it, therefore minimizing the number of literals is an acceptable criterion for optimization.

At the beginning of this section we reduced the number of literals in a Boolean expression using the postulates and Theorems of Boolean algebra. This method known as **algebraic simplification,** is not useful in practice as it is difficult to apply and it is not possible to guarantee that the reduced expression is minimal. Two methods of systematic simplification of Boolean expressions which guarantee a simplified expression with a minimum number of literals have been derived in the literature. These are known as the **Veitch-Karnaugh map method** and the **Quine-McCluskey chart method.** The Veitch-Karnaugh method is easy to apply for Boolean expressions with four or less variables. The Quine-McCluskey method is suitable for any number of variables. Besides this, it is adaptable to an algorithmic formulation and thus computer programs have been written to implement it.

We will discuss the Karnaugh map (abbreviated **K-map**) method first and the McCluskey method later in the following section.

## 2.8   VEITCH-KARNAUGH MAP METHOD

The Veitch-Karnaugh map is another method of representing a truth table. It is a diagram made up of a number of squares. Each square represents a minterm of the corresponding truth table. Thus, for functions of two variables the map will have four squares, for functions of three variables the map will have eight squares and for functions of four variables the map will have 16 squares. Each square in the map is labelled in such a way as to aid simplification of Boolean expressions by inspection of the map.

The Karnaugh map for three variables is non-trivial and we will consider it first. The map with the minterm represented by each square is shown in Figure 2.10. Note that the minterms are not arranged in the map in their natural ascending sequence, but in a sequence corresponding to a cyclic code with unit Hamming distance between adjacent squares (see Section 1.4.3). The map in Figure 2.10(ii) indicates the minterm (in terms of the literals) represented by each box and also the logic values of the triplet of variables.

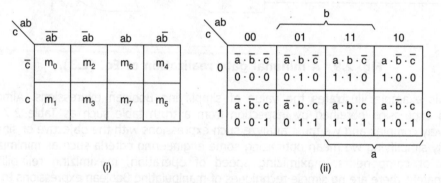

(i)                                            (ii)

**Fig. 2.10   A three-variable Karnaugh map.**

This labelling of the boxes in the map directly aids simplification of Boolean expressions. Observe that with this coding, adjacent squares in the map differ by only one variable which is complemented in one box and appears as it is (that is uncomplemented) in the next. From Postulate 5 of Boolean algebra it is evident that if we OR the minterms in adjacent squares, they may be simplified to yield a term with one less literal. For example, if we OR $m_2$ and $m_6$ we obtain:

$$m_2 + m_6 = \bar{a} \cdot b \cdot \bar{c} + a \cdot b \cdot \bar{c}$$

$$= (\bar{a} + a) \cdot b \cdot \bar{c} \qquad \text{By Postulate 4(a)}$$

$$= b \cdot \bar{c} \qquad \text{By Postulate 5(a)}$$

We will use this basic principle to simplify Boolean expressions.

*Example 2.5.* Consider the Truth Table 2.15. The table is first mapped on to the Karnaugh map as shown in Figure 2.11(i).

**TABLE 2.15**
**A Boolean Function for Simplification**

|  | $a$ | $b$ | $c$ | $z$ |
|---|---|---|---|---|
| $m_0$ | 0 | 0 | 0 | 0 |
| $m_1$ | 0 | 0 | 1 | 0 |
| $m_2$ | 0 | 1 | 0 | 1 |
| $m_3$ | 0 | 1 | 1 | 0 |
| $m_4$ | 1 | 0 | 0 | 0 |
| $m_5$ | 1 | 0 | 1 | 1 |
| $m_6$ | 1 | 1 | 0 | 1 |
| $m_7$ | 1 | 1 | 1 | 1 |

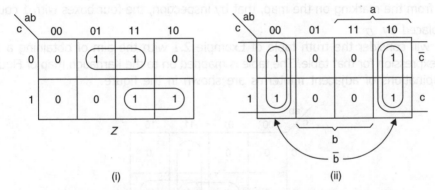

**Fig. 2.11   Simplification with three-variable maps.**

The mapping is straightforward. For each combination of $a$, $b$, $c$, with $z = 1$, a 1 is entered in the Karnaugh map. Thus, for $a\,b\,c$ = 0 1 0, 1 0 1, 1 1 0, and 1 1 1, we have 1s in the map. The next step is to identify adjacent 1s in the map. Two adjacent 1s may be combined to eliminate one literal. In this example, we have:

$$z = (\bar{a} \cdot b \cdot \bar{c} + a \cdot b \cdot \bar{c}) + (a \cdot b \cdot c + a \cdot \bar{b} \cdot c)$$

$$= (\bar{a} + a) \cdot b \cdot \bar{c} + a \cdot c (b + \bar{b})$$

$$= b \cdot \bar{c} + a \cdot c$$

The main merit of the Karnaugh map is the fact that terms which are logically adjacent, that is, minterms which differ in only one variable (such as $a \cdot \bar{b} \cdot c, a \cdot b \cdot c$) are also physically adjacent in the map. Thus, one can, by inspection, pick terms to be combined to eliminate variables. This is true except for the first and last columns of the map. They are logically adjacent; the terms $\bar{a} \cdot \bar{b} \cdot \bar{c}$ and $a \cdot \bar{b} \cdot \bar{c}$ are adjacent. Similarly, $\bar{a} \cdot \bar{b} \cdot c$ and $a \cdot \bar{b} \cdot c$ are adjacent. To ensure that they are all physically adjacent one may imagine the map to be wrapped on a cylinder with the first and last columns next to one another. We will illustrate minimization of a function in which they are physically adjacent.

***Example 2.6.***    Consider the K-map of Figure 2.11(ii). First we observe if the 1s in the first and second rows are adjacent. Thus,

$$z = (\bar{a} \cdot \bar{b} \cdot \bar{c} + \bar{a} \cdot \bar{b} \cdot c) + (a \cdot \bar{b} \cdot \bar{c} + a \cdot \bar{b} \cdot c)$$

$$= \bar{a} \cdot \bar{b} + a \cdot \bar{b} \quad \text{As } (\bar{c} + c = 1)$$

Now, we see that the first and the fourth columns are adjacent. Thus, they may be combined.

$$z = \bar{a} \cdot \bar{b} + a \cdot \bar{b} = (\bar{a} + a) \cdot \bar{b} = \bar{b}$$

Observe from the marking on the map, that by inspection, the four boxes with 1 could have been replaced by $\bar{b}$.

We will consider the truth table of Example 2.1 with the aim of obtaining a minimal Boolean expression for that table. The table is mapped on to the Karnaugh map of Figure 2.12. The combinations of adjacent minterms are shown in the figure.

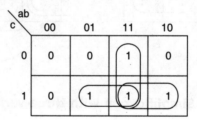

**Fig. 2.12   K-map for Example 2.1.**

Observe that the minterm $a \cdot b \cdot c$ is used thrice to facilitate minimization.

$$z = (\bar{a} \cdot b \cdot c + a \cdot b \cdot c) + (a \cdot b \cdot \bar{c} + a \cdot b \cdot c) + (a \cdot b \cdot c + a \cdot \bar{b} \cdot c)$$

$$= b \cdot c + a \cdot b + a \cdot c$$

***Example 2.7***    Consider the Karnaugh map of Figure 2.13(a). The reduced expression for $z$ is:

$$z = \bar{a} \cdot \bar{c} + b \cdot \bar{c} \tag{2.4}$$

which when realized with gates leads to Figure 2.14.

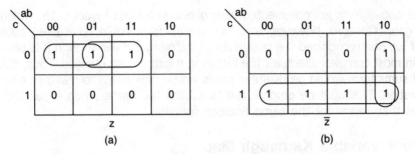

**Fig. 2.13 K-map for a three-variable function.**

Instead of getting the sum of product form, if we wish to obtain the product of sums form we may use the 0s in the map of Figure 2.13(a) and obtain Figure 2.13(b) from which

$$\bar{z} = a \cdot \bar{b} + c \quad \text{and} \quad z = (\bar{a} + b) \cdot \bar{c}$$

using De Morgan's theorem.

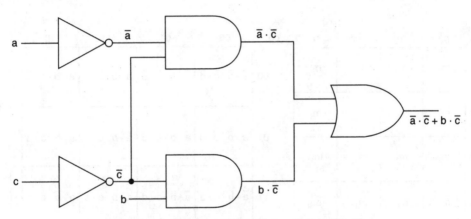

**Fig. 2.14 Gate realization of Eq. (2.4).**

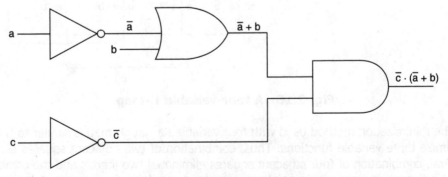

**Fig. 2.15 A minimal gate realization of Eq. (2.4).**

If the above form is implemented with gates we obtain Figure 2.15, which uses one less AND gate. Observe, however, that the second form could have been obtained from Eq. (2.4) if we had recognized the possibility of factoring $c$. Even though it is obvious in this example, in most complex examples the factoring might not be obvious. Thus, obtaining the product of sums form would be useful in cases where one wants to make sure of a minimal gate realization. It should be emphasized that both the forms when expanded should be identical as they represent the same Boolean function.

## 2.8.1 Four Variable Karnaugh Map

The Karnaugh map for Boolean functions of four variables is shown in Figure 2.16. The map on the left shows how the 16 minterms are represented in the map. The map on the right shows the coding used to indicate rows and columns in the map. Observe that adjacent squares differ by not more than one bit in their four-bit code representation. Further, the first and last columns are adjacent. The same is true for the top and bottom rows. One can imagine the map to be wrapped round on a surface in both directions to remember the logical neighbourhoods given above.

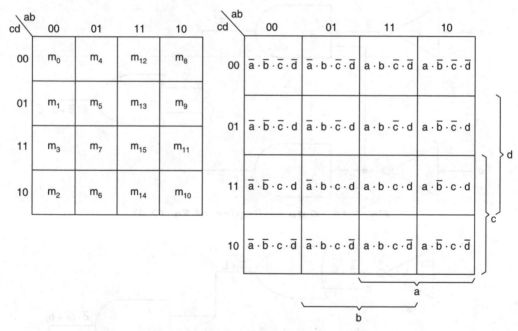

**Fig. 2.16 A four-variable K-map.**

The minimization method used with four variable Karnaugh map is similar to that used to minimize three variable functions. Thus, combination of two adjacent squares eliminates one literal, combination of four adjacent squares eliminates two literals and the combination of eight adjacent squares eliminates three literals. A number of examples of combining 1s in the Karnaugh map to eliminate literals is shown in Figure 2.17.

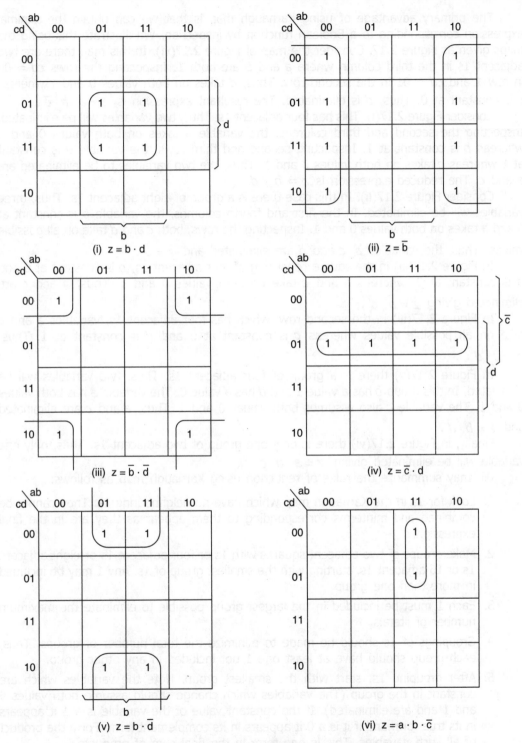

**Fig. 2.17  Simplification with four-variable maps.**

The primary advantage of using Karnaugh map is that we can obtain the minimal expression corresponding to a Boolean function by inspection. We illustrate this using the maps given as Figure 2.17. Consider the map of Figure 2.17(vi). In this map there are two adjacent 1s in the third column where $a$ and $b$ are both 1. Inspecting the rows $cd = 00$ in row 1 and $cd = 01$ in the second row. Thus, $d$ takes on both values 0 and 1 whereas $c$ is constant at 0. Thus, $d$ is eliminated. The resultant expression is $z = a \cdot b \cdot \overline{c}$.

Consider Figure 2.17(i). This has four adjacent 1s. Thus, two variables will be eliminated. Inspecting the second and third columns, the variable $a$ takes on both values 0 and 1 whereas $b$ is constant at 1. Inspecting second and third rows, the variable $d$ is constant at 1 whereas $c$ takes on both values 0 and 1. Thus, the two variables to be eliminated are $a$ and $c$. The reduced expression is $z = b \cdot d$.

Consider Figure 2.17(ii). In this case there is a group of eight adjacent 1s. Thus, three variables will be eliminated. In the first and fourth columns, the variable $b$ is constant at 0 and $a$ takes on both values 0 and 1. Inspecting the rows, both $c$ and $d$ take on all possible values. Thus, the variables $a$, $c$ and $d$ are eliminated and $z = \overline{b}$.

In Figure 2.17(iii) in the square consisting of four adjacent 1s, $b$ is constant at 0 and $d$ is constant at 0, whereas $a$ and $c$ take on both values 0 and 1. Thus, $a$ and $c$ are eliminated giving $z = \overline{b} \cdot \overline{d}$.

In Figure 2.17(iv) in the second row, which has four adjacent 1s, variables $a$ and $b$ take on all possible values whereas $c$ is constant at 0 and $d$ is constant at 1. Thus, $z = \overline{c} \cdot d$.

In Figure 2.17(v) there is a group of four adjacent 1s. Thus, two variables will be eliminated. In this group $b$ has a value 1 and $d$ has a value 0. The variable $a$ has both values 0 and 1. The variable $c$ also assumes both values 0 and 1. Thus, $a$ and $c$ are eliminated and $z = b \cdot \overline{d}$.

Finally, in Figure 2.17(vi) there is only one group of two adjacent 1s. Thus, only one variable will be eliminated giving $z = a \cdot b \cdot \overline{c}$.

We may summarize the rules of reduction using Karnaugh map as follows:

1. Look for 1s in the Karnaugh map which have no neighbouring 1s. They cannot be combined and minterms corresponding to them appear as they are in the final expression.

2. Make groups of two adjacent squares with 1s or four adjacent 1s or eight adjacent 1s or 16 adjacent 1s, starting with the smallest group of 1s. Any 1 may be included in more than one group.

3. Each 1 must be included in the largest group possible to eliminate the maximum number of literals.

4. Groupings of 1s should be made to minimize the total number of groups. Thus, each group should have at least one 1 not included in any other group.

5. After grouping 1s, start with the smallest group. Note the variables which are constant in the group (The variables which change should assume both values 0 and 1 and are eliminated). If the constant value of the variable is a 1 it appears in its true form and if it is a 0 it appears in its complement form. Form the product of all such variables. This is one term in the final sum of products.

Repeat this step and form a product for each group until all groups are exhausted. Thereafter, take the sum of the products to form the final expression.

A Boolean expression which cannot be further reduced is said to be in its minimal sum of products (or product of sums) form. Each term in the minimal expression is known as a **prime implicant. Minimization** is thus, the process of obtaining minimal set of prime implicants which "covers" all the minterms of the given Boolean function.

## 2.8.2 Incompletely Specified Function

So far we have considered completely specified functions namely, functions whose value is specified for all minterms. Quite often, in practice, we encounter situations in which some minterms cannot occur. We will illustrate this with an example.

*Example 2.8.* A switching circuit is to be designed to generate even parity bit for decimal numbers expressed in the excess-3 code. The truth table is given in Table 2.16. Observe that six code groups are illegal. No parity bit need be generated in these cases as these cases cannot occur. Thus, $P$ is marked with a $\phi$ in the truth table and in the Karnaugh map indicating that it could be either 0 or 1. In other words the value of $P$ is immaterial. These are known as *don't care conditions* and may be taken as 1 or 0 in the Karnaugh map depending on whether they aid in eliminating literals. The Karnaugh map for the Parity generator is shown in Figure 2.18.

### TABLE 2.16
### Even Parity Bit for Excess-3 Code

| A | B | C | D | P | |
|---|---|---|---|---|---|
| 0 | 0 | 0 | 0 | $\phi$ | |
| 0 | 0 | 0 | 1 | $\phi$ | Illegal codes |
| 0 | 0 | 1 | 0 | $\phi$ | |
| 0 | 0 | 1 | 1 | 0 | |
| 0 | 1 | 0 | 0 | 1 | |
| 0 | 1 | 0 | 1 | 0 | |
| 0 | 1 | 1 | 0 | 0 | |
| 0 | 1 | 1 | 1 | 1 | |
| 1 | 0 | 0 | 0 | 1 | |
| 1 | 0 | 0 | 1 | 0 | |
| 1 | 0 | 1 | 0 | 0 | |
| 1 | 0 | 1 | 1 | 1 | |
| 1 | 1 | 0 | 0 | 0 | |
| 1 | 1 | 0 | 1 | $\phi$ | Illegal codes |
| 1 | 1 | 1 | 0 | $\phi$ | |
| 1 | 1 | 1 | 1 | $\phi$ | |

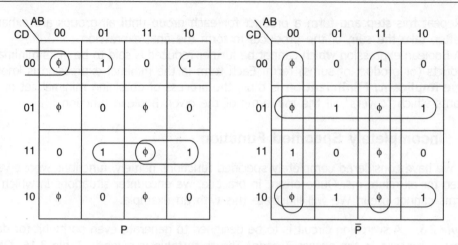

**Fig. 2.18  K-map for Parity generator.**

Observe that the number of terms in $P$ using don't care conditions, when they help in reducing literals and ignoring them when they do not help, leads to the expression:

$$P = \bar{A} \cdot \bar{C} \cdot \bar{D} + \bar{B} \cdot \bar{C} \cdot \bar{D} + B \cdot C \cdot D + A \cdot C \cdot D$$

If we look at the Karnaugh map for $\bar{P}$ we find that it can use all the don't care conditions optimally and we obtain:

$$\bar{P} = \bar{B} \cdot \bar{A} + A \cdot B + \bar{C} \cdot D + C \cdot \bar{D}$$

and using De Morgan's theorem,

$$P = (A + B) \cdot (\bar{A} + \bar{B}) \cdot (C + \bar{D}) \cdot (\bar{C} + D)$$

The expression is more economical to implement. The gate circuit is shown in Figure 2.19.

## 2.9  QUINE–McCLUSKEY PROCEDURE

The Karnaugh map method is a useful and powerful tool to minimize Boolean expressions. The construction of the map and its use depends on the coding scheme, which ensures that physically adjacent minterms in the map are also logically adjacent. This cyclic coding scheme is difficult to extend to a larger number of variables. Up to six variable maps can be constructed and used with some success but beyond that it is practically impossible to use this technique.

A method developed by Quine and extended by McCluskey is applicable to any number of variables. It is an algorithmic method and programs have been written to implement it on a computer.

McCluskey's procedure is similar to Karnaugh map procedure. The similarity is that in both methods groups of minterms, which will combine to eliminate the maximum number of literals, are first isolated. From these groups the smallest set of prime implicants which will cover all minterms is selected.

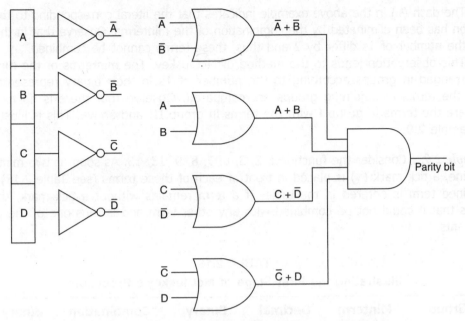

**Fig. 2.19  Gate realization of the Parity generator.**

The method of eliminating literals is based on the repeated application of the theorem:

$$a \cdot b + a \cdot \bar{b} = a$$

If two minterms are to be combined using the above theorem, then the number of 1s appearing in their binary representation must differ by one and only one 1. In other words, the Hamming distance between their binary representations should be 1. This is illustrated in Table 2.17.

**TABLE 2.17**
**Illustrating Combination of Minterms**

| Minterm | Binary Representation | Reduced Representation |
|---|---|---|
| | $a\ b\ c\ d$ | |
| $m_{10} = a \cdot \bar{b} \cdot c \cdot \bar{d}$ | 1 0 1 0 | $1\,0\,1 - (a \cdot \bar{b} \cdot c)$ |
| $m_{11} = a \cdot \bar{b} \cdot c \cdot d$ | 1 0 1 1 | |
| $m_8 = a \cdot \bar{b} \cdot \bar{c} \cdot \bar{d}$ | 1 0 0 0 | |
| $m_{12} = a \cdot b \cdot \bar{c} \cdot \bar{d}$ | 1 1 0 0 | $1 - 0\,0\,(a \cdot \bar{c} \cdot \bar{d})$ |
| $m_8 = a \cdot \bar{b} \cdot \bar{c} \cdot \bar{d}$ | 1 0 0 0 | |
| $m_{11} = a \cdot \bar{b} \cdot c \cdot d$ | 1 0 1 1 | Does not combine |

The dash (−) in the above example indicates that the literal corresponding to that bit position has been eliminated by the combination of the minterms. Observe that in the last case the number of 1s differ by 2 and thus, these terms cannot be combined.

This observation leads to the method of McCluskey. The minterms of the function are arranged in groups according to the number of 1s in their binary representation. Then the terms in adjoining groups are compared. Observe that there is no need to compare the terms in group I with the terms in group III and above. This is illustrated in Example 2.9.

***Example 2.9.***   Consider the function $\Sigma$ 2, 3, 6, 7, 8, 9, 13, 15. As soon as two minterms combine, a tick mark ($\sqrt{}$) is placed in front of each of these terms (see Table 2.18). The combined term is entered in the table. If a term remains without a tick mark, then it means that it could not be combined with any other term and is thus one of the prime implicants.

**TABLE 2.18**
**Illustrating the First Stage of McCluskey's Procedure**

| Group | Minterm | Decimal Rep. | Binary Rep. | Combination | Binary Rep. |
|-------|---------|--------------|-------------|-------------|-------------|
| I (One 1) | $m_2$ | $\sqrt{2}$ | 0 0 1 0 | | |
| | $m_8$ | $\sqrt{8}$ | 1 0 0 0 | | |
| | | | | 2, 3 | 0 0 1 − |
| | | | | 2, 6 | 0 − 1 0 |
| II (Two 1s) | $m_3$ | $\sqrt{3}$ | 0 0 1 1 | 8, 9 | 1 0 0 − |
| | $m_6$ | $\sqrt{6}$ | 0 1 1 0 | | |
| | $m_9$ | $\sqrt{9}$ | 1 0 0 1 | | |
| | | | | 3, 7 | 0 − 1 1 |
| | | | | 6, 7 | 0 1 1 − |
| III (Three 1s) | $m_7$ | $\sqrt{7}$ | 0 1 1 1 | 9, 13 | 1 − 0 1 |
| | $m_{13}$ | $\sqrt{13}$ | 1 1 0 1 | | |
| IV | | | | 7, 15 | − 1 1 1 |
| | $m_{15}$ | $\sqrt{15}$ | 1 1 1 1 | 13, 15 | 1 1 − 1 |
| (Four 1s) | | | | | |

Notice that after combining minterms the resulting combinations fall into groups which differ by not more than one 1. The minterms in each one of these groups can be further combined into sets of four minterms using the reduction theorem again. This second step is explained further. Observe that in this step terms will combine only if the positions of dashes in them coincide. This requirement is in addition to the requirement that all the other bits in the minterm, except one, also coincide. Notice that in this example, the pairs 2, 3 and 6, 7 as well as pairs 2, 6 and 3, 7 combine to produce the term 2, 3, 6, 7 with binary equivalent $0 - 1 -$.

No further combinations of minterms are possible in this example. The terms without a tick mark are the remaining uncombined terms (Table 2.19). These terms are the prime implicants of this Boolean function as shown in Table 2.20

### TABLE 2.19
#### McCluskey Procedure—Second Stage

| Combined Result | Binary Rep. | Second Combination | Binary Rep. |
|---|---|---|---|
| √2, 3 | 0 0 1 – | | |
| √2, 6 | 0 – 1 0 | | |
| 8, 9 | 1 0 0 – | | |
| | | 2, 3, 6, 7 | 0 – 1 – |
| √3, 7 | 0 – 1 1 | 2, 6, 3, 7 | |
| √6, 7 | 0 1 1 – | | |
| 9, 13 | 1 – 0 1 | | |
| 7, 15 | – 1 1 1 | | |
| 13, 15 | 1 1 – 1 | | |

### TABLE 2.20
#### Prime Implicants of the Boolean Function (Example 2.9)

| | | |
|---|---|---|
| A | 2, 3, 6, 7 | $\bar{a} \cdot c$ |
| B | 8, 9 | $a \cdot \bar{b} \cdot \bar{c}$ |
| C | 9, 13 | $a \cdot \bar{c} \cdot d$ |
| D | 7, 15 | $b \cdot c \cdot d$ |
| E | 13, 15 | $a \cdot b \cdot d$ |

The next step, after the prime implicants are found, is to find the smallest set of these which will cover all the minterms in the function. This set is said to consist of **essential prime implicants.** The selection of the essential prime implicants is facilitated by using Figure 2.20.

The prime implicants are listed in the first column with the minterms included in them written within parentheses. The minterms in the functions are listed along a row. A grid is formed as shown. The minterms included in each prime implicant are indicated by crosses. The idea is to cover all minterms using the minimum set of prime implicants.

Thus, we first look at columns with a single cross mark in them. This indicates that only one prime implicant can cover that particular minterm and it is thus essential. In this example prime implicant $A$ is essential to cover minterms 2, 3, 6. If it is included it also covers 7. $A$ and the minterms 2, 3, 6, 7 are ticked in the table. Next, we see that $B$ is essential to cover minterm 8. It also covers 9. Thus, 8 and 9 and $B$ are ticked. Only minterms 13 and 15 are left now. They can be covered by including prime implicants $C$ and $D$ or by $E$ alone. The choice of $E$ is obvious. Thus, the essential prime implicants are $A$, $B$ and $E$ and the reduced expression is:

$$f = \bar{a} \cdot c + a \cdot \bar{b} \cdot \bar{c} + a \cdot b \cdot d$$

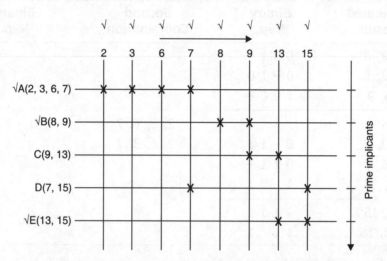

**Fig. 2.20   Selection of essential prime implicants.**

We will now consider another example to illustrate the use of Quine–McCluskey method. In this example there are five variables and some minterms which correspond to don't care conditions. The procedure followed is similar to that of the last example. The difference is that all the minterms (including the ones corresponding to don't care conditions) are used in combinations to obtain prime implicants. In finding the essential prime implicants, the minterms corresponding to don't care conditions need not be covered. Hence, they are not included in constructing the last table in the procedure.

*Example 2.10.*

$$f = \Sigma\ 4, 5, 10, 11, 15, 18, 20, 24, 26, 30, 31$$
$$+ \underset{\phi}{\Sigma}\ 9, 12, 14, 16, 19, 21, 25$$

where $\underset{\phi}{\Sigma}$ are the minterms corresponding to don't care conditions.

**TABLE 2.21**
**Reduction Steps for Example 2.10**

| | | | |
|---|---|---|---|
| √4 | 0 0 1 0 0 | √4, 5 | 0 0 1 0 – |
| √16 | 1 0 0 0 0 | *4, 12 | 0 – 1 0 0 |
| | | √4, 20 | – 0 1 0 0 |
| √5 | 0 0 1 0 1 | √16, 18 | 1 0 0 – 0 |
| √9 | 0 1 0 0 1 | *16, 20 | 1 0 – 0 0 |
| √10 | 0 1 0 1 0 | √16, 24 | 1 – 0 0 0 |
| √12 | 0 1 1 0 0 | | |
| √18 | 1 0 0 1 0 | √5, 21 | – 0 1 0 1 |
| √20 | 1 0 1 0 0 | *9, 11 | 0 1 0 – 1 |
| √24 | 1 1 0 0 0 | *9, 25 | – 1 0 0 1 |
| | | √10, 11 | 0 1 0 1 – |
| √11 | 0 1 0 1 1 | √10, 14 | 0 1 – 1 0 |
| √14 | 0 1 1 1 0 | √10, 26 | – 1 0 1 0 |
| √19 | 1 0 0 1 1 | *12, 14 | 0 1 1 – 0 |
| √21 | 1 0 1 0 1 | *18, 19 | 1 0 0 1 – |
| √25 | 1 1 0 0 1 | √18, 26 | 1 – 0 1 0 |
| √26 | 1 1 0 1 0 | √20, 21 | 1 0 1 0 – |
| | | *24, 25 | 1 1 0 0 – |
| √15 | 0 1 1 1 1 | √24, 26 | 1 1 0 – 0 |
| √30 | 1 1 1 1 0 | | |
| | | √11, 15 | 0 1 – 1 1 |
| √31 | 1 1 1 1 1 | √14, 15 | 0 1 1 1 – |
| | | √14, 30 | – 1 1 1 0 |
| | | √26, 30 | 1 1 – 1 0 |
| | | | |
| | | √15, 31 | – 1 1 1 1 |
| | | √30, 31 | 1 1 1 1 – |

| | |
|---|---|
| *4, 5, 20, 21 | – 0 1 0 – |
| *16, 18, 24, 26 | 1 – 0 – 0 |
| *10, 26, 14, 30 | – 1 – 1 0 |
| *10, 11, 14, 15 | 0 1 – 1 – |
| *14, 15, 30, 31 | – 1 1 1 – |

At the end of this we see that the terms marked with * are to be included in the essential prime implicant grid chart for this example shown in Figure 2.21. Observe that the don't care minterms are not listed at the top of the grid chart. The minimal expression obtained is also shown in the figure.

We summarise the Quine–McClusky method presented with Examples 2.9 and 2.10 as a step by step procedure below. This can be converted to a program using appropriate data structures.

1. Store in a matrix the binary equivalents of the minterms of the Boolean function to be minimized. (The number of columns in the matrix will be equal to the number

of columns in the truth table of the Boolean function and the maximum number of rows will be $2^n$.) Call the list of minterms to be covered A.

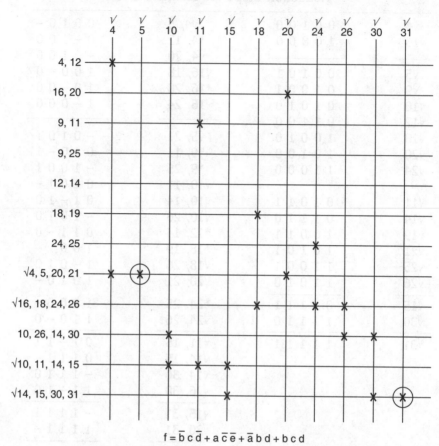

$$f = \overline{b}\,c\,\overline{d} + a\,\overline{c}\,\overline{e} + \overline{a}\,b\,d + b\,c\,d$$

**Fig. 2.21 Essential prime implicant grid chart.**

2. Sort the minterms into groups such that each group has minterms with one 1, two 1s, three 1s, etc. and the last one will have maximum *n* 1s. Number the group as 1, 2, ..., *m* indicating the number of 1s in each group.

3. There is a possibility that some minterms in adjacent groups will have a Hamming distance of 1. Select bit strings in groups 1 and 2 and compare them. Wherever all bits match except 1, replace this bit by a—indicating that the variable corresponding this position is eliminated. Group the minterms combined into one list. Repeat this for all groups 2, 3; 3, 4,..., (*m* − 1), *m*.

4. Put the list of minterms combined in adjacent groups. Put minterms which did not combine in a list of potential prime implicants. Call this list B.

5. Compare pairs of bit strings in adjacent groups which match the $k^{th}$ bit position (*k* = 1 to *n*). See if they have a Hamming distance of 1. If yes, combine them and put a − at the bit position which did not match. Put minterms which did not combine in list B.

6. Repeat step 5 till no further combinations are possible. Put all the remaining groups of minterms in the list of potential prime implicants namely, B.

7. The next step is to pick from list B the minimal set of prime implicants which will cover all the minterms in the function. This is done as follows:

Pick the lowest valued minterm from list A. Search list B sequentially and find if it is in any member of this list. If not, it is not a combinable minterm and stands alone in the final expression. Put it in the essential prime implicant list C. If it is found only in one group, that group is picked and added to the essential prime implicant list C. If it is in more than one group of minterms, pick the one with maximum number of minterms. Add it to the list C of essential prime implicants. Remove the minterms covered by this from list A.

8. Repeat step 7 with the remaining minterms till all the minterms in list A are accounted for. The list C of essential prime implicants found is the minimal cover of minterms. Obtain a Boolean expression corresponding to list C.

Use of C programs for minimization is necessary if the number of literals in the Boolean function exceeds eight. There are plenty of programs available in the open domain. One program can be found in http://bungled.net/~conrad/pi.c. You can also do a Google search with query "Quine McCluskey C Program" to get links to other C programs.

When the number of variables is very large, for example 32, the number of minterms will be of the order of $2^{32} \cong 10^9$. To search lists of minterms of this size the time taken by a computer can become too large. Thus, heuristic algorithms have been developed which will not gurantee optimality but will get a near optimal solution in a much smaller time. One popular program of this type which is commercially available is called **EXPRESSO** and is often used by designers of combinatorial circuits with a large number of literals. The references at the end of this book lists some of these.

## 2.10 CONCLUSIONS

In this chapter we introduced Boolean algebra and saw its usefulness in expressing two-valued functions and in simplifying such functions. We also illustrated the implementation of some Boolean functions with logic gates. The implementation aspects were discussed mainly to motivate the student to learn why minimization of the number of literals in a Boolean expression is useful. We gave methods which can be used for manual minimization of Boolean expressions. The manual methods are sufficient for small expressions with up to five or six variables. When the number of variables in a Boolean expression is above six, manual methods take considerable time and the possibility of making mistakes increases. Thus, computer programs have been developed and are widely available to aid minimization. These tools can be used on many computers including personal computers.

The hardware realization of the switching functions are also changing rapidly with the advent of large-scale integrated circuits. In the next chapter we will discuss the practical design of combinational logic circuits.

---
**SUMMARY**
---

1. A subset of a general algebra known as Boolean Algebra is called Switching Algebra. It is useful for designing digital switching circuits.

2. Switching algebra deals with a set of elements (0,1) together with two binary operators known as AND($\cdot$) and OR(+) and a unary operator called NOT (Shown as a bar – over a variable).

3. A set of Postulates define the functions of the operators and the result of applying these operators to binary variables (i.e. variables which can have a value 0 or 1).

4. Using these postulates a set of theorems can be proved. Table 2.4 gives a summary of all the postulates and theorems of Boolean Algebra.

5. A Boolean function $f(a, b, c)$ of three variables $a, b, c$ can be defined using a truth table. A truth table lists the value of the dependent variable for all possible values of the independent variables $a, b$ and $c$ starting with 000 and ending with 111. As the independent variables can have only one of two values (either 0 or 1), there can be only eight possible combinations of values of $a, b, c$. Thus, the Truth Table will have eight rows and each row gives one combination of values of $a, b, c$ and the corresponding value of $f(a, b, c)$.

6. A Boolean expression corresponding to any truth table representing $z = f(a_1, a_2, ..., a_n)$ can be obtained by inspecting the column corresponding to the dependent variable $z$ starting from the first column. A term in the Boolean expression corresponding to each row where $z = 1$ is obtained by applying AND to all the independent variables $a_1, a_2, ..., a_n$ in the truth table. The independent variable with a 0 entry appears in the complement form and that with a 1 entry appears as it is. For example, a row:

| $a_n$ | $a_{n-1}$ | ... | $a_3$ | $a_2$ | $a_1$ | $a_0$ | $z$ |
|---|---|---|---|---|---|---|---|
| 0 | 1 | ... | 1 | 0 | 1 | 0 | 1 |

will have a term in the Boolean expression for $z$ as $\bar{a}_n \, a_{n-1} \, ... \, a_3 \, \bar{a}_2 \, a_1 \, \bar{a}_0$. The expressions of all the rows with $z = 1$ are added (OR) to get the final expression for $z$.

7. The expression obtained as explained above is said to be in a standard form. Each term in the expression is called a minterm. A notation $m_0, m_1, ..., m_{2^n-1}$ is used to represent minterms starting from the row with all 0s to the row with all 1s. A Boolean expression for $z = f(a_0, a_1, ..., a_{2^n-1})$ represented by a truth table with 1s in rows 0, 3, 5, 6, 7 .... $2^n - 1$ is represented in the standard form as:

$$z = m_0 + m_3 + m_5 + m_6 + m_7 + ... + m_{2^n-1}$$

$$\Sigma = 0, 3, 5, 6, 7, ..., 2^n - 1$$

8. Another equivalent form for expressing the same truth table is obtained by examining the rows with 0. The term for the corresponding row is obtained by ORing independent variables. A variable with 0 entry is used as it is and a variable with a 1 entry is complemented. AND operation is then applied to individual terms. This form is called maxterm form. A Boolean expression for $z = f(a_0, a_1, ..., a_{2^n-1})$ represented with 0s in rows 1, 2, 4, 6, 8, ..., $2^n - 2$ is represented in this form as:

$$z = M_1 \cdot M_2 \cdot M_4 \cdot M_6 \cdot M_8 \cdot \ldots \cdot M_{2^n - 2}$$
$$= \Pi\ 1, 2, 4, 6, 8, \ldots, 2^n - 2$$

9. With two Boolean variables, 16 possible truth tables can be formed. Each truth table represents a Boolean function. Of these, eight can be used to represent binary operators. Of these eight operators, two operators called NAND (NOT of AND) and NOR (Not of OR) can be used to implement all Boolean functions and are called universal operators.

10. Electronic circuits called gates have been designed to realize Boolean operations. In these circuits two bands of voltages are used to represent 0 and 1. The band for 1, for example may be 5 V to 3.5 V and that for 0 to .5 V. The gap between the two bands is narrower in inputs to gates compared to output of gates. This provides noise immunity.

11. Boolean expressions in the standard form are not optimal for realization with gates. One commonly used criterion of optimization is minimizing the number of literals in the Boolean expression which also usually minimizes the number of gates used in realization.

12. There are two methods of minimizing the number of literals in Boolean expressions. Both of them repeatedly use the the theorem $ab + a\bar{b} = a$, which results in the elimination of one variable namely, $b$.

13. A method called Veitch-Karnaugh map method is a graphical aid to identify pairs of terms of the type $(a\bar{b} + ab)$ which allows elimination of one literal.

14. The Veitch-Karnaugh map is a diagram made up of a number of squares, each square representing a minterm of the corresponding truth table. A map for three variables has eight squares and a map of four variables has 16 squares. The labelling of the boxes is such that physically adjacent boxes are also logically adjacent, i.e. they differ in only one variable which appears in true form in one box and in its complement form in the adjacent box. Whenever the value of the dependent variable is 1, it is entered in a box corresponding to this minterm. By inspecting 1 entries in the box it is possible to identify the possibility of combining minterms to eliminate one or more variables.

15. The Karnaugh map is useful to minimize Boolean functions up to five variables, as it depends on the pattern recognition in two-dimensional maps. For functions of more variables an algorithmic method is needed.

16. Quine–McCluskey method of minimizing Boolean expressions is an algorithmic method which can be automated using a program. The basic idea used by the algorithm has been explained in this chapter.

---

## EXERCISES

1. Show that the three definitions in Section 2.3 satisfy the postulates of Boolean algebra.

2. Prove De Morgan's law for '$n$' variables.

3.  Using the postulates of Boolean algebra prove the following:

    (i)   $x \cdot y + \bar{x} \cdot z + y \cdot z = x \cdot y + \bar{x} \cdot z$

    (ii)  $(x + y) \cdot (x \cdot z + z) \cdot \overline{\bar{y}} + x \cdot z = \bar{x} \cdot y \cdot z$

    (iii) $x \cdot \bar{y} + y \cdot \bar{z} + \bar{x} \cdot z = \bar{x} \cdot y + \bar{y} \cdot z + x \cdot \bar{z}$

4.  Express the following in canonical sum and canonical product form:

    (i)   $\bar{a} \cdot b + a \cdot c + b \cdot c$

    (ii)  $\bar{a} \cdot b \cdot (a \cdot b + c) \cdot (b + \bar{c} \cdot d)$

5.  Exclusive OR operation is defined for two variables as $a\bar{b} + \bar{a}b$. Prove the associative law for exclusive OR operation.

6.  Simplify the following Boolean functions using the theorems of Boolean algebra:

    $f_1 (a, b, c, d) = \Sigma (0, 1, 2, 3, 6, 7)$

    $f_2 (a, b, c, d) = \Sigma (0, 4, 6, 10, 11, 13)$

    $f_3 (w, x, y, z) = \Pi (3, 5, 7, 11, 13, 15)$

7.  Repeat the problems in Exercise 6 using Karnaugh maps and verify your results.

8.  Using Karnaugh maps simplify the following Boolean functions:

    (i)   $f (a, b, c, d) = \Sigma (1, 3, 5, 8, 9, 11, 15) + \Sigma_{\phi} (2, 13)$

    (ii)  $f (w, x, y, z) = \Sigma (2, 3, 6, 7, 14, 15)$

9.  Minimize the following Boolean function using Quine–McCluskey's method. Check with Karnaugh map reduction method.

    $$f (a, b, c, d) = \Sigma (0, 1, 2, 3, 6, 7, 13, 14)$$

10. Add the following don't care condition to Exercise 9 and obtain the set of all prime implicants.

    $$\Sigma_{\phi} (8, 9, 10, 12)$$

11. Use Quine–McCluskey method to minimize the Boolean function:

    $$\Sigma_{\phi} 2, 5, 7, 9, 14, 21, 28, 31, 45, 48, 49, 50, 51, 62, 63$$

12. Use Quine–McCluskey method to minimize the following Boolean function with don't care conditions stated:

    $$\Sigma 2, 7, 9, 11, 13, 15, 19, 23, 26, 31$$
    $$+ \Sigma_{\phi} 3, 4, 14, 21, 25, 30$$

13. Use Quine–McCluskey method to minimize the following Boolean function:

    $$\Pi 3, 6, 8, 12, 14, 21, 28, 29, 31$$

## Chapter

# 3

# Combinatorial Switching Circuits

## 3.1  INTRODUCTION

Given the requirements, the next step is to analyze it and evolve a model of the system. The model is an abstraction of the essential features of the system. At the modelling stage we isolate the independent variables and the dependent variables. The next step in modelling is to assign binary values to the variables. This is essential as our primary aim is to design digital systems. During this step we develop the relevant truth table to model the input/

output relation of the system. The truth table may be represented by many equivalent Boolean expressions. Among these we can pick an appropriate one which will allow optimal logical realization of the required digital system. The meaning of "optimal" will depend upon the technology used to convert the logical to the physical realization of the system. Finally, we physically realize the required system with the technology available and appropriate at that time. It is important to understand that the logical realization is based on theory whereas the physical realization depends on the prevalent technology.

In this chapter we will first illustrate, using some examples, how requirements given as word statement may be analyzed and modelled as a truth table. We will then see how the minimal expressions obtained to represent the truth table may be realized by different gating circuits. Different types of gates could be used depending on the cost of such components prevailing at a particular time. At present, systems are designed using integrated electronic circuits. We will thus devote some attention to the design of such circuits.

The examples to be discussed in this chapter fall in the category of **Combinatorial Switching Circuits.** Combinatorial switching circuits (also called **combinational circuits**) consist of input variables, logic gates and output variables as shown in Figure 3.1. The inputs and outputs are two-valued. The values of output variables depend only on the present values of the inputs. The output does not depend on the previous history of inputs. In other words, time does not enter explicitly in the input-output relation of the system, that is, the system has no memory. The input-output relationship of such a circuit is given in Eq. (3.1).

$$z_1 = f_1 (x_1, x_2, ..., x_n)$$
$$z_2 = f_2 (x_1, x_2, ..., x_n)$$
$$\vdots \quad \vdots \qquad\qquad\qquad (3.1)$$
$$z_m = f_m (x_1, x_2, ..., x_n)$$

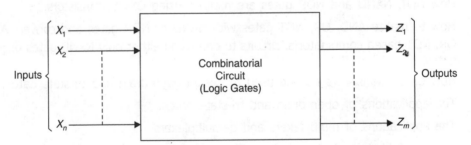

**Figure 3.1  Block diagram of a combinatorial circuit.**

## 3.2  COMBINATORIAL CIRCUIT DESIGN PROCEDURE

In this section we will illustrate the design procedure with a few examples.

*Example 3.1.*  A railway station with three platforms $A$, $B$ and $C$ is shown in Figure 3.2. A train coming to the station in the direction of the arrow is to be routed to platform $A$, $B$ or $C$. Normally, the train is to be routed to platform $A$ if that platform is empty. Only if both $A$ and $B$ are occupied, the train is to be routed to platform $C$. Each platform has a switch which will be turned ON if a train is standing at that platform. A signal light is to be green if a train is allowed to enter the station, otherwise it is red. A switching system is to be designed which will set points $S_A$, $S_B$ to route trains to the appropriate platform and to control the signal $S$.

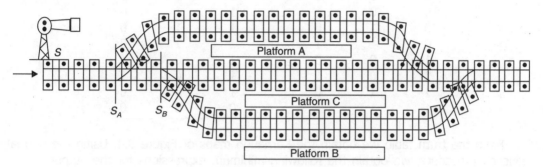

**Figure 3.2   Railway lines for Example 3.1.**

Analyzing this statement, we see that the inputs to the switching system are the platform occupancy signals which we will call $A$, $B$ and $C$ respectively. The outputs required are the signals to set the points and the green signal to let the train into the station. The switching system required may be modelled as shown in Figure 3.3.

**Figure 3.3   Switching system for Example 3.1.**

In this example it so happens that all inputs as well as output variables are inherently Boolean in nature. In other words, they assume one of two values. This need not always be the case as we will see at a later stage.

Now we make logical assignment to the variables. A '0' is assigned to variables $A$, $B$ and $C$ to indicate that platforms $A$, $B$ and $C$ respectively are empty and a '1' is used to indicate that the platform is occupied. For the output variables the assignment is a 1 if the particular signal is switched on (green signal) or the point is switched to allow entry to the appropriate line. A truth table (Table 3.1) is constructed keeping in view the requirement that the trains are to be routed to platform $A$ if that platform is vacant. Platform $C$ is to be used only when both $A$ and $B$ are occupied.

**TABLE 3.1**
**Truth Table for Track Switching**

| A | B | C | S | $S_A$ | $S_B$ |
|---|---|---|---|---|---|
| 0 | 0 | 0 | 1 | 1 | $\phi$ |
| 0 | 0 | 1 | 1 | 1 | $\phi$ |
| 0 | 1 | 0 | 1 | 1 | 0 |
| 0 | 1 | 1 | 1 | 1 | 0 |
| 1 | 0 | 0 | 1 | 0 | 1 |
| 1 | 0 | 1 | 1 | 0 | 1 |
| 1 | 1 | 0 | 1 | 0 | 0 |
| 1 | 1 | 1 | 0 | 0 | 0 |

From the truth table we obtain the Karnaugh maps of Figure 3.4. Using the normal reduction procedure, we obtain the following minimum expressions for the outputs:

$$S = (\bar{A} + \bar{B} + \bar{C}) \tag{3.2}$$

$$= \overline{A \cdot B \cdot C} \tag{3.3}$$

$$S_A = \bar{A} \tag{3.4}$$

$$S_B = \bar{B} \tag{3.5}$$

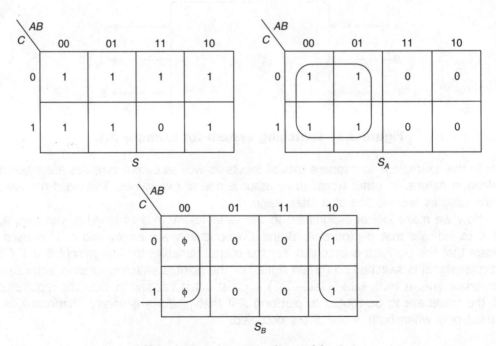

**Figure 3.4  K-maps for Table 3.1.**

We may interpret these in words as:

1. The signal for incoming train is turned green if platform A is not occupied or B is not occupied or C is not occupied. Equivalently, we may state that the signal is green if not all platforms A and B and C are occupied. In other words, turn S to green if any one of the platforms is not occupied.

2. The point to platform A is set if platform A is not occupied.

3. The point to platform B is set if platform B is not occupied.

The switching circuit is given in Figure 3.5.

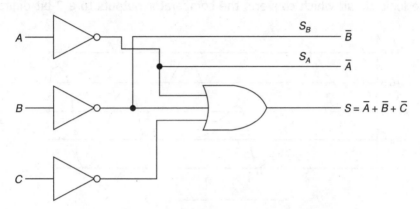

**Figure 3.5  Gate circuit for routing trains.**

As seen in Example 3.1, the design of combinatorial circuits begins with a statement of the problem and ends with a logic circuit diagram. The procedure used consists of the following steps:

1. State the problem.

2. Analyze the problem and model it using the following steps:

   (a) Find out the input and output variables.

   (b) Use an appropriate coding to represent the inputs and outputs with Boolean variables.

   (c) Assign letter symbols to represent input and output variables.

   (d) Obtain a truth table using the statements of the problem.

   (e) Represent each output variable in the truth table on a Karnaugh map or Quine–McCluskey chart.

   (f) Minimize the number of literals in the Boolean expression for each output variable.

   (g) Draw the logic circuit diagram corresponding to the Boolean expressions. This is the logical realization for the system.

   (h) Physically realize the system using appropriate technology.

We will now use this step-by-step procedure in another example.

***Example 3.2.*** An analog to digital converter converts an analog signal to digital form. Assume that the analog signal varies between +1 V and −1 V and is to be coded using two bits. If it is between −1 V and −0.5 V it is to be coded by 00, between −.05 V to 0 V it is to be coded by by 01, between 0 and 0.5 V it is coded by 10 and between 0.5 V and 1 V it is coded by 11. In order to find the voltage level of the input analog voltage, it is fed to three comparators as shown in Figure 3.6. The output of a comparator is 5 V if the analog signal exceeds the reference voltage and is 0 V otherwise. It is required to design the logic circuit which converts the comparator outputs to a 2-bit digital output.

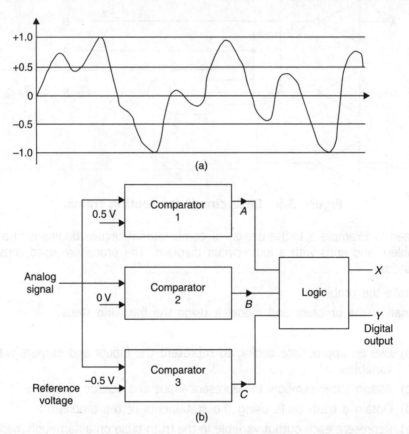

**Figure 3.6 (a) Analog signal (b) Block diagram for A/D conversion.**

After the problem is stated, the second step in solving the above problem is to recognize the inputs and outputs of the logic circuit. The inputs and outputs are as shown in Figure 3.6(b).

The next step is to code the inputs and outputs as two-valued variables. The comparators give binary outputs of 5 V and 0 V in this problem. Using a 1 to represent 5 V and a 0 to represent 0 V and using the letters A, B, C for inputs and X, Y for outputs, we may represent the requirements of the logic circuit by a truth table (Table 3.2). Observe that if comparator 3 gives an output of 0 V (that is, analog signal less than − 0.5 V) then comparator 2 cannot give an output of 5 V (as it will give 5 V only if the input is greater than 0 V). This set of input values cannot occur and thus, the outputs are coded as don't care values. Similar reasoning is used to obtain the full truth table.

**TABLE 3.2**
**Truth Table for A/D Converter**

| A | B | C | X | Y |
|---|---|---|---|---|
| 0 | 0 | 0 | 0 | 0 |
| 0 | 0 | 1 | 0 | 1 |
| 0 | 1 | 0 | $\phi$ | $\phi$ |
| 0 | 1 | 1 | 1 | 0 |
| 1 | 0 | 0 | $\phi$ | $\phi$ |
| 1 | 0 | 1 | $\phi$ | $\phi$ |
| 1 | 1 | 0 | $\phi$ | $\phi$ |
| 1 | 1 | 1 | 1 | 1 |

The truth table is next entered on Karnaugh maps in order to obtain minimal Boolean expressions for the outputs X and Y. Don't cares are optimally used to minimize the number of literals in the expressions for X and Y. The Karnaugh maps are shown in Figure 3.7(a) and 3.7(b). The minimal expressions are shown below the maps.

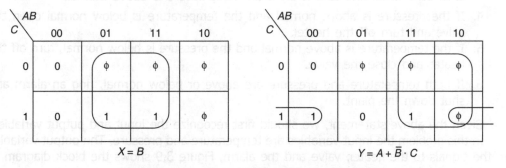

**Figure 3.7 K-map for A/D conversion.**

The minimal expressions are realized using AND, OR, NOT gates as in Figure 3.8. This is the logical realization of the required system.

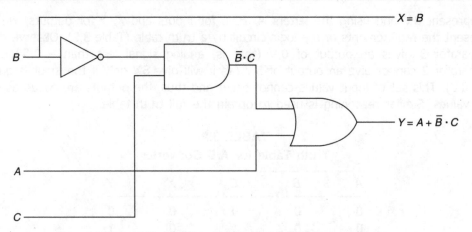

**Figure 3.8    Gate circuit for A/D conversion.**

*Example 3.3.*    A control unit is to be designed for a chemical process. Temperature and pressure are the two variables to be controlled. The control is exercised by switching on or off a heater and by opening or closing a valve. The control rules are given below:

1.  If temperature and pressure are in the normal range, switch off the heater and close the valve.
2.  If the temperature is normal, switch off the heater. Open the valve if the pressure is above normal and close it if it is below normal.
3.  If the pressure is normal, close the valve. Turn on the heater if the temperature is below normal and turn it off if the temperature is above normal.
4.  If the pressure is above normal and the temperature is below normal open the valve and turn off the heater.
5.  If the temperature is above normal and the pressure is below normal, turn off the heater and close the valve.
6.  If both temperature and pressure are above or below normal, ring an alarm and shut down the plant.

Given the above statement, we should first recognize the input and output variables.

In this problem the input variables are temperature and pressure. The output variables are the signals to the heater, valve and the alarm. Figure 3.9 shows the block diagram of the system.

The next step is to assign truth values to the inputs and the outputs.

The input conditions which determine controller action (namely the outputs) in this case are:

1. Temperature $\begin{cases} \text{above normal} \\ \text{normal} \\ \text{below normal} \end{cases}$

2. Pressure $\begin{cases} \text{above normal} \\ \text{normal} \\ \text{below normal} \end{cases}$

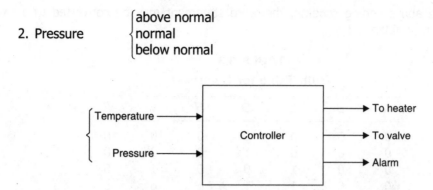

**Figure 3.9  Block diagram of a process controller.**

As there are three ranges for the input variables and we can represent only two-valued variables in a truth table, we need to code each one of these input variables by two Boolean variables in an appropriate coding as given below:

$$\text{Temperature} - \begin{cases} A - \begin{cases} \text{Above normal: 1} \\ \text{Not above normal: 0} \end{cases} \\ B - \begin{cases} \text{Below normal: 1} \\ \text{Not below normal: 0} \end{cases} \end{cases}$$

$$\text{Pressure} - \begin{cases} C - \begin{cases} \text{Above normal: 1} \\ \text{Not above normal: 0} \end{cases} \\ D - \begin{cases} \text{Below normal: 1} \\ \text{Not below normal: 0} \end{cases} \end{cases}$$

Observe that $A = 0$ and $B = 0$ indicates that the temperature is in the normal range; $A = 0$ and $B = 1$ indicates that the temperature is below normal; $A = 1$ and $B = 0$ indicates that the temperature is above normal and $A = 1$ and $B = 1$ is an impossible combination. The same interpretation may be given to the variables $C$ and $D$ indicating the pressure.

The output variables may be coded in a straightforward manner as given below:

$$\text{Signal to heater} - H - \begin{cases} 0 \text{ turn off heater} \\ 1 \text{ turn on heater} \end{cases}$$

$$\text{Signal to valve} - V - \begin{cases} 0 \text{ close valve} \\ 1 \text{ open valve} \end{cases}$$

$$\text{Alarm} - R - \begin{cases} 0 \text{ off} \\ 1 \text{ on} \end{cases}$$

Using the above coding scheme, the word statement may be converted to a truth table, as shown in Table 3.3.

**TABLE 3.3**
**Truth Table for Controller**

| A | B | C | D | H | V | R |
|---|---|---|---|---|---|---|
| 0 | 0 | 0 | 0 | 0 | 0 | 0 |
| 0 | 0 | 0 | 1 | 0 | 0 | 0 |
| 0 | 0 | 1 | 0 | 0 | 1 | 0 |
| 0 | 0 | 1 | 1 | φ | φ | φ |
| 0 | 1 | 0 | 0 | 1 | 0 | 0 |
| 0 | 1 | 0 | 1 | φ | φ | 1 |
| 0 | 1 | 1 | 0 | φ | φ | 1 |
| 0 | 1 | 1 | 1 | φ | φ | φ |
| 1 | 0 | 0 | 0 | 0 | 0 | 0 |
| 1 | 0 | 0 | 1 | 0 | 0 | 0 |
| 1 | 0 | 1 | 0 | φ | φ | 1 |
| 1 | 0 | 1 | 1 | φ | φ | φ |
| 1 | 1 | 0 | 0 | φ | φ | φ |
| 1 | 1 | 0 | 1 | φ | φ | φ |
| 1 | 1 | 1 | 0 | φ | φ | φ |
| 1 | 1 | 1 | 1 | φ | φ | φ |

Observe in the truth table that whenever $AB = 11$ or $CD = 11$, all the output variables have don't care values, that is, they may be either 0 or 1. In developing this truth table, it has also been assumed that when the alarm conditions exist the plant will be shut down and thus, the heater and valve signals may be undefined, that is, they may be either 0 or 1.

The Karnaugh map corresponding to the output variables $H$, $V$ and $R$ are shown in Figure 3.10(a), (b), (c) respectively. Using the don't care conditions, the minimal Boolean expressions shown below the maps are obtained. In order to see if they make sense, we interpret them into the following statements:

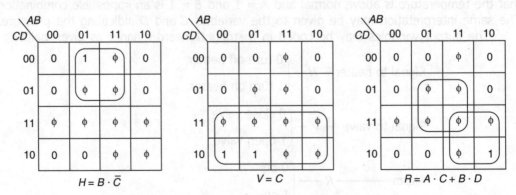

**Figure 3.10   K-maps for process controller.**

1. The heater is turned on if the temperature is below normal and the pressure is not above normal.

2. The valve is opened if the pressure is above normal.

3. The alarm is turned on if the temperature is above normal and the pressure is above normal or if the temperature is below normal and the pressure is below normal.

The statements made above are in fact a simplified but equivalent version of the original statement of the problem.

After obtaining the minimized expressions, they may be realized using AND, OR and NOT gates as shown in Figure 3.11.

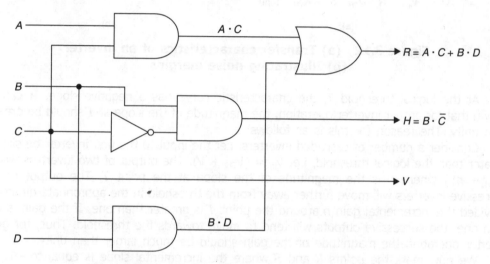

**Figure 3.11   Gate circuit for process controller.**

## 3.3   INTEGRATED NAND-NOR GATES

In Section 2.6 we presented gates which perform AND, OR and NOT operations. NAND/NOR gates are obtained by cascading an inverter with AND/OR gates respectively. Since the output is obtained from the inverter, let us look at the inverter characteristics in some detail.

Generally the input-output relationship (transfer characteristic) will have the form shown in Figure 3.12(a), where a low input voltage $V_{\text{in L}}$ gives a high output voltage $V_{\text{out H}}$, and a high input voltage $V_{\text{in H}}$ yields a low output voltage $V_{\text{out L}}$. This curve contains a lot of information as we shall see now. The operating points, $P$ and $Q$ on the curve are iteratively determined to satisfy this basic inverter function. Let us draw the line $OT$ of unity slope intersecting the curve at the point $T$. This point defines the **Logical Threshold** $V_{\text{TH}}$, corresponding to which the input and output voltages are equal. Now we see that when the input is higher than the logical threshold, the output is lower and vice versa. The logical threshold of an inverter is easily measured by connecting the output of an inverter to its own input thus forcing the equality condition between the two.

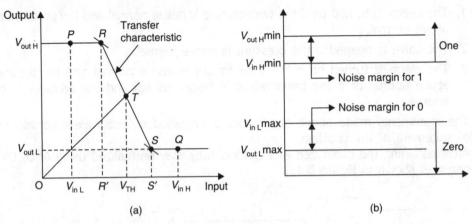

**Figure 3.12    (a) Transfer characteristics of an inverter
(b) Illustrating noise margins.**

At the logical threshold $T$, the characteristic curve has a negative slope. It can be shown that for proper inverter operation, the magnitude of the slope at $T$ should be greater than unity. The reason for this is as follows:

Consider a number of cascaded inverters. Let the input to the first inverter be slightly greater than the logical threshold, i.e. $V_{in} = (V_{TH} + V)$. The output of two inverters will be $(V_{TH} - nV)$ where $n$ is the magnitude of the slope at the point $T$. The output of the successive inverters will move further away from the threshold in the appropriate directions provided the incremental gain $n$ around the point $T$ is greater than one. If the gain is less than one, the successive outputs will tend to move towards the threshold. Thus, for good inverter operation the magnitude of the gain should be much larger than unity.

We now mark the points $R$ and $S$ where the incremental slope is equal to $-1$. We would naturally not like to operate an inverter with input lying in the region between $R'$ and $S'$ (see Figure 3.12(a)). The separation between these points $R'$ and $S'$ tends to be zero as the gain tends to be infinity, which gives the ideal threshold discriminator characteristics.

The manufacturers of gates specify the minimum $V_{in\,H}$ above which an input will be considered as logical one. Similarly, they also specify a maximum $V_{in\,L}$ below which an applied voltage will correspond to a logical zero. Further, they also guarantee a minimum $V_{out\,H}$ and maximum $V_{out\,L}$ that the gates will give as output over a specified temperature range when the loading rules are observed. The quantities $(V_{out\,H} - V_{in\,H})$ and $(V_{in\,L} - V_{out\,L})$ are defined as the noise margins (see Figure 3.12(b)). The larger the noise margin, the less the chance of a mistake or malfunction due to unwanted noise riding over the logic levels.

### 3.3.1    CMOS Transistor Gates

Before the advent of semiconductor switching elements, electronic tubes were used for switching and before that electromagnetic relays were employed. Semiconductor circuits revolutionized digital circuits by requiring much smaller space to fabricate, much lower power consumption and lower cost. By about 1960s we saw the introduction of the so-called semiconductor logic families. A **logic family** is a set of different integrated circuits that have similar input/output and internal circuits. Each member, however, performs a different logic function. Chips belonging to the same family can be interconnected to realize any desired logic function. Chips from different families may not be compatible as they may use different power supply values and their loading rules may differ.

Early digital circuits were designed using **transistor-transistor logic family** (TTL). This was popular from the 1960s to 1990s. Since the 1990s a family called **Metal Oxide Semiconductor Field Effect Transistors (MOSFET)** and its descendant **complementary MOSFET (abbreviated as CMOS)** circuits are universally used. CMOS circuits are used from medium-scale integrated circuits to very large-scale integrated circuits such as random access memories (RAM), processor chips, etc. which have several hundred million CMOS gates. The intention in this chapter is not to describe in detail the design of CMOS circuits, but to get a broad overview of their characteristics.

There are two types of MOS transistors called Negative-channel Metal Oxide semiconductor–**NMOS** and Positive-channel Metal Oxide Semiconductor–**PMOS.** Figure 3.13 is the circuit diagram of NMOS transistor. It has three terminals called drain, gate and source.

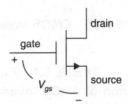

**Figure 3.13   NMOS transistor circuit symbol.**

Usually the source is at a low voltage and drain is kept at a positive voltage. If $V_{gs} > 0$, the gate "closes" making the resistance between drain and source almost 0. If $V_{gs} \leq 0$, the gate is open and the resistance between drain and source is very large (at least 1 mega-ohm). PMOS transistor has a similar behaviour except that the drain is at a low voltage and the source is at a + voltage.

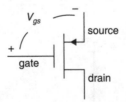

**Figure 3.14   Circuit symbol of PMOS transistor.**

In PMOS if gate is at a negative voltage, i.e. $V_{gs} < 0$, the gate closes and the resistance between source and drain is almost 0. If gate voltage $V_{gs} \geq 0$, gate is open and resistance of the gate will be high (> 1 mega-ohm). When the gate is open no current is drawn by the gate. It thus presents nearly infinite impedence at the input.

In computer applications NMOS and PMOS are used together in a configuration called CMOS. A CMOS inverter is shown in Figure 3.15. In this circuit if $V_{in} \leq 0$, the bottom NMOS gate will be open ($Q_1$ non-conducting state) and the PMOS gate will close. Thus, $Q_2$ will be shorted and thus, $V_{out}$ will be 5 V. On the other hand, if $V_{in}$ is + 5 V, $Q_1$ will close and $Q_2$ will be open. Thus, $V_{out}$ will be 0 V. This is shown in Table 3.4

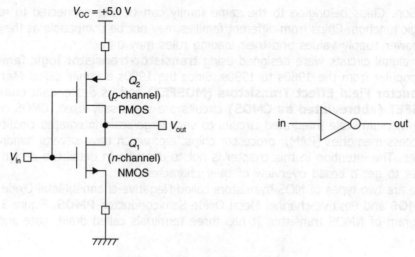

**Figure 3.15   CMOS inverter.**

**TABLE 3.4**
**Action of CMOS Inverter**

| $V_{in}$ | State of $Q_1$ | State of $Q_2$ | $V_{out}$ |
|---|---|---|---|
| 0 V(0) | Open | Closed | 5 V (1) |
| 5 V(1) | Closed | Open | 0 V (0) |

Thus, the circuit is an inverter. To show the logical behaviour of $p$ and $n$-channel MOS transistors, it is conventional to re-draw Figure 3.15 as shown in Figure 3.16. This illustrates the fact that when $V_{in}$ is 5 V, $Q_1$ will conduct and the bubble in input of $Q_2$ says that it has the opposite behaviour.

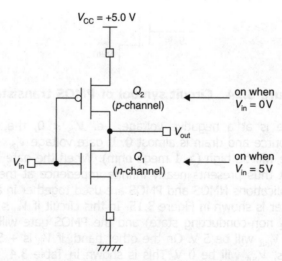

**Figure 3.16   CMOS inverter logical notation.**

## 3.3.2 NAND-NOR Gates with CMOS Transistors

CMOS gates can be connected in NAND configuration as shown in Figure 3.17. In Table 3.5 we show the status of various switches and the value of $C$ for various values of $A$ and $B$. We use 0 for 0 V and 1 for 5 V.

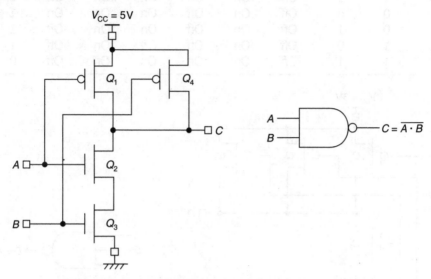

**Figure 3.17  A NAND gate using CMOS transistors.**

TABLE 3.5

**Action of CMOS configuration of Figure 3.17**

| Input $A$ | Input $B$ | Switch $Q_1$ | Switch $Q_2$ | Switch $Q_3$ | Switch $Q_4$ | Output $C$ |
|---|---|---|---|---|---|---|
| 0 | 0 | On | Off | Off | On | 1 |
| 0 | 1 | On | Off | On | Off | 1 |
| 1 | 0 | Off | On | Off | On | 1 |
| 1 | 1 | Off | On | On | Off | 0 |

We see from the Table 3.5 that the connection of CMOS gates of Figure 3.17 realizes a NAND gate ($C = \overline{A \cdot B}$). CMOS gates can be connected to realize NAND function for more than two inputs as shown in Figure 3.18.

TABLE 3.6

**Action of CMOS configuration of Figure 3.18**

| $A$ | $B$ | $C$ | $Q_1$ | $Q_2$ | $Q_3$ | $Q_4$ | $Q_5$ | $Q_6$ | $D$ |
|---|---|---|---|---|---|---|---|---|---|
| 0 | 0 | 0 | On | Off | Off | Off | On | On | 1 |
| 0 | 0 | 1 | On | Off | Off | On | On | Off | 1 |
| 0 | 1 | 0 | On | Off | On | Off | Off | Off | 1 |

(*Contd.*)

**TABLE 3.6 (Contd.)**
**Action of CMOS configuration of Figure 3.18**

| A | B | C | $Q_1$ | $Q_2$ | $Q_3$ | $Q_4$ | $Q_5$ | $Q_6$ | D |
|---|---|---|-------|-------|-------|-------|-------|-------|---|
| 0 | 1 | 1 | On    | Off   | On    | Off   | Off   | Off   | 1 |
| 1 | 0 | 0 | Off   | On    | Off   | On    | On    | On    | 1 |
| 1 | 0 | 1 | Off   | On    | Off   | On    | On    | Off   | 1 |
| 1 | 1 | 0 | Off   | On    | Off   | Off   | On    | Off   | 1 |
| 1 | 1 | 1 | Off   | On    | On    | On    | Off   | Off   | 0 |

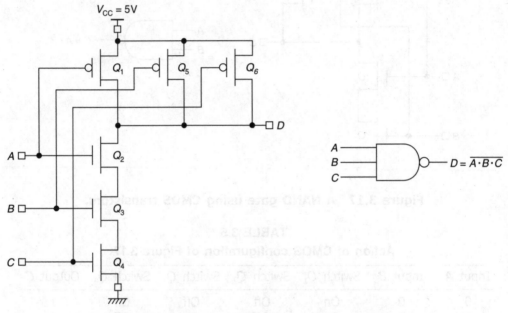

**Figure 3.18   A three input NAND gate.**

From the Table 3.6 we see that

$$D = \overline{A \cdot B \cdot C}$$

We can also use CMOS gates to configure a NOR gate. In Figure 3.19 we give a CMOS NOR gate. The functioning of this configuration is illustrated in Table 3.7.

**TABLE 3.7**
**Action of CMOS configuration of Figure 3.19**

| A | B | $Q_1$ | $Q_2$ | $Q_3$ | $Q_4$ | C |
|---|---|-------|-------|-------|-------|---|
| 0 | 0 | On    | On    | Off   | Off   | 1 |
| 0 | 1 | On    | Off   | Off   | On    | 0 |
| 1 | 0 | Off   | On    | On    | Off   | 0 |
| 1 | 1 | Off   | Off   | On    | On    | 0 |

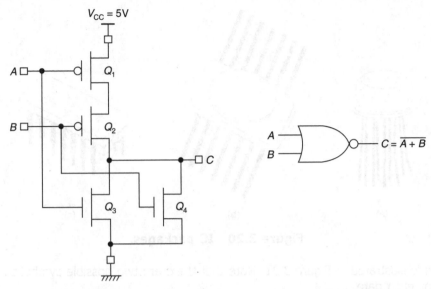

**Figure 3.19   A NOR configuration using CMOS gates.**

We see from the Table 3.7 that $C = \overline{A + B}$

The electrical characteristics of the configuration multi-input NOR and NAND differ. Multi-input NAND switches faster and thus, NAND is preferred over NOR in practice.

There are other families of integrated gate circuits. These are TTL (transistor-transistor logic) Schottky TTL, ECL, $I^2L$ and BiCMOS. A comparative study of these is available in the references cited at the end of this book.

A **small-scale IC (SSI)** consists of two to four gates in a package. A **medium-scale IC (MSI)** performs a complete logical function such as full binary addition. Typically, MSIs contain about a dozen gates. A **large-scale IC (LSI)** performs a fairly complex operation such as 10 digits BCD addition. Typically, LSIs contain 100 gates. A very extra large-scale IC (VLSI) contains a small system such as a calculator or a microprocessor on a single chip. Hitherto, we have been obtaining logic circuits using AND, OR and NOT gates to illustrate the principles. However, in practice many standard functions are readily available in the form of MSIs and LSIs. Thus, based on availability, the user has to judiciously select and use the appropriate ICs to design systems.

Some of the commonly available SSI packages are shown in Figure 3.20. They are the normal metal can, dual in-line package and the flat pack. Normally, they have 14 or 16 leads. Most SSI circuits incorporate a set of NAND/NOR gates. We will thus consider the use of these gates in detail.

As the NAND and NOR functions are complements of AND and OR respectively, the symbols used are those of AND, OR with additional small circles (called inversion circles) at the input or output of these gates.

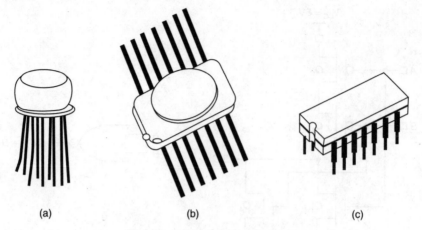

(a)                    (b)                    (c)

**Figure 3.20   IC packages.**

This is illustrated in Figure 3.21. Note that there are two possible symbolic representations for each gate.

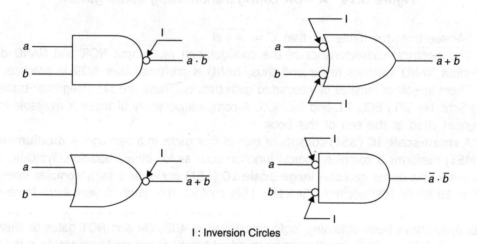

I : Inversion Circles

**Figure 3.21   Symbols for NAND/NOR gates.**

The NAND/NOR operators were defined for only two inputs in the last chapter. These operators are not associative.

$$(a \uparrow b) \uparrow c \neq a \uparrow (b \uparrow c) \tag{3.6}$$

This is shown below by evaluating both sides of Eq. (3.6).

$$(a \uparrow b) \uparrow c = \overline{\overline{a \cdot b} \cdot c} = a \cdot b + \overline{c} \tag{3.7}$$

$$a \uparrow (b \uparrow c) = \overline{a \cdot \overline{b \cdot c}} = \overline{a} + b \cdot c \tag{3.8}$$

Thus, we run into difficulties when more than two input variables are involved. To overcome this difficulty, we define the multiple input NAND/NOR gate as a complement of the corresponding multiple input AND/OR. This is shown in Figure 3.22. Using this modified definition (called **Associative NAND/NOR** indicated by the symbols $\curlywedge$ $\curlyvee$ respectively) we have:

$$a \curlywedge b \curlywedge c = \overline{a \cdot b \cdot c}; \quad a \curlyvee b \curlyvee c = \overline{(a + b + c)} \tag{3.9}$$

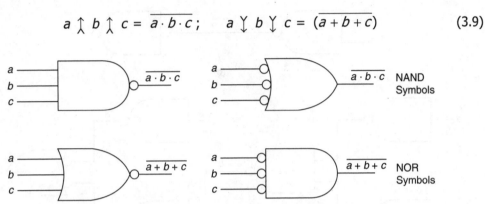

**Figure 3.22   Symbols for associative NAND/NOR gates.**

We showed in Figure 3.18 how we can realize multi-input NAND gate with CMOS transistors.

The NAND and NOR gates are universal gates since any Boolean expression can be implemented with these gates. To see this, we only have to show that AND, OR and NOT gates can be implemented with NANDs alone or NORs alone. This is shown as follows:

NOT: $$\bar{a} = \overline{a \cdot 1} = a \uparrow 1 \tag{3.10}$$

Also, $$\bar{a} = \overline{a \cdot a} = a \uparrow a \tag{3.11}$$

AND: $$a \cdot b = \overline{\overline{a \cdot b}} = (a \uparrow b) \uparrow 1 \tag{3.12}$$

OR: $$a + b = \overline{\bar{a} \cdot \bar{b}} = (a \uparrow 1) \uparrow (b \uparrow 1) \tag{3.13}$$

These realizations are shown in Figure 3.23. Note that complementation is straightforward. We can either NAND $a$ with 1 or connect the two inputs together as shown. With this understanding, we need not show the two inputs of the gate when the unary operation is performed. In fact, by only showing a single input we can immediately recognize that we are just performing the NOT operation using the NAND gate.

The AND operation using a NAND gate is straightforward as shown in Figure 3.23(b). The additional inversion needed is achieved using the second gate. But, the OR operation using the NAND gate is not so straightforward as shown in Figure 3.23(c) where both the diagrams (i) and (ii) are equivalent. The first diagram needs to be interpreted using DeMorgan's theorem, whereas in the second diagram the OR operation is more obvious. The symbol for the NAND gate which is based on that of OR is conveniently used to make the OR operation explicit. Thus, whenever OR operation is contemplated using a NAND gate, this symbol is conveniently used. This will be further illustrated later.

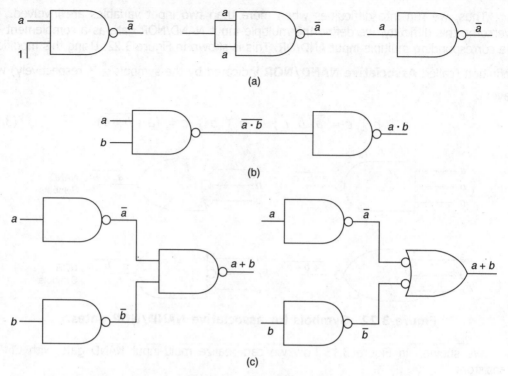

**Figure 3.23   Realization of NOT/AND/OR with NAND.**

We may realize AND, OR and NOT with NOR gates from the following equations:

NOT:
$$\bar{a} = \overline{a + 0} = a \downarrow 0 \tag{3.14}$$

Also,
$$\bar{a} = \overline{a + a} = a \downarrow a \tag{3.15}$$

AND:
$$a \cdot b = \overline{\bar{a} + \bar{b}} = (a \downarrow 0) \downarrow (b \downarrow 0) \tag{3.16}$$

OR:
$$a + b = \overline{\overline{a + b}} = (a \downarrow b) \downarrow 0 \tag{3.17}$$

These realizations are shown in Figure 3.24. Performing the NOT/OR operations using the NOR gate are straightforward. In performing the AND operation we use three NOR gates as shown in Figure 3.24(c). Once again the two diagrams are equivalent. However, the second diagram is more convenient since it makes the operation more explicit.

It is thus evident that all combinatorial circuits can be realized using only NAND/NOR gates. We will show in Section 3.4 how this is done systematically.

We have seen that all logical expressions can be realized using either NAND or NOR gates. In other words, they are universal gates. Thus, the variety of gates used to realize any combinatorial logic circuit is reduced to just one type of gate. This is of great value from the engineering point of view as design, testing and realization of combinatorial circuits are all simplified, as we have to deal with only one type of building block. This is the primary reason why NAND and NORs are the preferred gates in practice.

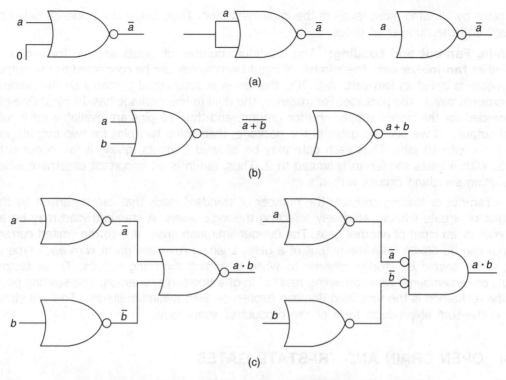

**Figure 3.24  Realization of NOT/OR/AND with NOR.**

The Karnaugh maps discussed earlier give Boolean expressions using AND, OR and NOT connectives with a minimum number of literals. This, in turn, leads to a circuit with a minimum number of gates and with each gate having the minimum number of inputs. When discrete components were being used, the realization with minimum number of gates also minimized the cost. This is not necessarily true when ICs are used. Since several gates are included in a single IC package, it may not cost more to use a few more gates provided they are all in the same package. The cost is determined not by the number of gates but by the number and variety of ICs used. In order to use ICs effectively we should keep in view the following factors:

**Propagation Delay and Number of Levels of Gating:**  In our discussions so far, we considered only the steady-state input and output of gates. In practice, each gate delays an input signal by a finite time period called the **propagation delay.** The delay introduced in a switching circuit is proportional to the number of gates in tandem through which an input signal has to travel before reaching the output terminal. The number of gates in tandem is also known as the number of levels in the logic circuit. For instance, the logic circuit of Figure 3.11 has a maximum of two levels from any input to output. If we assume the propagation delay of all gates to be identical, then this realization will introduce two units of delay.

A criterion in designing switching circuits is to minimize the propagation delay which is equivalent to minimizing the number of levels. Sometimes one can reduce the number of gates by allowing more levels in the implementation. Thus, there is a trade-off between speed and the number of gates.

**Fan-in, Fan-out and Loading:** The maximum number of inputs allowed for a gate is called its **fan-in.** Similarly, the number of input loads which can be connected to the output of a gate is called its **fan-out.** With ICs, the fan-in is determined primarily by the number of external pins in the package. For instance, the dual in-line package has 14 pins. One pin is needed for the power supply, one for ground, and thus 12 pins are available for inputs and outputs. If we put two gates in the package, then using two pins for two outputs will leave us with 10 pins. Thus each gate may be allowed 5 inputs, giving a fan-in per gate of 5. With 4 gates the fan-in is limited to 2. Thus, fan-in is an important constraint when designing switching circuits with ICs.

Fan-out or loading specifies the number of standard loads that can be driven by the output of a gate without adversely affecting the logic levels. A standard load may be an inverter or an input of another gate. The fan-out limitation arises due to the limited current which can be drawn from the output of a gate. Loading rules are given with each type of IC, which should be strictly adhered to while designing switching circuits. These factors must be remembered while obtaining realization of a Boolean expression. The starting point in the realization is the simplified Boolean expression with minimum literals. This will either be in the sum of products form or the product of sums form.

## 3.4 OPEN DRAIN AND TRI-STATE GATES

Consider the NAND of Figure 3.17. The *p*-channel transistors $Q_1$ and $Q_4$ are useful to actively pull up the output voltage at C to high in the low to high transition. In an open drain configuration these transistors are omitted. This configuration is shown in Figure 3.25.

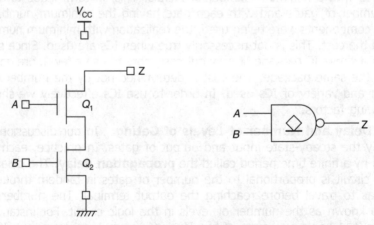

**Figure 3.25 An open drain gate and its symbol.**

Observe that the output of *N*-channel transistor is left unconnected internally. Thus, if *A* or *B* is low, $Q_1$ or $Q_2$ is open, then *Z* is left open (i.e. floating). The behaviour of this circuit is shown in Table 3.8.

**TABLE 3.8**

**Input-Output Behaviour of Open-Drain Gate**

| A | B | $Q_1$ | $Q_2$ | Z |
|---|---|-------|-------|---|
| L | L | Off | Off | open |
| L | H | Off | On | open |
| H | L | On | Off | open |
| H | H | On | On | L |

If we connect a resistor R, usually called a **pull up resistor,** to the output of the gate, it performs a NAND operation as the output voltage will be pulled up to nearly $V_{cc}$ when any or both inputs $A$ and $B$ is low (see Figure 3.26). The output voltage will be 0 if and only if both $A$ and $B$ are high. This is shown in Table 3.9.

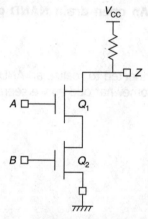

**Figure 3.26   An open drain NAND gate.**

**TABLE 3.9**

**Input-Output Behaviour of Open Drain Gate with a Pull Up Resistor**

| A | B | Z |
|---|---|---|
| L | L | H |
| L | H | H |
| H | L | H |
| H | H | L |

$$Z = \overline{A \cdot B}$$
$$H \rightarrow 1$$
$$L \rightarrow 0$$

Observe that this configuration saves two transistors when compared to the NAND gate of Figure 3.17. We, of course, get this at a price. The choice of $R$ is critical to maintain the high and low voltage levels of the gate within the allowed noise margins. A low value of $R$ is required to make the high level nearly $V_{cc}$ (5V). It will, however, drain too much current from the gate. Also, in the low state too the low value of $R$ will make low state rise up above the noise margin of L. Thus, $R$ has to be carefully chosen. The value of $R$ depends on the specific technology and one has to consult the appropriate data sheets. A different NAND gate symbol is used to depict an open drain NAND gate. This is shown in Figure 3.27.

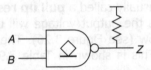

**Figure 3.27   An open drain NAND gate symbol.**

## 3.4.1   Wired AND Gate

Two open drain NANDs can be connected to realize an AND function (see Figure 3.28). This is called **wired AND.** This looks somewhat odd as we seem to be realizing an AND function at no cost.

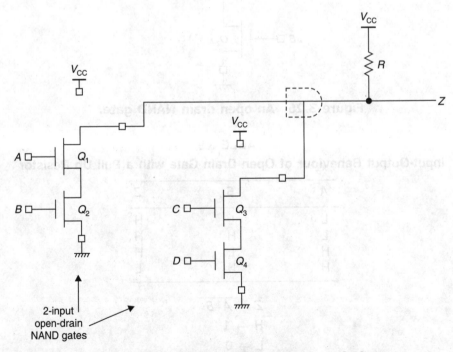

**Figure 3.28   A wired AND logic with open drain gate.**

It works with open drain gates only. This cannot be done with normal gates. In open drain configuration the pull up resistor effectively allows AND operation. This works because the output $Z$ will be high (i.e. one state ) if and only if **both** the open drain gates are high. If any one of the outputs is low, $Z$ will be pulled low.

## 3.4.2 Driving a Bus from Many Sources

Another useful application of an open drain gate is to drive a bus with one input at a time. This is illustrated in Figure 3.29.

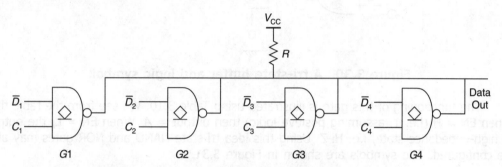

**Figure 3.29 Open drain gates driving a bus.**

In Figure 3.29 $C_1$, $C_2$, $C_3$, $C_4$ are control inputs and $\bar{D}_1, \bar{D}_2, \bar{D}_3, \bar{D}_4$ are complements of the data to be output. If all control inputs are low, all open drain gates will be in open state and the data output will be one. If we want to place $\bar{D}_2$ on the bus then we make control input $C_2$ high, and keep all other control inputs low. Thus, if $\bar{D}_2$ is high (or one) gate $G_2$ will close and the data output will become low. Thus, $D_2$ will be placed on the bus. If $\bar{D}_2$ is low (i.e. 0), data placed on bus is high (i.e. 1). In effect, the control bit determines which gate will open or close, thereby putting the data from the desired source to be placed on the bus.

## 3.4.3 Tri-state Gates

The two main disadvantages of open drain circuits are:

1. Problem in selecting value of $R$ to ensure proper functioning of gate.
2. Limited fan-out due to large current drain when $R$ is small and many outputs are connected.

Thus, another gate configuration is often used which is more expensive in terms of the number of gates used but is more robust. This is called a **three state gate circuit** (also known as **tri-state gate**). In tri-state gates there are three states as the name implies. They are low, high and high-impedance or Hi-Z state. The circuit diagram of a three state CMOS buffer is shown in Figure 3.30. Observe that this circuit uses an Enable (or control) input besides the data input to the buffer.

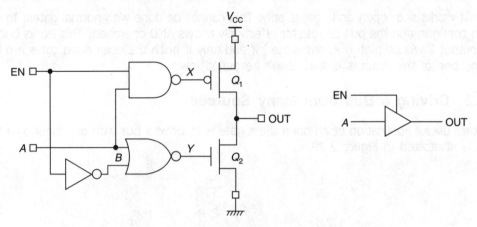

**Figure 3.30   A tri-state buffer and logic symbol.**

The functioning of this gate is illustrated using Table 3.10. We see from the table that when EN = H (i.e. 1, assuming positive logic) then output = A. When EN = L, the output is high-impedance state, i.e. Hi-Z. Using this idea tri-state NAND and NOR gates may also be configured. The symbols are shown in Figure 3.31.

**TABLE 3.10**

**Functioning of Tri-state Gate**

| EN | A | X | Y | $Q_1$ | $Q_2$ | OUT |
|----|---|---|---|-------|-------|-----|
| L | L | H | L | Off | Off | Hi-Z |
| L | H | H | L | Off | Off | Hi-Z |
| H | L | H | H | Off | On | L |
| H | H | L | L | On | Off | H |

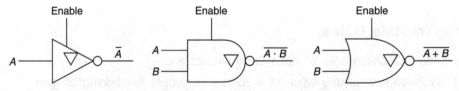

**Figure 3.31   Symbols for tri-state gates.**

The outputs of two or more tri-state gates may be connected together with the restriction that only one gate is allowed to be enabled at a time. This results in a restricted form of wired OR logic as illustrated in Figure 3.32. Either $E_1$ or $E_2$ may be high but not both. Table 3.11 illustrates the behaviour of the configuration of Figure 3.32.

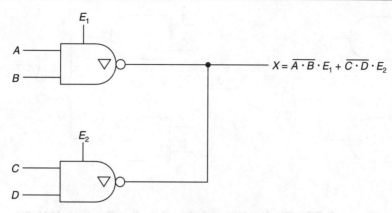

**Figure 3.32 Connecting two Tri-state gates.**

**TABLE 3.11**
**The Effect of Connecting the Outputs of Two Tri-state Gates**

| $E_1$ | $E_2$ | Output $X$ |
|-------|-------|------------|
| L | L | High impedance |
| L | H | $\overline{C \cdot D}$ |
| H | L | $\overline{A \cdot B}$ |
| H | H | Not allowed |

## 3.5 REALIZATION OF BOOLEAN EXPRESSIONS USING NAND/NOR GATES

Consider the expression $A \cdot C + B \cdot D$, which is in the sum of products form which we would have normally realized as shown in Figure 3.33(a). Now we wish to realize this using only NAND gates. We have to form the products and add them. With reference to Figure 3.33(b), we first concentrate our attention on the summing (OR) operation (second level). Naturally, we have used the appropriate symbol for this NAND gate. To get $A \cdot C + B \cdot D$ as output we need to feed $\overline{A \cdot C}, \overline{B \cdot D}$ as inputs into the gate. These complemented products are directly obtained (in the way we want) when we form products using NAND gates. This is a happy coincidence. Note that wherever there are two inversion circles connected together by a line, they cancel each other $(\overline{\overline{a}} = a)$. If we visualize their removal, the two diagrams of Figure 3.33 become identical. Thus, we see that the sum of products form of a Boolean expression naturally leads itself for implementation using NAND gates. Using uniform symbols of NAND gates and redrawing Figure 3.33(b) is straight forward. Consider, for example, another expression:

$$F = \overline{a} \cdot b + c \cdot \overline{d} + e \tag{3.18}$$

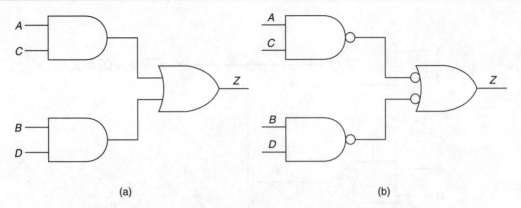

(a)          (b)

**Figure 3.33   Realization of *A · C + B · D* using NANDs.**

The AND-OR realization, assuming the complements to be available of Eq. (3.18), is given in Figure 3.34(a). The realization with NANDs alone, is shown in Figure 3.34(b).

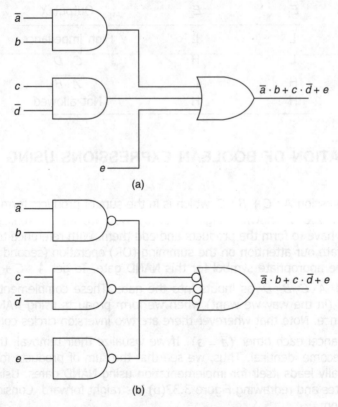

(a)

(b)

**Figure 3.34   Realization of a sum of products expression:**
**(a) With AND/OR (b) With NAND.**

Compare the two diagrams and again observe that the first two branches are identical when we ignore the pairs of inversion circles tied together. However, there is a difference in the third branch. In Figure 3.34(a), the literal 'e' is fed directly to the OR gate. We cannot do this in the NAND realization. We have to complement it before we feed it to the second level NAND gate. Having made this observation, we formulate the following rules for direct realization of a Boolean expression in the sum of products form with NAND gates:

1. For each product consisting of 'AND'ed literals in the Boolean expression, use the literals as inputs and draw a NAND gate.

2. Take the outputs of all such gates and feed them to a single NAND gate at the second level.

3. Any literal appearing alone as a term in the Boolean expression is complemented and fed to the NAND gate at the second level.

*Example 3.4.* The following Boolean expression $g$ in Eq. (3.19) is realized using NAND gates (see Figure 3.35) by following the rules given above:

$$g = a \cdot b \cdot \bar{c} + d + \bar{f} + a \cdot \bar{e} \tag{3.19}$$

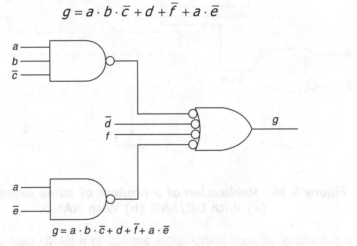

$$g = a \cdot b \cdot \bar{c} + d + \bar{f} + a \cdot \bar{e}$$

**Figure 3.35   NAND realization of Example 3.4.**

**Realization of the Product of Sums Form using NAND/NOR Gates:**  If a Boolean expression is in the product of sums form then the above rules do not apply. We can derive the appropriate rules after examining the realization of the following function:

$$g = (\bar{a} + \bar{b} + c) \cdot \bar{d} \cdot (\bar{a} + e) \cdot f \tag{3.20}$$

This expression is first realized using OR/AND gates (see Figure 3.36(a)). Figure 3.36(b) shows the realization using only NAND gates. Comparing these figures, we state the rules for NAND gate realization:

1. Each literal in a term is complemented and fed to a NAND gate. Since each one of the terms is a sum, the 'OR-based symbol' is used for the NAND gate.

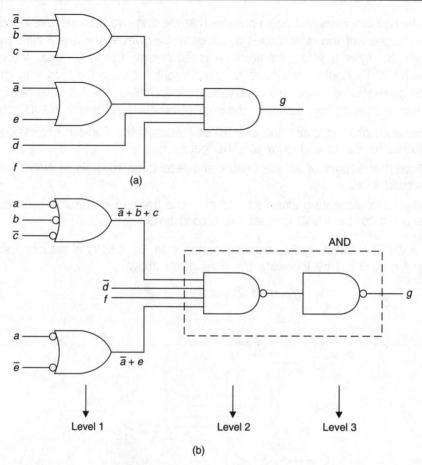

**Figure 3.36   Realization of a product of sums expression:
(a) With OR/AND (b) With NAND.**

2. The outputs of all such NAND gates are fed to a NAND gate at the second level.

3. Each literal appearing alone in the Boolean expression is fed as it is (i.e. uncomplemented) to the second level gate.

4. The output of the second level gate is fed to a NAND gate at the third level. The third level gate (an inverter) in conjunction with the second level forms an AND gate.

Thus, it is seen that three levels are required to realize product of sums with NANDs. It is, however, possible to realize a Boolean expression in the product of sums form with only two levels of NOR gating. This is illustrated in Figure 3.37 for the expression of Eq. (3.20). From the observation of this figure, we state the following rules for direct conversion of an expression in product of sums form to a two-level NOR realization:

1. For each sum term in the expression, use a NOR gate with the literals as inputs.
2. For each term in the expression which is a single literal, use its complement.
3. Feed the outputs of gates obtained in step 1 and the literals obtained in step 2 to a NOR gate. Since this level is used to form the product, the AND-based symbol is used for the NOR gate. The output of this second-level NOR gate is the required Boolean expression.

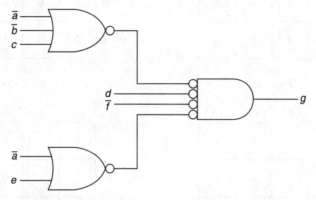

**Figure 3.37   Realization of a product of sums expression with NOR.**

In conclusion, we note that expressions in the product of sums form lend themselves naturally for NOR realization.

## 3.6   COMBINATORIAL CIRCUITS COMMONLY USED IN DIGITAL SYSTEMS

This section will illustrate the use of NAND/NOR gates to design a few combinatorial circuits which are used in digital systems.

*Example 3.5.*

**Code converter:**   Code conversion is a common function in digital systems. Suppose we want to convert digits in a given cyclic code to the 8-4-2-1 code. The procedure is to first express the conversion table as a truth table (Table 3.12). Next, Boolean expressions are obtained for each of the 8, 4, 2, 1 bits as a function of the cyclic code bits using K-maps (see Figure 3.38). Thus, we obtain

$$a = x \cdot \bar{z} \quad b = z \cdot x + y \quad c = z \cdot \bar{y}$$

$$d = \bar{x} \cdot \bar{y} \cdot z \cdot \bar{w} + \bar{x} \cdot \bar{z} \cdot w + \bar{z} \cdot \bar{w} \cdot x + x \cdot y + z \cdot w \cdot x \qquad (3.21)$$

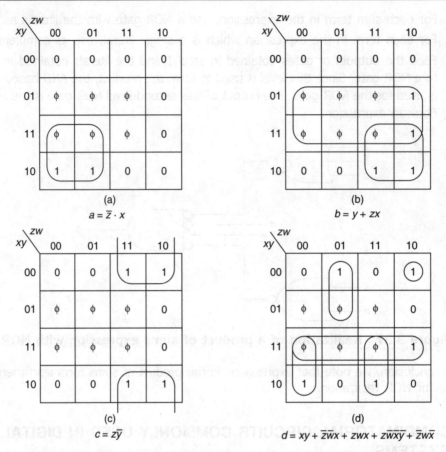

$$a = \bar{z} \cdot x$$

$$b = y + zx$$

$$c = z\bar{y}$$

$$d = xy + \bar{z}\bar{w}x + zwx + z\bar{w}\bar{x}y + \bar{z}w\bar{x}$$

**Figure 3.38 K-maps for code conversion—cyclic to 8421.**

**TABLE 3.12**
**Code Conversion: Cyclic to 8-4-2-1 Code**

| Cyclic code | | | | 8-4-2-1 NBCD code | | | |
|---|---|---|---|---|---|---|---|
| x | y | z | w | a | b | c | d |
| 0 | 0 | 0 | 0 | 0 | 0 | 0 | 0 |
| 0 | 0 | 0 | 1 | 0 | 0 | 0 | 1 |
| 0 | 0 | 1 | 1 | 0 | 0 | 1 | 0 |
| 0 | 0 | 1 | 0 | 0 | 0 | 1 | 1 |
| 0 | 1 | 1 | 0 | 0 | 1 | 0 | 0 |
| 1 | 1 | 1 | 0 | 0 | 1 | 0 | 1 |
| 1 | 0 | 1 | 0 | 0 | 1 | 1 | 0 |
| 1 | 0 | 1 | 1 | 0 | 1 | 1 | 1 |
| 1 | 0 | 0 | 1 | 1 | 0 | 0 | 0 |
| 1 | 0 | 0 | 0 | 1 | 0 | 0 | 1 |

These Boolean expressions are realized using NAND gates giving the circuit of Figure 3.39.

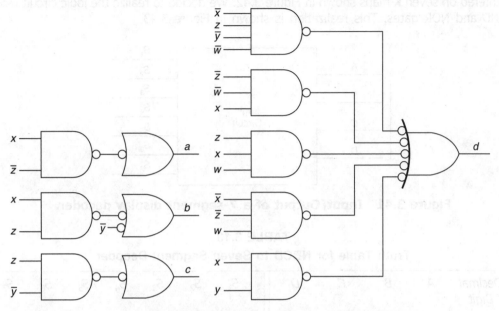

**Figure 3.39   NAND realization of cyclic to 8421 code converter.**

*Example 3.6.*

**Seven segment display realization with gates:** We will now consider an example of a BCD to seven segment converter and its realization.

A seven segment display consists of seven display lights arranged in a pattern shown in Figure 3.40. By selectively lighting a group of segments it is possible to display all digits from 0 to 9 as shown in Figure 3.40. We will now design a combinatorial circuit (see Figure 3.41) which will have as inputs a 4-bit NBCD code corresponding to the 10 decimal digits.

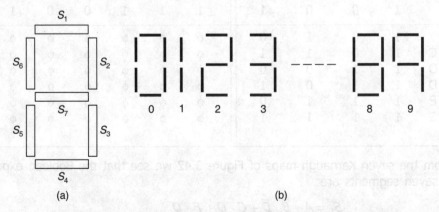

**Figure 3.40   Seven-segment display for numerals.**

The output of this circuit will be seven bits corresponding to the seven segments of the display. The bit corresponding to the segment to be lighted will be set to one. The truth table describing the requirements of the logic circuit is given as Table 3.13. This truth table is entered on seven K-maps shown in Figure 3.42. We decide to realize the logic circuit using NAND and NOR gates. This realization is shown in Figure 3.43

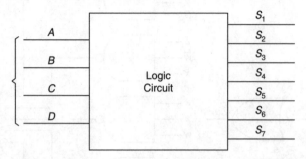

**Figure 3.41   Input/Output of a 7-segment display decoder.**

**TABLE 3.13**
**Truth Table for NBCD to Seven Segment Decoder**

| Decimal Digit | A | B | C | D | $S_1$ | $S_2$ | $S_3$ | $S_4$ | $S_5$ | $S_6$ | $S_7$ |
|---|---|---|---|---|---|---|---|---|---|---|---|
| 0 | 0 | 0 | 0 | 0 | 1 | 1 | 1 | 1 | 1 | 1 | 0 |
| 1 | 0 | 0 | 0 | 1 | 0 | 1 | 1 | 0 | 0 | 0 | 0 |
| 2 | 0 | 0 | 1 | 0 | 1 | 1 | 0 | 1 | 1 | 0 | 1 |
| 3 | 0 | 0 | 1 | 1 | 1 | 1 | 1 | 1 | 0 | 0 | 1 |
| 4 | 0 | 1 | 0 | 0 | 0 | 1 | 1 | 0 | 0 | 1 | 1 |
| 5 | 0 | 1 | 0 | 1 | 1 | 0 | 1 | 1 | 0 | 1 | 1 |
| 6 | 0 | 1 | 1 | 0 | 0 | 0 | 1 | 1 | 1 | 1 | 1 |
| 7 | 0 | 1 | 1 | 1 | 1 | 1 | 1 | 0 | 0 | 0 | 0 |
| 8 | 1 | 0 | 0 | 0 | 1 | 1 | 1 | 1 | 1 | 1 | 1 |
| 9 | 1 | 0 | 0 | 1 | 1 | 1 | 1 | 0 | 0 | 1 | 1 |
| I | 1 | 0 | 1 | 0 | φ | φ | φ | φ | φ | φ | φ |
| L    C | 1 | 0 | 1 | 1 | φ | φ | φ | φ | φ | φ | φ |
| L    O | 1 | 1 | 0 | 0 | φ | φ | φ | φ | φ | φ | φ |
| E    D | 1 | 1 | 0 | 1 | φ | φ | φ | φ | φ | φ | φ |
| G    E | 1 | 1 | 1 | 0 | φ | φ | φ | φ | φ | φ | φ |
| A    S | 1 | 1 | 1 | 1 | φ | φ | φ | φ | φ | φ | φ |
| L |   |   |   |   |   |   |   |   |   |   |   |

From the seven Karnaugh maps of Figure 3.42 we see that the Boolean expressions for the seven segments are:

$$S_1 = A + \bar{B} \cdot \bar{D} + C \cdot D + B \cdot D$$

$$S_2 = \bar{B} + \bar{C} \cdot \bar{D} + C \cdot D$$

$$S_3 = \bar{C} + D + B$$

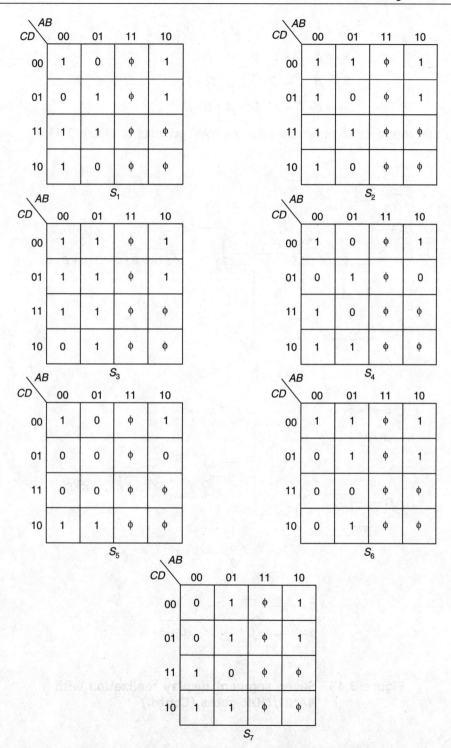

**Figure 3.42  K-maps for the truth table 3.13.**

$$S_4 = \bar{B} \cdot \bar{D} + \bar{C} \cdot D \cdot B + C \cdot \bar{D} + C \cdot \bar{B}$$

$$S_5 = \bar{B} \cdot \bar{D} + C \cdot \bar{D}$$

$$S_6 = B \cdot \bar{C} + B \cdot \bar{D} + \bar{C} \cdot \bar{D} + A$$

$$S_7 = B \cdot \bar{C} + B \cdot \bar{D} + A + C \cdot \bar{B}$$

We can realize these expressions by the NAND circuits of Figure 3.43.

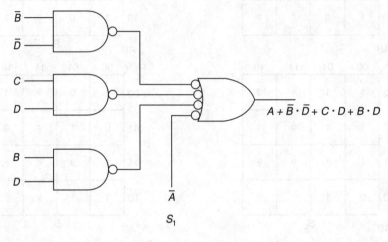

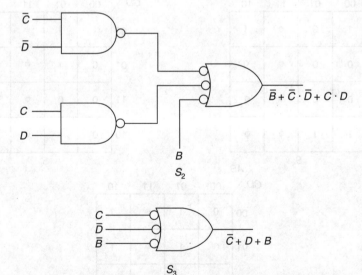

**Figure 3.43   Seven segment display realization with NAND/NOR gates (Contd.)**

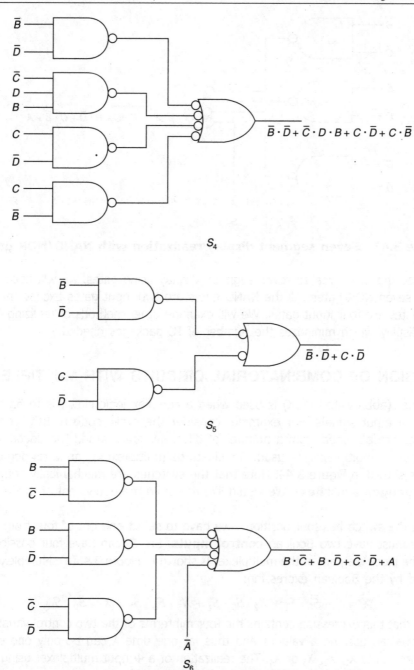

**Figure 3.43 Seven segment display realization with NAND/NOR gates (Contd.)**

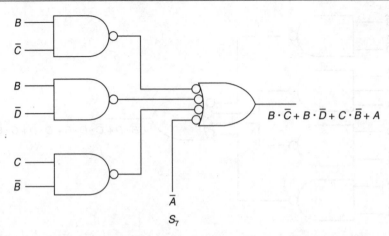

**Figure 3.43   Seven segment display realization with NAND/NOR gates.**

We see that if we realize seven segment display using gates, we will need 17 NAND gates and seven NOR gates. All the NAND gates are two input gates except one. Most of the NOR gates are four input gates. We will examine other methods of realizing the seven segment display which minimizes the number of IC packages needed.

## 3.7   DESIGN OF COMBINATORIAL CIRCUITS WITH MULTIPLEXERS

A multiplexer (abbreviated MUX) is used when a complex logic circuit is to be shared by a number of input signals. For example, consider the cyclic code to BCD converter. If cyclic codes are obtained from a number of different sources and the decoder is to be shared, then a multiplexer is used. To illustrate multiplexing, an arrangement using switches is shown in Figure 3.44. Note that the switches are mechanically coupled (also known as **ganged switches**). We would like to obtain the equivalent of this mechanical switch.

Since the switch has four positions, we have to select one out of four from these. To do this we must have two Boolean **control inputs.** So, $S_1$ can have four possible combinations. The block diagram of the multiplexer is shown in Figure 3.45(a). Multiplexing action is achieved by the Boolean expression:

$$X = X_1 \cdot \bar{S}_0 \cdot \bar{S}_1 + X_2 \cdot \bar{S}_0 \cdot S_1 + X_3 \cdot S_0 \cdot \bar{S}_1 + X_4 \cdot S_0 \cdot S_1 \qquad (3.22)$$

Note that this expression contains the four minterms of the two control variables. Only one of these can assume a value 1 and thus, at one time $X$ can be only one out of the four channel inputs $X_1$, $X_2$, $X_3$ or $X_4$. The realization of a 4-input multiplexer using AND and OR gates is shown in Figure 3.45(b).

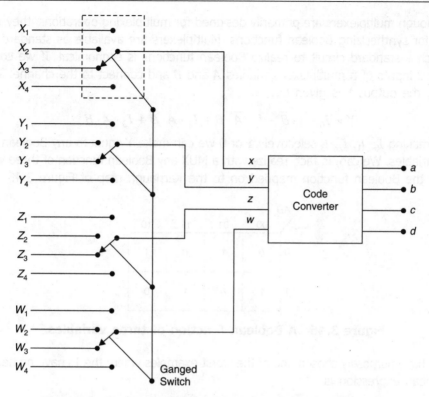

**Figure 3.44  Multiplexer using mechanical switches.**

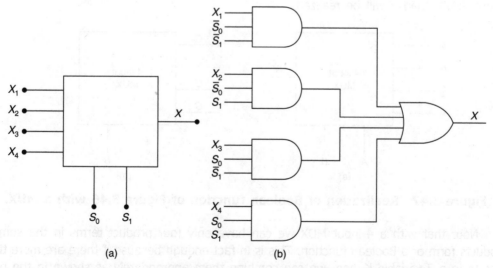

**Figure 3.45  (a) Block diagram of a multiplexer (b) Gate circuit.**

Although multiplexers are primarily designed for multiplexing operations, they may also be used for synthesizing Boolean functions. Multiplexers are available as standard ICs and using such a standard circuit to realize Boolean functions is economical. If we connect to the control inputs of a multiplexer variables $A$ and $B$ and connect to the channel inputs $I_0$, $I_1$, $I_2$, $I_3$, the output $Y$ is given by:

$$Y = I_0 \cdot \bar{A} \cdot \bar{B} + I_1 \cdot \bar{A} \cdot B + I_2 \cdot A \cdot \bar{B} + I_3 \cdot A \cdot B \qquad (3.23)$$

By making $I_0$, $I_1$, $I_2$, $I_3$ selectively 1 or 0 we can make $Y$ equal to any Boolean function of two variables. We can, in fact, realize with a MUX any Boolean function of three variables. Consider the Boolean function mapped on to the Karnaugh map of Figure 3.46.

| $C$ \ $AB$ | 00 | 01 | 11 | 10 |
|:---:|:---:|:---:|:---:|:---:|
| 0 | 0 | 1 | 0 | 1 |
| 1 | 1 | 0 | 1 | 0 |

**Figure 3.46    A Boolean function of three variables.**

We have purposely chosen one of the worst examples where the 1s have no neighbours. The Boolean expression is

$$Y = C \cdot \bar{A} \cdot \bar{B} + \bar{C} \cdot \bar{A} \cdot B + \bar{C} \cdot A \cdot \bar{B} + C \cdot A \cdot B \qquad (3.24)$$

If we make the $I_0$ input of the 4-input multiplexer $C$, $I_1 = I_2 = \bar{C}$ and $I_3 = C$ (see Figure 3.47), then $Y$ will be realized.

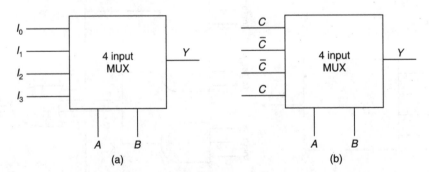

**Figure 3.47    Realization of Boolean function of Figure 3.46 with a MUX.**

Note that with a 4-input MUX we can have only four product terms in the sum of products form of a Boolean function. This is in fact enough because if there are more than four 1s in a 3-variable K-map, we can combine them appropriately as shown in the realization of the Boolean function mapped on the Karnaugh map of Figure 3.48. Observe that each of the columns in the K-map is a selection and routes $I_0$, $I_1$, $I_3$ and $I_2$ respectively.

Thus, instead of the usual K-map reduction we should inspect columns in the K-map to realize the Boolean function with a MUX optimally.

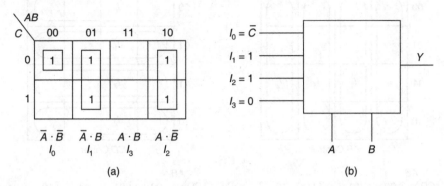

(a)                                              (b)

**Figure 3.48   Realizing a three-variable function with a 4-input MUX.**

A straightforward method to realize a Boolean function of four variables is to use an eight-input MUX. Sometimes it is possible to realize such functions with a four-input MUX. Consider the K-map of Figure 3.49(a). Taking *CD* as control variables for a MUX we obtain the realization of Figure 3.49(b). When attempting to realize a four-variable function with a four-input MUX the choice of control variables is crucial. Six different choices namely, *AB*, *AC*, *AD*, *BC*, *BD* and *CD* are possible. For each choice of control variables the K-map should be factored. The factorings are illustrated in Figure 3.50. The function given in Figure 3.51 is realized with a single 4-input MUX by realizing that *BD* should be picked as control variables. Sometimes it is not possible to realize a four-variable function with a 4-input MUX. However, it is possible to realize any four-variable function with additional gates and a 4-input MUX. This is illustrated in Figure 3.52.

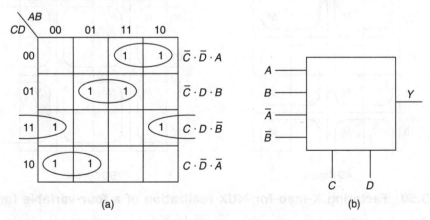

(a)                                              (b)

**Figure 3.49   Realizing a four-variable Boolean function with four-input MUX.**

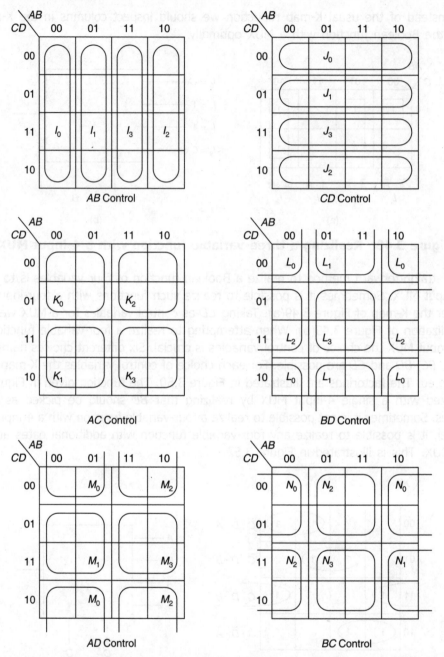

**Figure 3.50 Factoring K-map for MUX realization of a four-variable function.**

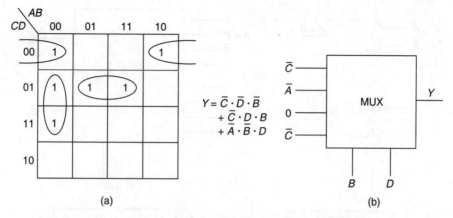

**Figure 3.51 MUX realization of a four-variable function.**

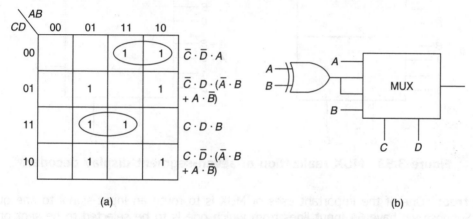

**Figure 3.52 Realizing with a MUX and a gate.**

*Example 3.7.*

***Seven segment display realization with MUX:*** We saw how a seven segment display was realized using gates in Example 3.6. We will realize it again this time using MUXs. We inspect K-maps of seven segment display given in Figure 3.42. By inspection we see that $S_3$ reduces to the simple expression $\bar{C} + D + B$. $S_1$, $S_2$, $S_3$, $S_4$, $S_5$, $S_6$, $S_7$ can be realized by one four input MUX each if $C$ and $D$ are used as control inputs. In commercially available MUXs, two four input MUXs are packaged in one IC. Thus, three dual input MUXs will realize $S_1$, $S_2$, $S_4$, $S_5$, $S_6$, $S_7$. The realization of the logic for the seven segment display is shown in Figure 3.53. Comparing this realization with that using gates (Example 3.6) we see that whereas gate realization needed 24 gates, the one with MUX needs only two gates and three dual MUXs. Further, MUXs-based realization is much simpler.

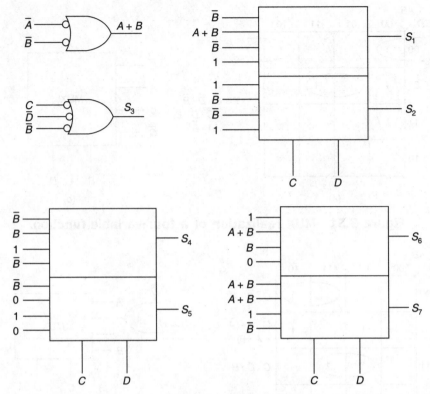

**Figure 3.53    MUX realization of seven-segment display decoder.**

**Mux tree:**   One of the important uses of MUX is to route an input signal to one output line. Suppose we have 64 input lines from which one is to be selected to be sent on the output line. We may either use a 64-input MUX, which is very expensive, or find a method of using a cascade of MUXs with a smaller number of inputs. A 64-line to one-line multiplexing may be achieved with a MUX tree as shown in Figure 3.54. This MUX tree may be used to realize any Boolean function of six variables.

**Demultiplexer:**   Demultiplexing is the reverse process. Data available on one line is steered to many lines based on the values of control variables. If, for example, we want to steer the signal on an input line to four output lines then the steering may be controlled by using two control variables. This is illustrated in Figure 3.55. The Boolean expressions for the demultiplexer are:

$$X = I \cdot \bar{C}_1 \cdot \bar{C}_0 \tag{3.25}$$

$$Y = I \cdot \bar{C}_1 \cdot C_0 \tag{3.26}$$

$$Z = I \cdot C_1 \cdot \bar{C}_0 \tag{3.27}$$

$$W = I \cdot C_1 \cdot C_0 \tag{3.28}$$

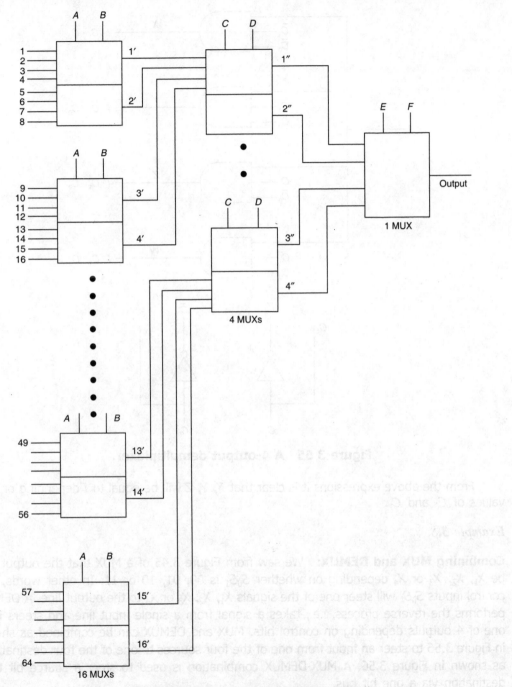

**Figure 3.54   A 64-input MUX tree.**

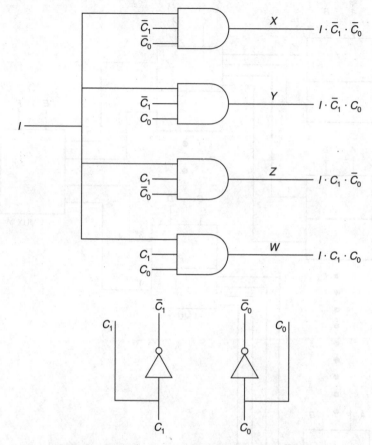

**Figure 3.55 A 4-output demultiplexer.**

From the above expressions it is clear that $X$, $Y$, $Z$ will be equal to $I$ depending on the values of $C_0$ and $C_1$.

*Example 3.8.*

**Combining MUX and DEMUX:** We saw from Figure 3.45 of a MUX that the output will be $X_1$, $X_2$, $X_3$ or $X_4$ depending on whether $S_0 S_1$ is 00, 01, 10 or 11. In other words, the control inputs $S_0 S_1$ will steer one of the signals $X_1$, $X_2$, $X_3$ or $X_4$ to the output line. A DEMUX performs the reverse process, i.e., takes a signal from a single input line and steers it to one of 4 outputs depending on control bits. MUX and DEMUX can be combined as shown in Figure 3.56 to steer an input from one of the four sources to one of the four destinations as shown in Figure 3.56. A MUX-DEMUX combination is used to steer a source bit to a destination via a one bit bus.

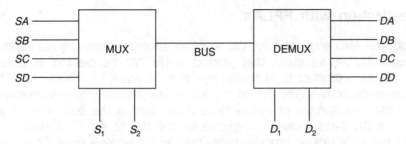

**Figure 3.56   A MUX-DEMUX combination.**

For example, if we want to send *SA* to destination *DC*, we will set $S_1 S_2$ to 00 and $D_1 D_2$ to 10. In general, any one of the sources can be selected by $S_1 S_2$ and any destination can be selected by $D_1 D_2$. Thus, to send *SB* to *DA* we set $S_1 S_2 = 01$ and $D_1 D_2 = 00$. Multiple MUX-DEMUX pairs can be used to send bits via a parallel bus with multiple lines.

## 3.8  PROGRAMMABLE LOGIC DEVICES

The examples of combinational circuits considered so far have a small number of input variables. Further, the number of outputs considered has been mostly one or two. In many real problems there are a large number of input and output variables. The number of gates used to realize such circuits will become very large. A cost-effective method of realizing such circuits is to use Programmable Logic Devices (PLDs). PLDs are medium-scale integrated circuits. MUXs also assist in building large combinational circuits. PLDs, however, allow much larger circuits to be designed.

PLDs fall into the following three categories:

1. Field Programmable Logic Array (FPLA)
2. Programmable Array Logic (PAL), and
3. Programmable Read Only Memory (PROM).

All these devices consist of an array of AND gates followed by an array of OR gates. A block diagram of a PLD is shown in Figure 3.57.

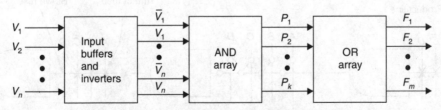

**Figure 3.57   Block diagram of PLD.**

There are *n* input variables fed to an input buffer and inverters. Both the true and the complement form of the variables are fed to an AND array. The maximum number of product terms which can be generated by the AND array with *n* variables is $2^n$. If *m* Boolean functions are to be realized as a sum of at most *k* products then an array of *m* OR gates, each with *k* inputs, are required.

### 3.8.1 Realization with FPLAs

In FPLAs both the AND array and the OR array are programmable. By stating that an AND array is programmable we mean that product terms can be created as required in an application with each product term having less than or equal to $2^n$ variables. The number of product terms depends on the size of the AND array. Similarly, programmability of an OR array means that the number of inputs to each OR gate in the array can be varied. The total number of OR gates, however, depends on the size of the FPLA device.

In PALs the AND array is programmable but the OR array is fixed. Thus, even though it is somewhat less flexible than FPLA, in most practical problems it is found to be adequate. Further, it is cheaper to fabricate and is widely available. It is thus currently preferred for realizing combinatorial logic circuits.

In PROMS the AND array is not programmable. Thus, all $2^n$ product terms are generated. The OR array is programmable. We will first consider FPLAs and clarify the notation we will be using. Consider the AND gate of Figure 3.58(a) which realizes the term $A \cdot B \cdot \bar{C} \cdot D$. Various methods of representing the product $A \cdot B \cdot \bar{C} \cdot D$ is shown in Figure 3.58(a), (b), (c) and (d). Figure 3.58 (d) shows the preferred notation. Observe that a single input line is shown as an input to an AND gate and a cross is shown on this line corresponding to each in the product term. A similar notation is used to indicate a programmable OR gate (see Figure 3.59).

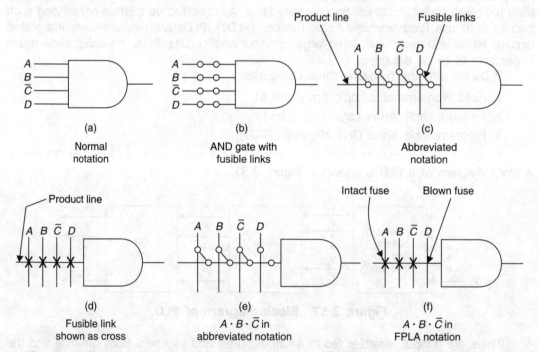

(a)
Normal
notation

(b)
AND gate with
fusible links

(c)
Abbreviated
notation

(d)
Fusible link
shown as cross

(e)
$A \cdot B \cdot \bar{C}$ in
abbreviated notation

(f)
$A \cdot B \cdot \bar{C}$ in
FPLA notation

**Figure 3.58 Various notations used to describe programmable AND gate.**

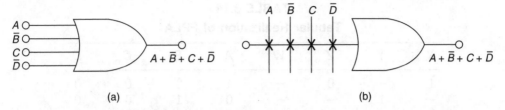

| (a) | (b) |

**Figure 3.59   Notation used to describe programmable OR gate.**

In Section 3.6, we obtained K-maps for a cyclic code to 8-4-2-1 code converter (Figure 3.38). This is realized using an FPLA in Figure 3.60. Observe the simplicity of obtaining an FPLA realization. The FPLA realization may also be shown as Table 3.14.

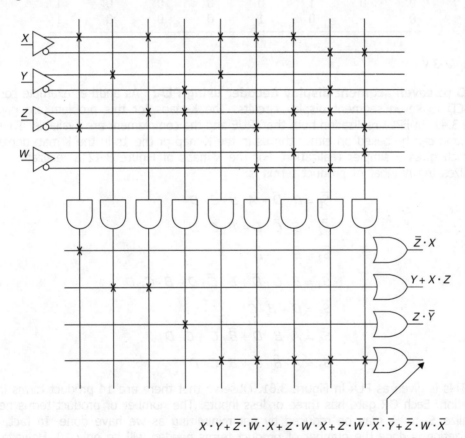

**Figure 3.60   PLA realization of cyclic code to 8-4-2-1 code converter.**

**TABLE 3.14**

**Tabular Realization of FPLA**

| X | Y | Z | W | A | B | C | D |
|---|---|---|---|---|---|---|---|
| 1 | – | 0 | – | 1 | 0 | 0 | 0 |
| – | 1 | – | – | 0 | 1 | 0 | 0 |
| 1 | – | 1 | – | 0 | 1 | 0 | 0 |
| – | 0 | 1 | – | 0 | 0 | 1 | 0 |
| 1 | 1 | – | – | 0 | 0 | 0 | 1 |
| 1 | – | 0 | 0 | 0 | 0 | 0 | 1 |
| 1 | – | 1 | 1 | 0 | 0 | 0 | 1 |
| 0 | 0 | 1 | 0 | 0 | 0 | 0 | 1 |
| 0 | – | 0 | 1 | 0 | 0 | 0 | 1 |

*Example 3.9.*

**A BCD to seven segment display decoder using PLA:** As another example consider the BCD to seven segment display circuits. The K-maps for this problem are given in Figure 3.42. In FPLA realization both the TRUE and the complement are available. Thus, the realization can be based on either the 0s in the K-map or the 1s in the K-map depending on which gives a simpler realization. For the K-maps of Figure 3.42 a realization which minimizes the number of product terms is:

$$\bar{S}_1 = B \cdot \bar{D} + \bar{A} \cdot \bar{B} \cdot \bar{C} \cdot D$$

$$\bar{S}_2 = B \cdot \bar{C} \cdot D + B \cdot C \cdot \bar{D}$$

$$\bar{S}_3 = \bar{B} \cdot C \cdot \bar{D}$$

$$\bar{S}_4 = B \cdot \bar{C} \cdot \bar{D} + \bar{B} \cdot \bar{C} \cdot D + B \cdot C \cdot D$$

$$\bar{S}_5 = D + B \cdot \bar{C}$$

$$\bar{S}_6 = \bar{A} \cdot \bar{B} \cdot D + \bar{B} \cdot C + C \cdot D$$

$$\bar{S}_7 = \bar{A} \cdot \bar{B} \cdot \bar{C} + B \cdot C \cdot D$$

This is given as PLA in Figure 3.61. Observe that there are 14 product terms in this realization. Each OR gate has three or less inputs. The number of product terms needed to realize $S_1$ to $S_7$ may be reduced by not minimizing as we have done. In fact, if no minimization is done the number of product terms needed will be only 10. However, the number of inputs to OR gates will go up to four. This is clear if we look at the standard sum of products given below (observe that $S_5$ instead of $\bar{S}_5$ is used below):

$$\bar{S}_1 = \Sigma\, 1, 4, 6; \quad \bar{S}_2 = \Sigma\, 5, 6; \quad \bar{S}_3 = \Sigma\, 2; \quad \bar{S}_4 = \Sigma\, 1, 4, 7, 9$$

$$S_5 = \Sigma\, 0, 2, 6, 8; \quad \bar{S}_6 = \Sigma\, 1, 2, 3, 7; \quad \bar{S}_7 = \Sigma\, 0, 1, 7$$

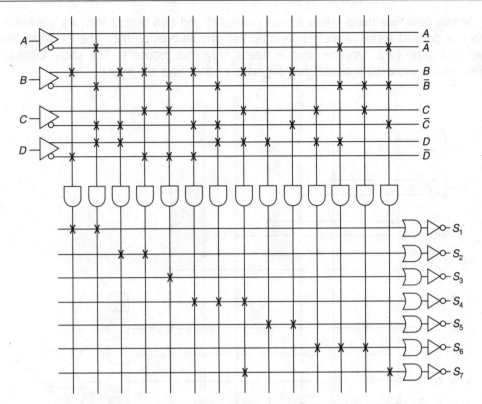

**Figure 3.61   BCD to seven segment decoder as a PLA.**

As can be seen terms 0 to 9 occur in the expressions. Thus, no more than 10 product terms need be considered. No sum has more than four terms. Thus, no OR gate will need more than four inputs.

## 3.8.2   Realization with PALs

The major difference between FPLAs and PALs is that in PAL the OR array is fixed and the AND array is programmable. Thus, the number of product terms allowed in a combinational circuit is limited by the type of PAL. This is not a major limitation in many cases. Non-programmability of OR array allows realization of more gates in a package at a lower cost. Thus, PALs are very popular.

A popular series of PALs is the 20 pin series in which there are total 20 pins for input and output. In the manufacturers' catalogue details of various types of PALs, number of inputs, outputs, number of product terms allowed per OR gate in the array, etc. are given. A user has to look at the catalogue before deciding what PAL is suitable for a given application.

Given the following functions we will show how it is realized with a PAL:

$$W = \Sigma\ 0,\ 2,\ 4,\ 6,\ 8,\ 11$$

$$X = \Sigma\ 1,\ 3,\ 5,\ 7,\ 9$$

In this case, we need a four inputs (variable) and two output PAL. As the maximum number of product terms is six the selected PAL should provide this. The PAL realization is shown in Figure 3.62. Observe that $X$ needs only five products. The sixth AND gate is marked with a cross to indicate that all fuses in that line are intact.

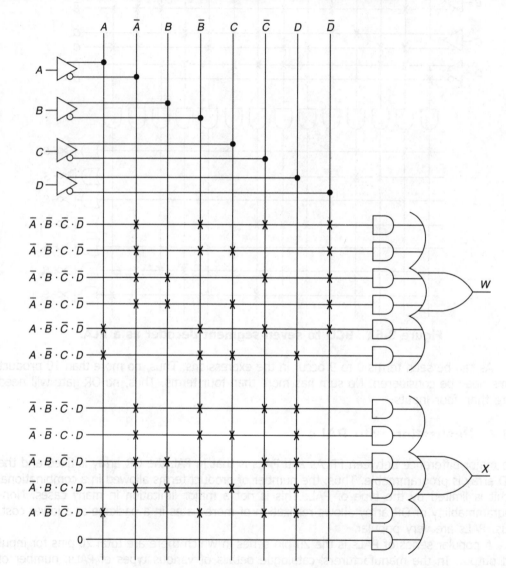

**Figure 3.62  PAL Programming of two sum of products.**

A BCD of seven segment display can also be realized using a PAL. This is shown in Figure 3.63. Observe that this can be directly done from sum of products form expressions. On the horizontal lines a cross is placed to obtain the binary equivalent of decimal minterm. For example, cases for one are at 0001 positions of vertical lines.

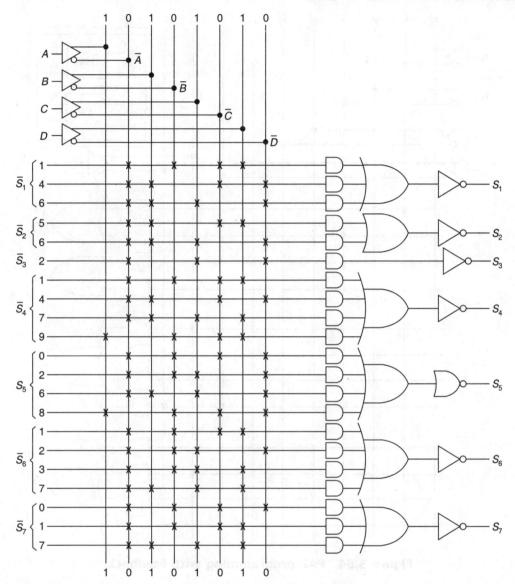

**Figure 3.63 Realization of BCD to seven-segment display decoder with a PAL.**

There are PALs with special features which are useful in certain applications. The features supported are:

1. Feedback from output back to AND array (see Figure 3.64).
2. I/O pins in some cases can be configured either as input or output.
3. Output can be active high or active low (i.e. 5 V can be considered either as 1 or 0).
4. Some PALs provide a one bit store at each output.

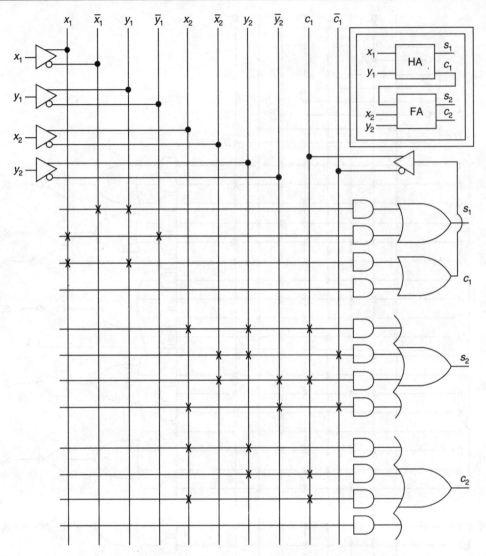

**Figure 3.64  PAL programming with feedback.**

PALs are economical and easy to configure for complex combinatorial circuits and are thus, widely used.

Programmable read only memory (PROM) is a storage device in which data can be permanently stored. Such a device can be used to realize a combinational circuit. We will discuss the use of such a device in a later chapter on memories.

──────────────────────( **SUMMARY** )──────────────────────

1. One of the most challenging problems in designing combinatorial switching circuits is analyzing and modelling a given requirement specification (usually given as a narrative).

2. Modelling involves identifying independent input variables and the dependent output variables. These variables are to be coded by two valued equivalents so that binary switching circuits can be used. Finally, it is essential to decide whether the problem lends itself to be realized by a combinatorial circuit, i.e. a circuit whose output depends only on current inputs and not on earlier values of the input. This is also known as *memoryless system.*

3. Modelling requires practice using a number of examples. This chapter presents three examples which illustrate the important aspects of the process of analyzing, modelling and realizing combinatorial switching circuits.

4. The inverter $V_{out} - V_{in}$ characteristics is called *transfer characteristics* of the gate and is useful to predict noise margin allowed in the 0 and 1 levels.

5. Early digital circuits were designed using Transistor-to-transistor logic family (TTL). Currently, complementary metal oxide semiconductor (CMOS) field effect transistors are universally used to design digital circuits.

6. There are two types of MOS transistors called NMOS and PMOS. These are three terminal devices with a gate (which controls the opening or closure of the gate), a source and a drain. PMOS and NMOS transistors are connected in series with a common input to configure a CMOS inverter shown in Figure 3.15 of this chapter.

7. CMOS transistors can also be connected to configure NAND or NOR gates.

8. NAND and NOR gates are universal gates in the sense that AND, OR and NOT operators can be realized with only NAND gates or only NOR gates.

9. Universal characteristics of NAND/NOR gates make them the preferred gates to design combinatorial circuits as variety is reduced with consequent advantages in design and maintenance.

10. Given a realization of a Boolean expression in a sum of products form, it is easy to realize it by a set of AND gates followed by an OR gate.

11. Such a configuration can be converted to a realization using only NAND gates by using some simple rules.

12. Similar rules apply to convert a product of sums realization by OR/AND gates to the one using only NOR gates.

13. An NMOS and a PMOS transistor can be connected in a CMOS configuration with an "open" drain. A resistor of appropriate value, when connected to the open drain, realizes a NAND gate. This configuration saves two transistors compared with the usual NAND configuration. However, this configuration's reliability depends on the right choice of the resistor.

14. Two open drain gates can be connected to realize an AND operation. This is called a "wired AND" logic.

15. Open drain gates can also be used to drive a bus with one selected input bit at a time.

16. CMOS gates can also be configured as a three state gate. The three states are low, high and high-impedance state. Such a gate is also known as a tri-state gate. The outputs of two or more such gates can be connected together to realize what is known as a wired-OR circuit.

17. A Multiplexer (abbreviated MUX) is a combinatorial circuit which steers one out of $2^n$ input signals to a single output line depending on the value of a $n$ variable control variable. Thus, a MUX with $n$ control variables can realize all the minterms of $n + 1$ variables, for example, if $A$ and $B$ are the control variables and the four inputs are $C \cdot \bar{C}, C, \bar{C}$ we can realize $\bar{A} \cdot \bar{B} \cdot C + \bar{A} \cdot \bar{B} \cdot \bar{C} + \bar{A} \cdot B \cdot C + \bar{A} \cdot B \cdot \bar{C} + A \cdot \bar{B} \cdot C + A \cdot \bar{B} \cdot \bar{C} + A \cdot B \cdot C + A \cdot B \cdot \bar{C}$. Thus, MUXs can be used to realize any combinatorial expression.

18. A Demultiplexer (abbreviated DEMUX) is a device which does the reverse of MUX. It steers data on a single input line to one of $2^n$ output lines depending on $n$ control variables.

19. A MUX-DEMUX combination can be used to steer a source bit to a destination via a one-bit bus.

20. A Progammable Logic Device (PLD) consists of an array of AND gates feeding an array of OR gates. The inputs to the AND array has both true and complements of input variables – If both the AND and OR arrays have fusible lines to select gates it is called a Programmable Logic Array (PLA). PLAs can realize any sum of products.

21. A PAL (Programmable Array Logic) has a fixed OR array and a programmable AND array with fusible links. Given a set of Boolean expressions in a sum of products form, it is easy to program a PAL after selecting an appropriate PAL.

22. Realizing with PAL is simple and does not require any minimization.

---

### EXERCISES

1. In Example 3.1 the platforms are marked *A*, *C* and *B* from top to bottom in Figure 3.2. Relabel the platforms as *A*, *B* and *C*. Obtain the truth table assuming that if the point is set to *A*, trains cannot go to *B* or *C*. Using Karnaugh maps, obtain a minimal combinatorial circuit for the switching system.

2. Assume that in Example 3.1, trains are allowed to enter from either direction. Assume again that trains are to be routed to platform *A* if empty, then to *B* if it is empty and to *C* only if *A* and *B* are occupied. Modify the switching system. Express in words the minimal Boolean expressions obtained after Karnaugh map reduction.

3. Obtain a logic circuit for an analog to digital converter with three-bit digital output.

4. Figure 3.65 depicts a tank with a float *F* and two valves $V_1$ and $V_2$. Valve $V_1$ is to be opened if the float reaches level $L_1$ and $V_2$ is to be opened if the float reaches level

$L_2$. Assuming that a sensor can sense the level of the float, obtain a switching circuit to control valves $V_1$ and $V_2$.

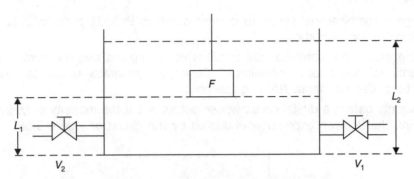

**Figure 3.65   A tank with float for Exercise 4.**

5. The entrance to a group of three flats has a light. The light is to be switched on or off independently by the tenants of the three flats using switches located in their flats. Design a switching circuit to implement this.

6. A company has four shareholders, Agarwal, Bhatia, Chamanlal and Daulat Ram. Agarwal owns 30 shares, Bhatia 40 shares, Chamanlal 10 and Daulat Ram 20 shares. In order for a particular measure in the shareholders meeting to be passed, shareholders holding more than two-thirds of the total shares should vote for it. Assuming that on the Board Room each shareholder has a switch which he switches on if he votes 'yes', design a switching circuit which will ring a bell if the measure passes.

7. A decoder is to be designed for a seven-segment display. The input to the display is a four-bit excess-three code. The output is to light one or more of the segments of the display as illustrated in Figure 3.40:

   (a) Design the decoder using all don't care conditions.
   (b) If one of the illegal four-bit pattern occurs what is the resulting display?
   (c) How can you avoid a false display? Redesign the decoder so that an illegal pattern of input bits does not produce a meaningful display.
   (d) Realize the decoder using four input MUXs.

8. Repeat above Exercise if the input is a 5421 weighted BCD number.

9. Obtain a combinatorial circuit to multiply two numbers each of which is three bits long, one bit being used as a sign bit. The output should have the right sign and magnitude.

10. Convert all the AND-OR combinatorial circuits obtained in Exercises 8 and 9 to circuits using only NAND gates.

11. Design a combinatorial circuit to obtain the nine's complement of decimal numbers represented in the 8421 code. Use only NOR gates to realize the circuit.

12. Obtain a circuit to convert numbers in 2421 weighted code to decimal. Use NOR gates to realize the circuit.

13. Design a combinatorial circuit to generate a parity bit for digits coded in 5421 code. Provide an error output if any illegal code is input to the circuit. Realize with NAND gates.

14. Design a combinatorial circuit to convert numbers in 5421 code to 2421 code. Use NOR gates for realization.

15. A comparator is a combinatorial circuit which compares two numbers *A* and *B* and determines their relative magnitudes. Design a comparator to compare two base 3 numbers. Use two input NAND gates only.

16. A majority gate is a digital circuit whose output is 1 if the majority of its inputs equal 1. Find the Boolean expression evaluated by the circuit of Figure 3.66.

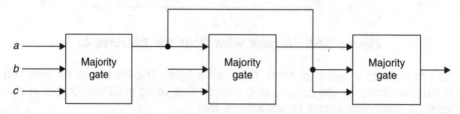

**Figure 3.66   Figure for Exercise 16.**

17. Reduce the following expressions to those using NAND, NOR, NOT operators:
    (a) $A \cdot B \cdot C \cdot D$
    (b) $A \oplus B \oplus C \oplus D$
    (c) $(A/B)/C$
    (d) $(A \uparrow D) \uparrow (C \uparrow D)$
    (e) $(A \downarrow B) \downarrow (C \downarrow D)$

18. A single communication line between a computer building and another remote building is to be used by 16 terminal users located in the remote building. Assuming that each terminal has a buffer register, design a MUX, DEMUX system which will allow the 16 terminal users to time share the communication line and use the computer.

19. Design a logic circuit using DEMUXs which will accept a seven-bit ASCII code for a character and energize one of 128 solenoids to activate a type bar corresponding to the appropriate character.

20. Repeat Exercise 14 using MUXs. Repeat with PALs and PLAs.

21. Repeat Exercise 12 and realize the logic circuit using a four input MUXs. Repeat with PALs and PLAs.

22. An Op-code decoder takes as input a set of bits and places a 1 on any one of a set of output lines. Is MUX or a DEMUX appropriate to realize it? Realize the circuit for a four bit of op-code.

# Chapter

# 4

# Sequential Switching Circuits

## Learning Goals

In this chapter we will learn:

☞ The difference between combinational and sequential switching circuits.

☞ What are asynchronous and synchronous sequential circuits.

☞ Different types of flip-flops and their characteristics.

☞ The use of flip-flops as building blocks of sequential circuits.

☞ How to model sequential circuits using Moore and Mealy models.

☞ How to design counters with various types of flip-flops.

☞ How to design sequential circuits from given requirements specification.

☞ The use of MSI to design sequential circuits.

## 4.1 INTRODUCTION

So far we have been concerned with combinatorial switching circuits in which the inputs were a set of independent variables and the outputs were Boolean functions of the inputs. An ideal combinatorial circuit acts instantaneously. Thus, the output, at any point of time, depends only on the input present at the instant. In other words, the output does not depend upon the past input.

In practical circuits, there is always some time delay between the application of the inputs and the appearance of the corresponding outputs. If we change the inputs, the new outputs will be available only after this delay period. Thus, the only difference between practical and ideal combinatorial circuits is that we have to wait a little to obtain the output.

However, even in practical combinatorial circuits the outputs do not depend upon the past inputs. The word 'past' here refers to time periods greater than the delay.

If we wish to have a circuit where the outputs depend upon the past inputs as well, then information regarding the past inputs must be stored. Information storage is performed in what are usually called **memory elements**. Thus, in this chapter we will consider another class of switching circuits that contain memory in one form or another.

In the new class of switching circuits some of the outputs of a practical combinatorial circuit, which appear after some time delay, are fed back as inputs as shown in Figure 4.1. An output when delayed can be thought of as stored for a period of time and made available at a later time. Remembering some conditions for a period of time and recalling these later means **memory.** Thus, these delays act as memories. The outputs then depend not only on the present inputs, but also on the past outputs which in turn were functions of the previous inputs. The word **history** is appropriately used to comprehensively refer to the past values or previous conditions which prevailed in the circuit. Since the history of inputs, as a sequence of events in time, forms an important factor in determining the behaviour of these circuits, these are known as **sequential switching circuits.**

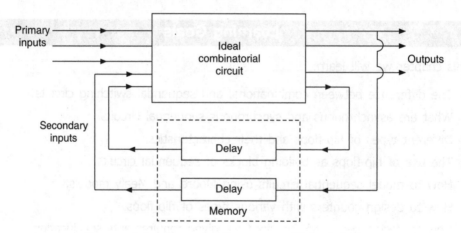

**Figure 4.1  A model for sequential circuits.**

With reference to Figure 4.1, we see that a sequential circuit is nothing but a combinatorial circuit with some feedback paths between its output and input terminals. The direct inputs into the combinatorial circuit which are externally controlled are called **primary inputs** and the ones that are fed back are called **secondary inputs.**

Systematic procedures are available for synthesizing sequential circuits needed to meet a set of specified tasks. However, we will use combinatorial circuit design and Boolean algebra, coupled with a heuristic approach, to analyse and synthesize sequential circuits.

Consider a NAND (or NOR) gate connected as an inverter. As the input crosses the threshold voltage in the positive direction, the output will cross the threshold in the negative direction after a time delay of $\tau_1$ as shown in Figure 4.2. Similarly, the upward transition of the output through the logical threshold takes place with a time delay $\tau_2$ with respect to the negative transition of the input through the threshold. The '0' to '1' upward transition of the logic level is called a **dynamic '1'** and the downward transition from '1' to '0' is known as **dynamic '0'**. The periods $\tau_1$ and $\tau_2$ are called **propagation delays** of the gate.

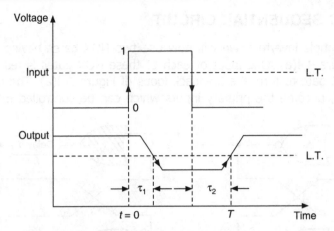

**Figure 4.2  Propagation delay of an inverter.**

Consider three inverters connected in tandem where the output is fed back to the input as shown in Figure 4.3(a). The circuit has no primary inputs. In order to understand the behaviour of the loop, assume that at $t = 0$, there is a noise-induced dynamic '1' occurring at the input as shown. This will propagate through the chain of gates in the time sequence shown in the figure and the output at $t = 2\tau_1 + \tau_2$ will get fed back as a dynamic '0' which will in turn cause another sequence. It can be easily seen that these changes will go on endlessly. Thus, the output of any gate will be oscillatory. An oscillatory output is also called **unstable**.

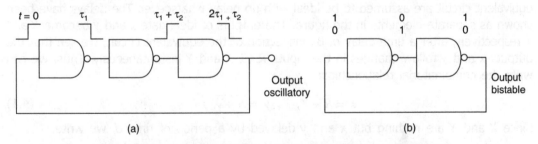

**Figure 4.3  Basic feedback loops formed by inverters.**

On the other hand, if we had an even number (two) of gates in the loop as shown in Figure 4.3(b), we can easily see that the output can only be either '0' or '1'. Generally, it is impossible to predict whether the output will be 0 or 1 since it depends upon the unknown conditions prevailing at the time of turning the power on in the circuit. We call these two states as **stable-states** of the circuit.

Note that the only input the circuit has is the feedback from the output. Hence, there is no simple way of making the circuit change from one state to the other because there are no primary inputs into the circuit which can be controlled externally. We will now examine an arrangement where we can cause a transition between the two stable-states by introducing primary inputs.

## 4.2   A BASIC SEQUENTIAL CIRCUIT

Instead of two simple inverters, we will now use two NOR gates having two inputs each as shown in Figure 4.4(a). One input of each of these NOR gates is fed from the output of the other NOR gate to form the feedback loops of Figure 4.4(a). The other two inputs, labelled *R* and *S*, become the primary inputs which can be controlled externally.

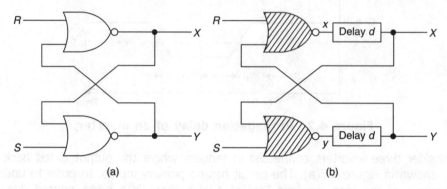

(a)                                        (b)

**Figure 4.4   A simple sequential circuit.**

To analyse the behaviour of this circuit, we should remember that any practical NOR gate cannot operate instantaneously. It will have a time delay between the application of a change in input and the appearance of the corresponding output. Thus, the circuit of Figure 4.4(a) is modelled by an equivalent circuit shown in Figure 4.4(b). The gates in the equivalent circuit are assumed to be ideal with no delay whatsoever. The delays have been shown as separate elements in the figure. The outputs of ideal gate *x* and *y* become *X* and *Y* respectively, after a time delay *d*. By inspection of the equivalent circuit, we see that the outputs *x* and *y* follow changes in the inputs *R*, *S*, *X* and *Y* instantaneously. Thus, we can write the combinatorial relationships:

$$x = \overline{R + Y}, \qquad y = \overline{S + X} \tag{4.1}$$

Since *X* and *Y* are nothing but *x* and *y* delayed by a period of time *d*, we write,

$$X(t) = x(t - d), \qquad Y(t) = y(t - d) \tag{4.2}$$

Observe that *x* and *y* are combinatorial functions of the primary inputs *R* and *S* as well as the previous values of *x* and *y* which are represented by *X* and *Y* respectively. The word 'previous' means *d* units of time earlier.

Now we represent *x* and *y* [Eq. (4.1)] in K-maps as shown in Figure 4.5(a) and (b) respectively. For convenience, the two maps are merged to form a single map as shown in Figure 4.5(c). We are aware of the fact that this K-map does not tell us anything whatsoever about the sequence of events in time. But we can make use of Eq. (4.2) to determine what happens after a time delay *d* by just saying '*X* becomes equal to *x* and *Y* becomes equal to *y* after the time delay'.

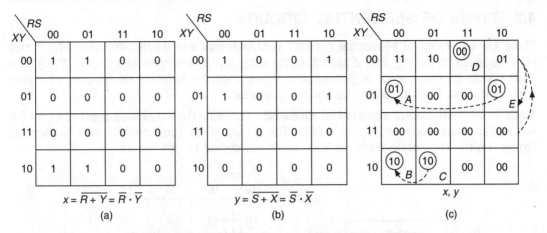

**Figure 4.5  K-maps for *x* and *y* of Eq. (4.1).**

If at any instant of time *X* and *Y* are not equal to *x* and *y*, then the circuit is unstable and therefore further changes must take place. The stable states of the circuit are characterized by *X* = *x* and *Y* = *y* when no further changes will take place. In the K-map the stable-states are easily identified by comparing the *XY* values of each row and the entries of *xy* in the same row of the map. The stable-states are distinguished by circling them.

Next, we will examine the sequence of events which take place if the circuit is in an unstable state at some point of time. For example, consider a situation where *RS* = 10 (fourth column) and *XY* = 11 (third row). From the map of Figure 4.5(c) we see that the value of *xy* at the intersection of the third row and fourth column is 00. Since *XY* assume the values of *xy* after a time delay, let us investigate what happens when *XY* = 00 (first row). Since *RS* value continues to be the same, we must focus on the fourth column but move to the first row. The entry in the map gives *xy* = 01. After another time delay, *XY* becomes 01 shifting our attention to the second row. Here *xy* is also 01. This is a stable-state and there will be no further changes. The sequence of events called **cycles** (or **transitions**) leading to this stable-state *E* are indicated by arrows in the K-map.

Let us now consider the situation where the primary inputs *RS* assume values 00 (1st column). The outputs *XY* can be in either one of the two stable-states 01 (*A*) or 10 (*B*). We will now show that the actual stable-state depends upon the previous history of the inputs *RS*.

The question that arises is, what were *RS* before they became 00. They could have been 01 or 10 from which, by a change of one variable, they could become 00. Let us first consider the input condition *RS* = 01 (second column) and assume that the circuit was in the stable-state *C*. Now, if we make *S* = 0, *RS* = 00 and move to the first column, we find the stable-state *B* adjacent to *C*.

If, on the other hand, we started with *RS* = 10 and the stable-state *E*, and made *RS* = 00, the circuit will move to the stable-state *A*. These transitions produced by changing the primary inputs are shown by the dotted arrows in the figure.

This clearly establishes the fact that this sequential circuit exhibits memory and this then is the essential difference between combinatorial and sequential circuits. Thus, the general schematic presentation of a sequential circuit given in Figure 4.1, is an abstraction in which the combinatorial part of the circuit is assumed to have no delay. The delay is shown separately in the feedback paths and labelled as memory.

## 4.3 TYPES OF SEQUENTIAL CIRCUITS

There are two types of sequential circuits: **synchronous** and **asynchronous.** The circuit considered above belongs to the asynchronous category. In asynchronous circuits, the inputs and outputs do not change at preassigned times since the inherent delays are not rigidly controlled. This leads to problems known as **races.**

**Race in asynchronous sequential circuits:** Consider the schematic presentation of a sequential circuit shown in Figure 4.6(a). The K-map of its combinatorial part is given as Figure 4.6(b). The stable-states of the circuit are circled in the K-map.

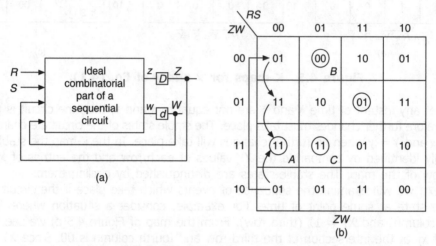

(a)

(b)

**Figure 4.6 Illustration of race conditions in any asynchronous sequential circuits.**

Assume that $RS = 00$ and $ZW = 10$. From the map, the corresponding value of $zw$ is 01. This is an unstable state. Thus, $ZW$ must change from 10 to 01. This means that $Z$ must change from 1 to 0 and $W$ from 0 to 1. In other words, both the variables must change their values. Notice that the time delays in the two feedback paths are not equal. These are hence marked differently as $D$ and $d$ (see Figure 4.6a). Assume that $d$ is smaller than $D$. This means that $W$ will change faster than $Z$. In other words, there will be a time when $W$ would have changed and $Z$ would not have changed. Thus, $ZW$, in going from 10 to 01, will go through an intermediate 11. If $ZW$ becomes 11, the circuit will reach the stable-state $A$.

If, on the other hand, $d$ is large than $D$, $Z$ will change first and $ZW$ in trying to change from 10 to 01 will go through an intermediate value 00. When $ZW = 00$, $zw$ is 01 and, therefore, $ZW$ will become 01. Corresponding to this, $zw = 11$. Now, $ZW$ becomes 11 and the circuit reaches the stable-state $A$ after three cycles as indicated by arrows on the K-map. Thus, we see that depending upon the relative magnitudes of the delays, the behaviour of the circuit is different. This is called a **race** condition. Fortunately, in this circuit the ultimate destination is the same stable-state $A$ regardless of which variable wins the race. Hence, this race is qualified as **uncritical.**

Consider now the second column in the map ($RS = 01$). For $ZW = 01$, $zw = 10$. Note that both variables have to change values. This is the root cause of the problem. If $d > D$, then *ZW*, in trying to become 10, assumes the intermediate value 11 and the circuit gets trapped in the stable-state *C*. On the contrary, if $d < D$, then *ZW* becomes 00 leading to the stable-state *B*. Now we see that the stable destination state critically depends upon which of the variables, *Z* or *W*, wins the race. Hence, this is called a **critical race.** Generally, the delays in the system are unknown and so the outcome in a critical race is unpredictable. This being highly undesirable, the designer of this type of sequential circuits must avoid critical race conditions. Let us see how races can be eliminated by using the synchronous design approach.

**Synchronous sequential circuits:** Synchronous sequential circuits do not depend upon unknown delays in the feedback path to give the memory function. Instead, they use bistable memory elements which can store a '1' or a '0'. Information regarding the outputs is stored in these memories. The transfer of information from outputs to memories is done only at preassigned discrete points of time in a systematic manner. The contents of these memories are fed back as secondary inputs.

We will explain the principle of operation of a synchronous sequential circuit using a simple arrangement where mechanical switches are used at the inputs of the memory elements as shown in Figure 4.7. Note that the switches $S_1$ and $S_2$ enable us to load the outputs *W* and *Z* into the memory elements $M_1$ and $M_2$ respectively. For the time being assume that these memory elements are capacitors as shown in the figure. If the switches are permanently closed, we essentially have an asynchronous circuit (see Figure 4.1). When the switches are open, the memory elements retain the values of *Z* and *W* which existed just before opening the switches.

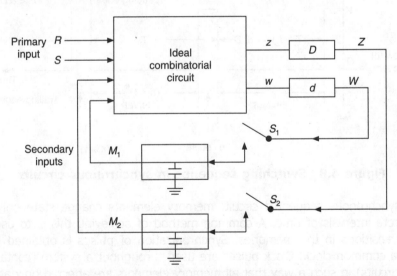

**Figure 4.7 Block diagram of a synchronous sequential circuits.**

We will assume that the switches are closed at time $t_n$ for a period of time $(T_p)$, which is smaller than both *d* and *D*. We will further assume that the memory elements can change state instantaneously.

If these conditions are satisfied at time $t_n$, the secondary inputs $(Z_n, W_n)$ are applied to the combinatorial circuit and $z_{n+1}$ $w_{n+1}$ are formed instantaneously. But before $Z_{n+1}$ and $W_{n+1}$ are available, the switches are opened. Enough time is allowed so that race, if any, between the variables is completed. Thus, two switches are kept open for a period greater than both $D$ and $d$ and during this period $M_1$ and $M_2$ maintain the secondary inputs $(Z_n, W_n)$. Once again the switches are closed storing $Z_{n+1}$ and $W_{n+1}$ in the memory elements. This process is repeated in a periodic manner making the behaviour of the circuit absolutely predictable.

For obvious reasons, we do not use mechanical switches in practical sequential circuits. Instead, we use gates and voltage pulses to obtain the switching action. The one-to-one correspondence between the mechanical switching and pulsed electronics switching is shown in Figure 4.8.

As the name suggests, a pulse is a short-lived level as shown in Figure 4.8. It lasts for a relatively short period of time called the **pulse-width** or **pulse duration** $(T_p)$. In positive logic, the high-voltage level, which lasts for the pulse duration, corresponds to '1' and the low-voltage level between the pulses corresponds to '0'. The front edge of the pulse (dynamic '1') is called the **leading edge** and the back edge (dynamic '0') is known as the **trailing edge.** Since a periodic pulse train marks time, it is popularly known as a **Clock.**

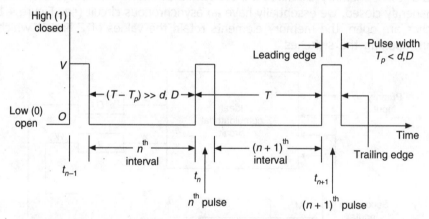

**Figure 4.8  Switching sequence in synchronous circuits.**

In a synchronous sequential circuit, memory elements change state only at preassigned discrete intervals of time. A common method of achieving this is to use pulses to effect the transitions in the memories. Synchronization of pulses is obtained by deriving them from a common clock. Clock pulses are used throughout a system (containing many sequential circuits) in such a way that all memory elements are affected only at the arrival of the clock pulse. Synchronous sequential circuits which use clock pulses at the input of memory elements are called **clocked sequential circuits.** As we have seen, such circuits do not exhibit race conditions. Their design is simpler and they operate reliably. Even though clocked circuits are inherently slower than asynchronous sequential circuits, they are more extensively used due to their higher reliability and easy design.

## 4.4 FLIP-FLOPS

Bistable memory elements, used in sequential circuits to store binary information, are called **flip-flops**. There are several types of flip-flops having different behaviour with respect to information storage and retrieval.

We analyzed the behaviour of a simple sequential circuit (Figure 4.4) using two NOR gates. The circuit known by the name *RS* Latch as well as its K-map [Figure 4.5(c)], are reproduced in Figure 4.9. Let us vary the primary inputs *R* and *S* in various sequences and observe the behaviour of the circuit. A typical sequence is shown in Table 4.1. We start with *RS* = 10, which means that the circuit has settled in the stable-state *E*. Looking at the sequence shown in the table, let us assume that after each change of *RS*, when we move to a different column in the K-map, sufficient time is allowed for the circuit to settle down in a stable-state.

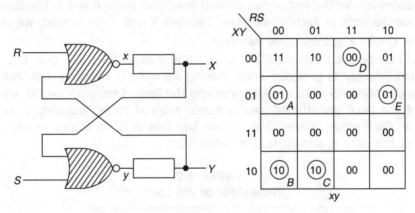

**Figure 4.9  Behaviour of *RS* latch.**

**TABLE 4.1**
**Behaviour of an *RS* Latch showing race condition**

| R | S | | Stable state | | X | Y |
|---|---|---|---|---|---|---|
| 1 | 0 | | E | | 0 | 1 |
| 1 | 1 | ← | D | → | 0 | 0 |
| 0 | 1 | | C | | 1 | 0 |
| 0 | 0 | | B | | 1 | 0 |
| 1 | 0 | | E | | 0 | 1 |
| 0 | 0 | | A | | 0 | 1 |
| 1 | 0 | | E | | 0 | 1 |
| 0 | 1 | | C | | 1 | 0 |
| 0 | 0 | | B | · | 1 | 0 |
| 1 | 0 | | E | | 0 | 1 |
| 1 | 1 | ← | D | → | 0 | 0 |
| 1 | 0 | | E | | 0 | 1 |
| 1 | 1 | ← | D | → | 0 | 0 |
| 0 | 0 | | Critical race | | 0 | 1 |
| | | | *A* or *B*? | or 1 | 0 | |

With reference to the table as well as the K-map, we note the following:

1. For the rows indicated by arrows in the table where $RS = 11$, $X$ and $Y$ are both '0'. In all the other rows, the outputs $XY$ are complements of each other.

2. When the circuit is in the stable-state $D$, where $RS = 11$, if we change $RS$ to 01 or 10, we move to the left or right into the adjacent columns of the map and the outcomes are predictable.

3. Again starting from $RS = 11$, if we change both the variables, $RS$ become 00 and we move to the first column of the map. Here, the circuit has two stable-states. Since both the variables $X$ and $Y$ have to change, there is a critical race condition and the outcome is unpredictable.

Thus, if we disallow the condition $RS = 11$, we have a predictable behaviour for the circuit. Furthermore, for the rest of the allowed combinations of $R$ and $S$, the outputs $X$ and $Y$ will be complements of each other. Thus, because $X$ and $Y$ are related, we rename the output $X$ as $Q$ and $Y$ automatically becomes $\bar{Q}$.

It can now be seen that if $RS = 10$, $Q = 0$ and when $RS = 01$, $Q = 1$. When $RS = 00$, $Q$ retains (stores) its previous value. Making $RS = 01$ is conventionally called *setting the latch* and making $RS = 10$ is called *resetting the latch*. Keeping $RS = 00$, we leave the contents of the latch undisturbed and is hence referred to as *operating it in the store condition* or *store mode*. When $Q$ is '1', we say that a '1' is stored in the latch. The behaviour of the latch is summarized in Table 4.2.

**TABLE 4.2**
**Behaviour of *RS* Latch**

| RS | X = Q | |
|----|-------|---|
| 10 | 0 | Resets |
| 01 | 1 | Sets |
| 00 | 0 or 1 | Stores previous value |
| 11 | | Disallowed |

As it is, the circuit is asynchronous. Synchronous operation is obtained as shown in Figure 4.10(a). The inputs $R$ and $S$ are applied along with clock pulses to two AND gates. The outputs of these gates become the inputs of the latch. Normally, the outputs of the gates are low and hence the latch is in the store mode. When the clock pulse (CP) arrives at time $t_n$, the primary inputs $R_n$ and $S_n$ of the $n^{\text{th}}$ interval (see Figure 4.8) are applied to the latch. After the pulse is gone, the $(n+1)^{\text{th}}$ interval starts. The output $Q_{n+1}$ during the $(n+1)^{\text{th}}$ interval depends upon $R_n$, $S_n$ as well as $Q_n$ as shown in Table 4.3. Thus, it becomes possible to express $Q_{n+1}$ as a Boolean function of $S_n$, $R_n$ and $Q_n$ given by

$$Q_{n+1} = S_n + \bar{R}_n \cdot Q_n \tag{4.3}$$

This is called the *characteristic equation* of an $RS$ latch.

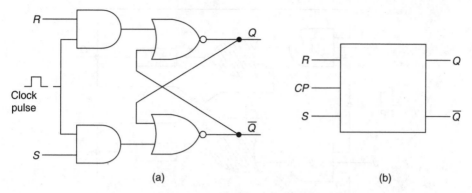

**Figure 4.10   Clocked *RS* flip-flop.**

**TABLE 4.3**
**Characteristic Table of *RS* Flip-Flop**

| $S_n$ | $R_n$ | $Q_n$ | $Q_{n+1}$ | | $Q_{n+1} = \bar{R}_n \cdot (S_n + Q_n)$ |
|-----|-----|-----|-----|---------|------------------------------|
| 0 | 0 | 0 | 0 | Stores | $Q_{n+1} = Q_n$ |
| 0 | 1 | 0 | 0 | Resets | $Q_{n+1} = 0$ |
| 1 | 0 | 0 | 1 | Sets | $Q_{n+1} = 1$ |
| 0 | 0 | 1 | 1 | Stores | $Q_{n+1} = Q_n$ |
| 0 | 1 | 1 | 0 | Resets | $Q_{n+1} = 0$ |
| 1 | 0 | 1 | 1 | Sets | $Q_{n+1} = 1$ |
| 1 | 1 | | Not allowed | | |

If we use the fact that $R_n = S_n = 1$ is disallowed, then the characteristic equation is

$$Q_{n+1} = S_n(\bar{R}_n + Q_n)$$

The reader should verify this using a K-map. We assume that the inputs $R_n$ and $S_n$ do not change within the pulse duration. The latch along with the AND gate (called loading gates) is called a **clocked *RS* flip-flop** the symbol for which is shown in Figure 4.10(b).

In an *RS* flip-flop, the condition $RS = 11$ is disallowed. The circuit of an *RS* flip-flop can be modified so that even when $RS = 11$, we can make the outputs $X$ and $Y$ to be complements of each other. Further, for this input condition, we can design the circuit in such a way that the output $Q_{n+1}$ at $t_{n+1}$ is the complement of $Q_n$ at $t_n$. In other words, for $RS = 11$ the content of the flip-flop gets complemented. In this way, we make use of all the four combinations $RS$ can assume to obtain useful transitions.

How can we make the flip-flop complement its content when $RS = 11$? Complementing its content means that we have to know what is contained in it so that we can bring about the appropriate transition. If a '1' is stored in the flip-flop, we must reset it. On the other hand, if a '0' is stored in it, we must set it. Now it becomes clear that we have to load the outputs into their own inputs to complement them as shown in Figure 4.11. Such a flip-flop is called a **JK flip-flop** and it is customary to label the primary inputs by the letters $J$ and $K$.

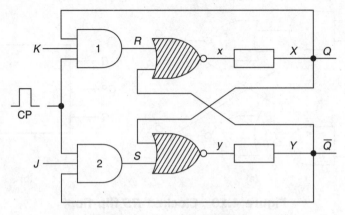

**Figure 4.11  *JK* flip-flop.**

For *JK* = 11, note that this feedback is such that if *X* = 1, the AND gate numbered one gets enabled. Now since *Y* = 0, gate number two gets disabled. Under these conditions, *R* = 1 and *S* = 0 during the clock pulse. Thus, if *X* = 1, at the end of a narrow clock pulse *X* becomes 0.

Using a technique similar to that used for analyzing an *RS* flip-flop, we can obtain an excitation map of this circuit (Figure 4.12) (assume that CP = 1). It is seen from the map that, in all its stable-states, *X* and *Y* are complements to each other. When the inputs *JK* change from 01 to 11, the inputs *RS* of the latch will be 01 which will set the latch. Thus, the content of the latch is complemented. However, this state is unstable if CP continues to be '1', because the complementation process will go on endlessly so long as CP is '1'. Thus, to see that complementation takes place only once, it is necessary that the width of the clock pulse is less than the delay in the latch.

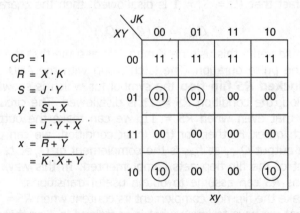

**Figure 4.12   K-map for explaining *JK* flip-flop action.**

In many commercially available ICs, the user does not have to worry about the pulse width. At the trailing edge of the external clock pulse, a new pulse of appropriate duration is generated internally in the IC. This is achieved by differentiating the back edge or by a charge control mechanism. When such a provision is incorporated, the flip-flop is called a **charge controlled *JK* flip-flop.** However, in such flip-flops one gets another restriction on the speed of the back edge of the clock. The minimum rate of fall of the back edge of the clock pulse is specified by the manufacturer.

**Sequential circuit with master slave memories:** Figure 4.7 explains how we could avoid critical races provided that the duration for which the switches were closed was smaller than the delays in the combinatorial circuit. The observation is analogous to the situation of pulse width control required in the *JK* flip-flop.

The problem of pulse width control in sequential machines is easily avoided by the arrangement shown in Figure 4.13. Now we have two sets of memory elements in tandem with a new set of switches ($S_3$, $S_4$) interposed between them. One set of memories is called **Master** and the other **Slave** as shown in Figure 4.13(a).

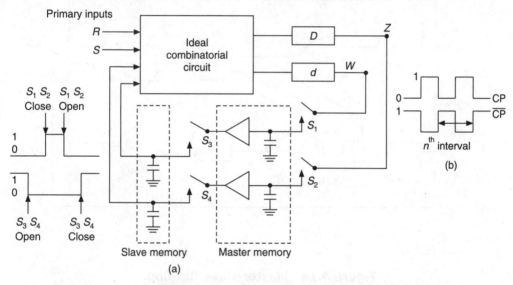

**Figure 4.13　Sequential circuit with master-slave memory.**

Assume that the switches $S_3$, $S_4$ are complements of $S_1$, $S_2$. By this we mean that when $S_1$ and $S_2$ are closed, $S_3$ and $S_4$ are open and vice versa. This is done by using a clock pulse (CP) to operate $S_1$, $S_2$ and $\overline{CP}$ [Figure 4.13(b)] to operate $S_3$, $S_4$. Now we explain the operation of this new arrangement as follows. When the clock is low in the $n^{th}$ interval, $S_3$ and $S_4$ are closed and $S_1$, $S_2$ remain open. Information from master stays connected to the slave. The outputs $W_n$, $Z_n$ of the $n^{th}$ interval are available, but these are not connected to the master memory. When the clock goes high, first we open the switches $S_3$, $S_4$ and then close $S_1$, $S_2$. This lets the information regarding $W_n$, $Z_n$ move into the master; the slave still contains $W_{n-1}$, $Z_{n-1}$. At the trailing edge of the clock pulse, $S_1$, $S_2$ are opened first and then $S_3$, $S_4$ are closed. This updates the contents of the slave memory to $Z_n$, $W_n$. Now $Z_{n+1}$ and $W_{n+1}$ are formed. Note that the new values of outputs are formed at the trailing edge of the clock pulse. Thus, we see that the duration of the clock pulse is immaterial from the point of view of the circuit operation.

To make such an approach to the design of sequential circuits possible, we put two flip-flops into a single IC package with appropriate gates so that a composite memory is obtained. Such flip-flops are called **master slave flip-flops.**

**Master-slave *JK* flip-flop:** A master-slave *JK* flip-flop with two NOR latches is shown in Figure 4.14. The loading gates at the inputs of the master and slave latches replace the mechanical switches of the example we discussed in the last section. Note that the input loading gates are operated with the clock pulse CP and the loading gates in between the latches are operated by $\overline{\text{CP}}$.

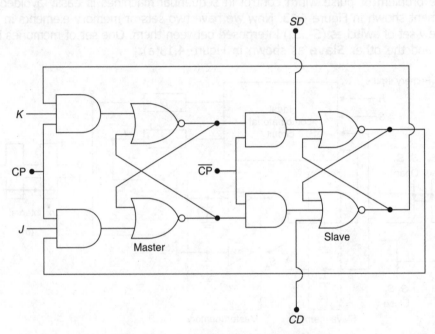

**Figure 4.14   Master-slave flip-flop.**

In order to make the flip-flop complement its own contents when *JK* = 11, the output of the slave is fed back to the master as shown in the figure. Now it is easy to see that the operation of the circuit does not depend upon the clock pulse duration. Since the pulse width is not critical any more, it becomes possible to even use square wave clocks which have a duty cycle of unity. Since the pulse width can be comparable to the period between the pulses, we should now carefully decide as to which interval the pulse duration belongs to. Since the transitions take place at the trailing edge of the pulse, the pulse duration is included in the previous interval as shown in Figure 4.13(b). The characteristic table of the flip-flop is shown in Table 4.4, where expressing $Q_{n+1}$ as a Boolean expression of $J_n$, $K_n$ and $Q_n$, we get,

$$Q_{n+1} = J_n \cdot \overline{Q}_n + \overline{K}_n \cdot Q_n \tag{4.4}$$

This may be verified by using K-map of Table 4.4. Equation (4.4) is the characteristic equation of master-slave *JK* flip-flop.

**TABLE 4.4**
**Behaviour of *JK* Flip-Flop**

| $J_n$ | $K_n$ | $Q_n$ | $Q_{n+1} = J_n \cdot \overline{Q}_n + \overline{K}_n \cdot Q_n$ | |
|:---:|:---:|:---:|:---:|:---|
| 0 | 0 | 0 | 0 | |
| 0 | 0 | 1 | 1 | Stores |
| 0 | 1 | 0 | 0 | |
| 0 | 1 | 1 | 0 | Resets |
| 1 | 0 | 0 | 1 | |
| 1 | 0 | 1 | 1 | Sets |
| 1 | 1 | 0 | 1 | |
| 1 | 1 | 1 | 0 | Complements |

With reference to Figure 4.14, note that there is provision to set and reset the slave latch asynchronously using the set direct (*SD*) and clear direct (*CD*) inputs. Normally, both the inputs *SD* and *CD* are kept low (0). *SD* = 1 and *CD* = 0 sets the slave latch. *SD* = 0 and *CD* = 1 resets the latch. Remember that *SD* and *CD* should never be made '1' simultaneously. The use of these inputs in entering asynchronous data into the flip-flop will be discussed later.

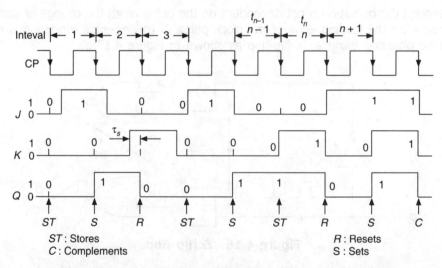

**Figure 4.15   Operation of master-slave *JK* flip-flop.**

Figure 4.15 explains how the *JK* flip-flop behaves when the inputs *J* and *K* are varied in a sequence. First, the time intervals are numbered as shown where the trailing edge of the clock pulse marks the beginning of an interval. During the first interval, the *J* input changes from 0 to 1. Since *JK* = 10 before the trailing edge of the clock appears, the flip-flop sets in the second interval. In the second interval, *J* becomes 0 and *K* becomes 1. Notice that the *K* input actually changes during the clock pulse. However, before the succeeding trailing edge of the clock, *JK* = 01 and hence the flip-flop resets. Observe that the $K$ input changed only $\tau_s$ units of time before the back edge of the clock as shown in Figure 4.15. If $\tau_s = 0$ the flip-flop will not reset. Instead it will store. Naturally, the question that arises is: how small can $\tau_s$ be? In fact, there is a minimum value of $\tau_s$ called the *setting up time* for which the changed input levels must be maintained in the $(n-1)^{th}$ time interval to obtain the correct outcome in the $n^{th}$ interval. In Figure 4.15, in the first three intervals, we have shown asynchronous changes in the inputs $J$ and $K$. If these inputs happen to be derived from other flip-flops operating in the system using the same clock, then $J$ and $K$ will change as shown from time $t_{n-1}$ onwards in the figure. Note that the behaviour of the flip-flop can be predicted by observing the $J$ and $K$ inputs in the previous interval just before the occurrence of the trailing edge of the clock pulse. Thus, in a system which uses such flip-flops all the outputs are guaranteed to change at the dynamic '0' of the common clock. Hence, the output of any flip-flop can be used as input into any other flip-flop making the outcome predictable in the next interval.

**D flip-flop:**   The flip-flop shown in Figure 4.16 is known as **D flip-flop.** It is a modification of the $RS$ flip-flop in which the combination $RS = 11$ is disallowed. A simple way to disallow $RS = 11$ is to impose the restriction that $R$ and $S$ will always be complements of each other ($R = \bar{S}$). Now note that the flip-flop has only one input. This input is called the $D$ input. The behaviour of this flip-flop is described in the characteristic table (Table 4.5). The characteristic equation of $D$ flip-flop is:

$$Q_{n+1} = D_n \tag{4.5}$$

Although the operation is not dependent on the pulse width the change of state takes place soon after the leading edge of the clock pulse. If trailing-edge triggering is needed, this can be obtained using a $JK$ flip-flop as shown in Figure 4.17(a).

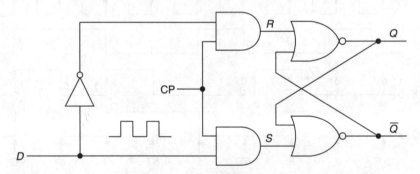

**Figure 4.16   D flip-flop.**

**TABLE 4.5**

**Characteristic Table of D Flip-Flop**

| $D_n$ | $Q_n$ | $Q_{n+1} = D_n$ |
|-------|-------|-----------------|
| 0 | 0 | 0 |
| 0 | 1 | 0 |
| 1 | 0 | 1 |
| 1 | 1 | 1 |

**T flip-flop:**  A $T$ flip-flop has the characteristic behaviour given in Table 4.6. This flip-flop also has a single input marked $T$ in the figure. The symbol $T$ stands for **toggling** which is a popular way of referring to complementation.

### TABLE 4.6
### Behaviour of T Flip-Flop

| $T_n$ | $Q_n$ | $Q_{n+1} = T_n \oplus Q_n$ | |
|-------|-------|------------------------------|-------------|
| 0 | 0 | 0 | |
| 0 | 1 | 1 | Stores |
| 1 | 0 | 1 | |
| 1 | 1 | 0 | Complements |

When $T = 0$, the content of the flip-flop is unaffected (store mode). When $T = 1$, it toggles. A trailing-edge triggered $T$ flip-flop is readily obtained by connecting the $J$ and $K$ inputs of a $JK$ flip-flop as shown in Figure 4.17(b). The characteristic equation of $T$ flip-flop is:

$$Q_{n+1} = T_n \oplus Q_n \qquad (4.6)$$

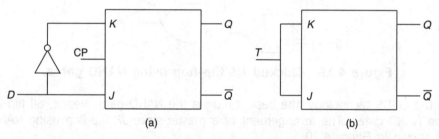

(a)                                    (b)

**Figure 4.17   Conversion of a *JK* flip-flop into (a) *D* flip-flop (b) *T* flip-flop.**

**The NAND latch:**   Hitherto we considered latches using NOR gates. We can make a latch using NAND gates also as shown in Figure 4.18(a). Although we can analyze the behaviour of the NAND latch in exactly the same way as we did for the NOR latch, we will try and do this by a shortcut approach.

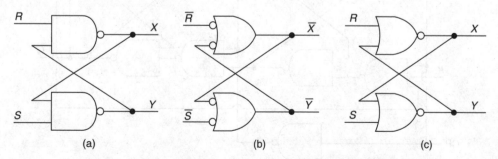

(a)                          (b)                          (c)

**Figure 4.18   NAND latch compared with NOR latch.**

The NAND latch is redrawn using the alternative symbol as shown in Figure 4.18(b). For comparison the NOR latch is reproduced in Figure 4.18(c). Comparing these two figures carefully, we see that the basic feedback loop in the two latches is the same. In order to obtain an exact one-to-one correspondence between the variables, start from the NOR latch and assign complemented variables in the NAND latch looking at the position of the inversion circles. Now we can obtain the characteristic table of the NAND latch from that of the NOR latch by replacing '0' by '1' and '1' by '0'. Immediately, in the NAND latch both the inputs assuming 00 has to be prohibited. When both the inputs are 11, the latch stores. It sets and resets when the inputs are 01 and 10 respectively.

Let us now make a clocked *RS* flip-flop using a NAND latch. For this, we have to use two loading gates. Instead of using AND gates, let us again use NAND gates as shown in Figure 4.19. We immediately recognize that the inversion circles at the output of the loading gate and the input of the latch cancel each other. Thus, at the inputs we get exactly the same conditions as in the *RS* flip-flop of Figure 4.4. Just the outputs have to be interchanged.

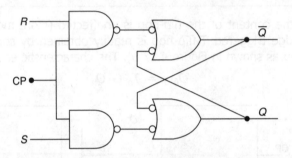

**Figure 4.19   Clocked *RS* flip-flop using NAND gates.**

In the CMOS technology, the basic circuit is the NAND gate. Hence, all flip-flops are based on NAND gates. The arrangement of a master-slave *JK* flip-flop using NAND gates alone is shown in Figure 4.20.

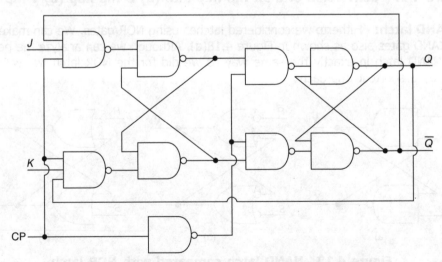

**Figure 4.20   Clocked master-slave *JK* flip-flop.**

For ready reference, we consolidate the characteristic equations of all the flip-flops in Table 4.7.

**TABLE 4.7**
**Characteristic Equations of Flip-Flops**

| Flip-flop type | Characteristic equation |
|---|---|
| RS latch (11 for RS not allowed) | $Q_{n+1} = S_n + (\bar{R}_n \cdot Q_n)$ |
| JK flip-flop (master-slave) | $Q_{n+1} = J_n \cdot \bar{Q}_n + \bar{K}_n \cdot Q_n$ |
| D flip-flop | $Q_{n+1} = D_n$ |
| T flip-flop | $Q_{n+1} = T_n \oplus Q_n$ |

## 4.5  COUNTERS

### 4.5.1  A Binary Counter

A **counter** is a sequential circuit consisting of a set of flip-flops which go through a sequence of states on the application of clock pulses. Counters form important building blocks in digital systems. They are used for counting the occurrence of events, frequency division and generating timing sequence to control operations in a digital system. This section illustrates how counters are constructed using flip-flops. Let us assume that all the flip-flops change state at the trailing edge of the clock pulses.

**Binary counters:**  Consider four JK flip-flops interconnected as shown in Figure 4.21. Note that the J and K terminals of each flip-flop have been connected together thereby making them T flip-flops. Since the T inputs are maintained at logical 1, each flip-flop will complement for every negative transition of the pulse applied to its CP input.

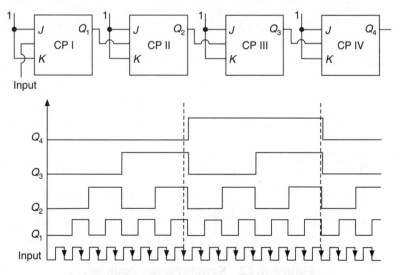

**Figure 4.21  A four-stage ripple counter.**

The first stage is fed by the clock. Observe that one output pulse is obtained for every two input pulses from the output of the first flip-flop. Thus, the frequency of the output $Q_1$ is half the frequency of the clock. The first stage may thus be thought of as a binary counter or as a frequency divider which divides by a factor of 2. Note that the output of the first stage is fed into the CP input of the second stage and so on. By cascading a number of such flip-flops, we can count by any power of two. The circuit of Figure 4.21 gives one output pulse for every 16 input clock pulses and is hence called a **modulo-16 counter.** Observe also that the contents of the flip-flops follow the natural binary counting sequence, namely from 0000 to 1111 and returns to 0000.

There will be a small delay between the clock input and the output of the first flip-flop. The output of the first flip-flop ripples through the other flip-flops in tandem. For instance, when the count is to change from 0111 to 1000, the trailing edge of the pulse from flip-flop I triggers flip-flop II. This in turn, triggers flip-flop III and the output of flip-flop III then triggers IV. Thus, the last flip-flop changes state only after a cumulative delay of four flip-flops. This counter is called **ripple carry counter.**

## 4.5.2  Synchronous Binary Counter

Section 4.5.1 shows how a ripple carry counter works, and the output is obtained after a delay. A counter in which all flip-flops change state simultaneously at the trailing edge of a clock pulse is called a **synchronous counter.** We will first analyze a given synchronous counter and understand its behaviour. Figure 4.22 is a synchronous counter. Observe that

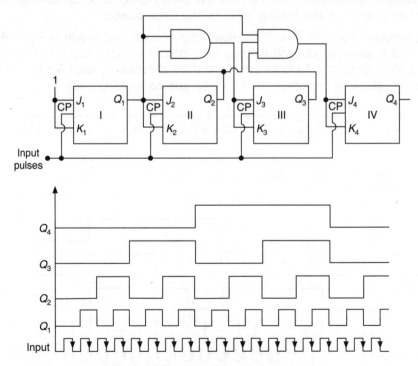

**Figure 4.22  Synchronous counter.**

all flip-flops are connected to a common clock. Thus, all of them will change simultaneously. Notice that the $J$ and $K$ inputs of all four flip-flops are tied together. All of them are thus $T$ flip-flops. The inputs to the four flip-flops are:

$$T_1 = 1, \; T_2 = Q_1, \; T_3 = Q_1 \cdot Q_2 \text{ and } T_4 = Q_1 \cdot Q_2 \cdot Q_3 \tag{4.7}$$

The outputs $Q_1$, $Q_2$, $Q_3$, $Q_4$ are as shown in Figure 4.22. $Q_1$ will toggle at trailing edge of each clock pulse as shown in Figure 4.22. As $Q_1$ is input to flip-flop II, it will toggle at each trailing edge of $Q_1$ as shown in Figure 4.22. As $T_3 = Q_1 \cdot Q_2$, flip-flop III will toggle when $Q_1$ and $Q_2$ are both 1 and transition from 1 to 0 as seen in Figure 4.22. Following the same argument $Q_4$ will become 1 when $Q_1$, $Q_2$, $Q_3$ are 1 and transition to 0 as seen in Figure 4.22. Using these wave forms Table 4.8 is obtained where the first row corresponds the first clock pulse, second row to the second clock pulse, etc. We see from this table that the output of four flip-flops follow the natural binary counting sequence. They start from 00000, go to 1111 and return to 0000. It is thus a modulo-16 counter.

**TABLE 4.8**
**Natural Binary Counting Sequence**

| $Q_4$ | $Q_3$ | $Q_2$ | $Q_1$ |
|-------|-------|-------|-------|
| 0 | 0 | 0 | 0 |
| 0 | 0 | 0 | 1 |
| 0 | 0 | 1 | 0 |
| 0 | 0 | 1 | 1 |
| 0 | 1 | 0 | 0 |
| 0 | 1 | 0 | 1 |
| 0 | 1 | 1 | 0 |
| 0 | 1 | 1 | 1 |
| 1 | 0 | 0 | 0 |
| 1 | 0 | 0 | 1 |
| 1 | 0 | 1 | 0 |
| 1 | 0 | 1 | 1 |
| 1 | 1 | 0 | 0 |
| 1 | 1 | 0 | 1 |
| 1 | 1 | 1 | 0 |
| 1 | 1 | 1 | 1 |
| 0 | 0 | 0 | 0 |

Figure 4.22 and the analysis process we followed show that we can abstractly model this sequential circuit by the block diagram of Figure 4.23. In this figure by a *state* we mean the state, i.e. 0 or 1, of the flip-flop constituting the sequential machine. **State memory** is the set of flip-flops and it stores the bits corresponding to those of the flip-flops. By next state logic we mean the combinatorial circuit whose inputs are the current state and the

outputs are those fed back to the inputs of the flip-flops constituting the counter. Transition from one state to the next takes place at each clock pulse. The next state logic of a synchronous four-bit binary counter is given by Eq. (4.7).

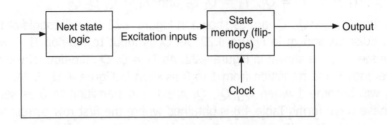

**Figure 4.23   Abstract model of a synchronous counter.**

This model is not a very general model but is appropriate to the synchronous counter we analyzed. More general models of synchronous sequential circuits have been proposed. These models are useful in synthesizing synchronous sequential circuits given the requirement specifications. We will now examine these models.

## 4.6   MODELLING SEQUENTIAL CIRCUITS—FINITE STATE MACHINES

There are two models to describe the behaviour of general sequential circuits. In one model the output of the sequential machine depends only on the current "state" of the machine, i.e. the states of the flip-flops constituting the machine. Such a machine is called **"Moore machine"** in honour of Moore who first proposed this model. In the other model, the output of the machine depends not only on the state of the sequential machine, but also on the inputs to the sequential machine. This is called the **"Mealy machine"** in honour of Mealy who proposed his model.

A block diagram of the two models are shown in Figure 4.24 and Figure 4.25 respectively.

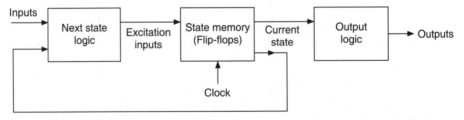

**Figure 4.24   Moore model of synchronous state-machine.**

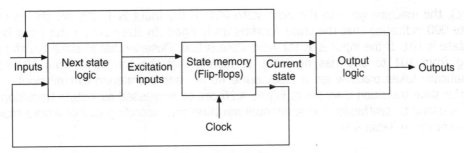

**Figure 4.25 Mealy model of synchronous state-machine.**

Observe the following common features of both models.

1. Both models have a block labelled "State memory". This represents the set of flip-flops which form an integral part of all sequential machines.

2. Both models have a feedback path connecting the output of the State memory (which represents the current state of the machine) to its input via a block named "Next state logic". This logic is a combinatorial circuit. This logic has in addition one or more inputs.

3. Both models have an output logic which is a combinatorial switching circuit. The only difference between the Moore machine and the Mealy machine is that the output of the Mealy machine depends on the current state as well as on the inputs, whereas the Moore machine's output depends only on the current state. The behaviour of both models is normally depicted by what is known as **state-transition diagram.** This diagram shows the initial state (i = 1), the input (if any), the next state (i + 1), the input which caused the transition, subsequent states and finally the return to the initial state. As we are concerned with machines with finite number of states at the end of a number of states, the machine has to return to the initial state.

The state-transition diagram of a Moore machine is shown in Figure 4.26.

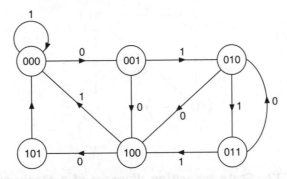

**Figure 4.26 State-transition diagram of a Moore machine.**

In the state-transition diagram of Figure 4.26 the states are inscribed within the circles. An arc with an arrow shows the next state. In state 000, if the input is 0 (shown as 0 above the arc), the machine goes to the next state 001. If the input is 1, the arc shown returns to state 000 indicating that the state remains unchanged. In state 100, if the input is 0 the next state is 101. If the input is 1, the next state is 000. Observe that in state 101 the arrow leading from 101 to 000 has no label. It means that the transition from 101 to 000 automatically takes place when a clock pulse occurs and is independent of input.

The state transition diagram of Figure 4.26 can be expressed as a state transition table which is useful to synthesize the sequential machine corresponding to this Moore machine. This is shown in Table 4.9.

### TABLE 4.9
### State-transition Table for Moore Machine of Figure 4.26

| Current state | | | Input | Next state | | |
|---|---|---|---|---|---|---|
| $A_n$ | $B_n$ | $C_n$ | | $A_{n+1}$ | $B_{n+1}$ | $C_{n+1}$ |
| 0 | 0 | 0 | 0 | 0 | 0 | 1 |
| 0 | 0 | 0 | 1 | 0 | 0 | 0 |
| 0 | 0 | 1 | 1 | 0 | 1 | 0 |
| 0 | 0 | 1 | 0 | 1 | 0 | 0 |
| 0 | 1 | 0 | 0 | 1 | 0 | 0 |
| 0 | 1 | 0 | 1 | 0 | 1 | 1 |
| 0 | 1 | 1 | 0 | 0 | 1 | 0 |
| 0 | 1 | 1 | 1 | 1 | 0 | 0 |
| 1 | 0 | 0 | 0 | 1 | 0 | 1 |
| 1 | 0 | 0 | 1 | 0 | 0 | 0 |
| 1 | 0 | 1 | $\phi$ | 0 | 0 | 0 |

The state transition diagram of a Mealy machine is shown in Figure 4.27

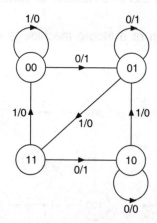

**Figure 4.27 State transition diagram of a Mealy machine.**

Observe the label 0/1 on the arc leading from state 00 to 01. It indicates that when this machine is in state 00 and an input 0 is applied, the next state is 01 and the output will be 1. The output depends on both the initial state 00 and the input 0 applied when the machine is in this state. Given this state-transition diagram we can write down a table which gives the current state, next state, input and output. Such a table is shown as Table 4.10 for the state transition diagram of Figure 4.27.

**TABLE 4.10**
**State-transition table for the Mealy Machine of Figure 4.27**

| Current state | | Input | Next state | | Output |
|---|---|---|---|---|---|
| $A_n$ | $B_n$ | | $A_{n+1}$ | $B_{n+1}$ | |
| 0 | 0 | 0 | 0 | 1 | 1 |
| 0 | 0 | 1 | 0 | 0 | 0 |
| 0 | 1 | 0 | 0 | 1 | 1 |
| 0 | 1 | 1 | 1 | 1 | 0 |
| 1 | 0 | 0 | 1 | 0 | 0 |
| 1 | 0 | 1 | 0 | 1 | 0 |
| 1 | 1 | 0 | 1 | 0 | 1 |
| 1 | 1 | 1 | 0 | 0 | 0 |

As we mentioned earlier, the state-transition table is useful to synthesize the corresponding sequential circuit.

In the Moore machine's state-transition diagram the output is not shown along the arcs as the output depends only on the current state and is independent of the input.

## 4.7 SYNTHESIS OF SYNCHRONOUS BINARY COUNTERS

This section explains how a counter can be synthesized with specified type of flip-flops given the state-transition diagram of the counter.

### 4.7.1 Modulo-5 Counter

A counter which counts five pulses and returns to its initial state is known as a **modulo-5 counter.** The counting sequence we use in this example is the natural binary counting sequence. The state-transition diagram of this counter is shown in Figure 4.28.

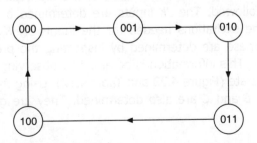

**Figure 4.28  State-transition diagram of modulo-5 counter.**

The data needed is the counting sequence and the number of counts. The synthesis procedure is to design combinatorial circuits to drive the flip-flops in such a way that they follow the specified counting sequence. The input drive needed to accomplish a particular transition in a flip-flop is obtained by referring to Table 4.11. This table, called **excitation table** of flip-flop, gives the input conditions $J_n$, $K_n$ required in the $n^{th}$ interval in order to obtain a desired transition from $Q_n$ to $Q_{n+1}$, where $Q_n$ is the current state of the flip-flop and $Q_{n+1}$ is its state in the next interval. Observe that this table is a re-statement of the characteristic table describing the behaviour of a *JK* flip-flop. We will now show the synthesis procedure for a modulo-5 counter.

**TABLE 4.11**
**Excitation Table for JK Flip-Flop**

| Current state | Transition $\rightarrow$ | Next state | Interpretation of the transition | Input conditions required in the $n^{th}$ interval | | Input conditions restated in a consolidated way | |
|---|---|---|---|---|---|---|---|
| | | | | $J_n$ | $K_n$ | $J_n$ | $K_n$ |
| 0 | $\rightarrow$ | 0 | Stores or resets | 0 0 | 0 1 | 0 | $\phi$ |
| 0 | $\rightarrow$ | 1 | Sets or toggles | 1 1 | 0 1 | 1 | $\phi$ |
| 1 | $\rightarrow$ | 0 | Resets or toggles | 0 1 | 1 1 | $\phi$ | 1 |
| 1 | $\rightarrow$ | 1 | Stores or sets | 0 1 | 0 0 | $\phi$ | 0 |

The counting sequence specified for this counter is given in Figure 4.28 and Table 4.12. As the number of states of the counter is five (greater than four), we need three flip-flops. Let us assume that *JK* flip-flops are to be used. Having made this choice, the next step is to determine the *J* and *K* inputs of each of the flip-flops such that the specified counting sequence is followed. The *JK* inputs are determined by using the information given in Table 4.11. The excitations needed for the inputs $J_A$, $K_A$ of the flip-flop *A*, are shown in Table 4.13. These are determined by inspecting the present state $A_n$ and the next required state $A_{n+1}$. This information is obtained by observing the sequence in which the flip-flop *A* changes state (Figure 4.28 and Table 4.12). Using this basic idea the inputs necessary for flip-flops *B* and *C* are also determined. They are given in Table 4.14.

**TABLE 4.12**

**Counting Sequence Required in Modulo-5 Counter**

| | *Outputs of flip-flops* | | |
|---|---|---|---|
| *Count* | *A* | *B* | *C* |
| 0 | 0 | 0 | 0 |
| 1 | 0 | 0 | 1 |
| 2 | 0 | 1 | 0 |
| 3 | 0 | 1 | 1 |
| 4 | 1 | 0 | 0 |
| 5 | 0 | 0 | 0 |

**TABLE 4.13**

**JK Inputs for Flip-Flop *A***

| $A_n$ | | $A_{n+1}$ | $J_{A_n}$ | $K_{A_n}$ |
|---|---|---|---|---|
| 0 | $\rightarrow$ | 0 | 0 | $\phi$ |
| 0 | $\rightarrow$ | 0 | 0 | $\phi$ |
| 0 | $\rightarrow$ | 0 | 0 | $\phi$ |
| 0 | $\rightarrow$ | 1 | 1 | $\phi$ |
| 1 | $\rightarrow$ | 0 | $\phi$ | 1 |

**TABLE 4.14**

**Excitation Table for Modulo-5 Counter**

| A | B | C | $J_A$ | $K_A$ | $J_B$ | $K_B$ | $J_C$ | $K_C$ |
|---|---|---|---|---|---|---|---|---|
| 0 | 0 | 0 | 0 | $\phi$ | 0 | $\phi$ | 1 | $\phi$ |
| 0 | 0 | 1 | 0 | $\phi$ | 1 | $\phi$ | $\phi$ | 1 |
| 0 | 1 | 0 | 0 | $\phi$ | $\phi$ | 0 | 1 | $\phi$ |
| 0 | 1 | 1 | 1 | $\phi$ | $\phi$ | 1 | $\phi$ | 1 |
| 1 | 0 | 0 | $\phi$ | 1 | 0 | $\phi$ | 0 | $\phi$ |

The next step is to express the *J* and *K* inputs as combinatorial functions of *A*, *B* and *C*. Observe that the three flip-flops *A*, *B* and *C* can give eight possible states of which three states, namely 101, 110 and 111 do not occur. These may thus be considered as don't care conditions. The information contained in Table 4.14 is entered in the K-maps (Figure 4.29) from which we obtain Boolean functions for $J_A$, $J_B$, $K_B$ and $J_C$. $K_A = 1$ and $K_C = 1$ are obvious from Table 4.14 and hence, the K-maps for these are not drawn. Knowing these functions we can directly draw the schematic of the counter as shown in Figure 4.30.

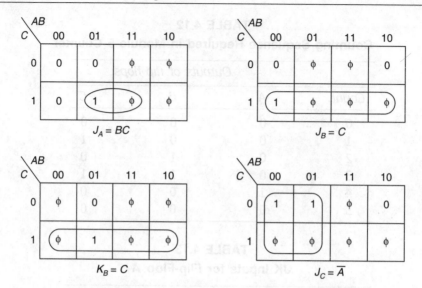

Figure 4.29   K-maps for modulo-5 counter.

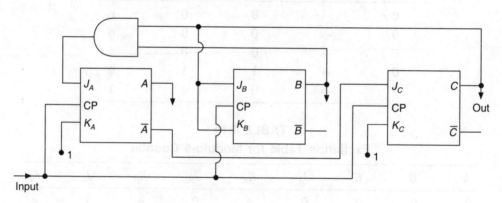

Figure 4.30   Modulo-5 counter.

## 4.7.2   Modulo-10 Counter

As another illustration, we will synthesize a 2421 decimal or modulo-10 or decade counter. The counting sequence of 2-4-2-1 counter follows the weighted 2-4-2-1 code shown in Table 4.16 (columns for $A$, $B$, $C$ and $D$). We will illustrate this counter design using $T$ flip-flops. The excitation table for a $T$ flip-flop derived from its characteristic table (Table 4.6) is shown in Table 4.15. The counting sequence and the inputs required for the four $T$ flip-flops to produce the sequence are shown in Table 4.16. The K-maps for the inputs $T_A$, $T_B$, $T_C$ and $T_D$ are now obtained as shown in Figure 4.31. From these maps we obtain the expressions:

$$T_A = \overline{A} \cdot B + B \cdot C \cdot D, \quad T_B = \overline{A} \cdot B + C \cdot D, \quad T_C = \overline{A} \cdot B + D, \quad T_D = 1 \qquad (4.8)$$

The counter is synthesized as shown in Figure 4.32.

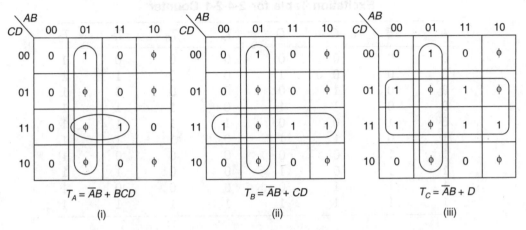

$$T_A = \overline{A}B + BCD$$

(i)

$$T_B = \overline{A}B + CD$$

(ii)

$$T_C = \overline{A}B + D$$

(iii)

**Figure 4.31   K-maps for modulo-10, 2-4-2-1 counter.**

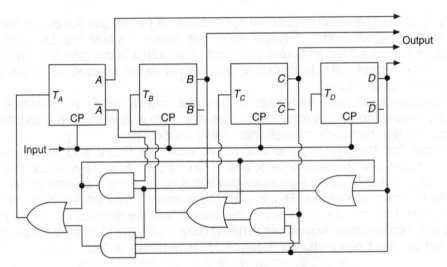

**Figure 4.32   2-4-2-1 Modulo-10 counter.**

**TABLE 4.15**

**Excitation Table of a *T* Flip-Flop**

| Transition $Q_n \rightarrow Q_{n+1}$ | Interpretation of the transition | Input required in the $n^{th}$ interval $(T_n)$ |
|---|---|---|
| $0 \rightarrow 0$ | Stores | 0 |
| $0 \rightarrow 1$ | Toggles | 1 |
| $1 \rightarrow 0$ | Toggles | 1 |
| $1 \rightarrow 1$ | Stores | 0 |

**TABLE 4.16**
**Excitation Table for 2-4-2-1 Counter**

| A | B | C | D | $T_A$ | $T_B$ | $T_C$ | $T_D$ |
|---|---|---|---|-------|-------|-------|-------|
| 0 | 0 | 0 | 0 | 0 | 0 | 0 | 1 |
| 0 | 0 | 0 | 1 | 0 | 0 | 1 | 1 |
| 0 | 0 | 1 | 0 | 0 | 0 | 0 | 1 |
| 0 | 0 | 1 | 1 | 0 | 1 | 1 | 1 |
| 0 | 1 | 0 | 0 | 1 | 1 | 1 | 1 |
| 1 | 0 | 1 | 1 | 0 | 1 | 1 | 1 |
| 1 | 1 | 0 | 0 | 0 | 0 | 0 | 1 |
| 1 | 1 | 0 | 1 | 0 | 0 | 1 | 1 |
| 1 | 1 | 1 | 0 | 0 | 0 | 0 | 1 |
| 1 | 1 | 1 | 1 | 1 | 1 | 1 | 1 |

## 4.7.3  Generation of Control Signals

The output of the sequential circuits we synthesized so far are the states themselves as shown in the abstract model of Figure 4.23. The Moore machine we described at the beginning of Section 4.6 has an output logic block. The output in this case is a combinatorial function of the current state. In this subsection we will design a sequential circuit with an output combinatorial circuit.

Sequential circuits are widely used to generate control signals in computers. These signals are required to start, execute as well as stop various operations in a specified time sequence. We illustrate such an application using an example.

Assume that the two sequences of pulses shown in Figure 4.33 are required. By inspection we see that the waveforms $S_1$ and $S_2$ have a periodicity. They repeat themselves after five clock pulses. Thus, we generate these sequences using a counter of five and an appropriate decoder as shown in Figure 4.34. The decoder inputs are fed from the outputs of the counter. The next step is to design the counter and the decoder. For the counter, let us use the design which we worked out earlier (Figure 4.30). The truth table for the decoder is obtained by direct observation of Figure 4.33. It is shown in Table 4.17.

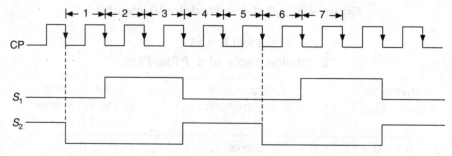

**Figure 4.33  Control signals to be generated.**

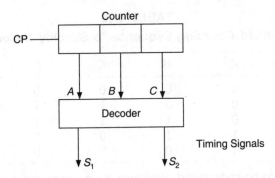

**Figure 4.34  The block diagram of a counter decoder.**

(The counter is the modulo-5 counter of Figure 4.30)

TABLE 4.17
**Truth Table for Counter Decoder**

| Clock Pulse | A | B | C | $S_1$ | $S_2$ |
|:-----------:|:-:|:-:|:-:|:-----:|:-----:|
| 1 | 0 | 0 | 0 | 0 | 0 |
| 2 | 0 | 0 | 1 | 1 | 0 |
| 3 | 0 | 1 | 0 | 1 | 0 |
| 4 | 0 | 1 | 1 | 0 | 1 |
| 5 | 1 | 0 | 0 | 0 | 1 |
| 6 | 0 | 0 | 0 | 0 | 0 |

The boolean expressions for the decoder are obtained using the K-maps of Figure 4.35. Observe that the unused counts are treated as don't care conditions. The Boolean expressions for the decoder are:

$$S_1 = B \cdot \bar{C} + \bar{B} \cdot C, \qquad S_2 = A + B \cdot C \qquad (4.9)$$

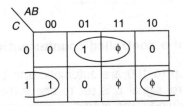
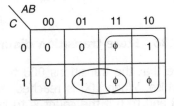

**Figure 4.35  K-maps for the decoder.**

The decoder can sometimes be made simpler if the counting sequence of the modulo-5 counter is appropriately chosen. Table 4.18 gives such a sequence. Now we see that the expressions for this decoder obtained by an inspection of Table 4.18 are $S_1 = C$, $S_2 = A$. In other words, the output of the flip-flops give the control signal directly without any need for decoding.

**TABLE 4.18**
**Modified Counting Sequence to Simplify Decoder**

| Clock pulse | A | B | C | $S_1$ | $S_2$ |
|---|---|---|---|---|---|
| 1 | 0 | 0 | 0 | 0 | 0 |
| 2 | 0 | 0 | 1 | 1 | 0 |
| 3 | 0 | 1 | 1 | 1 | 0 |
| 4 | 1 | 1 | 0 | 0 | 1 |
| 5 | 1 | 0 | 0 | 0 | 1 |

The counter has to be redesigned. However, it may need more gates than before. This is left as an exercise to the reader.

### 4.7.4 Controlled Counter

In this subsection we will design a more general sequential circuit that has some control inputs, which control the state transition in the system from one state to the next, and also has outputs. We will consider the design of a counter with a control input to meet the following specifications. The counter should normally count modulo-5. When a control input is set to one then it should count modulo-8. When the counter is in its initial state a red light should be on. A green light should be on when a count of six is reached.

A state diagram corresponding to the above specifications is shown in Figure 4.36.

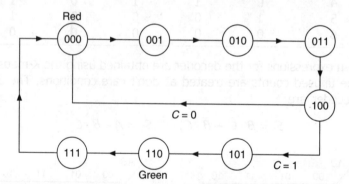

**Figure 4.36 State transition diagram of a controlled counter with output.**

Observe that the transitions 000 to 001 up to 100 are automatic and take place at each clock pulse. When 100 is reached, a control signal $C$ is set to one if the count is to be modulo-8 and to 0 if the count is to be modulo-5. The output is red when the system state is 000. It is green if the state is 110. This is also shown in the state diagram.

From the diagram one may obtain the state transition table and the inputs to the flip-flops as shown in Table 4.19. Using this table and K-maps the input equations of the three flip-flops are obtained as:

$$J_X = Y \cdot Z, \qquad K_X = Y \cdot Z + \bar{Y} \cdot \bar{Z} \cdot \bar{C} \tag{4.10}$$

$$J_Y = Z, \qquad K_Y = Z \tag{4.11}$$

$$J_Z = \bar{X} + Y + C, \qquad K_Z = 1 \tag{4.12}$$

## TABLE 4.19
### Table for Flip-Flop Excitation (Controlled Counter)

| Present State | | | Control | Next State | | | Flip-flop | | | | Inputs | |
|---|---|---|---|---|---|---|---|---|---|---|---|---|
| $X_n$ | $Y_n$ | $Z_n$ | $C$ | $X_{n+1}$ | $Y_{n+1}$ | $Z_{n+1}$ | $J_x$ | $K_x$ | $J_y$ | $K_y$ | $J_z$ | $K_z$ |
| 0 | 0 | 0 | $\phi$ | 0 | 0 | 1 | 0 | $\phi$ | 0 | $\phi$ | 1 | $\phi$ |
| 0 | 0 | 1 | $\phi$ | 0 | 1 | 0 | 0 | $\phi$ | 1 | $\phi$ | $\phi$ | 1 |
| 0 | 1 | 0 | $\phi$ | 0 | 1 | 1 | 0 | $\phi$ | $\phi$ | 0 | 1 | $\phi$ |
| 0 | 1 | 1 | $\phi$ | 1 | 0 | 0 | 1 | $\phi$ | $\phi$ | 1 | $\phi$ | 1 |
| 1 | 0 | 0 | 0 | 0 | 0 | 0 | $\phi$ | 1 | 0 | $\phi$ | 0 | $\phi$ |
| 1 | 0 | 0 | 1 | 1 | 0 | 1 | $\phi$ | 0 | 0 | $\phi$ | 1 | $\phi$ |
| 1 | 0 | 1 | $\phi$ | 1 | 1 | 0 | $\phi$ | 0 | 1 | $\phi$ | $\phi$ | 1 |
| 1 | 1 | 0 | $\phi$ | 1 | 1 | 1 | $\phi$ | 0 | $\phi$ | 0 | 1 | $\phi$ |
| 1 | 1 | 1 | $\phi$ | 0 | 0 | 0 | $\phi$ | 1 | $\phi$ | 1 | $\phi$ | 1 |

By inspection of the state transition diagram we get the outputs as:

$$\text{Red} = \bar{X} \cdot \bar{Y} \cdot \bar{Z} \tag{4.13}$$

$$\text{Green} = X \cdot Y \cdot \bar{Z} \tag{4.14}$$

The sequential circuit implemented with *JK* flip-flops is shown as Figure 4.37.

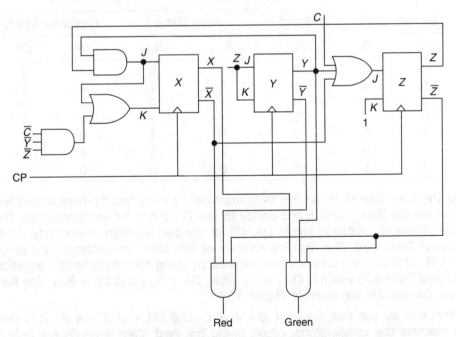

**Figure 4.37 Sequential circuit for controlled counter.**

## 4.8   SYNTHESIZING GENERAL SEQUENTIAL CIRCUITS

### 4.8.1   Synthesizing a Moore Machine

This section will explain how to synthesize general sequential circuits given their state-transition diagrams.

The state-transition diagram of a Moore machine is given in Figure 4.38. The corresponding state-transition and excitation table is given in Table 4.20. In this table $C$ is the input.

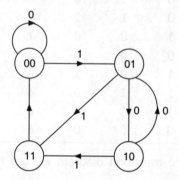

**Figure 4.38    State-transition diagram of a Moore machine.**

**TABLE 4.20**
**State-Transition and Excitation Table for Moore Machine**

| Current State | | Input | Next Status | | Excitation Inputs | |
|---|---|---|---|---|---|---|
| $A_n$ | $B_n$ | $C$ | $A_{n+1}$ | $B_{n+1}$ | $DA$ | $DB$ |
| 0 | 0 | 0 | 0 | 0 | 0 | 0 |
| 0 | 0 | 1 | 0 | 1 | 0 | 1 |
| 0 | 1 | 0 | 1 | 0 | 1 | 0 |
| 0 | 1 | 1 | 1 | 1 | 1 | 1 |
| 1 | 0 | 0 | 0 | 1 | 0 | 1 |
| 1 | 0 | 1 | 1 | 1 | 1 | 1 |
| 1 | 1 | ∅ | 0 | 0 | 0 | 0 |

As there are four states in this state machine we need two flip-flops to synthesize it. If we call the flip-flops $A$ and $B$ and decide to use $D$ flip-flop for implementation, then the state-transition and excitation inputs $DA$, $DB$ for the two flip-flops respectively is obtained as shown in Table 4.20. The first five columns of this table are obtained by inspection of Figure 4.37. The last two columns are obtained by using the characteristic equation of $D$ flip-flop (see Table 4.7) which is $Q_{n+1} = D_n$. Thus, $DA = A_{n+1}$ and $DB = B_{n+1}$. The Karnaugh maps for $DA$ and $DB$ are given in Figure 4.39.

From this we see that $DA = \bar{A}\cdot B + A\cdot \bar{B}\cdot C$ and $DB = \bar{A}\cdot C + A\cdot \bar{B}$. It is clear that in this machine the combinatorial circuit giving the next state depends not only on the current state, but also on the input. We have not drawn the synthesized circuit as it is a straightforward exercise left for the student.

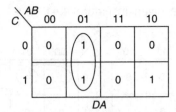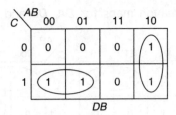

**Figure 4.39 Karnaugh maps for Table 4.19 excitation inputs of flip-flops for a Moore machine.**

## 4.8.2 Synthesizing a Mealy Machine

In Figure 4.27 we gave the state-transition diagram of a Mealy machine. It is reproduced below as Figure 4.40 for ready reference. The state-transition of this machine has been shown in Table 4.10.

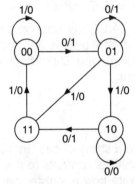

**Figure 4.40 State-transition diagram of a Mealy machine.**

We use Table 4.10 and extend the table by including the excitation inputs to the two flip-flops. We need to synthesize this machine, hence let us assume that $D$ flip-flops are used. The table is given as Table 4.21.

**TABLE 4.21**
**State-transition and excitation table of Mealy machine**

| Current State | | Input | Next State | | Output | Excitation Inputs | |
|---|---|---|---|---|---|---|---|
| $A_n$ | $B_n$ | $C$ | $A_{n+1}$ | $B_{n+1}$ | $X$ | $DA$ | $DB$ |
| 0 | 0 | 0 | 0 | 1 | 1 | 0 | 1 |
| 0 | 0 | 1 | 0 | 0 | 0 | 0 | 0 |
| 0 | 1 | 0 | 0 | 1 | 1 | 0 | 1 |
| 0 | 1 | 1 | 1 | 1 | 0 | 1 | 1 |
| 1 | 0 | 0 | 1 | 0 | 0 | 1 | 0 |
| 1 | 0 | 1 | 0 | 1 | 0 | 0 | 1 |
| 1 | 1 | 0 | 1 | 0 | 1 | 1 | 0 |
| 1 | 1 | 1 | 0 | 0 | 0 | 0 | 0 |

The Karnaugh maps for *DA*, *DB* and *X* are given in Figure 4.41

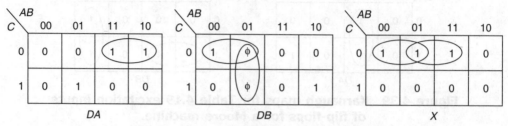

**Figure 4.41   K-maps for Table 4.21.**

From these maps we see that,

$$DA = A \cdot \overline{C} + \overline{A} \cdot B \cdot C \qquad (4.15)$$

$$DB = \overline{A} \cdot \overline{C} + \overline{A} \cdot B + A \cdot \overline{B} \cdot C \qquad (4.16)$$

$$X = \overline{A} \cdot \overline{C} + B \cdot \overline{C} \qquad (4.17)$$

From Eqs. (4.15), (4.16) and (4.17) we observe that next state logic as well as the output *X* depend on the states of both flip-flops and the input to the sequential machine. Drawing the sequential circuit diagram with *D* flip-flops and gates is straight forward and is left as an exercise to the student.

## 4.9   SHIFT REGISTERS

A **register** is a unit which can store a string of bits. In a number of algorithms it is required to enter bits into the register and shift its contents to the left or right by a specified number of bits. In this section, we will illustrate how a register can be constructed with flip-flops, and how its contents are shifted using control signals and gates associated with the flip-flops.

Generally, *D* flip-flops are used to construct registers. Recall that the behaviour of a *D* flip-flop is given by $Q_{n+1} = D_n$ (see Table 4.5). We assume that a *D* flip-flop changes state at the trailing edge of a clock pulse applied to it. Consider the four-bit register of Figure 4.42.

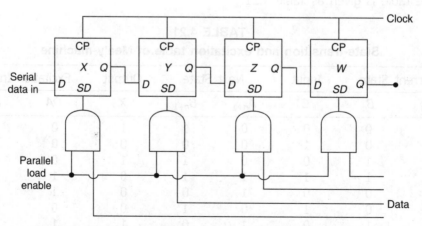

**Figure 4.42   Shift register using *D* flip-flops.**

The output of the first flip-flop is connected to the input of the second flip-flop. Thus, we get $Y_{n+1} = X_n$. In other words, the information moves from the flip-flop $X$ to $Y$ at the occurrence of the trailing edge of the clock. Simultaneously, information moves from $Y$ to $Z$ and $Z$ to $W$. In addition, information also moves in from the serial data input terminal into $X$ and the information contained in $W$ is lost.

Often it is necessary to enter information into all flip-flops in the register simultaneously. This is called **parallel data transfer.** This can be done independent of the clock (asynchronously) or the data may be constrained to enter only at the occurrence of the trailing edge of the clock pulse (synchronously). Asynchronous data entry is indicated in Figure 4.42, where the data is entered when the parallel load enable signal is '1'.

The method of interconnecting $JK$ flip-flops to form a shift register is shown in Figure 4.43.

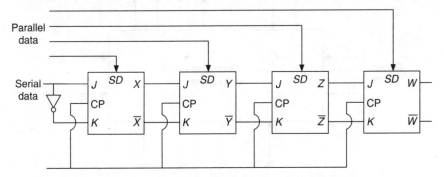

**Figure 4.43  Shift register using *JK* flip-flops.**

In order to shift the contents of the register left or right, the arrangement shown in Figure 4.44 is used. When SHR signal is '1' information is transferred from flip-flop 1 to 2, 2 to 3, etc. As each flip-flop gets triggered at the trailing edge of the clock pulse, there is no ambiguity in the transfer of information. In other words, we can simultaneously write fresh information in a flip-flop and read its previous content. This becomes possible since the new information does not get into the flip-flop till the trailing edge of the clock pulse arrives and the old content is safely transferred to the next flip-flop.

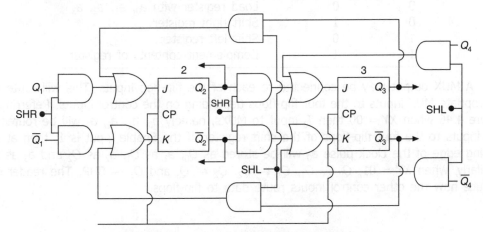

**Figure 4.44  Left-right shift register.**

Shifting left is achieved by making the SHL signal '1'. In this case, the content of flip-flop 3 is transferred to 2 and that of 2, into 1 (not shown in Figure 4.44). New information can also be entered into flip-flop 3 via the terminals marked $Q_4, \bar{Q}_4$ in Figure 4.44.

**Controlled shift register:**    Controlled shift registers can be made using MUXs and *JK* flip-flops. Such a shift register can be an integrated circuit in a single chip. A block diagram of such a shift register is given as Figure 4.45. Table 4.22 gives the functions to be performed by this shift register.

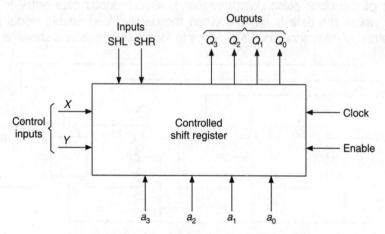

**Figure 4.45   A controlled shift register.**

**TABLE 4.22**
**Control Inputs to a Shift Register**

| Control inputs | | |
|---|---|---|
| X | Y | Function |
| 0 | 0 | Load register with $a_0, a_1, a_2, a_3$ |
| 0 | 1 | Shift right register |
| 1 | 0 | Shift left register |
| 1 | 1 | Complement contents of register |

A MUX output may be connected to each of the flip-flop inputs. This will route the appropriate MUX inputs to the four flip-flops depending on the control inputs. Referring to Figure 4.46 when $XY = 00$ then $I_0$ input to MUXs, namely $a_0, a_1, a_2, a_3$ will be routed as the inputs to the four flip-flops of the shift register. If the Enable input is 1, then at the trailing edge of the clock pulse $a_0$ will be stored as $Q_0$, $a_1$ as $Q_1$, $a_2$ as $Q_2$ and $a_3$ as $Q_3$. Similarly, when $XY = 01$, $Q_0 \leftarrow Q_1$, $Q_1 \leftarrow Q_2$, $Q_2 \leftarrow Q_3$ and $Q_3 \leftarrow$ SHR. The reader can deduce how the other control inputs route data to flip-flops.

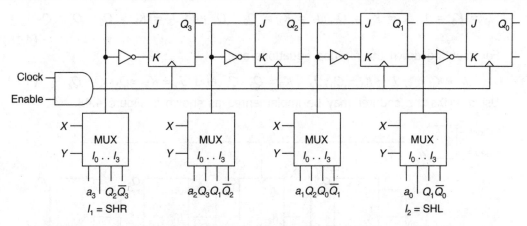

**Figure 4.46   Realization of controlled shift register with MUXs.**

**Controlled binary counter:**   We will now design a controlled binary counter which has the functions defined in Table 4.23.

**TABLE 4.23**
**A Controlled Counter**

| Control inputs | | |
|---|---|---|
| *X* | *Y* | *Function* |
| 0 | 0 | Stop counting |
| 0 | 1 | Count up |
| 1 | 0 | Count down |
| 1 | 1 | Complement state |

The block diagram of the counter to be designed is shown as Figure 4.47. The state diagram of the counter for counting up and down may be drawn and by its inspection we may deduce that for counting up,

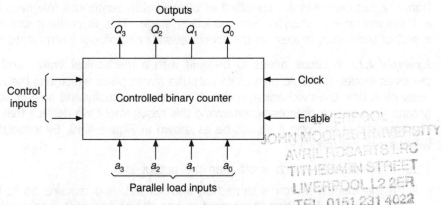

**Figure 4.47   Block diagram of a controlled binary counter.**

$$J_0 = K_0 = 1, J_1 = K_1 = Q_0, J_2 = K_2 = Q_0 \cdot Q_1 \text{ and } J_3 = K_3 = Q_0 \cdot Q_1 \cdot Q_2$$

$$(4.18)$$

For counting down the flip-flop equations are:

$$J_0 = K_0 = 1, J_1 = K_1 = \overline{Q}_0, J_2 = K_2 = \overline{Q}_0 \cdot \overline{Q}_1 \text{ and } J_3 = K_3 = \overline{Q}_0 \cdot \overline{Q}_1 \cdot \overline{Q}_2 \quad (4.19)$$

Using MUXs the counter may be implemented as shown in Figure 4.48.

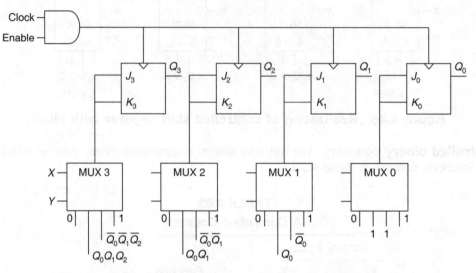

**Figure 4.48   MUX realization of a controlled counter.**

## 4.10   MODELLING, ANALYSIS AND DESIGN OF SEQUENTIAL CIRCUITS

Given the specifications to be met by a system, we introduced in the last chapter a four step process of analysis, modelling, selecting appropriate components to design a system and finally realizing the design with appropriate circuits. In this chapter also we will follow this four state procedure to realize some sequential circuits from given requirements. Normally, requirements are specified as plain English sentences. We have to interpret such a statement in the analysis and modelling stage. This is perhaps the most challenging aspect of the design process as the specifications need proper interpretation and judgement.

*Example 4.1.*   A circuit needs to be built with a mechanical switch and a train of clock pulses as inputs. It should give as its output a single pulse which has the width of the clock pulse each time the mechanical switch *M* is closed manually and held closed for an interval greater than one clock interval. Analyzing this requirement we deduce that the input-output characteristic of this circuit should be as shown in Figure 4.49. By inspection of this figure we observe the following:

1. If the manual switch is off then the output is 0.

2. If the manual switch is turned on and sensed, and remains on at the trailing edge of a clock pulse, then the output is one during the next clock pulse.

3. If the manual switch was on during two or more trailing edges of clock pulse, then only one pulse is given out.

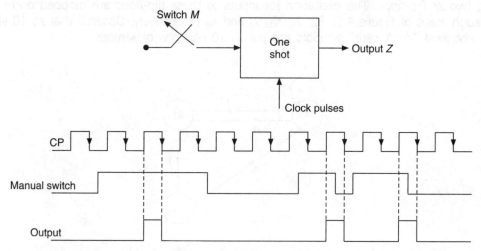

**Figure 4.49  Input-Output characteristics of a desired system.**

It is clear from the above analysis that we need a circuit with memory to implement this requirement, as the output depends on whether the manual switch was on during the previous clock pulse(s) or not. Based on this analysis we model it by the state diagram of Figure 4.50. As there are three distinct states, we need at least two flip-flops to realize the sequential circuit. As two flip-flops can give us four states one state will be unused. Assigning flip-flop states corresponding to Figure 4.50 we obtain the state transition diagram of Figure 4.51.

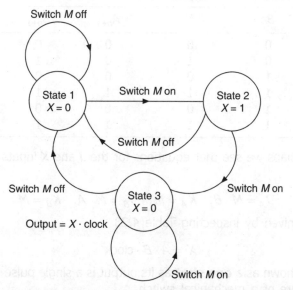

**Figure 4.50  State diagram for designing circuit with I/O characteristics of Figure 4.49.**

From this state diagram we obtain the state-transition table as Table 4.24. Observe from this table that state 10 does not exist in this system. We decide to realize this circuit using two *JK* flip-flops. The excitation for inputs to these flip-flops are mapped on to the Karnaugh maps of Figure 4.52 for $J_A$, $K_A$, $J_B$ and $K_B$ respectively. Observe that as 10 state does not exist "don't care" symbols are put in 10 columns of K-maps.

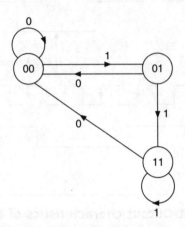

**Figure 4.51 State-transition diagram with state assignment corresponding to Figure 4.50.**

**TABLE 4.24**
**State-Transition Table for Figure 4.51**

| Current state | | Input | Next state | | Output |
|---|---|---|---|---|---|
| An | Bn | M | $A_{n+1}$ | $B_{n+1}$ | X |
| 0 | 0 | 0 | 0 | 0 | 0 |
| 0 | 0 | 1 | 0 | 1 | 0 |
| 0 | 1 | 0 | 0 | 0 | 1 |
| 0 | 1 | 1 | 1 | 1 | 1 |
| 1 | 1 | 0 | 0 | 0 | 0 |
| 1 | 1 | 1 | 1 | 1 | 0 |

From these K-maps we see that equations for the *J* and *K* inputs of the two flip-flops are:

$$J_A = M \cdot B, \quad K_A = \bar{M}, \quad J_B = M \cdot \bar{A}, \quad K_B = \bar{M} \qquad (4.20)$$

The output is given by inspecting Table 4.23

$$X = \bar{A} \cdot B \cdot \text{clock} \qquad (4.21)$$

This circuit is known as a **one shot** as its output is a single pulse with width of a clock pulse for each closure of a mechanical switch.

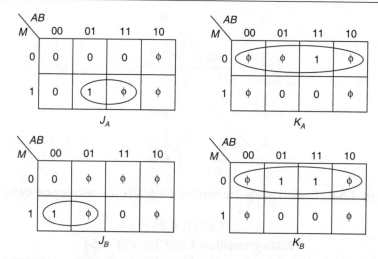

**Figure 4.52  K-maps for *JK* flip-flops corresponding to Table 4.23.**

We have given only the equations for *J* and *K* inputs of *A* and *B* flip-flops and not drawn their circuits as it is a simple straightforward exercise.

*Example 4.2.*

**A sequence detector:** It is required to design a sequential circuit which gives an output of 1 whenever input bit string has a four-bit sequence, 1001. As the first step in analyzing this requirement specification, we define the input and output and obtain a sample input and output of the desired circuit shown below:

|  |  |
|---|---|
| Input X | 10010100110101010100100110 |
| Output Z | 1   1       1  1 |

By inspection of the input and output strings it is observed that whenever an input bit is a 1 it is a prospective candidate for giving $Z = 1$. Further, as a sequence of four bits is to be detected, the sequential circuit will have four states. Based on this analysis we model the required system by the state diagram of Figure 4.53. As there are four states we need two flip-flops to realize the sequence detector. Assigning flip-flop states to each of the circuit states *P, Q, R, S* we obtain the state-transition diagram of Figure 4.54. We decide to realize this state-transition diagram using *JK* flip-flops. As the first step we obtain the state-transition table as Table 4.25.

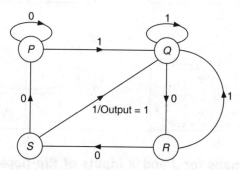

**Figure 4.53  State diagram for sequence detector.**

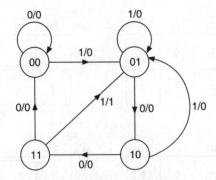

**Figure 4.54  Coded state-transition diagram for sequence detector.**

**TABLE 4.25**
**State-transition table for Fig. 4.54**

| Current State | | Input | Next State | | Output |
|---|---|---|---|---|---|
| $A_n$ | $B_n$ | $X$ | $A_{n+1}$ | $B_{n+1}$ | $Z$ |
| 0 | 0 | 0 | 0 | 0 | 0 |
| 0 | 0 | 1 | 0 | 1 | 0 |
| 0 | 1 | 0 | 1 | 0 | 0 |
| 0 | 1 | 1 | 0 | 1 | 0 |
| 1 | 0 | 0 | 1 | 1 | 0 |
| 1 | 0 | 1 | 0 | 1 | 0 |
| 1 | 1 | 0 | 0 | 0 | 0 |
| 1 | 1 | 1 | 0 | 1 | 1 |

From Table 4.25 we obtain the K-maps for $J$ and $K$ input of flip-flops $A$ and $B$ (Figure 4.55).

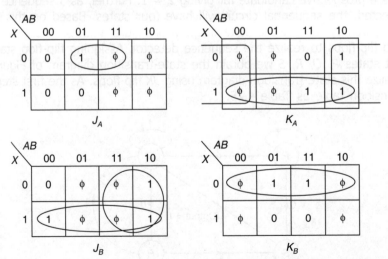

**Figure 4.55  K-maps for $J$ and $K$ inputs of flip-flops for Table 4.25.**

From these K-maps the equations for $J$ and $K$ inputs are given below as Eqs. (4.22) and (4.24).

$$J_A = B \cdot \bar{X}, \quad K_A = \bar{B} + X \tag{4.22}$$

$$J_B = X + A, \quad K_B = \bar{X} \tag{4.23}$$

$$\text{Output} = A \cdot B \cdot X \cdot \text{clock} \tag{4.24}$$

We have not shown the realized flip-flop diagram as it is a straightforward exercise. Observe that this machine is an example of a Mealy machine and is known as a **sequence detector.**

### Example 4.3.

**A four-bit comparator:** Given two strings $X$ and $Y$ of length four-bits each, it is required to design a circuit which would detect whether $X > Y$ or $X = Y$ or $X < Y$ (see Figure 4.56).

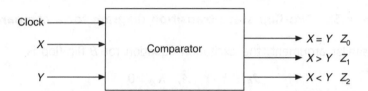

**Figure 4.56   Block diagram of a comparator.**

Let us analyze this requirement by assuming that the two bit strings $X$ and $Y$ are synchronized with a clock and are fed to a circuit. The circuit would compare the two most significant bits of $X$ and $Y$. If they are equal, then $X$ and $Y$ could be equal and further examination of bits in the input strings is necessary. If $X = 1$ and $Y = 0$ then $X > Y$ and if $X = 0$ and $Y = 1$ then $Y > X$. There are thus three states. We model the sytem by using the state diagram as shown in Figure 4.57.

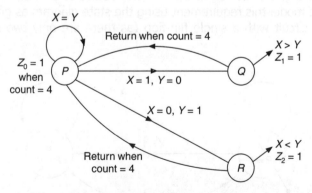

**Figure 4.57   State transition diagram for a comparator.**

In order to realize the behaviour depicted in this state diagram (Figure 4.57) we codify the states and obtain the state-transition diagram given as Figure 4.58. We need two flip-flops. Using *JK* flip-flops it is observed from Figure 4.58 that *A* is set when $\bar{X} \cdot Y$ is 1 and flip-flop *B* is in 0 state. Set *A* is cleared only when the count reaches 4. Thus, the excitation equations for *A* flip-flop is:

$$J_A = X \cdot \bar{Y} \cdot \bar{B}, \quad K_A = 0 \tag{4.25}$$

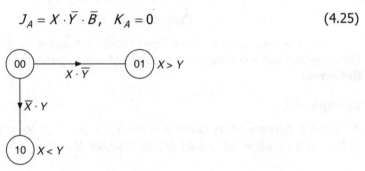

**Figure 4.58   Flip-flop state-transition diagram for a comparator.**

Using a similar argument, the excitation equation for *B* flip-flop is

$$J_B = X \cdot \bar{Y} \cdot \bar{A}, \quad K_B = 0 \tag{4.26}$$

We reset the flip-flops *A* and *B* to 00 state by setting $K_A = K_B = 1$ using a counter at the trailing edge of the fourth clock pulse. The outputs are $Z_0 = \bar{A} \cdot \bar{B} \cdot CP_4$, $Z_1 = \bar{A} \cdot B \cdot CP_4$ and $Z_2 = A \cdot \bar{B} \cdot CP_4$, where $CP_4$ is the fourth clock pulse derived from the counter.

*Example 4.4.*

**A parity generator:**   If four-bits are fed synchronized with a clock, the parity generator to be designed should give a fifth bit at the fifth clock pulse so that odd parity is maintained for the five bits. We model this requirement using the state diagram as given in Figure 4.59. The corresponding circuit with a single flip-flop (as there are only two states) is given as Figure 4.60.

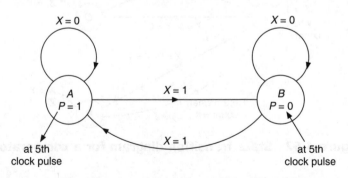

**Figure 4.59   State diagram for odd parity generator.**

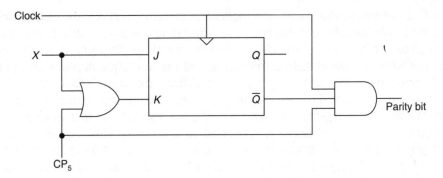

**Figure 4.60   Realization of an odd parity bit.**

One of the most difficult problems in sequential circuit design is to recognize the need for a sequential circuit and then design it. The following examples present complex problem statements that need to be analyzed for designing appropriate switching circuits.

*Example 4.5.*

**Toy train controller:**   A logic circuit needs to be designed to control the operations of a toy train. Referring to Figure 4.61, it is desired that the train should start at the starting point and go on track $A$, then on track $C$, then on track $B$ and then return to track $C$ and $A$. This cycle $A \rightarrow C \rightarrow B \rightarrow C \rightarrow A \cdots$ should then be repeated as long as power is applied to the engine of the train. The position of the train is sensed by three micro switches $A$, $B$ and $C$ which are activated when the train passes over them. These switches control points $W$, $X$, $Y$ and $Z$ on the track for routing the train. When the point $Y$ is set the train will go on track $B$. $X$ should be set for the train to return to track $A$. Point $Z$ should be set for the train to go on track $C$ and point $W$ is set for it to return to track $A$. After a train passes over a point set for it, the point automatically resets to its original position.

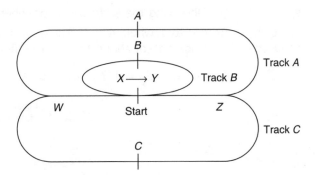

**Figure 4.61   Tracks of a toy train.**

By analyzing the requirement specification it is clear that the logic circuit required will be a sequential circuit as the movement of the train, when it passes on track $C$ on different occasions, would depend on the previous history of its movement.

We first determine the states and model the system using a state diagram as shown in Figure 4.62. We identify four distinct states (including the START state). The outputs $W$, $X$, $Y$ and $Z$ to set the points are also shown in the state diagram. It is clear from the diagram that when we are in state $C$ the output and the next state depends on the previous state. We now codify the states by two bits as there are four distinct states. The state diagram is given as Figure 4.63. As we have two bits to represent each state, we need two flip-flops. We will use $JK$ flip-flops for synthesis. We will also assume that when a microswitch is operated by the train this signal is converted to a pulse synchronous to the clock by a one shot (Figure 4.49). We convert the state diagram of Figure 4.63 to the state transition diagram of Figure 4.64. By inspection of this diagram (Figure 4.64) we see that $P$ goes from $0 \rightarrow 1$ with $Q$ fixed at 1 and $C = 1$.

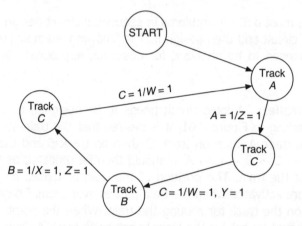

**Figure 4.62  State-transition diagram for controlling toy train.**

Thus, $J_P = C \cdot Q$. Flip-flop $P$ is reset when $PQ = 10$ and $C = 1$. In this case, $Q$ is fixed at 0 and $C = 1$. Thus, $K_P = C \cdot \overline{Q}$. Observing the state transition when $PQ = 00$, we see that $P$ is fixed at 0 and $Q$ is set from 0 to 1 when $A = 1$. Thus, $J_Q = A \cdot \overline{P}$. Similarly, $K_Q = B \cdot P$. Consolidating we get the excitaiton equations for $J$ and $K$ flip-flop as:

$$J_P = C \cdot Q, \quad K_P = C \cdot \overline{Q}, \quad J_Q = A \cdot \overline{P}, \quad K_Q = B \cdot P \tag{4.27}$$

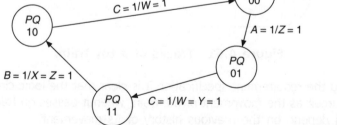

**Figure 4.63  State-transition diagram for toy train with flip-flop states.**

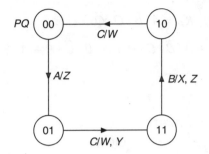

**Figure 4.64  State-transition diagram for toy train with flip-flop assignments.**

The equations for the output are:

$$X = P \cdot Q, \quad Y = \bar{P} \cdot Q, \quad Z = \bar{P} \cdot \bar{Q} + P \cdot Q, \quad W = \bar{P} \cdot Q + P \cdot \bar{Q} \tag{4.28}$$

*Example 4.6.*

**Plant starting sequence controller:**  In order to start a plant it is required to first start a water pump, next an air handling unit and lastly a compressor. If the above starting sequence is not followed then an alarm should be sounded as soon as the wrong unit is started. If the correct sequence is followed, then a green light should light. Let us assume that when a switch is turned ON it cannot be turned OFF manually. If an alarm is sounded then a controller will turn off all the switches automatically. The system, however, will remain in the alarm state until manual action is taken to turn off the alarm.

We will analyze the requirements statement now. As a first step identify the inputs to the logic circuit to be designed. These are the status of the switches to start the pump, air handling unit and compressor respectively. We will call these switches $A$, $B$ and $C$. The outputs are, of course, alarm and green light. As the output depends not only on present inputs, but also on the sequence of inputs leading to the present input, we need a sequential logic circuit. This is clear as an input of $A = 1$, $B = 1$, $C = 1$ will give a green light output only if it was reached in the sequence $A = 1$, $B = 0$, $C = 0$ and $A = 1$, $B = 1$, $C = 0$. If it was reached in the sequence $A = 0$, $B = 1$, $C = 0$ and $A = 1$, $B = 1$, $C = 0$ then an alarm should sound.

Having observed that a sequential circuit is needed we model the system by identifying the states of this circuit. These states are the START state with $A = B = C = 0$. At the START state we get the sequence of inputs $A$, $B$, $C = 0, 0, 1$ or $0, 1, 0$ or $1, 0, 0$. Of these possible sequences, the first two sequences should lead to an 'ALARM' state. The last sequence should lead to an intermediate non-alarm state. From this state one reaches the 'alarm' state if the inputs are $A = 1$, $B = 0$ and $C = 1$. Finally, if the inputs are $A = 1$, $B = 1$, $C = 0$, then as the sequence is correct we reach an 'OK' state. This state is not changed if the next input is $C = 1$. Thus, there are four states. State-transition diagram for this system is shown as Figure 4.65. From this diagram we obtain the flip-flop state-transition diagram of Figure 4.66 with the state assignments $PQ = 00$ for START, $PQ = 10$ for INTER, $PQ = 01$ for ALARM and $PQ = 11$ for OK. Assuming $JK$ flip-flops are used, the flip-flop excitation equations are derived by inspecting Figure 4.66 as:

$$J_P = A \cdot \bar{B} \cdot \bar{C} \cdot \bar{Q}, \quad K_P = A \cdot \bar{B} \cdot C \cdot \bar{Q} \tag{4.29}$$

$$J_Q = \bar{A} \cdot B \cdot \bar{C} \cdot \bar{P} + \bar{A} \cdot \bar{B} \cdot C \cdot \bar{P} + A \cdot B \cdot \bar{C} \cdot P + A \cdot \bar{B} \cdot C \cdot P, \quad K_Q = 0 \tag{4.30}$$

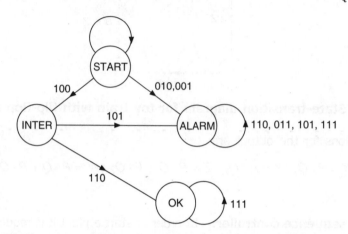

**Figure 4.65   State diagram for sequence controller.**

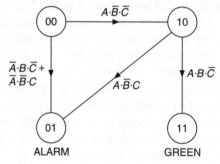

**Figure 4.66   Flip-flop state-transition diagram for Example 4.6.**

The outputs are:

$$\text{ALARM} = \bar{P} \cdot Q, \quad \text{GREEN} = P \cdot Q \tag{4.31}$$

*Example 4.7.*

**Revolution direction detector:**   A disc has three sets of slots as shown in Figure 4.67. A beam of light is positioned as shown in Figure 4.67(b) and it is picked up by two photodetectors on the other side of the disc. It is required to design a logic circuit which accepts the signals from the photodetectors and lights up a green light emitting diode (LED) if the disc is rotating clockwise and a red LED if the disc is rotating anti-clockwise.

From this requirements statement of the problem and by inspection of Figure 4.67 it is seen that if the photodetectors detect as inputs $AB = 11$, $AB = 10$, $AB = 01$, then the disc is rotating clockwise. If the disc is rotating anti-clockwise, then the photodetector output would be $AB = 11$, $AB = 01$ and $AB = 10$. Thus, the logic circuit should distinguish the input sequences 11, 10, 01, 11, ..., from 11, 01, 10, 11, ... As the output of the circuit to be designed depends upon its history of inputs the circuit would be a sequential switching circuit.

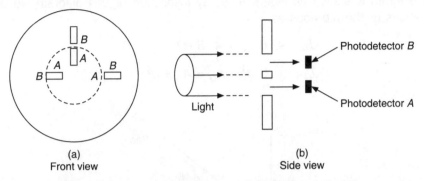

(a)
Front view

(b)
Side view

**Figure 4.67    Coded disc and lighting system.**

Let us assume that the outputs of the photodetectors are shaped and synchronized with a clock. To model a system using a state-transition diagram, one must identify the states of the logic circuit that is to be designed. It is clear that the sequence 11, 10, 01, 11, ..., should lead ultimately to a state which is distinct from the state reached when the sequence 11, 01, 10, 11, ..., is applied. Let us assume an existing starting state when the disc is not rotating. As the input 11 is common to both clockwise and anti-clockwise rotation, we will make the first state transition when this input is received. After this the input 10 signifies a clockwise rotation and 01 anti-clockwise rotation. Thus, these two inputs should take the system to two different states where they remain trapped. These two states are used to signal the direction of rotation.

The state diagram is shown as Figure 4.68. The four states of the circuit are Start, state $X$ to which the system goes if the input is 11, state Green which is reached when the rotation is clockwise and state Red which is reached when the rotation is anti-clockwise.

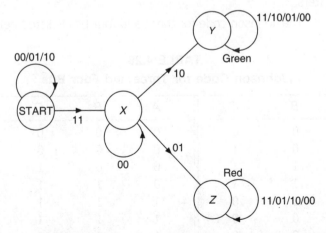

**Figure 4.68    The state-transition diagram for rotation direction detector.**

Now we code the four states by the codes Start = 00, $X$ = 01, Green = 11 and Red = 10. Assuming that we use $JK$ flip-flops to design the circuit the flip-flop state-transition diagram is shown as Figure 4.69. By inspection of this diagram we obtain the input equations of the flip-flops as:

$$J_P = A \cdot \overline{B} \cdot Q + \overline{A} \cdot B \cdot Q, \quad K_P = 0 \tag{4.32}$$

$$J_Q = A \cdot B \cdot \overline{P}, \quad K_Q = \overline{A} \cdot B \cdot \overline{P} \tag{4.33}$$

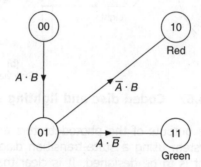

**Figure 4.69   Flip-flop state-transition diagram for the state diagram of Figure 4.68.**

The output equations are:

$$\text{Green} = P \cdot Q, \quad \text{Red} = P \cdot \overline{Q} \tag{4.34}$$

## 4.11   IMPLEMENTATION OF SEQUENTIAL CIRCUITS WITH MSIs

This section will help us design some useful sequential circuits using IC blocks for shift registers and counters.

**Johnson counter:**   The Johnson code for three and four bits is listed below as Table 4.26.

**TABLE 4.26**
**Johnson Code for Three and Four Bits**

| A | B | C | A | B | C | D |
|---|---|---|---|---|---|---|
| 0 | 0 | 0 | 0 | 0 | 0 | 0 |
| 0 | 0 | 1 | 0 | 0 | 0 | 1 |
| 0 | 1 | 1 | 0 | 0 | 1 | 1 |
| 1 | 1 | 1 | 0 | 1 | 1 | 1 |
| 1 | 1 | 0 | 1 | 1 | 1 | 1 |
| 1 | 0 | 0 | 1 | 1 | 1 | 0 |
| 0 | 0 | 0 | 1 | 1 | 0 | 0 |
| | | | 1 | 0 | 0 | 0 |
| | | | 0 | 0 | 0 | 0 |

Observe that it is a cyclic code. Using the controlled shift register (see Section 4.9 and Figure 4.45) and a modulo-8 counter the four-bit Johnson counter is implemented as shown in Figure 4.70. Observe that each clock pulse will shift the contents of the register right by one bit. The least significant bit is complemented and becomes the most significant bit in the next sequence as required by the code.

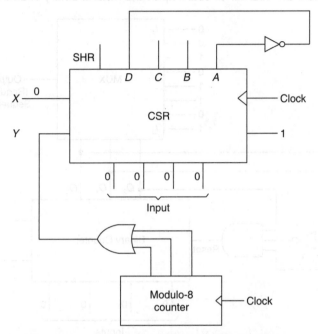

**Figure 4.70   A four-bit Johnson counter.**

**A sequence generator:**   It is required to build a circuit which will repeat the following binary sequence:

$$101101 \mid 101101 \mid 101101 \mid 101 \text{-----}$$

The repeating sequence is 101101. From the length of the sequence, namely 6, we conclude that we need a modulo-6 counter. Thus, we design a modulo-6 counter with a decoder (which is a MUX) to get the required sequence. A modulo-6 counter is designed by using a modulo-16 counter (which is a single MSI chip) and resetting it to 000 when the output count is 5 ($Q_2 = 1$, $Q_1 = 0$, $Q_0 = 1$). The circuit is shown as Figure 4.71.

**A controlled counter with output decoder:**   The state transition diagram for a sequential circuit is given as Figure 4.72. In this diagram a label above the arrow is used to indicate the Boolean variable which causes the transition. For example, the label $D$ indicates that the state transition 010 to 011 takes place when the Boolean variable $D = 1$. A label below the circle representing a state is the Boolean output when the circuit is in that state. For example, when the state of the sequential circuit is 011 the output is $P = 1$. In this section, we will design this sequential circuit using standard MSI chips.

The method is to implement the structure shown in Figure 4.73 which uses four standard MSI chips. The modulo-8 counter counts up in the natural binary counting sequence as long as the Enable signal is one. If the normal counting sequence is to be altered, then it is possible to alter the state of the counter by setting load equal to 1 in the counter and feeding a set of bits to direct input terminals. A MUX marked forward MUX (in Figure 4.73) must be used now to enable the counter to count up in the natural binary counting sequence. Thus,

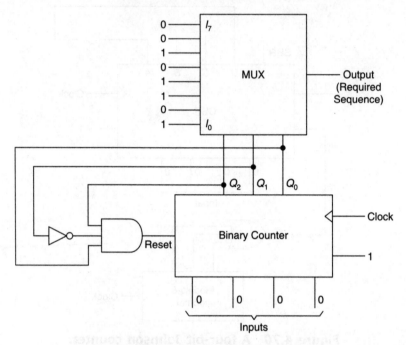

**Figure 4.71   A sequence generator.**

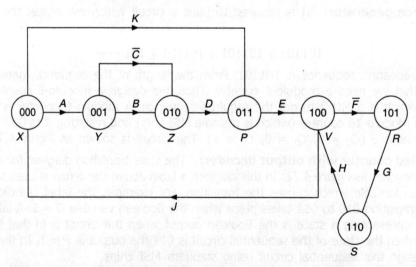

**Figure 4.72   State-transition diagram of a controlled counter
(Moore machine model).**

referring to Figure 4.73 when $Q_2 = Q_1 = Q_0 = 0$ and $A = 1$, the forward MUX output equals to 1 and the counter gets to state $Q_2 = 0$, $Q_1 = 0$ and $Q_0 = 1$. Next, the transition 001 to 010 takes place when either $B = 1$ or $\bar{C} = 1$. The $I_1$ terminal of the forward MUX is connected to $B + \bar{C}$. This takes the counter state to 010.

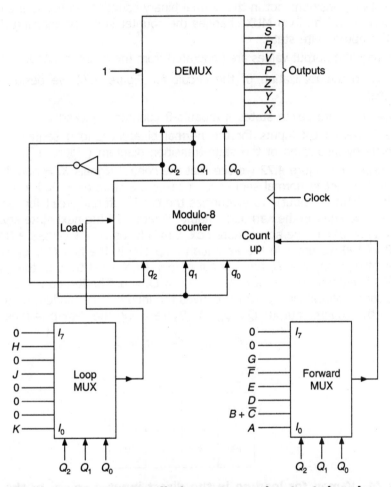

**Figure 4.73　A controlled counter and output decoder implemented with MSI chips.**

　　Whenever the normal counting sequence is to be altered the loop MUX is used. Thus, when $K = 1$ the counter state should go to 011 from 000. This is achieved by loading 011 into the direct input of the counter if $K = 1$ and $Q_2 = Q_1 = Q_0 = 0$, using the loop MUX output to enable loading. The direct inputs $q_2\, q_1\, q_0$ of the counter are made 011 by deriving them from $Q_2 Q_1 Q_0$ using a combinatorial circuit. Finally, the outputs of the sequential circuit are derived using a DEMUX at the output of the counter.

To summarize we see that the following steps are used in design using MSIs:

1. Depending on the number of states in the state-transition diagram a synchronous binary counter is selected.

2. The forward transitions of the counter states are controlled by a forward MUX.

3. The state transitions not in the normal binary counting sequence are controlled by a loop MUX. The loop MUX changes the counter state by enabling direct loading of the appropriate state.

4. The required output values are generated from the counter output using a DEMUX.

Returning to the realization of the circuit for Figure 4.72 we design it using the following steps:

1. Since there are seven states a modulo-8 counter is picked.

2. The forward MUX inputs for the normal binary counting sequence are entered directly by inspection of the state-transition diagram (Figure 4.72).

3. By inspecting Figure 4.72 we see that the control signals $K$, $H$ and $J$ lead to state transitions not in normal sequence. $K$ takes the state from 000 to 011. $K$ is input to loop MUX ($I_0$ input). To synthesize the combinatorial circuit for loading counter inputs, we enter in the Karnaugh map of Figure 4.74 the next state after 000 (when $K = 1$) as 011 in the appropriate box. Similarly, as $H = 1$ causes a transition from 110 to 100 we enter in the Karnaugh map 100 in the box $Q_2Q_1Q_0 = 110$. In the loop MUX, $I_6$ input is $H$, the $I_4$ input of loop MUX is set to $J$. In the Karnaugh map a 000 is entered for the box $Q_2 = 1$, $Q_1 = Q_0 = 0$. The K-map is reduced to obtain the combinatorial circuit, which derives the inputs to be loaded, namely $q_2$, $q_1$, $q_0$ from the counter output $Q_2$, $Q_1$, $Q_0$. By reducing the K-map entries we find:

$$q_0 = \bar{Q}_2, \quad q_1 = \bar{Q}_2, \quad q_2 = Q_1 \tag{4.35}$$

| $Q_2$ \ $Q_1Q_0$ | 00 | 01 | 11 | 10 |
|---|---|---|---|---|
| 0 | 011 | φ | φ | φ |
| 1 | 000 | φ | φ | 100 |

**Figure 4.74   K-map for loading in the direct input $q_2$ $q_1$ $q_0$ of the counter.**

4. Finally the output K-map of Figure 4.75 is filled by inspecting the state-transition diagram (Figure 4.72). The DEMUX of Figure 4.73 realizes these K-map requirements.

| $Q_2$ \ $Q_1Q_0$ | 00 | 01 | 11 | 10 |
|---|---|---|---|---|
| 0 | X | Y | P | Z |
| 1 | V | R | φ | S |

**Figure 4.75   K-map for outputs of the counter.**

---

$$\boxed{\text{SUMMARY}}$$

---

1. The outputs of an ideal combinatorial circuit depend only on the current inputs and not the past inputs.

2. The outputs of sequential circuits depend not only on the current inputs, but also on the past history of inputs. Thus, they have memory.

3. Sequential circuits can be modelled at a circuit level by an ideal combinatorial circuit some of whose outputs are fed back after a delay as secondary inputs to the combinatorial circuit. The delay acts as memory (see Figure 4.1).

4. A simple sequential circuit which exhibits memory is an *RS* flip-flop which is made using two NOR gates (see Figure 4.4).

5. An asynchronous sequential circuit is one whose inputs and outputs do not change at pre-assigned times. In other words, they spontaneously change their state whenever appropriate inputs are applied. They exhibit what is known as race condition, making the output state unpredictable. They are inherently faster but difficult to design. Thus, most practical circuits are synchronous circuits.

6. Synchronous circuits change state at predictable times as they are driven by a periodic sequence of pulses known as clock. Clocks determine whether system can change state.

7. There are four types of flip-flops, all based on clocked *RS* flip-flop. They are *JK, JK* master-slave, *D* and *T* flip-flop.

8. Behaviour of a flip-flop is determined by what is known as its characteristic equation. The characteristic equation gives the state of the flip-flop (i.e. its output) at clock time $(n + 1)$ given its output (or state) at the $n^{th}$ clock time. The characteristic equation of *RS, JK, D* and *T* flip-flops are respectively:

$$Q_{n+1} = S_n + \bar{R}_n \cdot Q_n \quad (R, S\text{-}1, 1 \text{ not allowed})$$

$$Q_{n+1} = J_n \cdot \bar{Q}_n + \bar{K}_n \cdot Q_n$$

$$Q_{n+1} = D_n$$

$$Q_{n+1} = T_n \oplus Q_n$$

9. A counter is a sequential circuit whose state changes to a predefined next state with application of a clock pulse and return to the starting state after the application of a finite number of clock pulses.

10. There are two broad classes of counters. They are:

   (i) Ripple counter in which the state of a succeeding stage changes when the previous stage changes state.

   (ii) Synchronous counter are more reliable and easy to design. Thus, they are widely used.

11. A synchronous counter is designed given it has to count modulo-$x$.

    If $2^n \geq x > 2^{n-1}$ then it needs $n$ flip-flops, as the total number of distinct states of $n$ flip-flops is $2^n$. The other information needed is the counting sequence and the initial state. Given these, the excitation inputs needed by each flip-flop to go to the next state is found such that the counter traverses all the desired states and returns to the initial state.

12. Synchronous counter is a special case of a general sequential circuit. Normally, a counter goes from an initial to a final state without any input.

13. There are two general models of a synchronous sequential machines. They are known as Moore model and Mealy model. Both these models have a state memory made up of a set of flip-flops. Given an input and the current state of the state memory as its inputs, a combinatorial circuit (called next state logic) gives as its output excitation inputs to drive the state memory to its next state. The output of the sequential machine in the Moore model is determined by a combinatorial circuit whose inputs are only the current state of the state memory. In the Mealy model, on the other hand, the output depends on both the inputs to the machine and the current state of the state memory. These models are useful in synthesizing sequential machines.

14. The behaviour of both Moore and Mealy machines are depicted by a state-transition diagram. This diagram shows the initial state, the input (if any) and the output which is a function of the current state, followed by the subsequent states with their respective inputs and outputs.

15. From this diagram a state-transition table with current state, input, next state and output is obtained. Given the type of flip-flop to be used it is easy to obtain the excitation inputs to the flip-flops to drive them from their current state to the next state. Given the current state of the flip-flop, a combinatorial circuit is synthesized to produce the excitation inputs. The output is obtained by synthesizing another combinatorial circuit whose input is the current state in the case of a Moore machine. In the case of the Mealy machine the inputs to the output combinatorial circuit is both the current state and the current inputs.

16. A more challenging problem is to model and synthesize appropriate sequential machines given the requirements specification. We have illustrated the methodology with a number of examples in the body of this chapter.

17. A commonly used sequential circuit is called a register. A register stores a string of bits and is made up of a set of interconnected $D$ flip-flops. An initial value can be loaded into all the flip-flops simultaneously (initiation step). The contents of a register can be shifted left or right. A string of bits can also be serially fed to a register. When bits are serially fed and the contents of register shifted, these bits replace the values stored earlier.

18. Shift registers of various sizes and controls are available as IC chips. Registers are common building blocks of many digital systems such as calculators and computers.

19. A sequential system to realize any state-transition diagram can be constructed using MSI counter of appropriate size and two MUXs which are used to control the state-transition of the counter to follow the state-transition diagram.

## EXERCISES

1. Modify an asynchronous *RS* flip-flop appropriately so that when *R* and *S* are both 1, the flip-flop is set.

2. Design an asynchronous ripple counter to count up to 10 in 8-4-2-1 code. Assume that the flip-flops have asynchronous set and reset terminals.

3. Design a modulo-6 synchronous counter using *T* flip-flops to count in a cyclic code.

4. Design a synchronous modulo-10 counter to count in the following codes: (1) 5-4-2-1 code, (2) a cyclic code, (3) in the sequence 1, 0, 2, 3, 4, 8, 9, 7, 6, 5. Use *JK* flip-flops.

5. Design a modulo-13 synchronous counter to count in natural binary counting sequence. Use *RS* flip-flops.

6. Design a synchronous decimal counter to count in Excess-3 code. Use *T* flip-flops. Can *D* flip-flops be used to design counters? If the answer is yes, repeat the design with *D* flip-flops.

7. Design a synchronous modulo-6 up-down counter. Use *JK* flip-flops for synthesis.

8. A counter is to be designed to count either in 5-4-2-1 code or in 8-4-2-1 code based on a control signal input. Draw the state diagram for such a counter and synthesize it using *T* flip-flops. Assume that the control signal cannot change in the middle of a counting sequence.

9. Redesign the counter of the above exercise to allow the change of the control signal in the midst of a counting sequence.

10. Design a counter which could count either in modulo-8 straight binary or in modulo-8 cyclic code based on a control signal.

11. Design a shift register which has one input, one output, one shift pulse input and a control input. If the control input is a 1, shift left once, else shift right once for each shift pulse.

12. Design a pulse distributor whose input/output characteristics are shown in Figure 4.76.

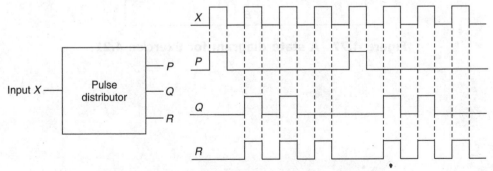

**Figure 4.76  Pulse distributor characteristics.**

13. Design a circuit to detect a sequence of four consecutive ones in an input bit sequence,

Input:          0110111011110111111011110
Output:              1     1        1

14. Natural binary coded decimal digits are serially transmitted. Design a circuit which will accept four bits of a number and detect whether they constitute a legal NBCD number.

15. Modify the toy train controller so that it will travel in the sequence track *C*, track *B*, track *A*, track *B*, track *C*, track *A* and repeat this sequence.

16. Design a circuit to check whether a five-bit sequence satisfies an even parity.

17. Design a circuit whose input is a mechanical switch and the output is a seven-segment display. The circuit is to be designed to simulate a dice. When the mechanical switch is pressed a counter is started. When the switch is released the display should display any digit between 1 and 6 randomly.

18. Design a counter to accept shaped and attenuated 50 Hz electrical mains voltage and give out one pulse every second. Use this to design an electronic stop watch which will measure up to 10 minutes. Use MSI counters for design.

19. Design a controlled four-bit register which can be controlled to perform the following four functions:

    Load, 1's complement, 2's complement, Clear.

20. Design an NBCD counter using MSI counter chip to (i) Load, (ii) 9's complement contents, (iii) count up and (iv) count down.

21. Realize the state transition diagram of the following Figure using MSI components.

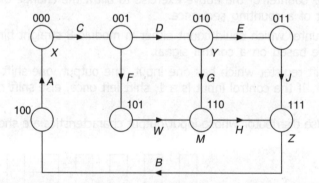

**Figure 4.77   A state diagram for Exercise 4.21.**

# Chapter

# 5

# Arithmetic and Logic Unit

## (Application of Combinatorial Circuits)

### Learning Goals

In this chapter we will learn:

☞ Algorithms for addition and subtraction.

☞ How to add/subtract numbers represented using one's and two's complement notation.

☞ Algorithms for multiplication and division.

☞ How Booth multiplication algorithm for multiplying numbers represented in two's complement notation works.

☞ Big endian and little endian representation of integers.

☞ How to store real numbers using floating point representation. Details of IEEE 754 standard for representing real numbers.

☞ Algorithms to add/subtract/multiply/divide floating point numbers.

☞ How to design logic circuits to add/subtract/multiply/divide integers and real numbers.

☞ Functions of MSI chips which perform arithmetic and logic operations.

## 5.1 INTRODUCTION

One of the important components of all computers is an **Arithmetic Logic Unit** (ALU). As the name implies, this unit is used to carry out all four arithmetic operations of add, subtract, multiply and divide and logic operations such as AND, OR, NOT, XOR, etc. on bit strings. This unit is also used to compare both numbers and bit strings and obtain the result of comparison to be used by the control unit to alter the sequence of operations in a program.

In this chapter we will be mainly concerned with the logical design of the ALU of computers. In order to design ALU we should first understand the algorithms for binary arithmetic operations. Arithmetic operations are carried out both on integers and reals. While integers are simple to deal with, some interesting problems of representation arise when large range of real numbers with adequate precision are to be stored and processed. We thus have to discuss the trade offs between various methods of representing real numbers.

Once we decide on the methods of representing decimal numbers and algorithms to process them, the next problem is of designing logic circuits to implement these operations. We will thus first examine the representation and algorithms for arithmetic operations and then realize them with logic circuits.

There are two distinct methods of realizing logic circuits to perform arithmetic/logic operations. One of them is using combinatorial circuits has two advantages: (i) ease of realization and (ii) potentially higher speed of operations of these circuits. On the negative side, these logic circuits use large number of gates and are expensive to realize. The other method is using sequential systems for realization. In such systems a single logic circuit (such as an adder) is used repeatedly on one bit or a group of bits to realize addition/ subtraction. For example, to perform arithmetic on two 32-bit operands we can design a four-bit unit and use it sequentially eight-times with appropriate clocking. This type of realization is economical in use of hardware but is inherently slower compared to combinatorial realization. A designer thus has to pick the appropriate realization based on cost/time trade-off. The decision will also be determined by the need for speed in a given situation.

There are significant differences between the methodology used for combinatorial design and sequential design. This chapter will describe combinatorial realization of ALUs.

## 5.2  BINARY ADDITION

**Counting** is a form of addition as successive numbers, while counting, are obtained by adding 1. In decimal addition, we start with 0 and by successively adding 1 reach 9. After 9, as the base of the system is 10 (ten) and as there are no further symbols in the system, we count 10 (one followed by zero). The 1 represents a *carry* to the tens position in the positional system. Similarly, in binary system the count progresses as follows:

$$0, 1, 1\ 0, 1\ 1, 1\ 0\ 0, 1\ 0\ 1, \ldots$$

Using the above idea, we may obtain Table 5.1 to represent addition of binary numbers.

**TABLE 5.1**

**A Half Adder Table**

| a | b | Sum | Carry |
|---|---|-----|-------|
| 0 | 0 | 0 | 0 |
| 0 | 1 | 1 | 0 |
| 1 | 0 | 1 | 0 |
| 1 | 1 | 0 | 1 |

We will now give some examples of binary addition:

*Example 5.1.*

| | | | |
|---|---|---|---|
| Carry | 1 1 | 0 1 | 1 1 1 . 0 |
| Augend | 1 1 | 1 0 1 | 1 1 . 1 0 |
| Addend | 0 1 | 0 0 1 | 0 1 . 1 1 |
| | 1 0 0 | 1 1 0 | 1 0 1 . 0 1 |

We see from the example that while adding two binary numbers, we have to add three bits; the carry bit and the bits of the two numbers being added. An addition table showing the values of sum and carry with three bits as inputs is developed in Table 5.2.

Table 5.2 is known as the "full adder" table in contrast with Table 5.1 which is known as a "half adder" table.

## TABLE 5.2
### A Full Adder Table

| a (augend) | b (addend) | Carry (carry) | Sum | Carry to next position |
|---|---|---|---|---|
| 0 | 0 | 0 | 0 | 0 |
| 0 | 0 | 1 | 1 | 0 |
| 0 | 1 | 0 | 1 | 0 |
| 0 | 1 | 1 | 0 | 1 |
| 1 | 0 | 0 | 1 | 0 |
| 1 | 0 | 1 | 0 | 1 |
| 1 | 1 | 0 | 0 | 1 |
| 1 | 1 | 1 | 1 | 1 |

## 5.3  BINARY SUBTRACTION

Binary subtraction is a special case of addition. In fact, the addition of a negative number to a positive number is **subtraction.** Thus, before discussing subtraction we should discuss how negative numbers may be represented in the binary system.

One method of representing signs of numbers is to use an extra bit at the left end of the number. A zero is by convention used to represent the + sign and a one to represent the − sign. For instance, +5 is represented by 0,101 and −7 is represented by 1,111. A comma is used to separate the sign bit from the number. (Please note that we use the comma only for readability. It is ignored in computation and data storage). If a number $x$ with a positive sign is to be added to a number $y$ with a negative sign, it is equivalent to subtracting $y$ from $x$. In order to subtract two binary numbers we may use a subtract table similar to the one used for addition. We will obtain a subtract table after looking at a few examples.

*Example 5.2.* Subtracting single bit

| | | | | |
|---|---|---|---|---|
| Borrow | | 1 | | |
| Minuend | 0 | 0 | 1 | 1 |
| Subtrahend | 0 | 1 | 0 | 1 |
| Difference | 0 | 1 | 1 | 0 |

*Example 5.3.*

| | |
|---|---|
| Borrow | 1 0 |
| Minuend | 1 0 1 |
| Subtrahend | 0 1 1 |
| Difference | 0 1 0 |

*Example 5.4.*

| | |
|---|---|
| Borrow | 1 1 1 |
| Minuend | 1 0 . 0 0 |
| Subtrahend | 0 1 . 1 1 |
| Difference | 0 0 . 0 1 |

Tables similar to the half adder table and full adder table may be obtained using the above examples. The tables are given as Table 5.3 and Table 5.4.

**TABLE 5.3**
**Half Subtractor Table**

| A | B | Difference | Borrow |
|---|---|---|---|
| 0 | 0 | 0 | 0 |
| 0 | 1 | 1 | 1 |
| 1 | 0 | 1 | 0 |
| 1 | 1 | 0 | 0 |

**TABLE 5.4**
**Full Subtractor Table**

| A (Minuend) | B (Subtrahend) | Borrow | Difference | Borrow to next position |
|---|---|---|---|---|
| 0 | 0 | 0 | 0 | 0 |
| 0 | 0 | 1 | 1 | 1 |
| 0 | 1 | 0 | 1 | 1 |
| 0 | 1 | 1 | 0 | 1 |
| 1 | 0 | 0 | 1 | 0 |
| 1 | 0 | 1 | 0 | 0 |
| 1 | 1 | 0 | 0 | 0 |
| 1 | 1 | 1 | 1 | 1 |

The sign and magnitude of the result of an add or subtract operation, when numbers are represented with a sign and a magnitude part, may be summarized as shown in Table 5.5. In this table $x$ and $y$ represent the two operands. The variable $x$ is taken to be the first number (augend/minuend) in addition or subtraction and the variable $y$ as the second number (addend/subtrahend). The magnitudes of $x$ and $y$ are represented by $m(x)$ and $m(y)$ respectively and their signs by $s(x)$ and $s(y)$. In Table 5.5 $\overline{s(y)}$ means complement of $s(y)$. In other words, if $s(y) = 1$, $\overline{s(y)} = 0$ and if $s(y) = 0$, $s(\overline{y}) = 1$.

**TABLE 5.5**
**Add/Subtract Rules**

| Conditions | Rule 1 | Rule 2 | Rule 3 | Rule 4 | Rule 5 | Rule 6 |
|---|---|---|---|---|---|---|
| Is $s(x) = s(y)$? | No | No | No | Yes | Yes | Yes |
| Operation? | Subtract | Add | Add | Subtract | Subtract | Add |
| Is $m(x) \geq m(y)$? | — | No | Yes | No | Yes | — |
| **Actions** | | | | | | |
| Sign of Result = | $s(x)$ | $s(y)$ | $s(x)$ | $\overline{s(y)}$ | $s(x)$ | $s(x)$ |
| m (Result) = $m(x) + m(y)$ | X | — | — | — | — | X |
| m (Result) = $m(y) - m(x)$ | — | X | — | X | — | — |
| m (Result) = $m(x) - m(y)$ | — | — | X | — | X | — |

The table used above (Table 5.5) is known as a **decision table.** It lists in a tabular form the conditions to be tested and the actions to be taken based on the results of the tests. Each column to the right of the vertical double line is called a **decision rule.** For example, the fifth rule in Table 5.5 is interpreted as: "If $s(x) = s(y)$, and if the operation is subtract, and if $m(x) \geq m(y)$, then the sign of the result is $s(x)$, and the magnitude of the result equals the magnitude of $x$ minus the magnitude of $y$". A dash against a condition indicates that the outcome of testing the condition is irrelevant. A dash entry for an action indicates that the corresponding action need not be carried out. An 'X' against an action indicates that the particular action is to be carried out. (A reader not familiar with decision table notation should read Appendix B.)

It is seen from Table 5.5 that when numbers are represented in the sign magnitude form we must have separate procedures or algorithms to add and subtract. It will be advantageous if another convention could be evolved for representing positive and negative numbers which allows us to use one basic algorithm for both addition and subtraction. The advantage will be that a single basic electronic circuit could then be used to implement addition as well as subtraction.

Two conventions for representing negative numbers which allow this are the one's complement representation and the two's complement representation of numbers.

## 5.4  COMPLEMENT REPRESENTATION OF NUMBERS

In the one's complement system, the representation of positive numbers is identical to that used in the sign magnitude system. The convention used to represent negative numbers is different. The number −5, for example, is represented by 1,010. The bit appearing in front of the comma is the sign bit. This representation is obtained by replacing every 1 by a 0 and every 0 by a 1 in the binary representation of the number +5 (0,101).

The process of replacing a 1 by a 0 and a 0 by a 1 is known as bit complementing. In general, for an $n$ bit number $x$ (excluding the sign bit) the one's complement is given by $(2^n - 1 - x)$. Thus, −14 is represented by $1111 - 1110 = 0001$ excluding the sign bit.

The two's complement representation of a negative number is obtained by adding a 1 to the one's complement representation of that number. Thus, the two's complement representation of −5, for example, is 1,011. In general, for an $n$ bit number $x$, the two's complement is given by $1, (2^n - x)$. Another method of obtaining a two's complement of a binary number is to scan the number from right to left and complement all the bits appearing after the first appearance of a 1. Thus, the two's complement of 0, 1110, for example, is obtained as 1, 0010. It is left to the student to understand why this is true.

Table 5.6 depicts the three methods of representing negative numbers.

**TABLE 5.6**
**Three Methods of Representing Negative Numbers**

| Sign and magnitude (binary) | Sign and magnitude (decimal) | One's complement (decimal) | Two's complement (decimal) |
|:---:|:---:|:---:|:---:|
| 0000 | +0 | +0 | +0 |
| 0001 | +1 | +1 | +1 |
| 0010 | +2 | +2 | +2 |
| 0011 | +3 | +3 | +3 |
| 0100 | +4 | +4 | +4 |
| 0101 | +5 | +5 | +5 |
| 0110 | +6 | +6 | +6 |
| 0111 | +7 | +7 | +7 |
| 1000 | −0 | −7 | −8 |
| 1001 | −1 | −6 | −7 |
| 1010 | −2 | −5 | −6 |
| 1011 | −3 | −4 | −5 |
| 1100 | −4 | −3 | −4 |
| 1101 | −5 | −2 | −3 |
| 1110 | −6 | −1 | −2 |
| 1111 | −7 | −0 | −1 |

The complement notation may be used to represent negative numbers in any number base. If the radix of a number system is $r$ then one may define an $(r - 1)$'s complement and an $r$'s complement. Thus, for representation of negative decimal numbers one may use the 9's complement or the 10's complement representation. For example, the 9's complement of a decimal number 3459 is $9999 - 3459 = 6540$, whereas its 10's complement is 6541.

## 5.5 ADDITION/SUBTRACTION OF NUMBERS IN 1's COMPLEMENT NOTATION

We will first illustrate with some examples addition and subtraction rules for binary numbers represented in the 1's complement notation. We will assume that the two numbers are four bits long. We would like to emphasize again that the comma used in the complement representation of binary numbers is intended only for easy readability and is not relevant in either storing the number or in computation.

*Example 5.5.*

$$
\begin{aligned}
+3 &= 0,0011 \\
+7 &= 0,0111 \\
\hline
+10 &= 0,1010
\end{aligned}
$$

*Example 5.6.*

$$
\begin{array}{ll}
+8 & 0,1000 \\
+9 & 0,1001 \\
\hline
& 1,0001 \quad \text{Incorrect}
\end{array}
$$

When positive numbers are added, the two binary numbers may be added including the sign bits and the result will be correct. This assumes that the sum should be less than or equal to 15. If the sum exceeds 15 this rule gives an incorrect answer as may be seen from Example 5.6.

If a number $y$ is to be subtracted from another number $x$, it is equivalent to adding $-y$ to $+x$. In one's complement arithmetic $-y$ is represented by its one's complement and it is *added* to $x$. Thus, subtraction operation is replaced by addition of a complement. This is the main reason why the complement notation is used. No separate electronic circuit is needed for subtraction in this case as addition and complementing circuits are sufficient.

In one's complement arithmetic if the two numbers including the sign bits are added and an overflow (beyond the sign bit) is obtained, then the overflow bit is removed and added to the result. This leads to the right answer with the right sign. Adding the overflow bit to the least significant bit of the sum is called **end around carry.** This is illustrated in Examples 5.7 and 5.8.

*Example 5.7.*

$$
\begin{array}{ll}
+5 & 0,0101 \\
-3 & 1,1100 \\
\hline
& 10,0001 \\
& \quad\ \longrightarrow 1 \\
\hline
+2 & 0,0010
\end{array}
$$

*Example 5.8.*

$$
\begin{array}{ll}
+15 & 0,1111 \\
-2 & 1,1101 \\
\hline
& 10,1100 \\
& \quad\rule{0pt}{0pt}\llcorner\!\!\longrightarrow 1 \\
\hline
+13 & 0,1101
\end{array}
$$

If a positive number is added to a negative number and no overflow is observed then the result is negative. The answer is correct as it is, and it is in one's complement form. The following examples illustrate this.

*Example 5.9.*

$$
\begin{array}{ll}
-5 & 1,1010 \\
+3 & 0,0011 \\
\hline
-2 & 1,1101
\end{array}
$$

*Example 5.10.*

$$
\begin{array}{ll}
-8 & 1,0111 \\
+8 & 0,1000 \\
\hline
-0 & 1,1111
\end{array}
$$

If two negative numbers are added then an overflow results and the overflow bit is added to the answer. The final answer has the right sign. We again assume that the magnitude of the sum (for four-bit operands) is less than or equal to 15 for the rule to work correctly.

*Example 5.11.*

$$
\begin{array}{ll}
-5 & 1,1010 \\
-8 & 1,0111 \\
\hline
& 11,0001 \\
& \quad\rule{0pt}{0pt}\llcorner\!\!\longrightarrow 1 \\
\hline
-13 & 1,0010
\end{array}
$$

*Example 5.12.*

$$
\begin{array}{ll}
-8 & 1,0111 \\
-9 & 1,0110 \\
\hline
& 10,1101 \\
& \quad\rule{0pt}{0pt}\llcorner\!\!\longrightarrow 1 \\
\hline
& 0,1110 \quad \text{Incorrect}
\end{array}
$$

Observe that if the sign of augend and addend are same and after addition the sign of the sum is not the same, then the result is incorrect.

The rule observed through the examples considered so far is summarized using two decision tables [see Table 5.7(a) and 5.7(b)]. In these tables it is assumed that $x$ and $y$ are the operands and $z$ is the result and that negative numbers are represented in their 1's complement form.

**TABLE 5.7(a)**
**Decision Table for One's Complement Addition**

| | | | | | | | | |
|---|---|---|---|---|---|---|---|---|
| $s(x) =$ | 0 | 0 | 0 | 0 | 1 | 1 | 1 | 1 |
| $s(y) =$ | 0 | 0 | 1 | 1 | 0 | 0 | 1 | 1 |
| Operation | Add | Subtract | Add | Subtract | Add | Subtract | Add | Subtract |
| Complement $y$ | — | X | — | X | — | X | — | X |
| Add numbers including sign bit | X | X | X | X | X | X | X | X |
| Add carry (if any) to the sum $z$ | X | X | X | X | X | X | X | X |
| Declare $z$ as answer | — | X | X | — | X | — | — | X |
| Go to Table 5.7(b) | X | — | — | X | — | X | X | — |
| Stop | — | X | X | — | X | — | — | X |

**TABLE 5.7(b)**
**Decision Table for One's Complement Addition**

| | | | | |
|---|---|---|---|---|
| $s(x) =$ | 0 | 0 | 1 | 1 |
| $s(z) =$ | 0 | 1 | 0 | 1 |
| Error (Result out of range) | — | X | X | — |
| Declare $z$ as answer | X | — | — | X |
| Stop | X | X | X | X |

In one's complement representation of numbers there are two possible representations of zero. The representation of $+0$ is 0,0000 and that of $-0$ is 1,1111. We saw the result of adding $+8$ and $-8$ in Example 5.10 which gave $-0$.

The rationale behind the rules given in this section may be derived using the definition of 1's complement of a number $x$ and systematically working out all cases. This is left as an exercise to the student.

## 5.6 ADDITION/SUBTRACTION OF NUMBERS IN TWO's COMPLEMENT NOTATION

When positive numbers are added the situation is identical to the one discussed for 1's complement notation in the last section.

When one of the numbers is positive and the other is negative the answer could be either positive or negative. The rule is to add the two numbers and ignore overflow if any. As before, the sign bit will be treated as though it is a part of the number. The bit in the sign bit position will be the correct sign bit after addition. If the answer is negative it will be in the 2's complement form. This is illustrated in Examples 5.13 and 5.14.

*Example 5.13.*

$$
\begin{array}{rl}
+5 & 0,0101 \\
-3 & 1,1101 \\
\hline
+2 & 10,0010 \\
& \quad\uparrow \\
& \text{Ignore}
\end{array}
$$

*Example 5.14.*

$$
\begin{array}{rl}
-5 & 1,1011 \\
+3 & 0,0011 \\
\hline
-2 & 1,1110
\end{array}
$$

When two negative numbers in two's complement notation are added an overflow bit will result and may be discarded. The sign bit will be correct if the sum is within the allowed range of the answer. For four-bit operands the answer should be $\leq 15$. If the answer is outside the permitted range, the sign bit would become 0 indicating an error condition.

*Example 5.15.*

$$
\begin{array}{rl}
-5 & 1,1011 \\
-3 & 1,1101 \\
\hline
-8 & 11,1000 \\
& \quad\uparrow \\
& \text{Ignore}
\end{array}
$$

*Example 5.16.*

$$
\begin{array}{rl}
-8 & 1,1000 \\
-9 & 1,0111 \\
\hline
& 10,1111 \quad \text{Incorrect}
\end{array}
$$

When two positive numbers are added and if the sum is outside the allowed range of numbers, then the sign bit would become 1 indicating an error condition. This is illustrated in Example 5.17.

*Example 5.17.*

$$
\begin{array}{rl}
+8 & 0,1000 \\
+10 & 0,1010 \\
\hline
& 1,0010 \quad \text{Incorrect}
\end{array}
$$

From these examples we can derive the two linked decision tables [Tables 5.8(a) and 5.8(b)] for addition/subtraction of two's complement binary numbers. In this table $s(x)$ and $s(y)$ are the sign bits of the two operands $x$ and $y$. The sign bit of the result is represented by $s(z)$. In Table 5.8(a), the first and the fourth column depict the situations when the result of the operation can possibly become too large to store. In the situations shown in columns 5, 6, 7 and 8 the result cannot become too large to store. In the former case, we use Table 5.8(b) to decide if the answer is correct or incorrect due to overflow. In the last four cases the result of addition may be declared as the answer.

**TABLE 5.8(a)**

**Decision Table for Add/Subtract Operation of Numbers in 2's Complement Notation**

| | | | | | | | | |
|---|---|---|---|---|---|---|---|---|
| $s(x) =$ | 0 | 1 | 0 | 1 | 0 | 1 | 0 | 1 |
| $s(y) =$ | 0 | 1 | 1 | 0 | 0 | 1 | 1 | 0 |
| Operation | Add | Add | Subtract | Subtract | Subtract | Subtract | Add | Add |
| Take 2's complement of $y$ and add $z = x + y$ | — | — | X | X | X | X | — | — |
| Ignore overflow | X | X | X | X | X | X | X | X |
| $z$ is answer | — | — | — | — | X | X | X | X |
| Use Table 5.8(b) | X | X | X | X | — | — | — | — |

**TABLE 5.8(b)**

**Decision Table for Add/Subtract Operation of Numbers in 2's Complement Notation**

| | | | | |
|---|---|---|---|---|
| $s(x)$ | 0 | 1 | 0 | 1 |
| $s(z)$ | 1 | 0 | 0 | 1 |
| Declare correct answer | No | No | Yes | Yes |
| Result too large to store | Yes | Yes | No | No |

The simplicity of the rules for adding or subtracting numbers in the 2's complement notation has made this the preferred method in a large number of computers.

## 5.7 BINARY MULTIPLICATION

Binary multiplication is nothing but successive addition. Thus, multiplication of 5 by 4, for example, is achieved by adding 5 to itself 4 times. This basic idea is refined to implement binary multiplication.

The method used to multiply two-signed binary numbers depends on the method used to represent negative numbers. If negative numbers are represented in the sign magnitude form, then the method of successive addition is easily implemented. If negative numbers are represented in the one's or two's complement form then multiplication becomes complicated. In this section we will discuss the multiplication of numbers in sign magnitude notation.

***Example 5.18.***    Consider the following long-hand multiplication method.

| | |
|---|---|
| Multiplicand | 1 1 0 1 |
| Multiplier | 1 0 1 1 |

| | |
|---|---|
| Partial Product | 1 1 0 1 |
| | 1 1 0 1 |
| | 0 0 0 0 |
| | 1 1 0 1 |

| | |
|---|---|
| Product | 1 0 0 0 1 1 1 1· |

The method used in Example 5.18 may be summarized as follows:

*Step 1:*    Examine the least significant bit of the multiplier. If it is a 1, copy the multiplicand and call it the first partial product. If the least significant bit is a zero, then enter zero as the first partial product and preserve (or store) the partial product.

*Step 2:*    Examine the bit left of the bit examined last. If it is a 1, do Step 3. Else do Step 4.

*Step 3:*    Add the multiplicand to the previously stored partial product after shifting the partial product one bit to the right. This sum becomes the new partial product. Go to Step 5.

*Step 4:*    Get new partial product by shifting the previous partial product one bit to the right.

*Step 5:*    Repeat Steps 2 to 4 till all bits in the multiplier have been considered. The final value obtained for the partial product is the product of the multiplicand and the multiplier.

From this long-hand or "paper and pencil" method of multiplying observe the following:

1. We need to preserve the multiplicand as it is added repeatedly to the partial products.

2. We need to preserve the partial product and shift it.

3. The number of bits in each new partial product is one bit more than the previous one. The maximum number of bits in the final product equals the sum of the number of bits in the multiplier and the multiplicand.

4. After each bit of the multiplier is used to develop a partial product, that bit is not used again. It may thus be erased or discarded.

These observations aid us to develop an appropriate algorithm for implementation in a digital system.

In order to multiply we need three registers. Assuming an '$n$ bit' multiplier and an '$n$ bit' multiplicand, we need an '$n$ bit' register to store the multiplier and a '$2n$ bit' register to store the final product and the intermediate partial products. We may reduce the length of the product register by remembering that, after each bit of the multiplier is used to develop a partial product, it may be discarded and that the length of partial product grows from $n$ to $2n$ in increments of one bit.

We thus implement multiplication using three registers: a multiplicand register which can store *n* bits, a multiplier-quotient register of *n* bits to store the multiplier (or the quotient during division), and an accumulator in which partial products are added and stored. This register needs $(n + 1)$ bits as the intermediate sum of two *n* bit numbers could be $(n + 1)$ bits long. For $n = 4$ the configuration of the registers and their initial contents (for the case of Example 5.18) is shown in Figure 5.1.

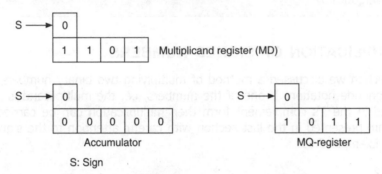

Figure 5.1 **Registers for multiplication.**

The accumulator and the MQ register are physically joined so that their contents can be shifted together either left or right.

Using three registers an algorithm for multiplication may be evolved using the ideas presented in the long-hand multiplication method.

ALGORITHM 5.1. **Procedure to multiply two *N* bit numbers**

*Const* N = 4; N1 = 5; NPLUSN1 = 9;

*Var*

MD : *array* [1. .N] *of bit* {MD is N bits long. Multiplicand stored in MD};

ACC : *array* [1. .N1] *of bit* {ACC is the accumulator where partial products are developed. It is N1 = N + 1 bits long};

MQ : *array* [1. .N] *of bit* {MQ is the multiplier-quotient register in which the multiplier is stored. It is N bits long};

SIGNMD, SIGNACC, SIGNMQ : *bit* {These are sign bits of MD, ACC and MQ respectively};

COUNT : *integer* {used as counter};

ACCMQ : *array* [1. .NPLUSN1] *of bit* {ACCMQ is obtained by concatenating MQ to the right of ACC};

*begin* {of algorithm}

*Input* SIGNMD, MD, SIGNMQ, MQ;

ACC:= 0;

ACCMQ:= *Concatenate to right* MQ *to* ACC;

*for* COUNT:= 1 to N *do*

*begin*

   *if* MQ [N] = 1 *then* ACC:= ACC + MD

{MQ [N] is the least significant bit of MQ};
        *Shift-Right* ACCMQ
   *end;*
   SIGNACC: = SIGNMD ⊕ SIGNMQ;
   *Output* SIGNACC, ACCMQ
*end* {of algorithm}.

## 5.8 MULTIPLICATION OF SIGNED NUMBERS

In the last section we discussed a method of multiplying two binary numbers represented in a sign magnitude notation. If one of the numbers, i.e. the multiplicand is negative and is represented in the 2's complement form then multiplication can be carried out by the same algorithm presented in the last section with careful attention to the sign bits. This is illustrated in Example 5.19.

*Example 5.19.*

| | | |
|---|---|---|
| | 1 0 0 1 1 | (−13) Multiplicand |
| | 0 0 1 1 0 | (+6) Multiplier |
| 0 0 0 0 0 | 0 0 0 0 0 | First partial product |
| 1 1 1 1 1 | 0 0 1 1 | Second partial product |
| 1 1 1 1 0 | 0 1 1 | Third partial product |
| 0 0 0 0 0 | 0 0 | Fourth partial product |
| 0 0 0 0 0 | 0 | Last partial product |
| 1 1 1 0 1 | 1 0 0 1 0 | (−78) Final answer in 2's complement form |

Observe that the leading bits of the negative partial products are made 1. This is known as **sign bit extension.** This is necessary if we remember that the leading zeros of a positive number would become one's when their two's complement is taken. For instance, 2's complement of 0, 001001110 (78) is 1, 110110010. For example, +5 = 00000101 and −5 = 11111011.

If the multiplier is negative and the multiplicand is positive we can interchange them and carry out the same algorithm or we can complement the multiplier and carry out the algorithm. If both are negative then both can be complemented and we can use the algorithm used for positive operands.

**Booth's method of multiplication:** Another method of dealing with operands in two's complement form was proposed by Booth. This method has two advantages. First, it deals with both positive and negative multipliers uniformly. Second, it reduces the number of addition operations in the multiplication in cases where the multiplier has a long sequence of ones.

This method replaces a multiplier by another coded string called a **Booth code.** This code for a multiplier is obtained by the following procedure:

1. Scan the bit string representing a multiplier from right to left.
2. Replace the right bit by −1 if it is 1 and by 0 if it is 0.
3. Replace $i^{th}$ bit by an appropriate code using Table 5.9.

**TABLE 5.9**
**Booth Coding**

| $i^{th}$ **bit** | $(i − 1)^{th}$ **bit** | **Code for** $i^{th}$ **bit** |
|:---:|:---:|:---:|
| 0 | 0 | 0 |
| 1 | 0 | −1 |
| 0 | 1 | +1 |
| 1 | 1 | 0 |

An example of the Booth coding is given below:

|  | *Binary number* | *Decimal equivalent* |
|---|---|---|
| Number: | 0 1 1 0 1 1 1 1 1 0 1 | 893 |
| Booth coded number: | +10 − 1 + 10000 − 1 + 1 − 1 | |

Observe that the coding effectively replaces each occurrence of a sequence of $n$ consecutive ones by the sequence 1 followed by $(n − 1)$ zeros and a minus 1. For example, the Booth code of 011111 is 10000 − 1 and their values are respectively $1 + 2 + 4 + 8 + 16 = 31$ and $32 − 1 = 31$. Thus, the multiplication by the coded number will be same as that by the original one.

The Booth coded representation of 01101111101 is + 10 − 1 + 10000 − 1 + 1 − 1. The decimal number equivalent of this code is found by beginning at the least significant bit position and giving the decimal equivalent of that bit. If it is preceded by −, then this number is subtracted from the resulting decimal equivalent. If it is + then it is added. Thus the decimal value of

$$+ 10 − 1 + 10000 − 1 + 1 − 1$$

is

$$+ 1024 − 256 + 128 − 4 + 2 − 1 = 893$$

which is the same as that of the original number. Observe that the number of 1s in the code is six compared to eight in the original number. As each 1 of a multiplier requires an addition, using Booth code reduces the number of additions in multiplication. We will consider another example of Booth coding.

Number: 000111110110 = 502 decimal
Booth Code: 00 + 10000 − 1 + 10 − 10
Equivalent decimal = +512 − 16 + 8 − 2 + 0 = 502 (decimal)

Observe that the number of 1s in Booth code is four compared to seven in the original binary number.

***Example 5.20 (a).***

We will now multiply 6 by 14 using Booth code.
Booth code of 14 = 001110 = 0 + 100 − 10
Multiplication using Booth code:

|  |  |
|---|---|
| 000110 | Multiplicand (+6) |
| 0 + 100 − 10 | Multiplier (+14) |
| 0100001 | First partial product |
| 1111111010 | Add 2's complement of multiplicand |
| 000000000 | Third partial product |
| 00000000 | Fourth partial product |
| 0000110 | Add multiplicand |
| 1 00001010100 | Product (= 84) |

└→ Shifted out

Observe that the 2's complement added as the second partial product has leading 1s extending to the $2^n$th bit of product.

***Example 5.20(b).***

|  |  |
|---|---|
| 010000 | Multiplicand (+16) |
| 0 + 10 − 100 | Multiplier (+12) |
| 000000 |  |
| 000000 |  |
| 1111110000 |  |
| 000000000 |  |
| 00010000 |  |
| 000011000000 |  |

|← 12 bits →|

The same coding scheme also works for negative numbers represented in the 2's complement notation. Some examples of negative numbers and their Booth coding are shown below:

|  | *Binary number* | *Decimal equivalent* |
|---|---|---|
| Two's complement number | 1 1 1 1 0 1 0 1 | (1 + 4 + 16 + 32 + 64 − 128 = −11) |
| Booth code | 0 0 0 −1 +1 −1 +1 −1 | (− 1 + 2 − 4 + 8 − 16 = −11) |
| Two's complement number | 1 0 0 0 0 1 1 0 | (2 + 4 − 128 = −122) |
| Booth code | −1 0 0 0 +1 0 −1 0 | (− 2 + 8 − 128 = −122) |
| Two's complement number | 1 1 0 1 1 1 1 1 | (1 + 2 + 4 + 8 + 16 + 64 − 128 = −33) |
| Booth code | 0 −1 +1 0 0 0 0 −1 | (− 1 + 32 − 64 = −33) |

The fact that Booth coding works correctly for negative numbers may be shown as follows:

**Case 1:** If $N = \dfrac{n \cdots 3210 \;\leftarrow\; \text{Bit number}}{1 \cdots 1111 = -2^n + (2^{n-1} + 2^{n-2} + \cdots + 2^0) = -1}$

Booth code $= 00 \cdots 00 - 1 = -1$

**Case 2:** Let $N = 1010101011$

The decimal equivalent is : $-2^9 + 2^7 + 2^5 + 2^3 + 2 + 1$

$$= -512 + 128 + 32 + 8 + 2 + 1$$
$$= -512 + 171 = -341$$

Booth coded $N = -1 + 1 - 1 + 1 - 1 + 1 - 1 + 1\; 0 - 1$

$$= -512 + 256 - 128 + 64 - 32 + 16 - 8 + 4 - 1 = -341$$

This can be generalized by noting that any negative number will have 1 as the most significant bit. The next bit can be 1 or 0. If it is a 0 then from Case 2 we see that the Booth coding for the substring 010101011 is $+1 -1 +1 -1 +1 -1 +1\; 0 -1 = 171$, which is the correct decimal value of the original substring. The leading 1 gives a Booth code of $-1$ for the most significant bits 01. This leads to a decimal value $-512$ to be added to 171 giving $-341$.

If there is a sequence of leading 1s as shown in Case 3 below (which is Case 2 with 2 extra bits at most significant positions), then substring 1010101011 when Booth coded gives a decimal value $-341$.

**Case 3:** 1110101010111. The two leading 1s code to 00 and do not change the value. The binary value of substring 10101010111 = 683. The leading 1s give $-2048 + 1024 = -1024$ which when added to 683 results in $-341$, the same as the value obtained by Booth coding. Thus, these three cases convince us that Booth coding for 2's complement numbers give the correct binary value.

We now multiply a positive number by a Booth coded negative number expressed in 2's complement form.

***Example 5.21.***

| | |
|---|---|
| 0 0 0 1 1 0 | (+6) Multiplicand |
| 1 1 0 0 1 0 | (−14) Multiplier |
| 0 − 1 0 + 1 − 1 0 | (−14) Booth coded |

| | |
|---|---|
| <u>0 0 0 0 0 0 0 0 0 0 0 0</u> | (0) |
| <u>1 1 1 1 1 1 1 1 0 1 0</u> | (−6 in 2's complement form with sign extension) |
| <u>0 0 0 0 0 0 0 1 1 0</u> | (+6) |
| <u>0 0 0 0 0 0 0 0</u> | (0) |
| <u>1 1 1 1 1 0 1 0</u> | (−6) |
| <u>0 0 0 0 0 0 0</u> | (0) |
| 1 1 1 1 1 0 1 0 1 1 0 0 | (−84 in 2's complement form) |

## 5.9 BINARY DIVISION

Binary division may also be implemented by following a procedure similar to that used in long-hand division with appropriate modifications. We will discuss in this section a method for dividing integers represented using the sign magnitude notation. It is called the **restoring method for division.** Another method called the **non-restoring method** is also popular. We will not discuss that method leaving it as an exercise to the student.

This section illustrates division by the long-hand method used for decimal numbers which can then be extended for binary numbers.

*Example 5.22.*

**Long-hand division of decimal integers:** We will explain the procedure for dividing by considering a three digit dividend and a three digit divisor. Let the dividend be 721 and the divisor be 025. In order to divide 721 by 25 we first see if 25 will "go into" the first digit 7 of the dividend. In other words, we subtract 25 from 7 and see if the answer is negative or positive. In this case the answer is −18 and is negative. Thus, 25 does not "go into" 7. The first digit of the quotient is thus zero. To proceed further we have to "restore" the negative answer −18 back to the original dividend. We do this by adding 25 and get back 7. The next digit of the dividend, namely 2, is now appended to 7. We now examine whether 25 can go into 72 and, if so, how many times. We see that 72 − 25 is positive. Thus, 25 can go into 72 at least once. Next we try if (2 × 25) can go into 72. As 72 − (2 × 25) = 22 is positive we see that 25 can go into 72 at least twice. We next try 72 − (3 × 25) and see that the answer is −3 and negative. Thus, 25 can go into 72 only two times. The quotient digit is 2. We restore the remainder back to −3 + 25 = 22. The last digit 1 of the dividend is appended to 22 giving 221. Repeating the same step, namely finding out how many times 25 will go into 221, we see that it can go eight times. Thus, the quotient digit is 8. As no more digits are left in the dividend, the division process ends. The quotient is thus 028 and the remainder is 21. The division process is illustrated below:

| Divisor | Dividend | Quotient |
|---------|----------|----------|
| 025) | 721 | (028 |
| | 25 | |
| | −18 | |
| | 25 | ← Restoring step |
| | 72 | |
| | 75 | |
| | −03 | |
| | 25 | ← Restoring step |
| | 221 | |
| | 225 | |
| | −004 | |
| | 25 | ← Restoring step |
| | 21 | ← Remainder |

Binary division is similar and in fact simpler. It is simpler as we have to only check whether the divisor will go into the dividend or not. The question of how many times the divisor will go into the dividend is irrelevant as the quotient bit can be either 1 or 0. Binary division is illustrated with an example below.

***Example 5.23.***

**Long hand division of binary integers:**

We illustrate below the division of 1011 by 11.

```
               Divisor        Dividend          Quotient
  Quotient
    bit        11 )            0 1 0 1 1        ( 0 0 1 1
                               1 1
                              _____
     0         Borrow →        1 1 0
               Restore         1 1
                              _____
                               0 1 0
                                 1 1
     0         Borrow           1 1 1
               Restore          1 1
                              _____
                               1 0 1
                                 1 1
     1         No borrow         1 0 1
                                 1 1
                              _____
     1         No borrow         1 0          ← Remainder
                              _____
```

The method used in Example 5.23 is expressed as the following step-by-step procedure:

*Step 1:*  Let $y$ be the most significant bit of the dividend.

Repeat steps 2, 3 and 4 four times (as the dividend in this example is four-bits long).

*Step 2:*  Subtract the divisor from $y$.

*Step 3:*  If a borrow is generated in subtraction then add divisor to the remainder to restore dividend. Quotient bit is 0. Else quotient bit is 1.

*Step 4:*  Append the next significant bit of the dividend to the remainder.

From the long-hand division presented above we see that,

1. The divisor is to be preserved as it is to be successively subtracted from the dividend.

2. The dividend bits are used starting from the most significant bit. Once a bit is used to develop a quotient it is not needed again. The bit to its right is appended to the remainder for developing the next quotient bit.

3. As each quotient bit is developed the corresponding most significant bit of the dividend may be discarded.

We may thus use three registers again as was done for multiplication. The three registers used are again an $N$ bit register to store the divisor, an $(N + 1)$ bit accumulator in which the dividend is originally stored and from which the divisor is subtracted in each step and an *N* bit quotient register (see Figure 5.2). The accumulator and the MQ register may be again physically joined so that their contents can be shifted together. Algorithm 5.2 gives the detail of implementation of division. Observe that we have used 2's complement addition instead of subtraction.

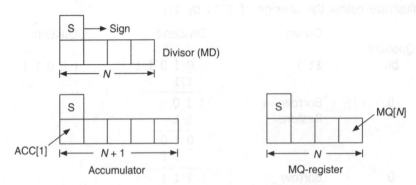

**Figure 5.2   Registers for division.**

ALGORITHM 5.2. **Procedure to divide two *N* bit numbers**

*Const*   N = 4; N1 = 5; NPLUSN1 = 9;
*Var*   MD: *array* [l..N] *of bit* {MD is N bits long. Divisor is stored in it};
   ACC: *array* [1..N1] *of bit* {ACC is the accumulator where the remainders are developed. N1 = N + 1};
   MQ: *array* [1..N] *of bit* {MQ stores the quotient during division};
   SIGNMD, SIGN ACC, SIGNMQ: *bit* {These are sign bits of MD, ACC, MQ respectively};
   COUNT: *integer* {used as counter};
   ACCMQ: *array* [1..NPLUSN1] *of bit* {ACCMQ is obtained by concatenating MQ to the right of ACC};
*begin* {of algorithm}
   *Input* SIGNMD, MD, SIGNMQ, MQ {Initially the dividend is stored in MQ};
   ACC: = 0;
   ACCMQ: = *Concatenate to right* MQ to ACC;
   *for* COUNT: = 1 to N *do*
   *begin Shift-Left* ACCMQ;
         ACC: = ACC − MD {This may be achieved by adding 2's complement of MD to ACC};
         if ACC [1] = 1 *then begin* MQ [N]: = 0; ACC: = ACC + MD *end else* MQ [N]: = 1;
   *end;*
         SIGNMQ: = SIGNMD ⊕ SIGNMQ;
   *Output* SIGNMQ, ACC, MQ {ACC has the remainder after division, MQ has the quotient};
*end* {of algorithm}.

We have traced algorithm 5.2 using the data divisor 1 1 and dividend 1 0 1 1 below:

**Initial state**

| ACC | MQ | MD |
|-----|-----|-----|
| 0 0 0 0 0 | 1 0 1 1 | 0 0 1 1 |

COUNT = 1

| | ACC | MQ |
|---|-----|-----|
| *Shift-Left* | 0 0 0 0 1 | 0 1 1 0 |
| ACC: = ACC − MD | 1 1 1 0 1 | |
| ACC [1] = 1 | 1 1 1 1 0 | |
| Set MQ [N] = 0 | | 0 1 1 $\boxed{0}$ |
| Restore | 0 0 0 1 1 | |
| | 0 0 0 0 1 | 0 1 1 $\boxed{0}$ |

COUNT = 2

| | ACC | MQ |
|---|-----|-----|
| *Shift-Left* | 0 0 0 1 0 | 1 1 $\boxed{0}$ $\boxed{0}$ |
| ACC: = ACC − MD | 1 1 1 0 1 | |
| ACC [1] = 1 | 1 1 1 1 1 | |
| Set MQ [N] = 0 | | 1 1 $\boxed{0}$ $\boxed{0}$ |
| Restore | 0 0 0 1 1 | |
| | 0 0 0 1 0 | 1 1 $\boxed{0}$ $\boxed{0}$ |

COUNT = 3

| | ACC | MQ |
|---|-----|-----|
| *Shift-Left* | 0 0 1 0 1 | 1 $\boxed{0}$ $\boxed{0}$ 0 |
| ACC: = ACC − MD | 1 1 1 0 1 | |
| ACC [1] = 0 | 0 0 0 1 0 | |
| Set MQ [N] = 1 | 0 0 1 0 1 | 1 $\boxed{0}$ $\boxed{0}$ $\boxed{1}$ |

COUNT = 4

| | ACC | MQ |
|---|-----|-----|
| *Shift-Left* | 0 0 1 0 1 | $\boxed{0}$ $\boxed{0}$ $\boxed{1}$ 0 |
| ACC: = ACC − MD | 1 1 1 0 1 | |
| ACC [1] = 0 | 0 0 0 1 0 | |
| Set MQ [N] = 1 | 0 0 0 1 0 | $\boxed{0}$ $\boxed{0}$ $\boxed{1}$ $\boxed{1}$ |

Remainder      Quotient

## 5.10    INTEGER REPRESENTATION

Normally, integers are represented using 16 bits, 32 bits or 64 bits in most computers. Each time such an integer is loaded in CPU, multiple bytes are transferred. In some CPUs, the most significant byte is stored in the numerically lowest memory address. This representation is called a **big-endian** representation. Thus, when four bytes of a 32-bit integer is taken to CPU it will be as shown in Figure 5.3.

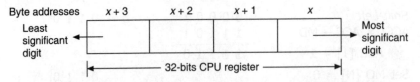

**Figure 5.3    Big-endian representation of 32-bit integer.**

In some other CPUs, (e.g. Intel 80 $\times$ 86 series) the least significant digit is stored in the numerically, least memory address. This is called a **little-endian** representation. This is shown in Figure 5.4

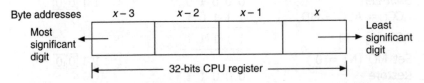

**Figure 5.4    Little-endian representation of 32-bit integer.**

There is no specific advantage of one method over the other. It is important for a systems programmer to know which method is used by the hardware of a given computer. Further, due to this non-uniformity, portability of programs between machines of two different manufacturers becomes unnecessarily difficult.

## 5.11    FLOATING POINT REPRESENTATION OF NUMBERS

A number with a fractional part (commonly known in the computer literature as a real number) may be stored and represented in several ways in a digital system. Consider, for example, the real decimal number 172.354. It may be written as:

1. 172.354
2. .172354 $\times 10^3$

Assume that a register is available which can store six digits and a sign bit. One way of storing the above number in the register is to imagine that the register is split into two parts: one part containing the integer portion of the number and the other fractional portion. The decimal point **is assumed** to exist between the two parts of the register and should be remembered by the user while manipulating the number in the register. Figure 5.5 illustrates this representation.

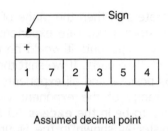

**Figure 5.5   Real number representation.**

Hardware implementation of arithmetic operations is simple if this representation is used. The two parts of the number may be treated independently. After the operation is performed one may transfer any carry or borrow generated in the fractional part to the integer part. The practical difficulty in using this scheme is the need for the user to keep track of the decimal point location and significant digits, particularly in multiplication and division operations. Further, the range of numbers that could be represented using this notation is limited. With the register configuration of Figure 5.5 the range is ± 999.999.

We will now consider another method of storing real numbers using the register of Figure 5.5. This is known as the **floating point representation.** Consider the second form of 172.354 at the beginning of the section. In this form the number is written as a fraction multiplied by a power of 10. The fractional part is known as the mantissa (also known as **significand**) and the power of 10 multiplying the fraction is known as the **exponent.** If other number systems are used, for example, octal, a number would be represented by a fraction in that base multiplied by a power of 8 (e.g. $.127 \times 8^4$).

If a number in this form is to be stored in a register with a capacity of six digits and a sign, then we should divide the register again into two parts: one part to hold the mantissa and one part to hold the exponent. If we arbitrarily allot two digits for the exponent and four digits for the mantissa, we may store the number in the register as shown in Figure 5.6. Two problems arise in doing this: first, all the six digits in the number cannot be stored in the register as two digits in the register have been taken out to store the exponent. Second, as only one sign bit is available it can be used with the mantissa only. We have to devise some other way to indicate the sign of the exponent.

As indicated in Figure 5.6 the most significant four digits of the number are stored in the mantissa part. The last two digits are truncated and are thus lost. This is the penalty for having a separate exponent. The gain in using a separate exponent is the increase in the range of numbers we can represent.

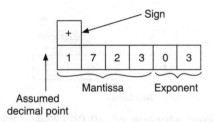

**Figure 5.6   Real number with mantissa and exponent.**

If the exponent has a separate sign then the range of numbers will be $10^{-99}$ to $10^{99}$. If we do not have the facility to store a separate exponent sign then in order to be able to store both positive and negative exponents it would be necessary to split the range of the exponent, namely 00 to 99, into two parts. If we shift the origin to 50, we may interpret all exponents greater than 50 as positive and all exponents less than 50 as negative. This is illustrated below. Thus, the range of the exponent will be $-50$ to $+49$. Exponents expressed in this notation are said to be in the **excess 50** form. Using this notation $.1723 \times 10^3$ may be stored in the register as shown in the Figure 5.7.

$$
\begin{array}{ccc}
00 & +50 & +99 \\
-50 & 00 & 49
\end{array}
$$

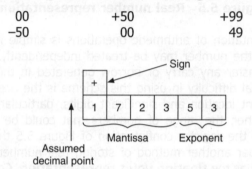

**Figure 5.7   Representation of $.1723 \times 10^3$ with excess 50 exponent.**

Assume that we want to store the number $-.001234 \times 10^{-5}$. If we blindly follow the procedure mentioned in the previous paragraphs we may store it as shown in Figure 5.8. A little thought shows that the information conveyed by the leading zeros in the mantissa may be included in the exponent. The number may be written as $-.1234 \times 10^{-7}$ and stored as shown in Figure 5.9 thereby preserving all the significant digits in the mantissa. This technique is called **normalization.** In the normalized floating point representation, the most significant digit of the mantissa is non-zero. Normalization is universally used in digital systems.

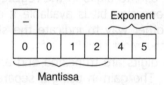

**Figure 5.8   Improper storage of $-0.001234 \times 10^{-5}$ in real format.**

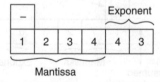

**Figure 5.9   Normalized storage of $-0.001234 \times 10^{-5}$ as $-.1234 \times 10^{-7}$.**

Using the normalized floating point representation of real numbers the range of numbers we can represent in a six digit register is: maximum magnitude $.9999 \times 10^{+49}$ and the minimum magnitude $.1000 \times 10^{-50}$. This should be compared with the magnitude range representable with a fixed (assumed) decimal point which is 999.999 to 000.001.

Thus, using a given six digit register with one sign bit, the normalized floating point representation is able to store a much larger range of numbers. The price paid, namely the loss of two significant digits in order to do this, is well worth it. Besides the loss of two significant digits, the use of normalized floating point numbers requires some specific rules be followed when arithmetic operations are performed with such numbers. We will discuss these rules later in this chapter.

Another question which arises in the normalized floating point representation is how to represent zero. If all the digits in the mantissa are zero then one may conclude that the number is zero. In actual computation, however, due to rounding of numbers which arises because of the finite number of digits in the mantissa it would be preferable to call a very small number, not exactly zero, as zero. This suggests that zero may be represented by all zeros for the mantissa and the largest negative number as exponent. In the excess 50 representation of exponent, the largest negative exponent is represented by 0. Thus, a zero will have both mantissa and exponent equal to zero. This is desirable as it will simplify the circuitry to test zero.

## 5.11.1   Binary Floating Point Numbers

We saw in the last section that given a fixed length register to store numbers, we can store a real decimal number (i.e. a decimal number with a fractional part) in two ways. One is to assume a decimal point to be fixed at a particular point in the number. The other is to divide the available digits into two parts: a part called the mantissa and the other called the exponent. The mantissa represents fraction with a non-zero leading digit and the exponent the power of ten by which the mantissa is multiplied. The main advantage of the first method, called **fixed point representation,** is that all the available digits are used to represent the number. The disadvantage is that the range of numbers which can be represented is severely limited. The second method called **floating point representation** of real numbers increases the range of numbers which can be represented by using an exponent. It, however, reduces the precision of numbers which can be represented as part of the available digits is used to store the exponent. On the balance the floating point representation of real numbers with normalized mantissa is the preferred method as the representation of larger range of numbers is more important in practical computation.

Binary floating point numbers may also be represented using a similar idea. If we extend the idea in the simplest possible way to binary numbers, then a binary floating point number would be represented by:

$$\text{mantissa} \times 2^{\text{exponent}}$$

where the mantissa would be a binary fraction with a non-zero leading bit.

Suppose a 32-bit register is available. We will now examine the methods which we may use to store real numbers in it. We will reject a fixed point representation as the range of real numbers representable using this method is limited. With a floating point representation we have to decide the following:

1. Number of bits used to represent the mantissa.
2. Number of bits used to represent the exponent.
3. Whether to use an excess representation for the exponent.
4. Whether to use a base other than 2 for the exponent.

The number of bits to be used for the mantissa is determined by the number of significant decimal digits required in computation. From experience in numerical computation it is found necessary to have at least seven significant decimal digits in most practical problems. The number of bits required to represent seven significant decimal digits is approximately 23 (1 decimal digit = $\log_2 10$ bits). If one bit is allocated for the sign of the mantissa then eight bits are left for the exponent. If we decide to allocate one bit of the exponent for its sign then seven bits are left for the magnitude of the exponent. In the normalized floating point mode the largest magnitude number which may be stored is:

$$0.1111 \ldots 1 \times 2^{1111111}$$
$$|\!\!\leftarrow\!\!\text{23 bits}\!\!\rightarrow\!\!|$$

$$= (1 - 2^{-23}) \times 2^{127}$$
$$\cong 10^{38}$$

The minimum magnitude number is:

$$0.100000 \ldots 0 \times 2^{-1111111} = 0.5 \times 10^{-38}$$
$$|\!\!\leftarrow\!\! \text{23 bits} \!\!\rightarrow\!\!|$$

If we use excess representation for the exponent, the range of the binary exponent would be 0 to 255. The minimum exponent would be –127 and the maximum would be 128. We thus do not gain exponent range. The main gain in using this representation would be the unique representation of zero. A zero will be represented by all 0 bits for mantissa as well as the exponent. Further, as exponents will not use any separate sign, it is easy to compare two floating point numbers by first comparing the bits of the exponent.

***Example 5.24.***   Represent –(0.625) decimal in binary floating point form.

***Solution:***

$$-(0.625) = -(0.101) \text{ in binary} = -0.101 * 2^0$$

Therefore, normalized mantissa = 0.101

As excess representation is being used for the exponent, exponent –0 = 127. Thus, exponent = 127 = 01111111.

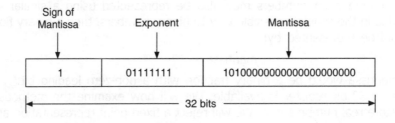

*Example 5.25.* Represent (4.21875) decimal in binary floating point form.

*Solution:*
$$(4.21875) = 100.00111 = 0.10000111 * 2^3$$

Normalized mantissa = 0.10000111.

As excess representation is being used for exponent, (exponent −3) = 127. Thus, exponent = 130.

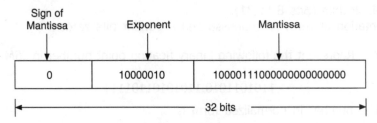

The range obtained by this representation is considerably larger compared to base 2 representation of exponents. The penalty is some loss of significance. If the exponent is increased by 1 the mantissa is to be shifted left by one hexadecimal digit, namely four bits. In contrast to this when 2 is used as the exponent base, increasing exponent by 1 will lead to shifting the mantissa left by one bit position.

Another way in which the exponent bits may be interpreted is to assume a base other than 2 for the exponent. If we assume a base of 16 for the exponent, then the largest magnitude floating point number that may be represented in this format would be:

$$0.111 \dots 1 \times 16^{127} \approx 10^{153}$$
$$\leftarrow 23 \text{ bits} \rightarrow$$

When 16 is used as the exponent base the most significant hexadecimal digit of mantissa should not be zero. Thus, the following representation would be valid.

$$0.00010100 \dots 1$$
$$\longleftarrow 23 \text{ bits} \longrightarrow \times 16^{1111111}$$

Thus, we can lose three significant bits in the mantissa. A compromise may be made and the mantissa bit may be increased by 1 to 24 bits. This would leave seven bits for the exponent. Allowing one bit for the exponent sign, the maximum number represented would be:

$$0.111 \dots 1 \times 16^{163} \approx 10^{76}$$
$$\leftarrow 24 \text{ bits} \rightarrow$$

and the minimum magnitude number:

$$0.10000 \dots 0 \times 16^{-64}$$
$$\leftarrow 24 \text{ bits} \rightarrow$$

This range is considered reasonably good. This idea was used in the floating point representation in IBM 370 series machines. The exact format used is:

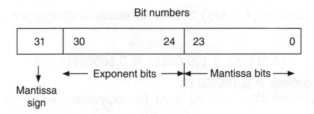

Exponent: Base 16. Excess 64 representation.
Mantissa: 24 bits (Bits 8 to 31).
Representation of zero: All mantissa and exponent bits zero.

***Example 5.26.*** Represent the following binary floating point number in *IBM floating point format.*

$$1101011010.11010101101111$$

*Solution:* The number in normalized form is:

$$.11010110101101010101101111 * 2^{10}$$
$$= 0.0011010110101101010101101111 * 2^4 * 2^4 * 2^4$$
$$= 0.0011010110101101010101101111 * 16^3$$

exponent $-64 = 3$. Therefore, exponent $= 67$.

| 0 | 1000011 | 0011010110101101010101011011 | 11 |
|---|---------|------------------------------|-----|

Sign ◄— Exponent —►◄———— Mantissa ————►◄—► Lost

The following Table 5.10 summarizes the various choices in floating point representation of binary numbers.

**TABLE 5.10**
**Binary Floating Point Number Representations**

| Mantissa | Exponent |
|----------|----------|
| 1. Binary point on left | 1. Sign magnitude notation |
| 2. Leading bit non-zero | 2. Excess notation |
| 3. 2's complement for negative mantissa | 3. Exponent base binary or hexadecimal |

## 5.11.2 IEEE Standard Floating Point Representation

The Institution of Electrical and Electronics Engineers, U.S.A. (IEEE) formulated a standard, known as **IEEE 754 floating point standard,** in the '80s for representing floating point numbers in computers and performing arithmetic operations with floating point operands. Such a standard is necessary to ensure portability of programs between different computers. In other words, a program using floating point numbers executed on some machine *A* will give the same result if run on machine *B* provided both machines *A* and *B* use the same standard representation of floating point numbers. Since its announcement most computers use this standard. The floating point co-processor designed for microcomputers also use this standard.

Most computers have separate hardware units to perform floating point arithmetic and integer arithmetic. The integer arithmetic unit is faster. Thus, operations such as comparison of numbers, increment and decrement are done using the integer unit. One of the aims of the IEEE 754 standard was to allow integer units to perform some aspects of floating point arithmetic. Thus, many decisions were taken in the standard to facilitate this objective. These decisions were:

1. To have the sign bit of the mantissa as the most significant bit.
2. The exponent bits are placed before the mantissa bits. When two floating point numbers of the same sign are compared, the magnitude of the exponents need only be compared first. This simplified sorting of floating point numbers.
3. Comparison of exponents with different signs pose a challenge. To simplify this a biased exponent representation is used. The most negative exponent is all 0s and the most positive all 1s.

Besides this, to increase the precision of mantissa, IEEE 754 uses a normalized mantissa representation. In this representation the most significant bit of mantissa must always be 1. As this is implied it is assumed to be on the left of the (virtual) decimal point of the mantissa. Thus, the general form of the representation is

$$\text{Sign } (1.0 + \text{mantissa}) \times 2^{(\text{Exponent-bias})}$$

using these general ideas IEEE 754 standard describes three formats for representing real numbers. They are:

1. Single precision
2. Double precision
3. Extended precision

We will explain these now.

**Single precision real number representation:** The format for single precision uses 32 bits to represent floating point numbers. The distribution of bits is shown below:

The standard specifies two formats: one for operands using 32 bits and another for 64-bits operand (known as **double precision**). The format for single precision is shown in Figure 5.10.

| 31 | 30          23 | 22              0 |
|----|----------------|-------------------|
| s  | Exponent       | Significand       |

**Figure 5.10  IEEE Single precision floating point representation.**

The term significand is used instead of the term mantissa in the IEEE standard. The sign bit is 0 for positive numbers and 1 for negative numbers. The exponent uses excess 127 format (also called **biased format**).

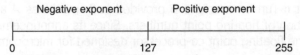

Negative exponent      Positive exponent

0     127     255

The IEEE 32-bit standard assumes a virtual 24th bit in the significand which is always 1. This assumption is valid as all floating point numbers are normalized and the leading bit should be 1. Thus, in the IEEE format the significand is 24 bits long; 23 bits stored in the word and an implied 1 as the 24th or the most significant bit. Thus, we get 24 bit for significand. The number is thus interpreted as:

$$(-1)^s * (1 + s_{22} 2^{-1} + s_{21} 2^{-2} + \cdots + s_0 2^{-23})*$$
$$2^{(\text{exponent} - 127)}$$

where $s_{22}$, $s_{21}$, etc. are bits at 22nd, 21st-0th bit position of the significand. Thus, the range of numbers is $\pm 2.0 \times 2^{-127}$ to $\pm 2.0 \times 10^{+128}$ which is approximately $\pm 2.0 \times 10^{\pm 38}$.

*Example 5.27.* Represent $-(.625)$ decimal in IEEE 754 floating format.

$$(-0.625)_{10} = -(0.101)_2 = -1.01 * 2^{-1}$$

The sign in IEEE format is 1. The significand is:

$\longrightarrow$ Bit number

22 21 20 19 18 17 16 15 14 13 12 11 10 9 8 7 6 5 4 3 2 1 0
0  1  0  0  0  0  0  0  0  0  0  0  0  0 0 0 0 0 0 0 0 0 0

The exponent is:

$$(\text{exponent} - 127) = -1$$

Thus, exponent = 126.

The floating point representation is thus:

$\longrightarrow$ Bit number

| 31 | 30 29 28 27 26 25 24 23 | 22 21 20 19 --------- 0 |
|----|-------------------------|-------------------------|
| 1  | 0  1  1  1  1  1  1  0  | 0  1  0  0 --------- 0   |

$\mid\leftarrow$ Sign $\mid\leftarrow$ ——— Exponent ———$\rightarrow\mid\leftarrow$ — Significand —$\rightarrow\mid$

**Double Precision Representation:** Double precision representation for floating point numbers uses 64 bits. The format is given in Figure 5.11.

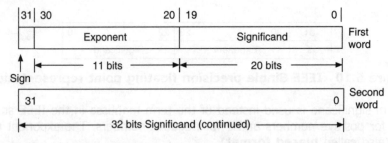

**Figure 5.11   IEEE Double precision floating point representation.**

*Example 5.28.*   Repeat +0.625 in double precision.

The number of significand bits in the fractional part of a double precision number is (1 + 20 + 32) bits where 1 is the implied most significand bit in normalized mode. This is approximately 16 decimal digits. The exponent range is $2^{-1023}$ to $2^{1024}$ which is approximately $10^{\pm308}$.

In double precision the number 0.625 will be represented as:

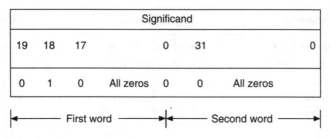

Exponent is $2^{-1}$ which is expressed as:

$$(\text{exponent} - 1023) = -1$$
$$\text{exponent} = 1022$$

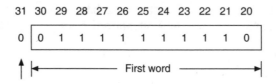

**Extended Real:**   This format uses 10 bytes (80 bits) to represent floating point numbers. It is usually not used to store numbers in memory. Its main purpose is for storing intermediate results obtained during computations to shield the final result from the effects of rounding errors and underflow/overflow during computation. In this format there is no hidden 1 in significand. It is physically present as part of the significand.

The format is as follows:

1. The bits are numbered from 0 to 79 with bit 79 as the most significant bit.
2. Sign of the number is 79th bit.
3. Exponent bits are from 78 to 64 (15 bits).
4. Exponent is represented using biased format. The bias value is $(2^{15} - 1) = 32767$. The exponent range is thus $10^{\pm4932}$.
5. Significand bits are 63 to 0. Thus, the precision of numbers is around 19 digits compared with 16 digits for double precision.

IEEE 754 floating point standard also specifies some bit patterns for cases such as exact 0 and numbers too large or too small to be accommodated in the number of bits available in a word. An exact value of 0 is represented by 0 for the exponent and 0 for the mantissa. An exponent of 255 and a zero for mantissa is used to represent infinity. An exponent of 255 and a mantissa not equal to zero is used to represent exception conditions which occur when one attempts to divide 0 by 0 or subtract infinity from infinity. This is called **NaN** (*not a number*). This is summarized in Table 5.11.

**TABLE 5.11**
**IEEE 754 Floating Point Representation**

(i) Single Precision (32 bits)

| Exponent | Significand | Value |
|---|---|---|
| e width = 8 bits | f width = 23 bits | |
| 1 < e < 254 | Any bit pattern f | $(-1)^s \, 2^{e-127} \, (1.f)$ |
| 0 | 0 | $(-1)^s \, 0$ |
| 255 | 0 | $(-1)^s \, \infty$ |
| 255 | $\neq 0$ | NaN |

(*s* is sign bit)

(ii) Double Precision (64 bits)

| Exponent | Significand | Value |
|---|---|---|
| e width = 11 bits | f width = 52 bits | |
| 1 < e < 2046 | Any bit pattern f | $(-1)^s \, 2^{e-1023} \, (1.f)$ |
| 0 | 0 | $(-1)^s \, 0$ |
| 2047 | 0 | $(-1)^s \, \infty$ |
| 2047 | $\neq 0$ | NaN |

(iii) Extended Real (80 bits)

| Exponent | Significand | Value |
|---|---|---|
| e width = 15 bits | f width = 64 bits | |
| 1 < e < 32766 | Any bit pattern f | $(-1)^s \, 2^{e-32767} \, (0.f)$ |
| 0 | 0 | $(-1)^s \, 0$ |
| 32767 | 0 | $(-1)^s \, \infty$ |
| 32767 | $\neq 0$ | NaN |

Similar to big endian and little endian in integers we also have the same situation where floating point numbers are stored in byte addressable machines. Single precision reals are stored in four bytes and double precision reals in eight bytes. If the most significant bits are stored in the smallest byte address it is called the **big endian representation** and when the least significant bits are stored in the smallest byte address it is called **little endian representation.** A little endian floating point representation is shown as follows:

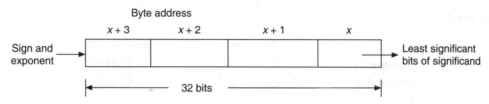

Byte address

Besides the representation of floating point numbers, the IEEE standard also specifies extra bits called **guard bits** to be carried during calculation using floating point numbers. This is to preserve the significance of the results. Rounding rules have also been specified in the standard. For greater details the reader is referred to reference [8] given at the end of this book.

## 5.12  FLOATING POINT ADDITION/SUBTRACTION

If two numbers represented in floating point notation are to be added or subtracted the exponents of the two operands must be made equal. In doing this an operand would need shifting. The points will be clarified by considering a few examples. Decimal numbers are represented using the format given in Section 5.11 (Figure 5.6).

*Example 5.29.*

|  | Number | Register form |
|---|---|---|
| Operand 1 | $.1234 \times 10^{-3}$ | 123447 |
| Operand 2 | $.4568 \times 10^{-3}$ | 456847 |
| Addition | $.5802 \times 10^{-3}$ | 580247 |

*Example 5.30.*

|  | Number | Register form |
|---|---|---|
| Operand 1 | $.1234 \times 10^{3}$ | 123453 |
| Operand 2 | $.4568 \times 10^{2}$ | 456852 |

Addition–Shift operand 2 right by one place and add

|  |  |  |
|---|---|---|
|  |  | 123453 |
|  |  | 045653 |
| Sum | $.1690 \times 10^{3}$ | 169053 |

*Example 5.31.*

|  | Number | Register form |
|---|---|---|
| Operand 1 | $.1234 \times 10^{3}$ | 123453 |
| Operand 2 | $.9234 \times 10^{3}$ | 923453 |
| Add | $1.0468 \times 10^{3}$ | 104654 |

Shift result right one digit 0. Increment exponent by 1.

*Example 5.32.*

|  | Number | Register form |
|---|---|---|
| Operand 1 | $.1234 \times 10^3$ | 123453 |
| Operand 2 | $.4568 \times 10^8$ | 456858 |
| Add |  |  |

Shift operand 1, five places right and add.

|  |  | 456858 |
|---|---|---|
| Answer | $.4568 \times 10^8$ | 456858 |

In this case the first operand is too small compared to the second operand and is not added.

*Example 5.33.*

|  |  |  |
|---|---|---|
| Operand 1 | $+.4568 \times 10^8$ | $+456858$ |
| Operand 2 | $-.1234 \times 10^8$ | $-123458$ |

Add nine's complement of mantissa of operand 2 to operand 1. If overflow add 1 to result. Declare result positive.

|  |  |  |
|---|---|---|
|  | 4568 |  |
|  | 8765 |  |
| Overflow (1) | 3333 |  |
|  | 1 |  |
|  | 3334 |  |
| Result positive |  | + 333458 |

*Example 5.34.*

|  |  |  |
|---|---|---|
| $+4568 \times 10^8$ | Operand 1 | $+456858$ |
| $-4566 \times 10^8$ | Operand 2 | $-456658$ |

Add 9's complement of operand 2 (mantissa) to operand 1 (mantissa). Add overflow $4568 + 5433 = 10001 + 1 = 10002$.

$$200055$$

Result    $.0002 \times 10^8$    (In register)

Shift right three digits to get 200055.

In this case the answer has three leading zeros. It is shifted to three spaces till the most significant digit is non-zero. For each left shift the exponent is reduced by 1.

*Example 5.35.*

|  |  |
|---|---|
| $.4568 \times 10^{49}$ | 456899 |
| $.8268 \times 10^{49}$ | 826899 |

Add

$$\text{Sum} = 1.2836 \times 10^{49}$$

$$.1283 \times 10^{50} \qquad 1238 \ (100)$$

In this example the sum exceeds $.9999 \times 10^{99}$ and is called an **overflow condition.**

*Example 5.36.*

$$+.4568 \times 10^{-50} \qquad +456800$$

$$-.4500 \times 10^{-50} \qquad -450000$$

Add

$$\text{Sum} = .0068 \times 10^{-50}$$

$$.6800 \times 10^{-52} \qquad -6800 \ (52)$$

In this case the answer is less than $.1 \times 10^{-50}$ and is called an **underflow condition.**

If there is a hardware feature in the machine for floating point addition and subtraction it should account for all the above conditions.

## 5.12.1 Floating Point Multiplication

Floating point multiplication is relatively simple. In this case the exponents are added and the mantissas multiplied. In the added exponents there would be an excess of 50. This is subtracted. If the exponent exceeds 99, overflow is declared. As both mantissas are normalized to less than 1, the product mantissa cannot exceed 1. The mantissa, however, can have leading zeros. Thus, normalization, after the product is obtained with adjustment of exponent, would be necessary.

## 5.12.2 Floating Point Division

In this case the divisor mantissa should be larger than the dividend mantissa to ensure that quotient is less than 1. If this is not true a divide stop will occur. To ensure that division does not stop we may shift the dividend right by one digit and add 1 to the exponent before the beginning of division. (This is a blind method and the ease of dividing is gained at the expense of one significant digit.)

The dividend is placed in the accumulator and the divisor in the MD register. Division of the mantissa parts proceed as usual. The fractional part of the answer is stored in MQ at the end of the division. The quotient is shifted left till the most significant digit is non-zero. The exponent part of the answer is equal to

(ACC exponent – MD exponent – Number of left shifts + 50).

Fifty is added as the excess 50 in accumulator and MD exponents would be cancelled in the subtraction operation.

We have seen floating point arithmetic in this section in decimal system. Same procedures can be followed when both exponent and mantissa are represented in binary form.

## 5.13 FLOATING POINT ARITHMETIC OPERATIONS

We saw in the last section how decimal arithmetic operations are performed on decimal floating point numbers. Multiplication and division are straightforward. To multiply we multiply the two significands of the numbers and add the exponents. We should take care of exponent overflow/underflow and normalize the significand of the product. Similarly, in division if we divide $x$ by $y$ we divide the significand of $x$ by that of $y$ and subtract the exponent of $y$ from that of $x$. Any exponent overflow/underflow has to be taken into account and significand normalized. We define first the notation we will be using in this section.

$$\text{Operand 1: } x: s_x, e_x, m_x$$
$$\text{Operand 2: } y: s_y, e_y, m_y$$
$$\text{Result: } z: s_z, e_z, m_z$$

where $s_x$ is the sign of $x$, $e_x$ the exponent of $x$ in excess 127 format, $m_x$ the significand of $x$. Similarly, $s_y$ is the sign of $y$, $e_y$ its exponent and $m_y$ its significand.

---

ALGORITHM 5.3. **Multiplication of two floating point members**

*Step 1:*   Read $x$, $y$

*Step 2:*   if $m_x$ or $m_y = 0$ *then* $z = 0$; exit

*Step 3:*   $e_z = e_x + e_y - 127$ /* Excess 127 assumed for exponents */

*Step 4:*   if $e_z > 255$ *then* overflow error; exit

*Step 5:*   if $e_z < 0$ *then* underflow error, exit

*Step 6:*   $m_z = m_x * m_y$ /* multiplication */

*Step 7:*   if most significant bit of $m_z = 0$ *then* left shift

$m_z$ ; $e_z \leftarrow e_z - 1$ /* Normalization step */

*Step 8:*   if $e_z < 0$ *then* underflow error; exit

*Step 9:*   $s_z = s_x \oplus s_y$

*Step 10:*  Result = $s_z, e_z, m_z$

---

In the above algorithm we have not rounded the result. Most machines will have at least two bits beyond the allowed number of bits in $m_z$. If two bits are there and they are 11, then a 1 is added to the least significant bit. If it is 00 or 01 nothing is done. If it is 10, then if the least significant bit is 1, a 1 is added. If it is 0 nothing is done. The idea is to round the number to an even number.

Division operation is similar. We give the algorithm for division as Algorithm 5.4.

---

ALGORITHM 5.4. **Division of two floating point numbers**

*Step 1:*   Read $x$, $y$ /* we need $x/y$ */

*Step 2:*   if $m_x = 0$ *then* $Z = 0$; exit

*Step 3:*   if $m_y = 0$ *then* $z \leftarrow \infty$; exit

*Step 4:*   $e_z = e_x - e_y + 127$ /* Excess 127 used for exponents */

*Step 5:*   if $e_z > 255$ *then* overflow error; exit

*Step 6:*     if $e_z < 0$ *then* underflow error, exit
*Step 7:*     if $m_x > m_y$ then {shift right $m_x$, $e_x \leftarrow e_x + 1$}
*Step 8:*     $m_z = m_x/m_y$   /*Division */
*Step 9:*     if most significant bit of $m_z = 0$ *then*
             leftshift $m_z$; $e_z \leftarrow e_z - 1$   /*Normalization */
*Step 10:*   if $e_z < 0$ *then* underflow; exit
*Step 11:*   if $m_z > 1$ right shift most significant
             bit of $m_z$; $e_z \leftarrow e_z + 1$   /*Normalization */
*Step 12:*   if $e_z > 255$ *then* overflow; exit
*Step 13:*   $s_z = s_x \oplus s_y$
*Step 14:*   Result = $s_z$, $e_z$, $m_z$

**Floating point addition/subtraction:** Floating point addition and subtraction will be considered together, as addition of a positive number to a negative number is actually subtraction. We will again assume that the operands are in sign magnitude form with normalized significand (most significant bit 1) and excess 127 representation for exponent. The algorithm is developed as Algorithm 5.5. As before the two operands are $x = s_x$, $e_x$, $m_x$ and $y = s_y$, $e_y$, $m_y$, and the result is $z = s_z$, $e_z$, $m_z$ where s is the sign, e the exponent and m the signficand.

---

ALGORITHM 5.5. **Addition/Subtraction of Floating point numbers**

*Step 1:*    Read $x = s_x$, $e_x$, $m_x$ and $y = s_y$, $e_y$, $m_y$
*Step 2:*    if operation is subtract *then* $s_y = \bar{s}_y$
*Step 3:*    if $y = 0$ *then* $z = x$, exit
*Step 4:*    if $x = 0$ then $z = y$, exit
            /* The following steps are needed to ensure the exponents of the two
              operands are equal before add/subtract */
*Step 5:*    $e_d = e_x - e_y$
*Step 6:*    {if $e_d \geq 0$ *then* right shift $m_y$ by $e_d$ bits;
                   $e_z = e_x$;
            if $m_y = 0$ *then* $z = s_x$, $e_x$, $m_x$, exit}
            else {if $e_d < 0$ *then* right shift $m_x$ by $e_d$ bits, $e_z = e_y$;
               if $m_y = 0$ *then* $z = s_y$, $e_y$, $m_y$, exit}
*Step 7:*    $s_z$, $m_z = (s_x \ m_x + s_y \ m_y)$ /*Add signed significands */
*Step 8:*    if $m_z = 0$ *then* $z = 0$, exit
*Step 9:*    if $m_z$ overflows by 1 bit *then* right shift $m_z$, $e_z \leftarrow e_z + 1$
*Step 10:*   if $e_z > 255$ *then* overflow error; exit
                *else* $z = s_z$, $e_z$, $m_z$; exit

> *Step 11:* *if* most significant bit of $m_z = 0$ then
>      *repeat*
>           {Left shift $m_z$ by 1 bit, $e_z \leftarrow e_z - 1$
>           *if* $e_z < 0$ *then* report underflow error, exit}
>      *until* most significant bit of $m_z = 1$
> *Step 12:* $z = s_z, e_z, m_z$
>      *End of algorithm*

We have discussed a number of methods of performing arithmetic operations in digital systems with a view to achieve simplicity and economy in implementing these with electronic circuits. We will now discuss the actual logic design of subsystems to perform these operations in the succeeding sections.

## 5.14  LOGIC CIRCUITS FOR ADDITION/SUBTRACTION

So far in this chapter we have examined methods of representing integers and real numbers and appropriate algorithms to perform the four basic operations of addition, subtraction, multiplication and division. In this section we will develop logic circuits to perform addition and subtraction. These are realized as hardware units which form part of an Arithmetic Logic Unit (ALU) of a computer. We will present first the basic circuits to illustrate how it is done. Nowadays these are integrated as part of a Medium Scale Integrated (MSI) circuit. We will also examine one of these MSI chips and what it provides.

### 5.14.1  Half- and Full-Adder Using Gates

**A half-adder:**  The truth table for a half adder was given as Table 5.1. It is reproduced here as Table 5.12.

**TABLE 5.12**
**A Half-Adder Truth Table**

| x | y | s | c |
|---|---|---|---|
| 0 | 0 | 0 | 0 |
| 0 | 1 | 1 | 0 |
| 1 | 0 | 1 | 0 |
| 1 | 1 | 0 | 1 |

The Boolean expressions for the sum s and carry c are given by

$$s = x \cdot \bar{y} + \bar{x} \cdot y, \quad c = x \cdot y \tag{5.1}$$

Using NAND gates, we obtain the circuit shown in Figure 5.12(a). It uses seven NAND gates. With some ingenuity we can obtain the circuit of Figure 5.12(b) which uses only 5 NAND gates. However, given the Boolean expression, there is no straightforward and simple method of obtaining the realization of Figure 5.12(b). The half-adder expression of Eq. (5.1) can also be expressed as Eqs. (5.2)

$$s = x \oplus y, \quad c = x \cdot y \qquad (5.2)$$

where $\oplus$ is the exclusive OR operator. This may be shown as the block diagram of Figure 5.12(c).

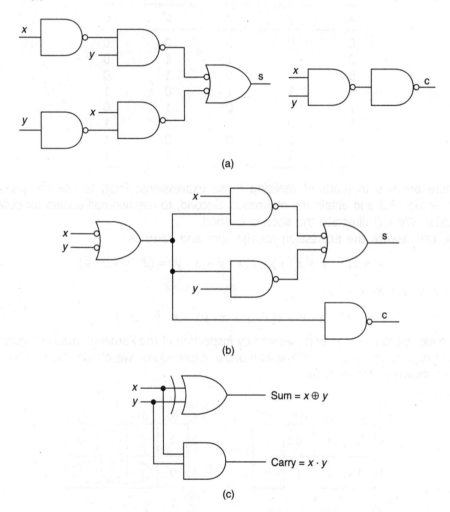

(a)

(b)

Sum = $x \oplus y$

Carry = $x \cdot y$

(c)

**Figure 5.12   Half adder using NAND and XOR gates.**

**A full-adder:** The truth table of a full-adder is shown in Table 5.13. From the table we obtain Boolean expressions for the sum $s'$ and carry $c'$ as:

$$s' = \bar{x} \cdot \bar{y} \cdot z + \bar{x} \cdot y \cdot \bar{z} + x \cdot \bar{y} \cdot \bar{z} + x \cdot y \cdot z \tag{5.3}$$

which can also be written as

$$s' = x \oplus y \oplus z \tag{5.4}$$

$$c' = x \cdot y + y \cdot z + x \cdot z \tag{5.5}$$

**TABLE 5.13**
**Truth Table of a Full-Adder**

| x | y | z | s' | c' |
|---|---|---|----|----|
| 0 | 0 | 0 | 0 | 0 |
| 0 | 0 | 1 | 1 | 0 |
| 0 | 1 | 0 | 1 | 0 |
| 0 | 1 | 1 | 0 | 1 |
| 1 | 0 | 0 | 1 | 0 |
| 1 | 0 | 1 | 0 | 1 |
| 1 | 1 | 0 | 0 | 1 |
| 1 | 1 | 1 | 1 | 1 |

There are two methods of realizing these expressions: First, to use the procedure given in Section 3.3 and obtain the realization. Second, to use two half-adders for obtaining a full-adder. We will illustrate the second method.

We can rewrite the expression for the sum and carry as:

$$s' = \bar{z}(\bar{x} \cdot y + x \cdot \bar{y}) + z(\bar{x} \cdot \bar{y} + x \cdot y) = (\bar{z} \cdot s + z \cdot \bar{s}) \tag{5.6}$$

where $s = \bar{x} \cdot y + x \cdot \bar{y}$

$$c' = x \cdot y + z(\bar{x} \cdot y + x \cdot \bar{y}) = x \cdot y + z \cdot s \tag{5.7}$$

The expression for c' may be verified by inspection of the Karnaugh map of Figure 5.13. Using the expressions above and the half-adder expressions, we obtain the circuit for the full-adder shown in Figure 5.14.

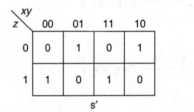
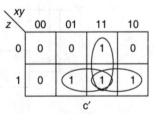

**Figure 5.13  K-maps for full-adder.**

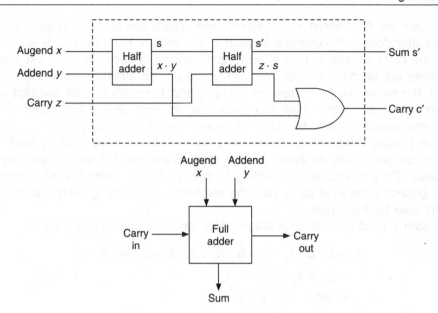

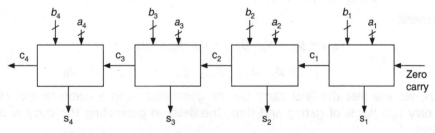

**Figure 5.14  Full-adder.**

## 5.14.2  A Four-bit Adder

In the last subsection we saw how a full adder can be constructed using two half adders. We obtained a full-adder with one bit augend, one bit addend and carry (from previous addition) bit giving sum and carry to be carried to the next bit position. We can use four such full adders to add two four bit numbers as shown in Figure 5.15. Observe that this is a combinatorial circuit. This is called a **ripple carry adder** as the carry generated in the least significant bit position is carried to the successive stages. In the worst case, the carry generated in the least significant bit position will be carried to the most significant bit position, for example, when 0001 is added to 1111. Thus, the answer will not be ready till the carry propagates through all four stages. The propagation delay is $3t_p$ per stage where $t_p$ is the gate delay per level of gating. Thus, the total delay for four stages will be $12t_p$.

**Figure 5.15  A four stage ripple carry adder.**

The case we considered is the worst case. There are other situations where the carry generator does not propagate beyond a bit position. For example, if we add 0001 to 1001, the carry generated in the least significant bit is added to the next significant bit and there are no more carries. We can speed up the addition process if at any bit position *i*, the same can be computed using $a_i$ and $b_i$ values in that position and the carry from the $(i-1)^{th}$ stage, namely $e_i$ only and not from any of the pervious stages. Similarly, one should be able to obtain the carry out of the final stage, $c_{n+1}$ for (for *n* stage adder) using values of $a_i$, $b_i$ for $i = 1$ to 4. This is called a **carry look ahead** adder. We can build such an adder whose carry propagation delay is fixed regardless of the value of *n* provided we are willing to construct fairly complicated combinatorial circuit to generate the final carry bit. The methods of designing such a combinatorial circuit will now be explained.

The sum $s_i$ of stage *i* of an *n* stage adder can be expressed as follows:

$$s_i = \bar{a}_i \cdot b_i \cdot \bar{c}_i + a_i \cdot \bar{b}_i \cdot \bar{c}_i + \bar{a}_i \cdot \bar{b}_i \cdot c_i + a_i \cdot b_i \cdot c_i \tag{5.8}$$

$$= a_i \oplus b_i \oplus c_i \tag{5.9}$$

$$c_{i+1} = a_i b_i + a_i c_i + b_i c_i \tag{5.10}$$

If we call $a_i \cdot b_i = g_i$ and $p_i = (a_i + b_i)$, we can rewrite Eq. (5.10) for carry out of the $i^{th}$ stage as Eq. (5.11).

$$c_{i+1} = g_i + p_i \cdot c_i \tag{5.11}$$

Thus, the sum and carry can be written using only $a_i$, $b_i$ and $c_i$. To see how we can generate carry with only a combinatorial circuit we can express the carries in stages 1, 2, 3, ..., etc., as follows:

$$c_1 = g_0 \text{ as } c_0 = 0 \tag{5.12}$$

$$c_2 = g_1 = p_1 \cdot c_1 = g_1 + p_1 \cdot g_0 = f_2(a_1\, b_1, c_1) \tag{5.13}$$

$$c_3 = g_2 + p_2 \cdot c_2 = g_2 + p_2 \cdot g_1 + p_2 \cdot p_1 \cdot g_0 = f_3(a_2, b_2, a_1, b_1, c_1) \tag{5.14}$$

$$c_4 = g_3 + p_3 \cdot c_3$$

$$= g_3 + p_3 \cdot g_2 + p_3 \cdot p_2 \cdot g_1 + p_3 \cdot p_2 \cdot p_1 \cdot g_0 \tag{5.15}$$

$$= f_4 (a_1, b_1, a_2, b_2, a_3, b_3, c_1)$$

and in general

$$c_{n+1} = g_n + p_n \cdot g_{n-1} + p_n \cdot p_{n-1} \cdot g_{n-2} + \cdots$$

$$+ p_n \cdot p_{n-1} \cdot p_{n-2} \cdot g_{n-3} + \cdots + p_2 \cdot p_1 \cdot g_0 \tag{5.16}$$

Thus, we see that the final carry can be generated using a combinatorial circuit. It requires only two levels of gating and thus, the delay in generating the carry is only two gate delays.

The circuit of a four-bit carry look ahead adder is given in Figure 5.16.

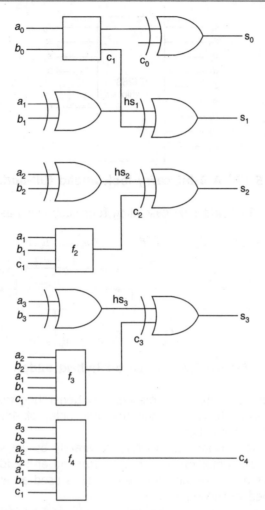

**Figure 5.16  Structure of a carry look ahead 4 stage adder. Blocks marked
$f_2$, $f_3$, $f_4$ are carry look ahead combinatorial circuits.**

Observe from Figure 5.14 that the delay in generating $s_0$ and $s_1$ is two gate delays each. If we call a gate delay $t_p$, the total delay is $2t_p$. The gate delays for generating $s_2$ and $s_3$ is, however, $3t_p$ as the combinatorial circuits $f_2$ and $f_3$ use two levels of gating thus leading to a delay of $2t_p$ each. The carry $c_4$ has only two levels of gating generated by $f_4$. Observe that the maximum delay is $3t_p$ and is not a function of the number of bits to be added.

Developments in integrated circuit technology have made it possible to put in one chip the entire combinatorial circuit of Figure 5.16. Such a chip is available commercially. It is called **4-bit carry look ahead full adder chip** (Also known as 74283 chip). It accepts 4 bits addend, 4 bit augend, the carry in and generates 4 bit sum and carry to next stage as shown in Figure 5.17. The maximum gate delay of the chip is $3t_p$ for obtaining the sums as was explained earlier.

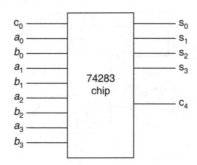

**Figure 5.17   A 4-bit carry look ahead full-adder chip.**

We can obtain a 16-bit adder by cascading four such chips as shown in Figure 5.18.

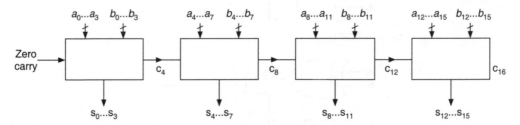

**Figure 5.18   A 16-bit hybrid adder**

When we cascade four chips, the time delay in generating the final carry $c_{16}$ will be $4 \times 2t_p = 8t_p$, which is much smaller than the time delay of $48t_p$ if 16 full adders are cascaded to add two 16-bit numbers.

There is no need to consider subtractors separately as we saw that subtraction in nothing but taking the 2's complement of the subtrahend and adding it to the minuend. Thus, no separate chips are made and the same unit is used as an adder/subtractor unit using the rules explained in section 5.5.

### 5.14.3   MSI Arithmetic Logic Unit

A MSI arithmetic logic unit (ALU) is a combinatorial circuit integrated in a single medium scale integrated circuit which can perform one of a set of specified arithmetic operations or logical operations on a pair of $n$ bit operands. A typical MSI ALU has two four-bit operands and five bits for operation selection. Thus, 32 different operations can be performed on a pair of four-bit operand inputs. In Figure 5.19 we give the logic symbol of model SW745181, four-bit ALU chip of Texas Instruments. The operation to be performed is selected by the bits $s_0$, $s_1$, $s_2$, $s_3$ and $m$. The input operands are $a_0$, $a_1$, $a_2$, $a_3$ and $b_0$, $b_1$, $b_2$, $b_3$ and $c_n$ (which is carry in). The outputs $f_0$, $f_1$, $f_2$ and $f_3$ are the result of performing the specified operations on the input operands. The other outputs are $c_{n+4}$ which is the carryout, $g$ and $p$ which generate and propagate outputs of addition corresponding to $g$ and $p$ of the carry look ahead adder explained in the last section. They are useful if a number of these chips are to be cascaded to add, for example, 16 bit operands. They can be used in a carry look ahead adder circuit to reduce propagation delay. The data sheets specify

4-bit add time of 11 ns if one of these is used and 18 ns if two of these are used with ripple carry from the first 4-bit chip to second chip. For 16-bit addition we use four of these chips and one carry look a head chip. This configuration produces sum and carry in 19 ns.

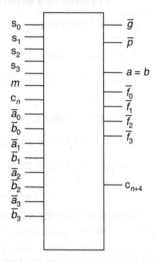

**Figure 5.19  Schematic of ALU SN745181 of Texas Instruments.**

In this MSI circuit observe that inputs $a_0$-$a_4$, $b_0$-$b_4$ and outputs $f_0$-$f_4$, $g$ and $p$ are complemented assuming active High as 1 (which we have used throughout this book). Another output $a = b$ will be asserted if $a = b$.

In Table 5.14 the functions performed by SN745181 ALU is adapted from Texas Instruments data sheet. In Table 5.13 $a$ and $b$ represent the two 4-bit input operands and $f$-represents the 4-bit output.

**TABLE 5.14**

**Functions Performed by ALU SN745181**

| Operation Code | | | | Functions Performed | |
|---|---|---|---|---|---|
| $S_3$ | $S_2$ | $S_1$ | $S_0$ | $m = 0$ (Arithmetic) | $m = 1$ (Logical) |
| 0 | 0 | 0 | 0 | $f = a$ plus $c_n$ | $f = \bar{a}$ |
| 0 | 0 | 0 | 1 | $f = (a$ plus $b)$ plus $c_n$ | $f = \overline{a + b}$ |
| 0 | 0 | 1 | 0 | $f = (a + \bar{b})$ plus $c_n$ | $f = \bar{a} \cdot b$ |
| 0 | 0 | 1 | 1 | $f = 0 - c_n$ | $f = 0000$ |
| 0 | 1 | 0 | 0 | $f = a$ plus $(a \cdot \bar{b})$ plus $c_n$ | $f = \overline{a \cdot b}$ |
| 0 | 1 | 0 | 1 | $f = a + b$ plus $(a \cdot \bar{b})$ plus $c_n$ | $f = \bar{b}$ |
| 0 | 1 | 1 | 0 | $f = a - b - \bar{c}_n$ | $f = a \oplus b$ |
| 0 | 1 | 1 | 1 | $f = a \cdot \bar{b} - \bar{c}_n$ | $f = a \cdot \bar{b}$ |
| 1 | 0 | 0 | 0 | $f = a$ plus $(a \cdot b)$ plus $c_n$ | $f = \bar{a} + b$ |

(*Contd.*)

**TABLE 5.14 (Contd.)**
**Functions Performed by ALU SN745181**

| Operation Code | | | | Functions Performed | |
|---|---|---|---|---|---|
| $s_3$ | $s_2$ | $s_1$ | $s_0$ | $m = 0$ (Arithmetic) | $m = 1$ (Logical) |
| 1 | 0 | 0 | 1 | $f = a$ plus $b$ plus $c_n$ | $f = \overline{a \oplus b}$ |
| 1 | 0 | 1 | 0 | $f = (a + \overline{b})$ plus $(a \cdot b)$ plus $c_n$ | $f = b$ |
| 1 | 0 | 1 | 1 | $f = a \cdot b - \overline{c}_n$ | $f = a \cdot b$ |
| 1 | 1 | 0 | 0 | $f = a$ plus $a$ plus $c_n$ | $f = 1111$ |
| 1 | 1 | 0 | 1 | $f = (a + b)$ plus $a$ plus $c_n$ | $f = a + \overline{b}$ |
| 1 | 1 | 1 | 0 | $f = (a + \overline{b})$ plus $a$ plus $c_n$ | $f = a + b$ |
| 1 | 1 | 1 | 1 | $f = a - \overline{c}_n$ | $f = a$ |

Observe from this table that $m = 0$ selects arithmetic operations and $m = 1$ logic operations. Thus there are a total of 32 operations. When logic operations are selected, the operations are carried out simultaneously on $a_0$-$a_4$ and $b_0$-$b_4$. The carry input, output, $g$ and $p$ are ignored. Observe that all the 16 binary operations on two Boolean operands (explained in Chapter 3) are available. When $m = 0$, to perform two's complement addition, we select the appropriate code from Table 5.13 to perform $a$ plus $b$ plus $c_n$ ($c_n$ will normally be 0). To perform two's complement subtracting, we select the code $s_3 - s_0 = 0110$ which gives $a$ minus $b$ minus $\overline{c}_n$ with $\overline{c}_n = 1$ as $c_n$ acts as the complement of the borrow during subtraction. The other operations such as $a$ plus $c_n$ and $a$ minus $\overline{c}_n$ are useful to increment (with $c_n = 1$) and decrement (with $c_n = 0$) input operand. There are many more arithmetic operations which are there as they come as bonus from intermediate variables. Many of them are rarely used. There is also simpler MSI ALU with only eight operations shown in Figure 5.20 and Table 5.15.

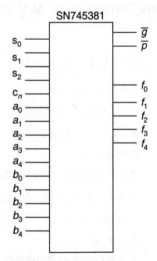

**Figure 5.20  A simpler MSI ALU chip SN745381.**

**TABLE 5.15**
**Function Performed by ALU SN745381**

| Operations Codes | | | Functions |
|:---:|:---:|:---:|:---|
| $S_2$ | $S_1$ | $S_0$ | |
| 0 | 0 | 0 | $f = 000$ |
| 0 | 0 | 1 | $f = b - a - 1$ plus $c_n$ |
| 0 | 1 | 0 | $f = a - b - 1$ plus $c_n$ |
| 0 | 1 | 1 | $f = a$ plus $b$ plus $c_n$ |
| 1 | 0 | 0 | $f = a \oplus b$ |
| 1 | 0 | 1 | $f = a + b$ |
| 1 | 1 | 0 | $f = a \cdot b$ |
| 1 | 1 | 1 | $f = 1111$ |

## 5.15 A COMBINATORIAL CIRCUIT FOR MULTIPLICATION

The algorithm for multiplication was presented in Section 5.7 as primarily sequential. Multiplication is not inherently sequential as all partial products can be added by combinatorial adders. This is illustrated in Figure 5.21 for $4 \times 4$ multiplication of $a_3$, $a_2$, $a_1$, $a_0$ by $b_3$, $b_2$, $b_1$, $b_0$. Final product is computed as follows:

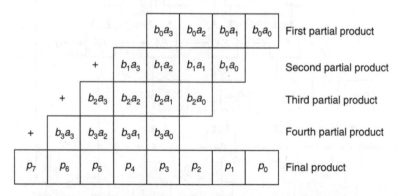

**Figure 5.21   Multiplication of two 4-bit operands.**

$p_0 = b_0 a_0,$    $p_1 = b_0 a_1 + b_1 a_0,$    $p_2 = c_{p1} + b_0 a_2 + b_1 a_1 + b_2 a_0$

$p_3 = c_{p2} + b_0 a_3 + b_1 a_2 + b_2 a_1 + b_3 a_0$

$p_4 = c_{p3} + b_1 a_3 + b_2 a_2 + b_3 a_1$

$p_5 = c_{p4} + b_2 a_3 + b_3 a_2$

$p_6 = c_{p5} + b_3 a_3$

$p_7 = c_{p6}$

The equations given above for products can be implemented by multipliers and full adders as shown in Figure 5.22. Remember that an AND gate is a multiplier of two 1-bit operands. Observe the regularity of the structure of this multiplier. Such regular structures are easy to implement as an integrated circuit. A total number of 16 AND gates and 12 full adders are used by this multiplier. For multiplying two 8-bit operands we need 64 AND gates and 56 full adders. In general, for $(4 \times 4)$ bit multiplication $n^2$ AND gate and $n(n-1)$ full adders are needed. This is very large and thus sequential multipliers are used which implement Algorithm 5.1. In this case the same adder is used repeatedly. It is, however, slower. We will discuss sequential implementation in the next chapter.

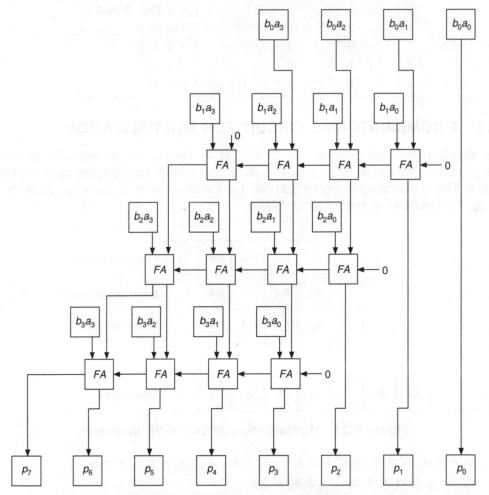

**Figure 5.22  A combinatorial multiplier to multiply two 4-bit numbers.**

We have implicitly assumed in this section that the two binary numbers to be multiplied are represented in sign magnitude form. Implementation of a Booth multiplier is left as a challenging exercise to the student.

---

### SUMMARY

---

1. An adder which adds two bits and finds the sum and carry (if any) is called a half adder. An adder which adds two bits and carry bit (if any) propagated by adding the bits to its right, finds the sum and carry bit (if any) is called a full adder.

2. How to represent negative numbers using one's and two's complement system is described in Section 5.4.

3. Subtraction can be performed by adding the one's or two's complement of subtrahend to the minuend.

4. Decision tables can be used to summarize rules to add/subtract two operands represented in one's or two's complement notation. Tables 5.7 and 5.8 are the appropriate tables.

5. Multiplication of two binary numbers is similar to long-hand multiplication. It can be implemented using a multiplicand register whose length equals number of bits $n$ in multiplicand, a register called ACCMQ of length $2n + 1$ to store the product. The $n$ least significant bits of ACCMQ is used to store the multiplier. Algorithm 5.1 gives details of this.

6. Multiplication of numbers represented using sign magnitude notation is simple. Magnitudes are multiplied using long-hand multiplication method. The sign of the result is the exclusive OR of the signs of the two operands.

7. If negative numbers are represented in two's complement form an algorithm proposed by Booth is useful. Booth's algorithm reduces the number of addition operations (on the average). Details are given in Section 5.8.

8. Division of two numbers is similar to long-hand division. Just like in multiplication it can be implemented using a $n$-bit register to store the divisor, a $2n+1$ bit register whose $n$ least significant bits store the dividend and later the quotient. Algorithm 5.2 gives the details.

9. Integers are normally represented using 16, 32 or 64 bits in most computers. When integers are loaded in CPU from memory multiple bytes are transferred. If the most significant bits are stored in lowest memory address it is called big endian representation and if the least significant bits are stored in the lowest memory address it is called little endian representation.

10. Real or floating point numbers are stored in computers using a representation with a fractional mantissa (also called significand) and an integer exponent. The fractional mantissa is normalized to make the most significant bit 1. The mantissa and exponent may have independent signs.

11. IEEE has standardized the number of bits to be used in the significand and exponent respectively. If 32 bits are used to store floating point numbers, 23 bits are used to represent the significand, one bit for its sign and eight bits for the exponent. It assumes a virtual $24^{th}$ bit as the most significant bit which is always 1 (normalization requirement). There is no separate sign for the exponent. It uses excess 127 format

in which all exponents greater than 127 are treated as positive and all exponents less than 127 are treated as negative. A set of bits stored in this format are interpreted as $(-1)^s * (1 + s_{22} 2^{-1} + s_{21} 2^{-2} + \cdots + s_0 2^{-23}) * 2^{(\text{exponent}-127)}$ where $s_{22}$, $s_{21}$, etc. are $22^{nd}$, $21^{st}$ bits. The range of numbers is $\pm 2.0 * 2^{-127}$ to $\pm 2.0 * 2^{128}$.

12. Standards for double precision (64 bits) and extended real (80 bits) have also been defined by IEEE. Details are given in Table 5.11.

13. Arithmetic on floating point operands is straightforward: the mantissas are multiplied and the exponents added. The mantissa is normalized adjusting the exponent. At the end, if exponent exceeds the maximum size of exponent, the result is declared incorrect due to exponent overflow. If the exponent is smaller than the smallest exponent which can be stored, then also the result is declared incorrect.

14. To divide, the dividend is divided by the divisor. The mantissa is normalized. If the exponent lies outside the allowed range the result is declared incorrect.

15. To add/subtract, the exponents of the two operands should be equal. If these are not, the mantissa of the number with the smaller exponent is moved right by the number of bits needed to make its exponent equal to the larger exponent. The mantissas are added/subtracted. The resulting mantissa is normalized adjusting the exponent. Overflow or underflow of exponents may occur (similar to multiplication) in which case an error is declared.

16. Detailed algorithms for floating point arithmetic operations is given in Section 5.13.

17. Combinatorial circuits may be designed to realize add/subtract operations. Starting point are the appropriate truth tables. From this truth tables logic circuits may be designed using the techniques discussed in Chapter 3.

18. A full adder circuit has as inputs two one-bit operands and carry if any. If two operands, each 4-bits long are to be added, 4 full adders may be cascaded to construct a 4-bit adder. This is called a ripple carry adder as a carry (if any) generated by adding lesser significant bits ripple through the more significant bits. Time to add $n$ bits will equal (in the worst case) $3nt_p$ where $t_p$ is the gate delay per level of gating.

19. To reduce the delay an adder called a carry look ahead adder may be designed. It uses a complex combinatorial circuit to generate the final carry simultaneously with the sum bits. For an $n$ bit adder the total delay is only $3t_p$ and is independent of $n$. However, the combinatorial circuit to generate the carry is very complex.

20. Integrated circuit chips have been designed to realize a carry look ahead adder.

21. Medium-scale integrated circuits are available to realize arithmetic (add/subtract) and logic operations on $n$ bit operands. The circuits become more complex and expensive as $n$ increases. In the text we have illustrated the functions of two such chips (ALU 745181 and 745381) which have two 4-bit operands as inputs.

22. Multiplication/division may be performed either using sequential circuits or combinatorial circuits. In Section 5.15 we have illustrated how a combinatorial circuit can be designed for multiplying two 4-bit operands.

## EXERCISES

1. Find the sum and difference of the following pairs of binary numbers:
   - (i) 111.01        + 10.111
   - (ii) 11.01         + 110.11
   - (iii) 110.11       − 111.01

2. Repeat Exercise 1 using 1's and 2's complement representation of numbers.

3. Multiply the following binary numbers using the algorithm developed in Section 5.7. Show all steps in the calculation.
   - (i) 1110 × 0111
   - (ii) 101 × 010
   - (iii) 101110 × 101011
   - (iv) 101010 × 01010

4. Multiply the following numbers represented in two's complement form. Use first the method of Section 5.7.
   - (i) 0011011 × 1011011
   - (ii) 110011 × 001100
   - (iii) 101101 × 110011
   - (iv) 011011 × 011101

   Repeat using Booth coding method.

5. Divide the following binary numbers using Algorithm 5.2. Show all steps in your computation.
   - (i) 110/111
   - (ii) 0011/1011

6. Subtract the following decimal numbers using: (a) 9's complement representation (b) 10's complement representation
   - (i) 23-12
   - (ii) 17-6
   - (iii) 23-29

7. A digital system is to store binary numbers in a 16-bit register. Assuming five-bits are reserved for the exponent and 11 bits are reserved for the mantissa and sign, how would the following decimal numbers be represented in this system?
   (Assume a normalized floating point representation is used.)
   - (i) 183.25
   - (ii) −12.4
   - (iii) .00048

8. A binary computer uses 36-bit registers to store numbers. Eight bits are used for the exponent and the exponent is represented in excess 128 form. Find the approximate range of decimal numbers handled by this computer.

9. A binary computer uses 48-bit registers to store numbers. If an exponent range of at least ± 999 and 8 significant decimal digits are needed for the mantissa find an appropriate scheme to represent floating point numbers in this system.

10. Represent the following decimal number in a 32-bit word in
    - (i) Normalized floating point mode in excess 128 form
    - (ii) IBM floating point format
    - (iii) IEEE 754 format
        - (a) 2500
        - (b) .25
        - (c) $35 * 10^{-3}$

11. Represent the following number in double precision IEEE format (64 bits).
    - (i) 0.654
    - (ii) $75 × 10^3$

12. Repeat Exercise 9 assuming the exponent is represented using hexadecimal base.

13. Algorithm 5.3 assumes that the most significant bit of the product should be 1 for normalization. Modify the algorithm using IEEE 754 floating point standard for 32-bit operands.

14. Modify Algorithm 5.4 for division using IEEE 754 floating point standard for 64-bit operands

15. Modify Algorithm 5.5 for addition/subtraction assuming IEEE 754 floating point standard for 32-bit operands.

16. Obtain a combinatorial circuit to multiply two numbers each of which is 3 bits long and has 1 bit for sign. The output should have the right sign and magnitude.

17. Repeat Exercise 16 for division of two 3-bit operands.

18. Obtain a combinatorial circuit using PAL to realize a 4-bit carry look ahead adder.

19. Obtain PAL realization of ALU 745181 function with operation code with $s_3, s_2, s_1, s_0$ = 1, 0, 0, 1 and $m = 0$. (Realize row 11 of Table 5.14 with $m = 0$)

20. Repeat Exercise 19 for row 7 of Table 5.14.

21. Obtain MUX realization of ALU SN745381 (Table 5.15) for row 4.

22. Repeat Exercise 4 for row 3.

# Chapter

# 6

# Application of Sequential Circuits

| Learning Goals |
| --- |

In this chapter we will learn:

☞ How to evolve Algorithmic State Machine (ASM) charts to express sequential algorithms relevant to the design of digital systems.

☞ How to develop ASM charts for common arithmetic/logic operations for their sequential implementation.

☞ How to express ASM charts in a Hardware Description Language (HDL).

☞ How to design logic circuits for common arithmetic/logic operations using ASM charts and corresponding HDL description.

## 6.1 INTRODUCTION

In the last chapter we explained various algorithms for performing arithmetic and logic operations in a computer, and how these operations can be realized using combinatorial circuits. Such circuits perform the operations fast but are expensive in terms of use of hardware resources. In this chapter we will explain how arithmetic and logic operations can be realized using sequential logic circuits. This method of realization is economical in use of hardware but takes a longer time to perform the specified operation. Which of these two alternatives is appropriate depends on the specific application and a designer has to use his judgement.

In general, digital systems (including ALUs) are built using building blocks which include registers, flip-flops, counters, decoders, multiplexers, adders, logic gates and clocks. The general methodology of design follows the steps enumerated below:

1. Given the requirements specification, an algorithm is evolved to perform the intended task.

241

2. From the algorithm the size and number of registers needed to store data is determined and the kind of operational units, such as adders, comparators, etc., which are necessary to perform the required processing, are specified.

3. For each step of the selected algorithm, the details of performing that step by using the operational units is obtained. The operations that could be performed simultaneously (i.e. in parallel) so as to minimize the overall time required to complete the steps are identified.

4. The timing signals which will control the sequencing of different steps of the algorithm are generated.

5. The controller to generate the timing signals is synthesized. The design is completed and the system is tested with appropriately selected test inputs.

In this chapter we will illustrate the design of some simple digital systems (in particular ALUs) following the above steps. Algorithms for digital data processing will be developed and presented using a chart known as **Algorithmic State Machine (ASM).**

## 6.2  ALGORITHMIC STATE MACHINE

The design of a digital system can be divided into two distinct parts. One part is to design a processor to process the data stored in registers, flip-flops, etc. and the other is to design a controller to correctly sequence the operations to be performed by the data processor. Thus, a general block diagram of a digital system is shown in Figure 6.1. It consists of a data processor which transforms given inputs to outputs. The sequence of operations carried out by the data processor is controlled by a controller. In clocked synchronous systems all operations are controlled by a central clock. The design of sequential circuits studied in the last chapter is primarily useful for designing the control signals. We will introduce another design method known as **Algorithmic State Machine Chart** which assists in developing digital systems.

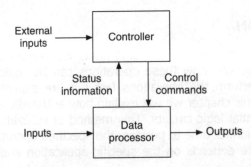

**Figure 6.1  Generalized block diagram of a digital system.**

Algorithmic state machine chart is similar to flow charts used to describe data processing algorithms. It is, however, interpreted differently to specify what operations are carried out simultaneously in a given state during one clock interval and when one advances to the next state.

An ASM chart is drawn using three types of blocks shown in Figure 6.2. The rectangular box is known as the *state box*. The state box is given a label which is written on its top left-hand corner. Each state box is assigned a binary code (normally during hardware realization) which is written at the upper right-hand corner. Inside the box, operations to be carried out on registers when the system is in this state are given. The box may also contain names of outputs which will be initiated during this state. For example, the state box shown in Figure 6.2(a) is labelled $T_2$ with binary code 010. The operations are clearing a register $A$ to 0 and incrementing register $B$ (Incr. $B$). A signal LOAD is initiated during this state. All these operations are carried out simultaneously.

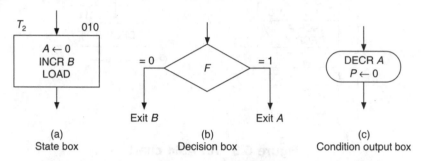

**Figure 6.2  Symbols used in algorithmic state machine.**

The diamond shaped box [Figure 6.2(b)] specifies a decision to be taken. It is called a *decision box*. The condition to be tested is written inside the box. If it is true one path is taken and if it is false the other path is taken. Usually, the condition to be tested is the contents of a flip-flop or the presence of a signal. The two paths are then indicated as 1 and 0 which correspond to the contents of the flip-flop. In Figure 6.2(b) the condition is the status of flip-flop $F$. When $F = 1$ exit $A$ is taken when it is 0 exit $B$ is taken.

The third type of box used in ASM is called a *condition output box* and is drawn as a rectangle with rounded sides [Figure 6.2(c)]. The input to a condition output box must come from the output of a decision box. Inside the condition output box operations to be carried out on registers in the digital system are specified. These operations are carried out when the condition output box is reached based on a decision taken in a preceding decision box. These operations are carried out simultaneously.

Consider the ASM chart of Figure 6.3. This chart uses all the symbols defined in Figure 6.2. Observe the dotted rectangle enclosing the state box $T_1$ and boxes connected to its exit up to the next state box. This is called a **block of** ASM. Observe that there are four blocks in the chart of Figure 6.3. Each block in an ASM chart describes events which take place during **one clock interval.** All the operations in a block are carried out simultaneously during this clock interval. For example, the operations $S \leftarrow 0$, $Q \leftarrow 0$, initiating START signal, setting $L \leftarrow 0$ if $P = 1$ or $E \leftarrow 1$ if $P = 0$ are all performed in one clock while the system is in state $T_1$ [see Figure 6.4(a)]. The end of this clock transfers the system to state $T_2$ or $T_3$ depending on the value of $P$. If $P = 0$, the next state is $T_2$ else it is $T_3$. In state $T_2$, $A$ is incremented and $X$ decremented during one clock (i.e. carried out simultaneously).

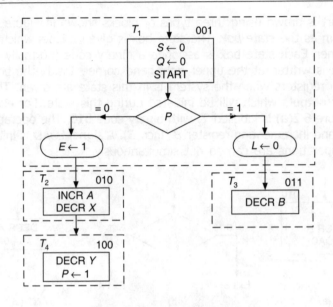

**Figure 6.3   An ASM chart.**

The ASM chart is a generalization of the state transition diagrams used in designing sequential circuits. The state transition diagram corresponding to the ASM chart of Figure 6.3 is shown in Figure 6.4(b). Sometimes a state transition diagram obtained from the ASM chart is useful in designing the control logic of the digital system.

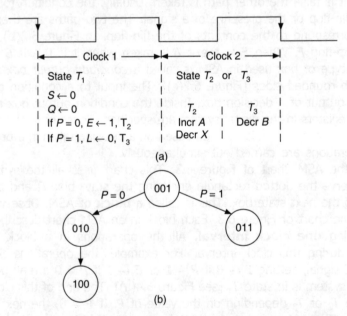

**Figure 6.4   State transition and operations during a clock interval.**

We will now consider an example to illustrate how an ASM chart is obtained from a problem specification.

*Example 6.1.* Two 4-bit registers $X$ and $Y$ are loaded with values. On a start signal $X$ and $Y$ are compared. If $X > Y$ a flip-flop $A$ is to be set to 1. If $X < Y$ a flip-flop $B$ is to be set to 1. If $X = Y$ a flip-flop $E$ is to be set to 1. The method is to load $X$ and $Y$, clear all flip-flops and give a start signal. On start the most significant bits of $X$ and $Y$, namely $X_3$ and $Y_3$ are compared. (It is assumed that the bits of $X$ and $Y$ are respectively $X_3 X_2 X_1 X_0$ and $Y_3 Y_2 Y_1 Y_0$.)

If $X_3 = 1$, $Y_3 = 0$ then $X > Y$. If $X_3 = 0$ and $Y_3 = 1$, then $X < Y$. If $X_3 = Y_3 = 1$ or $X_3 = Y_3 = 0$, then it is not possible to decide at this stage whether $X > Y = Y$ or $< Y$. We shift both $X$ and $Y$ left by one bit and compare the bits moved into $X_3$ and $Y_3$. At some stage if $X_3$ and $Y_3$ are not equal we can find out which is larger. If after three shifts there is no difference then $X = Y$. This method is specified as an ASM chart in Figure 6.5. This logic system is called a **comparator**.

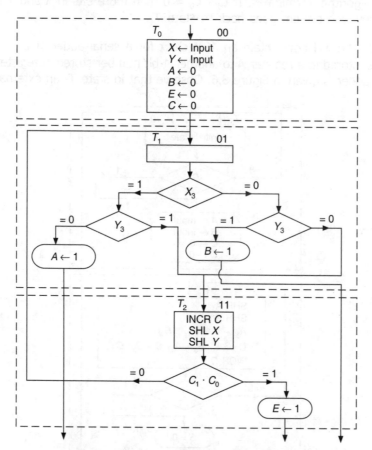

**Figure 6.5 ASM chart for a comparator.**

Observe that in State $T_0$ in the ASM chart $X$ and $Y$ registers are loaded with inputs, and the flip-flops $A$, $B$ and $E$ are set to 0. $C$ is a 2-bit counter used to count the number of shifts of registers $X$ and $Y$. It is also set to 0. All this takes place in one clock pulse interval. At the end of the interval the system transits to the state $T_1$.

Observe that the state box has no operations specified. This is allowed in ASM. This does not mean that nothing is done in state $T_1$. In fact in this state the most significant bits of $X$ and $Y$ registers are compared. Based on this comparison flip-flop $A$ is set to 1 if $X > Y$ and $B$ is set to 1 if $X < Y$. To show that the operation of comparison is done in state $T_1$, all these operations are enclosed in a dotted box. If the most significant bits of $X$ and $Y$ are equal then the other bits of $X$ and $Y$ should be checked. To do this the system transits to state $T_2$ at the end of the clock interval. In the next clock pulse the counter is incremented as one comparison has been completed. Registers $X$ and $Y$ are then shifted left by one bit and the most significant bits are compared again. If all four bits have been compared then $C$ will have 11 stored in it. This is checked by the condition box (see Figure 6.5). If $C_1 \cdot C_0 = 1$ then all the four-bits have been compared and found equal. Thus, $E$ is set to 1 and the algorithm terminates. If $C_1 \cdot C_0 = 0$ then more bits in $X$ and $Y$ are still to be examined. Thus, the system goes back to state $T_1$.

*Example 6.2.* We will now obtain an ASM chart for a serial adder. It is required to add a 4-bit number stored in a register $A$ to another 4-bit number stored in register $B$. The ASM chart for this adder is given in Figure 6.6. Observe that in state $T_0$ an externally generated

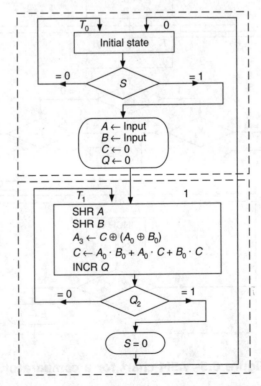

**Figure 6.6  ASM chart for a 4-bit serial adder.**

signal $S$ is tested. If $S$ is 1 then the numbers to be added are loaded into registers $A$ and $B$. The carry flip-flop $C$ and the counter $Q$ are cleared. $Q$ is a 3-bit counter. All operations indicated in the state box $T_0$ are carried out during one clock pulse. In the next clock pulse state box $T_1$ is executed. $T_1$ is executed repeatedly until $Q_2 = 1$. $Q_2$ equals 1 at the end of four pulses. Thus, $T_1$ is executed four times adding the four bits of the operands $A$ and $B$. As soon as counting is over signal $S$ is reset to 0 and control returns to $T_0$ and waits. When $S$ is set another addition starts.

*Example 6.3.* **Binary Multiplier:** Let us consider the design of a binary multiplier. The numbers to be multiplied are assumed to be represented in sign magnitude form with one bit for sign and four bits for magnitude.

We need two 5-bit registers to hold the multiplier and the multiplicand and their signs and a long register of five bits to hold the unsigned partial sums obtained during multiplication. We call the registers:

$MQ$ : Multiplier register,
$SMQ$ : Sign of MQ
$MD$ : Multiplicand register,
$SMD$ : Sign of MD
$AC$ : Accumulator register (Holds partial sum)
$R$ : $AC$ and $MQ$ registers concatenated and called $R$ (Holds partial products)
$SR$ : Sign bit of result

The result is stored with the four least significant bits in $MQ$ and the four most significant bits in $AC$ and the sign bit in $SR$.

A schematic of the registers used by the multiplier system is shown in Figure 6.7. The multiplication procedure itself is shown in the ASM chart of Figure 6.8. It is based on the long-hand multiplication method, explained in Section 5.6. The reader should observe the following three facts about this method:

1. In each step we add four bits of $MD$ to $AC$. This partial sum can be four bits or five bits long. Thus, $AC$ must be five bits long.

2. For every step we need the multiplicand and one bit of the multiplier (again from right to left) to generate the partial product. After that bit of the multiplier is used, we will not require it again. This suggests that $AC$ concatenated to $MQ$ could be a shift register and its contents could be shifted right after every step. The right shift by 1 bit of $AC$ and $MQ$ together is essential to mimic the long-hand multiplication method. This is the reason we give a name $R$ to $AC$ concatenated to $MQ$.

3. The steps are repeated four times where four is equal to the length of the register which is the same as the length of the multiplier or multiplicand.

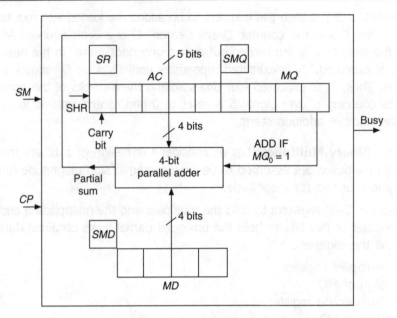

**Figure 6.7   Schematic of a four-bit multiplier.**

The above facts are taken into account in obtaining the ASM chart of the multiplier subsystem shown in Figure 6.8. The start multiplication signal *SM* is supplied by an external event and the clock input will be used to generate the timing signal. A three-bit counter *C* is used to count iterations.

In the ASM chart, in state $T_0$ when *SM* becomes 1 the operands and their signs are loaded, a counter is initialized and multiplication is started. A flip-flop BUSY is set to 1 to indicate that the multiplier is busy. In state $T_1$ the least significant bit of *MQ*, namely $MQ_0$ is checked. If it is 0 nothing is done. If it is 1 then the contents of *AC* and *MD* are added by a parallel adder (i.e. one which adds all the bits simultaneously in one clock cycle) and the result stored in *AC*. The clock period must be chosen in such a way that the slowest operation is completed within this period. In this example the parallel addition will take the maximum time. Thus, the clock period must be larger than this. In state $T_2$ the bits of *AC* and the bits of *MQ* (excluding its sign bit *SMQ*) are considered as a single unit and called *R* register. This is shifted right one bit. Thus, the least significant bit of *AC* is shifted into the most significant bit of *MQ* and the least significant bit of *MQ* (which has already been used to multiply) is lost. As one partial product had been computed the counter *C* is incremented by 1. When *C* = 4, the most significant bit of *C*, namely $C_2$ becomes 1 and multiplication is over. The sign bit of the result *R* is obtained by exclusive ORing the sign bits of *MQ* and *MD*. *SM* and BUSY are reset to 0.

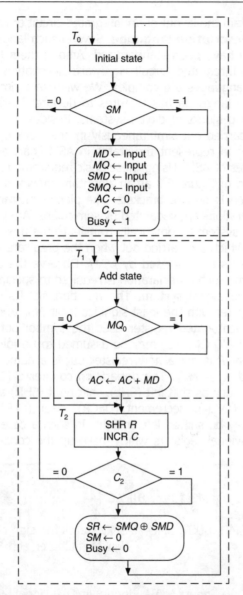

**Figure 6.8  ASM chart for multiplier.**

## 6.3  ALGORITHMIC REPRESENTATION OF ASM CHARTS

The ASM chart is similar to a flow chart and assists in developing and understanding digital systems. Its main disadvantage is that it is time consuming to draw and for large systems it will become cumbersome. Thus, usually a hardware-oriented programming language which has facilities to express specific features of hardware algorithms is used. Another advantage of such a language with strict syntax and semantic rules is that it will be possible to write a translator for a computer to translate it and obtain a schematic of the corresponding digital system or even obtain the layout of an integrated circuit to realize it. Such a language is known as **hardware description language**. Several such languages have been defined over the years and many have been standardized. Among them two languages known as **VHDL** (Very High Speed Integrated Circuit Hardware Description Language) and **Verilog** are very popular. These languages are complex. We will use a simple informal language to describe ASM charts. The language has features to declare flip-flops, registers, counters, etc., which are the building blocks of digital systems. Besides this, we provide methods of representing operations carried out simultaneously in one clock cycle and those which are sequential. We use labels to represent the states in ASM chart and *if then else* structure to represent decision boxes of ASM. Using these basic requirements of hardware description we express the ASM chart of Figure 6.8 as an algorithm shown in Figure 6.9. Observe that all the operations enclosed in square brackets take place simultaneously during one clock period. The individual operations are separated by semicolons. After completing the operation in the square bracket the system automatically transits to the next block. In the *if then else* construct the operations which are carried out when the predicate is true/false are enclosed in curly brackets. Comments are enclosed by /* */. Observe the declarations made at the beginning of the algorithm. Such a declaration is required to specify the registers, flip-flops, counters, etc. used in the digital system. The notation $MD$ [3 . . 0] indicated that the register $MD$ is a 4-bit register with the least significant bit $MD_0$ and the most significant bit $MD_3$. The declaration concatenated register uses the symbol dot (.) to indicate that the registers $AC$ [4 . . 0] and $MQ$ [3 . . 0] may be assumed to be joined together as one unit and called $R$. Observe that $R$ is not a new register but is a name used for convenience of description. $R_7 = AC_3$ and $R_0 = MQ_0$. The declaration counter $C$ [2 . . 0] declares that $C$ is a 3-bit counter. Operation such as shift left (SHL), shift right (SHR) are allowed with registers. Operations of increment (INCR), decrement (DECR), clear (CLR) are valid for counters. Concatenated registers may be shifted left or right. In such a case the system will shift the bits belonging to the individual registers which make up the concatenated register.

**Declarations**

Registers: MD [3 . . 0], MQ [3 . . 0], AC [4 . . 0]
Concatenated register: R [8 . . 0]: = AC [4 . . 0]. MQ [3 . . 0]
Flip-flops: SM, SR, SMD, BUSY, SMQ /* SMD stores the sign of multiplicand, SMQ the
                                        sign of multiplier and SR the sign of result */

Counter: C [2 . . 0]
**Procedure**
$T_0$: [*if* SM *then* {MD ← input; MQ ← input; AMD ← input, SMQ ← input AC ← 0;
          SR ← 0; C ← 0; *Busy* ← 1;}
      *else* $T_0$]
$T_1$: [*if* MQ$_0$ *then* AC ← AC + MD/* This is parallel addition. After completion the
    system goes to $T_2$ automatically */]
$T_2$: [SHR R; INCR C;
    *if* C$_2$ *then* {SR ← SMQ ⊕ SMD; SM ← 0; BUSY ← 0; $T_0$}
      *else* $T_1$]

**Fig. 6.9 ASM chart of multiplier expressed in a hardware description language.**

Observe that the algorithm of Figure 6.9 is a straightforward representation of the procedure depicted in the ASM chart of Figure 6.8. The most important additions are the set of declarations defining various registers, counters and flip-flops. This algorithm is very useful in synthesizing the logic diagram of the multiplier. We will do this later in this chapter.

We now express the ASM chart of Figure 6.5 as an algorithm in Figure 6.10.

**Declarations**

    Register: X [ 3. . 0], Y [3 . . 0]

    Counter: C [1 . . 0]

    Flip-flops: A, B, E

**Procedure**

    $T_0$: [X ← input; Y ← input;

        A ← 0; B ← 0; E ← 0; C ← 0]

    $T_1$: [*if* $X_3$ *then*

            {*if* $Y_3$ *then* $T_2$

                *else* A ← 1; exit}

           *else* {*if* $Y_3$ *then* B ← 1; exit;

                *else* $T_2$]

    $T_2$: [INCR C; SHL X; SHL Y;

       *if* $C_1 \cdot C_0$ *then* E ← 1; exit

            *else* $T_1$]

**Fig. 6.10  Algorithm for a comparator.**

The ASM chart for a 4-bit serial adder (Figure 6.6) is expressed as an algorithm in Figure 6.11.

**Declarations**

    Register : A[3..0], B [3..0]

    Counter:  Q [2..0]

    Flip-flops: C, S

**Procedure**

    $T_0$: [*if* S *then* {A ← input; B ← input; C ← 0; Q ← 0}

         *else* $T_0$]

    $T_1$ : [SHR A; SHR B; $A_3$ ← C ⊕ ($A_0$ ⊕ $B_0$);

       C ← $A_0 \cdot B_0$ + $A_0 \cdot C$ + $B_0 \cdot C$; INCR Q;

       *if* $Q_2$ {*then* S ← 0; $T_0$}

          *Else* $T_1$ ]

**Fig. 6.11  Algorithm for a 4-bit serial adder.**

## 6.4 DESIGNING DIGITAL SYSTEMS USING ASM CHART

**Synthesizing comparator from its ASM chart:** Designing a digital system from an ASM chart is straightforward. We illustrate the method using comparator ASM chart (Figure 6.5) as the first example. We perform the following steps:

1. Draw a controller box (see Figure 6.12). The inputs to the controller are the variables appearing in condition boxes of the ASM chart and the outputs are the labels of the state boxes. For the ASM chart of Figure 6.5 the inputs are $X_3$, $Y_3$ and $C_1 \cdot C_0$. The outputs are $T_0$, $T_1$ and $T_2$. The controller is synthesized using the method presented in Chapter 4. We will do the synthesis at the end.

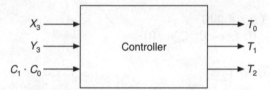

**Figure 6.12 Inputs and outputs of controller of a comparator.**

2. The data processor consists of the registers and the flip-flops which appear in state boxes and decision boxes. For the ASM chart of Figure 6.5 the registers are $X$ and $Y$. $C$ is a 2-bit counter. $A$, $B$ and $E$ are flip-flops.

3. The entire system is driven by a single clock. The operations on registers indicated in the state boxes in ASM are controlled by the controller output corresponding to that state. In Figure 6.10 which is the algorithm corresponding to the ASM chart the operations on the registers $X$ and $Y$, the counter $C$ and the flip-flops $A$, $B$ and $E$ are indicated.

4. The operations on the registers, flip-flops, etc. indicated in the decision boxes are controlled by both the state in which the operations take place and the path from the condition box. This is shown in Figure 6.13.

5. The controller is synthesized as follows. The controller outputs are $T_0$, $T_1$, $T_2$. They are the three states of the algorithmic state machine. The transitions from state $T_0$ to $T_1$ as well as from state $T_1$ to $T_2$ are governed by the ASM algorithm represented by the ASM chart of Figure 6.5 and the equivalent algorithm of Figure 6.10. In the chart we have coded the states $T_0$, $T_1$ and $T_2$ by the binary tuples 00, 01, 11 respectively. By inspection of the algorithm of Figure 6.10 we see that the transition from $T_0$ to $T_1$ is unconditional. The transition from $T_1$ to $T_2$ takes place either when both $X_3$ and $Y_3$ are true or when both $X_3$ and $Y_3$ are false. In other words, the transition from $T_1$ to $T_2$ takes place when $X_3 \cdot Y_3 + \bar{X}_3 \cdot \bar{Y}_3$ is true. Again by inspection of the algorithm (Figure 6.10) we see that $T_2$ to $T_1$ transition happens when $C_1 \cdot C_0$ is true. These state transitions are represented by the state

transition diagram of Figure 6.14. This is used to synthesize the controller. We need two flip-flops $P$ and $Q$ to represent states $T_0$, $T_1$, $T_2$. The controller is synthesized using the method explained in Chapter 4. We obtain the block diagram for the controller shown in Figure 6.15.

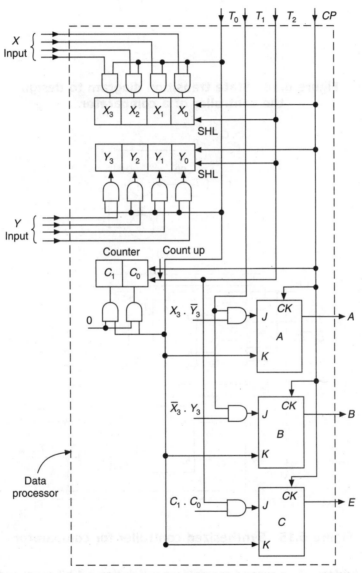

**Figure 6.13  Data processor block diagram for a comparator.**

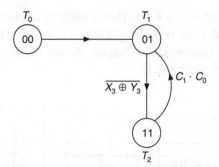

**Figure 6.14   State transition diagram to design the controller of a comparator.**

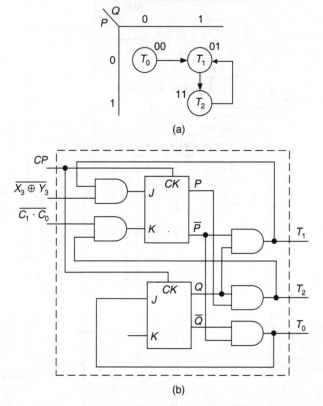

(a)

(b)

**Figure 6.15   Synthesized controller for comparator.**

**A 4-bit serial adder:**   As a second example we will design a 4-bit serial adder whose ASM chart is given in Figure 6.6. The algorithm for the adder corresponding to this ASM chart was given in Figure 6.11. By inspection of the algorithm we see that the synthesis of the data processing part of the algorithm is straightforward and is shown in Figure 6.16. Observe that a signal $T_0 = 1$ corresponding to state $T_0$ loads $A$ and $B$ registers, clears the carry flip-flop and the counter. The counter will have three bits as four clock pulses are needed for adding four bits and the fifth clock pulse indicates end of addition, resetting the system to start another add operation. Observe also that a full adder is used to add a pair of bits and carry (if any) during each clock pulse. The sum will have four or five bits. The carry bit (if any) will be in the carry flip-flop and the four bits of the sum will replace the augend bits in the $A$ register. During this state $T_1 = 0$. The addition operation takes place when $T_1 = 1$. $T_0$ is to be sent to 0 during this phase.

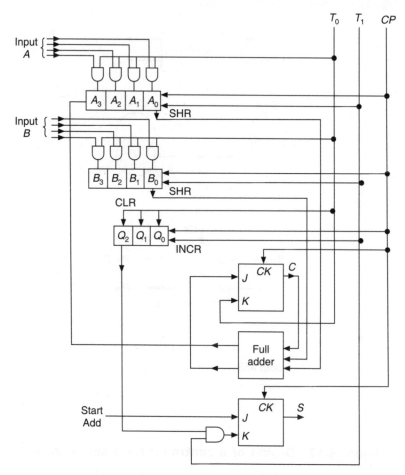

**Figure 6.16   A 4-bit serial adder.**

Once the data processor is designed, the next step is to design the controller to generate the control signals. In order to do this we observe that an external start signal will set flip-flop $S$. This flip-flop output is needed as an input to the controller. The end of the add operation is indicated when $Q_2$ (the most significant bit of the counter) becomes 1. This is also needed as the second control input. The controller of this adder has only two outputs $T_0$ and $T_1$ [see Figure 6.17(a)]. The state transition chart is very simple and is shown in Figure 6.17(b). As there are only two states we need only one flip-flop to synthesize the controller. This is shown in Figure 6.17(c). Observe that the flip-flop $P$ (which is the controller) is set when $S = 1$ making $T_0 = 1$ which loads registers $A$ and $B$ and clears flip-flops $C$ and $Q_2$. When $Q_2$ is cleared $Q_2$ becomes zero. The signal $\bar{Q_2}$ clears flip-flop $P$ making $T_1 = 1$ which initiates the addition process [see Figure 6.17(c)]. A flip-flop $S$ has as its $J$ input "Start Add" signal which initiates addition process. When addition of four bits is completed, $Q_2$ becomes 1 and $T_1 = 1$. This signal is used to reset flip-flop $S$. Till the next "Start Add" signal, the adder will be in idle state.

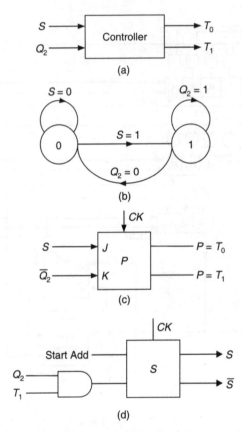

**Figure 6.17    Design of a controller for a serial adder.**

**A 4-bit Multiplier:**    We first refer to the schematic of a 4-bit multiplier (Figure 6.7). The ASM chart showing the sequence of operation is given in Figure 6.8. The corresponding algorithm is given in Figure 6.9. Using these we have to synthesize the multiplier.

The data processor without the control paths is obtained using the declarations. The controller has two inputs, namely SM the output of a flip-flop which is set when "Start Multiply" signal is given (Figure 6.18) and $C_2$. When flip-flop $SM$ is set and the multiplication operation starts in the $T_0$ state, another flip-flop called BUSY flip-flop is set to 1 to indicate that multiplication is in progress. This flip-flop is cleared at the end of multiplication operation which is indicated when $C_2$ bit of the counter becomes 1.

There are three more flip-flops, *SMQ* to store the sign of the multiplier, *SMD* that of the multiplicand and *SR* that of the result. The signs *SMQ* and *SMD* are loaded and *SR* cleared during $T_0$. In the diagram for data processor (Figure 6.7) parallel transfer of bits from registers is shown by putting a slash across the data path and putting a number 4 adjoining it to show that there are four lines running in parallel. The adder in this implementation is a parallel adder which adds the multiplicand bits with the partial product stored in *ACC · MQ* (concatenated) register.

The controller has two inputs *SM* and $C_2$, the predicates which cause transitions between states in the multiplication algorithm (see Figure 6.9). The outputs are $T_0$, $T_1$ and $T_2$. The controller is synthesized using the state-transition diagram shown in Figure 6.19. Observe that $T_1$ to $T_2$ transition is automatic and takes place with clock. This controller uses this flip-flop and its synthesis is straightforward using the procedure explained in Chapter 4. This is left as an exercise to the student. The multiplier logic diagram including the control paths is shown in Figure 6.18. Observe that during $T_0$ the operands are loaded and flip-flops

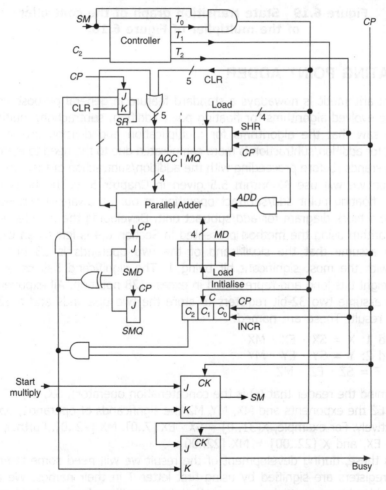

**Figure 6.18  A four-bit serial multiplier.**

cleared. During $T_1$ addition takes place and result stored in $ACC \cdot MQ$. During $T_2$ the sign of the result is set and the *SM* and BUSY flip-flops are cleared.

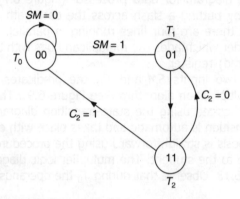

**Figure 6.19 State transition graph of the controller
of the multiplier of Figure 6.18.**

## 6.5 FLOATING POINT ADDER

Floating point arithmetic is nowadays a standard feature in general purpose computers. In Chapter 5 we evolved algorithms for floating point addition, subtraction, multiplication and division. We saw that the algorithms for multiplication and division are straightforward whereas that for addition/subtraction is more complicated due to the need to match exponents of the two operands (before proceeding with the addition/subtraction of the two significands). In this section we will use Algorithm 5.5 given in Chapter 5 as the basis to obtain an algorithm for floating point add/subtract operation in our hardware description language. We then give a block diagram for add/subtract unit. Developing the detailed logic diagram from the algorithm using the method presented in Section 6.4 is left as an exercise to the student. We assume that the significand of the two operands is 23 bits long and is normalized with the most significant bit being 1. The significand has its own sign. The exponent is eight bits long and represented in excess 128 notation. All exponents >128 are positive. We assume two 32-bit registers to store the two operands and a 32-bit register to store the result. These are named:

Operand 1: X = SX · EX · MX
Operand 2: Y = SY · EY · MY
Result: Z = SZ · EZ · MZ

(We remind the reader that (·) is the concatenation operator), SX, SY, SZ are the sign bits, EX, EY, EZ the exponents and MX, MY, MZ the signficands of operand1, operand 2 and result respectively. For example, X[31..0] = SX · EX [7..0]. MX [22..0]. Further, X[31] = SX, X[30...23] = EX, and X [22..00] = MX [22..00].

Besides these, during development of the result we will need some temporary registers. These registers are signified by using first letter *T* in their names. We assume sign magnitude add/subtract and also assume that the significands are added or subtracted using a parallel adder/subtractor. The algorithm is given in Figure 6.20.

**Declarations**

Registers:    MX[22..0], MY[22..0],
              TEMP [23..0], EX[7..0], EY[7..0], EZ[7..0],
              TED[7..0], TEXP[8..0]
              /*TEMP, TED and TEXP store intermediate results */

Flip-flops:   SX, SY, SZ, OP /*OP = 1 for Add, OP = 0 for subtract */
              SA, /*Start operation.*/ ERROR /* Set to 1 if overflow or
              underflow error */

Counter:      C[7..0] /* used to count shifts of significand */

Concatenated registers:    X = SX. EX. MX, Y = SY. EY. MY,
                           Z = SZ . EZ. MZ

**Procedure**

$T_0$: [*if* SA *then* { X ← input; Y ← input; TEMP ← 0;
                  TED ← 0; TEXP ← 0; C ← 0; ERROR ← 0;
                  BUSY → 1} *else* $T_0$]

$T_1$: [*if* MX = 0 *then* Z ← Y; SA ← 0; BUSY ← 0; $T_0$]

$T_2$: [*if* MY = 0 *then* Z ← X; SA ← 0; BUSY ← 0; $T_0$]

$T_3$: [TED ← EX − EY] /*Subtract exponents parallel subtractor */

$T_4$: *if* (TED > 0) *then* [{ SHR MY by TED bits; TEXP ← EX}
                        *if* (MY = 0) *then* {Z ← X; SA ← 0; BUSY ← 0; $T_0$}]
    *else if* (TED < 0) *then* [{ SHR MX by TED bits; TEXP ← EY}
                        *if* (MX = 0) *then* {Z ← Y SA ← 0; BUSY ← 0; $T_0$}]

/* we have not shown details of shifting register. It is done by first setting counter
C to a value equal to TED and shifting mantissa TED bits */

/*In $T_3$ and $T_4$ significands are aligned. Addition of signed significands can now
proceed */

$T_5$: [*if* (OP = 1) *then* SY ← $\overline{SY}$]

$T_6$: [*if* (SX = SY) *then*
      {TEMP[23..0] ← MX + MY; SZ ← SX}
          *else if* (MX > MY) *then* {TEMP(23..0) ← MX − MY; SZ ← SX}
                          *else* {TEMP (23..0) ← MY − MX; SZ ← SY}]

$T_7$: [*if* TEMP[23] = 1 *then* {SHR TEMP; TEXP ← TEXP + 1}]

$T_8$: [*if* TEXP[8] = 1 *then* {ERROR ← 1; SA ← 0; BUSY ← 0; $T_0$}
              *else* $T_{11}$

$T_9$: [*if* TEMP[22] = 0 *then* {SHL TEMP; TEXP ← TEXP − 1}]

$T_{10}$: [*if* TEMP [22] = 1 *then* $T_{11}$
                  *else if* (TEXP > 0) *then* $T_9$
                              *else* {ERROR ← 1; SA ← 0; BUSY ← 0; $T_0$}]

/* $T_9$ and $T_{10}$ are used to normalize result significand. If in this process TEXP < 0
it indicates underflow error */

$T_{11}$: [EZ ← TEXP; MZ ← TEMP; Z ← SZ . EZ . MZ; SA ← 0; BUSY ← 0; $T_0$]

**Fig. 6.20  Algorithm for floating point add/subtract using a
hardware description language.**

Block diagram for a floating point adder/subtractor is developed using the algorithm given in Fig. 6.20.

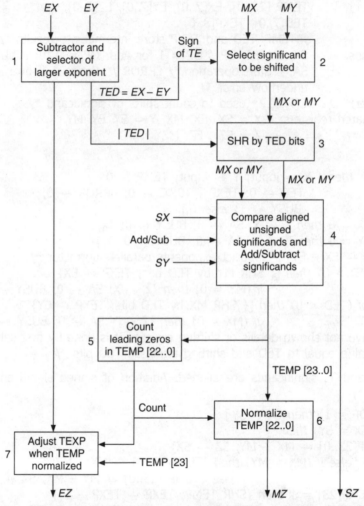

**Figure 6.21  Floating point add/subtract using block diagram.**

The major blocks of the hardware are numbered in Figure 6.21. Their functions are explained in what follows:

*Block 1:*   A subtractor which computes $TED = (EX - EY)$. From this computation we can find the larger exponent. The significand of the operand with the smaller exponent has to be shifted right a number of bits equal to the magnitude of the difference $TED$. $TED$ is added to its exponent. In the algorithms step $T_3$ finds $TED$.

*Block 2:*   The significand to be shifted right is picked in box 2. If $TED > 0$, $MY$ is shifted else $MX$ is shifted.

*Block 3:* This block shifts right the signficand of the operand with the smaller exponent by *TED* bits and adds *TED* to its exponent. The functions of box 2 and 3 are performed in the algorithm of Figure 6.20 in step $T_4$.

*Block 4:* The exponents have been made equal and thus add/subtract can proceed. The magnitudes of the two operands are compared and depending on whether the operation is add or subtract signfiicands are added/subtracted. Steps $T_5$ and $T_6$ perform this in the algorithm (Figure 6.20).

*Block 5:* At the end of add/subtract operation the result stored in TEMP[23..0] would be unnormalized. It may either have an overflow bit in TEMP[23] or TEMP [22, 21 .. etc.] may be 0s. In the former case, TEMP should be shifted right by 1 bit and 1 added to TEXP. In the latter case, the number of leading 0s in TEMP has to be found and TEMP shifted left till TEMP[22] is 1. Block 5 counts leading 0s.

*Block 6:* Normalization of TEMP is performed in this block. The output of this block is the normalized significand of the result of add/subtract.

*Block 7:* This block adjusts the value of TEXP. It adds 1 to TEXP if TEMP[23] = 1. It subtracts from TEXP the number of left shifts of TEXP to normalize it. Its output is the exponent of the result of add/subtract.

The functions of blocks 5, 6 and 7 are performed by steps $T_7$, $T_8$, $T_9$ and $T_{10}$ as given in the algorithm Figure 6.20.

We will not develop hardware algorithms for floating point multiplication and division as they are much simpler. They are left as exercises for the student.

─────────────────( **SUMMARY** )─────────────────

1. A digital system consists of a data processor, which performs a sequence of operations that transform given inputs to outputs, and a controller that sequences the operations performed by the data processor.

2. An Algorithmic State Machine (ASM) chart is useful in describing and designing digital systems.

3. ASM is similar to a flow chart. It uses three symbols. A rectangle represents a sequence of operations such as SHR, INCR, LOAD, STORE, etc. A rhombus is used to indicate decisions taken and their outcome and a rectangle with rounded edges depicts operations performed when decisions are taken. Figure 6.2 shows the symbols. Rectangles are labelled with a symbol $T_i$ to indicate the "state" in which the operations are performed.

4. ASM chart is a generalization of state transition diagram used in sequential systems design. State transition diagram derived from ASM chart is useful in designing control logic of digital systems.

5. Examples 6.1, 6.2 and 6.3 describe how ASM charts are obtained for a comparator, serial adder and a 4-bit multiplexer.

6.  ASM charts are useful to describe the algorithm used in a notation similar to a programming language. Such languages are widely used to design digital systems and are known as Hardware Description Language (HDL). Two of the widely used languages are known as VHDL (Very High Speed Integrated Circuit Hardware Description Language) and Verilog. They are quite complex.

7.  An algorithm in a hardware description language has two major parts: a declaration part which specifies registers used (with their lengths), flip-flops, counters and concatenated registers (if any), and a procedure part which specifies actions to be carried out one after the other. Each action is specified by a labelled statement which would take place normally in one clock period. The labels are clock times. An action has a number of operations which are carried out simultaneously. An operation is typically moving the contents of a register to another, SHR, SHL, Increment a counter, etc. Another important operation is carrying out an action (*if* condition *then* action 1 *else* action 2) which performs one of two alternative actions.

8.  The steps in design consists of:

    (i)   Obtaining an ASM chart using requirement specifications.

    (ii)  Expressing it using a HDL

    (iii) Design a controller whose inputs are conditions appearing in *if then else* statements and outputs are the clock times which are labels $T_0$, $T_1$, etc. of HDL statements.

    (iv)  Controller is synthesized using state-transition diagram.

    (v)   The timing signals obtained from the controller drive the data processor which consists of registers, counters, etc., specified in the declarations of HDL and used in each HDL statement.

9.  We have illustrated the above procedure by designing three sequential arithmetic and logic limits, namely a comparator, an adder and a multiplexer.

10. Floating point add/subtract unit is a challenging system to design. In this chapter we have developed a procedure in a hardware description language for such a unit using the algorithm described in Chapter 5. We also give a hardware block diagram which is evolved using the HDL description of a floating point adder/subtractor.

──────────────────────────( **EXERCISES** )──────────────────────────

1.  Obtain an ASM chart for a serial adder/subtract unit for 8-bit integers. Assume 2's complement for subtract.

2.  Obtain a HDL for Exercise 1.

3.  Obtain a logic circuit for adder/subtractor using Exercises 1 and 2.

4.  Obtain an ASM chart for an integer divider for 4-bit operands. Use registers used for multiplier.

5.  Obtain a HDL for Exercise 4.

6.  Obtain a logic circuit for a divider using results of Exercises 4 and 5.

7. Obtain an ASM chart for a floating point multiplier. Use 32-bit representation of floating point numbers used in the text for add/subtract.

8. Obtain a HDL corredponding to ASM chart of Exercise 7.

9. Obtain logic circuit for a floating point multiplier.

10. Obtain an ASM chart for a floating point divider with 32-bit floating point numbers using representation used in the text.

11. Obtain a HDL corresponding to ASM of Exercise 10.

12. Obtain logic circuit for a floating point divider.

13. Using HDL for floating point adder/subtractor given in Figure 6.20 of the text develop a logic circuit for the same.

14. Modify the HDL description for floating point adder/subtractor given in Figure 6.20 of the text if IEEE 754 representation for 32-bit floating point numbers is used.

15. Obtain a logic diagram for a floating point adder/subtractor using hardware description language algorithm of Figure 6.20.

# 7

# Computer Systems—Multiple Views

---

In this chapter we will learn:

☞ How to view a computer system from the perspectives of end users, system and application programmers, and hardware designers.

☞ How to view a computer system as a layered system with the facilities provided by lower layers being used by higher layers.

☞ How to measure the performance of computing systems.

## 7.1 INTRODUCTION

The ultimate goal of designing computers is to use them for solving problems. Today low cost personal computers are available in plenty at homes and work places. Powerful supercomputers can be accessed from remote terminals through communication networks. Computers are more widely used now than ever before, not only by specialists but also by casual users for a variety of applications. Because of the widespread use of computers, ease of use has become more important than efficiency of computation. Further, the complexity of application programs has increased enormously. Thus, many application programs consist of tens of thousands of lines of code and sometimes even millions of lines of code. From the end users' perspective, the number of lines of code is irrelevant. Users interact with the application program which is in a "black box" hidden from their view by using a user interface which is very often graphical. Thus, how easy it is to use an application with the given user interface is their greatest concern. Application designers, thus have to cater to this requirement. Hence the system software and hardware should have facilities to implement an appropriate user interface which in today's context may be graphical, audio or even video.

To solve problems using computers, we need two major entities: **data**—which suitably represent the relevant details of the problems to be solved in a form that is manipulatable by computers; and **algorithms**—which systematically transform the input data using a step-by-step method and give the desired output. We need a language to describe algorithms. We also need high level data structures. They are structured collections consisting of primitive data elements such as integers, reals, booleans, and/or ASCII characters described in Chapter 1. A language used for describing algorithms meant for execution on computers, is known as a **Programming Language**. It is a formal language which is very different from a natural language such as English. Every statement of a formal language is interpreted by the computer hardware in exactly one way. Thus such a language has precisely defined syntax and unambiguous semantics.

Programming languages are classified into two levels: lower level or systems programming level (also known as assembly language level) and higher level or application programming level. The system software is actually a collection of software subsystems, which includes language translators, linkers, loaders and supervising programs which are collectively known as **Operating Systems** or **OS**. An OS is responsible for the orderly management of diverse system resources that we will study in the following chapters. An algorithm expressed in a programming language is called a **program**. A program consists of several statements each of which performs an *operation* on some *data.* The operation is very primitive at the hardware level: add, subtract, compare, move data from one register to another, test if a particular bit is ON or OFF, etc. Using these primitive operations and well-organized data representations, an application software designer builds higher level operations. For example, when a computer system is used for railway reservation, a higher level operation could be "Book a one-way ticket from place A to place B by train C for the date D in first class". It is the responsibility of the application designer to develop a clear specification for all the relevant higher level operations pertinent to the domain of application.

Lastly, the application and system software execute using the hardware of the computer. The hardware designer must design the system in such a way that system and application programmers have available to them features which ease program and user interface development.

## 7.2    A LAYERED VIEW OF A COMPUTER SYSTEM

Often a computer system is viewed as consisting of several layers. Usually the higher layers depend upon the facilities provided by the lower layers. Each layer may be independently designed as their purposes are different. However, when higher layers are designed, the facilities provided by the lower layers should be clearly specified.

A computer system can be viewed as a layered system (see Figure 7.1). We will now examine the various layers and how they are to be taken into account while designing a digital computer system.

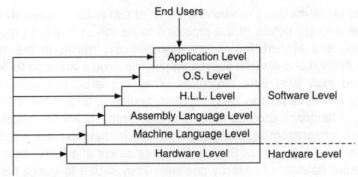

Special access to System Designers

**Figure 7.1   A layered view of a computer system.**

## 7.2.1  Hardware Level

The classical model of a computer hardware system consists of five basic subsystems:

1. Input
2. Output
3. Memory
4. Processor
5. Control

These subsystems communicate with each other by transferring data and control signals among themselves as shown in Figure 7.2. In this figure the solid lines denote the data flow and the dotted lines denote the control flow.

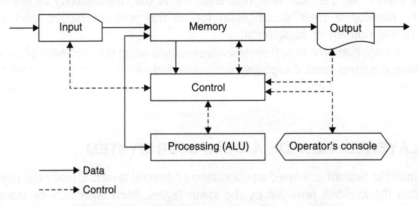

——→ Data

-----→ Control

**Figure 7.2   Block diagram of a computer.**

As a computer system is used to solve a problem, it is necessary to feed data relevant to the problem. This is done via the input unit. The results obtained by solving the problem must be sent to the person (or even a machine) who gave the problem. This is done by an output unit. The memory subsystem is needed to store data as well as the program. The processor is required to transform the data using the primitive operations which the hardware is designed to perform. The control subsystem is needed to correctly sequence the execution of various steps of the algorithm. It should be noted that the steps of an algorithm are stored in and fetched from memory. That is why we have the solid line in Figure 7.2, drawn from memory to control. The processing unit performs arithmetic and logic (AND, OR, NOT) operations and thus it is also known as **Arithmetic** and **Logic Unit** or **ALU**. Sometimes we refer to the combination of processing and control units as CPU.

We note in Figure 7.2 that memory is the "heart" of this hardware organization. A program is stored in memory and the data on which it operates is also stored in memory. Instructions from this program are fetched by the control subsystem one after another and executed by the ALU. Memory being at the heart of the organization, we can redraw Figure 7.2 as shown in Figure 7.3. In this memory-centred organization, we have explicitly shown communication media called **buses**. Two buses are shown in this figure and both of them are bi-directional. The I/O bus connects the input/output subsystems to memory and CPU. The processor bus connects the CPU to memory. CPU is made of LSI and VLSI electronic components and operates at the rate of tens of mega hertz. On the other hand, the I/O is made of electro-mechanical and electro-optical components and thus operates at several kilo hertz. Figure 7.3 brings out an important issue in computer design. We see that there are two entities which communicate with memory. Their speeds are very different (ratio of 1 to 1000). Both entities may require the services of memory (READ or WRITE) simultaneously. How should we deal with this speed mismatch? How do we resolve the conflict which may arise if both the units attempt to access memory simultaneously? The computer hardware designers and the system software designers together should address these two questions. We will see later in this book how these problems are satisfactorily solved.

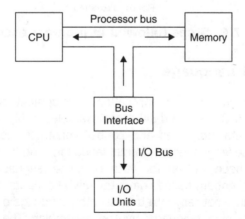

**Figure 7.3   Bus structure memory centred organization.**

## 7.2.2   Machine and Assembly Language Levels

The lowest level in the hierarchy of languages is the **machine language**. This language is specific to (dependent on) the hardware design of a computer. In the next chapter, we present in detail how to write a machine language program. The assembly language is one step higher in the hierarchy, and it allows symbolic references to data, operations, and memory addresses. The various steps followed in the translation and execution of a program are shown in Figure 7.4. The **assembler** is a system software that translates a symbolic assembly language program into a machine language format and produces what is called a **LINK module**. This form of program representation is convenient for linking selected pre-compiled programs with the currently translated link module to form one composite **LOAD module**. The job of Loader software is to load the given composite load module into the memory (RAM) starting from a specified starting address in memory. Once the machine language program is loaded into the main memory, it is ready for execution.

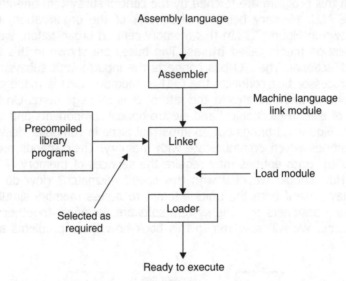

**Figure 7.4   Steps followed in program execution.**

## 7.2.3   Higher Level Language

The most widely used languages for application development are the higher level languages. FORTRAN, Pascal, C, C++ and JAVA are examples of higher level languages. Such languages have richer data structures and control constructs compared to assembly or machine languages. These languages are formal languages and hence automatic translators called **compilers** have been written for each of these languages. For example, the C compiler written for Intel Pentium-based computer will take inputs that are programs written in C and translate them automatically into the assembly language of Pentium which will then be translated to the machine language by the assembler. The translated or compiled program can be stored in memory and executed. The compilers are also programs, although a special class of programs. Hence, they are also stored in memory.

For a given computer system, there are several compilers to facilitate the users to develop application programs in the languages that are suitable for them. Compilers are thus one important software resource of a computer system. If we add up the storage needed by all compilers, it is quite large.

As the demand for storage is very high in a modern computer system, there are at least two kinds of memories: Primary memory or **Random Access Memory** (RAM) and Secondary memory (for example) disks. Disks are much cheaper than RAMs and hence it is cost effective to have billions of bytes (GB for giga bytes) of disk storage in a computer. When a large disk storage is available, several users of a computer system can keep their large data files in them. Thus, disk space is yet another resource that is shared by users. It should therefore be properly managed, that is, allocated and deallocated to users.

## 7.2.4 Operating System Level

The main purpose of an **operating system** (abbreviated OS) is to effectively manage the hardware and software resources of a computer system. Suppose a computer system is capable of executing one million "typical" instructions per second; and an average user requires execution speed of 100,000 typical instructions per second for his application. Then ten such users can, in theory, time share this computer. In such time shared computers, the processing power becomes another resource to be managed by the OS. In order to facilitate such time shared use, the size of the RAM of the computer should be large enough to store several programs at the same time. The CPU, under the control of the OS scheduler, will switch from the execution of one program to another program, possibly in a round robin fashion. When many programs have to be resident in memory and the system has to switch between programs, memory becomes yet another resource to be managed.

Consider a particular instant of time *t* during the operation of a time shared computer system. Assume that the system is shared by 4 users' programs A, B, C, and D. At this instant *t*, let us suppose C is running, A and B are blocked or waiting for some external events to take place, and D is ready to run if it gets the CPU. We will use the two terms program and process synonymously. A state diagram showing the state changes of a process is shown in Figure 7.5. In this diagram we have abstracted a large number of states

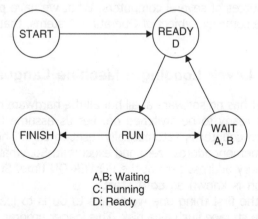

A,B: Waiting
C: Running
D: Ready

**Figure 7.5  State diagram of process.**

of a process into three major states: WAIT, READY, and RUN. Moreover, let us assume that programs A, B, C and D (in our example) together require 512 KB memory and they are mapped into the RAM as shown in Figure 7.6. The state of the system at *t* is: A-WAIT; B-WAIT; C-RUN; D-READY. The OS scheduler, according to some scheduling scheme will decide which process and when it should go into the RUN state. As there is only one CPU, only one process can be in the RUN state at a given time. One of the simplest scheduling policies is called **round-robin scheduling**. In this policy, each process in the READY state is cyclically given a fixed quantum of time for running. Irrespective of the scheduling policy used, the OS has to switch the execution from one process to another.

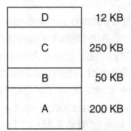

| D | 12 KB |
| C | 250 KB |
| B | 50 KB |
| A | 200 KB |

**Figure 7.6   A memory map.**

The process switching operation has to first save the state of the currently running process. After this, it should load a process in the READY state and make it ready to RUN. In the following chapters, we will study in detail what constitutes the process state and how to design the hardware to make process switching efficient.

So far we have examined a single isolated computer. Now-a-days it is rare to find an isolated computer. Computers in organizations are interconnected using a Local Area Network (LAN). Widely-dispersed computers are connected using a Wide Area Network (WAN). Often to solve compute intensive problems, the resources of several computers connected to a network are used. In such a case an operating system becomes much more complex as it has to manage the resources of several computers. What we have presented in this section is only the flavour of the complex subject of Operating Systems, that too of a single isolated computer.

## 7.2.5   Application Level: Loading a Machine Language Program

Consider a computer that has no software at all but all the hardware design and development are completed and it is ready to be switched on. Let us assume that when the power is switched on the program counter is automatically reset to zero. The computer would then fetch the instruction at memory address zero and execute it. So, what happens is determined by the contents of memory address zero at the POWER-ON time. Starting a computer from its POWER-OFF condition is known as **cold start**.

At the cold start, the first thing one would like to do is to load a program called the **loader** from the back-up storage such as a disk. This loader program will read the operating system software, which is also resident on the disk, and load it into the main memory. Then control will be transferred to the operating system software. The program that loads the loader is normally referred to as the **boot-strap loader**. A boot-strap loader is a simple machine language program that would read the loader program, sector by sector from a fixed place in the disk and load it in the memory, starting at some predetermined address.

The boot-strap loader itself could be loaded into memory in two ways. One method would be to store the boot-strap loader permanently starting at the address zero in a small ROM or non-volatile portion of the memory. Upon cold start this program can be automatically executed. The second method would be to enter a very small program, usually a few instructions, in machine language, through console switches of the machine, and execute them. This program would load the boot-strap loader from a standard input device, which in turn will take care of further loading. As ROMs are inexpensive, the latter method is not used any more.

In the case of many pocket computers or personal computers, the operating systems software or the loader is small enough to be stored in a ROM. Upon cold start this ROM-based program is executed and then the machine is fully active. A loader may be classified into any of the following categories according to its versatility and capabilities:

1. Absolute loader
2. Relocating loader
3. Linking loader

The absolute loader is the simplest of all the loaders. It can read a machine language program from the specified backup storage and place it in memory starting from a predetermined memory address (Figure 7.7). The machine language program so loaded will work correctly only if it is loaded starting from the specified address. In Figure 7.7(a) we have shown an example in which the absolute loader is in addresses 0000 to 00EE of memory and the loaded program starts at address 0100 and extends up to 01FF. If the only purpose of a loader is to load the operating system at cold start, one may be contented with an absolute loader. But multiprogramming makes it necessary to have relocatable loaders.

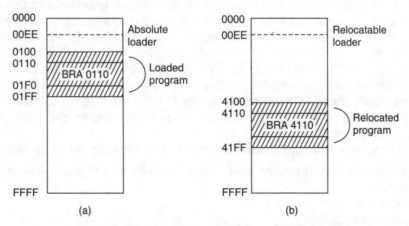

**Figure 7.7 Loading program in memory**

Consider a user program that was loaded in memory from the address 0100 to 01FF and was running. After some time for some reason it was moved from memory to a disk and then reloaded. But when reloading, the program is relocated in memory addresses 4100 to 41FF (see Figure 7.7(b)). A loader that can relocate programs is known as a **relocating loader**. When a program is relocated, a set of instruction addresses that are dependent upon the starting address of the program have to be properly modified. A dictionary consisting of such addresses is known as **relocation dictionary** or **RLD**. One such relocation table is shown in Figure 7.7(a). In this example, by adding 10 to the base address (0100) of the program, the branch address is correctly generated. The branch instruction itself is located at the F0-th address from the beginning address 0100 of the program. Hence the address F0 will be contained in the RLD. When relocatable programs are generated, the program translator (assembler or compiler) assumes the base address of the program to be 0, without loss of generality.

So far we have assumed the simple case of loading a program that existed as one unit. In developing a large application program, it is quite common that several modules will be developed independently and finally they are all linked together. Each such module is called an **object module** (Figure 7.8). The loader which can link several such object modules to obtain one relocatable program for loading is known as a **linking loader**.

**Figure 7.8   An object module.**

An object module contains the program code, RLD, and an **external symbol dictionary** or ESD. The ESD of the module M is a table of symbols (i.e., addresses of data, entry points, and subroutines) defined in M and accessed by other modules. It may also contain the symbols referenced in M but defined elsewhere in other modules. The linking loader will merge the ESDs of all the modules together, put the programs of the modules in some linear order, and then resolve the undefined addresses by referring to the ESDs. It will also combine and modify the RLDs into one composite RLD for the final relocatable module. The reader is encouraged to read the references given at the end of the book for detailed discussions on linking loaders.

The term system software is used to refer to the following set of software systems:

1. Operating system (memory management, scheduler, I/O management)
2. Compilers
3. Assemblers
4. Loaders and Linkers

The above list is not exhaustive. A software system to manage large files is also sometimes included in this list.

## 7.3 PERFORMANCE MEASURES

The cost of a computer for a specified performance is an important criterion when one buys a computer. Thus, a computer designer must understand performance measures used by industry and user community and try to obtain the best performance for a given cost. Measuring the performance of a computer system is not an easy task because a computer is a very complex system consisting of hardware (processor, memory, disk) and software (compilers, OS, etc.). The processor of a computer system has a master clock from which all timings are derived. The frequency of this clock is one simple parameter. A typical microcomputer of today has a clock frequency of 1 GHz (Giga Hertz per second). The time taken for one clock cycle in this case is 1 ns. The time taken to carry out an instruction is normally a multiple of clock cycles. It is very often quoted as x-cycles per instruction. Assume that a computer has $N$ instructions. Let $T_i$ be the time taken by the $i$th instruction. $T_i$ will be dependent on the instruction.

If we can determine, the frequency of usage of the various instructions, i.e. $f_i$ for $i = 1, 2, ..., N$, we can express $f_i$ as a fraction by the following equation

$$p_i = \left( f_i \middle/ \sum_{i=1}^{N} f_i \right)$$

The sum of all $p_i$s will be equal to 1. We can thus define the average instruction execution time $T$ as $T = \left( \sum_{i=1}^{N} p_i T_i \right)$ seconds. The main problem in using the above formula is the need to know $p_i$. The frequency of use of the $i$th instruction depends on the program chosen to measure it. The question to be addressed is: What sample program collections should we consider to measure these frequencies? Should we measure them statically by looking at the machine language programs, or should we measure them dynamically by counting the number of times various instructions are executed at the run-time? Questions like these are not easy to answer and they require extensive study. If we have a good idea of the type of applications for which a machine is to be designed, we can then estimate the $f_i$s and reduce $T_i$ for the most frequently used instructions. The reciprocal of $\overline{T}$ the average instruction execution time is commonly known as **MIPS rate** (Millions of Instructions Per Second). MIPS rate $= 1/\overline{T}$. The early PCs of the 1970s and 1980s had an MIPS rate less than 1 whereas the MIPS rates of current PCs of the 2000s range from 500 to 2000.

Although MIPS is easy to use as a measure, one should be careful in interpreting it. It is important to understand how $\overline{T}$ is obtained. If MIPS rates of two systems say C1 and C2 are compared, the larger MIPS does not automatically mean that it is a better machine. We should understand the similarities and differences of the instruction sets of C1 and C2 thoroughly and then examine the impact of their differences on the MIPS rate. To avoid problems of this type a System Performance Evaluation Cooperative, or SPEC, group was formed in 1988. SPEC has representatives of many computer companies such as DEC, HP, SUN, etc. Their objective was to "establish, maintain and endorse a standardized set of relevant benchmarks that can be applied to the next generation of high performance computers". They evolved a group of programs, typical of many computer applications, which are run to measure SPEC marks. SPEC marks measure not only the hardware efficiency of a machine but also the quality of compilers and system software. The SPEC group of programs is called **SPEC benchmark suite**.

In 1992 the SPEC benchmark suite was modified (called SPEC92) to provide separate sets of programs to measure integer and floating point performance. Currently these numbers are quoted by every computer manufacturer and often a manufacturer tries to design the hardware and software to obtain a high SPEC mark.

SPEC marks are appropriate for evaluating CPU power of programs run in a batch mode and do not consider the needs of interactive users such as clerks in railway booking offices working on-line with computers and databases to reserve tickets for customers. In this case several clerks share a computer and database. All of them require fast service. Each interactive request of a clerk and the response may be considered as a transaction. For such applications there are *transaction processing benchmarks.* Benchmarks known as TPC-A, TPC-B and TPC-C are commonly used by industry. These benchmarks have been evolved by the Transaction Processing Council (TPC) representing 40 computer and database vendors.

The availability of powerful computers has made it possible to simulate a proposed CPU. Benchmarks such as SPEC are used as data in the simulation. Results of simulation are used to optimise the design of CPUs.

We have given a brief introduction to the problem of performance evaluation in this section. The method used to evaluate performance must be remembered while designing computers.

In this chapter we brought out the point that the design of a computer involves examining a number of issues. These are the hardware components available to build the five subsystems, high level languages needed to use computers, the operating system which manages the computer's resources and the applications for which the machine will be used. Thus, while examining issues such as picking the instructions to be carried out by the machine and hardware features to be put in the machine, the close inter-relationship between applications, algorithms, programming languages, compilers, operating systems, performance and cost should be kept in view. This theme will recur throughout the rest of the book.

---

### SUMMARY

1. A computer system may be viewed from the perspective of end users, system and application programmers and hardware designers.

2. End users' primarily concern is ease of use and good user interfaces which may be graphical, audio and even video.

3. The main concern of system and application programmers is the facilities provided by the hardware which eases their task and enables them to develop error-free maintainable programs.

4. Hardware designer's concern is to provide the best design with currently available technology at reasonable cost.

5. A complex system such as a computer is usually viewed as consisting of several layers. Each layer may be independently designed. Higher layers depend on the services provided by the lower layers.

6. We can view a computer system as consisting of six layers. The lowest to highest layers are respectively hardware, machine language, assembly language, high level language, operating system and application programs.

7. A computer hardware system consists of five subsystems. They are Input, Output, Memory, Central Processing Unit and Control Unit. In the rest of this book we will describe each one of them in detail.

8. At the lowest level in the hierarchy of languages is machine language which consists of instructions provided by the hardware of the computer.

9. Assembly language uses mnemonics for hardware instructions and symbolic representation of memory address. It is a one-to-one representation of machine language.

10. High level languages provide users with facilities to express algorithms with ease.

11. An operating system is used to effectively manage hardware and software resources of a computer system. It has facilities to allow orderly execution of several users' programs concurrently in a computer system.

12. A loader is a machine language program which loads an initial program from a secondary store such as a disk to the main memory ready for execution. The loader itself is a small machine language program which is stored in a ROM.

13. CPU performance measures are used to assess the time taken to run application programs. Cost to speed ratio gives an indication of cost-benefit of a computer.

14. A set of typical programs representing a range of applications has been created as "benchmark programs" by a consortium of computer vendors and users. These are called SPEC benchmarks and are used to assess CPU speed.

15. SPEC application programs do not measure the efficiency of a computer system in transaction processing such as airline reservations, banking transactions, etc. For this class of problems another benchmark known as TPC (Transaction Processing Council) benchmarks are used.

---

## EXERCISES

1. What is the reason we view a computer system as consisting of several layers? What are the different layers?

2. What does a hardware layer consist of? What are the functions of the control unit of a computer?

3. What is the difference between a machine language and assembly language? What are the advantages of using assembly language instead of machine language?

4. When does one use a higher level language? When is assembly language preferred over a higher level language?

5. What is an operating system? Why is it needed? What are the functions of an operating system?

6. What is a loader? Why is it required?

7. What are the different categories of loaders? In what way do they differ?

8. What are the functions of a relocating loader? Why is it needed?

9. What are the main differences between a relocating loader and a linking loader?

10. What is a relocation directory? Why is it required? How is it used?

11. What is an object module? What does it consist of? Why is it necessary?

12. What is MIPS rate? Some professionals expand it as "meaningless index of processor speed". Are they justified in their interpretation? If yes explain.

13. What is SPEC marks? In what way is it different from MIPS?

14. How is SPEC marks used in designing CPUs of computers?

15. What is TPC benchmark? How does it differ from SPEC marks? When is it appropriate to use TPC benchmark?

# Chapter

# 8

# Basic Computer Organization

## Learning Goals

In this chapter we will learn:

☞ How stored program computers are organized.

☞ How machine language programs are stored in main memory, and how instructions are sequentially fetched and executed.

☞ Using a series of hypothetical computers, how an instruction set architecture is evolved based on application requirements.

## 8.1 INTRODUCTION

Real life, that is, commercially available computers are quite complex. In order to introduce the fundamentals of computer organization, it is traditional to start with a hypothetical small computer first and then systematically expand it to study the features of a real-life computer. Following this philosophy of learning, in this chapter we will introduce a hypothetical computer and call it SMAC (Small Computer). We will first introduce an elementary model of SMAC with minimum frills and a small set of instructions (S1). This introduction provides a programmer's view of a computer system at the level of the machine language. Trivial "machine language" programs may be written for SMAC using the small set of instructions, S1. The difficulties encountered in programming this computer to solve realistic problems will then become evident. In order to facilitate programming, we will expand the instruction set incrementally from S1 to S2 and then to S3. We will also add extra architectural features to SMAC organization in two steps and rename it as SMAC+ and then as SMAC++. Our objective is to make SMAC simple enough so that the students can build it in hardware in their hardware laboratory and make SMAC+ simple enough for students to simulate it using C++ or JAVA.

## 8.2 MEMORY ORGANIZATION OF SMAC (S1)

To start with, we will assume that the memory of SMAC is very tiny and consists of a number of addressable storage "boxes", also called **memory locations**. Each memory location will store 8 bits which we call a byte (8 bits). Let SMAC have only 16 bytes in memory and each byte is directly addressable by means of a 4-bit address ranging from 0000, 0001, 0010, ..., 1111. Later we will increase the size of the memory. There will be only two registers in SMAC called registers A and B.

Each byte in SMAC is treated as a word at this stage. One 8-bit word can store one "machine instruction" according to the following format:

1. Bits 0,1,2:    Represent one of the 8 possible instructions in the set S1.

2. Bit 3:         Denotes one of the two registers (0 means register A, 1 means register B)

3. Bits 4,5,6,7: Will address one of the 16 bytes in the SMAC memory.

The memory unit has an assembly of binary cells represented in Figure 8.1 as a matrix with 16 rows (one for each byte) and 8 columns (one column for each bit within a byte). There are two registers named MAR and MBR. The Memory Address Register (MAR) holds the address of the word in the memory to be accessed. In this case it will be a 4-bit register.

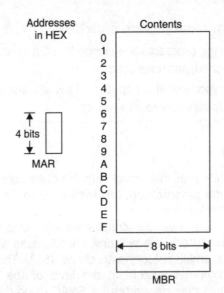

**Figure 8.1   A 16 byte memory.**

The data read from the memory or the data to be written in it, is held in the Memory Buffer Register (MBR) which is an 8-bit register. The operation to be performed, namely, reading from or writing into memory is initiated by a Read/Write signal which is sent by the Central Processing Unit (CPU). If the memory access is for READ, the CPU places the address of the location to be read in MAR and issues a Read control signal. The memory address decoder selects that particular address and the contents of that address are read and placed in MBR. We call this reading "non-destructive read", because after the contents of the selected memory location are read into the MBR, that location's contents remain the same. If data is to be written into memory, then the CPU places the data in MBR and places the address where the data is to be written in MAR. It then sends a Write signal to the memory unit. The memory unit writes the contents of MBR in the memory location specified by MAR. Writing into a memory location destroys the older contents of that location. Once the specified operation on memory (READ or WRITE) is completed, the memory system is ready for the next operation. Memory is accessed repeatedly for fetching either an instruction or a data item from the memory to the CPU for further processing.

## 8.3 INSTRUCTION AND DATA REPRESENTATION

An instruction for the hypothetical computer SMAC defines an operation that is native to the machine. An instruction is said to be native to the machine if it is implemented in the hardware by its designer. Each instruction will contain the following information:

1. The operation to be performed is denoted by means of a code (Op-code for short).

2. Address in memory where the operands will be found. The operation will be performed on these operands.

3. Address in memory where the result of the operation will be stored. The operand(s) may be stored either in the main memory or in registers and their addresses will be used for pointing to them. In general, the instructions may have zero, one, two or three addresses of operands and zero or one address for the result (if any).

Accessing the main memory which is a random access memory takes considerably more time compared to the data transfer to or processing in the CPU. Thus, the trend has been to keep more and more data stored in the CPU itself in **General Purpose Registers**. These are registers built with high speed flip-flops. Storing and retrieving data from these registers is much faster when compared to fetching from a large-sized memory. An instruction should be able to refer to these registers by using register addresses. In the case of SMAC, we have only 2 registers in the CPU and we symbolically call them A and B registers. One bit is enough to address them.

For the sake of simplicity, we will assume that a location of 8 bits in SMAC stores one instruction. All instructions of SMAC are assumed to be of the same length. The 8 bits of an instruction are formatted and coded. This instruction format is simple and consists of only 3 fields, namely, the Op-code field (3 bits), register address field (1 bit) and direct memory address field (4 bits). A simple uniform format for all instructions is not essential. Many commercial computers have variable instruction formats..

The data stored in an 8-bit byte of SMAC may be any of the following:

1. A positive or negative integer. The number is stored in binary form. Negative numbers are represented in two's complement form. The range of integers is thus $-2^7$ to $(+2^7 - 1)$.

2. An 8-bit ASCII character.

When a word is read from the memory of SMAC, it may represent an integer, an ASCII character or an 8-bit instruction. It is the responsibility of the programmer to keep track of the nature of the data stored in each location in memory.

With the 3-bits Op code field, we can represent 8 different instructions. The computer designer has the challenging task of choosing what should be this set of instructions. We choose the following set S1 of 8 instructions as the instruction set for SMAC:

1. **ADD meaning:** The contents of the memory location specified in this ADD instruction will be added to the contents of the register A or B depending on whether the Bit-3 is 0 or 1 and the result will be left in that register.

   *Example:* ADD A, X    A ← A + C (X)

2. **LOAD meaning:** Read the memory from the specified address in the LOAD instruction and put it in either register A or B as specified.

   *Example:* LOAD A, X    A ← C(X)

3. **STORE meaning:** Write the contents from register A or B into the memory address specified in the STORE instruction.

   *Example:* STORE A, X    C(X) ← A

4. **JUMP meaning:** The next instruction to be executed is located at the memory address specified in this JUMP instruction.

   *Example:* JUMP Y    PC ← Y

5. **JMIN meaning:** If the specified register (A or B) of this instruction is "minus", then the next instruction to be executed is the one located at the memory address specified in this JMIN instruction; otherwise the CPU should follow its flow of instruction execution.

   *Example:* JMIN A, Y    If A< 0 then PC ← Y

6. **INPUT meaning:** The 8-bits set on the input device of SMAC should be transferred to the memory address specified in the INPUT instruction. The register field is not used for this type of instruction.

   *Example:* INPUT X    C(X) ← INBUF

7. **OUTPUT meaning:** The 8-bit contents of the memory address specified in this OUTPUT instruction should be displayed on the output device of SMAC. The register field is not used for this type of instruction.

   *Example:* OUTPUT X    OUTBUF ← C(X)

8. **HALT meaning:** Stop program execution.

The above set of 8 instructions can be coded with the 8 combinations of the 3-bit Op-code field. The designer will have to choose which 3-bit combination will represent which instruction. In this encoding or the assignment of bit-combinations to Op-codes, the designer may optimize some criteria. At this stage let us say we make this assignment arbitrarily as shown in Table 8.1 and call this table as "Op-code Table".

**TABLE 8.1**

**Op-code Assignment for S1**

| Op-code | 3-bit code |
| --- | --- |
| HALT | 000 |
| ADD | 001 |
| LOAD | 010 |
| STORE | 011 |
| JUMP | 100 |
| JMIN | 101 |
| INPUT | 110 |
| OUTPUT | 111 |

## 8.4  CPU ORGANIZATION

The Central Processing Unit (CPU) consists of a set of registers, arithmetic and control circuits which together interpret and execute instructions. The CPU of SMAC has two registers A and B that are used in interpreting and executing certain instructions. They are accessible to programmers in the ADD, LOAD and STORE instructions.

There are three other registers in the CPU of SMAC which are not accessible to the programmers but are essential for program execution and hardware organization of the computer:

PC:      A 4-bit register that points to the memory address which contains the "next" instruction to be executed in the sequential flow of instructions. [PC—Program Counter register. It is also known as IP—for Instruction Pointer]

IR:       This 8-bit register holds the current instruction that is brought from the memory to be executed. [IR—Instruction Register]

OVFLOW: This 1-bit register holds 1 if the ADD instruction produces 9 bits as result when two 8-bit numbers are added.

Before a program is executed, the sequence of instructions of that program is to be stored or loaded into the memory. We call this the **program loading phase**. The instructions are then executed one after another, starting from the first instruction specified by the contents of PC. The execution of each instruction has two phases or cycles:

1. Instruction fetch cycle (I-cycle)
2. Instruction execution cycle (E-cycle)

The following is the sequence of operations carried out during I-cycle:

(I-1)  The address of the instruction to be fetched is found in the PC-register. The instruction is fetched from that memory address and placed in IR.

(I-2)  The PC-register is incremented by 1 to point to the next instruction in sequence during the succeeding I-cycle.

(I-3) The Op-code field of the current instruction in IR is decoded using the Op-code Table to determine which operation is to be performed. The execution of each operation needs a set of control signals which are initiated after this decoding.

The execution cycle (E-cycle) of an instruction involves the three steps given below:

(E-1) Decode the instruction into its constituent parts.

(E-2) The operands are fetched either from registers in the CPU or from the memory as determined by the Op-code and the control signals.

(E-3) Using these operands the operation is performed by the hardware of the processing unit.

The execution of an operation requires the processing unit which is also known as **Arithmetic and Logic Unit** (ALU), and a set of control signals. These control signals differ from one operation to another. Unlike others, there are some instructions which do not need fetching of an operand from memory during the execution cycle (example: JUMP and JMIN). At the end of an E-cycle, the execution of the next instruction, that is, the I-cycle of the next instruction begins. Thus, the I and E cycles alternate until the machine comes to a halt state.

## 8.5 INPUT/OUTPUT FOR SMAC

Every computer needs a mechanism to receive data from sources outside it for processing. Such a mechanism is called an **input** and the device used to feed the data is called the **input device**. After the data is processed the results are to be communicated to the outside world. This is performed by an **output device**. The devices used for input and output units are jointly referred to as I/O devices. A variety of I/O devices such as CRT display, keyboard, printer, mouse, speech recognizer and speech synthesizer are available. Besides these, back up storage systems such as magnetic tapes, and discs are also used as intermediaries in I/O operations. A computing system would normally consist of a variety of I/O devices besides the CPU and memory. Later in this chapter we will discuss this topic again. For the present we will give a rudimentary I/O capability to SMAC. As a simple input device, SMAC will be assumed to have a bank of 8 switches. Each switch can be turned ON or OFF denoting a binary 1 or 0. After setting all the 8 switches to denote one 8-bit data input, the human operator will push an INR or Input Ready switch. The INR will signal the SMAC CPU that the input data is ready to be taken in. Similarly, as an output device, SMAC will contain a set of 8 LEDs or light emitting diodes. An 8-bit output is sent in parallel to this array of LEDs. Each LED in this array will be lit or not lit depending on whether the corresponding bit is 1 or 0.

## 8.6 PROGRAMMING SMAC WITH INSTRUCTION SET S1

The instruction set S1 is very simple and it is kept that way so that a beginner can fabricate SMAC using MSI chips on a breadboard and test it. Now let us write a simple program using the instruction set S1.

**Program 8.1:** Write a program with the instruction set S1 to read two input binary numbers from the input device and store them in memory. Then add the two numbers and display the sum.

*Memory allocation:*

| | | |
|---|---|---|
| Data Item 1 (X) | read and stored at memory address 15 | (1111) |
| Data Item 2 (Y) | read and stored at memory address 14 | (1110) |
| The sum (Z) | computed and stored at the address 13 | (1101) |

The program itself will be stored starting from the memory address:     0000

*Symbolic form of the program:*

Program 8.1:  Program to add two numbers

| | |
|---|---|
| INPUT X | X is the symbolic name of the first data item |
| INPUT Y | Y is the symbolic name of the second data item |
| LOAD A,X | Read the value of X from memory into the register A |
| ADD A,Y | Add the second data item at address Y to A. The sum is thus in A |
| STORE A,Z | Store the sum. The symbolic name for the sum is Z |
| OUTPUT Z | Display the sum |
| HALT | Stop execution |

After the instruction OUTPUT Z the machine halts. We will assume that when power is switched ON, all registers are set to zero. This symbolic program is easily readable. But for SMAC it has to be in the binary form. By binding the symbolic names X,Y, Z to the addresses that we have "memory allocated" and using the Op-code Table 8.1, we can manually convert Program 8.1 into the machine language format shown in Program 8.2. In this format, each instruction is represented as a sequence of 1 and 0.

**Program 8.2:** Machine Language equivalent of Program 8.1.

*Assumption:* The program is stored in memory starting from the memory address 0000.

| Memory Address | Instruction Stored | Symbolic |
|---|---|---|
| 0000 | 110 0 1111 | INPUT X |
| 0001 | 110 0 1110 | INPUT Y |
| 0010 | 010 0 1111 | LOAD A,X |
| 0011 | 001 0 1110 | ADD A,Y |
| 0100 | 011 0 1101 | STORE A,Z |
| 0101 | 111 0 1101 | OUTPUT Z |
| 0110 | 000 0 0000 | HALT |

1. The programmer would find it convenient to write the program in symbolic form, although the hardware (machine) would interpret only zeros and ones.

2. There is one-to-one correspondence between the symbolic form and the machine language form.

3. The input and output data are determined by the programmer and they are allocated space suitably in memory.

4. Memory is systematically allocated. Starting from the lowest address, the program instructions are placed successively at increasing addresses. Similarly, the data items are located at successive memory addresses, starting from the highest address and progressing towards lower addresses.

5. It is the responsibility of the programmer to ensure that data and program do not overlap.

## 8.7 INSTRUCTION SET S2 AND SMAC+

The instruction set of a computer determines its power. One approach to designing computers is to introduce complex instructions and a large number of instructions. This is known as CISC (Complex Instruction Set Computers) approach. The instruction set of a CISC type computer contains powerful instructions which enable programmers to write efficient programs. Examples of CISC computers are Intel Pentium, Motorola 68040, etc. As there are several hundred instructions in CISC computers, programming them effectively is not simple and it requires a thorough knowledge of the instruction set and the semantics of various instructions.

In order to motivate the need for a better instruction set, let us slightly expand the problem considered in Program 8.1. Let us suppose that we want to repeat this problem, that is read five pairs of numbers, add them and store the five sums in memory. We can use Program 8.1 and modify it suitably to make the computer repeat it five times. This modification is represented in Figure 8.2. To solve this expanded problem we have introduced

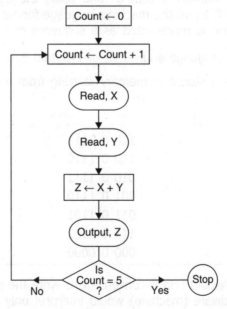

**Figure 8.2 Adding X and Y five times.**

a counter variable named COUNT. First this variable is initialized to zero outside of the iteration loop, then COUNT is incremented by 1 at the beginning of each iteration, and at the end of the iteration COUNT is compared with the limit (5 in this case) to decide if the next iteration is to be continued or not. This type of repeated execution of a segment of a computation commonly occurs in software systems. One question is: Can we achieve the three sub-tasks of initializing, incrementing, and comparing with a specified limit using the instruction set S1? The other question is, if this type of repetitive execution of program segments is common in software systems, how to realize it efficiently?

Now we will enhance the instruction set S1 to S2 so that a programmer can write non-trivial programs for SMAC. The enhancement of the instruction set S1 to S2 will be considered from the following four points of view. Each point of view will be further explained by means of Choice 1, Choice 2, etc.

1. To provide facilities at the instruction set level for iterative execution.
2. To support binary variables and Boolean operations (AND, OR, NOT).
3. To support other commonly used arithmetic operations subtract, multiply and divide and discover the limitations of the 8-bit "word" size.
4. To support the creation of "well written" programs.

First let us consider where the COUNT variable should be located. It could be located in memory or in register B of SMAC. For the CPU hardware, accessing a register is ten to hundred times faster than accessing the memory. On the other hand there are limited registers (around 8, 16 or 32) but a lot more memory locations exist (in the order millions or billions). Let us suppose the following enhancements are made in SMAC:

**Enhancement 1:** To support iterative executions, the COUNT variable is implicitly assumed to be in register B. We introduce the following three new instructions and additional flags in the CPU of SMAC:

INC B:      Meaning: increment register B by 1

CMP B,x:      Meaning: compare the contents of register B with the number x and set one of the three flags in the CPU namely EQ, GT, LT depending upon whether the result of the comparison is = x, > x or < x respectively. The data value x to be compared with contents of B is stored as a part of the instruction itself.

JLT BEGIN:      Meaning: if the flag LT was set in the CPU then jump to the instruction labeled BEGIN; otherwise continue the sequential flow of the execution. Also reset the flag.

To simplify the problem of initializing the COUNT to zero, we will introduce a change in the organization of SMAC. In the hardware design, we will force the memory location 0000 to permanently contain zero. The programmer is allowed to read it but cannot store anything at that location. LOAD B,0 instruction can be used to initialize register B to zero. With these modifications to SMAC, we can write a symbolic program corresponding to Figure 8.2 as shown in Program 8.3.

***Program 8.3:*** Repeat the Program 8.1 five times. The additions to Program 8.1 are shown in boldface.

| | | |
|---|---|---|
| | **LOAD B,0** | Register B is initialized to zero |
| **BEGIN** | **INC B** | Increment the COUNT by 1 |
| | INPUT X | X is the symbolic name of the first data item |
| | INPUT Y | Y is the symbolic name of the second data item |
| | LOAD A,X | Read the value of X from memory into register A |
| | ADD A,Y | Add the second data item to A |
| | STORE A,Z | Store the sum. The symbolic name for the sum is Z |
| | OUTPUT Z | Display the sum |
| | **CMP B,5** | Compare register B with 5 |
| | **JLT BEGIN** | Go to BEGIN if B < 5 |
| | HALT | Stop execution |

When we try to translate Program 8.3 into its machine language equivalent, we find that we cannot do it with the current coding scheme for instructions. The 3 bit Op-code field of SMAC is fully utilized and it is not sufficient to encode the additional instructions INC, CMP and JLT. We need more bits in the Op-code field. Increasing the Op-code field would increase the instruction length which in turn will increase the "word length" if we assume that one instruction is one "word". Thus, we will later redefine the organization of SMAC into SMAC+ to accommodate these three instructions.

**Enhancement 2:** Very often there is a need to use binary or Boolean representations of data. Then the 8-bit word could be treated as a binary vector with 8 components, each bit being 1 or 0 which can be also treated as TRUE or FALSE in Boolean logic. Just as we used the ADD operation on two integers, we can provide SMAC with the ability to do the traditional Boolean operations such as AND, OR, NOT. This would increase the instruction set S2 further.

AND A,B: Meaning: bit-wise AND of the contents of register A with that of register B is performed and the resulting 8-bits are stored in register A.

OR A,B: Meaning: similar to AND operation above, but instead of AND the operation OR is performed

NOT A: Meaning: the individual bits of the register A are complemented.

**Enhancement 3:** In SMAC we had only one arithmetic operation, namely, ADD on the 8-bit integer data. If we want to introduce in SMAC other commonly used arithmetic operations such as subtract (SUB), multiply (MULT) and integer divide (IDIV), these additional instructions would increase the instruction set S2. We also notice that the range of numbers represented by an 8-bit word using two's complement form of representing negative integers is +128 to −127. This is too small, particularly when we want to multiply numbers and solve realistic problems that involve numbers beyond the range −128 to +127. As a result of the need to extend the range of numbers that can be handled, it is worthwhile to increase the word length of SMAC from 8 bits to a larger size. Then, one question we can ask is, "How large"? Let us suppose that we increase it from 8 to 32 bits. This increase will allow us to store integers in the range $+2^{31}$ to $(-2^{31} + 1)$. This will also allow us to store floating point numbers in IEEE 745 floating point standard (Refer to Section 5.11.2). When the word length is increased then both registers A and B should be enlarged to hold 32 bits. The LOAD and STORE instructions are used to load or store the register contents in memory. Therefore, the memory can also be viewed as "locations" that contain 32 bits each. This results in the concept of a "memory word". In this example the 32-bit word could be considered to consist of 4 bytes of 8 bits each.

Having made registers A and B 32 bits long, we could also increase the length of the MAR and MBR to 32 bits giving us two major advantages. Since the MAR can be 32 bits long, we can now have a memory as large as $2^{32}$ (that is 4 GB) if we can afford large memory. The MBR being 4 bytes long, each memory READ or WRITE operation can read or write a group of 4 bytes. If we also increase the instructions length to 32 bits, the IR (instruction register) will become a 32-bit register. With an instruction of this length we can have longer Op-code fields and memory address fields. Increasing the instruction length to 32 bits can also lead to other improvements in SMAC. So far we have used 1-bit field in the instruction format of SMAC to denote register A or B. If we could use 4 bits for this register reference instead of 1 bit, we can accommodate as much as 16 registers instead of 2. This large set of registers can be used by the programmer for many different purposes. Then instead of naming these registers as A, B, etc we will use the convention R0, R1, R2, ..., R15. With all these modifications the original 8-bit SMAC has changed. We will call the modified SMAC as SMAC+.

**Enhancement 4:**  In addition to the above two types of extensions to the instruction set, we observe the need for a new kind of instructions that would help a programmer to write "better software". As an example, consider the situation when two 32-bit integers are added. The result can be 33 bits long. This overflow situation would cause the CPU hardware to turn the overflow flag OVFL to ON condition. It would be nice to provide an instruction to the programmer similar to the JMIN instruction but called Jump on overflow (JOFL). Using this instruction software can be written to provide a diagnostic message to the end user as, "An addition overflow has occurred". Of course, to provide such a diagnostic message a suitable output device must exist to display the text message and the computer must be able to store text in a standard format like the international standard ASCII code for alphabets.

*JOFL Message-text:*  This instruction means, IF the OVFL flag was set due to a previous arithmetic operation, then jump to the address in memory labeled "Message-text", after the jump reset the flag; otherwise follow the normal sequential flow of instruction execution.

Based on the above choices, we have extended the instruction set of SMAC+ and labeled the set as S2 (See Table 8.2). The organization of SMAC+ is summarized in the next section.

## 8.8  ORGANIZATION OF SMAC+

For the sake of simplicity, we assume that one 32-bit word of SMAC+ stores one instruction and all instructions of SMAC+ are of the same length. (This need not be the case in real machines when optimization is needed). The 32 bits of an instruction are formatted and coded to specify the operation performed by that instruction and point to (i.e., provide the address of) the operands needed for that operation. This format is known as an **instruction format** needed for that operation. There are three different instruction formats in SMAC+ , called **R-format**, **M-format** and **J-format**, and they are shown in Figure 8.3. Note that four bits are used to address one of the 16 registers. In these instruction formats, we have assumed the Op-code field to be 8 bits long. With 8 bits we can have $2^8 = 256$ different Op-codes or instructions which are more than sufficient for most purposes.

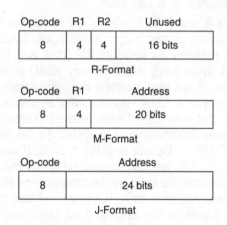

**Figure 8.3  Instruction formats of SMAC+.**

The R-format of SMAC+ specifies two operand addresses both of which are register addresses. An instruction such as AND R1,R2 is interpreted as the contents of R2 is ANDed to that of R1. To execute such instructions, the CPU need not access the memory during the E-cycle.

The M-format is useful to define instructions that will refer to one or two registers for the operands and store the result in memory. LOAD and STORE instructions could be of this type. In this format 8 bits are reserved for the Op-code, 4 bits are reserved for the register reference and the remaining 20 bits are reserved for memory reference. The 20-bit memory address of an M-type instruction can directly address any of the $2^{20}$ locations in memory. Each location is 32 bits long. Thus, we can address $2^{20}$ words, each 32 bits long (i.e., 1M words or 4 MB). Addressing each byte in a 32-bit word has several advantages particularly in processing character strings. Most modern computers use byte addressing. However, we will use word addressing for simplicity. A question arises, "if SMAC+ has a memory larger than 1 M word ($2^{20}$), how to address the other memory locations?"

The J-format is useful to define branch type instructions that are essential in programming. A simple jump instruction has 8-bit Op-code and a 24-bit memory address. According to this format, the jump instruction can branch control to any of the instructions in the addressing range of $2^{24}$ words. If we want to address each byte of 4-MB memory we need a 22-bit address.

Data stored in a word of SMAC+ may be any of the following:

1. A positive or negative integer. The number is stored in binary form. Negative numbers are represented in two's complement form. The range of integers is thus $-2^{31}$ to $(+2^{31} - 1)$.

2. A character string. Eight bits are used to represent a character in the standard ASCII format and thus 4 characters may be stored in each word or a register of SMAC+.

When a word is read from the memory of SMAC+, it may represent an integer, a character string or an instruction. It is the responsibility of the programmer to keep track of consistent interpretation for the 32-bit data stored in a memory word.

The CPU of SMAC+ consists of a set of registers, arithmetic and control circuits which together interpret and execute instructions (see Figure 8.4). It has a set of registers accessible to a programmer and another set of registers that are used in interpreting and executing instructions and not accessible to programmers. There are seven registers in the CPU of SMAC, which are not accessible to programmer is but are essential for program execution. In addition to the PC, IR, MAR, MBR and FLAG registers of SMAC introduced earlier, we introduce two more registers and they are the multiplier quotient register (MQ) and an arithmetic result register (MR). The MQ and MR registers are used during multiplication and division operations as explained in Chapter 5. The bits of the FLAG register are expanded and named C, V, Z, N, P, M and T (from left to right). The interpretation for these bits are as given below and they are automatically set by the CPU hardware at the end of each instruction execution depending on the status of the instruction execution:

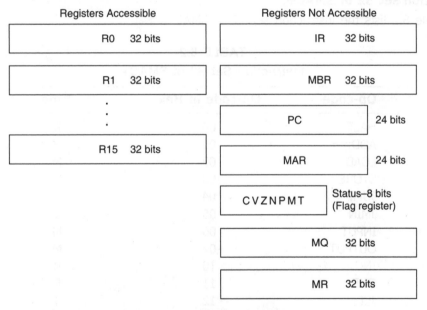

**Figure 8.4   SMAC+ registers.**

Bit 1, C: (carry bit)   Set to 1 if a carry is generated during an add operation or a borrow is generated during subtract operation. It is otherwise cleared to 0.

Bit 2, V: (overflow bit)   Set to 1 if an add or subtract operation produces a result that exceeds the two's complement range of numbers. Else it is 0.

Bit 3, Z: (zero bit)   Set to 1 if the result of an operation is zero. Otherwise it is 0.

Bit 4, N: (negative bit)   Set to 1 when the result of an arithmetic operation is negative.

Bit 5, P: (positive bit)   Set to 1 when the result of an arithmetic operation is positive. Else it is set to 0.

Bit 6, M: (compare)   Set to 1 if the "bit comparison operation" succeeds, else it is set to 0.

Bit 7, T: (Trace bit)   When this bit is set to 1 by a special instruction (not discussed in this chapter) program execution stops and special debug software is executed.

The hardware organization of SMAC+ at the level of registers is summarized as follows:

### Registers of SMAC+

1. All registers of SMAC+ are 32 bits long.
2. Registers accessible directly to programmers of SMAC+ are named: R0, R1, R2, ..., R15.
3. Registers which are not accessible to programmers directly but are in the hardware organization include: MAR, MBR, PC, IR, MR, MQ and the FLAG register.
4. The Flag register and its bits are explained above.

### Instruction set S2 of SMAC+

Table 8.2 lists the instruction set S2 of SMAC+.

**TABLE 8.2**
**Instruction Set S2 of SMAC+**

| Op-code | Op-code in Hex | Type |
|---------|----------------|------|
| HALT | 00 | R |
| ADD | 01 | R |
| LOAD | 02 | M |
| STORE | 03 | M |
| JUMP | 04 | J |
| JMIN | 05 | J |
| INPUT | 06 | M |
| OUTPUT | 07 | M |
| INC | 10 | R |
| CMP | 11 | R |
| JLT | 12 | J |
| AND | 20 | R |
| OR | 21 | R |
| NOT | 22 | R |
| SUB | 31 | R |
| MULT | 32 | R |
| IDIV | 33 | R |
| JOFL | 34 | J |

## Instruction Formats of SMAC+

The following are the instruction formats of SMAC+:

1. R-Type    Op-code, R1,R2

    *Example:* ADD R3,R4  [in Hex format: 01 34 00 00]

In ADD the two operands are available in R1,R2. In the case of CMPR3,5 the second operand is a constant and is available as part of the instruction. In this case there are two restrictions: (i) the constant cannot be changed during program execution and (ii) as only 4 bits are available is R field, the maximum value of the constant is 15.

2. M-Type    Op-code, R, mem-address [mem-address=20 bits-long]

    *Example:* LOAD R5,X [in Hex: 02 50 FF FF where 0FFFF is the address of the variable X in memory]

3. J-Type    Op-code, jump-address [jump-address=24 bits-long]

    *Example:* JLT BEGIN [in Hex: 12 00 16 40 where 001640 is the jump address BEGIN in memory]

In Table 8.3 we list the format of all the instructions of SMAC ++

### TABLE 8.3
### Instruction Format of Semantics of Instruction Set S2 of SMAC ++

| Instruction Hex form | | | Symbolic form | | | | Semantics |
|---|---|---|---|---|---|---|---|
| OP | REG | ADDR | OP | Reg1 | Reg2 | ADDR | |
| 00 | 00 | 0000 | HALT | | | | Stop execution |
| 01 | 34 | 0000 | ADD | R3, | R4, | 0000 | C(R3) ← C(R3) + C(R4) |
| 02 | 40 | FFFF | LOAD | R4, | 0, | X | C(R4) ← C(X) |
| 03 | 50 | EEEE | STORE | R5, | 0, | Y | C(Y) ← C(R5) |
| 04 | 00 | DDDE | JUMP | 0, | 0, | Z | PC ← Z |
| 05 | 00 | CCCF | JMI | 0, | 0, | D | If (N in status Register = 1) PC ← D |
| 06 | 00 | BBBE | INP | 0, | 0, | B | C(B) ← INPUT |
| 07 | 00 | AAAA | OUT | 0, | 0, | X | OUTPUT ← C(X) |
| 10 | 10 | 0000 | INC | R1 | | | C(R1) ← C(R1) + 1 |
| 11 | 12 | 0000 | CMP | R1, | B | | Compare C(R1) with B. Set LT, EQ, GT flag depending on result of comparison |
| 12 | 00 | 9999 | JLT | 0, | 0, | Z | If LT flag set PC ← Z |
| 20 | 34 | 0000 | AND | R3, | R4 | | C(R3) ← C(R3) ∧ C(R4) (∧ bitwise AND operator) |
| 21 | 56 | 0000 | OR | R5, | R6 | | C(R5) ← C(R5) ∨ C(C6) (∨ bitwise OR operator) |

(Contd.)

## TABLE 8.3 (Contd.)
### Instruction Format of Semantics of Instruction Set S2 of SMAC ++

| Instruction Hex form | | | Symbolic form | | Semantics |
|---|---|---|---|---|---|
| 22 | 40 | 0000 | NOT | R4 | $R4 \leftarrow \overline{R4}$ (bitwise complement) |
| 31 | 43 | 0000 | SUB | R4, R3 | $C(R4) \leftarrow C(R4) - C(R3)$ |
| 32 | 78 | 0000 | MULT, | R7, R8 | $C(R7) \leftarrow C(R7) * C(R8)$ |
| 33 | 67 | 0000 | IDIV | R6, R7 | $C(R6) \leftarrow$ Integer Quotient of $C(R6)/C(R7)$ |
| 34 | 00 | BBBB | JOFL | Z | If OVFL bit set $PC \leftarrow Z$ |

Now we will present four stages in the development and execution of programs in SMAC+, in particular we identify the following four stages:

1. **Programming stage:** [The program is developed by the programmer in symbolic form using a programming language]

2. **Assembly or Translation stage:** [The symbolic program is automatically translated into an equivalent machine language form by the System Software]

3. **Load stage:** [When the assembled and stored program is loaded into the main memory and made ready for execution]

4. **Execution stage:** [When the program is "run" or executed by the hardware one instruction at a time]

It is intuitively clear that these four stages are executed sequentially in the order specified here.

As an example case we have chosen the problem of computing $\sum_{i=1}^{5} (x_i + y_i)$ using SMAC+ assembly language. In assembly language, mnemonics are used to represent operation codes and symbols are used for addressing data and branch addresses. This stage will be referred to as *programming stage*. During this stage an appropriate algorithm is chosen and the programmer takes several other decisions about naming the data items and naming the instructions to branch to.

Following this, assembler software automatically translates the symbolic program into its equivalent machine language program. This phase is referred to as **assembly stage**. During this stage, the assembler software determines where to store the program and what memory addresses to assign to operands. It also constructs and uses several tables and takes other important decisions. One table used by the assembler is the Op-code table. See Table 8.2 where each Op-code is uniquely associated with 8-bit Op-code and this 8-bit code will be decoded and interpreted by the CPU hardware that is to be discussed later. Another table known as symbol table is also used which will be introduced later in this chapter. When the assembly process is completed, we have a machine language program that is ready to be stored in the main memory.

The process of storing the program in main memory ready for execution is called **loading** and this stage is called **load time**. A system software known as loader performs the job of loading the given machine language program, starting from a given start address in memory. Loading becomes simple if we assume that every instruction in the machine language format occupies exactly one word (or 4 bytes) in memory. At load time the loader decides where in memory free space is available and chooses a suitable memory region for loading. When loading is completed, the program is ready for execution.

The execution stage of the translated machine language program is known as **run time**. During this time the instructions are executed one at a time. The address of the first instruction to be executed is placed into the PC-register by the loader software and then the execution is started. Thereafter, instruction fetch and execution are repeated cyclically.

## 8.9 ASSEMBLING THE PROGRAM INTO MACHINE LANGUAGE FORMAT

In Program 8.3 which is reproduced as Program 8.4, we note three data variables (X,Y,Z) and reference to two registers (A and B). Our first task is to map these variables and registers to memory locations and registers in SMAC+. Let us suppose we use the mapping shown in which the data area starts from the highest address in memory (FFFFF) and gets filled backwards, that is towards decreasing memory addresses. Thus X will be stored in FFFF, Y in FFFE and Z in FFFD. Besides this R1 will be used to store X, R2 to store Y and R3 as a counter to control the number of iterations.

Our next task is to decide the starting memory address from where the translated machine language program will be located in the memory in successive words. We have conveniently assumed that every instruction will fit **exactly** into one memory word or 4 bytes. Let us suppose that the first instruction in memory will be located in 10000 in Hex. Then the next instruction will be located in 10001 and the next in 10002 and so on. This decision automatically makes the address of the instruction INC R3 to be 10001 and the address of HALT instruction to be 1000B. Based on the program's starting address, the *symbolic address* in the program, BEGIN, gets memory locations associated with it as 10001. A table showing all the symbols in a program and their associated memory addresses is called **symbol table**. The assembler software can automatically build a symbol table by scanning the assembly language program statement by statement. With these assignments we are now ready to translate the symbolic program in Program 8.3 to its equivalent machine language format by using the Op-code table in Table-8.2. Remember that in SMAC+ we have assumed that by its design the register R0 will always contain the number zero. The machine language of the assembly language program is given as Program 8.4.

***Program 8.4:*** Machine language equivalent of Program 8.3

|        |       |      |             |           |       |
|--------|-------|------|-------------|-----------|-------|
|        | LOAD  | R3,0 | 02 30 00 00 | stored at | 10000 |
| BEGIN  | INC   | R3   | 10 30 00 00 | stored at | 10001 |
|        | INPUT | X    | 06 0F FF FF | stored at | 10002 |
|        | INPUT | Y    | 06 0F FF FE | stored at | 10003 |

| | | | | |
|---|---|---|---|---|
| LOAD | R1,X | 02 1F FF FF | stored at | 10004 |
| LOAD | R2,Y | 02 02 FF FF | stored at | 10005 |
| ADD | R1,R2 | 01 12 00 00 | stored at | 10006 |
| STORE | R1,Z | 03 2F FF FD | stored at | 10007 |
| OUTPUT | Z | 07 0F FF FD | stored at | ·10008 |
| CMP | R3,5 | 11 30 00 05 | stored at | 10009 |
| JLT | BEGIN | 12 01 00 01 | stored at | 1000A |
| HALT | | 00 00 00 00 | stored at | 1000B |

We observe that the program occupies memory locations 10000 through 1000B, namely, 12 memory words and the data area occupies memory locations FFFFF, FFFFE and FFFFD.

## 8.10 SIMULATION OF SMAC+

In this section an algorithm to simulate SMAC+ will be developed. This algorithm can be easily converted by a student to a C or Java program and executed on a real computer, such as a PC. This simulated machine will behave as SMAC+. Thus SMAC+ machine language program can be fed as data to this SMAC+ simulator and executed. The physical end of the machine language program will be coded with a data FF for Op-code field.

ALGORITHM 8.1. **SMAC+ Simulator**

*Program loading phase*

PC ← starting address of program in main memory.
Instruction overflow ← false
   *repeat*
         Read, instruction
         Memory [PC] ← instruction
         PC ← PC + 1
         if (PC > FFFF) *then* memory overflow ← *true*
   *until* op-code of instruction = FF or memory overflow

*Execution phase*

PC ← starting address of program
Halt ← false

*Repeat*

   IR ← Memory [PC]
   PC ← PC + 1
   Op-code ← IR[31..24] /* bits 31 to 24 of IR*/
   Find op-code type as R, J or M

Case
  R-type:          Opr1 ← IR[23..20]
                   Opr2 ← IR[19..16]
  M-type           Opr1 ← IR[23..20]
                   Addr ← IR [19..0]
  J-type           Addr ← IR [23..0]

end of case

Case Op-code R type
  0: halt ← true
  1: R(opr1) ← R(opr1) + R(opr2)
  10: R(opr1) ← R(opr1) + 1
  11: *if* (R(opr1) > *x then* set of GT flag
      *else if* R(opr1) = *x then* set EQ flag
                        *else* set LT flag
        *endif*

   *endif*

  20: R(opr1) ← R(opr1) ∧ R(opr2) /* ∧ is bitwise AND */
  21: R(opr1) ← R(opr1) ∨ R(opr2) /* ∨ is bitwise OR */
  22: R(opr1) ← NOT R(opr1) /* NOT is bit wise NOT*/
  31: R(opr1) ← R(opr1) − R (opr2)
  32: R(opr1) ← R(opr1) *R(opr2) / Multiplication */
  33: R(opr1) ← R(opr1) / R(opr2) /* Integer division */

end case /* R type */

Case Op-code M type

  2 : R(opr1) ← Memory (addr) /* Load */
  3 : Memory (addr) ← R(opr1) /* store */
  6 : Memory (addr) ← Read input
  7 : Write Memory (addr)

end case /* M type */

Case Op-code J type

  4 : PC ← addr
  5 : *if* (N) *then* PC ← addr
  12 : *if* (LTflag) *then* PC ← addr
  34 : *if* (OFLO) *then* PC ← addr

end case /* J-type */

*until* Halt

The Algorithm 8.1 only gives a general idea of how SMAC+ can be simulated. We have left out a lot of details. The student should convert this algorithm to a C or Java program.

## 8.11 PROGRAM EXECUTION AND TRACING

In what follows we will examine in detail how the machine language program (Program 8.4) would be executed by SMAC+ instruction by instruction in a sequence. For this purpose we will use Algorithm 8.1 and the flow chart shown in Figure 8.5. The PC (also known as IP for instruction pointer) will be initialized to 100 00 as the first instruction of the program

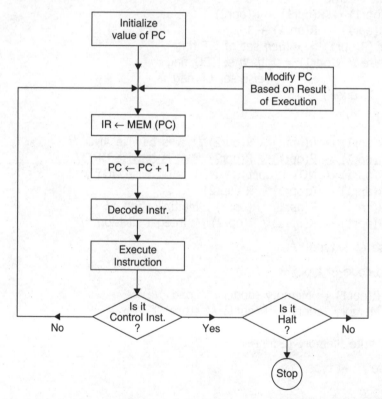

**Figure 8.5  Flow chart depicting the sequential execution of instructions.**

is located at that memory address. As stated in Section 8.4, every instruction execution has two phases or cycles: *instruction fetch cycle* and *instruction execution cycle*. In the fetch cycle the memory is read and the contents of memory at the address contained in the PC register is loaded into the instruction register or IR. Then, the execution cycle consists of three sub-cycles: *instruction-decode*, *operand-fetch* and *operation-execution*. In some arithmetic instructions there may be a fourth sub-cycle of storing the result of execution in either a register or memory. In Figure 8.6 we show these.

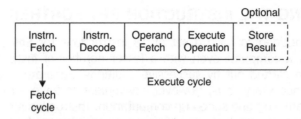

**Figure 8.6  Instruction fetch and execution cycles.**

After the fetch cycle of the first instruction in the above program, the contents of the IR will be 02 30 00 00. We will denote the effect of this fetch cycle as follows:

$$C(IR) \leftarrow 02\ 30\ 00\ 00$$

Immediately after the fetch cycle, the three sub-cycles of the execution cycle are followed one after another. Based on the coding of the Op-code, the SMAC+ hardware knows that this is an R-type instruction, and it must be decoded in the format that the first two hex-digits for Op-code, and this Op-code involves data move at the execution time, the third digit refers to the destination register, and the fourth digit refers to source register, and the remaining four hex-digits are to be ignored. The operand-fetch sub-cycle in this case is a *null cycle* because both operands are in registers and there is no memory reference. During the operation execution sub-cycle, the contents of R0, that is zero, is moved into the register R3 which is denoted as: $C(R3) \leftarrow 0$. From the flowchart of Figure 8.5 one notices that there are two paths and we have followed the path in which the contents of PC is incremented by 1. Thus the PC, after this increment will point to the next instruction in sequence. The next instruction is fetched and executed. The cycle keeps repeating. The *program trace* or instruction by instruction execution of the above program is shown in Table 8.4.

**TABLE 8.4**
**Program Trace of Program 8.4**

| Instruction-Address | Effect of executing that instruction |
|---|---|
| 10000 | $C(R3) \leftarrow 0$ |
| 10001 | $C(R3) \leftarrow 1$ |
| 10002 | $C(FFFFF) \leftarrow$ the data input for X |
| 10003 | $C(FFFFE) \leftarrow$ the data input for Y |
| 10004 | $C(R1) \leftarrow C(FFFFF)$ |
| 10005 | $C(R2) \leftarrow C(FFFFE)$ |
| 10006 | $C(R1) \leftarrow C(R1) + C(R2)$ |
| 10007 | $C(FFFFD) \leftarrow C(R1)$ |
| 10008 | Output $\leftarrow C(FFFFD)$ |
| 10009 | $C(R3) \leftarrow$ compared to 5 LT flag set to False |
| 1000A | LT flag is False; hence $C(PC) \leftarrow 10001$ |
|  | [when LT is True $C(PC) \leftarrow 1000B$] |
| 1000B | HALT |

## 8.12   EXPANDING THE INSTRUCTION SET FURTHER

In Section 8.9 we decided to have a set of 18 instructions for SMAC+. In principle it is possible to program a computer even with a lesser number of instructions. For example, multiplication can be carried out by successive additions. Separate instruction for multiplication is not really necessary. It is, however, convenient to have a multiply instruction as it will simplify programming and speed up computation. Instruction sets for computers have evolved with the primary goal of simplifying programming and the secondary goal of reducing computing time. At the same time, it should be pointed out that implementation of each instruction results in extra hardware and consequently higher complexity and cost. The designer thus has to trade off between programming convenience, computing speed and hardware cost.

With the growth of powerful and affordable computers, their applications in many problems have grown enormously. As a result of this, easy programming of a variety of applications is becoming an important factor in the design of computer systems.

From the sample program, we observe the need for supporting the following operations more efficiently. We can extend the instruction set of SMAC+ to include three new instructions explained as follows:

1. To be able to load a register with a constant other than zero, without having to read from the input device, because input operation is slow.

2. To be able to move the contents of one register to another.

3. Iterative execution of a program segment requires a counter to be used. This counter is initialized to some value, decremented after every iteration, compared against a limit value, and a conditional jump executed. These set of actions (except initializing) can be packaged into a single machine instruction. We call such an instruction BCT or branch and count. As looping in programs is frequently used, this type of instruction will ease writing loops in programs.

1. *Semantics of LDIMM*: Load immediate instruction

| | |
|---|---|
| *Symbolic form:* | LDIMM R2, + 4 [Op-code for LDIMM is 40; M-type] |
| *Machine language form:* | 40 20 00 04 |
| *Semantics:* | C(R2) ← + 4 |

2. *Semantics of MOVE instruction*

| | |
|---|---|
| *Symbolic form:* | MOVE R2, R4 [Op-code for MOVE is 41; R-type] |
| *Machine language form:* | 41 24 00 00 |
| *Semantics:* | C(R2) ← C(R4) |

3. *Semantics of BCT instruction*

| | |
|---|---|
| *Symbolic form:* | BCT R4, 0, NEXT [Op-code for BCT is 42 ; J-type] |
| *Machine language form:* | 42 40 478B (assuming the address of NEXT is 0478B) |
| *Semantics:* | C(R4) ← C(R4) − 1 |
| | If [C(R4) = 0] then PC ← NEXT |

4. *Modifications to I/O and arithmetic instructions of SMAC+*: When an I/O instruction is executed normally the data input is transferred from a peripheral register into the computer via a CPU register. Therefore, we will modify the semantics of the INPUT and OUTPUT instructions of SMAC+ to refer to a register as opposed to memory locations. As we have more registers in the CPU, we will modify the instruction formats of the ADD, SUB, MULT and IDIV to contain three register addresses instead of one register address and one memory address. Thus in Table 8.3 these instructions are marked as type R. This will make the execution of these instructions faster because there is no memory reference; but the programmer has to load the operands in proper registers before issuing such arithmetic operations. We give below an example with the SUB instruction in this 3-address format. The reader is urged to note the advantage of the three-address formatting in arithmetic operations by studying Program 8.5.

*Symbolic form:*     SUB R5, R4, R3

meaning $C(R5) \leftarrow C(R4) - C(R3)$ and the contents of R3 and R4 remain unchanged.

***Program 8.5:*** Read five input numbers one after another and find the largest among them; store the result in a location named LARGE.

*Storage allocation*

R1: used as a counter for loop
R3: contains the data Read, x
R4: holds the largest number, big
LARGE: is a memory location

*Symbolic Program*

```
            LDIMM     R1, 4          ; LOAD 4 INTO R1
            INP       R4             ; Read first number as big
LOOP        INP       R3             ; Read x
            SUB       R5, R3, R4     ; C(R5) ← x − big
            JMINUS    NO_CHANGE      ; if x < big go to NO-CHANGE
            MOVE      R4, R3         ; x > = big & so big ← x
NO_CHANGE   BCT       R1, LOOP       ; C(R1) ← C(R1) − 1
                                     ; IF (C(R1) > 0) go to LOOP
            STORE     R4, LARGE      ; C(LARGE) ← C(R4) = big
            OUT       R4             ; Output big
            HALT
LARGE       DW        1
```

By comparing Program 8.5 with Program 8.3, the reader should notice how writing an iterative loop in a program is facilitated by the BCT instruction. Not only the number of instructions is reduced but also execution will be faster. There is a wide range of other problems where these instructions will reduce program size and speed up execution. In Program 8.5 we have introduced a new type of instruction DW. This is not really an Op-code like ADD or MOVE. The purpose of the "LARGE DW 1" (define word) instruction is to inform the assembler to introduce a symbol by the name LARGE into the **symbol table** and assign a memory address for that symbol so that data can be stored is that address or accessed by the programmer. This type of instructions is known as **pseudo instructions** or **assembler instructions**.

Developing a good set of instructions for a computer is based on the designer's experience, existing technology and a good knowledge of the underlying architecture. What is meant by the term "architecture"? The term is well understood in the case of buildings. When we say the architecture of a building is excellent, its external appearance as well as its functionality are taken into account.

Let us consider the users of a computer system. There are several levels of users. Those who program a computer at the level of the assembly language are called **assembly language programmers** or **system programmers**. The term "**application programmers**" is used to refer to those who program for applications using *higher level languages*. A system programmer has to keep track of several low level details such as the memory allocation and register allocation. He/she should also remember the mnemonics, instruction types and their semantics. Viewing a computer system at this level of detail has come to be known as **instruction set architecture**. There is a lot more to instruction set architecture than the set of instructions. Some of the factors to be taken into account are as follows:

1. What are the different formats of the instructions?

2. How are the various registers classified and addressed?

3. How is the status register affected at the end of an instruction?

4. Organization of the memory system which is usually in the form of a hierarchy.

5. How is the memory addressed?

6. Speed of memory.

7. The organization of I/O devices and their interface to memory and central processing unit (see Chapter 12).

8. The control and data paths used in the execution of instructions for moving the bits from one place to another (called buses).

9. The organization of a collection of system software programs (Loaders, Linkers, Assemblers, Compilers, Operating Systems, etc.) in the form of a "coherent" system.

In essence, a thorough understanding of the instruction set architecture of a given computer system is like analysis of a system. A good analysis is prerequisite to any design. Thus, before designing a new computer system (whether hardware or software), we must develop a skill to analyze.

## 8.13 VECTOR OPERATIONS AND INDEXING

An ordered sequence of data items is known as a **vector**. The matrix is a two-dimensional vector in which each row (or each column) can be viewed as a vector. We can have a vector of integers, real numbers, or ASCII coded bytes. A sequence of bytes is also known as a **string**. Strings of bytes or characters occur commonly in word processing applications and in high level language programming. The basic operation we need with vectors is reading a vector of data items from an input unit and storing it in memory starting from a specified address. This starting address of the vector is called the **base address** of the vector.

Let us suppose that we want to read a vector of 20 integers and store it in memory with the vector base address as 300. This read operation is expressed using a *for* loop in Algorithm 8.2.

---

ALGORITHM 8.2.  **Reading a vector**

SA ← 299    {SA: Start address; because the *for* loop starts counting from 1 and increments the loop variable 'i' right at the beginning of the loop we initialize SA to (300−1)}

*for* i = 1 *to* 20 *do*

   *begin*

       Read D;        (D is the data item)

     .  Memory (SA + i) ← D;

   *end*;

---

In every iteration of the *for* loop of the above algorithm, the address where D is stored gets modified, that is SA (Start Address) gets incremented by *i*. Note that *i* is the *for loop* counter which gets incremented by 1 in successive iterations and it starts with an initial value of 1.

As *i* goes from 1 to 20 in the *for* loop, the addresses where D is stored, increases from 300 to 319. We need a mechanism in SMAC+ to realize such a variation of the address of an instruction in successive iterations of a loop. This *address modification* is achieved through the use of an index register. Consider the following instruction with indexed addressing.

STORE R2, R5, SA    [*indexed addressing*]

In the previous uses of the STORE instruction, we had only one register reference, but in indexed STORE we have two register references. R5 in this case plays the role of an *index* register. The effective address for the store operation is obtained by adding the contents of R5 to the address denoted by the symbol SA in the symbol table. If SA is given a value of 299 and R5 is initialized to zero, the effective address initially will be 299. As R5 is incremented by 1 in every iteration, the effective address will also get incremented in each iteration by 1. The data read can then be stored in successive locations in memory. The instruction format of SMAC+ has to be redefined in order to accommodate indexed addressing. We will do this later in this chapter and call the modified SMAC+ as SMAC++.

**Program 8.6:**  To read 20 data items, one data at a time and store them as a vector in memory with the vector base address of 300.

   *Storage allocation*

      R1: Loop counter register

      R2: Data is read into this register

      R5: Index register

*Symbolic program*

```
            LDIMM    R1, 20        ; Load R1 with 20
            LDIMM    R5, 0         ; Initialize R5 to zero
    LOOP    INP      R2
            INC      R5
            STORE    R2, R5, 299   ; Indexed address as two registers are used
            BCT      R1, LOOP      ; Repeat for Loop
            HALT
```

In the above program the effective address for the STORE instruction is calculated as follows:

Effective address = contents of the index register specified
+ the value of the address in the symbol field

Because, the register field of an M-type instruction can refer to any of the 16 registers, we can use any of them (except R0) for indexing. In certain other computers like 80486, separate registers are reserved only for the purpose of indexing. Since the registers of SMAC+ can be used for multiple purposes, they are sometimes known as **General Purpose Registers** (GPRs).

## 8.14   STACKS

A **stack** is a very useful data structure in computer software design. A pile of plates (or trays) in a cafeteria operates as a stack. Washed plates are added to the top of the stack, and a plate for use is removed from the top of the stack. Thus, in a stack structure both addition (known as push) and removal (known as pop) take place at the same end, usually called top of the stack. In software systems, a stack could be a stack of bytes, stack of words, or a stack of other structures (stack of stacks!).

A stack when implemented will have a finite capacity. Consecutive PUSH operations carried out without any intervening POP has a chance of causing a **stack overflow** condition. Similarly, consecutive POP operations without a PUSH operation can possibly lead to popping of an empty stack leading to a **stack underflow** condition. A computer designer has a choice of providing a set of registers in CPU as a stack or let the programmer use part of the main memory as a simulated stack. Register sets used as a stack would allow high speed operations (POP and PUSH) because no memory access is required. It is, however, expensive. If GPRs are used as a stack, the stack size will be very small as GPRs are addressable and the number of GPRs in computers rarely exceeds 256. Using the main memory of the computer as a simulated stack yields a low cost solution and the possibility for a large-sized stack. The size of the stack can be varied and may be as large as the memory. The method, however, will be slower as data storage and retrieval from main memory is much slower compared to register access. It would be desirable to combine both by storing certain number of top elements in registers and the rest in memory. Such a combination makes the stack faster.

Stack Pointer (SP) is a register which holds the address in memory where the top element of the stack is stored. This is useful in simulating the stack in memory. If we assume that the stack is stored from its top to bottom in successively increasing memory addresses, then every PUSH instruction would increase the SP by a constant and the POP instruction would decrease the SP by the same constant. This constant would be 1 if the data elements of the stack are one byte long and the memory is byte-addressed. Let us suppose that we make an arbitrary choice and designate the CPU register 15 (1111) as SP. PUSH and POP instructions would increment or decrement the SP register as shown in Figure 8.7. In certain computers like Pentium there is a separate register for SP, whereas in SMAC+ we have assumed Register 15 (R15) to be SP. This designation has certain advantages and some disadvantages. For example, because SP can be addressed like other registers, it can be incremented or decremented using INC or DEC instruction. The LOAD and STORE instructions in their indexed mode can be used to read or write the top element of the stack. A compare instruction can be used to check if SP has gone out of the stack boundary causing stack overflow or stack underflow conditions. On the other hand we are restricted in the use of R15 and it cannot be used for any other purpose. Thus, we have one register less for general-purpose use. Such trade-offs occur often in any system design, and computer design is not an exception.

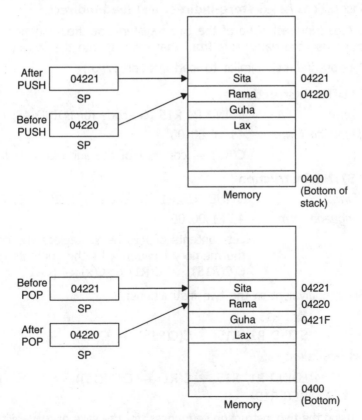

**Figure 8.7 Illustrating PUSH and POP instructions.**

When the stack is not implemented in the hardware, we have to realize it by software with other instructions. For convenience, let us assume that the bottom of the stack is at the memory address 04000. Let us also assume that the top of stack is at address 04FFF. Thus the stack size is FFF words (4K words). We also assume that the programmer is very careful so that stack underflow and stack overflow conditions do not occur (later we will relax these constraints in an exercise). Then PUSH R1 (push the contents of the register R1 into the stack) will be equivalent to the following two instruction sequence (R15 is assumed to store stack pointer):

INC R15

C(memory location whose address is in R15) ← C(R1)

Similarly, POP R1 (pop the top of stack into the register R1) is equivalent to:

C(R1) ← C(memory location whose address is in R15)

DEC R15

Note that SP is decremented after reading the top element of the stack from memory.

In order to realize the effect of the data transfers indicated above to implement a software stack, let us introduce a new mode of addressing called register-indirect addressing and two new instructions called **store-indirect** and **load-indirect**.

1. LDIND (Load indirect: One of the two registers specified contains the address of the data. Load the data value from that address into the second register.)

2. STIND (store indirect: Similar to load in addressing.)

### Semantics of LDIND instruction

*Symbolic form:*                        LDIND R1,R15 [Op-code for LDIND 45; R-type]

*Machine language form:*   45 1F 00 00

*Semantics:*                           C(R1) ← contents of the address stored in R15

### Semantics of STIND instruction

*Symbolic form:*                        STIND R15,R1 [Op-code for STIND 46; R-type]

*Machine language form:*   46 F1 00 00

*Semantics:*                           Let contents of R15 be x. Replace the contents of the memory location x by the contents of R1, i.e. C(C(R15)) ← C(R1) or C(x) ← (CR1)

Then PUSH is equivalent to the two instructions:

INC R15
STIND R1, R15     C(C(R15)) ← C(R1)

And POP is equivalent to:

LDIND R1, R15     C(R1) ← C(C(R15))
DEC R15

Instead of using the two instruction sequences, for the sake of readability of programs, we wish to be able to use PUSH and POP. Whenever the assembler software encounters

PUSH, we want the assembler to substitute PUSH by the corresponding two instruction sequences, and so also for the POP. Let us assume (for now) that the assembler has this capability. Thus, we can use PUSH and POP in the symbolic programs we write. But the corresponding machine language program will have two equivalent machine instructions substituted for one symbolic instruction.

In order to illustrate the concepts presented in this section, let us write Program 8.7 as given below.

**Program 8.7:** Read three data items each 4 bytes long, one at a time, in the sequence GUHA, RAMA, SITA and PUSH each item into the stack as the item is read. Then POP one at a time repeatedly as output.

*Storage allocation*

> R1:     Holds the data read
> R2:     Holds the counter for repeating 3 times
> R15:    Reserved for stack pointer

*Symbolic Program*

```
        LDIMM   R2, 3       ;
LOOP1   INP     R1          ;
        PUSH    R1, R15     ; Push in top of memory stack C(R1)
        BCT     R2, LOOP1   ;
        LDIMM   R2, 3       ;
LOOP2   POP     R1, R15     ; Pop data from top of stack and load it in R1
        OUT     R1          ;
        BCT     R2, LOOP2   ;
        HALT
```

The reader is urged to observe the following three points by simulating the execution of Program 8.7:

1. The readability of the symbolic program.

2. The two-instruction sequences indirect LOAD (LDIND) and DEC is substituted for POP and INC and indirect store (STIND) is substituted by PUSH in the machine language version.

3. What will be the sequence of output obtained? How is it related to the input sequence?

## 8.15 MODULAR ORGANIZATION AND DEVELOPING LARGE PROGRAMS

With the growth of computer application in all walks of life, some application programs have become so large that their sizes run into thousands or even millions of lines of code. Such large programs are usually developed by a team of programmers working together and sharing the total work. Each person develops a subsystem. All such subsystems are then combined into one large software. Modular organization is needed even within the task of one programmer to manage the complexity of the software. Each module is normally structured so that it carries out a well-defined quantum of work and is of manageable size. The organization of a program into modules while writing large programs (i.e. at the software level) is supported by the hardware design of a computer system by using a technique known as **subroutines and linkages**. Subroutines are also known as **subprograms**.

Organizing a program into subprograms has numerous advantages. Each subprogram can be separately programmed, assembled, tested and then interconnected. In general a large program would have to be broken down to a number of subprograms and held together by a main program which acts as the coordinator. A subprogram may be called (used) by the main program several times and in turn the subprogram may call other subprograms. Since a subprogram can be called or may call another subprogram, we will use the terms **calling program** (or **caller**) and **called program** (or **callee**). The main program is the coordinating program. It can never be a called program, that is, no subprogram may call the main program. The same subprogram may be a called program at one stage and a calling program at a different stage during execution. For example, in Figure 8.8, the main program calls Sub 1, Sub 2 and Sub 3. Sub 1 and Sub 2 in turn call Sub 4 to complete their task. The art of splitting a complex task into a set of subtasks requires careful analysis and experience. Usually factors such as logical independence and program-length would be the guiding factors.

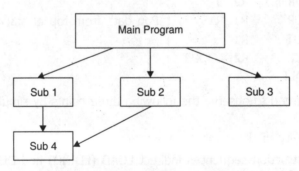

**Figure 8.8  Subroutine linkages.**

A calling program should transmit the following information to the called program:

1. The point of return, that is, where the control should be returned when the called program completes its task. For example, at the end of Sub 4 the control should return to Sub 1 or Sub 2 whichever was the caller at that time.

2. The addresses of the arguments are to be communicated. Suppose Sub 4 is a subroutine to compute $(x + y)^2$, then the storage locations of $x$ and $y$ are to be given by the caller to the called program. Similarly, the caller should know the location where the called program puts the result.

We should observe that between the caller and the called two kinds of transfers, *control transfer* and *data transfer*, should take place. In the sequel we will explain how these transfers can be achieved.

Suppose a subprogram is to be called from the main program a number of times. At the end of its execution, control should return to the appropriate location in the calling program, as shown in Figure 8.9.

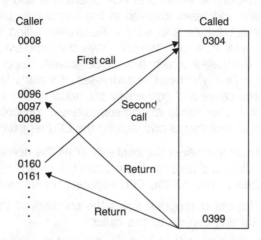

**Figure 8.9  Subroutine call and return.**

We observe that the return address can be easily obtained from the address of the instruction that transfers control to the called program. In the first call (see Figure 8.9) this address is 0096 and the return address will be the address of the next instruction, that is, 0097. We can introduce a new instruction to store the contents of the program counter in a specified register (remember that after the current instruction is fetched, the program counter contains the address of the next sequential instruction) and then transfer the execution to the first instruction in the called program or subroutine. The address of the first instruction of the called program is also known as the address of the callee.

We will enrich the instruction set by adding two new instructions:

1. CALL (to call a subroutine) and
2. RET (short for RETURN) (Return to the calling program)

## Semantics of CALL instruction

*Symbolic form:*             CALL POLY [Op-code for CALL is 43; J-type]

*Machine language form:*  43 30 2EFA (assuming POLY is located at address 2EFA)

*Semantics:*               Top of stack ← address of the memory location following that of the CALL instruction, that is, the addess for returning, i.e. PUSH PC (Save return address in top of stack)

                              PC ← 2EFA (the starting address of the subroutine)

## Semantics of RET instruction

| | |
|---|---|
| *Symbolic form:* | RET [Op-code for RET is 44; R-type] |
| *Machine language form:* | 44 04 00 00 |
| *Semantics:* | PC ← top of stack |

We note that the semantics of CALL and RET instructions (which are hardware instructions) are defined in terms of the PUSH and POP operations and a stack in the hardware is used to store the return addresses involved in the subroutine calls. A called subroutine can in turn call another subroutine and so on. Recursive calling to any depth becomes straightforward with the use of stacks. We still have the problem of passing parameters between the caller and the callee which has to be solved. Suppose we have written a subroutine to compute $z = (x + y)^2$ then the addresses of $x$ and $y$ known to the caller have to be communicated to the callee and conversely the address of $z$ known to the callee has to be communicated to the caller. While writing subroutines, conventions are established for passing these parameters or arguments and sharing the CPU registers for their computation.

**Convention 1:**   The caller saves the contents of all the needed registers in a known area in memory before calling and restores them when the control returns to the caller. This way the callee can be free to use all the CPU registers for its own computation.

**Convention 2:**   The called program saves the contents of the registers it uses and restores them before returning control to the caller.

To pass parameter addresses between the caller and the callee we have two options:

**Convention 3:**   Pass the values of arguments in mutually known registers (call by value).

**Convention 4:**   Store the arguments in a block of consecutive locations in a reserved part of the memory in an orderly fashion and pass only the starting addresses of that block (call by reference).

***Program 8.8:***   Read $x$ and $y$ one at a time and then compute $(x + y)^4$ using a subroutine that computes $(x + y)^2$. Parameters are to be passed by passing the base address through the stack.

*Storage allocation*

| | |
|---|---|
| R1: | internal working |
| R4: | Contains output |
| R6-R8: | Used by subroutine |

*Symbolic program*

```
MAIN    INPUT    R1        ; Read X
        STORE    R1,X
        INPUT    R1        ; Read Y
        STORE    R1,Y
        CALL     SUBR
X       DW       1          ; Parameters stored here
```

```
        Y        DW        1
        XYSQ     DW        1        ; Results stored here
        XY4      DW        1
                 LOAD      R1, XYSQ ; SUBR will return here
                 MUL       R4,R1, R1
                 STORE     R4, XY4
                 OUTPUT    XY4
- - - - - - - - - - - - - - - - - - - - - - - - - - - -
        SUBR     POP       R6       ; Store address from stack in R6
                                    ; R6 contains address of the data X
                 LDIND     R7, R6   ; R7 now has the value of X (indirect address)
                 INC       R6       ; R6 now points to Y
                 LDIND     R8, R6   ; R8 now has the value of Y
                 ADD       R7,R7, R8 ; (x + y) in R7
                 MULT      R8,R7, R7 ; (x + y)² in R8
                 INC       R6       ; R6 now points to XYSQ
                 STIND     R8,R6    ; result stored in XYSQ
                 INC       R6       ; R6 now points to XY4
                 INC       R6       ; R6 now points to return address
                 PUSH      R6       ; Top of stack has return address
                 RET                ; stack top points to the return address
                 END
```

The method of passing parameters as shown above is adequate but it is not elegant as data areas and program instruction areas are mixed in memory. After every CALL instruction, this method will place the arguments of the subroutine in the main memory immediately following the placement of the CALL instruction. This intermixing of program and data can be avoided by putting all the arguments (data) together at the end of the program and by passing their base address through the stack. We will leave rewriting Program 8.8 to follow this convention as an exercise to readers. In order to facilitate this rewriting process, we introduce a new instruction called **Load Effective Address** (LEA).

### Semantics of LEA instruction

*Symbolic form:*            LEA R2, R3, DELTA [Op-code for LEA 47; M-type; indexed addressing with R3]

*Machine language form:*    47 23 789A (assuming the address of DELTA is 0789A)

*Semantics:*                $C(R2) \leftarrow 789A + C(R3)$ {i.e. the effective address}

Note that the LEA instruction leaves the address of data (not the data value) in the specified register. This distinction must be clearly understood.

We have introduced eight new instructions into SMAC+ and three new types of addressing modes through indexing for vector operations, LDIMM for conveniently loading a constant into a register (load immediate), and indirect addressing through LDIND/STIND (load/store indirect). There has to be appropriate modifications in the hardware architecture of SMAC+ to accommodate these new features. This modified SMAC+ is summarized below and re-named as SMAC++ with its new instruction set called S3.

## 8.16 ENHANCED ARCHITECTURE—SMAC++

The architectural enhancement in SMAC++ when compared to SMAC+ is summarized below:

1. The instruction set is enriched to become S3

2. Three new addressing formats are incorporated (*indexing, immediate addressing* and *register-indirect addressing*). Hence, the instruction format has to be appropriately modified so that the decoding hardware can do its job properly.

3. The software architecture (the Assembler) has to be so designed as to distinguish the pseudo operations (like DW) from the machine operations and take appropriate actions.

4. The stack has to be supported with a special SP or dedicating a general purpose register for stack pointing.

5. The team of assembly language programmers makes suitable conventions in developing their subroutines (or modules) so that they can share each other's subroutines and pass parameters correctly while using the subroutines.

The instruction set S3 of SMAC++ is given in Table 8.5. In Table 8.6 we give the instruction format and semantics of the new added instruction set S3.

**TABLE 8.5**
**Instruction Set S3 of SMAC++**

| Op-code | Op-code in Hex | Type |
|---------|----------------|------|
| 1. HALT | 00 | R |
| 2. ADD | 01 | R |
| 3. LOAD | 02 | M |
| 4. STORE | 03 | M |
| 5. JUMP | 04 | J |
| 6. JMIN | 05 | J |
| 7. INPUT | 06 | R |
| 8. OUTPUT | 07 | R |
| 9. INC | 10 | R |
| 10. CMP | 11 | R |
| 11. JLT | 12 | J |
| 12. DEC | 13 | R |
| 13. AND | 20 | R |
| 14. OR | 21 | R |

(Contd.)

**TABLE 8.5 (Contd.)**
**Instruction Set S3 of SMAC++**

| Op-code | Op-code in Hex | Type |
|---------|----------------|------|
| 15. NOT | 22 | R |
| 16. SUB | 31 | R |
| 17. MULT | 32 | R |
| 18. IDIV | 33 | R |
| 19. JOFL | 34 | J |
| 20. LDIMM | 40 | R |
| 21. MOVE | 41 | R |
| 22. BCT | 42 | J |
| 23. CALL | 43 | J |
| 24. RET | 44 | R |
| 25. LDIND | 45 | R |
| 26. STIND | 46 | R |
| 27. LEA | 47 | M |

**TABLE 8.6**
**Symbolic Instructions and Semantics of New Instructions in SMAC++**

| Instruction Hex form | | | Symbolic form | | | | Semantics |
|------|-----|------|------|------|-----|------|-----------|
| OP | REG | ADDR | OP | Reg1 | Reg | ADDR | |
| 06 | 1 | | INP | R1 | | | $C(R1) \leftarrow$ INPUT (Modified from S2) |
| 07 | 2 | | OUT | R2 | | | OUTPUT $\leftarrow C(R2)$ (Modified from S2) |
| 40 | 40 | 4567 | LDIMM | R4, | 0, | Y | $C(R4) \leftarrow Y$ |
| 41 | 12 | | MOVE | R1, | R2 | | $C(R1) \leftarrow C(R2)$ |
| 42 | 40 | 8543 | BCT | R4, | 0, | XX | $C(R4) \leftarrow C(R4) - 1$, If $(C(R4) = 0)$ PC $\leftarrow$ XX |
| 02 | 12 | 4672 | LOAD | R1, | R2, | X | $C(R1) \leftarrow C(X + C(R2))$ [Indexed address] |
| 03 | 12 | 7432 | STORE | R1, | R2, | X | $C(X + C(R2)) \leftarrow C(R1)$ [Indexed address] |
| 10 | F | | INC | R15 | | | $C(R15) \leftarrow C(R15) + 1$ (R15 is assumed to be reserved as stack pointer) |
| 13 | F | | DEC | R15 | | | $C(R15) \leftarrow C(R15) - 1$ |

(Contd.)

**TABLE 8.6 (Contd.)**

**Symbolic Instructions and Semantics of New Instructions in SMAC++**

| Instruction Hex form | | | Symbolic form | | | | Semantics |
|---|---|---|---|---|---|---|---|
| OP | REG | ADDR | OP | Reg1 | Reg | ADDR | |
| 45 | IF | | LDIND | R1, | R15 | | $C(R1) \leftarrow C(C(R15))$ |
| 46 | IF | | STIND | R1, | R15 | | $C(C(R15)) \leftarrow C(R1)$ |
| 10 | F | } | PUSH | R1, | R15 | | [Equivalent to INC R15,STIND R1, R15] |
| 46 | IF | | | | | | |
| 45 | IF | } | POP | R1, | R15 | | [Equivalent to LDIND R1, R15; DEC R15] |
| 13 | F | | | | | | |
| 43 | 00 | 2EFA | CALL | POLY | | | [Equivalent to PUSH PC; PC ← POLY] Jump to subroutine lable POLY after storing return address in stack |
| 44 | 00 | | RET | | | | PC ← (Contents of top of stack) (Return to calling program) |
| 47 | 23 | 789A | LEA | R2, | R3, | DELTA | $C(R2) \leftarrow C(R3) + DELTA$ (R2 stores effective address) |

## 8.16.1 Modifications in the Instruction Formats for SMAC++

The following are the modifications in the instruction formats for SMAC++:

1. In the Op-code field of SMAC++ we have 8 bits. Let us use the two high order bits to denote the type of the instruction (R, J, M) and use the following coding. The remaining 6 bits in the Op-code field of an instruction are sufficient to code instruction set S3.

   - 01  M-type
   - 10  J-type
   - 11  R-type

2. In order to facilitate indexing, the format of the M and J type instructions will be modified by adding another register reference that is called **index register**. When registers in the CPU are general purpose, any available register can be used by the programmer or the assembler as an index register. In certain other machines like Pentium there are separate registers available for indexing. Allocating a separate field for index register specification reduces the number of bits available for the operand-address field in the address space to 16 bits.

3. The assembler software will use several tables. One table will contain the Op-codes and their corresponding hex-codes and it will be used in translation to the machine language. Another table will contain the list of all pseudo-ops so that they can be recognized for taking appropriate actions. Yet another table will be the symbol table that is constructed by the assembler during the assembly process and used for translation to machine language.

## 8.17  CONCLUSIONS

In this chapter, we introduced a pedagogical computer called SMAC and explained how a machine language program for SMAC is stored and executed. Then, we wrote several programs to bring out the issues involved in designing an instruction set for SMAC. We started with S1 and then progressively improved it from S1 to S2 and to S3. It is not a complete computer yet, because we need to study its memory organization and I/O organization. However, in succeeding chapters, we will not be focusing on SMAC or its derivatives. Our purpose in this chapter has been to explain basic concepts and not to make SMAC a real computer. We have introduced a number of basic concepts in this chapter and they are summarized as follows:

1. Concepts of stored programs, Instruction Fetch, Instruction execution and Instruction sequencing using the PC (IP) register.
2. SMAC and its derivatives are **not** real computers. They are used to explain the organizational concepts.
3. Simplicity in design—All instructions are 32 bits long and all Op-codes are 8 bits long.
4. Access to the main memory for operands are only with a few instructions: Load Store (in the case of SMAC++).
5. Simple modes of addressing data or instruction are introduced (indexing, immediate operands, direct addressing, register-indirect addressing).
6. The difference between word addressing and byte addressing of main memory.
7. Three simple formats for instruction—R, M, and J types (note the two left most bits of the Op-code determine the type).
8. In SMAC++ we introduced 3-address format for arithmetic instructions. All three addresses referred to registers.
9. The "instruction set" is driven by the application needs.
10. The basic principle of trade-off in design.
11. How to support subroutines. (Subroutines are needed for modular organization of large program).
12. The concept of stack and its uses.
13. Symbolic programs and their machine language equivalents.
14. An introduction to assembler instructions which are not machine language instructions (like Define Word or DW)
15. The need to write programs in an elegant manner.

---

$\boxed{\textbf{SUMMARY}}$

1. A computer's instruction has five parts. They are: operation to be performed, the address(es) where the two operands will be found, the address where the result is to be stored and the location where the next instruction will be found.

2. However most instruction sets have only operation code, and two or three address fields. The address of the next instruction to be executed is kept in Program Counter (PC).

3. The instruction length (or the word length) is the number of bits retrieved from the main memory in parallel in one cycle. Currently word lengths of 32 bits are common. However, machines with 64-bit words are currently entering the market.

4. The number of bits to be assigned to the various parts of an instruction depends on the instruction length, number of operations to be supported, the size of the memory, the number of registers in the CPU and how many of them need to be addressed in an instruction.

5. The choice of an instruction, the use of registers, and modes of addressing are all determined by the requirements of providing simple and convenenient method of writing a variety of application programs.

6. In this chapter we have used a series of hypothetical computers SMAC, SMAC+ and SMAC++ in which we introduced registers, new operations and addressing modes to illustrate how these features simplify programming.

7. It is seen that to implement loops, instructions such as branch on count, compare and various jump instructions are useful.

8. Using registers reduces access time to main memory and simplifies arithmetic, logic, and certain types and jump instructions.

9. Use of registers as index registers; instructions to increment/decrement values in registers, and immediate addressing simplifies operations with vectors.

10. Use of stack simplifies passing parameters and return from subroutines to calling programs. To implement stacks indirect addressing is useful.

---

$\boxed{\textbf{EXERCISES}}$

1. Write a simulator in C to simulate SMAC+. Using this simulator execute Program 8.3 given in text. Print a trace of the program generated by the simulator.

2. Assume ASCII codes for the letters A-Z. Represent the following sentence using these character codes "RAHUL FOUND A PEN". Write a SMAC+ program to count the number of As in this sentence.

3. A computer is to be designed with the following specifications:

   32K words of memory, each word to be addressable, 64 operation codes and 8 registers. Answer the following questions:

   (a) What is the format of an instruction for this computer?

   (b) What is the number of bits in an instruction?

   (c) If an integer is to be stored in a word using a two's complement representation, what is the range of integers which can be represented in this machine?

   (d) Can a floating point number be represented in this word? If not, what solutions would you suggest for floating point representation?

   (e) What CPU registers are needed and what are their lengths?

4. A byte addressed machine has 256 MB memory. It has 160 instructions and has 16 GPRs.

   (a) What is the instruction format if in an instruction 3 GPRs can be addressed?

   (b) What is the word length of the machine?

   (c) What is the largest integer which can be stored in a word?

   (d) Is the word size sufficient to represent floating point numbers? If yes, pick appropriate number of bits for the mantissa and exponent. Justify your choice.

   (e) What are the advantages of byte addressing over word addressing and what are their disadvantages?

   (f) If the number of registers is to be increased to 32 , discuss at least three choices you can make to redesign the instruction format. Discuss their respective advantages and disadvantages.

5. Write a program for SMAC+ to count the number of zeros in a given 32-bit word. Do you find the instruction set to be adequate? Comment. Trace your program and show that it is correct.

6. Write a program in SMAC+ assembly code to find the largest and the second largest integer from a set of 10 integers. Which instruction set is appropriate for this problem?

7. Write a subroutine to add the 5 data elements in a vector. Use this subroutine to add the elements of the columns of a $5 \times 5$ matrix. Scan your program carefully to assure the number of instructions cannot be reduced any further. Use SMAC++ assembly language.

8. Write an algorithm similar to Algorithm 8.1 in the text to simulate SMAC++.

9. Write a C or Java program to simulate SMAC++. Use this simulator to execute the program you wrote to solve exercise 7.

10. For Program 8.7 of the text write

    (a) The machine language equivalent to the assembly code.

    (b) If the contents of the stack has to be X, Y, Z, W from top to bottom, how should input data be presented?

    (c) In what order will the output characters be printed?

11. Is it possible to implement a stack using indexed addressing instructions instead of indirect addressing?

    (a) If yes write assembly programs for SMAC++ to simulate PUSH and POP instructions.

    (b) Rewrite Program 8.7 of the text using these new instructions.

    (c) Write the machine language equivalent of the assembly code of (b).

12. Re-write Program 8.5 using the two addressing format for the arithmetic operations. Compare your program with Program 8.5 and comment.

13. Illustrate how a stack can be used when a program calls a subprogram A which in turn calls another subprogram B. Show how the parameters and the return addresses will be transmitted.

14. Use logical instruction of SMAC++ to replace every occurrence of a byte A5 (in Hex) in a word by the byte B6.

15. Introduce instructions in SMAC++ to do the following and define their semantics:

    (a) Shift right the contents of a register by a specified number of bits.

    (b) Shift left the contents of a register by a specified number of bits.

    (c) Shift circular right the contents of a register by a specified number of bits.

    Expand the SMAC++ simulator to include these instructions.

16. Assemble Program 8.8 into its machine language equivalent using the instruction set S3.

17. In chapter 6 we gave an algorithm for floating point addition of two 32-bit numbers. Write that algorithm as an assembly language program for SMAC++ with the enhanced instructions of exercise 15.

18. Write assembly codes for floating point multiply and divide. Write machine language equivalent.

19. Rewrite program 8.8 using LEA instruction described in the text.

20. In SMAC+ we have defined the compare instruction as CMP R1, X where X is a constant. Modify it to CMP R1,R2 where R2 is a register address. Discuss the advantages and disadvantages of defining CMP in this manner. Modify the similator of Algorithm 8.1 appropriately. Rewrite Program 8.3 and 8.4 to reflect this changed definition.

**Chapter**

# 9

# Central Processing Unit

| Learning Goals |
| :--- |

In this chapter we will learn:

☞ What features are relevant to a typical Central Processing Unit.

☞ Encoding and decoding of Instructions and Addresses.

☞ How instruction formats and instruction sets are designed.

☞ Different modes of addressing the contents of a RAM and their applications.

☞ What determines the size of the register set.

☞ How clocks are used for timing a sequence of events.

☞ How buses are used for transferring the contents from one place to another.

☞ Data paths and control flow or sequencing in CPUs.

☞ Microprogramming of control unit of CPU.

## 9.1 INTRODUCTION

In any computer system, small or large, the central processing unit (also known as CPU) is the heart of the system. However, a powerful CPU alone does not make a powerful computer system. Memory sub-system and the I/O sub-system should also match the power of CPU to make a computer powerful. In Chapter 8, we presented a hypothetical computer and its organization from the point of view of the instruction set and assembly language programming. In this chapter we will examine what constitutes the central processing unit and how it is organized at the hardware or microprogramming level. In this case, micro-level operations such as "transfer a register-content to another register" play a major role. Strict timing and sequencing of micro-operations become important. The CPU of a computer system is characterized by many features such as: the set of instructions supported by that system (instruction set); how the Op-codes and addresses in these instructions are encoded (instruction format); the diverse ways in which the operands and instructions in memory can be addressed (addressing modes); the set of registers in the CPU and how the registers are functionally partitioned or divided for the programmer's use (register organization); how the various registers and the ALU are connected to each other by one or more buses; the data paths which facilitate efficient data flow from component to component in the CPU so as to enable correct instruction execution; the timed sequencing of micro operations in the form of a micro program and the control signals which facilitate it.

In Chapter 8, we evolved the instruction set of a hypothetical computer called SMAC++ in three successive iterations. The main focus was how to write concise programs to solve meaningful problems using a set of elementary instructions. In that process of simplifying programming, we needed more registers, more instructions and newer addressing modes. We will summarize below, the elements of the CPU of this hypothetical computer SMAC++:

1. In SMAC++ all registers were 32 bits long. A string of 32 bits was called a 'word'.

2. The instructions were of fixed length (32 bits). One instruction was stored in a word even if the instruction did not require all the 32 bits.

3. There were 16 registers in the CPU, this number was limited due to the 4-bit address field reserved for register references.

4. The registers were called General Purpose Registers (GPRs) because they were not pre-assigned to hold any specific data items nor reserved for any specific purpose. This is unlike the Pentium processor.

5. There were only 3 simple instruction formats (referred to as R, M, and J types).

6. Within an instruction, the Op-code field encoding an instruction was of fixed length of 8 bits for all instructions. Normally this is not true in many real computers which use variable number of bits in the Op-code field with the objective of optimizing coding efficiency.

7. The memory system was assumed to be organized into words of 32 bits each. Most real computers use byte addressing instead of word addressing used by SMAC++.

8. When a memory location was referenced in SMAC++, it was directly addressed or addressed using indexing. These were the two basic addressing modes provided.

9. Direct addressing restricted the range of memory addresses (in some cases SMAC++ used 16-bit address giving 64K word range and in other cases a larger address range).

10. The instruction set of SMAC++ had less than 30 instructions as opposed to hundreds of instructions in a Pentium like processor.

11. There were three registers: IR (instruction), FLAG (status) and IP or PC (instruction pointer or program counter), mainly used to control instruction sequencing.

In the following sections we will study in detail the various aspects of a typical CPU but will not restrict our study only to SMAC++. However, wherever appropriate we will use SMAC++ as an example.

## 9.2 OPERATION CODE ENCODING AND DECODING

In general an instruction for a computer should specify the following:

1. What operation is to be performed?
2. Where are the operands stored (in register or where in memory)?
3. Where will the result be stored (in register or where in memory)?
4. What is the address of the instruction to be executed next?

An instruction is designed to codify the information related to the questions given above. There is a large variety of ways in which the above information can be specified. Computer designers over the years have designed computers with a number of different instruction formats as there is no optimal way of selecting an instruction format. The selection is based on electronic and memory technology available at a specified time, the intended applications of the computer, the programming method and languages of relevance at that time, compatibility with the older computers designed by the manufacturer, etc.

An instruction in SMAC++ had an Op-code field that was 8 bits long and the codes for the 26 operations were assigned rather arbitrarily. With 8 bits we can represent $2^8 = 256$ different operation codes, but we used only 26 of these possibilities. This representation or mapping of a set of Op-code symbols to binary strings on a one-to-one basis is called **encoding**. This mapping could have been done in a systematic or hierarchical manner. For example, the first two bits of the 8-bit Op-code could have been used to identify the R-type, M-type, J-type instructions (see Figure 9.1). If we do so, then the code space consisting of the ($2^8$) combinations will be partitioned into 4 equal sets. Each set can then be assigned to denote one type of instruction. With this coding scheme, a 2-input decoder would determine the type of instruction being considered (see Figure 9.2). For an R-type instruction no memory access is needed whereas for an M-type instruction, memory access is required. The decoder output can be used to trigger the appropriate sequences of micro level operations for register access or memory access.

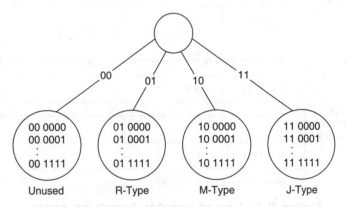

**Figure 9.1  Partitioning the code space.**

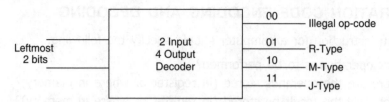

**Figure 9.2  Instruction type decoder.**

The type of hierarchical encoding explained above has one disadvantage. The number of instructions of each type is not the same. Recall the instruction set of SMAC++ where there are many more R-type instructions than other types. If we go beyond the limit of 64 instructions in one type we cannot use any available free space in another partition.

In the above encoding, all operation codes are of equal length. We can consider variable length codes instead of fixed length codes. Suppose 15 operation codes are used much more frequently than others. Call these 15 operation codes as belonging to group 11. We can encode these 15 operations with 4 bits. Out of the 16 combination of 4 bits we use the first 15 to code group 1 instructions. The unused 16th combination 1111 is used along with 4 more bits to encode 16 operation codes of group 2 (those that are not used frequently). The coding will thus be as shown in Figure 9.3. If the group 1 instructions were used 80% of the time by the different programs, then the "average Op-code length" with this encoding would be:

$$\text{Average length} = 0.8 \times 4 + 0.2 \times 8 = 4.8 \text{ bits}$$

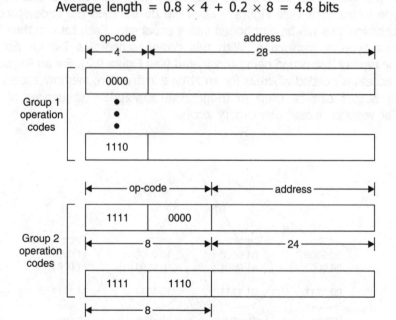

**Figure 9.3  Use of variable length op-codes.**

This is to be compared with 5 bits needed in simple fixed length encoding. Thus, there is not much gain in terms of saving bits. We have bought complexity in decoding without substantial gain. However, group 1 instructions may be used to directly address a larger address space. We will illustrate this with an example.

*Example 9.1.* A computer has 32-bit word length. It has 16 registers. There are 15 instructions which use 3 register (addresses) for operands. The other instructions have 2 register operands and bits address main memory. Suggest an instruction format for this computer.

*Solution:* *Option 1* To encode 16 register addresses, we need 4 bits. 15 instructions which use 3 register addresses for operands may be designed as half-word instructions as shown in Figure 9.4.

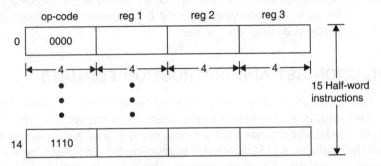

**Figure 9.4  Half word instructions (Example 9.1).**

The other instructions with 2 registers and memory address may be designed as full word instructions as shown in Figure 9.5. Observe that we use 8 bits for the Op-codes of the second set of instructions. The total number of instructions is limited to 31. Direct addressability is 64 KB (as 16 bits are used for address part of instruction).

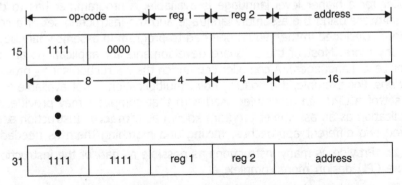

**Figure 9.5  Full word instructions (Example 9.1).**

*Option 2* Use all instructions as full word instructions. With this design, we can encode 128 Op-codes. Direct addressability is 128 KB (see Figure 9.6).

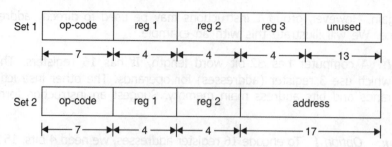

**Figure 9.6   Using full word instruction option.**

The reader is urged to observe how the various instructions are encoded in a computer they use. This can be done by observing the output generated by an assembler software when assembly language programs are written.

## 9.3   INSTRUCTION SET AND INSTRUCTION FORMATS

An instruction has several fields and each field may be encoded differently. The instruction decoder unit (hardware) in a computer decodes these fields individually. The instruction set is a collection of all the instructions that a computer designer has selected for hardware implementation. Normally, in a RISC (Reduced Instruction Set Computer) type computer, the designer chooses a small set so that the assembly language programmer or the assembler software can use this set more effectively. In a CISC (Complex Instruction Set Computer), the number of different instructions runs into three or four hundred.

### 9.3.1   Instruction Set

The instruction set of a CPU determines its power to do various operations on data items. If no compiler for a higher level language is available, a programmer has to develop the application software using the assembly language and the instruction set of a computer. In early machines (Designed in the 1960s) one had to program in assembly language, but this is not true any more. Most of the software developments for applications are done using HLLs (Higher Level Languages). A compiler can enrich the instruction set by providing *higher level operations*. For example, if a floating point multiplication is not available as part of an instruction set of a CPU; an assembler used with that computer may provide the floating point multiplication as an assembler program known as a **macro**. Instruction set designers have followed two different approaches, mixing and matching them as needed:

**Approach 1:**   Provide as many instructions as possible as part of the instruction set. This will make the CPU design more complex.

**Approach 2:**   Provide a minimal set of frequently used instructions as part of the instruction set. Additional support needed is provided through suitably designed HLL compilers or *macros*.

When we use the term *minimal* as above, we do not mean the theoretical minimum but small in the sense of engineering design. In order to understand this, let us enumerate the various classes of instructions needed in an instruction set. The reader is urged to use

SMAC++ as an example to appreciate the following classes and note that we have not introduced any instruction of the type C9 below in this textbook.

| Class-Name | Type of Instruction |
|---|---|
| C1 | Load register from and store register to memory |
| C2 | Move instructions (Register-to-Register) |
| C3 | Arithmetic instructions |
| C4 | Bit oriented instructions (Logical operations, etc.) |
| C5 | Branch instructions |
| C6 | Subroutine control instructions |
| C7 | Shift type instructions |
| C8 | I/O instructions |
| C9 | Instructions to support the Operating System |

When the instruction set is too large (how large is too large?), the assembly language programmer has to be smart enough to judiciously use them and optimize a chosen objective function. The objective function could be: minimize the execution time of the program; or minimize the storage occupied by the program, or minimize the human effort needed to understand/modify the program developed by a programmer. If the computer system is mostly used with HLL compilers, then the compilers have to be smart enough to do the above. From experience and statistical study, it has been observed that a core set of instructions are used very frequently and the remaining set of instructions are used rarely or not at all. This is the reason for some designers to promote approach 2 mentioned above.

Let there be $N$ instructions in the instruction set of a CPU and let $F_i$ be the frequency of the $i$-th instruction. Without loss of generality, let us assume

$$F_i \geq F_{i+1} \quad i = 1, 2, ..., N - 1$$

In order to estimate or compute $F_i$, we need a collection of representative programs, which represent the expected use of that computer system. Such programs are known as **benchmark programs**. We can evaluate a computer system that is in use by writing these benchmark programs and calculating the $F_i$s. But how can we estimate the $F_i$s for a computer system that is being designed? One way to do that would be to simulate the proposed computer system at the level of details of the instruction set and iteratively refine the instruction set.

While measuring the $F_i$s for a computer system in use, we are faced with a question: Should we consider the $F_i$s for the *static* case or for the *dynamic* case? In the static case, the benchmark programs are not executed and the frequencies are calculated from the compiled (or assembled) programs. To find $F_i$ for the dynamic case, we execute the benchmark programs using typical data sets as input data and observe the various instructions as they are executed. We could use the trace files, discussed in Chapter 8, for this purpose or instrument a program by putting counters at suitable places from which dynamic $F_i$s can be calculated. Researchers like Knuth have found that there is a good correlation between the dynamic and static $F_i$s. Using $F_i$s one may decide to provide hardware only for the first

$k$ instructions. Such that $\sum_{i=1}^{k} F_i \leq 0.95$ and implement the rest with macros.

Designing an instruction set for a computer system is not an algorithmic process and it requires extensive experience. A designer uses both scientific reasoning and intuition based on past experience. However, once an instruction set is designed, its usefulness can be evaluated through benchmark programs and static or dynamic $F_i$s. The reader is urged to study the complete instruction set of at least one computer system and examine it carefully. You may put those instructions into the classes (Class 1 through Class 9) presented in this section. Comment on the merits and demerits of classifying instructions using this idea. For the case study undertaken would you need another type called **miscellaneous**? Explain why?

## 9.3.2   Instruction Format

The instruction format of a given instruction reveals how the various fields or bits forming that instruction have to be interpreted by the hardware for execution and by the programmer to understand the meaning of that instruction. For SMAC++ we decided arbitrarily that the various instructions will fall into one of three formats: R-type, M-type, or J-type. In doing so, we followed the designers of a commercial RISC type computer, MIPS-R4000. From what we studied in Chapter 8, we now enumerate the various fields that might be present in an instruction format:

1. Op-code field.
2. Register reference (there may be zero, one, two, three operand references).
3. Memory reference (if one of the operands is located in memory).
4. A small integer constant (that may be present in some instructions).

At the least, an instruction format should have the Op-code field and nothing else. The HALT instruction could be of this type. Of the various fields of an instruction, the memory reference field is the longest and the register reference field is the shortest. A diadic operation such as ADD, SUB, MULT, DIVIDE or MOVE requires two operands (in some cases three if we count the destination or the result of the operation to be different):

$$ADD\ X,\ Y$$

which means $X \leftarrow X + Y$.

Consider a typical instruction of the above type. If both operands are in registers, the instruction will be shorter compared to the case when one of the two operands is in the main random access memory (RAM). In some computer organization (starting from IBM system 360), a short instruction occupied half of a word, that is 16 bits. In such cases two half instructions can be packed into a single word. In order to find the address of these instructions, every byte in the RAM must be addressable. The price one pays for making the RAM byte addressable is the increased address length for addressing the same size RAM. All modern computers are byte addressable even though machines built in the 1960s were word addressable. An early word addressable computer that was popular in the 1960s was IBM 7094.

*Example 9.2.*

| | |
|---|---|
| IBM | 7094 |
| Year | 1962 |
| Word length | 36 bits |
| Memory | Word addressable |
| | Maximum size 32K words |
| Number of index registers | 7 |
| Number of Op-codes | 185 |
| Memory cycle time | 2 micro seconds (Magnetic core memory) |

In a memory system, normally each memory access fetches one word and stores it in the MBR (memory buffer register). For an instruction fetch cycle the MBR will be moved to IR (Instruction Register). If two short instructions are packed into one word, we have the benefit of fetching two instructions in one memory access. Of course, there is some amount of book-keeping overhead to determine if the next instruction to be executed is already in the IR or not.

In the 1970s byte addressability became popular as it was realized that many applications, particularly in business data processing required manipulating character strings. Strings were packed in many words before storage and unpacked for processing. This slowed down processing. Short strings such as a single character had to be allocated a whole word which was wasteful. Thus, byte addressing became almost a universal standard during the 1970s for general purpose computers. Even though it increases the number of bits in the address field of an instruction, the convenience of byte addressing in writing both systems and applications software has induced computer designers to use byte addressing almost universally.

We had 16 registers in the CPU of SMAC++. In contrast to this, let us suppose, there is only one register for all arithmetic and logic operations. Let us call this register *accumulator register* (ACC). All operations of this computer will be performed using this ACC register. Thus, the higher level language construct like C = A + B will translate into

| | |
|---|---|
| LOAD A; | A's value is loaded into ACC |
| ADD B; | B's value is added to the contents of ACC |
| STORE C; | ACC is stored in C |

Such a computer organization is called **single address computer** because each instruction has (at most) one address. The second operand for diadic operations is implied to be in the ACC register. The assembly language programs for single addressed computers tend to be long; thereby occupying more RAM space and also making the program less readable. However, designing the CPU with a single ACC register made the hardware design simpler during the 1950s and 1960s when LSI chips were not available.

*Example 9.3.* The instruction structure of IBM 7090 that was popular in the 1960s which had an accumulator for all arithmetic operations was designed as follows:

| | |
|---|---|
| To address 32K words memory : | 15 bits |
| To encode 185 Op-codes : | 8 bits |

To address 7 index registers :                                   3 bits

To address 4 different index registers in a single instruction : 12 bits

It had indirect addressing and one bit called indirect bit for indicating it. Thus the instruction structure in IBM 7090 was as shown in Figure 9.7.

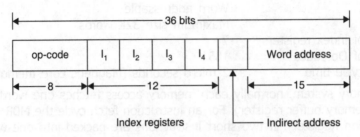

**Figure 9.7  Instruction structure of IBM 7090.**

Characters were encoded using 6 bits per character (lower-case letters were not used). Thus each word could accommodate 6 characters. An instruction format of this type for a modern processor is totally inappropriate. Can you list all possible arguments to show why it is inappropriate?

Another way to classify the instruction set of a computer system is based on the number of addresses associated with an instruction. There can be 0, 1, 2, or 3 addresses. Each address could be that of a register or of a memory location in the RAM. In CPUs that contain multiple registers, most instructions have two addresses. One of the two addresses refers to an operand in a register and the second address could refer to a register or a memory location. Computers based on such type of CPUs are called **two addressed computers**. What percentage of the instructions in Chapter 8 are two addressed?

Consider the task of copying a contiguous set of memory locations (say 125 words) from one region in memory to another region. This task has to be performed when programs are relocated for compacting fragmented free spaces in memory or when a copy of a data set is sent from one program to another. An instruction designed to perform this operation of memory to memory transfer will have the following three fields:

1. Start address (in memory) of the dataset to be copied.
2. Start address (in memory) of the place where the new copy is to be placed.
3. Word count of the data set.

An instruction of this kind is possibly the longest instruction due to the two memory references contained in it. In IBM 370 type computers such an instruction existed. Find out how to do this operation in the computer you are using.

*Example 9.4.*   IBM 370 SS-type instruction (see Figure 9.8)

| | |
|---|---|
| Op-code: | 8 bits |
| Function: | Copy a specified number of bytes from one place in memory to another place |
| Length of block: | 8 bits |

From address in memory:     16 bits (4 bits base register + 12 bits displacement)
To address in memory:       16 bits (4 bits base register + 12 bits displacement)
Total length of instruction:  48 bits
Word length:                32 bits

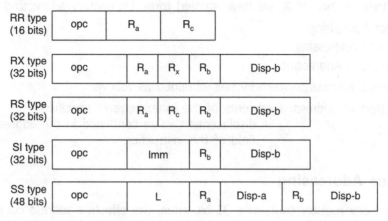

opc : 8-bit op-code field
$R_a$, $R_b$, $R_c$, $R_x$ : 4-bit register address
Disp-a, Disp-b : 12-bit displacement
Imm, L : 8-bit integer constant
$R_x$ : Refers to use as index register
$R_b$ : Refers to use as base register
$R_a$, $R_c$ : Refers to use as operand register

**Figure 9.8   IBM 370 instruction formats.**

We can treat an arithmetic instruction like ADD as a zero address instruction if the addresses of the two operands and the result are implicitly known to the implementing hardware. In *stack machines* (like HP 3000) there are special instructions called **stack instructions**. For example, ADD instruction of this type *pops* the top two elements of an *arithmetic stack* adds them and *pushes* the result back into the stack. Thus, all the required addresses are implied in this case. Besides stack instructions, a stack machine will have other instruction formats to load from and store into memory.

## 9.4   ADDRESSING MODES

Every instruction, except the immediate type instruction, is associated with addresses that point to an *operand* (data) or another instruction. Conditional jump, unconditional jump and subroutine CALL instructions contain memory address of another instruction. Arithmetic, logic, and shift instructions address one or more data items which may be located in memory or in registers. Thus, addressing is important for using computers. A memory system with 32-bit MAR can address 4 GB of memory. However, with today's technology most personal computers contain close to a GB of memory. If we have a 24-bit address field in the instruction format, we can *directly address* 16 MB of RAM. After allowing for the Op-code field and the register reference field, a 32-bit instruction length may not have 24 bits available for the address field. The remaining part of memory must be addressable based on addressing modes other than direct addressing. In this section, we will introduce some new modes of addressing such as base addressing, segmented addressing, relative addressing and indirect addressing.

Recall that in Chapter 8, we have studied three elementary addressing modes:

1. Direct Addressing
2. Indexed Addressing
3. Immediate Addressing

An indexed address to memory was obtained as follows:

Effective address = contents of the index register specified
+ displacement value contained in the address
field of the instruction

## 9.4.1 Base Addressing

Because the index register contains a 32-bit value, the effective address could be 32 bits long, thus allowing 4 GB addressability. This increases the addressable memory range. However, remember that index registers were introduced not for increasing the address range but for facilitating array-oriented calculation. We do not wish to mix these two roles. Hence, in IBM 370 computers, the concept of *base addressing* was introduced. This feature requires special registers called **base registers**. The effective address in the case of base addressing is calculated exactly like indexing:

Effective address = contents of base register referenced
+ the value in the displacement field

The base register contents is used as the reference point or the origin, relative to which the displacement field specifies the memory address (see Figure 9.9). The procedure

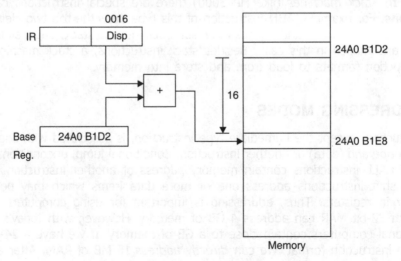

**Figure 9.9  Base register usage.**

by which the effective address is calculated is the same both for indexing as well as for base addressing. In both cases, an integer value contained as part of the instruction is added to the contents of a CPU register. This addition cycle is the extra time overhead in the execution of an instruction when indexing or base addressing is used. The base register contents refers to the *base address*. A 32-bit base register can point to any address in the 4 GB ($2^{32}$) address space as the base address.

The effective address generated in base addressing is *relative* to the base address. For example, in Figure 9.9 the displacement value of 16 refers to the 16th word from the origin 24A0B1D2, which is the base address. When the base value is changed, say to 24A0C90, the effective address will refer to the 16th word from the new base value. Base addressing is extremely useful when programs are relocated in RAM. Relocation of programs is very common in multiuser or multitasking operating systems.

## 9.4.2  Segment Addressing

In Pentium-based computers, a variant of base addressing is used and it is called **segmented addressing**. The similarity stops at the fact that the contents of the segment register is added to the displacement. The purpose of segmented addressing in Pentium is totally different from that of the IBM 370 computers. In this case the large address space ($2^{32}$) is segmented to serve logically different purposes such as to separately store the instructions or code, data, stack, etc. There are six segment registers (CS, DS, ES, SS, FS, GS) in the CPU of Pentium and they are 16 bits long. The segment register is used to select one of the *segment base addresses* stored in a special area in memory called **Segment Descriptor Table**. The segment descriptor table is managed by the Operating System. Then, the selected segment base address is added to the displacement (which is 32 bits in the case of Pentium) to get an effective address that is used to access the operand or instruction in RAM. Note that the effective address is also 32-bits long. This is depicted in Figure 9.10.

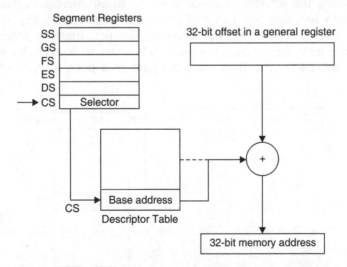

**Figure 9.10  Use of segment registers in Pentium.**

### 9.4.3  PC Relative Addressing

Let us turn our attention to another addressing mode known as **PC relative addressing** or simply **relative addressing**. Consider a part of a program shown below:

```
016    COMPARE    A,B
017    J MIN      *+2      Relative address * means the address of this instruction.
018    CALL       XYZ
019    OUT        A
01A
```

The instruction at address 016 compares two data values A and B and the instruction at address 017 causes jump to the address (017 + 2 = 019) if the result of the comparison is negative. The symbolic reference of * refers to the current PC value or the address where the instruction with * reference is located in RAM. In this example it is 017. The relative address +2 is with reference to the current PC value. This addressing mode has two major benefits. If the above program is relocated in some other place in RAM, the * +2 (PC-relative reference) would work correctly without any adjustments to the address field. Secondly, the address field has to store only a small constant like +2 which will require fewer bits. For example, if 8 bits are used to store such a constant and treated as a signed 2's complement integer, the relative address can range from −128 to +127. The positive constant refers to forward reference from the PC value whereas the negative constant refers to backward reference from the PC value. One of the early computers from the Digital Equipment Corporation (DEC) called PDP 11 popularized this kind of addressing mode.

### 9.4.4  Indirect Addressing

The final addressing mode that we will learn is known as **indirect addressing**. In this mode of addressing, the effective instruction points to an address in memory where the address of the data item (not the data itself) is stored (see Figure 9.11). Thus, data access will require not one, but two memory accesses. The first memory access will yield the address of the data item, using which the memory is accessed again to fetch the data. What is the gain one obtains for this time overhead paid as a price for indirect addressing?

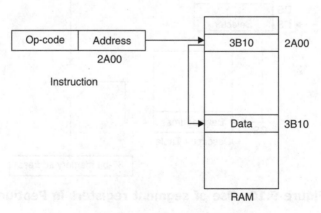

**Figure 9.11  Indirect addressing.**

Suppose the instruction shown in Figure 9.11 is part of an already compiled program and the data item has to be located at the address 3B10 for one execution, and at another address say 4B10 for the next execution. If we have addressed the data indirectly through the address 2A00, there is no need to modify the program at all. In the second execution one has to simply change the contents of the memory location 2A00 from 3B10 to 4B10. This kind of requirement arises often while writing system software, such as Operating Systems, I/O drivers, etc.

In the description given above we have used indirect addressing through another memory location (2A00 is an address in RAM). The indirect addressing could very well be through a register. Then it is called **register indirect addressing**. In this case we will address a data item **through** a register, i.e. the specified register will contain the address of the data item, and not the data itself. The concept of indirect addressing can be recursively extended beyond level 1. That is, in the example shown in Figure 9.11, the location 2A00 may be made to contain another address where the data is stored. Beyond one level, human understanding and tracking becomes quite difficult, and this multilevel indirection is mainly of theoretical value.

## 9.4.5 How to Encode Various Addressing Modes

In Table 9.1, we have summarized various addressing modes. The roles played by each of the addressing modes are also indicated in this Table. Note that some of the roles are played by more than one addressing mode. Not all the addressing modes will be present in a particular computer system. If indirect addressing feature is not present in a system, its effect could be simulated through software means. Simulation will be much slower than equivalent hardware implementation. A computer designer should first decide which addressing modes are to be included in the hardware design. The next question is "how to encode them in the instruction format"?

### TABLE 9.1
### Summary of Addressing Modes

| Addressing Mode | Role Played |
| --- | --- |
| 1 Direct | Simple and fast |
| 2 Indexed | For iterative vector type operations |
| 3 Immediate | Readability, faster access to data, small data range, better usage of bits |
| 4 Base | Extending addressable range; facilitate relocation of programs |
| 5 Segmented | Logical separation of the program from data and stack contents |
| 6 PC relative | Better use of bits, facilitate relocation, shorter range of relative address |
| 7 Indirect | Location independence, system software support |

The IBM 370 designers decided to uniformly associate base addressing in every memory address. Thus, except the RR-format (see Figure 9.8) all other formats have a 4-bit field to refer to the base register. The indexing mode is associated with the RX format, that too only with the first operand. Since any of the 16 GPRs in IBM 370 can be used as an index register or as a base register, 4 bits are reserved in the instruction format for register references. The register R0 is assumed to always hold a constant zero. Thus, 0000 in the index field or the base register field of an instruction denotes the absence of indexing or base addressing for that instruction. In this design, the encoding of Op-code field is kept separate from the encoding of the index and base address fields. Thus, every instruction in the instruction set can benefit from indexing and base addressing modes.

The Pentium processor did not include base addressing. For indexing only two special registers (ESI and EDI) are used. Indirect addressing is restricted to indirection through a register content and not through a memory content.

1. A designer has to select a subset of addressing modes. (The goal is to provide flexibility and power to programmers).

2. A designer has to encode the fields in an instruction so that the hardware can decode which addressing mode(s) are used in that instruction and appropriately compute the effective address for fetching the operand or another instruction from the RAM.

## 9.5   REGISTER SETS

Every CPU has a set of registers. IBM 370 had 16 registers, another popular computer in the 1970s called PDP 11 had 8 registers, and INTEL 80486 has 12 registers and Power PC has 32 registers. There is no universal acceptance among designers and manufacturers about the number of registers that must be in a CPU. In fact there is no agreement even on how these registers should be partitioned or grouped. For example, IBM and Power PC group them all as one set of GPR (general purpose registers). The Pentium partitions them based on their functions into three sets: arithmetic registers (EAX, EBX, ECX, EDX); segment registers (ESS, ECS, EDS, EES); index registers and pointer registers (ESI, EDI, EBP, ESP). At the other extreme PDP 11 has the flexibility of allowing the PC to be an explicitly addressable register available to programmers.

An assembly language programmer has direct control over various registers in developing the programs. On the other hand a programmer using a higher level language like JAVA does not have direct control over the use of registers, because the compiler is responsible for register allocation and management. A computer designer aims at providing a sufficiently large and flexible set of registers to facilitate efficient register allocation and management.

Registers are used as short term memory to store data values or address values during a computation. Accessing a register is one to two orders of magnitude (10 to 100 times) faster than accessing a memory location. Thus, one would believe that there must be a large number of registers in a CPU. However, the registers in CPU have to be effectively allocated and managed either by a programmer or by a compiler. Also, when the CPU switches from one process to another, all the registers must be saved in memory and they must be kept free for their use by the newly started process. The time needed to save registers can become a significant part of the "process-switching time" if the number of registers is increased without limit.

Yet another issue is that each register has to be connected through hardware and buses (data and control paths) to other registers as well as to other parts of the computer system like the ALU. As the number of registers grows, this connection complexity grows rapidly. The RISC type design philosophy believes in providing a large number of registers (32, 64, 128, etc.) and manages the complexity through regular structures in the VLSI design. The register allocation and management responsibilities are mostly done by well-designed compilers. In order to help in these activities, the instruction formats are kept simple and the instruction set is kept small. The R4000 CPU from a company called MIPS and the SUN Micro's SPARC architecture belong to this family of design.

For certain types of computer applications called **real time applications**, process switching has to be extremely fast; because the external stimuli (coming from outside the computer), require very fast response. Computer organizations like SPARC provide more than one set of identical CPU registers. When an external interrupt occurs, there is no need to save the register contents; instead the CPU will leave one set of registers intact and use another set of registers. If there are two sets of registers say $S_0$ and $S_1$, the CPU can switch between two processes $P_0$ and $P_1$ very fast. Moreover, if the address spaces of $S_0$ and $S_1$ overlap, as shown in Figure 9.12, the two processes using these two sets can communicate (data or control information) with one another by storing items in the shared address space (see the shaded region in Figure 9.12).

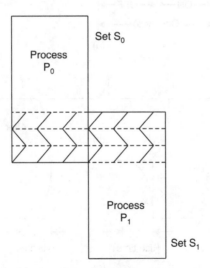

Process
$P_0$

Set $S_0$

Process
$P_1$

Set $S_1$

**Figure 9.12   Two sets of overlapping CPU registers.**

In some other computer systems, special instructions are provided to store (or to load) the CPU registers all at once. Thus by executing a single instruction, multiple registers can be saved in memory in contiguous locations, thereby reducing the process-switching time.

## 9.6   CLOCKS AND TIMING

The clock is a timing device needed to control the sequential activities that take place in a computer system. In a block diagram, we represent the clock as a rectangle with no input and single output (see Figure 9.13). It produces pulses at regular intervals, called **cycles**. Each cycle has an ON period and a following OFF period. In Figure 9.13 we have shown these two periods to be equal. There is a *rising edge* and a *falling edge* in each cycle. At the rising edge, the clock signal changes from the low signal level (0 voltage) to the high signal level (5 volts); and at the falling edge the reverse takes place. In Figure 9.13(a), we have shown these changes to be "instantaneous" which is not true in practice. As shown in Figure 9.13(c), the signal takes a finite time ($t_r$) to rise from low-to-high and finite time ($t_f$) to fall from high-to-low. When $t_r << T$ we approximate the cycle time by zero and assuming the change to be instantaneous. If a state change is initiated at the rising edge, this change will be initiated, in reality, only after a time period $t_r$. In Figure 9.13(b) we have shown how the pulse when differentiated by an electronic circuit will appear. The polarity of the differentiated pulse can be used easily to detect the rising and falling edges.

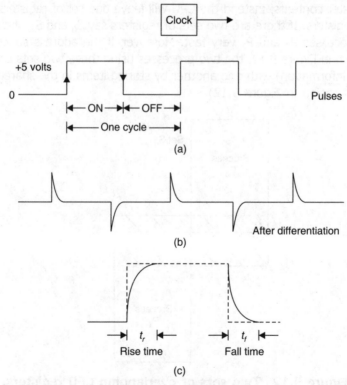

**Figure 9.13   Clock pulses.**

While studying time varying systems, we encounter two terminologies: "events" and "states". Events occur and their occurrence causes changes in the state of the system. An edge of a clock pulse (rising or falling) can be viewed as an event and the level of the signal (low or high) can be viewed as a binary state. As shown in Figure 9.13(b), the edge information can be extracted from a clock pulse through a device that performs differentiation.

Consider the example of an adder shown in Figure 9.14. There are 3 registers; A and B acting as input to the adder and C as the output register. Let us assume the following sequence of actions, so that the adder will perform its function within a system:

1. Before the event $t_1$ the input registers A and B are loaded with data.
2. At $t_1$ ($t_1$ = start) the start event occurs, which lets the adder start its adding operation.
3. The adder takes a *maximum* of ($t_2 - t_1$) units of time to perform addition.
4. At $t_2$ ($t_2$ = load) the result of addition is available from the adder and it is loaded into the register C.

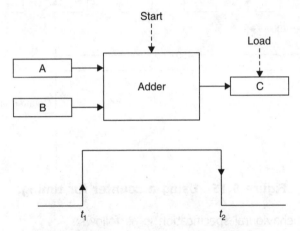

**Figure 9.14 An adder with timing.**

Through this example, we have introduced the need for *data* and *control* at a level lower than the programming level. The registers A, B and C hold data and data flows from one place to another. It flows from A to the adder (also from B to the adder) and then from the adder to C. The control signals start and load (shown above dotted lines in Figure 9.14) initiate the pre-determined  operations. Which control signals should trigger which events is pre-determined by the designer, and this information is encoded in the control flow. In the following two sections, we will study more about data flow and control flow and the paths they need which are known as **data path** and **control path**. In Figue 9.14 solid lines with arrows are *data paths* and dotted line with arrows are *control signals*.

When we use a clock, there is an inherent sequencing mechanism. For example, in Figure 9.15, the event $t_2$ occurs after the event $t_1$. The elapsed time between $t_1$ and $t_2$, in this example, is determined by the clock frequency. For a 10-MHz clock this time will be 100 ns or one-tenth-of a microsecond. Suppose, we use a 10-MHz clock. If the adder is fast enough to produce its output in a time less than 100 ns, the two events $t_1$ and $t_2$ could be timed with the rising and the falling edge of one clock pulse. However, if the adder requires 400 nanoseconds, this cannot be done. Note that 400 ns is an integral multiple of the clock period (100 ns). We can use a counter of 4, that will count 4 clock pulses, starting at $t_1$, and generate the $t_2$ event at the trailing edge of the 4th clock pulse. This is shown in Figure 9.15. For generating the various control signals in the CPU we will need many such counters and a master clock.

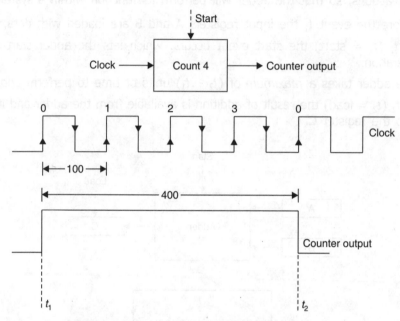

**Figure 9.15  Using a counter for timing.**

The counter's behavioural specification is as follows:

**Counter 4 specification**

1. Start counting the clock pulses after the "start" signal is given.

2. The counter value is incremented at the rising edge of the clock pulse.

3. After 4 clock pulses, that is at the fifth occurrence of the rising edge give the "counter output signal".

4. Immediately after that, reset the counter to zero and wait for the next occurrence of the start signal.

We have specified the counter behaviour using an informal language. This could be written in a formal language, like HDL (like ch. 6) to avoid any ambiguity. From such unambiguous specifications, hardware circuits can be synthesized and tested.

## 9.7  CPU BUSES

Buses are a set of parallel wires used to connect different subsystems of a computer. Buses may be broadly classified into two types. Those inside a CPU chip are called **internal buses** and those outside it are called **external buses**. Internal buses are conducting lines which are used to connect ALU with a set of registers and on-chip memory (called **caches** which we will describe in Chapter 10). External buses connect the CPU chip to the external memory and I/O devices. External buses are a set of parallel wires printed on an electronic printed circuit board. External memory, I/O interface chips, graphics chips, etc. are plugged to this bus.

We will mainly concentrate on internal buses in this chapter. We will also describe some aspects of CPU-Memory bus in this section. The organization of I/O buses is quite different because I/O devices are slow and there is a large variety of I/O devices. We will describe these buses in Chapter 12. There will be some repetitions. However, we make the two discussions self-contained to avoid frequent cross referencing. Data flow and control flow between subsystems can take place through buses. Several subsystems share a bus as the common link for the exchange of data or control. When a shared bus is used as a common link for interconnection, it becomes flexible; new connections can be established easily. The positive aspect of using a bus for interconnection is its low cost and flexibility. On the other hand, because a bus is shared by several subsystems and only one of them can control it at a time, its allocation and control has to be managed by proper protocols. Buses are slower when compared to dedicated data and control paths but are flexible and cheaper.

A bus in a processor board, in general, consists of three groups of wires, called **address lines**, **data lines**, and **control lines**. They are symbolically shown in Figure 9.16. The control lines are used to select who sends data on the bus and who all will receive it from the bus. Each bus design embeds a built-in procedure for determining who becomes the sender. This procedure is known as **bus arbitration** protocol. A meaningful activity on the bus is called a **bus transaction**. A transaction has two sub parts: sending the address on the bus and reading from or writing data in that address.

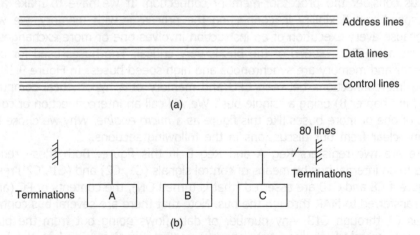

**Figure 9.16  A bus connecting multiple subsystems.**

Buses are classified as *synchronous buses* and *asynchronous buses*. In synchronous buses everything takes place at precise time instants specified by the designer of the bus.

The time instants are defined by a clock. This clock is transmitted through one of the control lines. The transaction protocol of a synchronous bus is straightforward and it is hardware realizable as a simple finite state machine.

An asynchronous bus, on the other hand, does not have a common clock and it uses a *hand-shaking* protocol. In Figure 9.17, we have shown an abstract representation of handshake protocol. This protocol can be viewed as a pair of finite-state machines working on two independent clocks and communicating with each other. The communication assures that one machine does not proceed beyond a particular state until the other machine has reached an anticipated state.

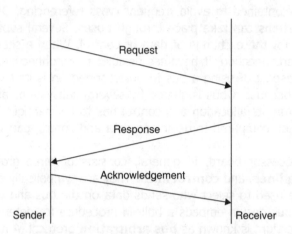

**Figure 9.17  Handshake protocol.**

Let us consider the processor-memory connection. If we have to make a trade-off between speed and flexibility in connecting the processor with memory, we will favour speed; because every execution of an instruction involves one or more exchanges between CPU and memory. Thus, speed of the bus is very critical. The buses used for connecting the processor and memory are synchronous and high speed buses. In Figure 9.18, we have shown the interconnections between CPU and memory of a hypothetical computer SMAC (described in Chapter 8) using a "single bus". We will call an interconnection of components by means of one or more buses like this figure as a *micro engine*. Why we chose this name will become clear from our discussions in the following sections.

There are two registers Reg A and Reg B in this figure. Both these registers are connected to an internal bus by means of control signals (C1, C2) and (C1', C2') respectively. In this figure if C8 and C10 are asserted (that is turned ON), the contents of PC (also known as IP) is transferred to MAR through the bus. Note that there are several bus control signals denoted as C1 through C13. Any number of data flows going out from the bus can be simultaneously asserted whereas only one bus control signal coming into the bus can be asserted at a time. This signifies multiple simultaneous transmissions from one source to several destinations but the bus can carry only one set of signals at a given instant of time. Observe also the broken lines which signify commands; add, subtract, mult, read and write which initiate actions.

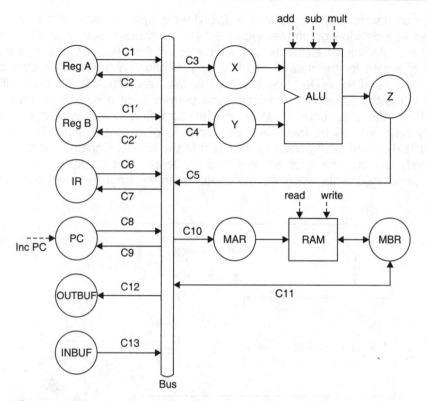

**Figure 9.18   An example of *micro engine* with a single bus.**

The processor memory buses are generally proprietary buses and they are specific to a particular computer system. An I/O bus is attached to such a bus through a *bus adaptor* or *interface chip*. Some designers wish to minimize the number of tappings made to connect a bus adaptor to the high speed processor-memory bus. With the development of microprocessors and personal computers several standards have come into existence in the design and re-use of I/O buses and *backplane* buses. They will be described in Chapter 12.

In Figure 9.18, we have used a single bus to connect all the entities inside a CPU. Instead we could use multiple buses to facilitate simultaneous activities. In Figure 9.18 although the data transfers Z → A, Z → B could take place at the same time data transfers Z → A and MBR → IR cannot be carried out simultaneously, that is in parallel, because only one source can transmit data on a shared bus. Multiple buses are needed for simultaneous independent data transfers.

## 9.8   DATAFLOW, DATA PATHS AND MICROPROGRAMMING

In a computer system data is stored in one out of three storage entities, namely, flip-flops (Flags), register, or RAM. We will exclude mass storages like disks at this stage. During computational process, data flows from one place to another, gets processed or reset to an initial value. For our understanding, we will denote this dataflow and data storage in the form of an abstracted graph and call it a **dataflow graph**. Observe that Figure 9.18 can be redrawn as a dataflow graph (see Figure 9.19). The nodes of such a graph (represented by circles) indicate storage elements, and a directed arc from node *i* to node *j* indicates the existence of a path for the data in *i* to flow to *j*. Although a path for dataflow may exist between *i* and *j* and the node *i* may contain the data ready to flow, the data will actually flow only when the appropriate control signal permits such a data flow from node *i* to node *j*. Thus, the data path is necessary for data flow but it is not sufficient. The sufficiency condition will be met when the corresponding control signal is asserted (see Figure 9.18). The interesting point to note is that the control signals have to be asserted in an orderly fashion, one after another in a sequence. This is interesting because, we gave the same arguments when we discussed assembly language level programming in Chapter 8.

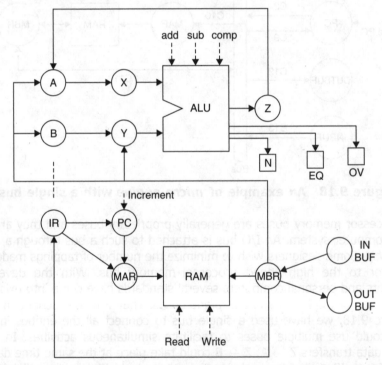

**Figure 9.19   A partial dataflow graph for SMAC instruction set S1.**

For the sake of simplicity, let us consider a subset S1 of the instructions of SMAC that we designed in Chapter 8. It included the following 8 instructions:

HALT, ADD, LOAD, STORE, JUMP, JMIN, INPUT, OUTPUT.

Further, we will assume the existence of two registers called INBUF and OUTBUF such that the INPUT and OUTPUT instructions simply transfer the data between these buffer registers and their respective I/O devices. When this transfer takes place, the previously stored data in OUTBUF is assumed to be already consumed so that the buffer is empty and ready to receive the data being moved. Similarly, the INBUF is assumed to hold the right data received from the input device. We make all these assumptions so that the dataflow graph can be simple enough for presentation in a textbook.

With the above assumptions we have drawn Figure 9.19. This is a preliminary dataflow graph to implement the instruction set S1. We have used the following conventions for the figure:

| | |
|---|---|
| Circles: | Denote registers or flip-flops (i.e. storage) |
| Rectangles: | Functional units like memory. |
| Small squares: | Denote flip-flops |
| Rectangle with V groove: | Denotes a two input adder (X+Y=Z) |

The nodes are labelled with appropriate register names, flag-names, or functional-unit names. A directed arc may or may not be labelled. When an arc is labelled, the name indicates a partial dataflow on which part of the data contained in the source is transferred to destination. For example, the label "addr" will indicate the address part of the register and so on. In Figure 9.19, a reader may notice that dotted lines in a path is used to indicate that it performs a control operation like selecting read or write or incrementing the PC by 1. The reader is urged to verify that the micro engine shown in Figure 9.18 can be modified to support the data paths shown in the graph of Figure 9.19.

Recall that there are two distinct sub-cycles in the execution of every instruction, namely, fetch cycle and execution cycle. The fetch cycle involves four ordered operations, which are:

1. Transfer the PC to MAR
2. Issue memory read
3. Increment the PC by 1 and
4. Transfer the MBR to IR.

Note that after the memory read operation is completed, the MBR will contain the instruction to be executed. This sequence can be expressed in the form of a step-by-step program. We will call such a program as **microprogram**. We introduced a hardware description language in Section 6.3. We will use the same notation to represent microprogram in what follows.

***Program 9.1:*** Microprogram for fetch cycle

$$T_0 : MAR \leftarrow PC$$
$$T_1 : Memory\ Read$$
$$T_2 : PC \leftarrow PC + 1$$
$$T_3 : IR \leftarrow MBR.$$

Every step in the microprogram is called a **microoperation**. There are 4 micro-operations in the above microprogram. Each step is labelled with time $T_0$, $T_1$, etc. Each label represents the time of occurrence of a pulse. The time taken for an operation equals the clock period. The sequencing implies that an operation at $T_1$ takes place after the operation at $T_0$ is completed. Steps at $T_2$ and $T_3$ do not cause any explicit data flow. Every micro-operation is executable if and only if there is a data path in the micro-engine that will facilitate that data flow. A micro-operation can be executed only when the control signal corresponding to that data flow or operation is asserted. The designer's objective is to make the microprogram as efficient as possible. In this case the microprogram can be considered efficient if it takes the least number of steps. Then, we ask: "Can two or more micro-operations be executed in parallel without any conflict?" In the microprogram shown above operations at $T_1$ and $T_2$ can be executed in parallel without any conflict. We will re-write the above microprogram in 3 time steps as shown below. Note that a symbol; is used to denote that those micro-operations can be executed in parallel as one single step.

**Program 9.1(a):**  Fetch cycle with parallel operations

$$T_0 : MAR \leftarrow PC$$
$$T_1 : Memory\ Read;\ Increment\ PC$$
$$T_2 : IR \leftarrow MBR$$

In some cases, a parallel execution of two micro-operations can be done meaningfully only if two independent simultaneous data paths are available in the micro-engine. It should be noted that in order to execute two or more micro-operations in parallel they should not be conflicting and it should be meaningful to perform these operations simultaneously. Data from two different sources cannot be routed into the same bus at a given time. Thus, multiple buses will be useful. Similarly, data from two different sources cannot be simultaneously routed into the same destination register.

*Typical ADD instruction of SMAC:*      ADD A,Y 001 0 1110

*Semantics:*   SMAC has two registers A and B. Register A is coded 0 and B as 1. The contents of memory at 1110 (Y) is added to the contents of register A and the result is in register A.

**Program 9.2:**  Microprogram for the execution cycle of the ADD instruction

$T_0$: MAR ← Address part of IR /*To read the second operand*/
$T_1$: *memory READ*; X ← A /*The first operand sent to X register of ALU*/
$T_2$: Y ← MBR; /*The second operand sent to Y register of ALU */
$T_3$: *add-control signal to ALU*;
$T_4$: A ← Z. /*The result goes to register A.*/

Observe that we have enclosed comments between /* and */.

The microprogram corresponding to the execution cycle of the JUMP instruction is the simplest of all: PC ← Address part of IR. However, for the JMIN (jump on minus) instruction the data transfer "PC ← Address part of IR" will be conditional upon the N (Negative) flip-flop being in ON state. Such a conditional transfer can be achieved using AND gates. Note that when the result of an arithmetic operation results in a negative number, the ALU will set the N flip-flop ON. It will remain ON until it is reset .

**Program 9.3:**  Microprogram for the execution cycle of JMIN instruction

$T_0$: *if (N) then* PC ← Address part of IR;
$T_1$: *Reset (N)* /*The Flag N is reset.*/

A typical LOAD instruction in SMAC appears as:

LOAD A,X [010 0 1111]

where the memory address of the data X is 1111 and the Op-code for LOAD is 010 and the bit-4 from left determines if the word read from memory is to be loaded into the register A or B in the CPU. We can view the Op-code decoding of this instruction in two different ways and both will have the same effect. In one way we can view that the decoder decodes the load instruction, fetches the memory contents and transfers the MBR into register A or B depending on whether bit-4 is 0 or 1. In the second way, we can view the decoder to be using the 3 Op-code bits along with the bit-4 to select one of the microprogram sequences shown in Program 9.4 below. Observe that the two sequences are identical except that the destination register of the micro-operation $T_2$ is either A or B depending on whether bit-4 of the IR register is 0 or 1.

**Program 9.4:** Microprogram for the execution cycle of LOAD instruction

Sequence 1

$T_0$: MAR ← Address part of IR /* To read the data from RAM*/

$T_1$: *memory READ*;

$T_2$: A ← MBR /*This sequence is selected if bit-4=0*/

Sequence 2

$T_0$: MAR ← Address part of IR /*To read the data from RAM*/

$T_1$: *memory READ*

$T_2$: B ← MBR /*This sequence is selected if bit-4=1*/

The two sequences in Program 9.4 can be combined into one microprogram as shown in Program 9.5.

**Program 9.5:** Microprogram to store MBR in register A or B

$T_0$: MAR ← Address part of IR /*To read the data from RAM */

$T_1$: *memory READ*

$T_2$: {*if (bit-4 of IR = 0) then* A ← MBR *else* B ← MBR}

The micro-operation at $T_2$ of the combined sequence can be executed in the micro-engine with the help of an AND gate by directing the destination of the data transfer from MBR to register A or B. If we have 16 registers instead of the two registers A and B, then we will need a decoder instead of one AND gate to select one of the 16 registers for the destination of this data transfer. Working out the details of this is left as an exercise to students.

Now let us consider the execution cycle of the INPUT and OUTPUT instructions. For simplicity we will assume that when the INPUT instruction is executed, the INBUF contains the right data ready to be transferred to the RAM. In real life this may not be the case. The hardware has to ensure that indeed the right input has been put in the INBUF when INPUT is executed. Else the microprogram should keep the system in a wait state till the data is ready in INBUF. We will reserve those details to the chapter on I/O organization. Similarly, when the OUTPUT instruction is executed we will assume that the OUTBUF is free to receive the data being transferred from the RAM into the OUTBUF. It means that whatever was put into the OUTBUF before has been consumed by the intended receiver and the buffer is free to receive new data.

***Program 9.6:*** Microprogram for the execution cycle of INPUT instruction

$T_0$: MAR ← Address part of IR /*To store the data into RAM*/
$T_1$: MBR ← INBUF /*Data is transferred to MBR for storing*/
$T_2$: *memory WRITE.*

In the above program the two micro-operations at $T_0$ and $T_1$ in step 1 and step 2 are independent of each other and they can be executed in parallel. However, in the micro-engine shown in Figure 9.18 there is only one bus which prevents this parallel execution. If we were to re-design a micro-engine with two buses instead of one, we could speed up the microprogram in Program 9.6. We may re-design the micro-engine with two buses. The two buses are named b1 and b2. Program 9.6 is now re-written using the two buses as Program 9.7. Note that, now we have two buses and we need to specify with each data transfer which bus is used. This is done in our programs by appending the left arrow with bus label.

We can connect MBR, INBUF, OUTBUF, IR and PC to bus b2 and not change the connections to existing bus we call b1. This will allow independent operation of ALU and RAM. Drawing the micro-engine with two buses is left as an exercise to the student.

***Program 9.7:*** Executions input instruction with 2 buses

$T_0$: MAR ← (b1) Address part of IR; MBR ← (b2) INBUF
$T_1$: *memory WRITE.*

## 9.9 CONTROL FLOW

In a computer system dataflow and control flow are complementary to each other. An electronic signal is viewed as *data* or *control* solely based on the manner in which it is used or interpreted. The simplest form of control is exercised in selecting one out of several options. An integrated circuit called **multiplexer** (described in Chapter 3) is shown in Figure 9.20, as a black box. The need for selection occurs very often in a computer system. We need to select one out of several registers when there are multiple registers; we need to select one out of several ALU functions from a set such as {*add, subtract, multiply, divide, compare, shift....*}; we need to select one out of several I/O devices for an I/O operation, etc. The term *control flow* is used to signify a sequence of elementary operations that are individually controlled. The sequence implies that operation $i$ is completed before operation $i + 1$ is started. Abstractly we can denote a sequence of operations as an ordered sequence of pairs $< d_1\ c_1 > < d_2\ c_2 > < d_3\ c_3 > ... < d_n\ c_n >$, where $d_i$ denotes the data associated with the $i$th operation and $c_i$ is the corresponding control signal. The subsequence, $d_1\ d_2$ ... $d_n$ can be viewed as the dataflow and $c_1\ c_2\ ...\ c_n$ can be viewed as the control flow. For an $i$th operation to take place, its data $d_i$ must be ready and its control signal $c_i$ must be asserted. Recall that the term *asserted* is used synonymously with setting a flip-flop to the ON condition. In this abstract specification, we have not discussed about the *atomicity* of an operation, or about its *granularity*. An operation is said to be atomic if the operation is either completed in full or not started at all; there is no possibility of doing it partly. We will examine granularity briefly in what follows:

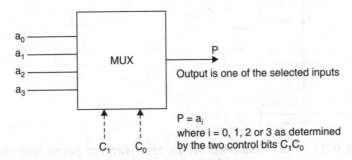

**Figure 9.20  A multiplexer.**

Consider a High Level Language (HLL) like Java or C++ and the programming constructs available in it. We will focus on three constructs:

1. Assignment (sequential flow of one statement after another is implied).
2. Conditional or IF ... THEN...ELSE (selection type control).
3. Iterative or FOR loops; REPEAT-UNTIL; (control is embedded in the computation either to repeat the loop or not).

The granularity of HLL instructions such as those given above is much larger than the machine or assembly language instructions. Each machine or assembly language instruction such as LOAD A, JMP can be treated as *atomic* whereas the blocks (enclosed between *begin ... end* in a high level language) are too big to be treated as atomic at the hardware level. An instruction execution is further divided into two parts: (i) instruction fetch and decode and (ii) instruction execution. The instruction fetch part and the instruction execution part of an instruction are realized through their corresponding microprograms. Let us suppose that the microprograms corresponding to the fetch cycle and the execution cycle of an instruction are executed without any interruption. This means the instruction is executed fully or not executed at all. The partial execution of microprograms corresponding to machine instructions is excluded and hence the partial execution of an instruction is not possible. In that case we ensure the atomicity at the instruction level. This is what is generally accomplished at the hardware level.

Let us consider the dataflow while executing the data transfer "PC ← address part of IR". This data path is activated for both the JUMP and JMIN instructions. For the JUMP instruction it is unconditional and for the JMIN instruction it is conditional. We can define the following Boolean expression to capture the control needed for this data path. When this expression is TRUE, we need to activate this data transfer.

$$\text{Transfer} = (\text{JUMP} \vee (\text{JMIN} \wedge \text{N}))$$

The Boolean variables JUMP or JMIN will be TRUE when the corresponding jump instruction is executed and the variable N (negative) would have been set to TRUE or FALSE by the ALU and stored in that flag. In Figure 9.21, we have realized the above Boolean expression with the *transfer-control signal* which indicates the time instant within the instruction cycle when this data path is to be asserted. From the above discussions we notice that Op-code decoding plays an important role in the generation of control signals.

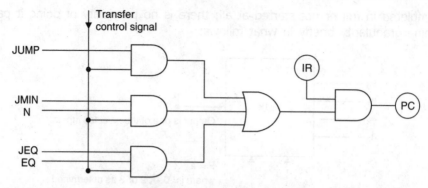

**Figure 9.21 PC ← address in IR transfer for jump instruction.**

In Figure 9.22, we have divided the instruction decoding into three parts: Op-code decoder, addressing mode decoder and one effective address calculator for each mode of addressing.

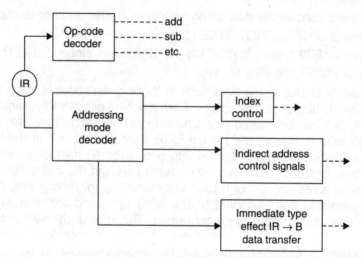

**Figure 9.22 Use of decoders.**

In order to generate certain types of control signals, we need to keep track of the timings of various inter-related events. This is achieved with the help of a clock. As an example, let us suppose that a clock runs at 20 MHz and one step of a microprogram is executed in one clock time. The resulting 50 ns may be too much time spent for some steps and too little time for other steps (example memory READ and WRITE). But let us ignore such fine details for now. From the study of the microprograms given above let us assume that the instruction fetch takes four clock cycles and the instruction execution of any instruction can be completed in a maximum of six cycles. Then a counter modulo ten can synchronously generate a control signal to start the instruction fetch cycle, one instruction after another. The instructions can be executed at a constant rate with a fixed instruction execution time of 500 ns per instruction. Such a design is simple to implement but it is not very efficient. In a real computer system both synchronous and asynchronous control need to be properly mixed for efficient implementations.

## 9.10 SUMMARY OF CPU ORGANIZATION

We have studied various aspects of a CPU in this chapter. Three main aspects are: (1) what makes the CPU of a computer system; (2) the instruction set view of a CPU, the semantics of each instruction and how microprogramming is used to realize this semantics at the hardware level; and (3) the atomicity of operations at the instruction level and what it means at the microprogramming level. Also we introduced the basic organization and the instruction set view of a computer using a hypothetical computer SMAC in Chapter 8 that was later expanded to SMAC++. In order to understand the CPU at the instruction set level, we list below 7 focus points. Under each focus point, we list some questions. Those questions are intended to enable a student to make a detailed analysis or study of the CPU of a given computer system. For the convenience of students, we have labelled these focus points as T1, T2, T3 to T7:

### T1. Registers

How many registers are there?

- What is the register length?
- Are they general purpose registers or are some of them special purpose registers?
- What are the special roles played by some registers?

### T2. Memory

How large is the memory address space supported? What is the basic unit of addressability (byte/word). Memory cycle time? Memory bandwidth? (number of bytes/access). How is the effective address calculated to access the RAM?

### T3. Addressing Modes Supported

What are the various addressing modes supported at the hardware level?

### T4. Instruction Format

What are the instruction formats used? Review the calculation of effective address for each addressing mode using the specific registers of this computer.

### T5. Instruction Set

Classify the instruction set based on different criteria such as, single address, double address; register reference, memory reference; based on operational characteristics JUMP, TEST, ARITHMETIC, etc. How large is the instruction set? Examine the instruction set to learn about its versatility, speed of execution, ease of its use, etc.

### T6. Support for Stacks

Stacks are very useful for programming, in compiling and OS run-time operations. How are stacks supported in the design?

### T7. Evolution

Is the CPU (computer system) a member of a family of evolving set of CPUs (computers)? If yes, what compatibility objectives are maintained from generation to generation?

---

### SUMMARY

1. In Chapter 8 the CPU organization of a hypothetical computer called SMAC++ was given. While SMAC++ provided a simple basic organization, real commercial computers over the years had a variety of instruction formats in their CPUs.

2. It is possible to design computers in which the number of bits assigned to Op-code is variable. Some instructions use a smaller number of bits allowing more bits for addressing memory.

3. It is also possible to design instruction sets in which instruction lengths can be 1 word, half word and one and a half word, 2 words, etc. It is primarily done to optimize memory utilization.

4. Besides direct, indexed and immediate address, there are several other addressing modes. They are: base addressing, segmented addressing, PC relative addressing and indirect addressing. Base addressing is useful to increase addressable space, segmentation is used by the Operating System, PC relative addressing allows jump within a small range of addresses, and indirect addressing is useful in subroutine linkages and parameter passing.

5. The number of CPU registers has increased in successive generations of computers with denser packing of ICs. A larger number of CPU registers speed up computation.

6. Clocks are used in CPUs to synchronize operations. The speed of execution of various operations is governed by the clock frequency. Currently processor use clocks in GHz range.

7. Buses are a set of parallel wires used to connect different subsystems of a computer. Internal buses are fabricated in the IC chip. They are short and can be driven at high clock speeds. Three buses, namely, address bus, data bus and control bus are common in all CPUs.

8. I/O devices are connected to CPU chip by external buses called I/O bus. This will be described in Chapter 12.

9. The control signals required to control and coordinate data flow among various sub-units of a CPU may be described using a high level hardware description language similar to the one we introduced in Chapter 6. This is called microprogramming.

10. We have obtained microprograms for a subset of the instructions of SMAC described in Chapter 8. This shows how the CPU of a small computer is designed.

---

### EXERCISES

1. A computer has 48 bits word length. It has 32 registers. There are 30 instructions which use 3 registers for operands and the others address main memory. Design at least two possible instruction formats for this computer. In each case give the range of directly addressable memory locations.

2. If SMAC++ is a byte addressable machine what will be the advantages and disadvantages?

3. IBM 370 has no indirect addressing. Explain how one would get the effect of indirect addressing on this machine.

4. Assume a memory cycle time of 250 ns, addition time of 90 ns and a gate delay of 5 ns. Make a table giving the time required to calculate the effective address in each of the different addressing modes. Assume any reasonable estimate of time for other operation (if you need it).

5. In Section 9.3 we have classified the instructions into 9 categories denoted as C1 through C9. For a computer system available to you list as many instructions as you can find in each of these categories. Comment on the relative execution times of these categories of instructions.

6. Explain in detail the advantages of PC being an addressable register in the CPU.

7. A PC-relative mode addressed branch instruction is stored in memory at the address 6AO. The branch is to be made to an address 59B. Show the address part of the instruction. Explain all the assumptions made by you clearly.

8. What are the justifications you can state:
   (i) For introducing several index registers in a computer.
   (ii) Index registers being a part of the GPRs in CPU and not as separate registers.

9. Give a set of instructions to address and manipulate bytes in word addressed SMAC++.

10. Using the instructions you have suggested for exercise 9, develop a program to reverse a string (reverse of 'abc' is 'cba') and then to verify if the string reads the same left to right as well as right to left. Will stacks be useful in developing this program?

11. Some CPUs include two sets of registers of identical registers for fast switching . In what situations are such duplicate sets very useful?

12. Distinguish between data flow and control flow in a processor design:
   (i) Give a complete data flow graph for the instruction set $S_0$ of SMAC++.
   (ii) Repeat for instruction set $S_1$.

13. Write data flow programs (such as Program 9.1, 9.2 etc., of the text) to:
   (i) Swap the contents of registers R1 and R2.
   (ii) Save the contents of all the registers R1 to R30 in main memory.
   (iii) Push and pop using R31.

14. Consider a single addressed, single register (only accumulator) machine HYCOM. Let HYCOM have a small instruction set (LOAD, STORE, ADD, COMPLEMENT, JUMP and JUMP ON MINUS). Recommend a micro-engine for realizing its instruction set. Draw a graph showing the essential data paths.

15. For the microprograms of Section 9.8, describe the control signals needed to maintain the control flow.

16. We have shown a micro-engine for SMAC with a single bus. Obtain for SMAC a micro-engine with two buses. The two buses must be configured to maximize parallel execution of micro-operations.

17. Obtain a single bus micro-engine for SMAC++. Compare this with SMAC microengine.

# 10

# Memory Organization

---

## Learning Goals

In this chapter we will learn:

☞ The different parameters of a memory system

☞ A memory cell as the building block of a semi conductor memory.

☞ Integrated circuit chips to fabricate memory systems.

☞ 2D and 2.5D organizations of memory systems using IC chips.

☞ Dynamic and Static Random Access Memories (RAM).

☞ Dual ports in a RAM and concurrency in memory access.

☞ Read Only Memories (ROM) and their applications.

☞ Importance of error detection and correction in memory systems.

☞ Locality in memory references under program executions.

☞ How to use the locality property to organize hierachical memory systems.

☞ Cache memory organization and three different mappings.

☞ Performance of cache memory systems.

☞ The need for addressing space larger than the main memory address.

☞ How to design a virtual memory by combining large capacity disc with a smaller main memory.

---

## 10.1 INTRODUCTION

In Chapter 6 we saw how flip-flops could be organized to form storage registers. Registers are normally used for temporary storage of a few items. For storing the bulk of data needed in digital computation a Random Access Memory (RAM) is used. A memory unit consists of a large number of 'binary storage cells' known as **bits** in which data is stored during data processing. Besides the billions of storage cells, a memory has a small number of registers to facilitate storage and retrieval of data in units of bytes or groups of bytes called **word**. A typical word consists of 4 bytes or 32 bits. The two typical registers used in a memory system are **memory address register** or MAR and memory data register which is also known as **Memory Buffer Register** or MBR.

In order that a physical device is usable as a binary storage cell in a memory unit, it must have the following desirable characteristics:

1. It must have two stable states. They are usually denoted as 0 and 1.
2. While it is in one of the stable states, it should not consume any power. If it does consume power, it must be small so that the total energy dissipated by the memory is small.
3. It should be possible to switch between the two stable states an infinite number of times.
4. The data stored in a cell should not decay with the passage of time.
5. Each binary cell should occupy very little space.
6. The cost of each cell must be low.
7. The time taken to read data from a group of cells (word) or for storing data in them must be small. This is also known as cycle time.
8. When power is turned OFF, the cell should not lose data stored in it.

Binary cells which are currently popular are semiconductor ICs used in RAMs (Random Access Memory) as the main memory of a computer system, and magnetic surfaces on a disk or tape and pits/lands on a laser disk.

There is also another type of semiconductor storage cells used in memories called **Read Only Memories** (ROMs). Semiconductor RAM cells lose the data stored in them when the power is turned off. This is called a **volatile memory**. On the other hand, cells used in ROMs do not lose the data stored in them when power is switched off. These are called **non-volatile memory cells**. Other non-volatile memories are magnetic surface recording and laser disks.

## 10.2 MEMORY PARAMETERS

A set of binary cells are strung together to form a unit called a word. A word is always treated as an entity and moves in and out of memory as one unit. The movement of words in and out of memory is controlled by signals called write and read signals. A word to be written in the memory unit is first entered in a register called the memory buffer register (MBR). A write signal is now initiated. The word in MBR is copied into the address specified in MAR. In order to read a word from memory, the address from where it is to be read is entered in MAR. When a read signal is sent to memory unit, the word is copied from the specified address and placed in MBR where it remains until it is transferred to another register in CPU.

From our discussions above it is clear that a memory unit is organized in such a way that it has a number of addressed locations, each location storing a word. The addresses normally start at 0 and the highest address equals the number of words that can be stored in the memory and is called its **address space**. For example, if a memory has 1024 locations, then the address ranges between 0 and 1023. In order to store the value of the address, the MAR register, in this example, should have 10 bits. 1024 is usually abbreviated as 1K.

Figure 10.1 depicts the block diagram of a memory system. This memory is assumed to store 1024 words (i.e., 1K words) with 32 bits per word. If a number 64 is to be stored in location 515, then this number is placed in MBR. The address where the number is to be stored is entered in MAR. The write signal is then initiated. This signal replaces the current contents of the location 515 by the contents of MBR.

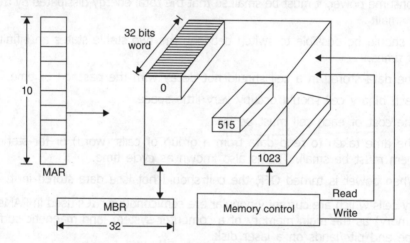

**Figure 10.1 Block diagram of a memory.**

If the contents of some location are to be read, then its address is entered in MAR. The read signal is initiated by the control unit. The contents of the specified location are copied into MBR and whatever data was in the selected location is left undisturbed. This is called **non-destructive read out**. Reading data from a memory must be non-destructive for the memory unit to be useful in a data processing system.

Whether read out is destructive or not depends on the device used as a binary cell in the memory. Flip-flop binary cells, for example, are non-destructive. Reading from binary cells made with capacitors is destructive. In this case, whatever was read from the selected memory cell must be written back to preserve its contents. The time interval between the initiation of a read signal and the availability of the required word in MBR is known as the **access time** of the memory. The time interval between the initiation of a write signal and the storing of the data in the specified address in the memory is called the **write time**. If reading data from memory is destructive, then it is necessary to write it back in memory. The time required for this combined read and write operations is known as the **memory cycle time**. Even if reading from memory is non-destructive, the time that should elapse between two successive references to memory read or write is larger than the access time. This time is the **cycle time** of the memory. Figure 10.2 illustrates these terms.

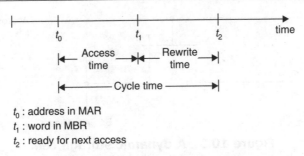

$t_0$ : address in MAR
$t_1$ : word in MBR
$t_2$ : ready for next access

**Figure 10.2  Read/Write time.**

The method of accessing memory depends on the particular device used to construct the binary cell and how the devices are interconnected to form a memory. Memory systems may be constructed with IC flip-flops in such a way that the access time is independent of the address of the word. Such a memory is known as a **random access memory** or RAM. In contrast to this, if the binary cells are on the surface of a magnetic tape or disk, then the access time would depend on its actual physical location.

## 10.3  SEMICONDUCTOR MEMORY CELL

In early days (1955–70) magnetic cores were used as the storage elements of the main random access memories of computers. With rapid development of integrated circuits, semiconductor storage elements have replaced magnetic cores. There are two types of semiconductor storage elements. One is a *dynamic memory cell* and the other a *static memory cell*. A dynamic cell uses a capacitor whereas a static cell uses an RS flip-flop fabricated with transistors to store data. Memories made using dynamic memory cells are called **Dynamic Random Access Memories** (DRAM for short) and those fabricated with static cells are called **Static Random Access Memories** (SRAM for short). SRAM cells are faster compared to DRAM cells. Memories fabricated using SRAM cells have an access time of around 20 ns whereas DRAMs have an access time of around 80 ns. The DRAM is, however, preferred for fabricating main memories as it is possible to realize an order of magnitude more memory cells per chip compared to SRAM. The cost per cell is thus an order of magnitude lower in DRAM. We will first see how the dynamic and static cells function.

### 10.3.1  Dynamic Memory Cell

Figure 10.3 illustrates a simple dynamic storage cell. It incorporates a transistor $T$ (called a pass transistor) which controls the charging of a capacitor $C$. The capacitor is of the order of 0.1 picofarad (pico = $10^{-12}$) and can hold a very small charge when it is charged. The pass transistor is connected to an address line and a bit/sense line (see Figure 10.3). A cell is selected for writing or reading by applying a voltage $V$ to the address line. To write a 1 in the cell a voltage $V$ is applied to the bit/sense line. This switches on $T$ and $C$ is charged to voltage $V$. If 0 voltage is applied to the bit/sense line, then if $C$ is charged it will discharge and a 0 is stored.

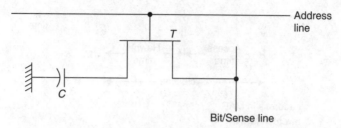

**Figure 10.3   A dynamic storage cell.**

Capacitance $C$ is not an ideal capacitance. It has a very large but finite leakage resistance. Thus the charge stored in $C$ when a 1 is written will slowly leak away (in a few milliseconds) and the data will be lost. It is therefore necessary to rewrite the data periodically. This is called **refreshing**.

As the charge stored in $C$ is very small, reading data from the cell is a little tricky. To read a cell, the address line is selected and a voltage $V$ is applied to it. This switches on the pass transistor $T$. If a 1 is stored in the cell, the voltage of the bit/sense line will tend to go up to $V$ and if a 0 is stored in the cell, it will tend to go down to 0. The direction of change of voltage in the bit/sense line is sensed by the sense amplifier. A positive change is taken as a 1 and a negative change as a 0. Observe that the read operation is destructive and a write should follow a read.

## 10.3.2   Static Memory Cell

A static memory cell is essentially a flip-flop. The cell is illustrated in Figure 10.4(a) within a circle. In this figure we have simplified the circuit to its essentials in order to explain the

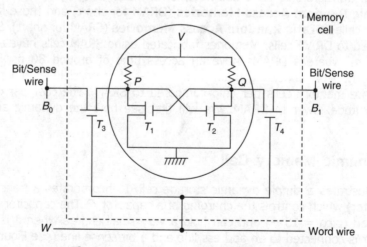

**Figure 10.4(a)   A static MOS cell.**

working of the cell. The cell works as follows: The flip-flop consisting of transistors $T_1$ and $T_2$ can be in one of the two stable states. One stable state is with $T_1$ conducting and $T_2$

non-conducting and other is with $T_2$ conducting and $T_1$ non-conducting. When $T_1$ is conducting the voltage at the point $P$ (Figure 10.4(a)) is nearly 0. This voltage is applied to the base of transistor $T_2$ which keeps it switched off. The voltage at $Q$ is thus at $V$. In this state the memory cell is said to be storing a 0. The opposite state is with $T_2$ conducting and $T_1$ non-conducting. In this case the voltage at $P$ would be $V$ (logic 1) and that at $Q$ will be 0 (logic 0). In this state the memory cell is said to store a 1. To summarize we observe that the two transistor memory cell can be in one of two stable states. One state with the voltage $P = V$ is (arbitrarily) called the 1 state and the other state with $P = 0$ is called the 0 state.

### 10.3.3  Writing Data in Memory Cell

In order to use this memory cell in a memory system, we connect this cell to a pair of bit wires $B_0$ and $B_1$ and a word wire $W$ via two transistor switches as shown in Figure 10.4(a). The transistor switches are necessary to select a cell for reading or writing. The two-bit wires $B_0$ and $B_1$ are normally kept at a voltage $V$ and the word wire $W$ is kept at 0. This keeps the two transistor switches $T_3$ and $T_4$ open. If a 0 is to be written in the cell, then the cell is selected by applying a voltage $V$ to the word wire $W$. The voltage on the bit wire $B_0$ is taken to 0. If the cell had a 1 stored in it, then the voltage at $P$ would have been at $V$. Applying a 0 to $B_0$ wire will switch on transistor $T_3$ and the point $P$ will be forced to 0 volt. This will switch off transistor $T_2$ taking point $Q$ to $V$ which will turn on $T_1$ and $P$ will go to 0. If $B_0$ now goes back to its normal voltage $V$ then, $T_3$ is switched off and the voltage at $P$ will remain at 0. Thus, the cell will have a 0 stored in it. If the cell had a 0 to begin with then taking $B_0$ to 0 will tend to keep $P$ at 0 and thus the state of the memory cell will not be altered. If a 1 is to be written in the cell, regardless of what is currently stored in the cell, the bit wire $B_1$ is taken to 0 volt. This will switch on $T_4$ (Figure 10.4(a)) and take point $Q$ to 0. When $Q$ goes to 0 transistor, $T_1$ will be switched off and $P$ will go to $V$. This will turn on $T_2$ and $Q$ will go to 0. Thus, the memory cell will be in 1 state. If the cell originally was in the 1 state, then $Q$ would have been at 0, and taking $B_1$ to 0 would not change the state of cell. Figure 10.4(b) summarizes the writing of 0 or 1 in the memory cell.

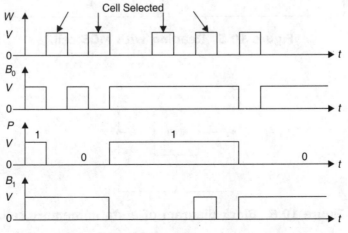

**Figure 10.4(b)   Writing 0 or 1 in a MOS cell.**

## 10.3.4   Reading the Contents of Cell

For reading the contents of a cell, a small voltage is applied to the word line keeping the voltage on the bit wires equal to $V$. This makes both transistors $T_3$ and $T_4$ tend to conduct. If the point $P$ is at 0 volts (in other words if the cell stores a 0) then a current flows through $T_3$ bringing down the voltage on line $B_0$ slightly. This wire is connected to a sense amplifier which will detect this change and store it as a 0 in the memory buffer register. If $P$ is at $V$, then $Q$ would be at 0 volts. In this case the small voltage applied to $W$ would cause transistor $T_4$ to conduct and the voltage on bit wire $B_1$ will dip slightly, and this will be detected by the sense amplifier. The sense amplifier output will be stored as a 1 in the memory buffer register. The sensing will be *non-destructive* since the word pulse only senses which state the cell is in without changing the state of the cell. Figure 10.5 illustrates the reading operation. The memory cell may be represented by the equivalent block diagram of Figure 10.6. We will use this block diagram to describe memory organization in the next two sections.

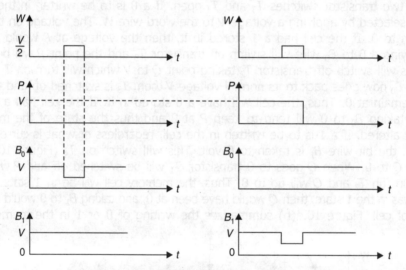

**Figure 10.5   Reading with MOS cell.**

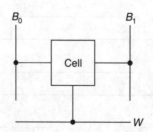

**Figure 10.6   Block diagram of a static memory cell.**

## 10.4  IC CHIPS FOR ORGANIZATION OF RAMs

The IC manufacturers package millions of memory cells into a chip which forms the building block for the organization of large size RAMs whose capacity can be in the order of several hundreds of mega bytes or a few GB. The block diagram of an example IC chip is shown in Figure 10.7. One of the limiting factors of such packaging has been the number of different pins which connect the internal circuitry of the chip to the external world. In this figure we have shown a chip that has 24 pins and internally contains 256 K addressable memory cells. Each of these cells, in this example, is one bit in size and is individually addressable. Thus, in this chip, we need 18 address pins (labelled $A_0$ to $A_{17}$) to select one out of 256 K cells. Each cell when read or written stores one bit. The data input pin and the data output pin are separate in the case of this chip (see Table 10.1) but in some other cases the same data pins are used for both input to as well as for output from the chip. In addition to this, a typical memory chip consists of other control pins such as CS (chip select or chip enable), R/W (read or write operation on the enabled chip), $V_{CC}$ for power and $V_{SS}$ for ground. This memory chip is packaged as a 24-pin integrated circuit.

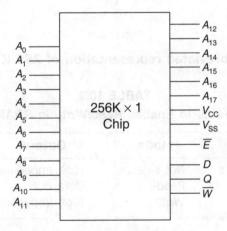

**Figure 10.7   256 K × 1 RAM chip pin out representation.**

**TABLE 10.1**
**Pin Assignment for 256 K × 1 SRAM Chip**

| Pin Names | Functions | Pin Names | Functions |
|-----------|-----------|-----------|-----------|
| $A_0$–$A_{17}$ | Address input | $Q$ | Data output |
| $\overline{E}$ | Chip enable | $V_{CC}$ | + 5V supply |
| $\overline{W}$ | Write enable | $V_{SS}$ | Ground |
| $D$ | Data input | | |

The truth table for selecting a chip when it is used as a part of a large memory and for reading and writing is given in Table 10.2. This chip's access time is around 15 nano seconds.

For the sake of drawing the organization of a large size RAM using such chips as building blocks, it is customary to abbreviate Figure 10.7 as shown in Figure 10.8. The reader should note the convention used to indicate the multiple lines by means of a single line with a '/' mark and an associated integer. As an exercise the reader is urged to draw an abbreviated diagram for an IC chip that has 16-M addressable elements where each element is a 4-bit group (half of a byte). Typically we denote such a chip as 16 M × 4.

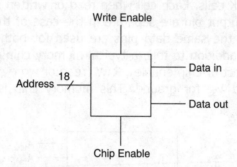

**Figure 10.8   Abbreviated representation of 256 K × 1 SRAM chip.**

**TABLE 10.2**
**Truth Table to Enable, Read/Write in SRAM Chip**

| $\bar{E}$ | $\bar{W}$ | Mode | Output | Cycle |
|------|------------|--------------|----------------|-------|
| High | Don't care | Not selected | High impedance | — |
| Low  | High       | Read         | Data out       | Read  |
| Low  | Low        | Write        | High impedance | Write |

## 10.5   2D ORGANIZATION OF SEMICONDUCTOR MEMORY

Let us suppose that we want to organize a 4 MB (4 Mega Bytes) memory using the chips 256K × 1 described in the previous section. How many such chips will we need? Conceptually, if we put 8 such chips in a **row**, each chip contributing one bit of a byte then we can construct a 256 KB memory system. This 256 KB memory will need a 18 bit address. The address lines can be fed as $A_0$ to $A_{17}$ to each of the 8 chips in a row so as to select one out of 256 K elements. Since we need 4 MB sixteen such rows can be used together to make up the total memory. A memory with 4 MB capacity will need a 22-bit address, as $2^{22} = 4$ MB. The high order 4 bits of the 22-bit address can then be used to select one out of 16 rows in the memory organization. In a 2D organized memory system the chips are laid out as several rows and several columns. Figure 10.9 illustrates the organization of what we described above in the form of 16 rows and 8 columns. A 4-bit decoder is used to decode the high order 4-bits of the MAR. The decoder output will select one (exactly one) of the 16 rows. Hence, the 16 decoder outputs are connected to the 16 rows of chips, one output for each row. The decoder will select one out of the 16 rows and all the chips in the selected row will be enabled for reading or writing. The 8 bits coming from the 8 chips (one bit from each chip) in the selected row are routed to the 8 bits of the MBR of this memory system.

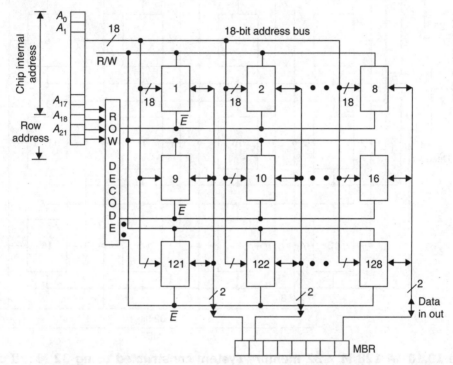

**Figure 10.9   A 4 MB memory constructed using 256 K × 1 chips**

Let us consider another example. In this example we are asked to organize a memory 128 M × 32, that is, it should have 128 M addressable units where each unit (word) is 32 bits long. We will assume that we are given the IC chips of size 32 M × 8 or 32 MB which has 32 M addressable units with each unit being a byte. The IC chip will have 25($2^{25}$ = 32 M) address pins and 8 data pins shared for both input and output. Our first step is to determine the number of chips required. In this case we will need 16 IC chips. These 16 chips will be organized in the form of a matrix with 4 rows and 4 columns as shown in Figure 10.10. The memory system will need a 27-bit address to address one of 128 M words where each word is 32 bits long. The 2 higher order bits of the memory address will be used to select one of the 4 rows and the 4 chips in the selected row together will supply the 32 bits of that word. The principle of operation in this example is similar to the previous example.

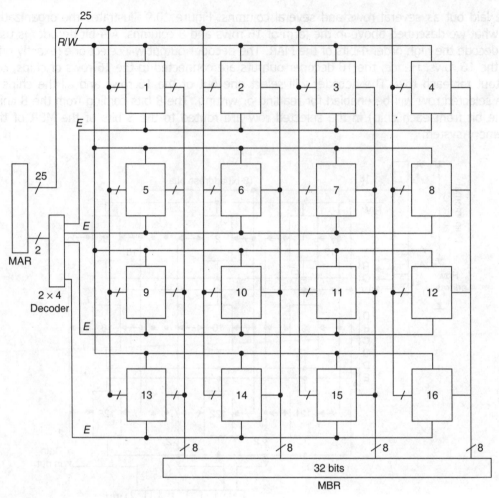

**Figure 10.10  A 128 M × 32 memory system constructed using 32 M × 8 chips.**

## 10.6  2.5D ORGANIZATION OF MEMORY SYSTEMS

In the 2D organization an address decoder is used to select one out of *W* addressable units which we called words. Let us call the decoder outputs the **word wires**. The electrical signals through the word wires perform the function of chip selection. The number of word wires in 2D organized memory systems is equal to the number of words in the memory. Obviously the number of word wires in a memory system will depend upon the chip size given and the size of the memory system required. When the number of word wires runs into hundreds and thousands, the address decoder can become too complex. Another organization called 2.5D (read as "two-and-half-D") organization  allows the use of simpler decoders. In this case the bits to be decoded are divided into *row decoder bits* and *column decoder bits*.

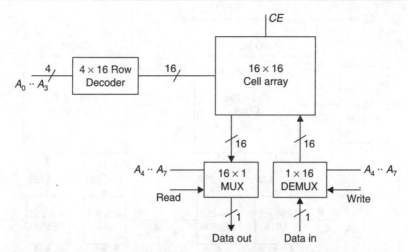

**Figure 10.11   A semiconductor 2.5D memory (256 W, 1 b/w).**

We will illustrate this organization by examining a 256 words, 1 bit/word memory. Figure 10.11 illustrates the way the cells are arranged in the memory. Again the 256 words are organized in the form of a $16 \times 16$ matrix. The 16-bit word address required for the 256 words is split into 4 bits for row address and 4 bits for column address. The row bits are decoded by a decoder which has 4 inputs and 16 outputs in this example. During the memory READ operation the 4-bit row address will select one of the 16 rows. All the 4 bits in the selected row will be passed to the column MUX/DEMUX unit. This unit does multiplexing in one direction and demultiplexing in the other direction. The 4-column address bits from the 16-bit address of the memory system will be used as the selector bits for the MUX/DEMUX unit. The memory system output is the one bit output from this unit. During the WRITE operation, the row address bits select one of the 16 rows. The bit to be written is input to the MUX/DEMUX unit. The bit will be routed only to the appropriate column in the selected row as determined by the 4-column address bits that are used as the selector bits for this multiplexer/demultiplexer unit. This form of selection of a word is also known as **coincidence selection**. In the above example, we have used a trivial case of 1bit/word. When more than one bit per word is required, identical matrix and selection units can be modularly constructed as one unit per bit. We will illustrate this by showing how 64 KB SRAM is organized as a 2.5D memory. The 64 KB memory is made up of an array of eight $256 \times 256$, 1 bit output memory chips (see Figure 10.12). The organization uses a $8 \times 256$ row decoder to select one of the rows. Having selected this row, if a read signal is initiated all the 256 outputs in this row will be read. To select one of these, we need $256 \times 8$ MUX to which a 8-bit column address is fed. Observe that there are 8 such arrays to get 1 byte output. Writing is by placing 1 bit to each of eight ($8 \times 256$) DEMUXes. Observe that 256 outputs of each decoder are simultaneously fed to all eight $256 \times 256$ chips. Similarly $A_8$ to $A_{15}$ is applied simultaneously to all MUX/DEMUXes. The organization is illustrated in Figure 10.12.

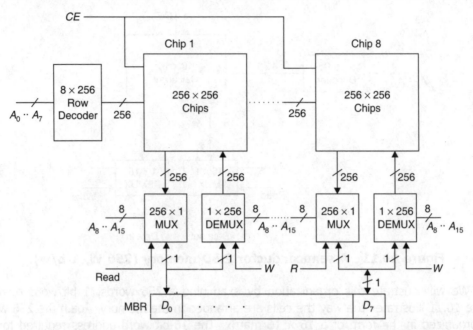

**Figure 10.12 A 64-KB memory using eight, 256 × 256 bit chips organized as a 2.5D memory.**

In commercial applications further reduction in the number of pins can be achieved if we can time multiplex the same number of pins for both row selection and column selection. Then READ/WRITE will be done as a two step process: In step 1 the pins will be used to carry the row address bits and in step 2 the same pins will be used to carry the column address bits. This can greatly reduce the complexity of the chip by reducing the number of pins but will increase the memory cycle time, thus resulting in a trade-off.

The design considerations in memory systems using IC chips are chip count, pins per chip and ease of expansion. It is quite often advisable to use chips such as 64K × 1 or 256K × 1 which give a 1-bit output. For example 64K × 1 chip has 16 address lines, 1 chip enable, 1 read/write line, a data in line and a data out line, 1 power supply line and 1 ground line for a total of 22 pins. In contrast an 8K × 8 chip which has the same memory capacity of 64K bits has 13 address lines, 8 bidirectional data lines, 1 chip enable, 1 read/write, 1 power supply and 1 ground line for a total of 25 pins. It would thus involve less soldered connections and hence higher reliability to use 64K × 1 chips. In contrast if a 64KB memory is to be built, we can use 2 chips of 32K × 8 as opposed to 8 chips of 64K × 1. Commercially available memories are packaged with multiple IC chips on a printed circuit board in such a way that all the pins form a single line. They are known as **SIMM** or **single in-line memory module** (see Figure 10.13). They can be easily plugged into the motherboard of a computer system connecting the memory system to the system bus.

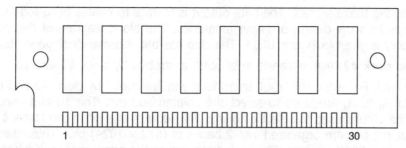

**Figure 10.13   30 pin single in-line memory module (SIMM).**

## 10.7   DYNAMIC RANDOM ACCESS MEMORY

In this section we will examine the organization of a typical Dynamic Random Access Memory (DRAM). The main differences between DRAM and the staic RAM or SRAM are as follows:

1. DRAM is a destructive read-out memory.
2. DRAM needs periodic refresh (to keep the contents from being lost).
3. DRAM has a slower cycle time than SRAM.
4. DRAM is much cheaper than SRAM and allows denser packing of bits per chip. In fact, up to 256M bit-cells have been realized on a single chip and this number keeps increasing as the technology advances.

Due to its lower cost DRAMs are commonly used as main memories in PCs and workstations. We will consider a typical commercially available DRAM chip and how it is organized (Motorola MCM51100A). This chip is a 1 Mbit (1M × 1) CMOS DRAM. It has 18 pins whose assignment is given in Table 10.3. The access time of this chip is 70 ns.

**TABLE 10.3**
**Pin Assignment of 1M × 1 DRAM**

| | |
|---|---|
| $A_0$–$A_9$ | Address bits |
| | (Row and column addresses multiplexed) |
| $D$ | Data input |
| $Q$ | Data output |
| $\overline{W}$ | Read/Write enable |
| $\overline{RAS}$ | Row Address strobe |
| $\overline{CAS}$ | Column Address strobe |
| $V_{CC}$ | +5V power |
| $V_{SS}$ | Ground |
| $T_F$ | Test function enable |

Observe that 20 bits are needed to address 1M bit whereas this chip uses only 10 bits for address. These bits are used to apply 10 row addresses and 10 column addresses by time multiplexing these signals. The data output is tristate to enable tying together outputs of many chips to allow design of larger memories. The block diagram of the organization of this memory is given in Figure 10.14. The chip has two internal clock generators. We call clock #1 and clock #2. Active transition of $\overline{RAS}$ is strobed by clock #1 and 10 row address bits are selected. Following this $\overline{CAS}$ transitions and is strobed by clock #2 and the 10 bits appearing in $A_0$ to $A_9$ are used to select the column address. The 10 bits used to select a row and the 10 bits used to select a column will address one bit in the (1M × 1) memory. Observe that the bits are organized into 2 banks of (512 × 1024) bits. Thus, there are 512 physical rows and 2048 columns. This is done to reduce the number of rows which facilitates refreshing as we will see later in this section. (Observe in Figure 10.14 that 1 bit of row address buffer is diverted to the column decoder.)

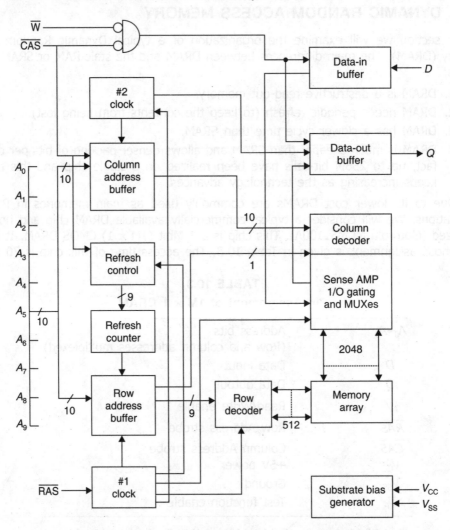

**Figure 10.14(a)  A dynamic random access memory.**

Bit/Sense lines (column address)

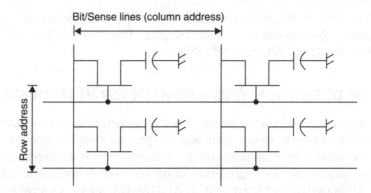

**Figure 10.14(b) Typical arrangement of bits in memory array.**

For reading, $\overline{W}$ is set high and the row and columns of the bit to be read are strobed. The bit is read out into the buffer. When $\overline{CAS}$ transitions to inactive the output goes to high impedance state. For writing, the data in D buffer is referenced by column address line and written at the end of strobing row and column by $\overline{RAS}$ and $\overline{CAS}$ signals.

The other modes are Read/Write cycle in which write follows read and a *page mode*. The page mode allows fast successive data access on all 2048 cells of a selected row in the two banks of the 1M bit DRAM. Page mode operation keeps $\overline{RAS}$ active and toggles $\overline{CAS}$ between $V_{HI}$ and $V_{LO}$ while selecting successive columns on the selected row. Page mode is useful to read a chunk of a program or data from DRAM and store it in SRAM (called a cache memory) from which individual words can be accessed faster. (We will see this use in greater detail later in the book.)

### Refresh cycle

As data is stored as charge on capacitors in DRAM, periodic recharging of capacitors known as **refresh cycle** is necessary. The maximum time allowed between memory cell refreshing depends on the specific design of DRAM. Typically it is a few milliseconds. The DRAM is refreshed by cycling through the 512 rows within the specified refresh time (which is 8 ms in the MCM511000A DRAM). If the number of rows is larger it is difficult to cycle through all of them within the specified time and that is the reason the memory cells are arranged as two (1024 × 512) banks. When a row is selected for refresh all 2048 cells in that row are refreshed. Observe also that a normal read, write or read/write operation will also refresh all the 2048 cells in the selected row. There are other modes of refreshing which we will not discuss.

A more recent chip is Infineon's 256 Mb Double Data Rate SDRAM (DDR 400A). This is called **double data rate** (DDR) as two data transfers take place per clock. The clock rate is 200 MHz. It has 66 pins out of which 13 pins are for address. With 13 pins we can address only 8192. These bits are used for 13 row and 13 column addresses by time multiplexing these, giving a maximum of $2^{26} = 64$ Mb address space. The memory is internally organized in 16 planes of 8192 rows and 512 columns. There are 4 such planes which can be accessed to give 4-bit output per address specified. The 256-Mb chip can be configured as 64M × 4b, 32M × 8b or 16M × 16b. The particular configuration is selected by using 2 bits available to external pins. This memory has 7.8 μs maximum average refresh interval (8192b row refresh).

## 10.8    ERROR DETECTION AND CORRECTION IN MEMORIES

Memory is an important part of a computer. It is thus essential to ensure that the data read from a memory do not have errors. Can you imagine what will happen if one bit of an instruction or one bit of important data stored in the memory is incorrect? Sometimes data read/stored in a memory are corrupted due to noise or hardware faults. When data read has an error, it should be detected and if possible corrected. Various error detection/ correction techniques have been used in designing memories. Most of the commonly used techniques are based on the principles of the Hamming Code (discussed in Chapter 1). If the number of bits in a memory unit is $i$ (for a 32 bit word $i = 32$) add $k$ error detecting/ correcting bits to $i$ information bits and write $(k + i)$ bits in each addressable word in memory. The $k$ bits are called **parity bits**. When a word is read the $(k + i)$ bits stored in it are read. The $k$ bits read are used to find out whether there were any errors in the $i$ information bits.

In the simplest case, to detect a single error in the data read, a single parity bit is sufficient. However, if we want to detect and correct a single error, we have shown that the number of parity bits $k$ required must be such that $(2^k - 1)$ must be greater than or equal to $(i + k)$. Thus for a single error correction in a 32-bit word, the number of parity bits needed is 6. Usually in memory systems one uses a code for Single Error Correction Double Error Detection (SECDED). For this at least 7 parity bits are needed when 32 bits are used in a word. This amounts to an overhead of 21.8%. The overhead goes down if the word length is larger. For a 64-bit word the number of parity bits needed for SECDED is 8, resulting in an overhead of 12.5%.

## 10.9    READ ONLY MEMORY

Read only memory, abbreviated ROM, is one in which data is permanently stored. Switching the power OFF in a computer system does not erase the contents of a ROM. Data stored in a ROM can be accessed as fast as in RAM made with similar storage cells. Writing of data into a ROM memory is impossible after it is stored. There are four types of ROMs which we will describe later in this section and in some of them the user can erase and re-write the contents of a read only memory in a special manner.

ROM is a specific case of a Programmable Logic Device discussed in this book. In ROM the AND array of the PLD is fixed and the OR array is programmable. A 3-bit input, 4-bit output, Read Only Memory (ROM) is shown in Figure 10.15. Observe that all the 8 *minterms* corresponding to the 3 input bits are generated. These can be thought as addressing 8 words in the ROM. The output bits are programmed by blowing fuses selectively in the OR array. The contents of the ROM of Figure 10.5 are shown in Table 10.4.

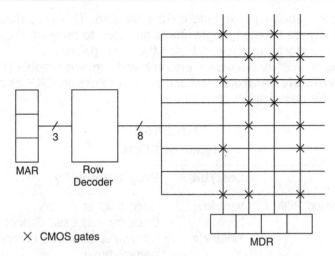

**Figure 10.15 A Read Only Memory (ROM).**

**TABLE 10.4**
**Contents of ROM of Figure 10.15**

| MAR | | | MBR | | | |
|---|---|---|---|---|---|---|
| $I_2$ | $I_1$ | $I_0$ | $0_3$ | $0_2$ | $0_1$ | $0_0$ |
| 0 | 0 | 0 | 1 | 0 | 1 | 0 |
| 0 | 0 | 1 | 0 | 1 | 1 | 1 |
| 0 | 1 | 0 | 1 | 0 | 1 | 1 |
| 0 | 1 | 1 | 0 | 1 | 1 | 0 |
| 1 | 0 | 0 | 0 | 1 | 0 | 1 |
| 1 | 0 | 1 | 1 | 0 | 0 | 1 |
| 1 | 1 | 0 | 0 | 0 | 0 | 0 |
| 1 | 1 | 1 | 1 | 1 | 0 | 1 |

We pointed out in the beginning of this section that there are 4 types of ROMs. The four types of ROMs differ in the way the link is programmed. In the factory-programmed ROM the links are placed during fabrication and cannot be altered later. Thus, in this ROM the stored data is permanent. Unless a ROM is to be mass produced with identical content, this would be uneconomical. The primary advantage of this type of ROM is its excellent reliability. It is also the least expensive of all ROMs.

The second type of ROM is called **user programmable ROM** (PROM). In this the factory supplies the PROM with fusible links. Wherever a 0 is to be stored, the link may be fused by the user by sending a high current through the link. Once a link is fused, it is permanent. Thus programming has to be done with care.

The third type of ROM is called an **ultraviolet erasable programmable ROM** (UVEPROM). This ROM is supplied by the manufacturer with links which can all be disconnected by shining intense ultraviolet light. Links can then be grown selectively by the user by selecting a word and applying a voltage on the bit wire. This procedure is called **ROM programming**. Software-assisted programmers are used to program these ROMs. Among the ROMs this is the most expensive but also the most flexible.

The last type of ROM is electrically erasable and reprogrammable (EEPROM). This is also known as a **writable control store** and is used to design CPUs of computers. Table 10.5 summarizes the classification of ROMs.

**TABLE 10.5**

**Types of ROMs**

| Type | Cost/bit | Programmablity |
|------|----------|----------------|
| Factory Programmed ROM | Very low | Once only at factory |
| PROM | Low | Once by end user. Cannot re-write |
| UVEPROM | Moderate | Ultraviolet erasable. Programmable several times |
| EEPROM | High | High voltage erasable and programmable several times |

The primary advantage of a ROM is that, unlike a RAM, the data stored in it is not lost when power fails and is applied again. In other words it is a non-volatile memory. Thus computer programs can be safely stored in them. Another advantage is the higher density of packing memory cells in it. The cost per bit of ROM storage is cheaper than RAM storage. 64KB per ROM chip are now commercially available.

ROMs are very useful in designing digital systems and some applications are given below.

### Code converter

This application is the most obvious use of a ROM. For instance, the ROM of Figure 10.15 implements the truth table given in Table 10.4.

ROMs for common code conversions such as NBCD code to 7-segment display code are readily available. Other code converters may be made to order. In general a ROM with an $n$-bit MAR and $m$-bit MBR can realize any $n$ input, $m$ output combinational circuit.

### Function generators

Tables for commonly used functions such as sine, cosine, and arctangent may be stored in ROMs. The arguments are entered in MAR and the function values appear in the output register.

### Character generators

Character displays in dot matrix form use ROMs for decoding and activating the display. Consider a $5 \times 7$ dot matrix shown in Figure 10.16. If each of the dot positions is a lamp, then a letter B, for instance, may be displayed by selecting a set of lamps and turning them ON as shown. If ON lamps correspond to 1 and OFF lamp to 0, then a character may be displayed by setting a subset of 35 bits to 1. Usually a $5 \times 7$ matrix is used for displaying characters from a 64-character set. The 6-bit code for a character is fed as the input to the ROM. The output is a 35-bit number which selects the correct dots to be lighted.

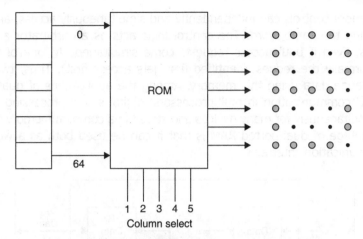

**Figure 10.16  A ROM character generator.**

The ROM may be simplified if, instead of requiring all 35 bits to be retrieved in parallel, we require that only 7 bits belonging to a specified column of the dot matrix be available. The column address in such a case is fed as an additional input to the ROM (Figure 10.16).

In microcomputers ROMs are used to store programs, particularly those which are for dedicated applications, such as washing machines, motor cars, etc.

To summarize, it is emphasized that a number of functions performed by combinational switching circuits may now be delegated to systems which incorporate ROMs.

### Flash memory

A variant of EEPROM which uses a special CMOS transistor (which has a second gate called a floating gate) is called a **flash memory**. Use of this special CMOS gate makes flash memory non-volatile and allows erasing and re-writing almost a million times. Flash memory has become extremely popular (because their storage capacity has increased and cost has remained moderate) since the late 1990s. Currently (2006) flash memory capacity has reached a maximum of 16 GB. It is fast replacing floppy disks in PCs, and even hard disks in portable devices such as portable music players and laptops. The main reasons for this is they are non-volatile, energy efficient and can be battery operated. The read time of flash memories is tens of nanoseconds per byte and write time is several microseconds. They are compact and are made in several shapes such as pens (a few centimetres long) and flat disks (2.5 cm$^2$). They are very commonly used in digital cameras. In PCs they are used by plugging them to Universal Serial Bus (USB) ports.

## 10.10  DUAL-PORTED RAM

The RAM we have discussed so far in this chapter has a set of memory cells which can be addressed using a memory address register (MAR) and the data stored in the specified address appears in a memory data register (MDR). It has only one address port and one data port. A dual-ported RAM, on the other hand, has two sets of addresses, data and read/write control signals, each of which accesses a common set of memory cells (see Figure 10.17).

Each set of memory controls can independently and simultaneously access, any word in the memory including the same word. The control logic acts as an arbitrator and allows one of them access. Even if both access requests come simultaneously, one of them is given access first (normally the request identified first gets access first). Thus, two devices can store and exchange data using this memory. Among the applications of dual-ported RAMs are CPU to CPU communication in multiprocessors, digital signal processing in which data are received simultaneously for many devices and stored in a common memory for processing. The main advantage of dual-ported RAM is that it can be used both as a working storage and as a communication interface.

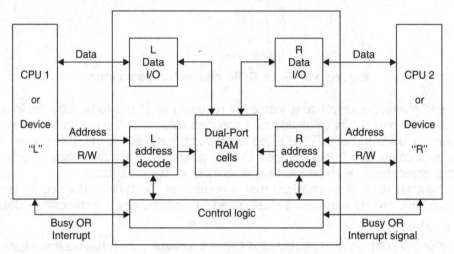

**Figure 10.17   Block diagram of a dual-port memory.**

## 10.11   ENHANCING SPEED AND CAPACITY OF MEMORIES

So far in this chapter we have described the technology used to design main RAMs of computers. We saw that DRAMs have access times of around 50 ns while their cost/bit is lowest in the semiconductor RAM family. DRAMs also need periodic refreshing. SRAMs, on the other hand, are designed using flip-flops. Their access time is lower (around 10 ns) and they are 10 times more expensive compared to DRAMs. Another device used as secondary memory (not the main RAM) is magnetic disk (to be described in detail in Chapter 11). They have very high capacity (around 100 GB), but their access time is in millisecond range. Their cost is 1000 times lower than that of DRAMs. Over the years the capacity of all these memories have increased (semiconductor memories' size doubles every 18 months and disk capacity doubles every 12 months) with no increase in cost. Thus, the relative sizes and cost ratios have remained almost constant. Over the years the applications of computers have become very complex and diverse. With this increase in complexity, application programmers have been demanding higher capacities of memories. Many applications are also on-line requiring fast response time which in-turn demands faster memories. Thus, a memory system designers challenge is to provide as large a size of memory as possible, as fast as possible and keep the cost as low as possible. This objective is fulfilled by appropriately designing computer systems as a combination of SRAMs, DRAMs and disks. In the rest of this chapter we will explore how this is achieved.

There are two methods used to meet the objectives explained in the last para. They are *cache memories* and *virtual memories*. Both these are dependent on the *principle of locality* which will be described in the next section. The cache memory idea is to combine a small expensive fast memory (such as a Static RAM) with a larger, slower, cheaper memory (such as Dynamic RAM) in such a way that the combined system has the capacity of the DRAM and the speed of SRAM at a cost slightly higher than DRAM. The virtual memory idea, on the other hand, is to provide a user with a large logical memory address space to write programs even though the available physical memory (DRAM) may be small. This is achieved by combining DRAM and a disk in such a way that the memory cycle time of the combined system is closer to DRAM cycle time while a large storage space is provided by the disk. The cost per byte of the combined system is slightly larger than the DRAM cost. While a cache memory provides a higher speed memory, a virtual memory provides a higher capacity memory. The cost-effectiveness is an important engineering design aspect in the design of both cache and virtual memory. In order to appreciate this, we give Table 10.6 which shows the cost, speed and typical capacities for three popular memory technologies.

**TABLE 10.6**
**Memory Technology Cost vs. Speed**

| Technology | Typical Access Time | Economical Size | Approximate relative Cost per byte |
|---|---|---|---|
| Static RAM (for cache) | 10 ns | 1 MB | $x$ |
| Dynamic RAM (for main memory) | 50 ns | 1 GB | $(x/10)$ |
| Disk | 10 ms | 100 GB | $(x/1000)$ |

## 10.12 PROGRAM BEHAVIOUR AND LOCALITY PRINCIPLE

Let us suppose that we execute a sample program and observe the sequence of memory addresses accessed by the CPU. Recall that memory is accessed both for instruction fetch and for operand or data fetch. The sequence of memory addresses accessed by a program for a given data set is known as its **trace**. For the same program different traces will be generated when different data sets are used. A program trace can be visualized as a graph in one dimension, that is, as a straight line on which the x points denote the neighbouring addresses in memory. In Figure 10.18, we have shown an example trace in which two distinct clusters are seen: one around the memory address where the instructions are stored and the other around the memory address where the data set is stored.

It has been found that many programs exhibit good or strong *locality* by dwelling in small parts of the memory address space (e.g. 128 or 256 bytes) when we consider rather long sequences of addresses in their address traces. To illustrate this point, let us consider a sample program given in Program 10.1 and its trace. This program is written in the language of SMAC++ to find the largest of one hundred numbers stored in memory, starting at the symbolic address A. The first data item at the address A is compared with the last data item at A+99 and the larger of the two numbers is kept in R1. This comparison is iterated with other numbers of the data set. A program loop is used for the iterative execution. For convenience all instructions and data are assumed to be of one unit in length. At location 0014 the conditional branch instruction will transfer control either to address 0015 or to 0016. For the sake of presenting the trace, let us assume a trivial data sequence of 100 numbers in which the two integers 60 and 50 alternate as: 60, 50, 60, 50, 60, 50...etc. Thus, after the branch instruction at the address 0014 the control branches to 0015 or to 0016 in alternative iterations of the loop. Let the data set be stored from 2000 to 2099 in memory. The address trace for Program 10.1 would be as follows:

When instructions are accessed the memory addresses read are in the following sequence:

10,11,12,13,14,16,  12,13,14,15,16,  12,13,14,16,  12,13,14,15,16  12,13,14,16, ...etc.

When data are accessed the memory addresses read are in the following sequence:

2001, 2099, 2098, 2097, 2096, ..., 2002.

In arriving at this trace we have used decimals and omitted leading zeros.

**Program 10.1:** To find the largest of 100 numbers stored in memory from the address A.

| Instruction address | | Instruction | Remarks |
|---|---|---|---|
| 0010 | | LDIMM R3, 99 | Load register R3 with 99 (63) Hex |
| 0011 | | LOAD R1, A | Load the first number in R1 |
| 0012 | LOOP | LOAD R2, R3, A | Load the last number in R2 when C(R3) = (63) Hex. R3 is the index register. |
| 0013 | | SUB R2, R1 | C(R2) ← C(R2) − C(R1) |
| 0014 | | JMIN * + 2 | Here, C(R1) is larger than C(R2) |
| 0015 | | LOAD, R1, R3, A | Here, C(A indexed by R3) is larger |
| 0016 | | BCT R3, LOOP | decrement R3 and branch if zero |
| 0017 | | HALT | |

In the address trace described above, we notice that the addresses (12,13,14) followed by either 15 or 16 are repeatedly addressed 100 times for the instruction fetch, and the data addresses are accessed sequentially one after another. We can conveniently present this address trace in the form of a *scatter diagram* as shown in Figure 10.18.

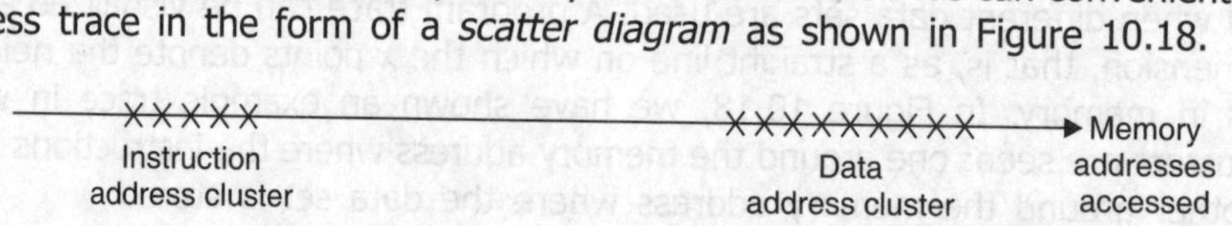

**Figure 10.18 Program trace represented as clusters.**

In this figure along the linear scale of memory addresses, we find two *clusters* one pertaining to instructions and the other pertaining to data. Normally there will be several clusters in a typical program trace. The locality principle implies that there are clusters. Each cluster has an associated cluster length. If we can keep a copy of that part of the memory pertaining to a cluster of addresses in a high speed buffer (see discussions on cache in Section 10.13) we can effectively increase the speed of memory accesses. The knowledge of the average cluster length could be used to determine how large such a buffer memory should be. It is also obvious that the control or access to memory, during program execution, will jump from one cluster to another. In Program 10.1 the program block following the conditional jump instruction, JMIN included only one instruction that is at the address 015. In large programs such a program block can be wider and thus separating the instruction cluster into multiple clusters. Similarly, a CALL instruction when executed could branch to a far away address and will thus create a jump from one cluster to another.

Empirical studies have shown that the clustering of addresses produced by the address trace of a program depends on the following factors:

1. The nature of the algorithm and the data structures used to solve the problem.
2. The programming language and its compiler.
3. The data set on which the program is run.
4. The programming style employed by the programmer

Since a majority of programs are written in a high level language, the compilers can play an important role in how storage is referenced. In some cases the programmer can control the locality by proper programming. As an example, consider the problem of summing all the elements of a large two-dimensional matrix. Suppose the matrix is stored in column major form that is one column after another. A program written to sum the elements column by column will exhibit more locality than the program written to sum the elements row by row. The latter program would give rise to an address trace in which the references would jump between two clusters in a systematic way (e.g. <u>101, 401</u>; <u>102, 402</u>; <u>103, 403</u>; <u>104, 404</u>; ... etc.).

The following programming techniques are recommended by Hellerman and Conroy to obtain good locality:

1. Placing data near the instructions that reference it, whenever possible.
2. Placing the instruction of the frequently called subroutines in line rather than using a CALL.
3. Separating exception handling routines (like error routines) from the main section of a program.
4. Organizing programs into modules and specifying the frequencies of use of these modules and the module interaction patterns. Such details can then be used by a linking loader to place the modules in a preferred order to enhance locality.

The principle of locality in programs can be summarized as follows. Programs during execution access a relatively small portion of their address space in small intervals of time. In programs, we can notice two types of localities.

1. *Temporal locality*:   If an item is referenced, it will tend to be referenced again soon.

2. *Spatial locality*:   If an item is referenced, there is a good chance that items whose addresses are near it will tend to be referenced soon.

In an iterative loop an instruction inside the loop is repeatedly accessed. See the BCT instruction in SMAC++ and its branch address. This is a good example of temporal locality. Consider the addition of two vectors A and B. $A_i$ and $A_{i+1}$ normally occupy two adjacent locations. During the addition process the adjacent locations are accessed in an orderly fashion as a sequence. This is a good example of spatial locality. In the following section we will learn how to make good use of this principle of locality in increasing the speed of a memory system with only a small increase in cost.

## 10.13   A TWO-LEVEL HIERARCHY OF MEMORIES

Temporal and spatial locality are properties of sequential programs. This property can be exploited in designing what is known as **two-level memories**. In two-level memories a memory system is designed by combining memories of two types. They are a very large but slow memory combined with a smaller fast memory. The adjectives large, slow, small and fast are relative. Their absolute values continuously increase with technology doubling of size almost every 18 months at the same absolute cost per byte. The important point is their relative cost difference per byte has remained almost invariant.

We will now examine how a two-level memory system is able to exploit locality of memory reference. In this organization the main RAM is combined with a fast small cache memory.

Let us suppose a cache memory of 256 bytes besides a RAM in a memory system. We will call it a **cache block** (also called a cache line). Let the system software store a duplicate copy of the contents of the RAM pertaining to a cluster in the cache block. When the computer accesses an address in RAM, first it looks for it in the cache. If the required item (instruction or data) is found in the cache, it is taken from there. This condition will be called *hit*. The opposite of *hit* is *miss*. When an item is not found in the cache memory, RAM will be accessed which is much slower than accessing the cache. A hit item will have two copies existing, one copy in the RAM and the other in the cache. The hit and miss can be expressed as a percentage of the total number of memory accesses in the execution of a program and will be normalized to fall in the range of 0 to 1. Thus, we can write:

Hit ratio ($h$):    $1 \geq h \geq 0$

Miss ratio = $(1 - h)$

Figure 10.19 is the schematic representation of a two-level storage model. Let $C$ and $T$ be the effective cost per bit and effective access time of the combined two-level system. If $h$ is the hit ratio, then

$$C = \frac{S1 \cdot C1 + S2 \cdot C2}{S1 + S2} \text{ units/bit}$$

$$T = hT1 + (1 - h)T2 \text{ units/byte access}$$

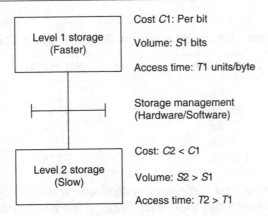

Cost $C1$: Per bit

Volume: $S1$ bits

Access time: $T1$ units/byte

Storage management
(Hardware/Software)

Cost: $C2 < C1$

Volume: $S2 > S1$

Access time: $T2 > T1$

**Figure 10.19   A model of a two-level storage.**

Let us define two more terms **access time ratio** $r$, and **access efficiency** $e$ as below:

$$r = \frac{T2}{T1} \text{ (ratio greater than 1)}$$

$$e = \frac{T1}{T} \text{ (desired to be 100\%)}$$

Substituting for $T$

$$e = \frac{T1}{hT1 + (1 - h)T2}$$

$$= \frac{T1}{T2 + h(T1 - T2)}$$

$$= \frac{1}{r + h(1 - r)}$$

In Figure 10.20 the access efficiency $e$ is plotted as the function of the hit ratio $h$ for different values of the access time ratio $r$. For all values of $r$, when $h = 1$, the efficiency is 100%. But $h = 1$ is not obtainable in practice because the size of the faster memory will be many orders of magnitude smaller than the slower memory. Typically in the modern computers, the cache memory size is of the order of KB whereas the RAM size is in the order of GB. When $r = 1$, efficiency is 100% for all values of $h$. No one would choose a two-level storage system when $r = 1$ and hence this case is only of academic value. In all other cases, the access efficiency is very poor if the hit ratio goes below 80%. This could be used as a good rule-of-thumb in designing a two-level storage system. The hit ratio is dependent upon many factors such as the size of the storage in level 1, the access pattern or the locality exhibited and the mapping between the two levels of storages. In a memory system based on a 10 MB RAM and cache, a particular type of mapping between the contents of RAM and that of the cache called **direct mapping** (to be discussed later) gives the results shown in Table 10.7 for different sizes of the cache.

**TABLE 10.7**
**Cache Size vs Hit Ratio in Direct Mapped Cache**

| Cache Size | Hit Ratio |
|---|---|
| 8 KB | 91.3% |
| 16 KB | 93.2% |
| 32 KB | 95% |
| 64 KB | 96% |
| 128 KB | 97.5% |

So far we have presented a memory system with a two-level hierarchy. There is no reason why we cannot extend this to multiple levels, if there is a clear benefit at the system level. The reader should observe that as we increase the number of levels in a hierarchy, the complexity in accessing increases and the designer will not choose this complexity unless the benefits outperform and justify such a complexity.

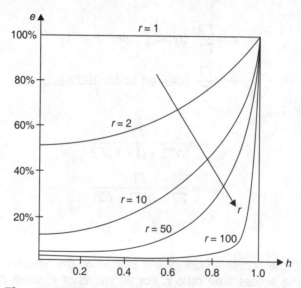

**Figure 10.20  Access efficiency vs hit ratio.**

## 10.14  CACHE IN MEMORY ORGANIZATION

*Cache* is a very high speed small capacity memory introduced as a buffer between the CPU and the main memory (RAM). Millions of instructions are executed every second in a computer system. Each instruction requires one access to memory for fetching the instruction and zero, one or more memory accesses to fetch the data for execution of that instruction. Thus, the speed with which memory can be accessed is important for reducing the execution time of an instruction. On the other hand the demand for large size memory is ever growing with the more sophisticated operating systems, real time and interactive applications, and networking of computers. The ubiquitous use of computers also demands that the cost be as minimal as possible.

The locality property in memory accesses, during program execution, makes the use of cache effective in reducing the access time to main memory without unduly increasing the cost of the memory system. Parts of the current program (and data) are copied from the main memory into the high speed cache. When the CPU refers to an instruction (or data), it is fetched from the cache if it is already there. If the required item is in cache, it is called a **hit**. If the required item is not in cache, it has to be fetched from the main memory. When the probability of hit is very high the CPU will be reading an instruction or data most of the time from the cache. There should be enough cache memory to store a large enough "cluster" about which we discussed in the previous section. However, there are two problems. The clusters vary in length and are dependent on several factors. Secondly when the program control jumps from one cluster to another, there is a need to flush the cache (that is save it in main memory) and reload it with the contents of this new cluster from RAM. Cache memory organization deals with solving such problems.

When a cache is to be reloaded, first its contents must be copied back to the RAM. During a memory WRITE operation if there was a hit, the contents of the cache memory would have been changed and its copy in the RAM would not have been updated. Hence, there is a need to write the contents of cache back in main memory before it is reloaded with new contents from the main memory. This is sometimes called **flushing** the cache to main memory. In a cache memory organization, to facilitate management, the available cache is divided into equal sized *cache blocks* and the RAM is also divided into *memory blocks* of the same size. The terminology *cache line* is also used by some authors instead of *cache block*. One of the management issues is to decide which memory block should be mapped to which cache block. Since there will be many more memory blocks than the number of cache blocks, this mapping will be many-to-one. The operating system with hardware support does cache management operations such as flushing a cache block, reloading a memory block into its cache, determining if an access to memory is a hit or miss. The memory design is such that the existence of cache is "transparent" or invisible to a programmer.

When a memory READ is initiated by the CPU, the address is automatically checked by the hardware to find if its contents are already in the cache. If so the word is read from the cache. See the path a-b-c in data flow diagram shown in Figure 10.21(ii). If it is not in the cache, then the contents of the specified address is read directly from the main memory (path d-b-c) and the word so read (or a block containing it) is also stored in the cache (path d-b-a) for future reference. If the same address is referenced again in the near future, it will be found in the cache leading to a hit.

Let the hit ratio $h$ be defined as follows:

$$h = \frac{\text{number of times the item is found in cache}}{\text{(sufficiently large) number of addresses referenced}}$$

The hit ratio is a fraction less than unity and is expressed as percentage and $(1 - h)$ is called *miss ratio*. If $T_e$ and $T_m$ are the cycle times of the cache and main memory respectively, effective memory cycle time is given by:

$$T = hT_e + (1 - h)T_m$$

For a case with $h = 90\%$ and $T_e$ and $T_m$ are 10 ns and 50 ns respectively, the effective cycle time $T$ would be 14 ns. This is a substantial improvement in memory speed. A hit ratio of 90% is usually achieved with strong locality exhibited by programs. Thus, the additional cost of cache and that of the associated cache-management-hardware is worth the speed improvement.

As stated earlier the cache capacity is very much smaller than that of the main memory and could be smaller than a user's program. Thus, every time something new has to be stored in the cache, something else already in the cache has to be copied back into the main memory and its space vacated. Data is moved between the cache and the main memory in integral number of blocks. Block size of 128 or 256 bytes is normally used. Assume that a command is received to write a word in the memory. If that word is in the cache, both the cache contents and the memory contents have to be changed. If both are updated simultaneously, it is known as *store through* or *writes through* method (see Figure 10.21(i)).

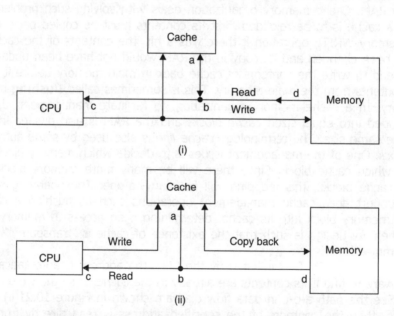

**Figure 10.21   Data flow in cache: (i) Write-through, and (ii) Copy back.**

The alternative method updates the cache location only and flags the corresponding cache block by setting a flag called **altered-bit**. Some authors call the altered-bit **dirty bit**. Whenever a cache block has to be reloaded by a newly read memory block, the altered bit of that cache block is checked. If the bit is ON, the cache block is copied back to the corresponding memory block to permanently store the updates; otherwise it is simply over-written. See Figure 10.21(ii). The disadvantage of this method is that there are time periods when the cache block is updated but the corresponding memory block is not updated. This inconsistency may be unacceptable in some operational environments. This inconsistency between the two copies (one copy in the RAM and another copy in the cache) is called **cache coherence problem**.

In the above paragraph we have used the term "corresponding memory block" more than once. We will illustrate the concept of a *mapping* between the main memory blocks (denoted as MB) and the cache blocks (denoted as CB) through an example. Consider Figure 10.22 wherein we have assumed the following block sizes and the unit of memory to be a word. It could very well have been bytes:

Block size: 16 words (4 bits to address a word inside a block)

Main memory size: 64 K words (4 K memory blocks; $2^{12}$ = 64 K)

Cache memory size: 1 K words (64 cache-blocks; $2^6$ = 64)

Address length: 16 bits ($2^{16}$ = 64 K)

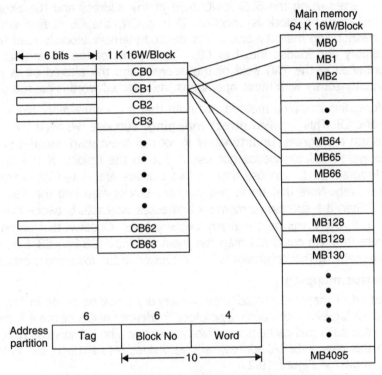

**Figure 10.22  Direct mapping of cache.**

The 4096 memory blocks are mapped into the 64 CBs and hence it is a many-to-one mapping. Dividing the 4096 memory blocks equally into 64 groups yields 64 memory blocks in a group. Any one of the 64 memory blocks belonging to a group can map into one CB and which one of these is resident in the given CB at any one time is indicated by the 6-bit ($2^6$ = 64) *tag field* associated with each cache block. Hence, the 16-bit memory address is first divided into two parts: 6-bit tag field and 10-bit cache address (Figure 10.22). The 10-bit cache address itself is further divided into a 4-bit word address (because there are 16 words per block) and a 6-bit block address (64 cache blocks is the total cache size and we need 6 bits to address one of the 64). The sequence of actions that takes place in accessing the memory can be summarized as follows:

## Memory access with cache

**Operation:**   Read word from main memory. Address given.

*Step 1:*   First, the BLOCK-NO field of the address is used to select a cache block and then its tag bits contents are compared with the TAG field contents of the given address.

*Step 2:*   If the two match, the required memory block is already in the cache and it is a hit. The required word (1 out of 16) is selected from the cache using the word field of the address.

*Step 3:*   If the two tag bits do not match, the required memory block is not in the cache and it is a miss. Hence a main memory read has to be initiated. A cache block is selected using the BLOCK-NO field of the address and the altered-bit of the selected cache block is checked. If it is ON, the CB is first written into the corresponding memory block. The desired memory block is read from the main memory and loaded into this CB. The tag bits of the CB are set to the value contained in the TAG field of the address and the altered bit is reset to zero. Simultaneously with these operations the selected word is passed on to the CPU.

In the foregoing mapping method, we note that a given memory block can map into only one specific CB. This is called **direct mapping**. Suppose we need two main memory blocks to execute a program. Unfortunately if both of them map into the same CB, even if another CB were available we cannot use it due to the rigidity of the direct mapping. Referring to Program 10.1, suppose that its two clusters are stored into memory blocks 0 and 128 respectively. Note that these two memory blocks map into the same cache block namely CB-0. When the successive memory addresses alternate between the two memory blocks 0 and 128, there will be too many cache misses. Observe that, even if the cache block CB 1 were free, we could not map the memory block 128 into CB-1 according to the direct-mapping method. This constraint is "fully" relaxed in the following method of mapping.

## Fully associative mapping

A flexible method of mapping should allow a memory block to reside in any cache block. Then we need 12 tag-bits with each cache block to identify which of the 4 K memory blocks is presently contained in that cache block. This type of mapping is known as **fully associative mapping**. In this case a 16-bit address will be divided into a 12-bit tag field and a 4-bit word field as shown in Figure 10.23.

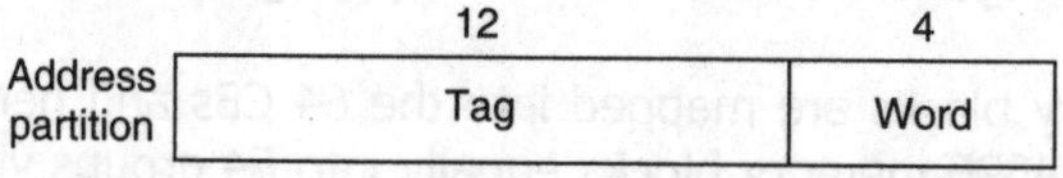

| | 12 | 4 |
|---|---|---|
| Address partition | Tag | Word |

**Figure 10.23  Address partition for fully associative mapping.**

In order to find if the required address is in the cache or not, first we have to find if the access is a hit or a miss. Since a memory block could be in any one of the 64 CBs and we have no way of knowing which one it is, we have to compare the tag field contents of the given address with the 12 tag bits of every one of these 64 cache blocks. If sequential comparison of the 64 entries is performed, the time taken will be too much to make the method worthwhile. In the case of direct mapping we do not have this problem of searching because a given main memory block goes into a fixed cache block. In the example above the memory block $n$ can possibly go only into the cache block $m$ where $m = n$ modulo 64 because there are 64 cache blocks. To make the associative mapping worthwhile, the search or comparison with 64 entries must be done in parallel using 64 different comparators. This is called **associative searching** which makes this method costly. However, the fully associative mapping provides complete freedom in placing a memory block into any available cache block whereas the direct mapping provides no freedom at all. Intermediate methods exist between these two extremes which are known by the name **block-set-associative mapping**.

### Block-set-associative mapping

The block set associative mapping is a combination of both the direct mapping and associative mapping. In this case, cache blocks are grouped into a number of sets and the number of blocks grouped in a set is a design parameter.

In Figure 10.24 we have chosen four blocks per set. Hence, for the above example there are 16 sets. Let us number them from 0 to 15. Dividing the 4096 memory blocks

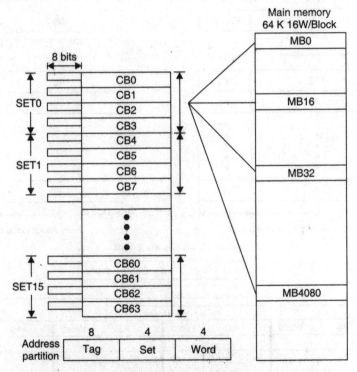

**Figure 10.24  Block-set-associative mapping.**

equally among these 16 sets, we find that 256 memory blocks can be mapped into one set. Figure 10.24 shows those memory blocks that are mapped into set 0, namely 0, 16, 32, 48, 64, 80, ..., 4080. In this sense, the mapping resembles the direct mapping. But the 256 memory blocks that are mapped into set 0 can be placed into any of the four cache blocks within the set 0, namely CB0, CB1, CB2, or CB3 indicated in the figure. In this way it resembles the associative mapping. Note that in this figure the number of tag bits is determined as:

Tag bits = address length − (number of bits needed to address a word in block
+ the number of bits needed to address one of the sets)

When accessing the memory, one of the 16 sets is selected by the 4-bit SET field of the given address. The 8-bit TAG field contents are matched with the tag bits of every block in that set. In this example there are 4 blocks in a set and a parallel comparison with 4 entities is relatively simpler. If a match occurs with the tag bits of any one of the 4 blocks of the set, the access is a hit. If the match fails with every block of the selected set, it is a miss. Then one of the four blocks of the set is chosen according to a *replacement rule*. As a preparation for re-load, the contents of the chosen block are first written into the main memory, if it was altered since it was brought from the RAM last time. Then the desired memory block is read from the RAM and placed into that cache block of that set. In Figure 10.25 we compare the three methods of mapping memory on to a cache.

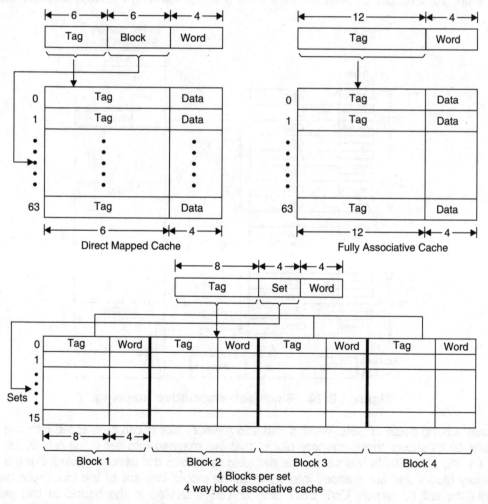

**Figure 10.25 Comparing the three methods of mapping memory on to a cache.**

Table 10.8 gives some specific implementation of caches by computer manufacturers. The values shown in this table show how technology has progressed. As memory technology improves the cache access time decreases and the cache size used in computer systems is much larger but it will always be a fraction of the main memory size.

### TABLE 10.8
### Caches in Real Computers

|  | 360/195 | PDP 11/70 | VAX 11/750 | 80486 |
|---|---|---|---|---|
| Block size | 64 bytes | 4 bytes | — | 16 bytes |
| Cache size | 32 KB | 2 KB | 4 KB | 32 KB |
| Memory size | 4 MB | 2 MB | 16 MB | 16 MB (typical) |
| Cache access time | 50 ns | 300 ns | 320 ns | 45 ns |
| Memory access time | 750 ns | 1 μs | 800 ns | 100 ns |
| Hit ratio | 99% | 90% | 90% | 99% |
| Mapping | Block-set-assoc. 4 Blocks/set | Block-set-assoc. 2 Blocks/set | Direct | Direct |
| Replacement | LRU | Random | — | LRU |

The hit ratio (or miss ratio) depends on many factors such as, the cache size, block size, replacement rule, program locality and so on. Figure 10.26 shows how the choice of block size affects the miss ratio, that is (1–hit ratio) for various values of the cache memory size. A good design will exhibit low sensitivity or variation in the miss ratio and also a very low value for the miss ratio.

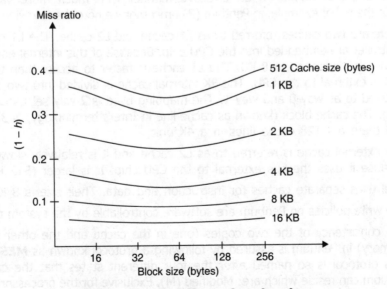

**Figure 10.26   Effect of cache size.**

When the cache size is reasonably large (8K or 16K), the choice of block size is not too critical. Because of high miss ratios, small cache sizes like 512 bytes are not effective.

As we have seen in earlier chapters, memory is accessed both for instruction and data. One can consider using two separate *caches*, one as *data cache* and the other as *instruction cache*. In Pentium processors , two separate 8 KB caches are used. Obviously, then we need two separate cache controllers. Experience with such twin systems has shown that patterns in memory access differ between the memory access during instruction fetch and during data fetch or store. Pipelined processors require access to both caches simultaneously and thus they are independently controlled.

With the reduction in cost of memories, main memories have become very large (around 1 GB is now common). Also CPU chips have reached very high level of integration allowing hundreds of millions of transistors on a chip and the chip sizes have increased. This increased capacity has led to incorporating 8 KB data and 8 KB instruction caches in the CPU chip itself. Accessing this cache is very fast. For instance Pentium V processors have two 8 KB caches in CPU one called instruction cache and the other data cache. Both of them are labelled as Level 1 (or L1) caches. Besides this, on the CPU board there is another SRAM memory of around 512 KB capacity called L2 cache. This is in turn connected to the DRAM main memory. Thus when an instruction or data is to be retrieved, one first looks up L1 cache whether it is in it. If not then L2 cache is examined. Only if there is a miss in 2 also there is a need to access the main memory. Usually there is 99% probability of the required data being found in either L1 or L2 cache and thus the average access time is quite small— a few nanoseconds.

## Cache memory in Pentium processors[1]

The above discussions on cache memory organization are broken into neat little categories for pedagogical simplicity. In real life computer systems like the Pentium processor these neat categories are combined in an effective manner with much more variations and adaptations in them. For example, in Pentium (R) processor we note the following adaptations:

1. There are two caches referred to as L1 cache and L2 cache. The L1 cache and its controller are embedded into the CPU chip. Because of this internal embedding the cache size is limited to 8 KB. The L1 cache is faster to access than the L2 cache that is external to the CPU. The 8K internal cache is divided into two 4K units and referred to as way-0 and way-1. The mapping used is 2-way set associative mapping. The cache block (known as cache line in Intel's terminology) is 32 bytes long and there are 128 cache lines in a 4K unit.

2. The external cache is referred to as L2 cache and it is relatively slower to access because it uses the bus external to the CPU chip. It is larger (512 KB).

3. Intel uses separate caches for instruction and data. Their size is 8 KB each.

4. The write policies on Pentium are software controllable by the system programmer.

5. The consistency of the two copies (one in the cache and the other in the main memory) in Pentium is assured by following a protocol known as **MESI protocol**. This protocol is so named after the four different states that the cache line in Pentium can reside which are: Modified (M), Exclusive for the processor (E), Shared access to other processors (S) and Invalid (I).

---

[1]See http://www.intel.com/design/intarch/papers/cache6.pdf

# 10.15 DESIGN AND PERFORMANCE OF CACHE MEMORY SYSTEM

In the design of cache memory systems, apart from choosing the right block size and cache memory size, two policy decisions are relevant: (1) When a cache "miss" happens leading to a main memory access, which cache block will be replaced? This is known as the **replacement rule** or **policy**; (2) upon hit, when a memory WRITE takes place, does the system update only the copy in the cache leaving the copy in the main memory to be un-updated (inconsistency) or does the system update both the copies? This is called **write policy**. When the data is updated in the cache but not in the main memory, the data in the cache is called **dirty**. Similarly, when the data in main memory is updated but not in the cache block its data is called **stale**. Keeping the cache consistent without being stale or dirty is an important responsibility of the cache controller hardware.

In the case of direct mapping, a main memory block can be loaded only to the pre-determined cache block and the question of choice does not arise. But, in the case of other two mappings the question of which cache block should be replaced becomes important. The simplest replacement rule is to select a block within the set randomly. This rule is simple to implement but not the best. The best replacement rule would be to select the block in that set that has not been referenced for the longest time. Such a block is called LRU block (least recently used) and the algorithm used to select a LRU block is called **LRU algorithm**. The implementation of LRU algorithm is not that simple.

There are two common write policies. Let us assume that the memory access is a hit and the operation is memory WRITE. One policy is known as **write-back** policy. According to this policy, when a memory WRITE is performed, the contents of the cache are updated and the processor is allowed to proceed without waiting. The cache controller will initiate a main memory write later to update the copy of the block residing there. In this case the cache controller is more complex as it has to handle memory write operation separately. The other policy is known as **write-through** policy. According to this policy the data is updated both in the cache block and in the memory block at the same time. This will slow down the processor. A similar analysis holds good during the memory READ operation. Let us suppose that the memory READ is a miss. In this case, the main memory block is accessed. There are two options. One is to transfer the memory block into the destination cache block and then forward the required item from the cache to the processor. This policy is known as **look aside** policy. In the second case, as the desired item is read from the main memory block it is immediately sent to the processor. The selected cache block is reloaded after this. This is called **look through** policy.

Cache performance can be studied experimentally or empirically, using approximate models. An experimental study requires typical programs and typical data from which address traces can be generated. For a given cache memory design, using such address traces hit ratio and miss ratio can be calculated. Recall that the hit ratio would vary from one program to another and again within a program from one data set to another data set. Therefore, a benchmark of programs and data sets are needed to obtain an average of such numbers so that one can compare the performances of two different cache designs. In what follows, as an exercise, we will use the example program and the data set given in Program 10.1 earlier and compute the hit and miss ratio. For this exercise let us assume the following:

1. The computer is word organized.
2. One instruction occupies one word.
3. The block size for cache is 5 words (so that we can highlight important points).
4. There are two separate caches, one for instruction and one for data.
5. Direct mapping is used for cache design.
6. The operating system has allocated one cache block for instructions and one cache block for data and they are called CB0 and DB0 respectively.
7. When the program is started the caches are properly loaded.
   - CB0—contains the contents of memory from 10 to 14
   - DB0—contains the contents of memory from 2001 to 2004

By observing Program 10.1 we note that there are 18 instructions loaded in the address range 10 to 17 and there are 100 data items loaded in the address range 2000 to 2099. As the block size is 5, the program and its data will occupy 4 blocks for instructions and 20 blocks for its data in the main memory. The program trace for this program was described earlier and is reproduced as follows:

For instruction access the memory addresses READ are in the following sequence:

10,11,  12,13,14,**16,**  **12,**13,14,**15,**16,  **12,**13,14,**16,**  **12,**13,14,**15,**16,
**12,**13,14,**16,** ...etc.

For data access the memory addresses READ are in the following sequence:

2001, **2099,** 2098, 2097, 2096, 2095, **2094,** 2093, 2092, 2091, 2090, **2089** ..., 2002.

Note the bold and underlined addresses indicated in the above sequences. When these memory addresses are accessed there is a "miss". The reason for this is explained in Table 10.9. The total number of memory accesses and the total number of "misses" can be easily calculated by observing the sequences and the addresses which cause the miss.

### Total number of memory accesses

| | | | |
|---|---|---|---|
| One time addresses 10,11: | 2 | Number of misses: | 0 |
| First time (12,13,14,16): | 4 | Number of misses: | 1 |
| 49 times (12,13,14,16): | 196 | Number of misses: | 98 |
| 50 times (12,13,14,15,16): | 250 | Number of misses: | 100 |
| One time address 17: | 1 | Number of misses: | 0 |
| Data accesses: | 100 | Number of misses: | 20 |
| Total | 553 | Total misses | 219 |

Hit ratio = (553 − 219)/553 = 0.6

The hit ratio of 0.6 in the above example is a pathological case and it is not a realistic case. This simple example was chosen to show how a program trace can be used to calculate the hit ratio. In this example if we were to make a moderate improvement of an increased cache block size of 10 words instead of 5 words, there will be no misses during instruction accesses and there would be only 10 misses during the 100 data accesses giving a hit ratio of (553 − 10)/553 = 0.98. An important point for the reader to observe from this example is the factors which cause a cache miss and how a programmer can minimize the chances of causing a miss.

**TABLE 10.9**

**Hit and Miss for Program 10.1**

Instruction Addressing → Followed by → Data Addressing

| | | | | | |
|---|---|---|---|---|---|
| 10 | CB0 | hit | | | — |
| 11 | CB0 | hit | 2001 | DB0 | hit |
| | | | | | |
| 12 | CB0 | hit | 2099 | DB0 | miss [loaded 2095 to 2099] |
| 13 | CB0 | hit | | | |
| 14 | CB0 | hit | | | |
| 16 | CB0 | miss [loaded 15 to 19] | 2099 | DB0 | hit |
| | | | | | |
| 12 | CB0 | miss [loaded 10 to 14] | 2098 | DB0 | hit |
| 13 | CB0 | hit | | | |
| 14 | CB0 | hit | | | |
| 15 | CB0 | miss [loaded 15 to 19] | 2098 | DB0 | hit |
| 16 | CB0 | hit | | | |
| | | | | | |
| 12 | CB0 | miss [loaded 10 to 14] | 2097 | DB0 | hit |
| 13 | CB0 | hit | | | |
| 14 | CB0 | hit | | | |
| 16 | CB0 | miss [loaded 15 to 19] | | | |
| | | | | | |
| 12 | CB0 | miss [loaded 10 to 14] | 2096 | DB0 | hit |
| 13 | CB0 | hit | | | |
| 14 | CB0 | hit | | | |
| 15 | CB0 | miss [loaded 15 to 19] | 2096 | DB0 | hit |
| 16 | CB0 | hit | | | |
| | | | | | |
| 12 | CB0 | miss [loaded 10 to 14] | 2095 | DB0 | hit |
| 13 | CB0 | hit | | | |
| 14 | CB0 | hit | | | |
| 16 | CB0 | miss [loaded 15 to 19] | | | |

## 10.16 VIRTUAL MEMORY—ANOTHER LEVEL IN HIERARCHY

In large computer applications, there is a need for storing and addressing very large amount of data. With the advent of multimedia and the World Wide Web, there is a need to store data that runs into hundreds of giga ($10^9$) or terra ($10^{12}$) bytes. **Virtual memory** is a method used in many computer systems to give a programmer the illusion that he has a very large addressable memory at his disposal although the computer may not have a large main memory. Consider the following scenario. A program or data (object) to be handled is too large to fit into a given main memory. The programmer, normally, divides such an object into segments so that no segment is too large for the main memory, stores them on a disk, dynamically loads and overlays the segments, as needed, during program execution.

In a similar situation, earlier we exploited the "locality" property to design a cache memory system. Using the same idea, we can define another level of hierarchy that is between the main memory and the very large disk space. In comparison to the cost and speed of main memory, the disk memories are cheaper, larger and slower by a factor of 100. A virtual memory system resembles the cache memory system. The cache is one level closer to the CPU than the main memory, and similarly the main memory is one level closer to the CPU than the disk memory. Using the notion of virtual memory system, large application software can address and manipulate objects stored on disks as if they were stored in main memory. Yet, there is one important difference. The cache management is done in hardware and it is completely transparent to all programmers including the system software developers whereas the virtual memory is managed by the system software that is a part of the Operating System. The application programmer is freed from the management of virtual memory system. The virtual memory system provides the following benefits to the application programmer:

1. It frees the application programmer from the chore of dividing an object into segments and managing the transfer of segments between the disk and the main memory. It provides the user with a large virtual memory which is a combination of memory space in a disk and main memory. This memory can be used as though it is all main memory.

2. It helps to develop programs that are independent of the configuration and capacity of memory systems because the virtual memory management is part of the system software.

3. It permits efficient sharing of memory space among different users of a multiuser system.

Consider a computer system like 80486 that has a 32-bit effective address. It can support a maximum memory capacity of $2^{32}$ or 4 GB. It is not economical to have a main memory as large as 4 GB. Let us suppose the memory system designer has chosen to have a 512 MB ($2^{29}$) main memory. The *physical address* space is then 512 MB and 4 GB is called *virtual address space*. Note that we must have a disk that is at least 4 GB in size to store the objects. A programmer can use an addressable memory as large as the virtual address space, as if it were fully available for program or data in main memory. The virtual memory management system will take care of the mapping between these two address spaces. For the sake of this management, the address spaces are partitioned. When this partition is into arbitrary but equal sizes it is called **paging**. When partitioning is based on logical reasoning leading to variable size partitions, it is called **segmentation**. In what follows we will focus only on paging. The concepts introduced in paging are quite similar to what we studied under cache memory systems.

## 10.16.1   Address Translation

We will use the terms VM page and MM page to refer to the partitions of the virtual memory and main memory respectively. The VM page and MM page are assumed to be of the same size. The conceptual mapping between them is shown in Figure 10.27.

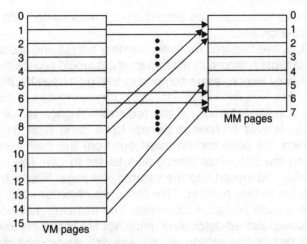

**Figure 10.27 Conceptual mapping from VM pages to MM pages.**

An example of organization and virtual memory address translation are shown in Figure 10.28. In this example, the page size is assumed to be 2 KB (needs 11-bit address).

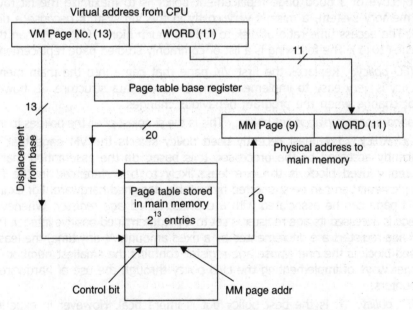

**Figure 10.28 Virtual address translation.**

A $2^{24}$ bytes virtual memory (16M bytes) is divided into $2^{13}$ (8K) VM pages; and $2^{20}$ bytes (1M bytes) main memory is divided into $2^{9}$ (512) MM pages. A *page table* is used in this case for mapping a VM page into an MM page. The page table contains one entry corresponding to each VM page and the page table can be relocated in main memory with the use of the page-table-base register. Each page table entry contains some control bits and a 9-bit MM page address where the corresponding VM page is stored, if it is presently stored in the main memory. The control bits are used to indicate if the VM page is in main memory or not, whether the page was altered after it was loaded into the main memory, the page-access frequency, etc.

From Figure 10.28, we find that for every memory access one access to the page table is needed. If the page table is stored in main memory, it would reduce the effective memory speed by a factor of two. Hence, some computers use high speed buffers to store part of a page table.

When the CPU accesses memory, if the required VM page is not found in the main memory, a *page fault* is said to have occurred. Upon page fault the *page replacement algorithm* selects which MM page can be rolled out from the main memory. The selected MM page is copied on the disk, if its altered-bit was set to ON. The required VM page is then read from the disk and loaded into the vacated MM page. Finally, the page-table-entry bits are properly set for further reading. This sequence of actions are similar to those we had discussed in the section on cache memories. The mapping methods discussed earlier, namely direct, associative, and set-associative mappings are applicable also to virtual memory management. In the rest of this section we will examine some page replacement policies.

## 10.16.2   Page Replacement

A major objective of a good page replacement policy is to maximize the hit ratio. Unlike the cache memory system, a miss is very costly in the VM system because a disk access is required. The access time ratio of disk to RAM is much higher ($10^4 : 1$) than that of the RAM to cache ($10:1$). The following is a list of commonly studied page replacement policies:

(a) *FIFO policy:*   Replaces the first VM page that came into the main memory. This policy is very easy to implement using a queue data structure. It, however, does not change when the program behaviour changes.

(b) *Random page replacement policy:*   This is the simplest of all the policies to implement.

(c) *LRU policy:*   The least recently used policy selects the VM page that was least recently accessed by the processor. It is based on the assumption that the least recently used block is the one least likely to be referenced in the future. Its implementation can be supported by suitably designed hardware. For example each MM page can be associated with a counter, called *age register*. Whenever an MM page is accessed its age register is set to a predetermined positive integer. Periodically all age registers are decremented by a fixed amount. At any time, the least recently used block is the one whose age register contains the smallest number. There are other ways of implementing the LRU policy through the use of hardware/software counters.

(d) *MIN policy:*   It is the best policy but is impractical. However in experiment and design, the MIN algorithm gives a useful comparison for replacement algorithms being considered. When replacement is required, MIN considers each page with respect to the address trace of that program and selects that page for replacement whose next reference is furthest in the future. Although available in simulation and design studies, such knowledge is not available during program execution.

(e) *Working set policy:*   Earlier we have introduced the notion of address trace. It is a sequence of addresses corresponding to reference to memory locations. Since each address falls into one MM page, the address trace can also be represented using MM page numbers instead of memory addresses. Let us assume such a method is used. *Working set* is defined over a window $T$ at a reference point $t$ and is denoted as $W(t, T)$. It is a set of all unique page numbers appearing in the window $T$ pages, looking back in the address trace from the page at reference point. Figure 10.29 gives an example of a working set. Since the working set is a set of page numbers, we can refer to its cardinality denoted as $|W(t, T)|$. The mean working-set size is obtained by taking the average of $|W(t, T)|$ over $t$ and it is denoted as $\bar{W}(T)$.

Time $t$

Address Trace:      1      2      3      4      5      6      7      8      9      10

(Page Numbers)   21    22    26    27    26    22    26    25    31    32 · · · ·

Working Set at $t = 8$ for $T = 6$
$W(t = 8, T = 6) = \{25, 26, 22, 27\}$ (Observe that page 26 repeats and
                                                                thus included only once)
$|W(t = 8, T = 6)| = 4$

**Figure 10.29   Explanation of working set.**

The mean working set size is a function of the window size $T$. It has been found that the mean working-set size possesses the following properties:

(a)  $1 < \bar{W}(T) <$ minimum of $(T, N)$ where $N$ is the number of MM pages in the system.

(b)  $\bar{W}(T) \le \bar{W}(T + 1)$

(c)  $\bar{W}(T + 1) + \bar{W}(T - 1) < 2\bar{W}(T)$  (implies concave down)

The above properties yield the general shape of the curve shown in Figure 10.30.

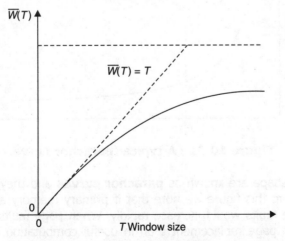

**Figure 10.30   Shape of working set curve.**

Smaller the working set of a program better it is from the point of view of the virtual memory system. It is the locality property of programs that makes their working sets much smaller than the respective program sizes.

In the working set policy of page replacement, pages that are not in the working set are replaced to release their MM pages. Such replacements are done at page fault times. The choice of window size is a design parameter that one optimizes by keeping the general shape of the curve (Figure 10.30) in mind. Because the working set model is based on the dynamic behaviour of memory references, this kind of policy can be expected to be better than other methods. Also working set measurements are useful in comparing programs from the point of view of their suitability for virtual memory systems.

Space-time product (SP) is sometimes used as a measure of goodness for evaluating various page replacement policies. It may be defined as follows:

$$SP = M(n + f\overline{T_2})$$

where

$M$ = primary memory allocated to that program. (This will not be constant for working set policy.)

$n$ = No. of memory references made by the program. (This is an indirect measure of time.)

$\overline{T_2}$ = Average time required to transfer a VM page to an MM page (Time should be expressed in the same unit as $n$).

$f$ = No. of page faults.

It is easy to visualize that when $M$ increases, $f$ should decrease. The general trend of the relation between $M$ and $f$ is shown in Figure 10.31.

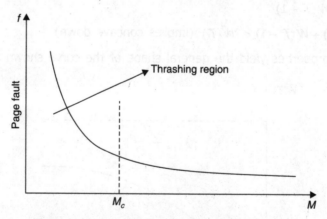

**Figure 10.31  A typical parachor curve.**

Graphs of this shape are known as **parachor curves** and they are very common in design problems. From this figure we note that if primary memory allotted for a program is less than $M_c$, page faults would increase rapidly. When page faults are too many, more time will be spent in page replacement than in useful computation. This phenomenon is known as **thrashing** and one should avoid chances of thrashing. In a particular performance evaluation study eight different benchmark programs were used and the average space-time products were computed for the following three page replacement policies (Baer):

| Policy | Average SP |
|--------|-----------|
| MIN | 12.84 units |
| Working Set | 15.63 units |
| LRU | 16.82 units |

## 10.16.3 Page Fetching

Let us consider the problem of fetching a VM page from the high speed disk. There are two strategies for fetching a VM page. These are: *Demand Paging* and *Pre-Paging*. In demand paging, a page is brought only when a page fault occurs. Until the virtual memory operating system completes page replacement, the process has to wait. Pre-paging is a technique in which a page is pre-fetched in anticipation. Since a pre-fetched page occupies an MM page, one will not choose this strategy unless he is reasonably sure about his predictions on the use of the pre-fetched page. In the processing of large arrays, one may predict with reasonable accuracy that a page required would be the next page.

Throughout this section we have seen many similarities between paging and cache memory concepts. Difference between them are summarized in Table 10.10.

**TABLE 10.10**

**Differences Between Cache and Virtual Memory**

| Description | Cache | Virtual Memory |
|-------------|-------|----------------|
| Access time ratio, $r$ (typical) | 10:1 | 10000:1 |
| Memory management by: | Special hardware | Mainly software |
| Typical partition size | $\simeq$ 100 bytes | Several kilo bytes |
| Processor's access to slower memory | Can access directly | Can access only through main memory |

## 10.16.4 Page Size

Page size is yet another design parameter in virtual memory systems. Small pages lead to large page table and increase the complexity of memory management. On the contrary, they minimize what is known as **internal fragmentation**. Suppose a program occupies $m$ complete pages and one byte in the $(m + 1)$th page. If the page size is $p$ bytes, $(p - 1)$ bytes are unused because of this program. It cannot be allotted to another program. This type of main memory fragmentation is known as internal fragmentation. When the page size is small, every page replacement brings from the disk only a small amount of code/data. This also affects the hit ratio. Large page sizes have the converse properties. As a compromise between these two opposing factors, a designer has to choose an optimal page size. We will not go into the details of the design. The page size used in some of the commercial computers popular during the 1990s was 4 KB. Current computer systems favour much larger page size of the order of 16 KB or 64 KB.

## 10.16.5 How to Make Address Translation Faster

When we use virtual memory, for every memory access we have to perform the translation from virtual address to physical address. If we use the fully associative mapping between VM pages and MM pages, it gives us a flexibility to replace any of the MM pages by a newly fetched VM page. However, searching in a fully associative memory can be quite expensive. To solve this problem of associative searching, we introduced the page table idea as shown in Figure 10.28. In this case a page table entry is directly accessed. The control bit in a page table entry tells if that VM page is in RAM or not. If it is in RAM then the address of the MM page which contains this VM page is found in the page table. Suppose we have a small fast buffer which stores the relevant part of a page table. If the required VM page entry is in this buffer, the address of the MM page is immediately found. Let us call this buffer TLB (Translation Look aside Buffer). Recall the principle of locality (temporal locality). If this same virtual address is accessed again in the near future, we could look into the TLB and obtain the MM page address without going through the slow process of address translation and page table access. Because TLB is a fast and small buffer which is a part of the hardware system, the TLB access time is practically negligible when compared to the address translation time. Design experience has shown that a TLB size of as small as 64 entries could give a TLB hit ratio ranging from 90% to 99.9%.

### An Example

| | |
|---|---|
| Virtual address: | 32 bits |
| Page size of 4 KB: | 12 bits (address) |
| Therefore VM pages ($2^{20}$): | 20 bits (address) |
| TLB entry contains: | |
| VM Page address: | 20 bits |
| MM Page address: | 20 bits |
| Valid bit (present/absent): | 1 bit |
| Dirty bit: | 1 bit |
| Other bits (for example usage frequency etc.): | 22 bits |
| TLB word length: | 64 bits |
| TLB size: | 64 entries |
| TLB access time: | 1 clock cycle |

In the above example, when a VM page address is given as an input to the TLB, it must be matched with all the VM page address entries to determine if it is in TLB. If it is in TLB, the corresponding MM-page address is read (see Figure 10.32).

All these activities are completed in 1 clock cycle. In order to achieve this speed, the given VM-page is compared simultaneously (by appropriate hardware) with all the 64 entries of TLB. Such a fully associative search cannot be done if the TLB size is very large. Recall that TLB is used in a way similar to the main memory cache. Thus, we need a replacement strategy for the TLB entries. The TLB controller determines what is to be replaced. Usually a simple strategy like random replacement is used.

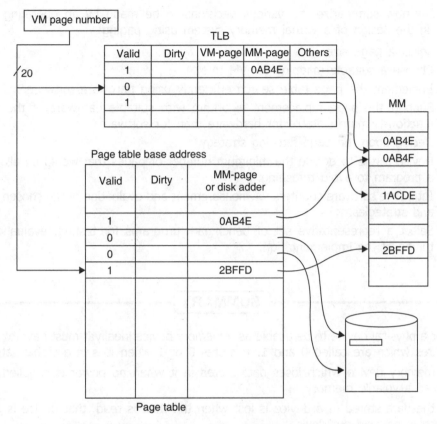

**Figure 10.32    TLB use in Address Translation.**

## 10.16.6    Page Table Size

In computer systems having a large virtual address space (4 GB or $2^{32}$), even when we use a large page size like 4 KB the page table size becomes quite large, $2^{20}$ or 1 million entries. From one task to another the page table mapping will be different and hence the page table has to be stored and retrieved as tasks or programs are switched from one to another. This could be very expensive needing both, more time in process switching as well as large memory. The computer system designer has to take steps to minimize this cost. Although the virtual address space is as large as 4 GB, a single task may not be using this large address space. One way to reduce the page table size is to include the page table entries for a limited address space and let this limit be allowed to grow dynamically. This would require the interaction between the system hardware and the operating system software. The reader is referred to advanced textbooks for details of this type. With hardware and OS interactions such as this, a user task can be prevented from writing into the page tables but permitted to read them. Thus, we could implement memory protection using the virtual memory and paging.

Let us now summarize the various decisions to be made by an operating system designer in the design of a virtual memory system using paging:

1. Select a page size.
2. Choose a suitable mapping for VM to MM.
3. Implement the page table search efficiently using hardware/software.
4. Support the page replacement algorithm with suitable hardware, if the support function is more suitable for hardware than for software.
5. Decide upon the page fetching strategy.
6. Devise a rule to decide the minimum number of pages that would be allotted for a program to avoid thrashing.
7. Introduce software counters for measurement and evaluation of the chosen policies and strategies.
8. Select a representative set of benchmark programs for testing, evaluation, and tuning of the implementation.

---

## ( SUMMARY )

1. For a physical device to be usable as a memory device ideally it must have two stable states which are called 0 and 1. It stores 0 or 1 when it is in a stable sate.

2. A memory device which loses data stored in it when no power is supplied to it is called a volatile memory.

3. If the data stored in a device is lost when the data is read, that device is called a destructive read out device.

4. There are three major devices used in memories. They are: a capacitor, a flip-flop and magnetic surface.

5. Several million storage devices are organized as the main memory of computers. The organization used is to arrange several cells to make a word which is addressable. Millions of addressable words are assembled to make up a main memory.

6. A word is written in the memory by placing its address in a register called Memory Address Register (MAR) and data to be written in a register called Memory Buffer Register (MBR) and a write command is issued. To read, the address is placed in MAR and Read command is issued. The data is placed in MBR by the memory circuits.

7. If the Read/Write time is independent of the address of the word accessed, the memory is called a Random Access Memory (RAM).

8. A memory made using flip-flop is called a Static Random Access Memory (SRAM). It is volatile, reading from it is non-destructive.

9. A memory made using capacitors and MOS switches is called a Dynamic Random Access Memory. DRAM is volatile and the read out from it is destructive. Further as capacitors lose their charge, it is necessary to periodically refresh the memory, that is, re-write data stored in it.

10. Memory cells are arranged as 2D or 2.5D organizations inside IC chips called RAM chips.

11. Standard chips such as 256K × 1 bit, 1M × bits etc., are available. Several of these chips can be organized to construct memory systems of required size.

12. Read Only Memory (ROM) is random access memory which is made using non-volatile, non-destructive read out devices. Once data is written, it is difficult to alter it but the data can be read.

13. There are several types of ROMs. The cheapest ones have data written in them permanently. There are ultra violet erasable and electrical erasable ROMs. Once data is erased, new data can be stored in such ROMs.

14. A variety of electrically erasable ROM called flash memory has recently become popular. Flash memories of size 256 KB to 4 GB are now available.

15. Memory system for computers uses a hierarchy of memories appropriately organized to provide applications cost effective overall memory with high capacity and fast access.

16. The main RAM uses DRAMs which are low cost, high capacity solid state memory. Their access time is around 50 ns. To get a faster access it is combined with a small SRAM memory called cache memory. Cache is smaller but faster than DRAM main memory.

17. Programs usually follow a pattern of memory access in which instructions stored in a small range of addresses are frequently referenced. The same is true for data accesses. Instructions accesses and data accesses are clustered in two distinct range of addresses. This is called locality of reference. This fact is used to keep frequently referenced instructions and data in small fast memories called caches. Normally there is a data cache and an instruction cache. The size of caches has increased to 32 KB over recent years and caches are integrated in the CPU chip. Besides these, many new computers have second level caches called – L2 (level 2) caches outside the CPU chip whose sizes are around 1 MB. They are usually SRAMS.

18. When CPU wants to access an instruction or data, it first accesses the cache. If the data is there, it is called a cache hit. In the case of a hit the access time is that of cache. Else the access time is the main memory access time which is around 10 times larger. Thus a designer tries to increase the hits.

19. Cache hit ratio is defined as : $h$ = (the number of times a required data is found in cache/total number of data accesses to main memory). The maximum value of $h = 1$. Usually a good cache design and policy of placing data from main memory in it gives $h > 0.95$.

20. A cache is much smaller than the main memory (~ 1000 times smaller) because their cost per byte is high. Therefore, we need to follow a policy which anticipates the requirement of data and places it in cache. The data must be removed from the cache and put back in main memory when it is not needed.

21. The cache can store only a small part of the contents of main memory. When CPU specifies an address from which data is to be retrieved, one should be able to quickly find out whether the data in that address is in cache or not by searching the cache. To expedite this search blocks of memory addresses should be systematically mapped to blocks of cache addresses. This mapping is an important design decision. Three mapping strategies known as direct mapping, associative mapping and set associative mapping are available. Figure 10.25 in the text summarises these three strategies.

22. Two other design decisions are: (1) When is data updated in the cache? Should it be updated in the main memory also immediately? If it is updated immediately it is called a write through policy and if it is done later it is called write back policy. (2) When the required address is not in the cache what should be removed from it and replaced with the required addressed data from the main memory? Several policies have been used.

23. Use of cache memory is now the standard in all computer organizations.

24. Another commonly used method in the design of memory systems is called virtual memory. A virtual memory provides a user with a large logical memory address space to write programs even though the available physical main memory (DRAM) may be small. This is achieved by combining a DRAM and a magnetic disk memory in such a way that the memory cycle time of the combined system is closer to DRAM cycle time while a large storage space is provided by a magnetic disk.

25. Virtual memory design also uses the locality principle and is designed broadly using ideas similar to cache design. However, the details are quite different. In other words, the ideas of mapping, and replacement strategies between DRAM and disk are used but the detailed methods differ significantly.

---

### EXERCISES

1. A computer memory has 8M words with 32 bits per word. How many bits are needed in MAR if all words are to be addressed? How many bits are needed for MBR? How many binary storage cells are needed?

2. What is the difference between a volatile and a destructive read out memory? Are destructive read out memories necessarily volatile?

3. What is the difference between access time and cycle time of a memory? Which is larger?

4. What are the differences between a static memory cell and a dynamic memory cell? Which of these cells can be non-destructively read out? Which technology allows larger memories to be fabricated? Which of these is faster?

5. Is DRAM or SRAM more expensive per bit of storage? Justify your answer.

6. What is refreshing? Which type of memory needs refreshing? How is refreshing done?

7. Illustrate 2D organization of 2M words, 16 bits/word SRAM memory.

8. Illustrate 2.5D organization of 2M words, 16 bits/word SRAM memory.

9. What is the advantage, if any, of 2.5D organization over 2D organization?

10. Draw a detailed diagram of a small DRAM which has 16 words 4 bits/word. Show the configuration of dynamic cells used and the detailed layout of cells in rows and columns.

11. Illustrate 2D organization 2M words, 16 bits/word dynamic memory cells.

12. Illustrate 2.5D organization 2M words, 16 bits/word DRAM memory.

13. Illustrate how a 16M, 32bits/word SRAM may be constructed using 1M × 1 chips as a 2D organization.

14. Illustrate how a 16M, 32bits/word SRAM may be constructed using 1M × 1 chips as a 2.5D organization.

**15.** Illustrate with a block diagram 4M × 1 DRAM organization using a 8192 column 512 row cell array.

**16.** Why do the memory cell arrangement in DRAMs use cell organization with more columns and smaller number of rows as in exercise 14.

**17.** Draw the block diagram of a 2M × 8 DRAM which uses sixteen (1M × 1) chips. Show how they are organized as a SIMM module.

**18.** Show how a ROM may be used as a 8421 to excess 3 code converter.

**19.** Draw a block diagram of a dual-ported RAM of (1M × 8) capacity.

**20.** Draw a block diagram of a (2M × 4) dual-ported memory constructed using (1M × 1) DRAM chips.

**21.** How would you simulate a FIFO memory using dual-ported RAM? Design (4K × 8) FIFO with 4K × 1 dual-ported RAM.

**22.** Design a (2K × 8) LIFO memory using shift registers. How many shift registers do you need?

**23.** Can you use a dual-ported RAM to construct a LIFO memory. If yes, explain how you would do it.

**24.** Write a program to add two 5 × 5 matrices. Let the matrices be stored column by column in the memory and let the program address be elements of matrices row by row. Obtain the address trace for your program. Comment on the program locality. Could this program be bad for a cache memory system? If so, under what conditions?

**25.** A block-set associative cache consists of a total of 128 cache blocks with two blocks per set. The main memory contains 4K blocks with 16 words per block. Draw a figure explaining the mapping and show the partitions of an address into TAG, SET and WORD.

**26.** What is the disadvantage of write-through policy in a cache memory system? Similar to write-through, there is a notion of *read through* in which case CPU is given the accessed word without waiting for the entire block to be written into the cache. Will you recommend read through in a system? Explain.

**27.** Explain clearly, as a designer when will you recommend the virtual memory system?

**28.** A virtual memory system has a page size of 2 K words and contains 8 VM pages and 4 MM pages. The page table contents at some instant of time is as shown below: What addresses will result in page faults? VM page: 0, 1, 2, 3, 4, 5, 6, 7, MM page: 3, 0, –, –, 1, –, 2, –, (– means not in main memory).

**29.** Consider the address trace given in the text for Program 10.1. Let the page size of a virtual memory system on which this program is run be 32 words. The program is allocated one page for instructions and one page for code. Calculate the space-time product SP for (a) FIFO, (b) LRU, (c) MIN replacement policies. Comment.

**30.** Would you recommend prefetching the "data page" in the above problem? How will your recommendation differ if the data array is accessed iteratively for some computation?

---

## Learning Goals

In this chapter we will learn:

☞ Various input/output devices which are attached to a computer and their characteristics.

☞ Video display devices and how they display characters and pictures.

☞ Input devices used with video displays—keyboard and mouse.

☞ Output devices which print results obtained by data processing.

☞ Hard disks for data storage and how data is organized and retrieved from these.

☞ Other secondary memories, namely, floppy disks, CD-ROMs, DVD-ROMs, Ultrium tapes and DATs and their applications.

## 11.1 INTRODUCTION

In this book, so far, we have discussed at length the design of the central processing unit and the memory of computers. In this chapter we will describe a variety of input-output devices (abbreviated I/O devices) which are attached to computers.

Input devices are used to feed manually prepared data and programs to computers and output devices to print or display computed results and messages. One of the major problems in designing computers is the speed mismatch between the CPU, memory and I/O devices. Mechanical I/O devices are thousands of times slower compared to the speed of main memory of computer. To alleviate this speed mismatch magnetic mass storage devices are used as buffers between mechanical I/O devices and main memory. These devices are known as peripheral devices or secondary memories. Often data is directly entered on magnetic media such as flash memory or disks by off-line data entry equipment. These media are then mounted on the peripheral devices connected to the computer and they act as input. Thus, we will discuss the characteristics of both mechanical I/O units and magnetic peripheral storage devices together in this chapter.

## 11.2 VIDEO DISPLAY TERMINAL CHARACTERISTICS

A video display terminal (Figure 11.1) is now very commonly used as an input/output device. The terminal consists of four parts:

1. A **display device** which is either Cathode Ray Tube (CRT) used in television sets or a Liquid Crystal Display (LCD) also called **flat panel display**.

2. A **keyboard** which is similar to a typewriter keyboard with additional *control* and *function keys.*

3. A **video memory and a processor** to control the terminal and display characters and pictures.

4. A device called a **mouse** used to point to an arbitrary position on the video screen.

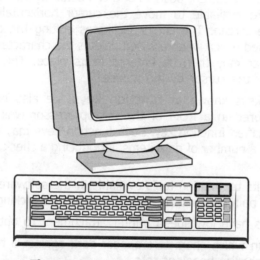

**Figure 11.1  A video terminal.**

There are two types of video terminals: cathode ray tube displays and liquid crystal displays. CRT displays are normally used with desktop terminals whereas LCD displays are used in portable laptop and hand held computers. However, with decreasing cost and better quality, LCD displays are replacing CRT displays. LCD displays are thin, consume less power and occupy less desk space compared to CRT but are more costly.

Video terminals normally have the following features:

1. A keyboard with 96 characters (ASCII Code) which include lower- and upper-case English letters, digits, special characters and control characters. The keyboard is arranged with the English character set as in a typewriter keyboard. Usually a separate set of keys is provided for numbers and is known as a **numeric keypad**. This facilitates rapid entry of numbers by a professional data entry operator. The

control keys in the keyboard are used for various purposes such as to halt computation, interrupt the display process etc.

2. A screen with the length of its diagonal ranging from 15" to 21".

3. A small plastic device called a mouse with a light source at its bottom which emits pulses when it is moved on a flat surface such as a table top. The mouse also has two buttons which can be pressed with one's finger. As the mouse is moved, an arrow moves on the screen whose position can be controlled by position of the mouse. The screen displays either icons (small graphical figures) or strips with names of some programs which are stored in the computer. The arrow is pointed at an icon or a program name (in a strip) by moving the mouse and the left button on it is clicked. This invokes a program to carry out some specified functions. The mouse is also used to move the cursor to any desired position on the video screen. It is also used to manipulate windows which appear on the screen when application programs are invoked.

4. A **cursor** which is normally a small vertical line is displayed on the screen. It is used to indicate the current position of a character on the screen. In the keyboard, special keys are available to move the cursor horizontally or vertically to any position on the screen. The cursor facilitates editing the data entered. A key is normally provided which when pressed deletes the character pointed by the cursor. A new character may then be entered in its place. This is an addition to the manipulation of the cursor by the mouse.

5. Some special keys known as **function keys** are also provided. Programs are written and stored in a ROM of the microprocessor which may be invoked by pressing a specified function key. Such function keys may be used for operations such as adding a number of data items, introducing a check digit for important data items, etc.

6. A **tool bar** at its top stating tools available in the software being used which can be invoked by pointing to them with a mouse and clicking the left button.

7. Some terminals have low speed printer attachment to obtain hard copy output.

8. Inverse video in which characters appear dark against a bright background. This is used to emphasize headings, etc.

The primary advantages of video terminals are their low cost, reliability, silent operation and zero paper consumption. Their main disadvantage is their tendency to cause fatigue (especially eyes) with long continuous use. No hardcopy is available from a video terminal unless a hard copy unit is attached to it.

## 11.3 CATHODE RAY TUBE DISPLAY

The most commonly used display device in computer graphics is a cathode ray tube (CRT). A simplified diagram of a CRT showing its essential part is given as Figure 11.2. It consists of an evacuated glass tube enclosing a source of electrons , an electrode to accelerate the electrons emitted by the source, a focussing system to constrain the accelerated electrons in a narrow beam, a horizontal and vertical deflection system to deflect the beam, and a phosphor-coated screen which glows when an electron beam strikes it. There are two methods used to focus and deflect the electron beam. One of them is an electrostatic method using voltages applied to sets of conducting plates. The other is an electromagnetic method which uses electrical currents passed through focussing and deflection coils. Electromagnetic deflection system is easier to fabricate and cheaper and is in common use.

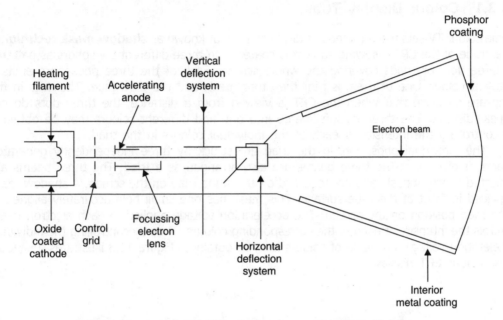

**Figure 11.2   Simplified diagram of a CRT display.**

Referring to Figure 11.2 an oxide-coated metal called a **cathode** is heated by a heating filament. The cathode emits a large number of electrons when heated. These electrons are accelerated by applying a positive voltage to a **control grid**. The control grid voltage determines the number of electrons which ultimately strike the phosphor coated fluorescent screen. If the grid voltage is negative then no electrons are allowed to pass the grid and the beam is said to be **blanked**. A large positive voltage applied to the grid attracts many electrons which will ultimately strike the screen. This increases the intensity of the emitted light when the electron beam strikes the screen. Thus, the voltage applied to the grid controls the beam's intensity. This is called **Z-axis control**.

The electrons accelerated by the grid are further accelerated by an accelerating anode to which a positive voltage is applied. These are focussed by a focussing electron lens assembly which consists of a cylindrical metal enclosure with a hole (Figure 11.2) through which the electron beam proceeds towards the screen. The assembly of electron source, accelerator and focussing system is known as an **electron gun**.

The beam from the electron gun passes through a vertical deflection system consisting of an appropriately wound coil on the neck of the CRT. By controlling current in this coil, the beam can be made to trace along the vertical or *Y*-direction.

Following this vertical deflection system is a horizontal deflection system which works on the same principle. The beam can be made to trace a line along the horizontal or *X*-direction.

The electron beam, when it emerges from the deflection system, is further accelerated by applying a high positive voltage to a metallic coating inside the sides of the conical part of the CRT. When the focussed and accelerated electron beam hits the phosphor-coated screen at a high velocity at one point, this point lights up.

## 11.3.1  Colour Display Tube

Home colour TV sets use a method of displaying colour known as **shadow mask technique**. The inside of the CRT's viewing surface is coated with three different phosphors as patterns of three dots or triads covering the whole screen. Each of the three phosphors emits a different colour. One of them is red, the other green and the third blue. The dots in the triad are so close that when the CRT is viewed from a distance, the three dots do not appear distinct. The three colours merge into one and different colours may be obtained by controlling the intensity of each of the individual colours in the triad.

The individual phosphors in the triad are struck by three independently generated beams of electrons. The three beams are also arranged as a triad. The three beams are deflected synchronously and are focussed on the same triad on the screen. A shadow mask is placed in front of the tube surface. This mask has one small hole accurately aligned at each triad position on the screen. The acceleration voltage applied to each electron beam controls the intensity of each of the corresponding colours. Thus by controlling the individual acceleration voltages, a range of colours may be obtained. Figure 11.3 illustrates a shadow mask colour CRT display.

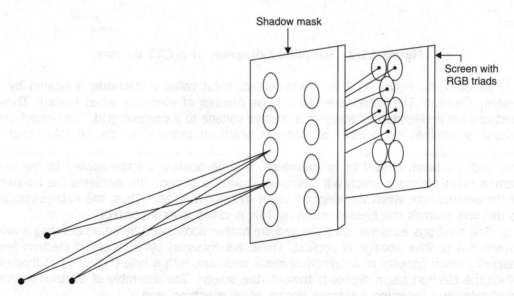

**Figure 11.3   Shadow mask colour CRT display.**

The resolution of a colour display tube is limited by the need to precisely align the shadow mask. In high resolution displays, the distance between the centres of triads is 0.35 mm whereas in home TV tubes this distance is 0.6 mm. The cost of colour tubes has come down rapidly. Users have a marked preference for colour displays. Thus, the majority of VDUs today are colour displays.

## 11.4 RASTER-SCAN DISPLAY DEVICE

Almost all current displays are known as **raster-scan displays**. In these displays the electron beam of the CRT sweeps and draws a line from the left edge of the screen to the right edge of the screen (see Figure 11.4), returns to the next line and again sweeps across the face of the tube. During the return sweep the beam is blanked as shown by the dotted lines of Figure 11.4. After the bottom line of the display has been traced, the beam returns to the top left corner of the screen. During this return also, the beam is blanked. A medium resolution display will have 480 scan lines and a high resolution display around 1000 lines. The scanning rate of modern displays is around 60 times/second.

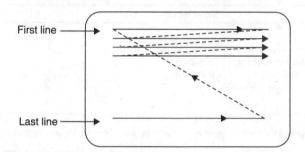

**Figure 11.4  Principles of a raster-scan display.**

A line drawing generated by a graphics program is sliced along the parallel horizontal scan lines generated by the raster-scan CRT. All the points where the drawing cuts the horizontal scan line is called a pixel which is an abbreviation for a picture element (see Figure 11.5). This procedure is called **scan conversion**. In a monochrome terminal 8 bits are used to represent a pixel. The value of the byte controls the brightness of the pixel and

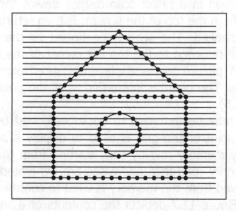

**Figure 11.5  Scan converting a picture to a set of pixels.**

gives 256 levels of intensity from black to white. The coordinates of each pixel is stored. If it is a colour display, the pixel will have 24 bits to represent colour and intensity—8 bits per colour. The pixels are stored in a memory called a **frame buffer**. The frame buffer may be an independent memory called a **display memory** or it may be part of the main memory of the computer.

The data stored in the display memory is retrieved by a video controller which drives the CRT display. The pixels are used to illuminate corresponding points on the VDU with appropriate colours. A general block diagram of the components of a graphic display system is given in Figure 11.6

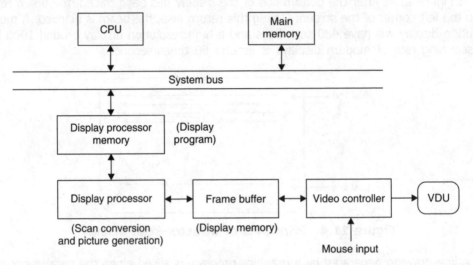

**Figure 11.6 Block diagram of an interactive computer graphics system.**

## 11.5 RASTER-SCAN DISPLAY PROCESSING UNIT

As we saw in the last section in a raster-scan display device the electron beam is swept from left to right starting from the top of the screen. It then returns to the next line. During the return the beam is blanked. The scan is continued till the bottom of the screen is reached. The beam is then returned to the top left corner of the screen again for the next scan (see Figure 11.4). A picture to be displayed is sliced along parallel horizontal line corresponding to the raster. The beam is intensified at all the points where the picture cuts the raster (see Figure 11.5).

The screen of VDU may be assumed to be superscribed by a grid of $1024 \times 1024$ points. Each intersection point of the grid is used to display a pixel. The video controller cycles through the display memory row by row, starting from the top row, at the rate of 60 times per second. Memory reference addresses are generated in synchronism with the raster-scan. The bit retrieved from the memory is used to control the intensity of the beam striking the CRT screen. Figure 11.7 depicts the contents of a small frame buffer and the corresponding picture displayed by the raster-scan display.

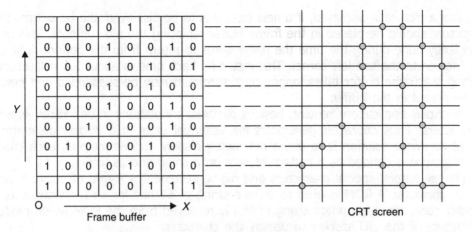

**Figure 11.7** **A frame buffer and the picture generated by it in a raster-scan display.**

The organization of a video controller is shown in Figure 11.8. The raster-scan generator produces the appropriate deflection signals to generate the raster. It also controls the $X$ and $Y$ address registers, which are used to fetch from the frame buffer the pixel value to control the beam intensity.

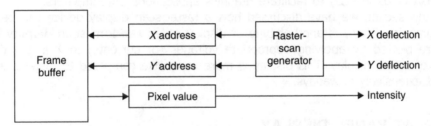

**Figure 11.8** **A raster-scan video controller.**

Assuming that a $1024 \times 1024$ points display is used, the $X$ and $Y$ addresses of the frame controller buffer will each range between 0 and 1023. At the start of the refresh cycle, the video will set $X$ address register to zero and the $Y$ address register to 1023 (the top scan line). The raster-scan generator, besides generating the first scan line, increments $X$ address register in synchronism. These $X$ addresses and the $Y$ address are used to fetch the appropriate pixel to control the beam intensity. At the end of the first scan line, $X$ address is reset to zero and $Y$ address is decremented by one. The next scan line is then generated and corresponding pixels are displayed. The process continues until the bottom scan line ($Y$ address = 0) is generated.

The top to bottom scanning is repeated 60 times a second, for a flicker-free display. With 60 repetitions of the picture per second, one scan line is retrieved in $1/(60 \times 1024)$ second. The time available to retrieve and display one pixel (8 bits for monochrome and 24 bits for colour) is thus $1/(60 \times 1024 \times 1024)$ second, which is about 15 nanoseconds. Consequently very fast memory and high bandwidth amplifiers are required which are very expensive.

After a picture is displayed, if a new picture is to be displayed, the bit pattern for the new picture should be placed in the frame buffer replacing the old contents. This may be conveniently done during the time the raster takes to return from the bottom right corner of the screen to the top left corner. This raster fly back time is about 1.3 milliseconds. If replacing the frame buffer takes longer, picture refresh may be suspended and new data may be placed in the buffer.

All display applications require, besides pictures, annotations to be written as a string of characters. Thus *character generators* are essential units in a display generator. The simplest hardware solution is to use a dot matrix display. In this method, each character to be displayed is defined as a pattern of dots on a small grid as in Figure 11.7. In order to display all letters, special characters and digits, at least 7 × 9 grid of points is needed for each character. A ROM is used to store a string of 63 bits for each character. Given a character code, the appropriate string of bits is retrieved from the ROM which modulates the intensity of the CRT display to display the character.

In our discussion so far we have assumed that a separate display processor, display memory and frame buffer are added to a computer to give it graphics capability. This is not essential. A part of the main memory may be used as both display memory and frame buffer. Similarly, CPU may execute graphics programs and perform scan conversion. This, even though feasible, would put too much demand on the CPU and memory of a general purpose computer and consequently slow down computation as well as graphics speed. Thus, nowadays, even Personal Computers use special purpose graphics systems (such as VGA, SVGA cards in PCs) to facilitate graphics applications on computers.

In this section we have discussed how a raster-scan display device can be used to display graphics. There is another type of display called **random scan display** in which points are plotted by applying appropriate voltages (or currents) to *X* and *Y* deflection systems of a CRT display. This display is more expensive compared to raster scan and is not used extensively nowadays.

## 11.6  FLAT PANEL DISPLAY

So far we have described Video Display Terminals which use cathode ray tubes. This continues to be extensively used, but recently display devices known as **flat panel displays** are gaining in popularity. All displays used in portable laptop computers are flat panel. Almost 40% of new Video Display Units sold now for desktop computers use flat panel displays. The reasons for the popularity of flat panel display are:

1. It consumes less power and does not need high voltage required in CRTs.
2. Its screen is flat whereas most CRT screens are slightly curved disturbing the image at its boundaries.
3. It is thin (less than 3 inches depth) and occupies less desk space. It is also light.

The main disadvantages of flat panel displays compared with CRT are:

1. Currently they are more expensive—almost three times costlier than CRTs. (Prices are, however, expected to reduce.)
2. They have a narrower viewing angle. In other words if you see the display from the side rather than straight, you may not see what is displayed.

## 11.6.1   Principles of Operation of Liquid Crystal Displays

The main active material used in flat panel displays is *liquid crystal*, and hence these displays are also known as **Liquid Crystal Displays** (LCD). The liquid crystal used is called a **twisted nematic crystal**. The molecules of the liquid crystal have electronic charges on them. By applying an electric field the liquid crystal can be twisted by an amount proportional to the applied field. This is the main physical principle used to make this display.

We will now describe how a display is constructed. This display requires individual pixels to be controlled, independent of one another. The liquid crystal is filled between two transparent glass plates marked 2 and 3 in Figure 11.9. Plate 1 has vertical grooves to align

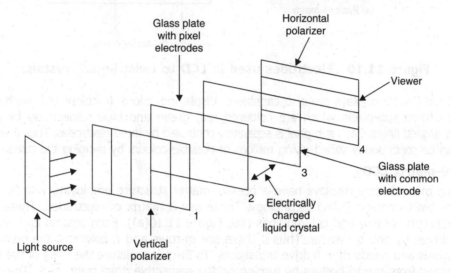

**Figure 11.9   Principles of operation of Liquid Crystal Displays.**

the crystals along the vertical direction. This plate also has electrodes printed on it—one electrode per pixel (see Figure 11.10(a)). By applying appropriate voltage to these electrodes the orientation of the liquid crystal of each pixel can be controlled. Referring to Figure 11.9, a film (marked 1) which polarizes the light entering it in the vertical direction is placed on glass plate 2. Consequently light entering glass plate 2 is polarized in the vertical direction. This light will pass through the liquid crystals without any change of orientation and reach the horizontally polarized film (marked 4 in Figure 11.9) which will block it and a dark pixel will result. To let the light through, it is necessary to twist the light to the horizontal direction. This twisting can be achieved by twisting the liquid crystals to align to the horizontal direction so that light passing through it is allowed to pass by film 4. By applying appropriate voltage to the electrode controlling the liquid crystals corresponding to this pixel, the liquid crystals can be twisted continuously from 0 to 90°. A full 90° twist will give the brightest light. The intensity can be varied depending on the amount of twist, which in turn, depends on the electrode potential. Thus, various brightness levels can be perceived. Each pixel can be independently controlled to display any bit mapped picture.

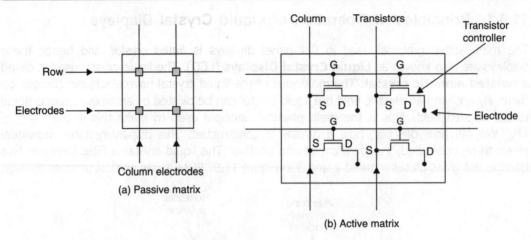

**Figure 11.10   Electrodes used in LCD to twist liquid crystals.**

Liquid Crystal displays are also capable of displaying colour. In colour LCD each pixel is split into three sub-pixels which are coloured red, green and blue respectively by placing precisely aligned filters. Each sub-pixel is separately controlled by three electrodes. Thus their intensities can be continuously varied giving millions of possible colours by merging the three colours.

### Passive-matrix LCDs

Low cost monochrome displays have a passive-matrix structure employing what is known as super twist nematic (STN) technology. These use a matrix of electrodes. These are at the intersection of row and column lines (see Figure 11.10(a)). Each column and each row line is driven by one transistor. Thus if there are *m* rows and *n* columns, the display has *m* × *n* pixels and needs *m* + *n* drive transistors. To display a picture the rows of the display are scanned from top to bottom by turning on the respective drive transistors. The column transistors are then turned on, one by one, and voltage based on the intensity of pixel to be displayed is applied to them. The main problem with this display is low intensity and narrower angle allowed to view the screen. They are normally used for smaller size displays (up to 8" diagonal).

### Active-matrix LCDs

These displays give much brighter, higher resolution images. They are the ones used in computer displays. For (*m* × *n*) pixel display a matrix of (*m* × *n*) Thin Film Transistor (TFT) is added next to the glass plate 2 (see Figure 11.9 and Figure 11.10(b)). As in STN display rows are selected one by one and correct voltage is applied to each column depending on the brightness needed. The selected transistor controls the brightness of the pixel. In colour displays three drive transistors, one each for red, blue and green respectively, are used to independently control their brightness. It is thus thrice as complex and thus expensive compared to STN displays.

## 11.7   INPUT DEVICES

There is a variety of devices used as input devices to computers. These devices may be logically divided into two classes: locators and keyboards.

A **locator** is used to move a *cursor* or a *pointing arrow* around the CRT screen to locate a desired point on the screen. A cursor is a small cross or underline or a small vertical line which may be placed anywhere on the screen and can be separately controlled. The main purpose of a locator is to locate a place at which typed characters will appear or to point to a window on the screen to involve an action by the computer. The most popular pointing device is called a **mouse**. It is a hand-held device fitted with one or more *buttons* and shaped to sit conveniently under one's hand. Currently (2005) the most commonly used mouse is the **optical mouse**. This mouse has light-emitting diodes to illuminate a flat surface (such as a table top) on which the mouse is moved. An optical sensor senses the relative motion of the mouse as it is moved on the table which is processed by a powerful special purpose image processing chip which translates the movement of the mouse on the surface into the movement of the pointer on the screen.

Most popular mice have two buttons, the left button is pressed (commonly called clicking) to invoke actions by the computer. The right button's use depends on the operating system. It is mostly used to manipulate windows on the screen.

Most mice are connected to a serial port of the computer by wire. Recently wireless mice are being manufactured and they are convenient to use.

### Keyboard

A keyboard is the most common input unit used for manual data entry. A picture of a keyboard is shown in Figure 11.11. This keyboard has been standardized for use in all types of computer such as PCs, workstations and laptop computers. It is called a QWERTY keyboard as these are the first six letters in the third row from top. The arrangement of letters was standardised for mechanical typewriters in the last century but has continued as most typists are used to it and there is unwillingness to change. The keyboard consists of the following major categories of keys:

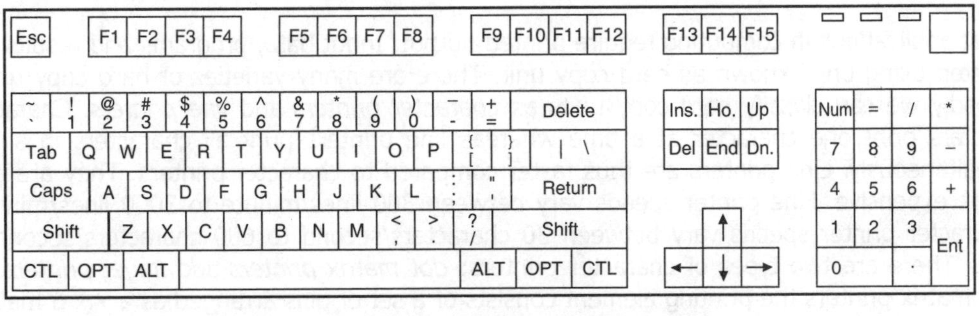

**Figure 11.11   A typical keyboard.**

1. *Letter keys:*  These are the 26 letters of English alphabet arranged as in a type-writer.

2. *Digit keys:*  There are two sets of digit keys; one on the second row from the top (see Figure 11.11) of the keyboard just as in a typewriter, and the other is a numeric key pad at the bottom right which allows quick entry of numbers using the fingers of one hand.

3. *Special character keys:* These are characters such as <, >, ?, /, {, }, [, ], (,), .., ", \, !, @, #, $, %, ^, &, *, _, +, =, -. Most of them are printed when the shift key in the keyboard is pressed down and the key on which it is written is pressed. For example, when the shift key and the key with digit 2 in the second row from top are pressed together, @ is printed.

4. *Non printable control keys:* These are used for backspacing, going to next line, tabulation, moving cursor up or down, insert, delete characters, etc. There is also a *space bar* at the bottom for leaving a space.

5. *Function keys:* These are labelled F1, F2, up to F15 and when pressed will invoke programs stored in the computer.

The functions of some of the non-printable control keys are listed below:

1. *Backspace key:* This key backs the cursor to the previous character and deletes the current character. If it is pressed 3 times, the 3 previous characters are deleted.

2. *Enter key:* At the end of a line of typing, this key is pressed to go to the next line.

3. *Arrow keys:* These keys move the cursor up, down, back or forward.

4. *Tab key:* This key moves the cursor to the next tab stop.

5. *Shift key:* When kept pressed and a letter key is pressed, the upper-case (i.e., capital) letter is printed. When a digit key, for example 5, on top line is pressed the character above the digit, namely % is printed. This can be locked by pressing the caps key again. When caps is locked a light on the keyboard is lit. This indicator light is to remind the user of the locked/unlocked status of caps key.

## 11.8  HARD COPY OUTPUT UNITS

Most applications in computing require printed output. Input data, programs and results are printed using units known as hard copy unit. There are many varieties of hard copy units. Broadly we can classify hard copy units as *character printers* and *line printers*. Character printers print one character at a time whereas line printers print all characters in a line simultaneously. Line printers are thus faster compared to character printers. They are also more expensive. Line printer speeds vary between 300 lines/minute to 3000 lines/minute. Character printer speeds vary between 30 characters/second to 600 characters/second.

There are two types of character printers: *dot matrix printers* and *inkjet printers*. In dot matrix printers the printing element consists of a set of pins arranged as a $7 \times 5$ matrix. Characters are formed by selecting an appropriate set of pins from this matrix. The printer head is kept in contact with paper and a black ribbon is sandwiched in between. The selected pins move out and impact on the ribbon making a black impression of the character on the paper. In dot matrix printers the character to be printed is fed to a character generator ROM. The appropriate bits of the $7 \times 5$ matrix of bits are retrieved from the ROM. These bits are used to activate solenoids in the print head which push the specified pins. These pins print the character on the paper as a set of dots.

Having seen how a single character is printed, we will examine how a whole line is printed. The characters to be printed fill up a buffer in the printer. For an 80 characters/line printer the buffer holds 80 coded characters. The character codes are successively sent to the ROM address register. The ROM output activates the print head pins. After printing a character, the print head is moved one position to the right. The next character from the buffer is sent to ROM address register and the next character is printed. This continues till the last character is reached. The buffer is now filled with the next line and the printer carriage advances the paper up by one position. The next line is printed from right to left starting from the 80th character and going to the first character. Such printing is called **bi-directional printing** and expedites printing. Not all character printers have this feature. Slow inexpensive printers are unidirectional and do not have a line buffer. In such a case the printer has a single character buffer which receives from the computer's memory one character at a time and prints it. After printing a line the print head advances to the first character position on the next line.

Dot matrix printers can be designed with a great amount of flexibility. More expensive printers have 24 pins in a vertical line and give very good print quality. With a line buffer and a built-in microprocessor control, many character printers accommodate varying sizes and styles for characters. Besides this, the microprocessor enables flexible control of printer carriage and head movements coupled with head pin selection. This allows the printer to be used as a low resolution, low speed graphics output device. Pie charts, bar charts and simple graphs can be drawn with such printers. Many special features such as selective multiple printing of some words to make them look bold, selection of a subset of pins placed together to produce better quality printing in which individual dots are not seen and printing multicolour outputs by controlling multicolour ribbons are now available.

The dot matrix printer is called a **contact printer** as the print head comes in contact with the ribbon while printing. By adjusting the force with which the head hits the ribbon, multiple carbon copies of a printed output may be taken. As discrete number of dots are used to form a character, the quality of the printing is not excellent.

Non-contact printers have been designed which provide much better resolution and print quality. Two such printers are now popular. One is called an **inkjet printer** and the other a **laser printer**.

## 11.8.1 Inkjet Printer

An inkjet printer consists of a print head which has a number of small holes or nozzles (Figure 11.12). Individual holes can be heated very rapidly (in a few microseconds) by an integrated circuit resistor. When the resistor heats up the ink near it vaporizes and is ejected through the nozzle and makes a dot on paper placed near the head. A high resolution inkjet printer has around 50 nozzles within a height of 7 mm and can print with a resolution of 300 dots per inch. A fairly complex microprocessor-based system selects the holes to be heated based on the character to be printed. The head is also moved rapidly across the paper. The operation is similar to the laser printer in the sense that more than one line rather than a single line is taken as a unit by the driver circuitry. The printer has enough memory to print an entire page accommodating different fonts. Latest inkjet printers have multiple heads, one head per colour which allows printing using multiple colours and hues by mixing colours. The print speed is around 120 characters/second.

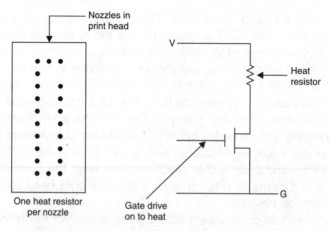

**Figure 11.12   Inkjet printer—print head.**

## 11.8.2   Laser Printers

In a laser printer an electronically controlled laser beam traces out the character to be printed on a photoconductive drum. The drum attracts a fine powder of graphite (called toner) on to the exposed area. A paper is then passed over the drum (just like in a xerox machine) and the toner is transferred to the paper thereby printing the characters. Unlike a character printer, lines to be printed on an entire page are temporarily stored in the laser printer and transferred to the drum. One revolution of the drum thus transfers the entire page on to paper. A low cost desktop laser printer prints about 8 pages per minute and costs about Rs.10,000. The main advantage of a laser printer is the excellent quality of printed output. The main disadvantage of a laser printer is that multiple copies cannot be taken on the printer. Inkjet printers also have the same disadvantage.

## 11.8.3   Line Printers

Line printers may be classified as *drum printers* and *band* or *chain printers*. A drum printer consists of a cylindrical drum whose length equals the length of a printed line. Normally there are 132 characters in a printed line. The drum has 132 parallel tracks along its circumference. Each track has embossed on it all the characters in the character set. Character sets of 48, 64, 96 and 128 are marketed. The 64 character set is the most popular set. A set of 132 print hammers, one per track, are positioned so that printer ribbon and paper are sandwiched between the drum and the hammers. The computer stores in the printer buffer the codes of the 132 characters to be printed. The drum is rotated at a high speed. Assume that a character in the $i$th position is to be printed. The character code in the $i$th buffer is compared with the position of each character in the $i$th track of the drum surface as it rotates. When the appropriate character is positioned in front of the print hammer, the hammer is activated and it hits the drum. The character is printed on the paper by this impact. In one rotation all the 132 hammers are activated and a full line is printed.

In a chain printer (see Figure 11.13), printing elements are chained together to form a continuous loop. In a loop character sets are repeated 4 to 6 times. In other words a printer with 48 character set will have each set of 48 characters repeated 4 times so that a total of 192 characters are on the chain. The chain is spooled on two spools and is rotated at a fast speed horizontally. A carbon ribbon is mounted in front of the chain touching it. Paper is mounted over the ribbon. A set of hammers equal to the number of print positions in the printer are mounted touching the paper. The characters to be printed on a line are entered in a buffer register in the printer. Assume that the character R is to be printed in the 20th position. When the character R of the chain is positioned in front of the 20th hammer, the hammer is fired and it hits the paper, carbon ribbon and the character embossed on the chain. The character R is thereby printed on the paper. In order to print all the characters on a line without many revolutions of the chain, it is essential to duplicate character sets on the chain. The primary advantage of a chain printer is the interchange-ability of chains which allows the use of different character sets depending on the appli-cation. Chain printer output quality is usually better than that of a drum printer as all characters are aligned on one line. Chain printer speeds vary between 300 lines/minute to 2400 lines/minute.

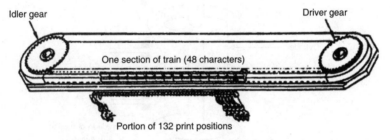

**Figure 11.13  Chain printer mechanism.**

## 11.9  HARD DISK DRIVES

Increasing the capacity of the main memory in computers is not cost effective for sizes beyond a few GBs. For mass storage of data of the order of 100s of GBs magnetic disk memories are used.

Magnetic disks are smooth metal plates coated on both sides with a thin film of magnetic material. A set of such magnetic plates are fixed to a spindle one below the other to make up a disk pack (Figure 11.14). The disk pack is mounted on a disk drive. The disk drive consists of a motor to rotate the disk pack about its axis at a speed of about 7,000 to 10,000 revolutions per minute. The disk pack and a set of magnetic heads mounted on arms are sealed in an enclosure. Such a disk is called a **Winchester hard disk**. The arm assembly is capable of moving in and out in a radial direction (Figure 11.14). The magnetic film coated on the disk surface has a square loop hysteresis characteristics so that it can maintain a residual magnetization in one out of two stable directions. These two directions correspond to the storage of a binary 1 or a 0. The head is made of a high permeability magnetic material. A coil is wound round the head and a current is sent through this coil (Figure 11.15). An intense magnetic field is created in the gap of the head. This field magnetizes the coating on the disc surface. The field strength should exceed the coercive field of the surface material for stable magnetization of the material. The direction of the field depends on the polarity of the current through the head coil. Current of one polarity magnetizes the surface in one direction which corresponds to writing a 1. The opposite polarity current magnetizes the surface in the opposite direction which corresponds to writing a 0.

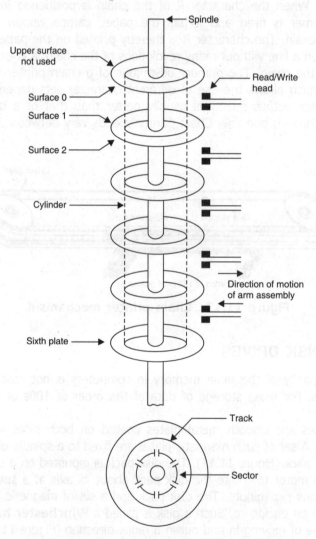

**Figure 11.14   A magnetic disk memory.**

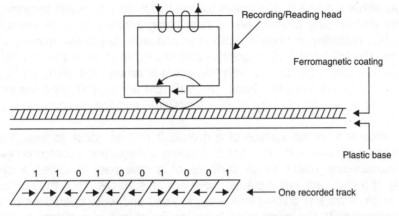

**Figure 11.15  Recording on a magnetic surface.**

Data recorded on the disk is read by the another head called **read head**. The read head uses a *magneto-resistive* material. The resistance of this material becomes low when a magnet with say S $\rightarrow$ N alignment passes below it and high when a magnet of opposite alignment N $\leftarrow$ S passes below it.

A constant current $i$ is passed through the head (see Figure 11.16) . This current value changes depending on the polarity of the magnetic spot below the head. When a 1 (S $\rightarrow$ N alignment) moves below the head, the resistance of the head reduces and consequently the current through the head increases. When a 0 (N $\leftarrow$ S alignment) moves

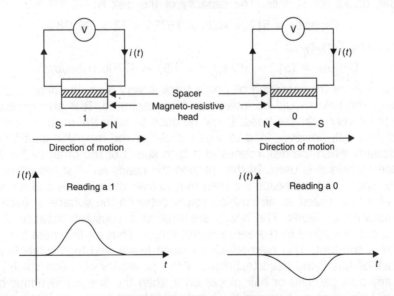

**Figure 11.16  Reading bits from a magnetic recording using magneto-resistive head.**

below the head, the resistance increases and the head current decreases (see Figure 11.16). The increase or decrease of the head current is detected by a sense amplifier and is interpreted as either a 1 or a 0. The magneto-resistive head (MR head) technology was first introduced by IBM in early nineties and is now being adopted by other manufacturers of magnetic surface recording memories. Both read and write heads use thin films of material on a tiny head. The MR head is very sensitive and has led to an increased density of packing bits on magnetic surface. Bit density with MR heads is around 150 Mbits/cm$^2$ compared to 30 Mbits/cm$^2$ with earlier inductive head. In 1998 IBM announced giant magneto-resistive heads which give a packing density of 400 Mbits/cm$^2$ and this is continuously increasing every year.

Data is recorded on the surface of a disk as it rotates about its axis. Thus, it is on circular *tracks* on each disk surface. A set of concentric tracks are recorded on each surface. A set of corresponding tracks in all surfaces of a disk pack is called a *cylinder* (see Figure 11.14). If a disk pack has $n$ plates, there are $2n$ surfaces. Thus the number of tracks per cylinder is $2n$. A track is divided into sectors. Read and write operations on a disk start at sector boundaries. If the number of bytes to be stored in a sector is less than the capacity of a sector, the rest of the sector is padded with the last byte recorded. Assume $s$ bytes are stored per sector, $p$ sectors are there per track, $t$ tracks per surface and $m$ surfaces. The capacity of the disk is:

$$\text{Capacity} = s \times p \times t \times m \text{ bytes}$$

If $d$ is the diameter of the disk, the density of recording is:

$$\text{Density} = (s \times p)/(\pi \times d) \text{ bytes/inch}$$

***Example 11.1.*** A 3.5 inch diameter disk pack has 6 plates, 512 bytes per sector, 1024 sectors, 16384 tracks per surface. The capacity of the disk is:

$$\text{Capacity} = 512 \times 1024 \times 16384 \times 12 = 96 \text{ GB}$$

The recording density is:

$$\text{Density} = (512 \times 1024)/(\pi \times 3.5) = 47706 \text{ bytes/inch}$$

As the density of the recording bits on a track is very high, the dimensions of a head must be small. The field should be intense and concentrated. It is also necessary for the disk surface to be very near the head. It will be good to have the head in contact with the disk surface. This will, however, lead to wearing out of the magnetic coating on the disk surface particularly when the disk rotates at a high speed of the order of 7200 rpm. Thus a **flying head** technique is used. In this method the heads are first retracted. The disk is brought to full speed and the heads are then moved over the surfaces and released. As the disk rotates at a high speed an air cushion forms between the surface of each of the disk and the corresponding heads. The heads are kept at a constant distance of about one micron from the disk surface by the aerodynamic forces. Thus air thickness between a head and a surface is constant. This method allows small heads and high rotation speeds. The main drawback of this flying head technique is the possibility of "head crash". If the disk surface has any dust particles or hair pieces on it, then the fine aerodynamic balancing of the head over the surface is upset and the head would crash on the surface which is moving at a high speed. It would be analogous to an aircraft suddenly encountering a mountain in its path as the thickness of a dust particle is of the order of ten microns. A head crash damages both the head and the magnetic coating on the surface. Data recorded on the disk is lost. Sudden power failure can also lead to head crash unless the heads are retracted before the disk slows down. It is thus essential to seal the disk pack in an airtight cover free from dust particles and other foreign matter. The surfaces of winchester disk have a lubricated layer that prevents wearing of the surface during head "take-offs" and "landings". The weight of the heads are also low which reduces possibility of damage due to crashes.

Associated with each disk drive is a small special purpose computer called a **disk controller**. The disk controller accepts commands from the computer and positions the read/write heads ready for reading or writing. In order to read or write on a disk pack the computer must specify the drive number, cylinder number, surface number and the sector number. The drive number is specified, as a controller normally controls more than one drive. Figure 11.17 shows the disk address format. Normally one or more tracks are reserved on a disk with permanent recording to provide timing pulses to aid the controller to position the heads at the specified address.

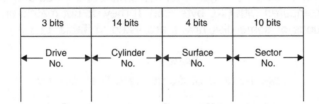

**Figure 11.17  Disk address format for a controller for 8 drives, 16384 cylinders, 12 surfaces and 1024 tracks.**

There are two popular controllers which are used to interface a disk to the CPU/ Memory of the computer. The ATA100 interface is used in Personal Computers. The SCSI (Pronounced SCUZZY) interface is used to interface disks to Servers and Workstations. The interface electronics determines the maximum speed at which data from the disk may be transferred to the main memory.

When read/write command is received by the disk controller, the controller first positions the arm assembly so that the read/write head reaches the specified cylinder. The time taken to reach the specified cylinder is known as the **seek time** $T_s$. The seek time depends upon the position of the arm assembly at the time read/write command is received by the controller. The maximum seek time is the time taken by the head assembly to reach the innermost cylinder from the outermost cylinder or vice versa. The minimum seek time is 0 if the head assembly happens to be positioned on the selected cylinder. The average seek time is usually quoted and it is of the order of 6 to 10 milliseconds. The actual seek time may be only 2 to 4 ms as the head may be near the required track.

Once the head assembly is positioned on the specified cylinder, the head corresponding to the specified surface is switched. This switching is electronic and is almost instantaneous. Having reached a surface there is a further delay before the specified sector reaches the read/write head. This rotational delay again is a variable. The average rotational delay is one half the time taken by the disk to rotate once. This time is known as *latency time* $T_1$. For a disk rotating at 7200 rpm, $T_1$ is 0.5/7200 minutes = 4.15 milliseconds. The sum of average latency and seek time is known as the **average access time**.

When the desired sector is reached data in it is read at a speed determined by the rotation speed of the disk. One full rotation of the disk takes 1/7200 minute. In one revolution one track which has 1024 sectors are read. The number of bytes read per revolution is thus $1024 \times 512 = 524288$ bytes. The transfer rate is thus $524288 \times 7200/60$ bytes/second = 60 MB/s. The time to read one sector is $512/(60 \times 10^6) = 8.5$ microseconds. Thus the average time to access a sector is $10 + 4.15$ ms and the time to read the data in it is 8.5 microseconds. Observe that the seek and latency times dominate the time to read data.

Besides moving the head to the correct sector for read/write and initiating read/write the disk controller also checks whether the data sent from the main memory of the computer is correctly written on the disk. It is done by appending a *cyclic redundancy code byte* (CRC) to the data written in a sector. The CRC byte is obtained by adding all the bytes in a sector and appending the least significant byte of the sum to the data bytes. When data is read back from a sector, the individual bytes read are added and the least significant byte of the sum is compared with CRC byte read. If they do not match, an error is signalled.

The specifications of some disk drives are listed in Table 11.1.

**TABLE 11.1**
**Specification of Some Hard Disk Drives**

| Model | Maxtor Atlas 15K | Seagate Barracuda 5400.1 | Seagate Barracuda 7200.7 | Samsung OEM |
|---|---|---|---|---|
| Formatted capacity (GB) | 80 | 40 | 160 | 120 |
| No. of heads | 8 | 1 | 4 | 2 |
| Interface controller | Ultra SCSI | Ultra ATA 100 | Ultra ATA 100 | Ultra ATA 100 |
| Average seek time (ms) | 3.4 | 12.5 | 8.5 | 8.9 |
| Sector size (bytes) | 512 | 512 | 512 | 512 |
| Rotation speed (rpm) | 15,000 | 5400 | 7200 | 5400 |
| Average rotational latency (ms) | 2 | 5.56 | 4.16 | 5.56 |
| Transfer rate to host (MB/s) | 100 | 100 | 100 | 100 |
| Cache (MB) | 8 | 2 | 8 | 2 |
| Diameter of disk (inches) | 3.5 | 3.5 | 3.5 | 3.5 |

## 11.9.1  Redundant Array of Inexpensive Disks (RAID)

We have seen that the rate of data transfer from a disk depends upon its speed of rotation and recording density. The speed of rotation and density cannot be increased due to mechanical limitations. Further, only one read-write head can read data at one time from a disk. Thus data access is serial.

In RAID technology a number of low cost disks are arranged as an array with a common array controller. The array of disks work in parallel to reduce read/write time of data (see Figure 11.18(a)). When data is to be written, it is distributed to different disks

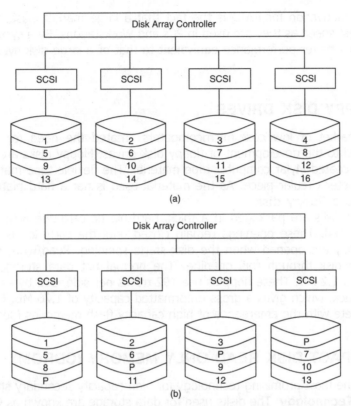

(a)

(b)

**Figure 11.18   Redundant array of inexpensive disks (RAID).**

by the array controller. This technique is known as **disk striping**. Reliability of such a group of disks, however, will become poor if the number of disks is increased. Reliability is increased by including some extra disks which contain redundant data. This idea was proposed by Patterson who has identified six levels of RAID.

**RAID 0:** Only disk striping

**RAID 1:** The data in each disk is duplicated in another redundant disk. This is called **disk mirroring**. This provides 100% redundancy and is thus expensive.

**RAID 2:** Data bits of a byte are written in parallel on disks of the array along with parity bits. In case of a disk failure the data is re-created using parity bits.

**RAID 3:** A single disk called a parity disk is used to recover data if one disk fails.

**RAID 4:** Instead of data bits being interleaved, data blocks are interleaved across disks. A parity block is created and it is also distributed in one of the disks. There is no single parity disk (see Figure 11.18(b)).

**RAID 5:** Offers excellent fault tolerance by writing parity data uniformly across all disks in an array. In the event of a disk failure, the system continues to run on the remaining drives using the parity data to reconstruct missing data. This method is much more cost effective compared to mirroring used in RAID 1.

The main motivation for RAID is the fact that a large market exists for inexpensive disks with modest speed as they are used in PCs and Workstations. By a system architecture approach a much better performance equivalent to that of a large disk system is obtained at low cost.

## 11.10   FLOPPY DISK DRIVES

The growing market of low cost microcomputers created the need for low cost mass storage. This led to the development of floppy disk drives. Floppy disks are created out of magnetic oxide-coated Mylar computer tape material. The flexible tape material is cut into a 3.5 inch diameter circular piece. As the material used is not a hard plate but a flexible tape, it is called a **floppy disk**.

The floppy disks are packaged in a thick, hard-plastic cartridge with an opening for the read-write head. These openings remain closed until the cartridge is inserted into a floppy drive. They are opened when the disk starts spinning. Read/write head reads the contents of the disk through this opening. The normal net data storage capacity of a 3.5 inch floppy is 1.2 MB. These floppies use 192 tracks per side, 512 bytes per sector and 9 sectors per track, which gives a gross unformatted capacity of 1.76 MB. Floppy disks are becoming obsolete with the emergence of high capacity flash memories (see section 10.9).

## 11.11   COMPACT DISK READ ONLY MEMORY (CDROM)

The latest and the most promising technology for high capacity secondary storage is known as **Laser Disk Technology**. The disks used for data storage are known as **Compact Disk Read Only Memory** (CD-ROM). The CD-ROM disk also known as a **laser disk** is a shiny metal like disk whose diameter is 5.25 inches (12 cm disk). It can store around 650 MB (equivalent to 250,000 pages of printed text).

Data in CD-ROM is written along a spiral track (see Figure 11.19(a)) by creating pits on a spiral groove on the disk surface by shining a laser beam on the disk. The sharply focused beam creates a circular *pit* of around 0.8 micro-metre diameter wherever a 1 is to be written and no pit (also called a *land*) if a zero is to be written. From a master disk many copies can be reproduced by a process called stamping a disk.

The CD-ROM with pre-recorded data is read by a CD-ROM reader which uses a laser beam for reading. As in a magnetic floppy disk the CD-ROM disk is inserted in a slot. It is rotated by a motor at a speed of 360 revolutions per minute. A laser head moves in and out to the specified position. As the disk rotates the head senses pits and lands (see Figure 11.19(b)). This is converted to 1s and 0s by the electronic interface and sent to the computer.

In recent models of CD-ROM, the rate of reading data is 7.8 MBs. CD-ROM disk speed is indicated by the notation *nx*, where *n* is an integer indicating the factor by which the original nominal speed of 150 KB/s is to be multiplied. Thus a 52x CD-ROM reading speed is 52 × 150 KB/s = 7800 KB/s. It has a buffer to keep the data temporarily. The buffer size is 256 KB. It is connected to a computer by an appropriate Interface adapter.

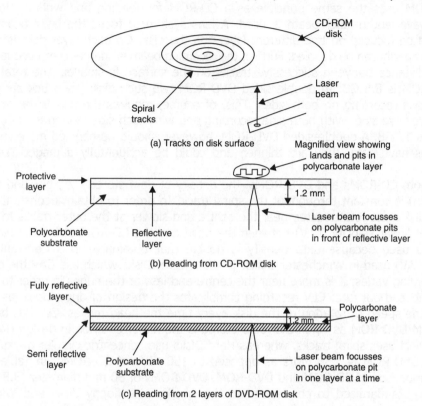

(a) Tracks on disk surface

(b) Reading from CD-ROM disk

(c) Reading from 2 layers of DVD-ROM disk

**Figure 11.19    CD-ROM and DVD recording.**

A standard has been evolved for recording data on CD-ROM. This is essential to allow CD-ROMs to be widely distributed and read by different computers. The standard used is called ISO 9660, standardized by the International Standards Organization. It is accepted by all CD-ROM vendors. This standard defines a Volume Table of Contents (VTOC) which allows opening any one of 140,000 files with a single seek using directories in the CD-ROM. Recording in ISO 9660 format is facilitated by a piece of software developed by Microsoft Corporation known as MSCDEX (Microsoft CD Extension). This software makes a CD-ROM look like a large hard disk to a programmer using a PC. All large software such as operating system and software updates are nowadays supplied on CD-ROMs. It is thus essential to have a CD-ROM drive on all computers.

Another major application of CD-ROM is in distributing large texts. For example the entire Encyclopedia Brittanica could be stored and distributed in one CD-ROM. Abstracts of articles appearing in scientific journals are also distributed in CD-ROM. Recently bitmaps of images are stored in CD-ROM for display with a PC. The current booming market is multimedia CD-ROMs in which text, audio and video are stored. Along with appropriate software these CD-ROMs can be used for education and entertainment.

## 11.11.1   Digital Versatile Disk Read Only Memory (DVD-ROM)

A DVD-ROM uses the same principle as a CD-ROM for reading and writing. However, a smaller wave length laser beam is used. A lens system to focus the laser beam is used which can be focused on two different layers on the disk. On each layer data is recorded. Thus the capacity can be doubled. Further, the recording beam is sharper compared to CD-ROM and the distance between successive tracks on the surface is smaller. The total capacity of DVD-ROM is 8.5 GB. In double sided DVD-ROM two such disks are stuck back to back which allows recording on both sides. This, of course, requires the disk to be reversed to read the reverse side. With both side recording and with each side storing 8.5 GB, the total capacity is 17 GB. A double-sided DVD-ROM, however, should be handled more carefully as both sides have data, they are thinner, and could be accidentally damaged (see Figure 11.19(c)).

In both CD-ROMs and DVD-ROMs, the density of data stored (i.e., pits and lands per unit length) is constant throughout the spiral track. In order to obtain a constant read-out rate the disk must rotate faster, near the centre and slower at the outer tracks to maintain a constant linear velocity (CLV) between the head and the CD-ROM/DVD-ROM platter. CLV scheme is used because data density is double that obtainable in a Constant Angular Velocity (CAV) used in Winchester Disks. In Winchester Disks which use CAV the density of data recording varies; it is more near the centre and less at the edges in order to maintain a constant read-out rate. CLV recording complicates the design of drive motor as it should readjust the speed of rotation of the disk every time the head moves. CLV has been used in CD-ROM/DVD-ROM as volume of data stored is the major criterion in design (Remember that CD-ROM uses spiral tracks, whereas Hard Disks use concentric circular tracks). The 1x speed of DVD-ROM is 1.38 MB/s as opposed to 150 KB/s of CD-ROMs. In Table 11.2 we give a comparison of CD-ROM and DVD-ROM. DVD-ROMs of 80 mm diameter (3.5 inch) are also being standardized to correspond to the smaller size floppy disks and Winchesters which are there in the market. Even though the physical formats of DVD-ROMs are different the **logical format** for storing and retrieving data uses a format called **Universal Disk Format** (UDF) is the same. UDF is standardized by the International Standards Organization.

**TABLE 11.2**
**CD-ROM and DVD-ROM Comaprison**

|  | CD-ROM | DVD-ROM |
|---|---|---|
| Pit length (micron) | 0.834 | 0.4 |
| Track pitch (micron) | 1.6 | 0.74 |
| Laser beam wavelength (nanometre) | 635 | 780 |
| Capacity 1 layer/1 side | 650 KB | 4.7 GB |
| 2 layer/1 side | No | 8.5 GB |
| 1 layer/2 sides | No | 9.4 GB |
| 2 layers/2 sides | No | 17 GB |
| Speed 1x | 150 KB/s | 1.38 MB/s |

## 11.11.2    CD-R (Recordable CD-ROM or Write Once CD-ROM—WOROM)

The medium used for recordable CD-ROM is a 12 cm writable disk. Such a disk made of polycarbonate already has a groove cut in it. It is covered by a photosensitive dye. This layer is covered with a thin layer of gold (called reflecting layer). The final layer is a protective layer. A laser beam is used to write data. The disk is rotated by a motor. For writing a 1 the laser beam is turned on. The laser beam fuses the dye to the substrate forming a pit which can be read by any CD-ROM reader. The entire image of the files to be recorded is first stored in a hard disk in ISO 9660 format. It is streamed at 300 KB/s to the CD-ROM which continuously records the data in one shot. Writing cannot be done in multiple sessions. The recorded CD can be read on any ordinary CD-ROM drive.

Early models of writable CD-ROM could write only once. If incorrect data is written, the CD is useless. It thus will be advantageous to have erasable-rewritable CD-ROM. Such a medium is now available. It is called CD-R/W. A CD writer in a PC can be used to write on this medium also. The medium, however, is more expensive (around 5 times) compared to write-once CD-ROM. Data may be written in this disk in multiple sessions.

Writable DVD-ROMs called DVD-RW are also being introduced and are being standardized.

## 11.12    MAGNETIC TAPE DRIVES

Magnetic tape memories are similar to the commonly used audio tape recorders. The tape medium in which data is recorded is sealed in a cartridge. The method of recording data is magnetic surface recording using a magnetic recording head, similar to the one used in hard disk. There are two major technologies which are currently popular. One of them called **Ultrium** uses 12.5 mm width tape of length around 650 metres storing 400 GB in compressed mode. The other uses 8 or 4 mm width tape of length around 150 metres with maximum capacity of around 20 to 100 GB compressed. We will describe these in what follows.

### 11.12.1    Ultrium Cartridge Tape Drive

Ultrium is an industry standard 12.5 mm width tape in a cartridge. A tape recorded using the drive of say IBM can be read by a drive manufactured by HP and vice versa. Data is fed to a set of eight recording heads. As the tape moves below this head, data is recorded along 8 parallel tracks. When the end of the tape is reached, the tape reverses direction and the heads move to a new position. Now eight tracks are recorded in the opposite direction. A total of 512 tracks are recorded in Ultrium 2 technology. In Ultrium 1 technology 384 tracks are recorded. This type of recording is called **serpentine recording**. Data can be recorded as is or may be compressed using a standard compression algorithm. In this system compression/decompression is done by a built-in hardware unit. The hardware uses a lossless compression algorithm. In Ultrium 2 the uncompressed capacity is 200 GB and compressed capacity is 400 GB. Ultrium 1 stores 100 GB uncompressed and 200 GB compressed. The reading rate of Ultrium 2 is 70 MB/s and that of Ultrium 1 is 35 MB/s. This technology is also known as **LTO tape technology**. This medium (namely, the tape) is usually certified for 1 million passes or 100 full backups and has 30 years shelf life.

## 11.12.2   Digital Audio Tapes (DAT)

DAT uses either a 4 mm or an 8 mm width tape enclosed in a cartridge. A **helical scan**, read after write recording technique is used which provides reliable data recording. Helical scan records at an angle to the tape. The head spins at a high speed while the tape moves. Very high recording densities are obtained. The tape length ranges from 75 metres to 225 metres. It uses a recording format called Digital Data Storage (DDS) which provides three levels of error correcting code to ensure excellent data integrity. The capacity of 8 mm tape is up to 60 GB with a data transfer speed of 3 to 6 MB/s. This tape uses SCSI interface. As in Ultrium tape, standard format and interface are used to allow data exchange in this medium. In Table 11.3 we summarize the characteristics of various tapes discussed above.

### TABLE 11.3
### Characteristics of Some Tape Drives

| Tape drive (Type and model) | Tape width (mm) | Data transfer rate MB/s | Mode of recording | Capacity GB |
|---|---|---|---|---|
| DAT IBM 7332/110 | 4 | 1 (Native) 2 (Compressed) | Helical scan | 12 (Native) 24 (Compressed) |
| DAT IBM 7208/345 | 8 | 12 (Native) 30 (Compressed) | Helical scan | 60 (Native) 150 (Compressed) |
| Ultrium 1 IBM 3580 | 127 | 15(Native) 30 (Compressed) | Serpentine, 8 heads, 384 tracks | 100 (Native) 200 (Compressed) |
| Ultrium 2 HP 460 | 127 | 30 (Native) 60 (Compressed) | Serpentine, 8 heads, 512 tracks | 200 (Native) 400 (Compressed) |

Magnetic tapes are used nowadays in computers for the following purposes:

1. Backing up data stored in disks. It is necessary to regularly save data stored in disk in another medium so that if by accident the data on disk is overwritten or if data gets corrupted due to hardware failure, the saved data may be written back on the disk.
2. Storing processed data (e.g., files of students' examination results) for future use. This is called **archiving**.

The most appropriate tape for backing up data from a disk today is Ultrium or DAT tapes. Archiving is best done on DAT or Ultrium. Software or data distribution is best done on CD-ROMs. The best medium for storing individual files and retrieving them easily is either floppy disk or flash memory today. Floppy disk will be superceded by flash memory in the near future.

The advent of CD-RW has broken the monopoly of tapes for backing up files from hard disks. DVD-RWs are also emerging with enormous storage capacities in gigabyte range. Thus, optical disks are an attractive alternative for backing up data from hard disk drives.

So far we have discussed a number of devices used to store data in computers. In Table 11.4 we have summarized the average capacity of each of the devices, the access times of each and the relative cost per byte of storage of each.

**TABLE 11.4**

**Comparative Characteristics of Secondary Memories**

| Memory type | Average capacity in bytes | Technology | Average time to access a byte | Purpose in a computer system | Relative cost per byte in units |
|---|---|---|---|---|---|
| Disk memory (hard disk) | 100G | Magnetic surfaces on hard disks | 8 ms | Large data and program files requiring fast access. | 1 |
| Flash memory EEPROM | 256M | Integrated circuit | 1 µs | Data entry. As input unit. Data and program files in micro-computers. | 10 |
| Ultrium | 200G | Long ½" tape wound on cartridge | NA | Historical files. Backup for disk. Data and program exchange between installations. | 1/100 |
| CD-R and CD-RW | 650M | Laser disk | 500 ms | Store large texts, pictures and audio. Software distribution. | 1/100 |
| DVD-ROM | 8G | Laser disk | 500 ms | Video files | 1/1000 |

---

## SUMMARY

1. The most common output device used with PCs and desktop computers is a Video Display Unit (VDU).

2. There are two types of VDUs: Cathode Ray Tube (CRT) display and Liquid Crystal Display (LCD).

3. CRT uses a display tube similar to a TV screen. It is heavy, needs high voltage and consumes considerable power. It cannot be operated using batteries.

4. LCD is a flat screen display. It uses electrically charged liquid crystal molecules filled between two glass plates. A film polarized in the vertical direction is placed over one glass plate. A horizontally polarized film is placed over the other plate. Vertically

polarized light enters the liquid crystal layer. It can be allowed to pass the horizontally polarized film by twisting liquid crystals by applying an appropriate electrical field to them. The amount of light passing the liquid crystal layer can be controlled by varying the field. Thus liquid crystals act as light valves controlled by an electrical field applied to them.

5. LCDs are of two types: Super Twisted Nematic (STN) displays and Thin Film Transistor (TFT) displays. STN displays use electrodes to generate electric field to twist liquid crystals whereas TFT displays use transistors. TFT displays are superior to STN displays. They are capable of colour displays and give brighter image whereas STN displays are monochrome and dimmer. Each pixel is independently controllable in both STN and TFT displays. TFT displays will soon replace STN displays.

6. LCDs occupy much smaller space compared with CRT displays, use much less power and are light weight. They are thus used in laptop computers and more expensive desktop machines. Currently they cost 30% more than CRT displays.

7. To display an image in an interactive graphics system, a graphics program is first written to represent it using the primitives of a graphics language. This program is translated into a set of instructions and stored in the display memory of a display processor. In cheaper computers such as a PC, a part of the main memory is used as display memory.

8. Almost all current computer displays are raster-scan displays in which the electron beam of CRT sweeps and draws a set of lines from top to bottom. The number of lines varies between 480 to 1000 depending on the cost of the VDU.

9. The image drawn by the display program (stored in display memory) cuts the scan lines generated by the raster at a number of points. Each point is called a pixel (picture element). The number of bits used to represent a pixel depends on the number of intensity levels used to represent it. In monochrome CRT, it is around 8 bits and in colour CRTs it is around 24. The number of pixels stored depends on the resolution of the display required. In high resolution display it is (1024 × 1024) pixels.

10. The conversion of a display program to a set of pixels is called scan conversion.

11. The memory where the pixels are stored is called a frame buffer (or a refresh memory). The pixels in the frame buffer are retrieved in synchronism with the raster of the CRT display (60 times a second) and used to control the intensity of the beam(s), thereby displaying the picture.

12. LCDs can also use the same principles as in CRT displays. However, a raster is not essential as each pixel on the display can be independently controlled and displayed. Once the pixels corresponding to a picture are stored in a display memory, they can be displayed in any order.

13. Input devices used with displays may be logically divided into two categories: keyboards and locators.

14. Alphanumeric keyboards have around 108 keys. Besides alphanumeric keys, they have keys for special characters and a number of control keys for back spacing, deleting, etc. They have also keys called function keys which are pre-programmed to carry out specific actions.

15. The most common locator is a mouse. It is an opto-electronic device which is placed on a flat surface (table top) and as it is moved an arrow moves on the screen. The arrow can be pointed to a location and a button on the mouse clicked to invoke a pre-defined action by the computer.

16. The most common output devices which are used to give hard copies of results of computation are inkjet printers, laser printers, and dot matrix printers. Inkjet and laser printers give good quality prints whereas a dot matrix printer is usually used for heavy duty printing and getting multiple print copies.

17. Line printers unlike character printers print complete lines in a page one by one. They are very fast (1000 lines/minute) and are used for bulk printing.

18. A bit may be stored on a magnetic surface by magnetizing the surface in either one of two directions. The surface is magnetized using a write-head. A read-head is used to retrieve a stored bit.

19. Magnetic surface recording devices commonly used in computers are hard disks, floppy disks, and magnetic tapes.

20. A hard disk consists of a number of hard platters mounted on a spindle. The platters are coated with magnetic material. Data is organized along tracks on each platter; each track is divided into sectors. Each sector on the disk has a unique address. Hard disks can store about 100 GB. Retrieval time is of the order of tens of milliseconds. Hard disks are used in computers to store user program files and data.

21. To obtain large capacity low cost hard disks, a technology called RAID (Redundant Array of Inexpensive Disk) is used. In this a number of low cost disks are arranged as an array with a single controller. Several disks work in parallel and redundant parity bits are written for error control.

22. A floppy disk is a circular flexible disk made of magnetic tape material. Data are stored on a floppy disk along concentric tracks. Each track is divided into sectors. Tracks and sectors on a floppy disk may be assigned unique addresses. Floppy disks are used to exchange small files. The storage capacity of a floppy disk is about 1 MB, retrieval time is of the order of fraction of a second.

23. A CD-ROM uses a laser beam to record and read data along spiral tracks on a 5.25" disk. A disk can store around 650 MB data. CD-ROMs are normally used to store massive text data (such as encyclopaedias) which is permanently recorded and read many times. CD-ROMs which can be written in the user premises are called writable CD-ROMs. They are used as archival store and for software and data distribution.

24. DVD-ROMs are similar to CD-ROMs but allow storage of data on 2 layers on each side of a laser disk giving a maximum capacity of 17 GB. They can store full length video recording of up to 3 hours. Writable/erasable DVD-ROMs are now available.

25. A magnetic tape is a serial access memory. It is a non-addressable memory. The time taken to store and retrieve data from tapes is of the order of seconds which is slow. Tapes are mostly used as a backup storage device and for archiving data.

26. A computer system is organized with a balanced configuration of different types of memories. The main random access memory is used to store program being currently executed by the computer. Disks are used to store large data files and program files awaiting execution. Tapes are used to backup the files from disk. CD-ROMs and DVD-ROMs are used to store user manuals and large text, audio and video data. CD-R/W is also used to backup and archive data.

---

## EXERCISES

1. A 25 line 80 characters monochrome VDU is refreshed 60 times per second. Each character uses (16 × 24) dots including inter-character spacing.

   (i) What should be the size of display memory?

   (ii) At what rate should the processor send data to fill the display memory?

2. A colour monitor has (1200 × 900) pixel display, at 60 dots/inch. It uses 24 bits/pixel to display colour. The refresh rate is 60 Hz.

   (i) Estimate the diagonal size of the monitor.

   (ii) What should be the bandwidth of the display memory in bytes/second. Assume 24 bits can be accessed in parallel.

3. A TFT colour monitor has (1800 × 1200) pixel display at 90 dots/inch. It uses 8 bits/ colour to display varying intensities of colour.

   (i) Estimate the diagonal size of the monitor.

   (ii) How many transistors are required to display pixels?

   (iii) How many transistors/cm$^2$ should be fabricated on one plane?

4. Does a TFT LCD monitor require raster-scan as a CRT monitor does? If not give the reason.

5. A TFT colour monitor displays (640 × 480) pixels. It uses 8 bits per colour.

   (i) What is the size of the display memory

   (ii) If a high quality video clip is to be displayed on this display what should be the speed of display memory? Assume that 24 bits are accessed simultaneously from the display memory.

6. Study in detail the specifications of a 17", TFT LCD monitor given by any manufacturer (one possible website is www.samsung.com) and give a technical summary of the product in your own words.

7. Explain the differences between the monochrome LCD used in an inexpensive mobile phone and a computer monitor

8. An STN monitor displays (320 × 240) pixels. It displays 60 dots/inch.

   (i) Estimate the diagonal size of the monitor.

   (ii) How many electrodes need to be printed to control the display?

9.  A line printer prints 1200 lines/minute with 132 print positions/line. At what rate should data arrive to the printer which has a 132 byte buffer?

10. A drum printer has a 96 character set and prints at the rate of 1200 lines per minute. At what speed should the drum rotate?

11. An inkjet printer prints 4800 dots/s Its resolution is 300 dots/inch. The print area is 9" × 6" (length × width). At what rate should data arrive to the printer head? Assume data arrives serially one bit at a time.

12. A bi-directional dot matrix character printer has 132 characters/line and prints 120 characters/second. Each character has 9 vertical dots and 7 horizontal dots.

    (i) What is the linear speed of the print head if the paper width is 14 inch?

    (ii) If all vertical pins strike the ribbon simultaneously what should be the speed of a serial communication line which sends data to a printer for printing?

13. A chain printer prints 132 characters/line, has a 64 character set repeated 4 times on the chain. If the printer speed is 800 lines/minute at what speed should the printer chain rotate?

14. A 6" × 8", 24 bit colour picture is to be printed on a laser printer which prints 600 dots/inch. How many bits should the processor send to print the picture? If bits travel at 2400 bits/second on a serial line, how much time will it take to send the data to the printer?

15. The characteristics of disk are given below:

    > speed: 7200 rpm, average access time: 10 ms, 12 surfaces,
    > 8000 tracks, 512 byte per sector, 800 sectors

    Using the characteristics, answer the following questions:

    (i) What is the capacity (in bytes) of a cylinder?

    (ii) Determine the average time needed to transfer a track of data to a buffer area.

    (iii) What is the minimum time and what is the maximum time needed?

16. A Winchester disk pack has 8 surfaces. The innermost track diameter is 5 cm and the outmost track diameter is 8 cm. The maximum storage density along any track is 12000 bits /cm and the minimum space between tracks is $0.75 \times 10^{-3}$ cm.

    (i) What is the maximum number of bits per track?

    (ii) Estimate the maximum number of tracks per surface.

    (iii) How many cylinders are there in the disk pack?

    (iv) Estimate the maximum unformatted capacity of the disk.

    (v) Estimate the formatted capacity of the disk.

    (vi) Give an address format to retrieve information from the disk.

    (vii) If the disk speed is 5400 rpm, estimate the latency time of the disk.

    (viii) Estimate the data transfer rate in bytes/second.

    (ix) If the average access time of the disk is 16 milliseconds, estimate the seek time of the disk.

17. Assume that a payroll file for 10,000 employees is to be stored on a disk. The file is arranged in ascending order of employee number and is to be processed in this order. The file can be stored in one or two ways:

   (i) Successive records occupy successive tracks on one surface from outermost track to the innermost track. After one surface is filled the next is recorded.

   (ii) Successive records are stored in tracks on the same cylinder. After a cylinder is filled the next succeeding cylinder is used.

   Which of the two organizations would you prefer and why?

18. A floppy disk has the following characteristics:

   Diameter of outermost track:     3 inch

   Diameter of innermost track:     1.5 inch

   Bits/inch on each track:         64000

   Distance between tracks:         0.00025 inch

   Rotation speed of disk:          360 rpm

   (i) Estimate the unformatted capacity of floppy disk.

   (ii) Estimate the formatted capacity.

   (iii) Estimate the latency time.

   (iv) Estimate data transmission rate (in bytes/second).

   (v) Estimate the time to read all the data on one side and the floppy disk.

19. A 5.25 inch CD-ROM stores 650 MB along a spiral track. It records data at constant linear velocity. It is a 52x CD-ROM and rotates at 360 rpm.

   (i) Estimate the time needed to read the contents of the entire disk.

   (ii) Estimate the track length.

   (iii) What is the density of recording data along the spiral track?

   (iv) What is the linear velocity along a track?

20. A 5.25 inch DVD-ROM stores 8.5 GB on 2 layers on one side. Its read/write speed is 1.38 MB/s. It is also CLV recording and the rotational speed of DVD-ROM is 360 rpm. Its track pitch is 0.74 micron.

   (i) Estimate time needed to read the entire disk contents.

   (ii) Estimate the track length.

   (iii) What is the density of recording of data along the spiral track?

   (iv) What is the linear velocity of the track?

21. An Ultrium1 tape uses 127 mm width tape. 384 tracks are recorded in parallel. The data transfer rate is 15 MB/s. Its capacity is 100 GB (uncompressed). The recording is serpentine with 8 read/write heads.

   (i) What is the track pitch?

   (ii) What is the length of the tape?

   (iii) What is the number of bits/inch along a track?

   (iv) Estimate the time needed to record 100 GB.

   (v) What is the primary use of this storage medium?

**22.** Repeat exercise 21 for Ultrium 2 tape using the data given in Table 11.3.

**23.** The speed of reading from a DAT is 10 MB/s. Compare this speed with the following:

   (i) Speed of reading from a keyboard

   (ii) Speed of reading from main memory

   (iii) Speed of reading from a floppy disk

   (iv) Speed of reading from a Winchester disk

   (v) Speed of reading from a CD-ROM

**24.** Make a comparison table for all the types of memories studied so far in this book in the following format.

| Memory type | Estimated max. capacity (in bytes) data | Average time taken to locate desired data | Transfer rate (bytes/second) | Cost per byte |
|---|---|---|---|---|

The memories to be considered are: RAM, flash memory, hard disk, floppy disk, CD-ROM, DVD-ROM, Ultrium tape and DAT.

# 12

# Input-Output Organization

---

## Learning Goals

In this chapter we will learn:

☞ How Input/Output (I/O) devices are interfaced with CPU and memory systems of a computer.

☞ How the speed mismatch between CPU speed and I/O device speeds influences I/O organization.

☞ How the three major methods of I/O data transfer to memory called program controlled, interrupt controlled and Direct Memory Access based are designed and their major differences.

☞ Why special I/O processors are needed and their connection to the computer system.

☞ The need for buses to interconnect CPU, Memory and I/O devices and details of some standard buses.

☞ The need for serial data communication between computers located at different geographic locations.

☞ Methods of interconnecting computers within a small geographic area as a Local Area Network.

## 12.1 INTRODUCTION

In the last chapter we discussed the characteristics and operation of some input devices, output devices and mass storage devices. Mass storage devices are connected to a computer in a manner similar to input and output devices. We will thus discuss the principles used in interconnecting input/output devices and mass storage devices with the CPU and memory in a unified manner.

When I/O devices are to be connected to CPU and memory, we should remember the following important facts:

1. There is a vast variety of I/O devices. Some devices such as keyboard and mouse are very slow (nearly 100 bps) whereas others such as disks and flash memory are much faster (nearly $10^8$ bps).
2. The method of data transfer differs from device to device. There is no uniformity.
3. All I/O devices transfer data at a rate much slower than the rate at which CPU and memory can process them.
4. The number of data bytes and their formats differ from one device to another. For example, data from a keyboard is sent byte by byte asynchronously whereas that from a disk is a sector which is usually 512 bytes and is sent as a stream.

It is thus necessary to have an I/O interfacing unit which acts as an interface between I/O devices and CPU/Memory. In Figure 12.1 we sketch this interconnection.

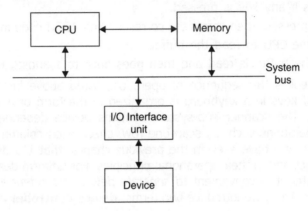

**Figure 12.1  I/O Interface unit to connect a device to CPU/Memory.**

The main functions of this I/O interface unit are as follows:

1. To receive instructions from CPU for Read/Write, interpret them and send appropriate commands to the specified I/O device.
2. For a write command, store temporarily the data received from the main memory. The specified device is then informed and made ready to accept the data. When the device is ready, it accepts the data from the buffer.
3. For a read instruction received from the CPU, send a command to the specified device. When the requested data is received from it, put the data in a buffer and inform the CPU that the data is ready. CPU should now start accepting data from the buffer.
4. It is the responsibility of the interface unit to monitor errors, if any, during data transmission, correct it (if possible) and inform CPU if data is corrupted.
5. Control all I/O operations using information such as read/write priority sent by CPU.

The I/O interface unit should communicate the following information to the CPU/ Memory system for correct transfer of data:

1. When data is ready in the interface unit buffer to be read by the memory/CPU system.
2. During write whether the interface buffer is ready to accept data.

In the rest of this chapter we will describe in detail the design of I/O interface unit and the means of communicating to and from I/O devices to CPU/Memory system.

## 12.2  DEVICE INTERFACING

Let us suppose that an I/O device has an integrated programmable unit. As an example, we will assume a dedicated processor to be resident in a computer keyboard device that constantly scans the rows of keys in a keyboard and does the following:

1. Determines if any key is pressed.
2. If a key is pressed, then stores the corresponding ASCII code in a "buffer storage".
3. Requests the CPU to read the buffer.
4. Waits till the buffer is read and then goes back to scanning the keyboard.

Figure 12.2 depicts the sequence of operations listed above in the form of a state diagram. The set of keys in a keyboard is organized in the form of a matrix with several rows and columns. The scanner sub-system contains device dependent operations that perform the sub-operations such as, scan one row, check each column of that row, move to the next row, etc. We have seen in the previous chapter that I/O devices differ widely in their characteristics and in their operational principles. For uniform design of the I/O sub-system of a computer, it is convenient to *separate device dependent aspects from device independent aspects*. Thus, we introduce two terms: **device controller** and **interface unit**.

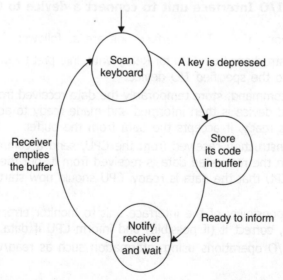

**Figure 12.2   A state diagram for the keyboard scanner.**

The device controller performs device-dependent electro-mechanical or electro-optical functions. The interface unit, on the other hand, performs the logic of communicating with the receiver of the input read or with the sender of the output to be displayed. An I/O organization based on this division of responsibilities is shown in Figure 12.3. A computer

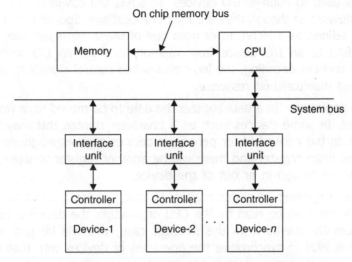

**Figure 12.3 Communication between CPU and peripheral devices.**

system contains many I/O devices and each of them will be assigned a unique address for identification. The interface units of the various I/O devices are connected using a *system bus* to the rest of the computer system as shown in Figure 12.3. In order to perform its functions interface unit should have the following features (see Figure 12.4):

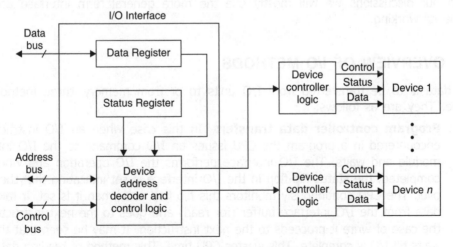

**Figure 12.4 Parts of an I/O Interface.**

1. **A device address decoder and control logic:**  Each device has a unique address. When the CPU wants to send data to a device or receive data from it, it places the device's address on the I/O bus. This address is decoded by the address decoder in the interface unit. In some microcomputers part of the memory address space is used to address I/O devices. This has the advantage of allowing access to I/O devices as though they are memory locations. Special I/O instructions need not be defined as a MOVE to or from one of these addresses will, by implication, move data to an I/O device from memory or from an I/O device to memory. Besides address decoding, the logic also sends control signals to devices to read/ write and monitor their response.

2. **A data register:**  In a data register the data to be moved to or from the memory is stored. In some devices such as a character printer, this may be a one byte register. In the case of faster peripheral devices such as magnetic disks, it would be a one word register and there will be another register to store the number of words to be moved in or out of the device.

3. **A status register:**  A status register is used to specify when the data from the device is ready to be read by the CPU or whether the device is ready to receive data from the memory. In the simplest case, this will be just a flip-flop. This register is vital to synchronize the operation of devices with that of the CPU.

The I/O interface unit varies in complexity depending on the number and type of I/O devices it controls. In large computers with powerful CPU, the complete control of all devices and I/O operations is delegated to the I/O module. In such a case the I/O module is a full fledged special purpose computer which is usually called **I/O processor** or **channel**. In smaller machines the CPU does fair amount of the device control functions. In such cases the I/O interface is a VLSI chip called an **I/O** or **device controller**.

In our discussions we will mostly use the more general term interface unit and describe its working.

## 12.3  OVERVIEW OF I/O METHODS

When data is to be transferred from I/O units to or from memory, three methods are possible. They are as follows:

1. **Program controller data transfer:**  In this case when an I/O instruction is encountered in a program the CPU issues an I/O command to the I/O interface module and waits. The I/O interface performs the I/O operation and when it is completed, the status flip-flop in the I/O interface is set indicating that the job is over. The CPU continuously monitors this flip-flop and when it is set, it takes the data from the I/O interface buffer (for read) and goes to the next instruction. In the case of write it proceeds to the next instruction. It may be seen that the CPU waits till I/O is complete. This wastes CPU time. This method of reading data from device is summarized in the flow chart of Figure 12.5.

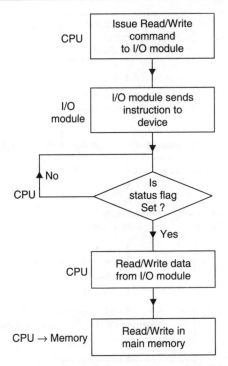

**Figure 12.5  Program controlled I/O transfer.**

2. **Interrupt driven data transfer:** In this case when an I/O instruction is encountered, the CPU issues an I/O command to the I/O interface. It then continues with the next instruction in the program. When the interface is ready with the data needed by the CPU, it sends an interrupt signal to the CPU. The CPU now suspends the program it is executing, retrieves the data from the I/O interface and places it in memory. It then returns to program execution. Observe that in this case CPU does not wait. The assumption is that the program does not require the data to be read from the device immediately. This method is summarized in the flow chart given in Figure 12.6.

3. **Direct memory access:** In the previous two methods CPU is involved directly in I/O operation. Data is stored in memory via CPU. In DMA the CPU issues I/O command to I/O interface unit and proceeds with the rest of the program. It has no further role in data transfer. The I/O interface assembles in its buffer register the data read from the device. When data is ready it transfers the data directly to the specified address of memory.

We thus see that in the first two cases data is transferred to memory via CPU whereas in DMA it is directly transferred to memory. We will now describe these three methods in greater detail.

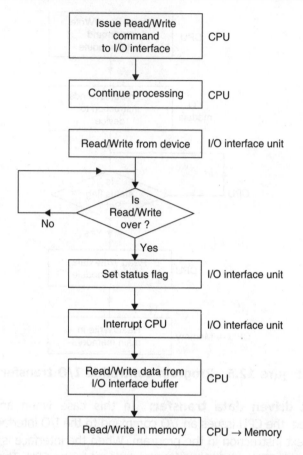

**Figure 12.6  Interrupt controlled I/O transfer.**

## 12.4  PROGRAM CONTROLLED DATA TRANSFER

Let us view the I/O operation as a process and the main computation performed in the CPU as another process and call them **I/O process and computation process** respectively. (The state diagram shown in Figure 12.2 depicts the I/O process.) These two processes communicate with each other in order to exchange information, such as data, coded commands, control signals or status signals. As we saw in Section 12.3 the information transfer between them can take place in several ways. This is one of the major aspects of I/O organization.

In this section we describe in greater detail program controlled data transfer between I/O process and computation. In Figure 12.7 we give a block diagram of the major units of a computer. The interface unit has the following registers:

IBR:        Interface Buffer Register (one byte)

Data-Ready: Flip-flop that indicates that data is ready in the IBR

Busy:       Flip-flop that indicates that the I/O interface unit is engaged (or busy)

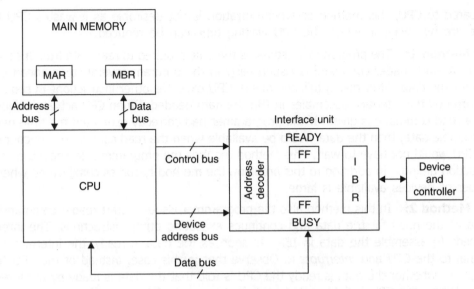

**Figure 12.7  Details of CPU-I/O-memory communication.**

The various buses connecting the units are also shown. A series of steps used for actual data transfer is given as follows:

*Step 1:*  An I/O instruction is encountered in the program being executed. The instructions may be of the form: I/O operation code, device address, device command.

*Step 2:*  The CPU sends on I/O bus the device address and command to be executed, namely, read or write.

*Step 3:*  The device address on the I/O bus is recognized by the address decoder of the desired I/O device interface unit. (It is assumed that the programmer knows that the device is free before issuing the command.)

*Step 4:*  The interface unit commands (for a read command) the concerned device controller to assemble a word in the interface buffer register (IBR) and at the same time it turns on an *interface busy* flip-flop. As long as this busy flip-flop is set, the interface will not entertain any other I/O requests. A data ready flip-flop in the interface unit is reset to 0.

*Step 5:*  The device controller fills the IBR. As soon as the data is ready in IBR the data ready flip-flop of the device interface is set to 1.

*Step 6:*  The CPU continually interrogates the data ready flip-flop in a wait loop. It gets out of the loop as soon as the data ready flip-flop is set to 1. When this happens the contents of IBR are transferred to the specified CPU register through the data bus.

This method of transfer of data from I/O to CPU is called **program controlled transfer**. In this method synchronization of the I/O device and CPU is achieved by making CPU wait till the data is assembled by the device. As I/O devices are normally much slower compared to CPU, this method of synchronization is not desirable as it wastes CPU time. There are two ways in which the CPU waiting time can be reduced.

**Method 1:** The programmer estimates the time required to read data from a specified device. A start reader command is issued early in the program several steps ahead of the need for the data. After giving this command, CPU executes other instructions in sequence. Concurrently the interface assembles in IBR the data needed. When CPU actually needs the data a read command is given. If the programmer had correctly estimated the time needed to assemble data, then the data would be available when the read command is encountered and CPU would not have to wait. This method requires the programmer to know the correct instruction timings. In addition to this problem, the method becomes complicated when the number of devices available is large.

**Method 2:** In this method also the programmer issues a start reader command well ahead of the need for the data and continues executing other instructions. The interface proceeds to assemble the data in IBR. As soon as the data is ready, the interface sends a signal to the CPU and *interrupts* it. Observe that in this case, instead of the CPU trying to find out whether the data is ready the CPU is told that the data is ready by the interrupt signal. When the CPU is interrupted, it jumps to a special sub-routine which reads the contents of IBR and stores it in the specified location in memory. This method is called **program controlled interrupt transfer**. This method is better than the previous method as a programmer need not carry out detailed timing calculations. If many devices are active, then the CPU will receive many interrupt signals and a method should be evolved to handle them systematically. We will consider this aspect in detail in the next section.

## 12.5 INTERRUPT STRUCTURES

In the last section we introduced the idea of transferring data between peripheral and CPU using an interrupt. We will expand on this idea in this section.

The interrupt process may be compared to the action of a housewife when she hears a doorbell while she is working in the kitchen. She may have been boiling milk when the bell rings. She would then shut the flame and go to the door to attend to the call. After receiving the visitor and attending to him or her, she will return to the original job she was doing, namely, boiling milk. We can extend this analogy recursively. When she is interrupted while boiling milk and she is walking towards the door to open it, if the telephone rings she rushes to pick up the phone. That is, the interrupting process is now interrupted by a higher priority event.

There are two processes, one is the **interrupted process** and the other is the **interrupting process**. In the case of I/O transfer between CPU and I/O the CPU is the interrupted process and the I/O interface is the interrupting process. An interrupt signal is sent by an I/O interface to the CPU when it is ready to transfer data to (or from) the memory. Normally, the CPU completes the current instruction it is executing and then attends to the interrupt. The interrupt request is serviced by executing a pre-written *interrupt-service program*. After the interrupt is serviced, the CPU will return and restart the interrupted computation. In order to restart computation, the CPU should store (possibly in a stack) the *process state* before branching to the interrupt service program. Restarting computation can then be achieved by a simple *process-switching*.

If we assume there is only one interrupt, the sequence of steps involved for interrupt processing is as shown below:

### 12.5.1 Single Level Interrupt Processing

*Step 1:* Interrupt signal is received by CPU.

*Step 2:* CPU completes current instruction.

*Step 3:* CPU stores the contents of program counter, processor status word and other general purpose registers in a reserved area in the main memory or in a stack.

*Step 4:* CPU sends acknowledge signal to I/O interface and jumps to an interrupt service routine.

*Step 5:* The interrupt service program carries out the required transfer of data from or to I/O. The last instructions in the service program restores the contents of the general purpose registers. The content of the program counter is then restored to that stored in step 3 and CPU returns to execute the original program it was executing.

These steps are summarized in Figure 12.8. Figure 12.9 depicts the status of memory during interrupt processing.

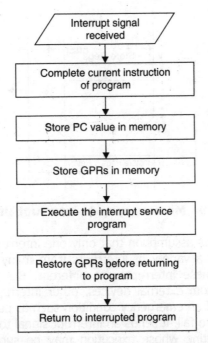

**Figure 12.8 Sequence of events in interrupt processing.**

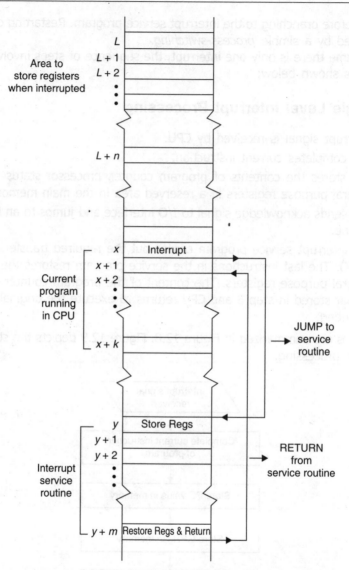

**Figure 12.9   Memory map in interrupt processing.**

**Interrupt levels:**   The assumption that only one interrupt occurs is not realistic. In practice CPU should handle a variety of interrupts from many I/O devices. The order of importance or priority of these interrupts are different. Besides interrupts from device interface to transfer data from external devices, other interrupts are also generated. An example is the occurrence of an emergency condition such as power failure. When a sensor detects that power is about to fail, it sends an interrupt signal to the CPU. The CPU initiates a power failure service routine whose execution may be supported by a small battery backup power. This routine would store all important registers in non-volatile memory so that the program may be resumed when power is restored. Interrupts caused by I/O devices and emergency events outside CPU's control are called **external interrupts**.

Another class of interrupts, **internal interrupts** (also known as **traps**) can occur when there is a mistake in a user's program. Common mistakes which lead to traps are: attempt to divide by zero, accumulator overflow or use of an illegal operation code. When such a mistake is detected by CPU, it interrupts the user's program and branches to a trap routine, which usually prints out the place where a trap occurred and the reason for the trap. The CPU may then resume the program if the mistake is not a serious one or suspend execution in case it is meaningless to continue with the interrupted program.

Another type of interrupt is caused if the hardware of a computer develops a fault. When the error detecting circuitry detects a fault, the CPU is informed of the location and the nature of the fault. The CPU then jumps to a fault service routine which determines if it is a correctable fault (such as when error correcting codes are used) and carries out the correction and resumes the user's program. If it is a noncorrectable fault, operation is suspended after printing an appropriate message.

Interrupts generated by a real time clock in a computer are used to regulate allocation of CPU time to users. Such interrupts are necessary to ration time to different users and to throw out jobs stuck in endless loops.

As there are many types of interrupts it is necessary to have a method of distinguishing types of interrupts. Further, if during an interrupt processing another interrupt occurs, a procedure to attend to this is to be formulated. The number of types of interrupts that can be distinguished by a CPU is called **interrupt levels** or **interrupt classes**. The relative importance given to an interrupt is called its **priority**.

## 12.5.2 Handling Multiple Interrupts

All interrupt systems use similar procedures to request CPU attention. A simple model of this is shown in Figure 12.10. Two flip-flops are used in the I/O interface unit. The interrupt request flip-flop R is set by the device controller when the device needs the attention of the CPU. When the CPU is ready to accept the interrupt, it sends a signal to the interrupt acknowledge flip-flop A and sets it. As soon as A is set, the device can transfer data to the CPU. This procedure of exchanging signals between processes to communicate each other's state is known as **handshaking**.

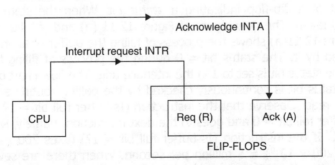

**Figure 12.10 Handshaking between CPU and I/O interface unit.**

The model shown in Figure 12.10 is simplified and shows only one device. Let us suppose that several I/O devices of the same interrupt class are involved. Then two problems arise:

1. How to connect the INTR (interrupt request) lines of these devices to the CPU?

2. How will the CPU determine which of the many devices has sent the interrupt so the INTA (interrupt acknowledge) can be given to the right device?

## 12.6    INTERRUPT CONTROLLED DATA TRANSFER

There are two ways to connect INTR line(s) to CPU. A simple method would be to use one INTR line and one INTA line per device and connect them to the CPU. The other is to OR all the INTR lines and send only one INTR line to CPU. Even though handling interrupts using the first method is simple, it is impractical as bus widths are limited and computers normally have a large number of I/O devices. It is thus necessary to group sets of devices and service devices within each group. In this case INTR of each group is ORed. A smaller number of lines are thus used to connect to CPU. Within each group one has to assign priority for servicing. Thus, the second method is essential and we will describe it now. In this case only one signal is received on INTR line. CPU should find out which device interrupted and service it. If several devices interrupt simultaneously, the CPU should decide in which order (or priority) the devices should be serviced. There are four major methods of servicing interrupts. They are as follows:

1. Software polling
2. Bus arbitration
3. Daisy chaining which is a hardware arrangement
4. Vectored interrupt handling (which uses one component of a vector of interrupt routine addresses)
5. Use of multiple interrupt lines

We will describe each one in turn.

### 12.6.1    Software Polling

Polling is a method in which a process periodically checks the status of an object. Usually the status is that of a flip-flop indicating a *status bit*. When the status bit changes, a specified action is taken. The flow charts of Figure 12.11 (a) and (b) illustrate polling. The flow chart of Figure 12.11(a) shows the process of filling the buffer of an interface unit from a device controlled by it. The status bit = 0 during the process of filling the buffer. When the buffer is full the status bit is set to 1 in the interface unit. The flow chart of Figure 12.11(b) shows how the status bit is continuously checked by the polling routine and when it is set to 1, the buffer is read. Observe that the instruction (Is buffer full bit = 1?) returns to itself as long as the buffer full bit = 0 and goes to the next instruction, namely, Read Buffer, when the bit is set to 1. If the instruction (Is buffer full bit = 1?) takes 200 ns to execute, the polling rate is $1/(200 \times 10^{-9}) = 5$ million per second. When there are several I/O devices capable of interrupting the CPU, a method should be found to arbitrate among them and service one of them. This is done by polling INTR flags of all the I/O units one after another cyclically to find which unit's INTR flag is set. If more than one INTR is set, then the unit with a higher priority, should be serviced first. The sequence in which the INTR of units are polled is based on its priority.

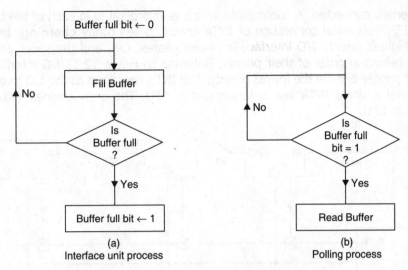

**Figure 12.11   Polling of interface unit.**

## 12.6.2   Bus Arbitration

Polling is time consuming. To reduce the time a method called **bus arbitration** is used. In this case an interrupting unit gains access to the data bus and posts its device address in a **device address register** in the CPU (see Figure 12.12). The interrupt service routine reads this address thereby uniquely identifying the device. This scheme is quite flexible. The CPU may choose to ignore an interrupt by setting an interrupt mask bit to 1 in CPU using an appropriate instruction. Thus, a program would set the mask bit to 1 if it does not want to attend to an interrupt from that device immediately. It can choose when it wants to service an interrupt by resetting the mask bit to 0.

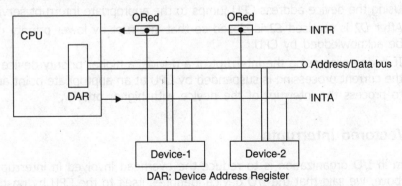

DAR: Device Address Register

**Figure 12.12   Use of address bus for device identification.**

## 12.6.3   Daisy Chaining

Daisy chaining is a hardware method used to assign order of priority in attending to interrupts. In this scheme the interrupt acknowledge lines (INTA lines) of the I/O interface units are serially connected. A controllable switch is incorporated in each of the blocks (see Figure 12.13). This serial connection of INTA lines is called **daisy chaining**. In the daisy chain the highest priority I/O interface is placed nearest CPU and the lower priority ones are placed behind in order of their priority. Referring to Figure 12.13 I/O interface *D1* has the highest priority and *Dn* the lowest priority. The INTR lines from all the I/O interface units are ORed and a single INTR line is terminated in CPU. The daisy chained INTA line also terminates in CPU.

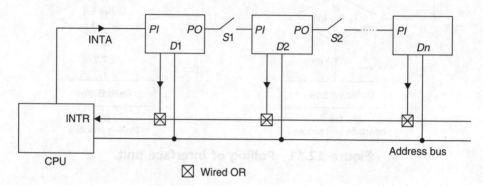

**Figure 12.13   Daisy chaining.**

**Arbitration method** used is described as follows. (It is assumed that all switches *S1*, *S2* ... *Sn*−1 are initially closed.)

Step 1:   When a device, say *D2*, needs interrupt services it sends a signal on INTR line. The CPU recognizes INTR and sends INTA signal which is captured by *D2*. It opens the switch *S2* so that no lower priority device can send a signal on INTA line.

Step 2:   *D2* now places its address on the address bus. This address is sensed by CPU.

Step 3:   Using the device address CPU jumps to the appropriate interrupt service routine.

Step 4:   After *D2* is serviced *S2* is closed so that interrupt by lower priority devices can be acknowledged by CPU.

Step 5:   If during processing the interrupt of a device, a higher priority device interrupts, the current processing is suspended by CPU at an appropriate point and it jumps to process the interrupt of the device with higher priority.

## 12.6.4   Vectored Interrupts

A major aim in I/O organization is to reduce the overhead involved in interrupt handling. In step 2 above, we said that the I/O device identifies itself to the CPU by posting its own address on the bus. This idea is extended in **vectored interrupts**. We will explain this with an example.

Let us suppose there are four different I/O devices connected to a CPU. Assume that the system programmer or the operating system designer has written the interrupt service routines for each of these devices and stored these routines in the reserved area of memory as shown in Figure 12.14.

The *vector of addresses* stored starting from address 1000 in Figure 12.14, contain the starting addresses of the four interrupt service routines. Let us associate the vector of addresses (1000, 1004, 1008, 1012) with the four devices (#1, #2, #3, #4) respectively. When the I/O device #3 is ready it posts the code 1008 on the bus. This information can be used by the CPU to straightaway branch to the corresponding interrupt service routine stored starting in address 7300. The interrupt service routines may be *relocated* at some other areas of memory but the vector of addresses must reside in the same place; otherwise this method will not work correctly.

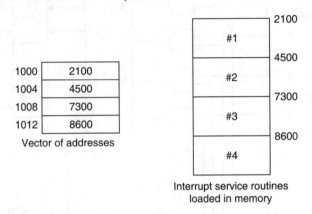

Vector of addresses

Interrupt service routines
loaded in memory

**Figure 12.14   Vector of addresses.**

## 12.6.5   Multiple Interrupt Lines

So far, we have considered models of interrupt systems in which we had only one interrupt request line entering the CPU and one interrupt acknowledge line leaving the CPU. If there are many devices, we assumed that the INTR of different devices are ORed together. We can extend this model to associate multiple pairs of (INTR, INTA) with the CPU. This model is shown in Figure 12.15. The INT register has one bit reserved for each INTR line which registers the interrupt requests from various lines. We already pointed out that it is impractical to have a pair of INTR and INTA for each device. We thus group I/O devices and each group has a pair of INTR and INTA lines. For example, the I/O devices may be grouped into 4 classes and connected through 4 separate INTR lines, as shown in Figure 12.15. In this scheme two or more simultaneous interrupt requests from different lines can be registered in the INT register. However, only one interrupt service routine can be executed at a time. Thus, the CPU has to assign priorities among multiple requests and select one of them at a time for service. Such a selection may be done using hardware devices called **priority encoders** or by software means with the help of an interrupt analyzer software.

Referring to Figure 12.15 we have shown a block diagram of a *priority encoder* and bus grant. We have shown in this example four devices $D1$, $D2$, $D3$ and $D4$. If a device wants to be serviced, it sets a bit corresponding to it in an Interrupt Register to 1. A mask register has 1 bit corresponding to each device. Depending on the priority to be assigned in a particular situation, the interrupt handling software will set mask bit of devices not to be serviced to 0 and those to be serviced to 1. The interrupt register bits are ANDed with mask register bits and the result is input to a *priority* encoder. The priority encoder is designed to give as its output the device address to be placed on the address bus. It also has an output to forward IR Interrupt Request (INTR) signal to the CPU. The interrupt acknowledgement (INTA) from the CPU is used to capture the address bus and put the device address on it.

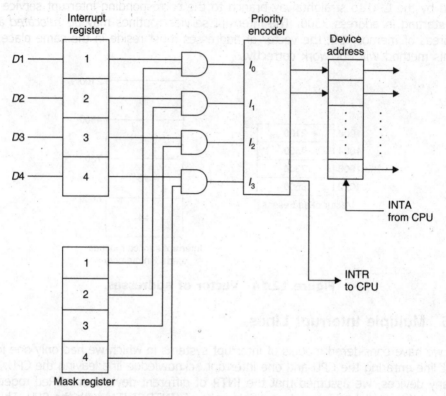

**Figure 12.15   Priority encoder for multiple interrupts.**

## 12.6.6   VLSI Chip Interrupt Controller

Microprocessor families such as $80\times86$ have as a support chip an external interrupt controller. One such controller is 82C59A which is in turn used with Intel 80386. External devices are connected to this chip. A simple controller can control up to eight devices. Eight controllers may be connected to a master controller to allow control of up to 64 devices (see Figure 12.16). The primary function of this chip is the management of interrupts. It accepts interrupts from devices, determines which has the highest priority and forwards INTR from this device to the microprocessor. The processor accepts the interrupt (when it is ready) and acknowledges via INTA line. This signals the controller to place the device's address on the data bus (which acts as device address bus) of 80386. The processor now proceeds to process the interrupt and communicates directly with the I/O interface unit to read or write data.

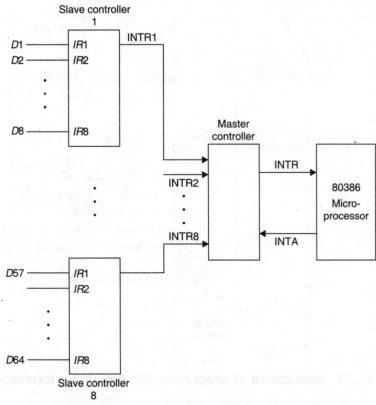

**Figure 12.16   VLSI chip interrupt controller.**

The 82C59A is a programmable chip. The priority scheme to be used is conveyed by 80386 by sending information to a control word in 82C59A. Three interrupt modes are available.

1. **Fully nested** in which priority order is $IR1$ to $IR8$.
2. **Rotating** in which after a device is serviced, it is put last in the queue for the next servicing.
3. **Masked** in which a mask is used to alter priority by inhibiting interrupts of specified devices.

## 12.6.7   Programmable Peripheral Interface Unit

There are also VLSI chips available as I/O interface unit. These are called **Programmable Peripheral Interface Unit** (PPIU) and can be used for program controlled as well as interrupt controlled data transfer from/to devices to the processor. A block diagram of such a device is shown in Figure 12.17. This figure shows two devices, namely, a keyboard and a Video Display Unit connected to the PPIU which is in turn connected to the microprocessor. Observe that in this example 8 data bits each from the two devices are fed to the PPIU. Also appropriate control bits for the devices are sent by PPIU. Interrupt request from the devices is also forwarded to the interrupt controller which forwards it to the microprocessor.

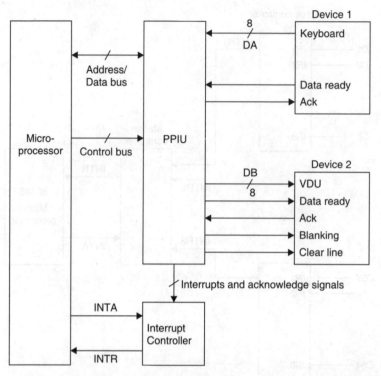

**Figure 12.17 Application of programmable peripheral interface unit.**

PPIU communicates to the microprocessor using data/address bus and the necessary control bits. We have highlighted only the main principles. For detailed configuration of chips the reader should refer to the data sheets of microprocessor manufacturers such as INTEL or AMD.

## 12.7 DMA BASED DATA TRANSFER

In both program controlled data transfer and interrupt controlled transfer of data, data is transferred to or from I/O devices to the memory via a CPU register. This is slow as data is transferred byte by byte. For the transfer of each byte, several instructions need to be executed by the CPU. Input or output of a block of data from a fast peripheral such as a disk is at high speed. These devices operate synchronously using their own internal clock and are independent of CPU. The combination of high speed of such devices and their synchronous operation makes it impractical to use program controlled transfer or interrupt controlled transfer via CPU to read or write data in such devices. Another method which uses a **Direct Memory Access (DMA)** interface eliminates the need to use CPU registers to transfer data from I/O units to memory or vice versa.

We could consider DMA based I/O to be memory centred, that is, memory is the main entity for whose service both I/O and CPU compete. Of course, it is necessary for the DMA device to know from the CPU where in memory the data should be stored and how many bytes are to be transferred. Thus, the CPU is also connected to the DMA device as shown in Figure 12.18.

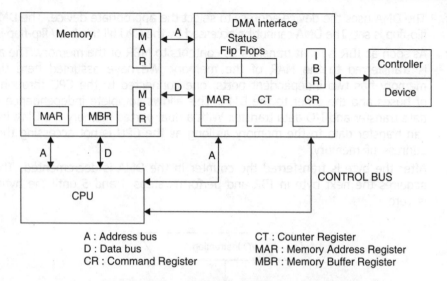

**Figure 12.18    Block diagram explaining DMA interface.**

A DMA interface contains the following registers to facilitate direct data transfer from I/O devices to memory.

1. A Memory Address Register (MAR) which contains the address in memory to which data is to be transferred or from where data is to be received.

2. A Memory Buffer Register (MBR) which contains the byte to be sent to the memory or that received from memory.

3. A counter register which contains the count of the number of bytes to be sent or received from memory. With the transfer of each byte the counter is decremented by 1.

4. A status register indicating DMA busy/free, data ready and other status information.

5. A register containing the I/O command to be carried out. This command is received from the CPU and stored in DMA to enable the DMA interface to carry out the command independent of CPU.

The configuration of the DMA interface and its connection to the CPU through buses is shown in Figure 12.18. The DMA interface functions as follows:

**DMA operation**

*Step 1:*    When an I/O instruction is encountered by the CPU, it sends the device address and the I/O command to the DMA interface. The address in memory where a byte is to be stored or from where a byte is to be received is also sent to the DMA by the CPU. If several bytes are to be stored or retrieved, then the address of the first byte in the group and the count of the number of bytes is sent by the CPU to the DMA interface. All the information sent by the CPU to the DMA interface is stored locally in the appropriate registers by DMA.

*Step 2:*    After sending the above information to the DMA interface the CPU continues with the next instruction in the program. CPU resources are not required hereafter.

*Step 3:* The DMA uses the device address to select the appropriate device. The DMA busy flip-flop is set. The DMA cannot be accessed by the CPU till this busy flip-flop is reset.

*Step 4:* As soon as IBR is full it transfers its contents to MBR of the memory. The address is transferred to the MAR of the memory. We have assumed here that the memory has two independent ports, one connected to the CPU through a pair of buses and the other to the DMA. This allows complete independence of CPU data transfer and I/O data transfer. With a dual ported memory the DMA interface can transfer data to the memory as long as the CPU is not accessing the same address of memory.

*Step 5:* After the byte is transferred the counter in the DMA is decremented. The DMA acquires the next byte in IBR and performs steps 4 and 5 until the byte count is zero.

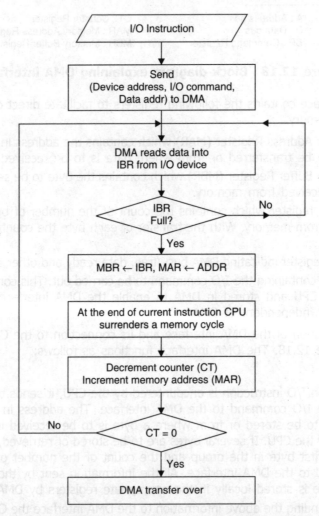

**Figure 12.19 DMA interface procedure (for I/O read).**

In step 4 we assumed that the main memory is dual ported. Dual-ported memories are however small in size. Main memory of computers are thus not dual ported. CPU and DMA interface must thus share the data and address bus. Only one of them can access memory at a time. Thus if the DMA does not have access to a separate port of memory, then it shares the MAR and MBR with CPU. In such cases when IBR in the DMA interface is filled and ready to be transferred to memory, the DMA sends an interrupt signal to CPU. The CPU completes the execution of the instruction it is currently carrying out and yields the next memory cycle to DMA. During this memory cycle IBR is sent to MBR of memory and the address to MAR and a byte is transferred to memory. After the byte is transferred, the counter in DMA is decremented. This method of transfer of a word from I/O to memory in which a memory cycle is taken away from CPU by DMA is known as **cycle stealing**. This procedure is illustrated in the flow chart shown in Figure 12.19.

This method of transferring data byte by byte to memory by DMA is appropriate for slow I/O devices such as a keyboard. If data being transferred is from a fast I/O device such as a disk, a burst of bytes (e.g., contents of a sector) is to be sent to the main memory. In this case the data and address buses are taken over by DMA for several cycles till all the bytes are transferred. In Figure 12.18 we showed two separate buses: one from CPU to memory and the other from DMA to memory. This was mainly done for ease of explanation. A more accurate block diagram of a DMA interface is shown in Figure 12.20.

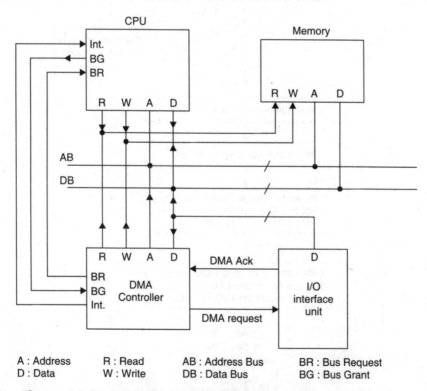

| A : Address | R : Read | AB : Address Bus | BR : Bus Request |
| D : Data | W : Write | DB : Data Bus | BG : Bus Grant |

**Figure 12.20  Details of CPU, memory, DMA, I/O interface unit interconnections.**

This figure shows a single pair of address and data buses being shared by CPU and DMA. The DMA controller has three control lines to CPU, an interrupt line, a bus request line and a bus grant line. When DMA wants to send data to memory, it requests the address and data buses from CPU by sending a signal on the BR line. CPU after completing the current instruction logically disconnects the buses from itself and sends a signal to DMA on BG line. DMA now uses the buses to transfer a burst of data. At the end, it informs the CPU by sending a signal on interrupt line. The CPU now gets back the buses. This method is illustrated in the flow chart of Figure 12.21. In this flow chart we have assumed that the I/O instruction is a "read" instruction. If it is a "write" instruction to a fast device, the starting address and the number of bytes to be transferred to I/O device is sent by CPU to DMA. The DMA now requests the CPU to yield the buses for reading from memory by sending a signal on BR line. The CPU grants the buses by sending a signal on BG line. Now the DMA reads data from memory and writes it on the fast I/O device.

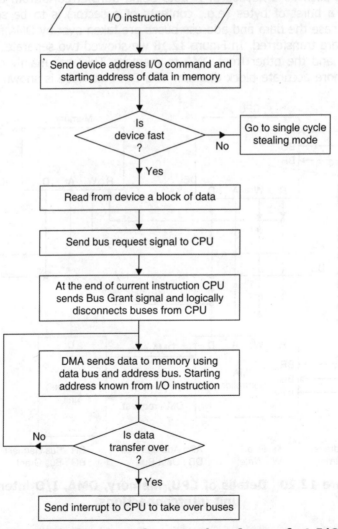

**Figure 12.21    DMA data transfer procedure from a fast I/O device.**

Observe that this entire process of data transfer is performed by the hardware without any program intervention. In other words the programmer does not have to worry about the detailed transfer of data. In computer literature such hardware procedures which are hidden from or *not visible* to the programmer are known as **transparent** to programmers.

This method of data transfer between I/O devices and memory is **non-program controlled**. The programmer must, however, give a read instruction sufficiently in advance so that the data is available in memory when needed for use in the application program.

Before we conclude this section we will compare DMA data transfer with transfer of data via CPU. The DMA transfer is faster and convenient to use. The CPU does not unnecessarily waste time. This advantage is gained by providing extra hardware in the DMA and also by introducing extra information paths.

## 12.8 INPUT/OUTPUT (I/O) PROCESSORS

So far we have assumed that each I/O device has a controller and is connected to an I/O interface unit. We have also seen that I/O interface units may be program controlled, interrupt controlled or may provide direct memory access (DMA). Nowadays computers have several I/O devices. For example, many computers have a keyboard, VDU, hard disk, floppy disk, flash memory, printer, scanner, audio I/O, video camera, CD-ROMs, tapes, etc. Very often it is more economical to consolidate the functions of several I/O interface units into one special unit called an **I/O processor**. An I/O processor is a full fledged special purpose processor with an instruction set optimized for reading from and writing in I/O devices. To distinguish I/O processor instructions from those of the CPU, these instructions are called **commands**. I/O processors are connected to the main memory of the computer just like a DMA interface. This allows them to perform I/O operations without loading the CPU. A block diagram of a computer reorganized with an I/O processor is shown in Figure 12.22. The CPU and I/O processor work independently communicating using the memory bus. The following gives the sequence of steps followed for I/O transfer using I/O processor.

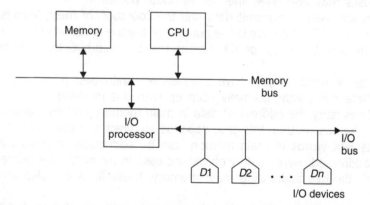

**Figure 12.22  Block diagram of a computer system with an I/O processor.**

*Step 1:*  CPU tests if I/O processor is available to read/write data. This information is available in a I/O processor status word stored in the main memory by I/O processor.

*Step 2:*    If I/O processor is available, CPU sends a request to I/O processor for service. The starting address of the appropriate I/O program stored in memory is sent to I/O processor. CPU having delegated the I/O tasks, continues its work.

*Step 3:*    I/O processor uses the I/O program to read/write data in specified I/O device. It communicates with memory in DMA mode.

*Step 4:*    At the end of I/O, I/O processor stores its status word in main memory and interrupts CPU.

*Step 5:*    CPU checks the status word to confirm I/O task is over. If all OK it continues with processing.

Observe that I/O processor and CPU work concurrently doing their own assigned tasks. They, however, compete for the main memory. Normally I/O processor works with devices which are relatively slow. Therefore CPU will not be significantly slowed down unless there are several high speed I/O devices handled by the system.

## 12.9    BUS STRUCTURE

In the chapter on CPU we described two types of buses: an internal bus within a chip which connects the processor with cache memory and an external bus which connects CPU chip with external memory chip. Another external bus is one which connects I/O interface units with CPU/memory. In this section we will describe in greater detail the external buses.

### 12.9.1    Structure of a Bus

A system bus usually has around 50 to 100 parallel wires which are normally printed on a printed circuit board. This is called a **back plane system bus**, because component boards such as CPU board, memory board and I/O processor board are plugged to the back plane to connect them to the bus. The bus usually has *data lines, address lines* and *control lines*. Some buses may also have lines to distribute power.

Data lines are used to transmit data and the collection of these lines is also called a **data bus**. The width of a data bus is the number of parallel wires which carry data. Usually data bus widths are 8, 16, 32 or 64. Larger the bus width better will be the system performance.

Microprocessor word lengths have progressively increased from 8 to 16 to 32 and currently 64. Data bus widths normally keep up with this increase.

Address lines carry the address of data in main memory and are collectively called an **address bus**. The bus width in this case depends on direct addressability of memory. With 16 address bits 64K words of main memory can be addressed whereas with 32 bits 4G words can be addressed. Here again with the increase in memory sizes address bus widths have increased. Besides addressing main memory, these lines are also used to address I/O devices.

The **control bus** is used to control the access to and use of data and address buses by various units which share the bus. Besides this, they carry command signals to specify operations such as memory write, memory read, I/O write, I/O read, data acknowledge, bus request, bus grant, interrupt request, interrupt acknowledge and clock signal to synchronize operations on the bus.

Apart from bus width and controls, there are three other characteristics of buses which are important. They are: type of bus, transaction type, method of timing and method of arbitration for bus use. We will explain them now.

## 12.9.2 Types of Bus

There are two major types of buses. They are: dedicated bus and multiplexed bus. In a dedicated bus, address and data lines are two sets of independent lines whereas in multiplexed bus the same set of lines are time shared. For a specified period they are used to transmit an address and for another specified period they carry data. The primary advantage of multiplexing is that the bus is cheaper as it uses fewer lines. Dedicated buses, on the other hand, are faster. Earlier microprocessor families used multiplexing whereas current high performance processors use dedicated buses.

## 12.9.3 Bus Transaction Type

A **bus transaction** can be read or write. The terms *read* or *write* are used for transaction with or to memory. Thus, read will transfer data from memory to the I/O device, and write from the I/O device to memory. Because the bus is shared by several units, the unit intending to read or write must first acquire the bus before transmission can begin. The unit then becomes the bus master and remains the bus master until the control transfers to another unit. The bus transaction has two distinct parts: (i) send the address to identify the receiver and (ii) transmit the data. Some buses also permit block transfer of data. In this case the first transaction gives the start address $k$ of $n$ data words to be stored. Subsequently $n$ words are transmitted in a burst and stored from the starting address $k$. This is useful for transferring data from/to fast I/O devices.

## 12.9.4 Timings of Bus Transactions

Another characteristic of buses is the presence or absence of a *clock*. A bus in which transactions are controlled by a clock is called a **synchronous bus** else it is an **asynchronous bus**. The operation of a synchronous bus is based on a clock which is an integral part of the bus. The **bus protocol** is based or timed by the number of clock pulses between events. Such protocols based on counting the clock pulses can be easily implemented in a small finite state machine and can be fast. When the length of a bus increases, clock skewing becomes high. Thus long buses are designed without clocks. Such buses are called asynchronous buses. They use a hand-shaking protocol rather than a clock for correct operation.

### Synchronous transfer

Let us consider a sequence of events in a synchronous data transfer. Transfer of one unit of data (normally an 8-bit byte or 32-bit word) takes place in each bus cycle. For convenience, we will assume the address lines and data lines to be different. First the bus master acquires the control of the bus, and the read/write control line is set to either read or write mode. In read mode the following four events take place in the order given and the sequence repeats thereafter cyclically (see Figure 12.23).

$t_0$: Address of the device to be read is posted on the address lines of the bus by the bus master. This information is kept on the address lines throughout the bus cycle. At the end of the cycle the address lines are reset.

$t_1$: This event refers to the data *being* placed on the data lines by the addressed device.

$t_2$: The signals on the data lines have settled and the data is ready for strobing (or reading) by the master.

$t_3$: Cycle is completed.

The above sequence of events are represented in the timing diagram in Figure 12.23. The events $t_0$, $t_1$ and $t_3$ are recognized in this diagram by the rising edge, or the falling edge of the bus clock-pulse. The event $t_2$ occurs during the OFF period of the clock. Data must be posted by the device on the data lines after $t_1$ and removed at $t_2$. The OFF period of the clock should be so selected that it is long enough for the device to put the data on the bus, data to propagate to the receiver, and be read by the receiver. This choice should not be unusually large, otherwise the frequency of data transfer will be reduced. If a wide variety of devices with differing speeds is used, the period will be selected to meet the needs of the slowest device.

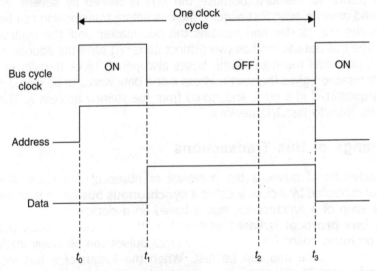

**Figure 12.23  Events represented as a timing diagram (synchronous data transfer—input).**

## Asynchronous Transfer

Consider two finite state machines communicating with each other in such a way that one does not proceed until it knows that the other has reached a *certain* state. This handshaking is achieved by following a well-defined *protocol* in the execution of both machines. As an example, let us consider the CPU and I/O as two machines and let us say that the CPU wants to read a data unit (byte or word) from the I/O.

In Figure 12.24 we have shown the sequence of 7 events marked 1 to 7 that take place during asynchronous read. The two vertical lines denote the time as it progresses in the two machines. A directed horizontal line denotes the occurrence of an event in one machine and its communication to the other machine. Note that zero slope horizontal line implies, zero propagation delay. The events (Figure 12.24) are:

1. CPU being the bus master sends the address of the device on the address lines.
2. After a delay D1 it sends the READY signal for accepting data.
3. The I/O unit receives the READY signal, notifies the acceptance for data transfer and transmits data.
4. The CPU reads data.
5. The READY signal is removed to indicate that the data is read.
6. The CPU de-asserts the address lines indicating the end of the cycle.
7. The I/O acknowledges the receipt of the signal by de-asserting ACCEPT and DATA lines.

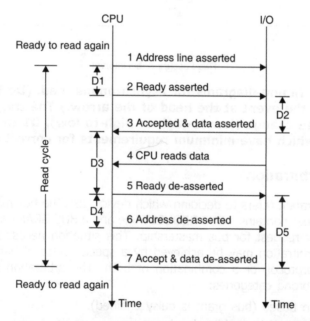

**Figure 12.24 Event sequence diagram showing the handshake protocol for read (D1 to D5 are delays; 1 to 7 are events).**

In practice it is unrealistic to assume zero delay. Delays occur due to bus skew, interface circuits, etc. In Figure 12.25 we have taken into account delays. The events and delays are shown in the form of a timing diagram. The events are represented by the rising or falling edges of the timing pulses. The "read data" strobing occurs during the time interval D3 as shown in the last line in the figure.

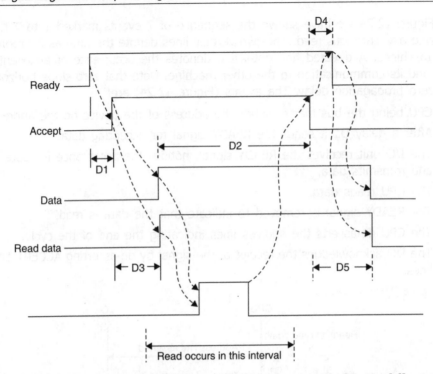

**Figure 12.25 Timing diagrams for asynchronous read. (Dotted line arrow means trigger the event at the head of the arrow.) The triggered event is simply a state change (low-to-high or high-to-low). D1 to D5 are time intervals which have minimum requirements for correct operation.**

## 12.9.5 Bus Arbitration

The term *bus arbitration* refers to deciding which device gets the bus mastership next. The set of bus control lines contains a BUS REQUEST line and a BUS GRANT line. Several devices may simultaneously request for bus mastership. This situation necessitates an arbitration mechanism. The arbitration may be achieved by a special piece of hardware or by using a bus arbitration protocol, or a combination of both. The arbitration techniques can be divided into three broad categories:

1. Daisy chain based (bus grant is daisy chained).
2. Based on central bus-arbiter hardware.
3. Distributed arbitration scheme based on a protocol.

We have described the *daisy chain* concept in an earlier section. The same concept is applicable here with respect to giving the BUS-GRANT line to one of the "daisy chain" contenders. In order to deal with the request and grant lines, we need a *bus controller* hardware unit. All the bus-request lines from the various devices will be connected to this controller. In the case of the *centralized-arbiter* scheme, the bus controller is the sole arbiter. It receives the bus requests, perhaps through a set of multiple and parallel request lines. According to some priority, it determines who gets the bus next and gives the bus mastership to that device. In both these methods, if the central unit (arbiter or bus controller) fails, the bus operation fails. Thus, the reliability of the bus system depends on the reliability of the central unit.

The distributed arbitration scheme can be divided into two categories, one category based on pre-assigned priorities and the other on collision detection. In the first case, each device that is capable of becoming a bus master is assigned a priority code. Lower priority codes will be lower in binary value. For example, in a group of 4 devices, the highest priority device may be assigned the code 1000 and the next successive priority devices codes 0100, 0010 and 0001 respectively. When a device requests for the bus-mastership, it posts its code onto a set of *bus-arbitration* lines that are shared by all the devices. If there are multiple codes posted, the design is such that the code values will be ORed. After placing its code on the arbitration lines, the device compares the bit values on the lines with its own code in order to decide if any other device with higher priority is requesting the bus. If yes, the device will *back-out* and request for the bus at a later time.

The distributed arbitration scheme based on collision detection is commonly known as CSMA/CD (CS-carrier sense; MA-multiple access; CD-collision detection). This is the protocol used by Ethernet a Local Area Network. We will discuss this scheme in detail in Section 12.12.

The choice or design of a bus will depend on several factors. We list them below.

1. The number of devices, connected to the bus, their speed or bandwidth and the range of their speeds.
2. Desired bus protocol (synchronous—simple, higher speeds, but accommodates low range of speeds; asynchronous—allows wide range, relatively slow, need to support handshaking).
3. Desired bus organization (bus width or the number of address lines, data lines, control lines, single bus master or more).
4. Desired bus arbitration scheme (centralized, or distributed).
5. Required bus bandwidth.
6. Cost (bus cost must be commensurate with the cost of the total computer system).

## 12.10  SOME STANDARD BUSES

Over the years many standards for buses have been proposed and used. As technology of processors, memory and I/O devices have evolved so have buses. Intel designed a bus called **PCI bus** (Peripheral Component Interconnect bus) for Pentium-based systems. To proliferate use of this bus they developed several VLSI chips to support several configurations of processors, memory and peripherals. Further, they made the specifications of the bus public knowledge and made it available to peripheral developers and chip designers. They also developed chips to connect this bus to older buses and systems. These decisions made PCI bus popular and currently it has become a standard used by several manufacturers.

PCI bus standard allows 32 or 64 bits for data or address lines. These lines are multiplexed for data/address. The standard specifies a synchronous-clocked bus with a clock speed up to 66 MHz. Thus the raw data transfer rate is $66 \times 64 \times 10^6 = 4.224$ Gbps. The other major characteristics of PCI bus are:

1. Multiplexed data and address
2. Centralized arbitration
3. Transaction types allowed: read, write, burst transfer
4. Error detection with parity bit

The details of the number and purpose of PCI bus lines is given in Table 12.1.

**TABLE 12.1**

**PCI Bus Lines and Their Purpose**

| Purpose of lines | Number of lines | Remarks |
|---|---|---|
| Data and Address | 64 | 32 mandatory<br>64 optional<br>Multiplexed |
| System | 2 | Clock and Reset |
| Interface control | 6 | Control and timing of transactions. Coordination |
| Arbitration | 4 | Centralized arbitration. Bus request and grant lines 2 extra for 64-bit transfer requests. |
| Error reporting | 2 | Parity and system error<br>2 optional for 64-bit data |
| Multiplexing commands | 8 | 1 bit/byte indicating which bytes carry meaningful data |
| Interrupt commands | 4 | Used by PCI devices that must request for service |
| Cache support | 2 | To support memory on PCI which can be cached |
| Testing bus | 4 | Optional—uses IEEE Standard 1149.1 |

The standard has 49 mandatory lines primarily for supporting 32-bit data and address and 50 optional lines to support 64-bit address and data version.

In Figure 12.26 we show a typical configuration of a desktop system using a PCI bus. Observe that the system shown is a two-bus system. The CPU-main memory bus is a proprietary high speed bus to support fast CPUs and memory. As CPU speeds increase, this bus can be improved. This bus is connected to the PCI bus by an integrated circuit called **PCI bridge**. High speed devices such as graphics board and high speed disks with SCSI controllers are directly connected to the bus. Another integrated circuit called **ISA bridge** connects devices supported on the ISA bus to PCI bus. The ISA (Industry Standard Architecture) bus was the previous standard used by personal computer manufacturers.

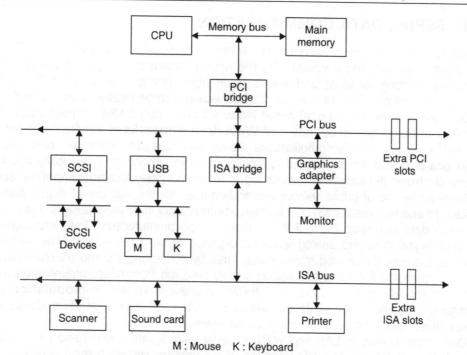

**Figure 12.26   Bus architecture (using PCI bus) of Intel Pentium based desktop computers.**

Thus ISA bus is useful to permit connecting older peripherals to the new PCI bus. Another innovation is an adapter to connect devices using **Universal Serial Bus** (USB). USB is a standard evolved by industry group to allow connecting lower speed I/O devices such as mouse, keyboard, flash memory, etc. to the PC. We now briefly explain the USB interface. The USB standard is designed to allow the following:

1. Users to connect a new device with a standard socket while a computer is working. This is known as **hot pluggable**.
2. Recognition of a newly plugged device and allocate it an address.
3. The I/O devices on USB to get their power from the computer using one of the USB lines.
4. Up to 127 devices to be connected.
5. Support real time operation of devices such as a telephone.

The USB cable has four wires; two for data, one for power (+5v) and one for ground. The USB cable hub is connected to the PCI bus and a serial port is brought to the back of the PC cabinet. A device connected to PC via a USB in turn has some USB ports. This allows more devices to be daisy chained. The USB plug is standardized for easy plug and play.

## 12.11 SERIAL DATA COMMUNICATION

The widespread use of personal computers at homes and desktop computers in offices have created two important requirements: (1) the need to share resources (data, disk storage, high quality printing facilities) and access them from remote sites and (2) the need for computer *networking*. Computer networks connecting people located within a radius of a few kilometres are known as **Local Areal Networks** or simply **LANs**. Computers all around the globe can be connected by means of **Wide Area Networks** or **WANs**. Such networks are used for several end-user applications. Some examples are: electronic mail, electronic bulletin boards, computer-supported collaborative work among geographically distributed workers, electronic file transfers, remote log-in to use remotely located computing facilities, etc. WANs make use of public *telecommunication* lines for the transfer of digital data from one place to another. Historically, public telecommunication lines were designed primarily to carry voice data in *analog form*. But the modern telecommunication lines are digital and carry both digital data and analog voice (in digitized form, if necessary). The digital data can be carried over the analog transmission lines by converting 1's and 0's transmitted by computers to analog form and the analog signals received from telecommunication lines to 1's and 0's for use by computers. The former process is known as **modulation** (while transmitting) and the latter as **demodulation** (while receiving). A physical device which achieves these two processes is known as **modem**.

Data transmission, in LAN and WAN, is serial as it is rather expensive to run parallel lines over long distances. The I/O interface of a computer system transmits or receives 8 bits or 32 bits at a time (see PCI bus for examples). Thus, it is necessary to group 8 bits arriving serially and present them as parallel inputs to a computer and serialize the output of a computer for transmission. Specialized integrated circuit chips are available to perform serial-to-parallel or parallel-to-serial conversions. As serial communication is very slow (in comparison to the CPU speed), asynchronous mode is used for serial communication. In the following paragraphs we describe an IC-chip known as Asynchronous Communication Interface Adapter (ACIA) and the concepts involved in the operation of a modem. We will first describe the nature of an asynchronous serial data communication.

### 12.11.1 Asynchronous Serial Data Communication

In asynchronous transmission there is no clock to time bits. Thus, for each frame of 8 bits there must be a special start bit to signal its start and a stop bit to indicate the end. A parity bit (either odd or even) may be appended as a ninth bit as an optional bit. The time-interval between successive bytes is arbitrary. The receiver must know the configuration of the frame and the speed at which bits are being transmitted. In Figure 12.27 we show an asynchronous data frame.

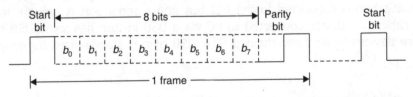

**Figure 12.27 An asynchronous serial communication bits.**

## 12.11.2 Asynchronous Communication Interface Adapter (ACIA)

Many I/O units such as keyboards accept and send data only serially. The data bus of a microprocessor has a width of 8 or 16 bits and receives and transmits data of 8 or 16 bits in parallel. Thus, an interface circuit is needed which would receive serial data from serial devices, assemble groups of 8 or 16 bits and send them in parallel to the CPU. In the output mode the interface should accept 8 bits in parallel from the CPU, store the bits in a register and send them serially to the I/O device at a rate determined by the I/O device. Chips for this serial to parallel and parallel to serial conversion and synchronization are marketed by microprocessor manufacturers. The chip marketed by INTEL Corporation is called UART chip and Motorola has a chip which it calls asynchronous communication interface adapter (ACIA). Figure 12.28 gives the functional characteristics of such a chip. As seen from this figure the chip has two logical parts, the receiver part and the transmitter part. The receiver part receives a series of bits serially at a predetermined rate called the **bit rate** (bits per second). A clock at a frequency equal to the bit rate synchronizes the received bits. The receiver recognizes the start and stop bits sent by the input peripheral unit, strips them, and checks whether the parity of the received group of bits is correct. If parity fails, an error indicator is set. If parity is correct, then the information bits are stored in a buffer register. The buffer register usually stores a byte. As soon as the buffer is full an indicator is set to inform the processor that the data is ready. The processor can interrogate the indicator and then receive the 8-bit data via the data bus.

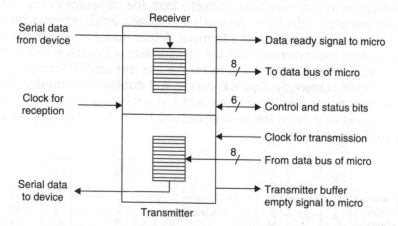

**Figure 12.28  Functional diagram of asynchronous communication interface adapter (ACIA).**

The transmitter part of the chip performs the following functions:

1. Receives 8 bits in parallel from the processor and stores them in a buffer register.
2. It prefixes a start bit to the group of 8 bits, shifts the 8 bits from the buffer at a preassigned clock rate, generates and appends a parity bit and follows this with stop bit. These bits are sent out serially via an output port.
3. When the buffer is emptied and serialized, an indicator is set to inform the processor that the buffer is empty.

When the processor wants to send out a word, it reads the status register (e.g., by polling) to check whether the transmit buffer register is empty. If empty, then the processor sends the 8 bits to the interface adapter and continues with its program. The interface adapter serializes and sends the data on the output line. If the buffer is full, processor must wait by either looping or by jumping to another part of the program and returning when the transmit buffer is empty.

We have not given in detail all the error controls performed by the chip (which are extensive). Besides this, the chip can be programmed for different clock speeds and different byte sizes. The reader is urged to consult such details in the manufacturers' data sheets.

### 12.11.3   Digital Modems

Serial transmissions of data and programs to terminals situated at long distances through telephone lines is useful to time share computers, and for networking. Telephone links are designed to carry analog signals over a frequency range of 50 Hz to 3500 Hz. Thus, it is necessary to convert dc voltages corresponding to 0 and 1 to audio frequency signals. Usually two sine waves at two different frequencies are used to represent 0 and 1. This is known as frequency shift keying (FSK). Digital outputs from a computer are serialized by a device such as ACIA. The serial bits are *modulated* to signals at two frequencies, 1070 Hz for a 0 and 1270 Hz for a 1 and sent on the telephone line. At the receiving end these frequencies have to be converted back to 0 and 1. This is done by a *demodulator*. As we need communication in both directions, namely, from the computer to the I/O device and vice versa each end of the telephone line needs a modulator and a demodulator. Figure 12.29 shows a link between a computer and a terminal. A user normally logs on the terminal and requests service from the computer. Thus the terminal side of the link is called the **originate end** and the computer end of the link is called the **answer end**. Information is to be sent in both directions simultaneously. This is known as **full duplex communication**. To enable such a communication, the frequencies for 0 and 1 at originating end are chosen as 1070 Hz and 1270 Hz respectively. From the answer end the 0 and 1 are transmitted by signals of frequencies 2025 Hz and 2250 Hz.

**Figure 12.29   Use of modems with telephone lines.**

Devices to modulate 0 and 1 to sine waves and demodulate the received sine waves to 0 and 1 are known as modems. As modems are extensively used special IC chips are marketed to replace a large number of discrete circuit elements. These chips have the following functional characteristics:

1. Modulation of 0 and 1 to two audio frequencies and demodulation from two audio frequencies to 0 and 1.

2. Two sets of frequencies for the transmitting and the receiving ends to enable full duplex communication.

3. Flexibility to be used either at the originating or at the answering end.

4. With the method of using only two frequencies the speed of the modem will be limited as the bandwidth available on telephone lines is limited. Thus a method called **phase modulation** is used. In this method the phase of a sine wave is shifted by $\pi/4$, $3\pi/4$, $5\pi/4$ and $7\pi/4$ and each phase is used to represent 00, 01, 11, 10 of the input bit string. With this coding the bit rate is doubled. With 8 phase to represent 3 bits in the input the speed is tripled. In recently manufactured modems (2006) a standard known as V92, redundant bits are used to correct errors in data transmission together with data compression to obtain speeds of 56.6 Kbps on ordinary voice grade telephone lines.

5. Controls to allow automatic answering and disconnecting.

A block diagram of a modem is given in Figure 12.30.

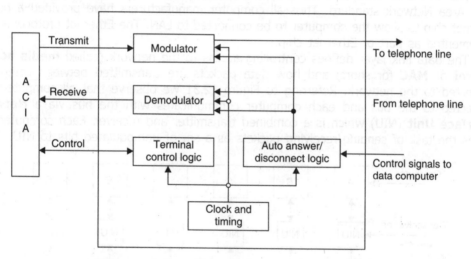

**Figure 12.30  Block diagram of a MODEM.**

## 12.12  LOCAL AREA NETWORKS

When computers located within a small geographical area such as an office or a university campus (within a radius of 10 km) are connected together we call it a Local Area Network (LAN).

There are four important aspects which characterize different types of LANs. They are as follows:

1. Topology of the networks, i.e. way in which the individual computers are interconnected.

2. The type of transmission medium used to interconnect the individual computers.

3. The protocol used to access the physical medium by a computer connected to a LAN. This is called **Media Access Control** (MAC).

4. How smaller LANs called **subnetworks** are interconnected to form a network encompassing the whole organization which may have thousands of computers.

There are two major topologies of connecting computers using Ethernet protocols. They are respectively; a bus structure (see Figure 12.31), a star interconnection (Figure 12.35). We will first describe the bus topology.

## 12.12.1 Ethernet Local Area Network—Bus Topology

Ethernet is a standard developed by Digital Equipment Corporation, Xerox and Intel for interconnecting computers within a small geographic area. This was later refined and standardized as IEEE standards 802. The original standard was for interconnection of computers using a bus. The physical layer was specified as a shielded coaxial cable supporting a data rate of 10 Mbps. Ethernet has advanced much beyond the earlier standard. Many versions have appeared and we will discuss them later in this section.

Due to the simplicity of Ethernet protocol and its flexibility, it is the most widely used Local Area Network standard. Thus all computer manufacturers have provided a built-in Ethernet chip to allow the computer to be connected to LAN. The Ethernet protocol is thus implemented as part of Ethernet chip.

The data link layer defines controlling access to the network (called **media access control** or **MAC** for short) and how data packets are transmitted between computers connected to the network. Referring to Figure 12.31 we observe that all computers are connected to the bus and each computer communicates with the bus via a **Network Interface Unit** (NIU) which is a combined transmitter and receiver. Each computer delegates the task of sending/receiving packets as a set of unmodulated bits to NIU.

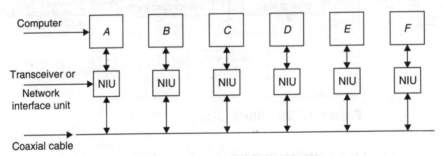

**Figure 12.31 An Ethernet LAN.**

Modulation is not necessary as the maximum length of the cable is small. Transmission of bits on the cable without modulation is known as **base band transmission**. Exchange of data between NIUs proceeds as per the following protocol. When a NIU wants to send data, its receiver listens to the bus to find out whether any signal is being transmitted on the bus. This is called **Carrier Sense** (CS). If no signal is detected, it transmits a data packet. As the bus is accessible to all NIUs connected to it, another NIU could also find no signal on the bus at that instant and try to transmit a packet. If both NIUs transmit a packet on the bus, then these packets will collide and both packets will be spoiled. Thus the receiver part of the transceiver of a NIU must listen to the bus for a minimum period $T$ to see if any collision has occurred. The period *T* is the time which the packet will take to reach the farthest NIU in the bus and return back to the sender. Collision is detected if the energy level of signal in the bus suddenly increases. Once a collision is detected, the NIU which detected the collision sends a *jamming* signal which is sensed by all other NIUs on the bus so that they do not try to transmit any packet. The NIU also stops transmitting and waits for a random time and retransmits the packet. As it waited for a random time the probability of another collision is low. If there is again a collision, it waits for double the previous random period and transmits. By experiments and analysis it is found that this method is quite effective and collisionless transmission will take place soon. This method of accessing the bus and transmitting packets is known as **Carrier Sense Multiple Access** with **Collision Detection** (CSMA/CD) system. It is called **Multiple Access** as any of the NIUs can try to send a packet on the bus or receive a packet from the bus. The protocol is explained in Figure 12.32 as a flow chart.

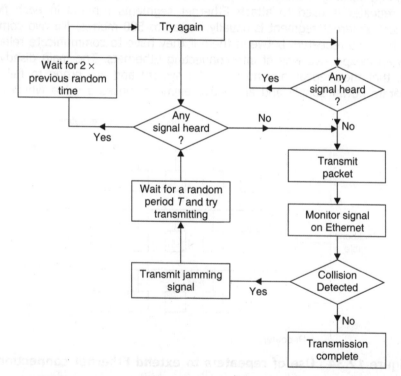

**Figure 12.32  CSMA/CD protocol used in Ethernet.**

The format of a packet consists of some bits for clock synchronization followed by the address of sender, address of the receiver, data packet and check bits (Figure 12.33). Ethernet is a broadcast medium. A packet sent by an NIU is monitored while it is in transit by all other NIUs on the bus and the NIU to which it is addressed receives the packet and stores it. Other NIUs ignore it. It is possible to *broadcast* a packet to all NIUs. A packet can also be *multicast,* that is, sent to a subset of NIUs.

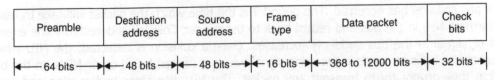

| Preamble | Destination address | Source address | Frame type | Data packet | Check bits |
|---|---|---|---|---|---|

|←—— 64 bits ——→|←— 48 bits —→|←— 48 bits —→|←— 16 bits —→|←— 368 to 12000 bits —→|←— 32 bits —→|

**Figure 12.33   The format of a frame or packet in Ethernet LAN.**

The length of the data packet is between 46 and 1500 bytes. The length is based on the length of the bus and the number of NIUs connected to the bus. Currently Ethernet is one of the most popular Local Area Network protocols used as it is well proven, standardized and supported by all vendors of computers.

Ethernet may be extended using a hardware unit called **repeater**. A repeater reshapes and amplifies the signal and relays it from one Ethernet segment to another. A typical use of repeaters in a building is shown in Figure 12.34. A backbone cable runs vertically up the building. A repeater is used to attach Ethernet segments running in each floor to the backbone. Each Ethernet segment is usually limited to 500 metres. No two computers can have more than two repeaters between them if they have to communicate reliably. Use of repeaters is an inexpensive way of interconnecting Ethernets. The main disadvantages of repeaters is that they repeat any noise in the system and are prone to failure as they require separate power supply and are active elements unlike a cable which is passive.

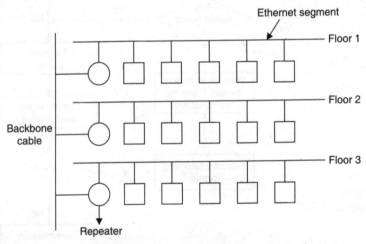

**Figure 12.34   Use of repeaters to extend Ethernet connection.**

## Transmission media

Recently several options have emerged for the physical layer of Ethernet. The first standard using a coaxial cable is called **10 Base 5 Ethernet**. The number 10 stands for Mbps, BASE indicates base band transmission and 5 stands for a coaxial cable with 50 ohm impedance. A cheaper version is called **10 Base 2** where the coaxial cable is thinner and cheaper. It is also known as **thin-wire Ethernet**. This Ethernet supports a fewer computers over a shorter distance compared to the Ethernet standard (see Table 12.2).

**TABLE 12.2**

**Physical Wiring of Ethernet**

| Type of Wiring | IEEE Standard | Maximum cable length (metres) | Topology |
|---|---|---|---|
| Shielded coaxial cable RG-8u (Thicknet) | 10 Base 5 | 500 | Bus |
| Shielded coaxial cable RG-8u (Thinnet) | 10 Base 2 | 185 | Bus |
| Unshielded twisted pair (telephone cable) | 10 Base T | 100 | Star with hub |
| Unshielded cat 3 twisted pair | 100 Base T | 100 | Star with hub |

## 12.12.2 Ethernet Using Star Topology

A star topology for interconnecting computers which logically follows the same principle for media access as a bus-based Ethernet has now become the preferred method for LANs. The topology is shown in Figure 12.35. The physical transmission medium used is unshielded

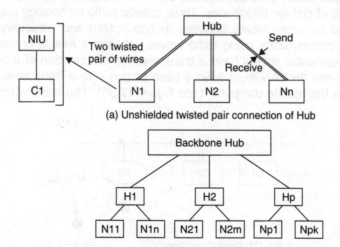

(a) Unshielded twisted pair connection of Hub

**Figure 12.35  Ethernet using unshielded twisted pair of wires and hub.**

twisted pair of copper wires normally used in telephone networks. This is called **10 Base T**. In this topology each node (i.e., a computer with an NIU) is connected to a central *hub* using twisted pair of wires (see Figure 12.35(a)). The hub has electronic circuits which receive signals from the twisted pair connected to it, amplifies and reshapes it and broadcasts it to all the other connections. The protocol is the same as Ethernet, namely, (CSMA/CD). The hub detects collisions and sends this information to all the nodes connected to it. Each hub can normally handle up to 16 nodes. (This number is increasing with improvements in technology.) The distance between a node and hub must be less than 100 metres. The main advantage of this type of connection compared to cable connection is higher reliability and ease of trouble shooting. Unlike a cable connection where if there is a fault in cable all nodes are affected and troubleshooting is time consuming, in a hub connection, if a node fails it can be isolated and repaired while other nodes work. Other advantages are that most buildings are wired with twisted pair telephone lines and it is easy to connect them to hub. Hub-based wiring is much more flexible compared to cable wiring. Adding new computers to the LAN is easy. If the capacity of hub is exhausted more hubs may be used as shown in Figure 12.35(b). Currently 100 Base T, Local Area Networks (100 Mbps) using CAT3 unshielded twisted pairs UTP and gigabit Ethernet LANs using fibre optic cables are available.

### 12.12.3  Wireless LAN

The use of wireless media to transmit digital information started in the late 1960s with the ALOHA Project at the University of Hawaii. The motivation was the requirement of communication between computers located in a number of scattered islands of Hawaii. ALOHA network which was set up used an early version of CSMA protocol. The situation changed dramatically in the 1990s with the emergence of portable computers and better wireless technology. Executives moving around with their laptops wanted to be connected to the computers in their organizations to look at their email and retrieve information from databases and also send email, purchase orders, etc. Wireless technology also improved leading to widespread use of cellular telephones. Thus, cellular radio technology used by telephones has been adopted to communicate between mobile laptops and stationary local networks.

In order to communicate using radio waves between a mobile computer and a fixed LAN, the mobile computer should have a transceiver (a combination of a wireless transmitter and receiver) and the LAN must have a base station with a transceiver to transmit and receive data from the mobile computer (see Figure 12.36). The transmitter uses frequency

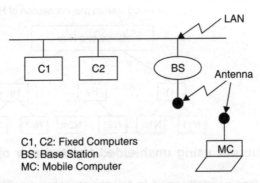

C1, C2: Fixed Computers
BS: Base Station
MC: Mobile Computer

**Figure 12.36  Wireless communication with LAN.**

in the so-called unlicensed band (2.4 MHz) which is not used for commercial radio and other purposes. The power should be low to avoid interference with other transmitters. This technology currently provides a peak bandwidth in the range of 1 to 11 Mbps.

Early systems used *narrowband* technology in which a low power carrier signal was modulated by digital data using amplitude modulation. It was necessary for the transmitter power to be low to avoid interference with other systems using this frequency. It was thus affected by noise and special coding methods and error detection/correction algorithms were implemented. To reduce error while maintaining low power transmission, a newer method called **spread spectrum** is now being used. In this method the input signal is transmitted (at a low power level) over a broad range of frequencies. This spreading of frequencies reduces the probability of jamming of the signal and makes it difficult for unauthorized persons to acquire and interpret data. Thus it is more reliable and secure.

There are three standards for wireless connection which are currently prevalent. They are IEEE 802.11a which works at 5.4 GHz and gives data rates of up to 54 Mbps; IEEE 802.11b which works at 2.4 GHz band and gives a data rate up to 11 Mbps and IEEE 802.11g which is just now emerging and works at 2.4 GHz and a data rate of 54 Mbps. As equipment at 5.4 GHz is expensive, IEEE 802.11b is more popular. Both 2.4 GHz and 5.4 GHz band are so called "free" or unlicensed wireless bands in USA. Only 2.4 GHz is currently a free band in Europe, Japan and India. Normally a wireless transmitter/receiver in a fixed spot (called **wireless hotspot**) is connected to a wired backbone (such as Ethernet LAN). This hotspot is accessed from a mobile computer. In 2003, Intel announced a new processor called Centrino which has Pentium IV architecture with built-in wireless interface using IEEE 802.11b standard. Thus, a mobile laptop with Centrino chip can access hotspots maintained by ISPs at airports, hotels and many public places. This is the most common use as of now. IEEE 802.11g standard is now becoming popular as it gives a higher speed of up to 54 Mbps.

## 12.12.4   Client-Server Computing Using LAN

We described I/O processor organization in Section 12.8. That organization is primarily used in mainframe computers where the CPU is very powerful and expensive. With the proliferation of powerful desktop computers and rapid reduction of the cost of microprocessors, the scenario has changed. I/O systems such as high speed laser printers, large RAID systems, etc. cost more than 10 times the cost of a desktop processor. Thus, we have now an additional method of catering to I/O requests. This method of performing I/O consists of one or more client computers connected to a LAN to which are also connected several server computers (see Figure 12.37). Clients request services such as printing and access to large files which are provided by servers. Servers are full-fledged computers and are programmed to cater to requests coming from several clients, queue them, and carry them out. For example, a print request will be accompanied by a file to be printed which will be transmitted by the LAN, received by the server and queued along with other requests. A specialized print program stored in the server will print the file. Observe that a client having delegated the print job proceeds with the rest of its computing.

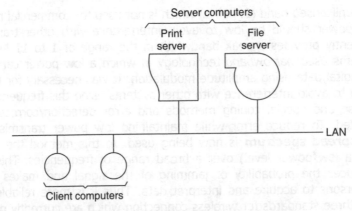

**Figure 12.37   Client-server computing.**

───────────────────────────── **SUMMARY** ─────────────────────────────

1. I/O Systems organization deals with methods of connecting I/O devices to the CPU-memory system of a computer.

2. The major challenge in I/O organization arises due to the fact that there is a large variety of I/O devices which vary in their speeds and data formatting.

3. To provide uniform I/O access each I/O device has a controller which is device dependent. This is connected to an I/O interface unit which has a uniform logical structure independent of devices' specific characteristics.

4. The speed of data transfer from an I/O device is at least 1000 times slower than CPU speed. Thus I/O transfer methods are required which reduce the impact of this speed mismatch on a computer's performance.

5. There are three methods used to transfer data to/from I/O devices to the main memory. They are: (i) program controlled data transfer, (ii) interrupt controlled data transfer and (iii) DMA based data transfer.

6. In program controlled data transfer the CPU after sending an I/O request is idle till I/O transfer begins at which stage it transfers data to or from the main memory. This method wastes CPU time.

7. In interrupt controlled I/O the CPU issues the command to the I/O interface unit and continues with the program being executed. When I/O data is ready the I/O interface unit sends an interrupt signal to CPU informing it that I/O is ready to transmit/receive data. CPU suspends its current activity and attends to I/O using an I/O procedure which sends/receives data to/from main memory. CPU idle time is thus reduced or eliminated.

8. In a DMA based I/O, a special unit called Direct Memory Access controller is used as an intermediary between the I/O interface unit and the main memory. The CPU after

issuing the I/O command proceeds with its activity. When I/O is ready, it requests CPU to yield the data and address buses for use by DMA controller. The DMA controller now directly sends/receives data to/from main memory. CPU has no role to play in data transfer other than yielding the buses.

9. As computers have several I/O devices, more than one device may need to transact I/O simultaneously. Thus they should be attended one by one based on their priority. Either software or hardware methods are used to assign priorities to devices and give them access to the main memory.

10. Some computers have separate I/O processors to which the CPU delegates I/O. I/O processors have a specialized instruction set to perform efficient I/O. They work in parallel with the main CPU and perform I/O using DMA mode.

11. The main units of a computer, namely, CPU, memory and I/O are interconnected with buses. A set of parallel wires which carries a group of bits in parallel and has an associated control scheme is called a bus.

12. A bus called Peripheral Component Interconnect (PCI) bus has been standardized by industry for higher speed Pentium class of computers. In this class of computers an internal bus connects the CPU to main memory. PCI bus is attached to this bus using a special IC chip. All I/O interface units of fast peripherals are connected to PCI bus. To allow older I/O devices (used with Intel 80486, etc.) to be used, the PCI bus is connected with a special chip to the ISA bus used by the older I/O devices. Another bus called Universal Serial Bus (USB) is connected to PCI bus. USB is standardized for use with slow and cheaper I/O devices such as keyboard, mouse, etc.

13. To carry out transactions on buses specially designed timing signals are needed which are discussed in detail in the text.

14. The lengths of buses are limited to tens of centimetres because in buses the number of parallel lines are large and their capacitance increases with length affecting their speed. Thus to connect a computer to a terminal or another computer a few metres away we use standard telephone lines (such as twisted pair of wires) which carry bits serially. An IC chip called Asynchronous Communication Interface Adapter (ACIA) is designed to take a byte (8 bits) appearing in parallel and convert it to serial data and vice versa.

15. When serial digital data is to be transmitted using the telephone lines provided by a Public Switch and Telephone Network (PSTN), we need a device called a modem because PSTNs are designed to transmit analog telephone conversation whose frequency in the band 50 Hz to 3500 Hz and not digital data. A modem converts 1's and 0's to two distinct sinusoidal signals of frequency in the 1000 Hz range to 2000 Hz.

16. To increase the speed of transmission via modems serial data is grouped (3 bits) per group. Each group is represented by a single sine wave with a phase shift of $\pi/8$. This is called Phase Shift Keying . PSK signals can be transmitted at a higher speed.

17. Computers located within a small geographical area may be connected to constitute a Local Area Network (LAN).

18. Ethernet is a very popular LAN. Ethernet uses a multidrop coaxial cable or unshielded twisted pair of wires to interconnect computers. Speeds of 10 to 100 Mbps are

supported by Ethernet. Ethernet uses a protocol called CSMA/CD (Carrier Sense Multiple Access with collision detection) to communicate between any two computers connected to it.

19. Earlier Ethernets used coaxial cable to interconnect machines. With coaxial cables it is difficult to add new computers to the network and also to troubleshoot if there is any problem in the LAN. Nowadays individual computers are connected using unshielded twisted pair of wires to a hub as a star connection. The hub is an electronic circuit which helps in implementing Ethernet protocol in such a LAN.

20. Communication between a mobile computer (such as a laptop) and computers on a LAN is established by using wireless communication. Wireless transceivers are added to a mobile computer. A wireless transceiver is connected to the LAN as a base station. Mobile machines establish communication to computers on the LAN via the base station. The protocol used is Ethernet protocol. 2.4 GHz wireless band is used. IEEE standard 802.11b with a data rate of 11 Mbps and IEEE 802.11g, a data rate of 54 Mbps are currently prevalent.

---

## EXERCISES

1. (i) Add instructions to SMAC++ to enable it to use the program controlled transfer to transfer a word from an I/O buffer register to a specified location in memory.

   (ii) Use these instructions in an illustrative machine language program.

2. Make a comparative chart comparing the hardware and software features of programmed information transfer, interrupt based information transfer and DMA information transfer.

3. Distinguish between traps and external interrupts. What are the major differences in handling these in a computer system?

4. A DMA interface receives 8-bit bytes from a peripheral, packs them in a 48-bit word and stores the word in memory. Draw a block diagram of the DMA registers and obtain a sequence of microoperations of the DMA.

5. Draw a comparative chart showing the differences between the five methods of servicing interrupts discussed in Section 12.6.

6. Draw a priority logic and encoder for an interrupt with six interrupt sources.

7. Enumerate the programming steps necessary in order to check when a device interrupts the computer while it is serving the previous interrupt from the same device.

8. Give the steps which would be taken by an I/O processor that byte multiplexes one high speed device which can transfer 4 bytes in parallel in 500ns (once every 0.5 microseconds), with 10 low speed devices that can each transfer 1 byte in 5 μs (once every 100 μs).

9. For a Pentium V based desktop PC find out the following:

   (i) Peripheral devices attached to the computer.

   (ii) How is each peripheral device logically connected to the computer?

(iii) How is the information represented and coded in the peripheral device?

(iv) What is the speed of data transfer from the peripheral device to the computer's memory?

**10.** In a LAN used at your institution find out the following:

(i) How many computers are connected to the LAN?

(ii) What is the distance between the farthest computers connected to the LAN?

(iii) How is each computer logically connected to the LAN? Is it a hub? If it is a hub, how many computers are connected to a Hub?

(iv) If any modems are used what are their characteristics?

**11.** Observe that in Figure 12.20 giving interconnections between DMA controller, CPU and Memory the R and W control lines are bi-directional.

(i) Why are bi-directional lines used?

(ii) When does read signal go to DMA and when does it go to Memory?

(iii) When does the DMA controller send write signal to memory?

**12.** A disk sector with 512 bytes are to be sent to the main memory starting in address 258. The computer is byte addressable.

(i) What information is to be sent by CPU to the DMA controller when it initiates a read command?

(iii) Draw a flow chart explaining how the sector is stored in the main memory.

**13.** In Figure 12.13 we have shown daisy chaining of devices which interrupt a CPU. Assume that $D2$ interrupts CPU at $t_1$ and INTA signal comes at $t_2 > t_1$. If $D1$ interrupts before INTA is initiated by CPU, which device will be attended? If $D1$ interrupts after INTA reaches $D2$, which device will be attended by CPU?

**14.** A message ABRACADABRA is sent from a keyboard to be stored in main memory. Which method of data transfer will be appropriate and why? If it is interrupt controlled, how many times will the CPU be interrupted?

**15.** Assume a computer uses software to assign priority to devices. Explain how interrupt servicing programs assign priorities. Draw a flow chart to explain priority interrupt servicing.

**16.** Is DMA given higher priority to access the main memory of a computer compared to CPU? If so why?

**17.** A DMA device transmits data at the rate of 16 KB/s a byte at a time to the main memory by cycle stealing. CPU speed is 100 mps (million instructions per second). By how much is CPU slowed down due to DMA?

**18.** In exercise 17 assume interrupt controlled data transfer is used. An interrupt processing program needs 50 machine instructions. Estimate by how much CPU is slowed down due to data input.

# 13

# Case Study of a Real Computer System

---

## Learning Goals

In this chapter we will learn:

☞ How to put the various concepts learnt in previous chapters in perspective.

☞ How a real computer system is organized.

☞ How to integrate the various components into a system.

☞ About Pentium-based computer system.

## 13.1 INTRODUCTION

Intel's Pentium is one of the latest microprocessors that has been successfully integrated into millions of computers all over the world. The heart of a computer is its processor, but the processor alone does not make a computer. The various subsystems such as CPU, memory, disks, and I/O devices are interconnected by a collection of low speed and high speed buses. The functions of the various subsystems are coordinated by means of their "controllers" and the operating system or OS. Memory controller, disk controller, video display controller, bus controller and I/O controllers are some examples. The hardware manufacturers develop specialized VLSI chips or chip-sets for interconnection of these devices to the bus and for integration into a full-fledged computer system. In the industry, several standards are constantly evolved so that computer designers can integrate products from different vendors in a compatible manner into a single system. Hardware of a computer system is only part of the whole. Without the software and the OS, the system is not readily usable. However, in this chapter we will restrict our discussions primarily to the system hardware aspects.

## 13.2   VIEWING PENTIUM AS A MEMBER OF A FAMILY OF COMPUTERS

Pentium is one member of a family of processors designed, developed and marketed by the Intel Corporation. The underlying hardware architecture is called IA-32 architecture which includes both 16-bit and 32-bit processors. Ever since the first microprocessors were introduced as Intel 4004 in 1969 which was a 4-bit processor, developments in microprocessors have grown steadily in many ways. The 4-bit processors became 8-bit processors, 16-bits, 32-bits and so on. Intel 8086 was one of the successful microprocessors. It was followed by other processors such 80186, 80286, 80386, 80486, Pentium and then Xeon. Professional applications developers have invested large amount of effort and money in developing software for a variety of applications and used the computers based on such processors in thousands of applications. As new processors were introduced into the market as technology advanced, Intel realized that it is essential that the software developed for earlier processors in the sequence must run on the newer processors. This is known as **backward compatibility**. Otherwise, the large investments on software would be wasted and people will be reluctant to move and use new advanced processors.

Intel 8086 had 16-bit registers and 16-bit data bus external to the processor, and Intel 386 was the first 32-bit processor in the family. The 8086 memory is organized into segments of 64 KB ($2^{16}$) and 4-segment registers are used to point to four different segments giving a total of 256 KB addressability. This is much smaller when compared to that of the Pentium. In 8086, they used a unique way of combining the 16-bit segment register pointer and the 16-bit address to give a 20-bit effective address which gave 1-MB address space. As the number of applications and the complexity of the operating system grew, 16-bit registers and 1 MB address space proved to be inadequate. The Intel 386 introduced 32-bit registers, 32-bit instructions and operands, 32-bit bus, and an ability to support 4-GB address space with its 32-bit effective memory address. The lower half of the 32-bit register retained the properties of the earlier 16-bit processors. A new mode of operation called **virtual-8086** was introduced in which the programs written for earlier 16-bit computers could run on the 32-bit processor more efficiently. The IA-32 architecture and Intel 386 as its member introduced several features to support the development of good quality operating systems. These features include: memory protection, paging support (4 KB fixed page size) and a large address space. The paging was transparent to programmers.

The term *micro-architecture* is used to refer to the hardware details at the microprogramming level where one is concerned about how every machine instruction is realized or interpreted in terms of micro-level operations in the hardware circuitry. Advances in fabrication technologies of the VLSI and parallel processing are used by the manufacturers to produce faster and high performance processors. In the IA-32 architecture, parallel processing is introduced in six different stages: bus interface unit accessing memory and I/O, the code pre-fetch unit which brings the instruction in advance and puts it in a 16-byte long queue, instruction decode unit, instruction execution unit, the segmentation unit which translates the logical address given in a program to a linear address and performs memory address protection checks, and finally in the paging unit which translates the linear address into the physical address, performs page protection checks and makes use of the hardware cache.

The Intel 486 processor introduced pipelining in the execution stage to support temporal parallel execution. A five stage pipeline was used with the aim of executing one instruction per clock cycle which is called **scalar performance**. In order to support such high speed execution and parallelism, Intel 486 introduced an 8-KB on-chip first level or L1 cache. Also this processor, for the first time integrated the floating point arithmetic unit on to the same processor chip. This could be achieved because of the fact that the fabrication technology by then had vastly improved to accommodate more gates per unit area of the chip than ever before.

The Intel Pentium introduced several more improvements to achieve super scalar performance. It introduced two pipelines instead of one. The on-chip first level cache was doubled from 4 KB to 8 KB and two separate caches were introduced, one for instruction and another for data. Cache consistency was assured in an efficient manner by means of special protocols; branch-prediction was added in the hardware to obtain better performance in the execution of program loops. An advanced programmable interrupt controller was added to facilitate computer system design with multiple Pentium processors. In a notable processor in the Pentium series Intel introduced, a special technology known as MMX technology. In **MMX technology**, single-instruction multiple-data stream (SIMD) type of parallelism was incorporated to perform parallel computations. Such computations performed on the packed decimal data types facilitated image processing, data compression and advanced media type data processing. Several versions of Pentium with different improvements have been introduced. The Intel Pentium 4, for example, added features to support multimedia applications ranging from 3 dimensional graphics, video encoding and decoding and speech applications. The Xeon processor is also based on the IA-32 architecture and it is based on the advanced micro-architecture called **NetBurst** micro-architecture which is designed to suit the needs of high performance workstations and server systems in client-server computing and web applications. The technological developments do not stop. At the same time, people are careful in system design so that the rapid changes and developments brought from technological innovations do not invalidate the efforts invested in the software application development.

## 13.3  MEMORY SYSTEM VIEW

The memory system and addressing the memory constitute the central features in a computer system. In this section we provide a brief overview of the memory and its addressing for Intel processor-based computer systems. The terms *physical memory* that is connected to the bus of a computer system and *physical address* refer to the hardware level of the memory system. The physical address ranges from 0 to ($2^{32} - 1$) that is 4 GB. Every byte has its own address. The physical memory is addressed through a "memory management system" that is a hardware unit which maps the virtual addresses into a physical address. This unit ensures efficient and reliable access to memory. In this case, the memory management unit includes segmentation and paging. The addresses generated by a program are called **logical addresses** and they are in the segmented address space. For safe operation, the address space is segmented into data segment, code segment, stack segment, etc. Segmentation hardware translates a logical address into a linear address. The paging hardware translates a linear address into a physical address which is then used by the memory hardware to access a memory location. Paging is a mechanism which supports a large "virtual address space in RAM" using a comparatively small amount of RAM and a large disk storage.

In the segmented model of memory, the logical address space is divided into segments (see Figure 13.1). For example, a program code can be put into a separate segment other than its data so that the two are kept separate. In the figure we have shown, the logical view of three segments, namely, code, data and stack. They are of different lengths and their length can be defined by the programmer as needed. In the physical memory reside several such segments and one of them in "each category" (code, data, stack, etc) will be the current segment. A logical address in the program is specified as a pair, the segment base and a 32-bit long offset value. A segment length can vary to a maximum of $2^{32}$ bytes. Each segment has a segment descriptor which contains the base or starting address of the segment in the physical memory and the segment size in bytes. A 16-bit segment selector is contained in the segment register. There are six segment registers: CS (code), DS (data), SS (stack), ES, FS, and GS (for other data types). The segment selector, loaded into the segment register, automatically selects one of the possibly many segments. The offset value is added to the base address to get the linear address.

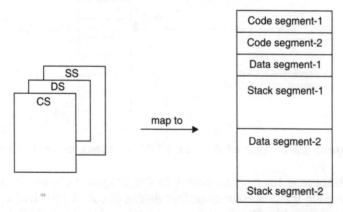

**Figure 13.1  Segmental view of memory in Pentium.**

Memory is addressed in units of bytes. Both data and instructions are stored in memory. Instructions vary in length and so also do data. The principal data types are: byte, word (2 bytes), double word (4 bytes) and quad word (8 bytes). Consecutive memory locations are used to store a data item. A word, for example, has two bytes: low order byte or the least significant 8 bits and high order byte. The low order byte is stored in the lower memory address (say *n*) and the high order byte is stored in the consecutively higher address in memory (*n* + 1). The low order byte of a word can be at any memory address and does not have to be aligned at an even or odd address. This applies to all data types.

Stack is a specially addressed memory. In the case of Intel the stack is managed and stored in the RAM. Three registers are provided to facilitate stack operations and its management: stack segment register (SS), stack pointer (ESP), and stack-frame base pointer (EBP). There can be any number of stacks but only one stack is available at a time. The SS register is automatically used in all the stack operations (PUSH/POP) and it points to the base of the current stack. The current stack is simply called **stack**. When the offset contained in the ESP is added to the base, it points to the top of the stack. The ESP register is decremented or incremented depending on whether it is a PUSH or POP operation on the stack. When the stack grows, it grows to occupy progressively lower addresses in memory. In other words it grows from higher order address towards lower order address. The EBP is used to store a *copy of the ESP* before the called subroutine starts its execution so that a programmer can conveniently access the data structures passed in a subroutine call using the safe copy in the EBP while the subroutine can use the stack (PUSH and POP) for temporary storage. Remember that the PUSH and POP will affect the ESP contents. In Figure 13.2 the stack registers are depicted.

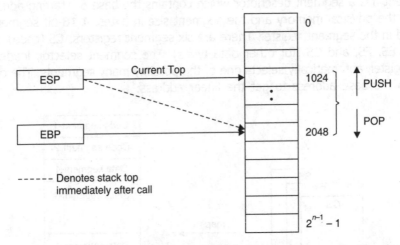

**Figure 13.2   Use of ESP and EBP in stack organization.**

Cache in Pentium is totally transparent to the programmers and is managed by the hardware integrated in the processor chip. Discussions about L1 (on chip) cache and L2 (off chip) cache can be found in Chapter 10.

## 13.4   THE PROGRAMMER'S VIEW OF PENTIUM PROCESSOR

In general a programmer can write programs in a machine independent higher level language like Java or in a machine dependent assembly language. For our discussions here, we assume the programmer to be an assembly language programmer. In his or her view the processor is hardware that processes data or executes machine or assembly language instructions. The *primitive data types* supported at the hardware level are signed or unsigned integers, binary coded decimal or BCD integers, Boolean or binary, floating point numbers, and character strings. Higher order data structures like arrays, lists and trees are supported in a higher level language, which are realized in terms of the primitive data types. Unsigned integers are used not only for specialized computations but also as address pointers that point to a memory location and the associated index arithmetic. The support for the primitive data types at the hardware level comes in two ways. A standard internal representation is followed at the bit level for each of these primitive data types and then one or more machine instructions are provided to operate upon such data types. For example, a signed integer is represented in the standard two's complement format and it has a fixed length in computations. In the case of Pentium the length can be fixed as one byte long, two bytes or word long, four bytes or double word long. If a machine instruction for Add Signed Integers or ADD is executed with one of the two operands as a 16-bit register (AX), the data size added is automatically understood by the hardware to be 16 bits or two bytes long. Similarly, the floating point data type follows the IEEE recommended standards and there are floating point arithmetic instructions to manipulate such data. Memory address pointers or simply called pointers are unsigned integers. Below we list the various data types supported in the case of Pentium:

1. Byte integer      1 bit sign and 7 bit magnitude
2. Word integer      1 bit sign and 15 bit magnitude
3. Double word integer      1 bit sign and 31 bit magnitude
4. BCD integer      One digit in one byte (4 bits unused)
5. Packed BCD      2 BCD digits packed in one byte
6. Byte ordinal      8 bit magnitude; one ASCII character
7. Word ordinal      16 bit magnitude; can store 2 ASCII char.
8. Double word ordinal      32 bits long magnitude; can store 4 ASCII char.
9. Near pointer      32 bits long offset value; can be added to a base
10. Far pointer      48 bits long; 16 MSBs are from a segment register
11. Bit data or Boolean      Up to 32 bits long
12. Byte string      Up to 4 GB
13. Bit string      Up to 4 GB
14. Real-single precision      32 bits long with 8 bits for exponent, 1 bit sign
15. Real-double precision      64 bits long with 11 bits for exponent, 1 bit sign
16. Real-extended precision      80 bits long with 15 bits for exponent, 1 bit sign

An assembly language programmer is concerned with the primitive data types, the machine instructions available to manipulate them and then the various CPU registers available in a computer system. The CPU registers of Pentium have been introduced in earlier chapters and they are summarized here in Figure 13.3. For a quick overview we have categorized the registers into four classes explained as follows:

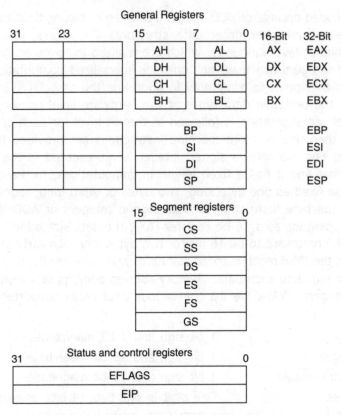

**Figure 13.3 Registers of Pentium.**

## 13.4.1 General Registers: EAX, EBX, ECX, EDX

The general registers are used to hold logical and arithmetic operands or for address calculations. They are 32 bits long. Their names are derived from the popular predecessor which used AX, BX, CX and DX. In fact the low order 16 bits of EAX, for example, can be addressed as AX. Similarly, BX, CX and DX are *sub-registers* of EBX, ECX and EDX respectively. Further, the low order 8-bits of AX can be addressed as AL and the high order 8-bits of AX can be addressed as AH for byte operations. This is true for other general registers as well. Some machine instructions use some specific registers for pre-determined purposes. For example, the string instructions and LOOP instruction use the register ECX in a special way to count. Similarly, the integer divide instruction (IDIV) uses the EDX register in a special way. If the integer divide instruction uses the EAX to hold the numerator of the division operation, the EDX before the division operation holds the sign extension of EAX and after the division is completed the remainder. One of the tasks of the assembly language programmer is to learn about such special uses of the registers with various instructions.

## 13.4.2 Pointers and Index Registers: ESP, EBP, ESI, EDI

The use of stack pointer (ESP) and base frame pointer (EBP) were explained in the previous section. The source index register (ESI) and destination index register (EDI) are used in string manipulations for indexing the source and the destination data. They are 32 bits long. The corresponding registers in 8086 were called SI and DI. SI and DI are sub-registers of ESI and EDI. Although the general registers can be of use for indexing, these two registers have special role in string data processing.

## 13.4.3 Segment Registers: CS, DS, SS, ES, FS, GS

The segment registers are 16-bits long. The use of segment registers in segmented addressing of the address space has been explained in the previous section.

## 13.4.4 Program Flow Control Registers: EIP and EFLAGS

The 32-bit EIP or extended instruction pointer holds the address of the instruction to be fetched from memory. This is constantly updated after every instruction is fetched from the memory. The instruction length in Pentium is not constant and it varies from one instruction to another. Thus, after an instruction fetch, the EIP is incremented by a number equal to the length of the instruction fetched so as to point to the next instruction in sequence. In the case of 8086 this register was called IP or Instruction Pointer. The 32 bits long EFLAGS register stores the status or conditions that occur during the execution of a program. Several arithmetic and other instructions can result in a condition such as overflow, the result being negative (or positive), etc., which will be stored in EFLAGS in the bit places reserved for them. Conditional branch instructions can test if such a flag is "set" or not and branch accordingly. Other conditions external to the CPU such as the failure of a parity check in memory read operation or an interrupt from an external device can also be stored in EFLAGS. The conditions or status stored in EFLAGS are used by the programmer or the hardware to make changes in the control flow of the program sequences. Table 13.1 shows some of the status flags to give a flavour to the students.

### TABLE 13.1
### Sample Status Flags

| Name of the Bit | Purpose | Conditions Reported |
|---|---|---|
| OF | Overflow | Arithmetic operation resulted in a number too large to store |
| SF | Sign | The operation resulted in the sign bit being 1 (Negative) |
| ZF | Zero | Result is zero |
| AF | Auxiliary Carry | Carry out of bit position 8—used in BCD arithmetic |
| PF | Parity | Parity check |
| CF | Carry Flag | Carry out of most significant bit of the result |
| IF | Interrupt Enable | The interrupt is disabled if this bit is Reset |

## 13.5  INSTRUCTION FORMAT

The Pentium processor is a very complex processor. It can be run in several different modes. In *real address mode* the Pentium processor runs programs written for its 8086, 8088, 80186, or 80188 predecessors. This also corresponds to the *real address mode* of later members of the family such as 80286, 80386 or 80486 processors. In this mode the architecture of the processor is almost identical to that of the predecessor processors. To a programmer, the 32-bit Pentium appears as a high speed 16-bit 8086 processor. The high speed is due to the advanced technology used in fabrication of the different components of the system. The reader might know that in the case of 8086, the effective address used to refer to the memory is only 20 bits long which gave rise to 1 MB addressability which was considered big in the 1970s. For details about how this compatibility is achieved, the reader is referred to the sources published by Intel (see http://www.intel.com/design/pentium4/manuals/index-new.htm). The Pentium processor is designed to support *multitasking*, a concept that will be covered in "Computer Software" courses. It is sufficient for our purpose, to know that "task" is a program that is waiting in a queue to run while another program is running on the processor. The processor may switch from one task to another when an interrupt or an exception condition occurs. In order to support multitasking, the Pentium processor includes several features. These features are supported by specialized registers and special instructions. Examples of such features include memory protection, task state description for fast task switching, memory management, multiprocessing, etc. The Pentium processor supports running one or multiple 8086 programs in *Virtual-8086 mode* when multitasking can be used profitably. The interesting point to note is that virtual-8086 tasks can be intermixed with other Pentium processor tasks. The virtual machine is a concept that supports complete hardware and software of 8086 inside a Pentium. In the EFLAGS register one bit is named VM-bit. When this bit is set by a system programmer, the Pentium processor runs in virtual-8086 mode. The processor constantly checks this VM bit under two general conditions:

1. When loading segment registers
2. When decoding instructions

The general instruction format of the IA-32 architecture is shown in Figure 13.4. Referring to this figure the reader can contrast the complexity of Pentium instruction format

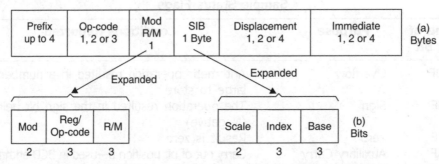

**Figure 13.4  General instruction format of Pentium.**

with that of SMAC++. For simplicity, we will view the "Op-code part" of the Pentium instruction format in three parts: *instruction prefix bytes, the primary Op-code bytes,* and *addressing-form-specifier bytes.* The primary Op-code is a must and the other two are optional depending on the type of instruction. The primary Op-code field itself is not constant across all instructions. It can be one, two or three bytes long. An instruction-prefix is one byte long and there can be as many as 4 prefixes to an instruction. The set of all prefixes is classified into 4 groups and an instruction may be prefixed by selecting one choice from each group. For the sake of completeness, without much detail, these four groups are mentioned below:

1. Group-1    Lock and repeat prefixes (repeat is useful for string operations)
2. Group-2    Segment override prefixes and hints on branching
3. Group-3    Operand size override (useful in SIMD type instructions)
4. Group-4    Address size override prefix

The *addressing-form-specifier* consists of two bytes called **ModR/M byte** and **SIB byte** and any one of the two bytes may optionally be present in an instruction. Many instructions which refer to the memory do have the ModR/M byte associated with them. The 8 bits of ModR/M byte is further subdivided into three fields as follows and similarly the 8 bits of the SIB byte is also divided into three fields. This is illustrated in Figure 13.4.

Three fields of ModR/M byte are:

1. 3-bit *r/m* field
2. 3-bit *reg/Op-code* field
3. 2-bit *mod* field

Three fields of SIB byte are:

1. 2-bit *scale*
2. 3-bit *index*
3. 3-bit *base*

The 3 bits of *r/m* field give rise to eight combinations. They are used for three different purposes. One purpose is to specify a register as an operand. Register addressing is not simple because we can view parts of the 32-bit EAX also as AX, AH, or AL. Besides, for multimedia data processing, many other registers are present in Pentium that we have not introduced here. Certain combinations of the *r/m* field are used in conjunction with the *mod* field to encode the addressing modes. Recall the various addressing modes that we have discussed in Chapters 8 and 9, such as base, indexing, base plus index, etc. In serving the third purpose also it is combined with the *mod* field to give additional Op-code information for certain types of instructions. As a result, the instruction decoding is made quite complex in Pentium. The *reg/op-code* field is used to specify a register or to supply additional Op-code information. The *mod* field in combination with *r/m* field is used to specify one of the 8 registers (see Sections 13.4.1 and 13.4.2) or one of 24 different addressing modes.

The index field specifies the register to be used for indexed addressing and similarly, the base field specifies the register to be used for base addressing. The basic unit of addressing being a byte, indexing can be scaled as 1, 2, 4, or 8 bytes long to facilitate processing arrays of different primitive data types. This scale factor is indicated by the scale field of the SIB byte. The displacement when present can be one, two or four bytes long as indicated by the displacement field. If the displacement is present, 1, 2 or 4 bytes that immediately follow the SIB byte, in the instruction format, contain the displacement value. This is depicted in Figure 13.4 (b). When an instruction uses immediate addressing the data value is stored as an integral part of the instruction. The immediate data can be 1, 2, or 4 bytes long. If it is present in an instruction, immediate data value follows the SIB byte as shown in Figure 13.4 (b).

We illustrate this complex instruction encoding with a small example below but we do not present the complete information of encoding of all the bits:

| mod field | r/m field | reg/op-code | Set selected |
|-----------|-----------|-------------|--------------|
| 00 | 001 | 000 | {AL, AX, EAX..} |
| 00 | 001 | 001 | {CL, CX, ECX.. } |
| 00 | 001 | 010 | {DL, DX, EDX..} |
| 00 | 001 | 011 | {BL, BX, EBX.. } |

The *mod* field being 00 and *r/m* being 001 specifies the addressing mode to be used is [BX+DI] in which the contents of BX and DI registers are added to get the effective address of the operand [1]. The *reg/op-code* field being 000 selects the subset of registers {AL, AX, EAX..}, one of which is involved in the instruction execution. The op-code field specifies the register.

## 13.6 INSTRUCTION SET VIEW

When we discussed a small hypothetical computer like SMAC++ in Chapter 8, we introduced a small instruction set of 26 instructions. A real computer system like Pentium which belongs to the family of processors called **CISC (Complex Instruction Set Computer)** has several hundred instructions. They can be studied at the machine language level or at the assembly language level where mnemonics and symbolic names are used instead of bits and hex digits. In this section we provide only a brief overview of the instruction set of Pentium and do not cover their details at the machine language level nor at the assembly language level. In Section 9.3, we stated that the instruction set can be grouped into classes for convenient study and we will follow the same approach here to provide an overview of the instruction set.

### 13.6.1 Classes of Instructions

The following are the classes of instructions:

1. Load register from memory and store register to memory
2. Arithmetic instructions
3. Bit-oriented instructions (AND, OR, NOT, etc.)
4. Branch instructions
5. Subroutine control instructions
6. Shift type instructions
7. I/O instructions
8. Instructions to support the operating system.

An assembly language programmer is usually interested in finer details like the length of an instruction and the number of cycles it takes to execute an instruction. This information is used by him/her to optimize the storage required for the program or the execution time of the program.

Pentium supports a wide variety of addressing modes and four types of data sizes (byte, word, double word and quad word). This results in many different instructions within one *category*. For example, consider the category of ADD instructions. If we consider the general template of "ADD X,Y" there are 7 types of ADD instructions (see http://www.paulcarter.com):

1. ADD register1 to register2 (result is in register2)
2. ADD register2 to register1 (result is in register2)
3. ADD *immediate* to register
4. ADD *immediate* to accumulator (EAX is the accumulator)
5. ADD *immediate* to memory
6. ADD memory to register
7. ADD register to memory

Generally, instructions which refer to memory take more cycles than others. In this case the ADD instructions referring to memory take 3 clock cycles as opposed to others which take one cycle. If we count all different ADD instructions as one category and not count real arithmetic and special processing instructions, there are about 130 categories of instructions in the case of Pentium. In each category there are a maximum of eight different instructions and a minimum of one instruction, giving rise to several hundred instructions. In what follows, we will use the assembly language mnemonics to refer to different instructions (see Intel website).

## C1. Load register from memory and store register to memory.

*Sample instructions:*

| | |
|---|---|
| MOV | move data |
| MOVSB | move byte |
| MOVSW | move word |
| MOVSD | move double word |
| MOVSX | move signed |
| MOVZX | move unsigned |
| LEA | load effective address into a register |
| LAHF | load FLAGS into AH register |

The "move" type instructions move the data from the source (second operand in an instruction) to the destination (first operand in the instruction). Loading a register from memory and storing a register into memory are duals of each other. Both are simple move instructions.

## C2. Arithmetic instructions

*Sample Instructions:*

| | |
|---|---|
| ADD | add integers |
| ADC | add with carry |

| | |
|---|---|
| SUB | subtract |
| MUL | unsigned multiply |
| IMUL | signed multiply |
| DIV | unsigned divide |
| IDIV | signed divide |
| FADD, FSUB, FMUL, FDIV | Floating point instructions |
| INC, DEC | increment or decrement by 1 (computationally faster) |

## C3. Bit-oriented instructions (logical instructions)

*Sample instructions:*

| | |
|---|---|
| AND, OR, NOT | instructions |
| XOR | exclusive OR instruction |
| CMP | compare two integers |
| CMPSB | compare bytes |
| CMPSW, CMPSD | compare words, double words |
| CLC, STC | clear carry, set carry |
| CLD, STD | clear direction flag, set direction flag |

## C4. Branch instructions

*Sample instructions:*

| | |
|---|---|
| JMP | jump unconditional |
| JE, JNE | jump on equal, jump on not equal |
| JG, JNG | jump on greater, not greater |
| JL, JNL | jump on less, not less |
| JZ, JNZ | jump on zero, not zero |
| JS, JNS | jump on sign, not sign |
| JO, JNO | jump on overflow, no overflow |
| JPO, JPE | jump on parity odd, parity even |
| LOOP mm | decrements CX, loops back to 'mm' until CX=0 |

Several combinations of branch conditions are also available.

## C5. Subroutine control instructions

*Sample instructions:*

| | |
|---|---|
| CALL | subroutine call |
| RET | return |
| PUSH, PUSHA | push onto stack, push all registers |
| PUSHF | push the flag register |
| POP, POPA | pop the stack into specified register |
| POPF | pop into the flag register |

## C6. Shift type instructions

*Sample instructions:*

| | |
|---|---|
| SAL, SAR | arithmetic shift left, right |
| SHL, SHR | logical shift left, right |
| RCL, RCR | rotate left with carry, right |
| ROL, ROR | rotate left, right |

## C7. I/O instructions

Although we introduced INP and OUT instructions into SMAC for simplicity, I/O in real computers are more complex. It is usually carried out with the help of specialized programs at the "system software level". INT instruction which generates an interrupt is generally used to assist the application programmer for input and output.

## C8. Instructions to support the operating system

A real computer system nowadays has to support multiprogramming, time sharing by multiple users, high speed computing, parallel processing and a massively large amount of storage. The operating system of such a computer is very complex and requires a considerable support from the processor hardware. Several architectural features, instructions and registers supporting all of them become necessary. Pentium is not an exception. Features included in this respect are: memory protection, segmentation, paging, virtual memory, high speed cache, 4-GB address space, fast process switching, and specialized instruction. We specify some such instructions without much explanation below.

| | |
|---|---|
| INVD | Invalidate cache |
| INVLPG | Invalidate TLB entry |
| LAR | Load access right byte |
| LIDT, SIDT | Load Interrupt Descriptor Table Register, store |
| LMSW, SMSW | Load machine status word, store |
| LTR, STR | Load task register, store |
| RDTSC | Read from time stamp counter |
| RSM | Resume from system management mode |
| VERR | Verify a segment reading |
| XLAT | Table look up translation |
| WBINVD | Write back and invalidate data cache |
| WAIT | Wait |

## 13.7  INTERCONNECTING THE COMPONENTS INTO A COMPUTER SYSTEM

The processor is the heart of a computer system but other components are also needed to support it. Memory and I/O are two other subsystems which together make a complete computer system at the hardware level. Chip manufacturers make several support chips to modularly build a computer system. As a particular technology matures, the industry introduces several standards in support of inter-operability of products from different manufacturers.

In order to make a memory subsystem, we know that, several memory chips are to be connected together. As we discussed in Chapter 9 under buses, these component chips are connected together on a Printed Circuit Board (PCB) on which sockets are provided to plug the memory chips. When computers based on 80286 and 80386 processors became popular, a new form of packaging the memory subsystem called **SIMM (Single In-line Memory Module)** emerged. In this packaging several memory chips are integrated together as a single pluggable unit that had, for example, 72 pins. SIMM became an industry standard. The SIMM card can be directly plugged into the motherboard (see Figure 13.5) to interconnect with other subsystems. The 72-pin configuration of the SIMM supported 32 bit data in and out. Pentium-based computers used the bus that was extended from 32 to 64 bits wide and thus required two matching SIMM cards for its memory subsystem. As Pentium-based computers became popular, an enhanced standard of SIMM called **DIMM (Dual In-line Memory Module)** emerged and it supports 64-bit data in and out.

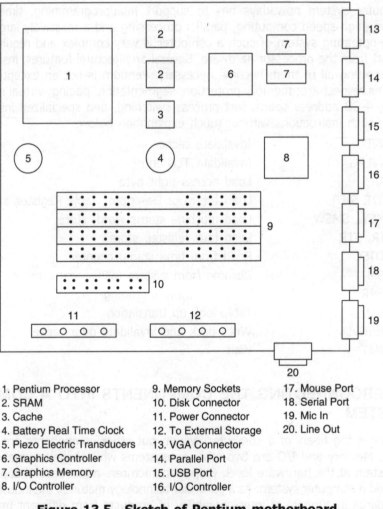

| 1. Pentium Processor | 9. Memory Sockets | 17. Mouse Port |
| 2. SRAM | 10. Disk Connector | 18. Serial Port |
| 3. Cache | 11. Power Connector | 19. Mic In |
| 4. Battery Real Time Clock | 12. To External Storage | 20. Line Out |
| 5. Piezo Electric Transducers | 13. VGA Connector | |
| 6. Graphics Controller | 14. Parallel Port | |
| 7. Graphics Memory | 15. USB Port | |
| 8. I/O Controller | 16. I/O Controller | |

**Figure 13.5  Sketch of Pentium motherboard.**

As the speed and versatility of CPU increased, the memory capacities increased and the variety and speed of peripheral devices grew, the buses also have evolved. Today's buses are more like a network of several buses interconnected, each catering to different speed requirements of different groups of subsystems within a computer system. For example, at the I/O level two buses are emerging and they are called **local bus** and **external bus**. One is suitable for high speed devices and the other for low speed devices. The PCI (Peripheral Component Interconnect) is an example of the former category. PCI bus supports a new concept called **plug-and-play**, according to which a new peripheral device can be plugged into the system through a port available for plugging and the system will automatically configure with appropriate device drivers. Of course, there are certain requirements for plug-and-play, for example the device must be plug-and-play type and the OS and the BIOS must support such a concept. Some new plug-and-play buses include, USB and Firewire. Some plug and play compatible devices are CD-ROM, DVD drives, printers, mouse, network card, graphics card and modem. Typically, the PCI bus operates at 33.3 MHz with synchronous data transmission. Bus widths of both 32 and 64 bits are supported. With a 32-bit wide bus the maximum data transfer rate can be 133 MB/s.

One can identify four different buses in a modern computer:

1. Processor bus which the processor uses to communicate with the world outside of the processor.

2. Memory bus that connects the processor and memory.

3. Local I/O bus used for high speed peripherals like video cards, disk storages. The PCI bus belongs to this category.

4. Standard I/O bus which connects devices like the modem, network cards, mouse, keyboard etc. A common bus of the type 4 is the ISA (Industry Standard Architecture) bus.

In a typical 266 MHz processor, memory bus speed could be 66 MHz (266/4), PCI bus could be 33 MHz (66/2) and the ISA bus speed could be 8.25 (33/4) MHz. Note that the various clock speeds are generated from a single master clock as multiples or sub-multiples. In complex processors where on-chip cache is used, a separate and dedicated bus connects the cache and the processor. This processor-cache bus runs at its own speed. For instance in the example of 266 MHz processor, this dedicated bus would run at 133(266/2) MHz.

The term **booting** in computers refers to the process of starting a computer from scratch when power is turned ON. Specialized software that is stored starting from a fixed address in memory, called **bootstrap loader** is first executed. To do this, the EIP is initialized with the address of the first instruction of the bootstrap loader and instruction execution is started. The bootstrap loader will normally load a more sophisticated loader from a boot-device and transfer control to that loader. This loader in turn will load the complete operating system and from then on the OS will take control. **BIOS** or basic input/output system is a collection of all the software needed to initialize the computer and start the operating system which included the loaders, device drivers for the I/O devices like the keyboard, mouse, display device, and disks. Once the OS takes control, the BIOS in olden days had no further role to play. In recent days the BIOS has taken additional responsibilities, such as the "power management" and configuring the parameters of the motherboard, etc. It is kept active throughout. Modern computers manage the power consumed and optimize its consumption by switching the system to a low power consumption state when no activities are taking place. Thus BIOS these days are much more complex and several vendors started marketing it. Standards like ACPI (Advanced Configuration and Power Interface) are being evolved to facilitate compatibility among the BIOS from different vendors.

A motherboard in a computer system is the underlying printed circuit board that interconnects various components into a system (see Figure 13.5). Typically it includes, the CPU, some amount of on-board RAM, video controller, disk controllers, a battery for real time clock, power connection, connectors for external I/O devices like mouse, keyboard, video display unit, speech devices, network connection, printer connection, etc. Different vendors make motherboards using which computer systems can be assembled. Each brand of motherboard is designed to support a processor from a specific vendor. Apart from that, there are other variations such as the amount of maximum RAM and the type of RAM supported on board, the number of PCI slots available, and the power requirements.

$$\boxed{\text{SUMMARY}}$$

In this chapter we provided a brief overview of a real computer system based on the Pentium processor. The purpose was not to explain how to build a computer system but it has been to make the reader to relate in his/her mind the various conceptual ideas learnt in the previous chapters to the components of a real computer system. In this attempt we followed the pattern of the chapters of the book by presenting the instruction set view, the view of memory and addressing, input-output and the integration of components into a system.

$$\boxed{\text{EXERCISES}}$$

1.  By reading the literature or browsing the Internet answer the following:
    (i) The need for compatibility among the generations of computers
    (ii) Upward and downward compatibility
    (iii) What architectural features in Pentium make it compatible with 8086

2.  Reviewing this chapter with other chapters of the book write critical notes on the following:
    (i) Comparison of the data types in SMAC++ and Pentium
    (ii) Similarities between SMAC++ and Pentium in register set
    (iii) The instruction sets of SMAC++ and Pentium

3.  If you have to make SMAC++ as a real computer, what minimal changes will you recommend? Make a list of the changes you recommend and comment on the need for each of them.

4.  What are the benefits and disadvantages of standards? What standards have been mentioned in this chapter? Browse the Internet and find more details about these standards.

5.  PUSHA and POPA are extensions of PUSH and POP instructions in Pentium. Read more about them. Compare and contrast their functions. Explain how PUSHA and POPA would be useful in optimizing the execution time of certain programs.

6.  From the Intel manuals find out the number of cycles taken by different instructions for their execution. Consider at least one instruction for each data type.

---

**Appendix** —————————————

# A

# Suggested Hardware Lab Experiments

———————————————————————————

While teaching the course on Computer Logic and Organization, we have found it pedagogically sound, and an engaging experience for students if we give them laboratory exercises to complete. Depending on the local needs, constraints, and limitations, the teacher may be able to organize such lab experiments in more than one way. In what follows, we describe our practice. The students in our case do not have much electronic background except the basic high school level Physics course where they would have learnt the basics of electricity, i.e., Ohm's law, voltage, current, power ground, and electrical circuits. We require the students to work in groups of two and complete the lab experiments described below. Each group is given a "Lab-Kit" which contains all the necessary components to complete the list of experiments. At the end of the 13-week semester, the students are expected to return the Lab-Kits for their re-use in the following semesters. Of course, our technician has to check the kits for completeness before giving them to the students. At the beginning of the term, the students are given a Lab Manual that contains description of the individual lab-experiments, necessary data sheets for the IC chips that they will be using, the concepts that are reinforced through that experiment and the expected week by which the students should have completed that experiment. The lab-work by students is supervised by a lab-instructor who is also the evaluator of the students' performance in the laboratory.

Each lab session is two hours long. At the beginning of the term, the students are given an orientation session. In this session they are told about the common mistakes students make in circuit connections, how to connect a circuit using the breadboard, how to identify the various pins of an IC chip and read the information contained in a data sheet, how to test their circuits for correctness and completeness, and how to write a laboratory report, and what they are expected to learn.

Students' learning through the Lab experiments is verified by the lab-instructor in two ways: (1) through the lab reports the students submit, and (2) the lab-instructor giving an individual quiz to one student at a time, any time during the semester. In this quiz, the selected student will be asked to re-do any of the lab experiments that were covered until then on his/her own. Depending on the time and resources, we ensure that every student will take a certain minimum number of quizzes in a semester.

Based on our curriculum needs, the pace with which the classroom lectures go, the synchronization needs between the lecture class and the labs, and the students' prior knowledge, we have devised six lab experiments that are described below. The first four experiments are simple enough to be completed in one lab session by the team of two students. The last two experiments will take multiple sessions to complete. Modular construction and testing should be encouraged for completing the last two experiments. Students are expected to come prepared for the lab-class. They are expected to show their design and a neatly drawn circuit diagram before they are permitted by the lab-instructor, to do an experiment each week in their lab-class. After they complete, the two students are expected to discuss among themselves how they have tested the circuits and what they have learnt. Then they display the working of their experiment to the lab-instructor before leaving the lab.

For the sake of simplicity, we have used DIP switches for binary input and LED indicators for binary output. Both these devices plug conveniently into the breadboard. Restricting to this type of simple I/O devices has also made our experiments very simple and small. In some universities or colleges, the teacher may be able to use more sophisticated I/O devices such as hex-keyboards or ASCII LED displays, and accordingly raise the complexity of the lab experiments they wish to follow. We suggest re-designing of the lab experiments in such cases. The bottom line, we recommend is, that there should be some sort of laboratory work attached to this course for students to get engaged in a hands-on learning.

## Lab #1—Introduction

- Learn about the lab-kit, data sheets, lab-rules, preparation for the lab work and how to write a lab report.
- Familiarization with the breadboard, the power supply, colour-coding in wiring, test methods, IC pins, two-terminal devices, logic levels.
- Use IC 7408 and 7432, learn 2-input AND and OR gates.

**Concepts:** Binary, voltage, current, power supply, DC, ground, breadboard layout, logic level, AND, OR, NOT functions, locating IC-pins, using LEDs, and DIP switches, Testing a logic circuit.

## Lab #2—Multi-level Gates

- Learn Boolean expressions for example SUM and CARRY of 1-bit half adder and full adder.
- Use IC 7405 and 7408 to implement the above.

**Concepts:** Boolean expressions, sum of products form, fan-in, fan-out, binary addition rule (one bit), SUM and CARRY Boolean functions, minimization (of what?)

# Lab #3—Flip-Flops and Buffer Registers

- NAND gates, sequential circuits, memory, using a control signal.
- Use IC 7475 to store one bit and extend it to store a 4-bit number (for example, 1011). The data input for a register is given through the dip switches. The contents of a register are displayed using LEDs. Let there be two 4-bit registers, A and B. When the control signal $T_{transfer}$ is true, transfer the contents of register A into register B.

**Concepts:** Universal gates, NAND function, flip-flop, register, store and read, enabling signal, voltage levels and transitions, 4-bit registers, extending to 32 bits and beyond.

# Lab #4—Clock, Counter and Decoder and Control signals

- Basic and atomic unit concept, clock and binary counting
- Construct a circuit to develop control signals called $T_0$, $T_1$, $T_2$, $T_3$, ..., $T_7$ using the clock, counter and decoder chips given to you.
- Learn the use of the inverter chip for complementing a signal

**Concepts:** Clocks, period, ON time and OFF time, frequency, atomic unit and settling time, counting the clock pulses, cyclic nature, edge triggering, binary counter, decimal counter, state diagram for counters.

# Lab #5—Memory and Datapath

- The notion of bus, tri-state buffers
- A micro-memory unit with 4 words, each 4 bits long
- 2-bit MAR and 4-bit MBR registers
- 2-bit IP and 4-bit IR registers
- Use data path of 4-bit width for movement of data
- Use three timing signals $T_0$, $T_1$ and $T_2$ to perform three consecutive micro-operations: (a) 2-bit IP is put into MAR, (b) IP is decoded to select one out of 4 words from the micro-memory unit and store that in MBR and (c) transfer MBR into IR.

**Concepts:** MAR and MBR, address decoding, READ and destructive WRITE, tri-state buffers, control signal, data path, BUS, transfer from one register to another register, phases involved in the transfer.

# Lab #6—A Toy Computer Project

- *Specifications for a toy computer:* It has a micro-memory of 4 words with each word having 4 bits. The memory unit has a 2-bit MAR and a 4-bit MBR. There is an IP register 2 bits long and an IR register that is 4 bits long. There are two 4-bit registers in the CPU. They are called A and B registers. The instruction format has 2-bit Op-code field and 2-bit address field. There is one 4-bit bus used in the toy computer for transferring bits from one place to another. The four possible instructions are encoded as follows:

1. 00: clear register A
2. 01: Move register A to B
3. 10: increment B by 1
4. 11: unconditional branch to the address specified

- Since there is no 'output' instruction in the toy computer, the specification requires that the contents of A and B registers are constantly displayed on two 4-bit LEDs respectively.

- Construct the toy computer on the breadboard.

- Load the following 4-instruction programs into the micro-memory of the toy computer.

  1. At address 00 load 0000    [clear register A to zero]
  2. At address 01 load 0100    [move A to B]
  3. At address 10 load 1000    [Increment B]
  4. At address 11 load 1110    [Branch to 10]

- Let there be one bit called RUN (Dip switch). When it is ON, the instructions starting from address 00 in the memory will be executed one after another at a very slow speed. Execute the program, observe the outputs and verify the expected behaviour.

**Concepts:**   Simple input/output for the toy computer, switches, LEDs, program loading, manual loading for toy computer, execution—one step at a time.

In Figures A.1 and A.2 an overall block schematic for the toy computer is given to help the students. The students are encouraged to develop a circuit diagram of their own for the toy computer based on their learning from the previous lab experiments, before looking into these figures.

**Suggestion to the teachers:**   You may like to expand this toy computer specification as you see fit to challenge the students depending on the context of your teaching and your students' background. You can modify the instruction set, the I/O, expand the memory, add complexity to instruction decoding, etc.

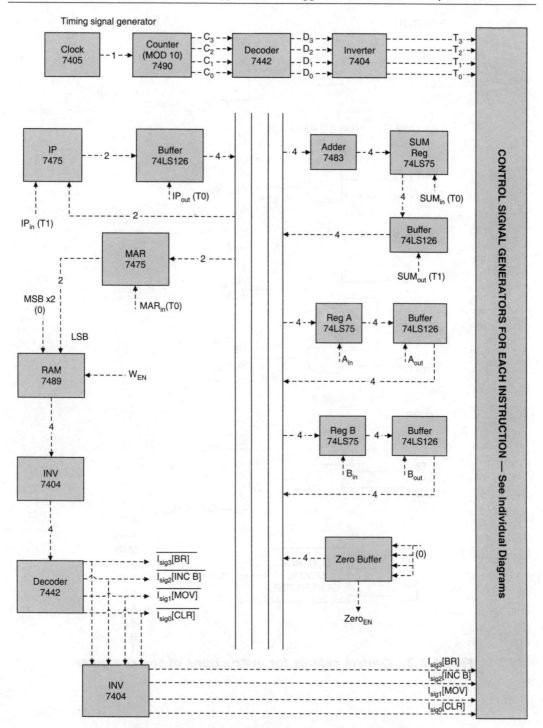

**Figure A.1   Block diagram of toy computer.**

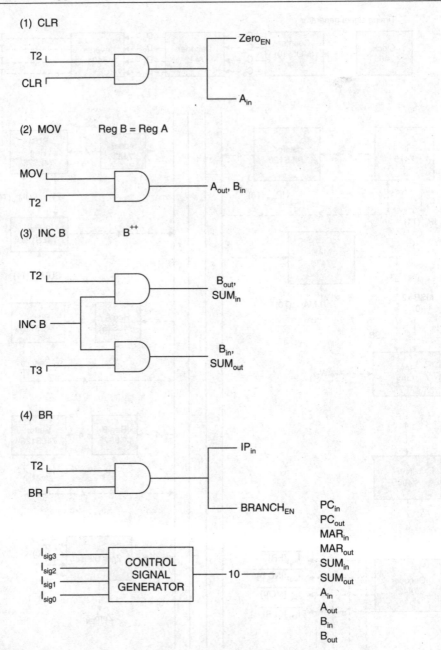

(1) CLR

T2

CLR

$Zero_{EN}$

$A_{in}$

(2) MOV    Reg B = Reg A

MOV

T2

$A_{out}$, $B_{in}$

(3) INC B    $B^{++}$

T2

INC B

T3

$B_{out}$, $SUM_{in}$

$B_{in}$, $SUM_{out}$

(4) BR

T2

BR

$IP_{in}$

$BRANCH_{EN}$

$I_{sig3}$
$I_{sig2}$
$I_{sig1}$
$I_{sig0}$

CONTROL
SIGNAL
GENERATOR

10

$PC_{in}$
$PC_{out}$
$MAR_{in}$
$MAR_{out}$
$SUM_{in}$
$SUM_{out}$
$A_{in}$
$A_{out}$
$B_{in}$
$B_{out}$

**Figure A.2  Control signals for instructions of toy computer.**

# Appendix

# B

# Decision Table Terminology

A decision table defines a logical procedure by means of a set of *conditions* and their related *actions*. The table is divided into four quadrants by double lines (see Figure B.1). All the

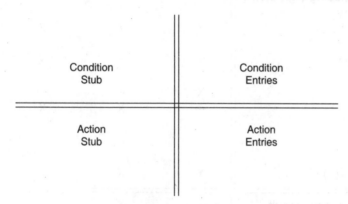

| Condition Stub | Condition Entries |
| --- | --- |
| Action Stub | Action Entries |

**Figure B.1  Decision table notation.**

conditions relevant to the procedure are listed in the *condition stub* and all the actions to be performed by the procedure are listed in an *action stub*. The construction of a decision table begins with the listing of all the conditions relevant to the procedure and all the actions to be performed. The actions are listed in the order they have to be performed. The next step is to determine which conditions, taken together, should lead to which actions. These are recorded on the right half of a decision table as a series of *decision rules*. The decision table (Table B.1) has 4 rules. The first rule is interpreted as follows:

If the operation is add as $s(x) = s(y)$ (i.e., sign bit of $x$ and $y$ are equal), then add $x$ and $y$ including the sign bit and call it $z$. If $z$ overflows, add the overflow bit to $z$ and go to Table T2. In Table T2 we go to rule 1 which states "if sign bit of the sum $z$, namely, $s(z)$ equals $s(x)$, declare $z$ as the answer and stop else declare the answer as wrong "out of range" and stop. Observe that $X$ as an action entry indicates that the action specified must be carried out. On the other hand, a − as an action entry indicates that the specified action is not carried out. Also observe that in rule 1 one of the actions is to go to Table T2 for further checking. As another example, we will consider rule 3. This rule states that if the operation is subtract and if $s(x) = s(y)$, then complement $y$ (namely take the 1's complement of $y$), add the complement of $y$ to $x$ including the sign bit. To this sum, carry (if any) is added and the sum obtained (including the sign bit) is the answer $z$. In this case there is no need to go to Table T2.

## TABLE B.1
### A Decision Table for One's Complement Addition

| | Rule 1 | Rule 2 | Rule 3 | Rule 4 |
|---|---|---|---|---|
| Operation | Add | Add | Sub | Sub |
| $s(x) = s(y)$ | Y | N | Y | N |
| Complement $y$ | — | — | X | X |
| $z = x + y$ (Add including sign bit) | X | X | X | X |
| Add carry (if any) to $z$ | X | X | X | X |
| Declare $z$ as answer | — | X | X | — |
| Go To T2 | X | — | — | X |
| Stop | — | X | X | — |
| | | | | |
| T2: | | | | |
| $s(z) = s(x)$ | Y | X | | |
| Answer wrong (result out of range | — | X | | |
| Declare $z$ as answer | X | — | | |
| Stop | X | X | | |

# References

[1] Agarwala, A.K. and Ranscher, T.G., *Foundations of Microprogramming Architecture*, Academic Press, New York, 1976.

[2] Blakeslee, T.R., *Digital Design with Standard MSI and LSI*, Wiley-Interscience, New York, 1975.

[3] Brey, B.B., *The Intel Microprocessors*—(8086/88, 80186/80188, 80286, 80386, 80486), Pentium and Pentium Proprocessor Pentium II, Pentium III, Pentium 4: Architecture, Programming and Interfacing, 7th ed., Prentice-Hall of India, New Delhi, 2006.

[4] Carter, Paul, "Assembly Language", http://www.paulcarter.com/

[5] Clare, C.R., *Designing Logic Systems Using State Machines*, McGraw-Hill, New York 1973.

[6] Denning, P.J., *Virtual Memory*, ACM Computing Survey, vol. 2, Sept. 1970, pp. 153–187.

[7] Dhamdhere, D.M., *Introduction to System Software*, Tata McGraw-Hill, New Delhi, 1990.

[8] Hamacher, V.C., Vranesic, Z.G., and Zaky, S.G., *Computer Organization*, 3rd ed., McGraw-Hill, 2000.

[9] Hayes, J.P., *Computer Architecture and Organization*, McGraw-Hill, New York 1978.

[10] Hennessy, J.L. and Patterson, D.A., *Computer Organization and Design: The Hardware/ Software Interfaces*, Morgan Kauffman Publishers, San Mateo, CA, 1994.

[11] Heuring, V.P. and Jordan, H.F., *Computer Systems Design and Architecture*, 2nd ed., Prentice-Hall of India, New Delhi, 2005.

[12] IA32 Intel architecture—Software developer's manual, http://www.intel.com/design/pentium4/manuals/index_new.htm

[13] IEEE 754 Floating Point Standard, *Computer*, vol. 14, No. 3, March 1981.

[14] "Indian Script Code for Information Interchange–ISCII", Electronics Information and Planning (Dept. of Electronics, Govt. of India), Feb. 1992 (pp. 221–239).

[15]  Kohavi, Z., *Switching and Finite Automata Theory*, Tata McGraw-Hill, New Delhi, 1970.

[16]  Kurtz, R.L., *Interfacing Techniques in Digital Design*, John Wiley & Sons, New York, 1988.

[17]  Lala, P.K., *Digital System Design Using Programmable Logic Devices*, Prentice Hall, New Jersey, 1990.

[18]  Mano, M. and Kim, C.R., *Logic and Computer Design Funamentals*, 2nd ed., Prentice Hall, New Jersey, 2001.

[19]  PC guide, http://www.PCGuide.com

[20]  Peterson, W.W., *Error Correcting Codes*, MIT Press, Cambridge (USA), 1961.

[21]  Rajaraman, V. and Radhakrishnan, T., *Essentials of Assembly Language Programming for the IBM PC*, Prentice-Hall of India, New Delhi, 2000.

[22]  Rajaraman, V. *Introduction to Information Technology*, Prentice-Hall of India, New Delhi, 2002.

[23]  Rajaraman, V., *Fundamentals of Computers*, 4th ed., Prentice-Hall of India, New Delhi, 2004.

[24]  Silberschatt, A. and Galvin, P.B., *Operating Systems*, 5th ed., Addison-Wesley, Reading, MA, USA, 1998.

[25]  Stallings, W., *Computer Organization and Architecture*: *Designing for performance*, 7th ed., Prentice-Hall of India, New Delhi, 2006.

[26]  Stallings, W., *Operating Systems*, 5th ed., Prentice-Hall of India, New Delhi, 2005.

[27]  Steinmetz, R. and Nehrstedt, K., *Multimedia: Computing, Communication and Applications*, Pearson Education, New Delhi, 2001.

[28]  Wakerly, J.F., *Digital Design—Principles and Practices*, 3rd ed., Prentice-Hall of India, New Delhi, 2001.

# Index